Conservation of Glass

Butterworth-Heinemann Series in Conservation and Museology

Series Editors: *Arts and Archaeology*

Andrew Oddy
British Museum, London

Architecture

Derek Linstrum
Institute of Advanced Architectural Studies, University of York

US Executive Editor: **Norbert S Baer**
New York University, Conservation Center of the Institute of Fine Arts

Consultants: **Sir Bernard Feilden**

David Bomford
National Gallery, London

C V Horie
Manchester Museum, University of Manchester

Colin Pearson
Canberra College of Advanced Education

Sarah Staniforth
National Trust, London

Published titles: Artists' Pigments c. 1600–1835, 2nd Edition (Harley)
Care and Conservation of Geological Material (Howie)
Care and Conservation of Palaeontological Material (Collins)
Conservation and Exhibitions (Stolow)
Conservation and Restoration of Ceramics (Buys and Oakley)
Conservation and Restoration of Works of Art and Antiquities (Kühn)
Conservation of Building and Decorative Stone, Volumes 1 and 2
(Ashurst, Dimes)
Conservation of Historic Buildings (Feilden)
Conservation of Library and Archive Materials and the Graphic Arts
(Petherbridge)
Conservation of Manuscripts and Paintings of South-east Asia (Agrawal)
Conservation of Marine Archaeological Objects (Pearson)
Conservation of Wall Paintings (Mora, Mora, Philippot)
The Museum Environment, 2nd Edition (Thomson)
The Organic Chemistry of Museum Objects, 2nd Edition (Mills, White)
The Textile Conservator's Manual, 2nd Edition (Landi)

Related titles: Manual of Curatorship, 2nd Edition
Materials for Conservation
Museum Documentation Systems
Manual of Heritage Management

Conservation of Glass

Roy Newton OBE, DSc, HonDSc (Tech), HonFSGT, FSA
Honorary Professor of Glass Technology,
School of Materials, University of Sheffield, UK

Sandra Davison FIIC
Ceramics and glass restorer
The Conservation Studio, Thame, UK

Butterworth-Heinemann Ltd
Linacre House, Jordan Hill, Oxford OX2 8DP

 A member of the Reed Elsevier plc group

OXFORD   LONDON   BOSTON
NEW DELHI   SINGAPORE   SYDNEY
TOKYO   TORONTO   WELLINGTON

First published 1989
Paperback edition 1996

British Library Cataloguing in Publication Data
Newton, Roy
  Conservation of glass.
  1. Glass painting and staining – Conservation and restoration
  I. Title
  748.5 NK5432

ISBN 0 7506 2448 5

Library of Congress Cataloguing in Publication Data
Newton, R. G. (Roy G.)
  Conservation of glass.
  Bibliography.
  Includes index.
  ISBN 0 7506 2448 5
  1. Glassware – Conservation and restoration.
  2. Glass painting and staining, Medieval – Conservation
  and restoration. I. Davison, Sandra. II. Title.
  NK5104.5.N4   748'.028   87–17862

Photoset by Scribe Design, Gillingham, Kent
Printed in Great Britain at the University Press, Cambridge

Series editors' preface

The conservation of artefacts and buildings has a long history, but the positive emergence of conservation as a profession can be said to date from the foundation of the International Institute for the Conservation of Museum Objects (IIC) in 1950 (the last two words of the title being later changed to Historic and Artistic Works) and the appearance soon after in 1952 of it journal *Studies in Conservation*. The role of the conservator as distinct from those of the restorer and the scientist had been emerging during the 1930s with a focal point in the Fogg Art Museum, Harvard University, which published the precursor to *Studies in Conservation, Technical Studies in the Field of the Fine Arts* (1932–42).

UNESCO, through its Cultural Heritage Division and its publications, had always taken a positive role in conservation and the foundation, under its auspices, of the International Centre for the Study of the Preservation and the Restoration of Cultural Property (ICCROM), in Rome, was a further advance. The Centre was established in 1959 with the aims of advising internationally on conservation problems, co-ordinating conservation activities and establishing standards and training courses.

A significant confirmation of professional progress was the transformation at New York in 1966 of the two committees of the International Council of Museums (ICOM), one curatorial on the Care of Paintings (founded in 1949) and the other mainly scientific (founded in the mid-1950s) into the ICOM Committee for Conservation.

Following the Second International Congress of Architects in Venice in 1964 when the Venice Charter was promulgated, the International Council of Monuments and Sites (ICOMOS) was set up in 1965 to deal with archaeological, architectural and town planning questions, to schedule monuments and sites and to monitor relevant legislation.

From the early 1960s onwards, international congresses (and the literature emerging from them) held by IIC, ICOM, ICOMOS and ICCROM not only advanced the subject in its various technical specializations but also emphasized the cohesion of conservators and their subject as an interdisciplinary profession.

The use of the term *Conservation* in the title of this series refers to the whole subject of the care and treatment of valuable artefacts both movable and immovable, but within the discipline conservation has a meaning which is distinct from that of restoration. *Conservation* used in this specialized sense has two aspects: firstly, the control of the environment to minimize the decay of artefacts and materials; and, secondly, their treatment to arrest decay and to stabilize them where possible against further deterioration. Restoration is the continuation of the latter process, when conservation treatment is thought to be insufficient, to the extent of reinstating an object, without falsification, to a condition in which it can be exhibited.

In the field of conservation conflicts of values on aesthetic, historical, or technical grounds are often inevitable. Rival attitudes and methods inevitably arise in a subject which is still developing and at the core of these differences there is often a deficiency of technical knowledge. That is one of the principal *raisons d'être* of this series. In most of these matters ethical principles are the subject of much discussion, and generalizations cannot easily cover (say) buildings, furniture, easel paintings and waterlogged wooden objects.

A rigid, universally agreed principle is that all treatment should be adequately documented. There is also general agreement that structural and decorative falsification should be avoided. In addition there are three other principles which, unless there are overriding objections, it is generally agreed should be followed.

The first is the principle of the reversibility of processes, which states that a treatment should normally be such that the artefacts can, if desired, be returned to its pre-treatment condition even after a long lapse of time. This principle is impossible to apply in some cases, for example where the survival of an artefact may depend upon an irreversible process. The second, intrinsic to the whole subject, is that as far as possible decayed parts of an artefact should be conserved and not replaced. The third is that the consequences of the ageing of the original materials (for example 'patina') should not normally be disguised or removed. This includes a secondary proviso that later accretions should not be retained under the false guide of natural patina.

The authors of the volumes in this series give their views on these matters, where relevant, with reference to the types of material within their scope. They take into account the differences in approach to artefacts of essentially artistic significance and to those in which the interest is primarily historical or archaeological.

The volumes are unified by a systematic and balanced presentation of theoretical and practical material with, where necessary, an objective comparison of different methods and approaches. A balance has also been maintained between the fine (and decorative) arts, archaeology and architecture in those cases where the respective branches of the subject have common ground, for example in the treatment of stone and glass and in the control of the museum environment. Since the publication of the first volume it has been decided to include within the series related monographs and technical studies. To reflect this enlargement of its scope the series has been renamed the Butterworth-Heinemann Series in Conservation and Museology.

Though necessarily different in details of organization and treatment (to fit the particular requirements of the subject) each volume has the same general standard which is that of such training courses as those of the University of London Institute of Archaeology, The Victoria and Albert Museum, the Conservation Center, New York University, the Institute of Advanced Architectural Studies, York, and ICCROM.

The authors have been chosen from among the acknowledged experts in each field, but as a result of the wide areas of knowledge and technique covered even by the specialized volumes in this series, in many instances multi-authorship has been necessary.

With the existence of IIC, ICOM, ICOMOS and ICCROM, the principles and practice of conservation have become as internationalized as the problems. The collaboration of Consultant Editors will help to ensure that the practices discussed in this series will be applicable throughout the world.

Preface

This volume is intended as a textbook for conservators working with glass artefacts and painted medieval glass windows. The field of conservation is becoming increasingly scientific, and yet those of us working on the preservation of antiquities, are, of necessity, also required to have considerable manual dexterity, and, in many cases, artistic ability. It is therefore pertinent perhaps that *Conservation of Glass* has been compiled from a number of sources by two authors of differing but complementary backgrounds: Professor Roy Newton, a scientist who has worked both in the glass manufacturing industry and in the field of medieval painted window restoration; and Sandra Davison, a conservator of antiquities of many years' experience.

Chapter 1 defines the nature of glass in terms of its chemical structure and physical properties. Chapter 2 contains a short history of glass-making from its beginnings 5000 years ago. A knowledge of glass history in conjunction with the technology of its production, the subject matter of Chapter 3, is valuable background information. This chapter is divided into two sections: part one deals with the raw materials and manufacturing techniques, and part two with the development of furnaces and melting techniques. Chapter 4 discusses the deterioration of glass in its many forms. As will be explained, a great deal of information regarding durability of glass is derived from modern research on glass of known compositions. Conservators should bear in mind, therefore, that ancient glasses of more complex and varying compositions may deteriorate differently under natural conditions than modern glasses used in laboratory research. The materials used in all aspects of glass conservation are discussed in Chapter 5. It is essential that conservators should be aware of the properties of materials, and of the effects which they will have when applied to glass antiquities. By the careful examination of glass before and during conservation, as described in Chapter 6, many details of its history and manufacture may become apparent, thus it is important for examination and conservation to be undertaken together, or vital evidence may be lost.

Compared with many other materials, relatively little has been published in the field of archaeological and decorative glass conservation. The majority of the literature concerning glass has been devoted to the conservation and restoration of architectural glass, and in particular, medieval painted ecclesiastical windows. However, standard glass conservation and restoration procedures for archaeological and decorative glass artefacts have evolved over the past decade or so, pioneered by Rolf Wihr in West Germany and Raymond Errett in the United States of America. Conservation techniques are discussed in Chapter 7 which, due to the nature of the subject, is divided into two sections: part one covers archaeological and decorative glass, illustrated where possible by case histories;

part two covers architectural glass. The term *painted glass* is used throughout this book to describe what are commonly referred to as stained glass windows, the reason being that many medieval windows are simply painted with enamels, whilst others are painted *and* stained with silver.

The authors are indebted to a number of conservators and restorers for providing information for this book, or for allowing their work to be published. In particular, the valuable assistance of the following persons is acknowledged: Robert Charleston BA, FSGT, FSA (Chapter 3, Part 2); Velson Horie BSc, The Manchester Museum (Chapter 5); Janey M. Cronyn BSc, FIIC, Research Associate, Textile Conservation Centre; Patricia R. Jackson BA(Hons), Institute of Archaeology, University College, London; Raymond Errett, the Corning Museum of Glass, Corning, New York (Chapter 7, part one); Alfred Fisher FMGP, Chapel Studio, Kings Langley, Hertfordshire; and Peter Gibson OBE, MUniv *h.c.*, FSA, FRSA, lately York Glaziers Trust (Chapter 7, part two).

R.G.N.
S.D.

Acknowledgement

The sources of illustrations (other than those by the authors) are briefly stated in the captions. Please note that the British Museum photographs reflect their practice in the 1970s. The publishers gratefully acknowledge the kind permission, granted by individuals, museum authorities, publishers and others, to reproduce copyright material.

Contents

Colour plates 1 to 5: between pages 130 and 131

Introduction

The conservation of glass, as of all antiquities, falls into two main categories: *passive conservation*, the control of the surrounding environment to prevent further decay; and *active conservation*, the treatment of artefacts to arrest decay and to stabilize them where possible. Depending upon the nature and condition of an artefact, a repository may involve one of the following environments: natural climatic conditions (painted glass windows and mosaics *in situ*); modified climatic conditions, especially those where some air-conditioning has been introduced to individual cases or galleries; or controlled climatic conditions where temperature and relative humidity are held within carefully defined limits. The stabilization of the environment is often outside the area of a conservator's immediate responsibility. He should however be consulted as to the most suitable environment for antiquities, and should thus be in a position to advise upon the correct conditions and methods of storage or display. It stands to reason that antiquities will continue to deteriorate if incorrectly housed, however thoroughly they may have been conserved.

The prevention of further damage and decay represents the minimum type of treatment, and may be the ideal type of conservation, especially if reversible techniques are not available at the time. Prevention of decay may only entail the removal of glass from an unsatisfactory environment. However, some further action is usually necessary, such as cleaning, consolidation, reconstruction or even restoration. These processes usually involve interference with the glass surface and the addition of synthetic materials which, it must be remembered, will be impossible to remove completely in practice, however reversible they remain.

A general discussion of the ethics of conservation and restoration is outside the scope of this book. Ethical considerations are and no doubt will continue to be controversial (see, for example, Pease, 1964; Lancaster, 1976; Pevsner, 1976). References to publications concerning ethics may be found by consulting *Art and Archaeology Technical Abstracts (IIC)*, published semi-annually by the Getty Trust in association with the International Institute for Conservation of Historic and Artistic Works, London (US ISSN 0004-2994).

Returning to the subject of glass, the use of synthetic materials and improvements in land and underwater archaeological excavation techniques have resulted in the preservation of ancient glass which it was formerly not possible to retrieve. For example, much early medieval potash glass was inherently unstable and did not survive burial, or the fragments, when found, were so friable that they disintegrated upon exposure to the atmosphere. Consequently the preservation of archaeological glass is of paramount importance in order to extend the knowledge of glass history and technology. As archaeology and its associated techniques develop further, more evidence will be obtainable from archaeological glass; therefore all fragments should be retained wherever possible, and some initially preserved untreated for laboratory analysis should this seem desirable.

Unweathered inorganic glasses are smooth, dense substances. Their surfaces are covered with layers of adsorbed water so that few materials will adhere satisfactorily to them. In addition, glass artefacts and windows are extremely fragile and difficult to handle. Consequently it was not until comparatively recently with the advent of clear, cold setting synthetic materials, with greater adhesive properties, that glass conservation began to be undertaken on any regular basis with consistent success. The earliest materials on record for use in the preservation of glass were animal glues and natural resins such as shellac, natural waxes and plaster of Paris ($CaSO_4.2H_2O$)

(Davison, 1984). These materials have subsequently deteriorated, becoming unsightly due to discoloration, or have caused the reconstruction to collapse as a result of their shrinkage. Wax and plaster of Paris used to replace missing areas of glass (i.e. used as gap fillers) could be cast into gaps in relatively thin layers, and were to a degree self-supporting and not unduly heavy. However, as they were opaque, they detracted from the appearance of the glass to which they had been applied.

Later, plastic materials such as poly(methyl methacrylate) in sheet form, for example Perspex (US Plexiglas), were applied to glass restoration. These materials possessed certain obvious advantages: they were transparent, did not discolour significantly and were resistant to embrittlement with age. Being rigid, they had to be cut to size, but being thermoplastic they could be softened by being heated, and shaped by pressing over prepared forms, although not over the glass itself because of the risk of cracking the glass. The edges were abraded and polished and the pieces were then secured to the glass with adhesive. The process was time-consuming, and the result sometimes inaccurate and not particularly attractive since coloured Perspex could not often be matched to the colour of the glass. Eventually it was found that more accurate and aesthetically pleasing results could be obtained by repairing and restoring glass with epoxy, polyester and acrylic resins whose properties enable them to be of use in glass conservation. Chief among these properties are clarity, transparency, and an improved ability to adhere to glass and to polymerize *in situ* at ambient temperature with little or no shrinkage occurring. However, since these materials have not been formulated with the special requirements of conservation in mind, they have to be fully tested by conservation scientists before being applied to glass.

Restoration implies replacement of missing areas of glass such as the addition of handles, rims etc. with another material. Restoration may be considered necessary to render the glass safe for handling, storage or display, or to further improve its appearance for display. Since restoration implies additions to the glass, these must only be made according to sound archaeological or art-historical evidence, to the design of comparable artefacts, or to descriptions in authentic documents. Before the decision to restore glass is taken, consideration must be given as to whether this is really desirable and opinions sought of those responsible for the glass, that is owners, custodians, trustees. Restoration of vessels will only be feasible if the glass body and its decoration are sound since the process will involve moulding and casting techniques. The present and future environments of the glass will also have a bearing on the feasibility of the work. Replacements of missing or decayed parts must integrate harmoniously with the whole, but must be distinguishable on close inspection so that restoration does not falsify the artistic or historic evidence. (Purists will argue that no additions should be made, or that additions will inevitably be misleading in some respect since the added material is modern.)

There is much room for controversy regarding the extent to which archaeological and decorative glass may be restored. In the case of architectural glass, however, the situation may be far more complicated for two reasons. Firstly, painted glass windows differ from most other ancient artefacts in continuing to be functional; they were intended to let light into a building and are generally still required to do so. Second, because the windows are still functional they, like the buildings of which they are a part, have suffered from previous, often misguided, restorations. Returning to the first point, the functional value of the window must be taken into consideration when restoration is being contemplated. Two quite different situations which illustrate the problems are the cleaning of badly crusted windows and the replacement of missing heads of figures in medieval windows.

Much early painted glass, especially of the twelfth and thirteenth centuries in Germany and Austria, but to some extent also in France and elsewhere, has the high-potash, high-lime composition which deteriorates with the formation of opaque crusts. As a result of this, some churches and cathedrals which have medieval painted glass windows are rather dark inside because the windows have ceased to be functional. There has been, and continues to be, controversy over whether such weathering crusts should be removed or not. On the one hand, removal exposes the original colour and brilliance of the windows; on the other, the dimensions of the glass are irretrievably altered. This same dilemma, of course, faces the conservator of archaeological glass.

Adaptive reuse is a term which recently has been introduced in connection with the conservation of historic buildings, and it is sometimes the only way that their historic and architectural values can be saved economically; as in the use of redundant churches as museums, homes, exhibition centres etc. The removal of painted glass windows from a redundant church, in order to replace plain glazing in another church, and the reuse of original leads and original pieces of coloured glass are examples of adaptive reuse.

In the field of glass vessel restoration, flakes of iridescence are occasionally found adhered to the surface of an artefact in order to create the impression of greater age; and fragments of glass from one (presumably irreparable) vessel were sometimes inserted in the missing areas of another to effect a repair.

It is often argued that the best action to take with important painted glass windows is to put them in museums and replace them in the cathedrals by good copies. This *may* be the only method of preventing, for example, a window from decaying irretrievably, *in situ*, and yet maintaining the architectural harmony of the place from which it was removed.

The Corning Museum of Glass in the United States of America has established a special collection of reproductions *and* forgeries (reproductions intended to deceive) of glass artefacts, in order that their methods of manufacture can be determined, with the aim of detecting forgeries in the future. Reproductions are valuable for educational and cultural purposes, and are often produced as souvenirs. However, they should be marked in some way to distinguish them as reproductions.

In summary, therefore, it can be seen that active conservation entails some form of alteration to the glass even if this is merely surface cleaning or consolidation. It is therefore important that certain conservation principles are adhered to in every case. These include the concept of reversibility of treatments and the maintenance of adequate records of treatment which should be placed in the archives of the institution in which or for which the conservation is undertaken. The record should contain a general description of the glass artefact before conservation, along with measured drawings and photographs. The conservation objective should be determined—for example stabilization, aesthetic improvement—and subsequent treatment carried out with respect for the integrity of the glass. Work should be kept to the minimum required to achieve the objective consistent with ensuring the safety of the glass. This point is particularly significant in the case of field conservation. No excavation should begin unless arrangements have already been made for conserving the finds and for storing the records. A report must eventually be published but this need rarely be as detailed as the record; the published reports should contain all the necessary references and detail conclusions, and should indicate where the unpublished records can be found. In the case of immovable objects such as mosaics and painted glass windows, it may be necessary to draw up a schedule of maintenance by instituting a regular (e.g. quinquennial) inspection, and to call for special inspections, for example by a curator after periods of high winds or heavy rain. Conservators must be ever aware that treatments must be adapted to meet the requirements of each individual artefact since no two artefacts have exactly the same problems. Bearing this point in mind it is essential that conservators keep abreast of developments in their field and that they maintain good working relationships with other conservators, art historians, technologists and scientists both within and outside their own institutions. In this way conservation experiences can be exchanged and advice sought or given when a new or difficult problem presents itself. Since conservators' *raison d'être* is the preservation of artefacts in their care there should be no room for professional jealousy or rivalry or for secrets. It is no weakness to ask for assistance nor to admit to a failed treatment, which may prevent a similar occurrence elsewhere. Conservators should not undertake complicated procedures for which they are not properly trained or in which they are not experienced, without obtaining competent advice.

1

The nature of glass

A knowledge of the nature of glass, that is to say its chemical structure and physical properties, is essential in order to understand the processes of deterioration which may make conservation a necessity. A wide variety of glass is known, both inorganic and organic (such as barley sugar), but this book is concerned only with *inorganic* glasses and then only with certain *silicate* glasses. Thus there are many important industrial glasses (such as borosilicates and calcium aluminates) which will not be discussed. The term *ancient glasses* is that used by Turner (1956a,b) to define glasses which were made before there was a reasonable understanding of glass compositions, that is, before the middle of the seventeenth century (see also Brill, 1962).

Before the discovery of how glass could be manufactured from its raw ingredients, man had used naturally occurring glass for many thousands of years. Natural *silica* (the basic ingredient of glass) is found in three *crystalline* forms: *quartz*, *tridymite* and *cristobalite*; and in its *amorphous* form, that is, glass, as *tektites*, *obsidian*, *pumice* and *lechatelierite*, as the result of melting at very high temperatures.

Tektites are thought to be of meteoric origin, as their form suggests that they have been heated by passage through the atmosphere while rotating. They are small, ellipsoidal, pear- or lens-shaped pieces of glass, which occur isolated on or just below the ground surface in many parts of the world, for example, Tasmania, Australia, Bohemia and South America. Their composition is similar to that of obsidian, but they have a higher proportion of iron and manganese (Cohen, 1963).

Sudden volcanic eruptions followed by rapid cooling cause highly siliceous lava to form natural glasses of various kinds. *Obsidian* is a glassy volcanic rock having the composition of a complex silicate of sodium, potassium, aluminium and calcium; it shows a typical conchoidal fracture. Obsidian occurs in all the volcanic areas of the world. Obsidian was, and

Figure 1.1 Since prehistoric times, obsidian has been used to fashion tools. This particularly fine arrowhead or spear of smoky-grey obsidian was formed by pressure-flaking. H 105 mm. Oregon, California. *Circa* AD 1000–1500. Corning Museum of Glass, New York.

still is, used by primitive peoples to fashion into tools and weapons by chipping in a manner similar to that used for making flint implements (*Figure 1.1*). *Pumice* is a natural foamed glass produced by gases being liberated from solution in the lava before and after rapid cooling. *Lechatelierite* is another naturally fused silica glass sometimes formed in desert areas by lightning striking a large mass of quartz sand. The heat produced may be sufficient to melt the sand and

1

entrapped air is suddenly expelled, resulting in the formation of irregular tubes (fulgurites) of crude silica, sometimes of considerable length. Lechatelierite has also been discovered in association with meteorite craters, for example at Winslow, Arizona (USA).

In order to understand the nature of man-made glass it is first necessary to define a number of terms used to describe vitreous materials, some of which have been used ambiguously or incorrectly (Bimson and Tite, 1987). There are four vitreous products: *glass*, *glaze*, *enamel* and *faience*, which consist of silica, alkali and small amounts of calcium. Glass, glaze and enamel always contain large quantities of sodium oxide, that is, *soda glass,* or another alkali, usually potassium oxide, that is, *potash glass*; whereas faience contains only very small amounts of alkali. In the manufacture of ancient vitreous materials there was an intermediate product, a powder (i.e. frit) which was the result of heating, raking and pulverizing (fritting) the raw materials before they were subsequently melted.

A glaze is a vitreous coating applied to a core or base of another material either to make it impermeable and/or for decorative effect. The glaze was sometimes mixed with the body-material before firing, but more often it was applied to the core after firing, after which the artefact was refired to form the glazed surface (*Figure 1.2*).

Faience is composed of fritted silica with about 2 per cent calcium oxide and about 0.25 per cent sodium oxide lightly held together with a binding medium such as water. The resulting paste (sometimes given the French nomenclature of *pâte de verre*) was shaped by hand or in an open mould, and then heated until the lime or soda had sufficiently reacted and fused to hold the silica particles firmly

Figure 1.3 Glazed siliceous ware. Broken *ushabti* figure, showing a white fritted silica interior in contrast to a copper-green coloured exterior of similar composition. Egypt. Dynastic period.

together. The body of the object thus formed could then be coated with a similarly produced glaze if required, usually coloured with copper and ranging in appearance from green to dark blue (Lewis 1953, 1954). (Strictly speaking the term faience is incorrect in this context since it is derived from the name of the Italian town of Faenza, and refers to the tin-glazed earthenware made there which was popular in sixteenth century France.) In order to avoid confusion, the vitreous material is sometimes referred to as *Egyptian faience* since it has been found to have been formed by nature on some Egyptian monuments, and because the material was in widespread use in Egypt for producing amulets and figurines. However, a more correct term for such objects would be *glazed siliceous wares* (*Figure 1.3*) (Tite *et al.*, 1983).

The pigment *Egyptian blue* was first used in Egypt during the third millennium BC, and during the subsequent 3000 years its use as a pigment in wall paintings and in the production of small objects such as beads, scarabs, inlays and statuettes spread throughout the Near East, the eastern Mediterranean, and to the limits of the Roman Empire (Chase, 1971). Chemical analysis of four pieces of Egyptian blue from Egypt and Mesopotamia has shown that the compositions were such that the material could contain a maximum of between 45 and 65 per cent of the *stoichiometric* crystalline Egyptian blue mineral ($CaO.CuO.4SiO_2 = CaCuSi_4O_{10}$), and that there

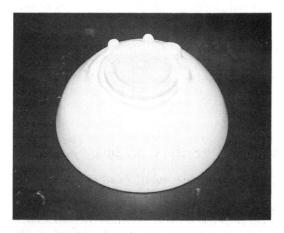

Figure 1.2 Glazed earthenware dish.

was an excess of between 30 and 50 per cent of silica present. The results were comparable with the compositions of other pieces of Egyptian blue which had been analysed, except that higher alkali contents up to 8 per cent have also been observed. X-ray diffraction analysis showed that, in addition to Egyptian blue, quartz and tridymite were the only crystalline phases present in significant quantities. Unlike glass, therefore, which has a variable composition, Egyptian blue is a specific crystalline compound: copper calcium tetrasilicate (Tite *et al.*, 1981).

A *true enamel* resembles a glaze in that it is also fused to a body of a different material, in this case a metallic surface (see *Figures 3.35–3.40*). However, the term enamel is also used to describe vitreous paint used to decorate ceramics and glass. It should be noted that not all vitreous substances applied to metals were true enamels, for many never actually fused to their metallic backing, and this is particularly true of many early so-called enamels. These were, instead, easily fusible glasses which were ground, applied to the metal and heated until they fused. Being basically either potash or soda glass, their contraction on cooling was such that, unless the backing was designed to prevent it, they would fall away from the metal. A true enamel in fact, must be so formulated as to satisfy two conditions: it must have a coefficient of expansion roughly equivalent to that of the metallic backing; and its melting point must be slightly lower than that of its backing to ensure fusion with it. For these reasons most true enamels were a lead-soda or lead-potash glass with or without colourants and opacifiers; the material being applied as a dried frit (powder) and fused in an enamelling oven. On cooling, the surface of the enamel was often polished flat with a fine abrasive.

True glass is a material normally formed from silica, alkali and lime when these ingredients have been heated to a temperature high enough to form them into a homogeneous substance ambiguously termed glass metal (Strauss, 1977). Chemically, glass, glaze and enamel can be identical, but there is one fundamental difference in their use which militates against this being so in antiquity: the coefficient of expansion of glass on cooling was unimportant since it was used alone to form the body of the artefact, whereas in a glaze or enamel any such difference between the vitreous coating and the body it covered would cause the former to craze or peel. As a result, the makers of glass tended to use a different set of criteria when formulating their material (albeit as a result of trial and error). For ease of working, a glass with a low melting point and one which remained plastic as long as possible was usually to be desired. Also, whereas in early glazing of earthenware, sufficient opacity to mask the body it covered was the normal aim, glassmakers soon began to produce translucent, and later transparent, glasses. The temperature to which the ingredients of a vitreous material were heated determined whether or not they actually melted to form a homogenous non-crystalline structure. In antiquity the glass batch was often insufficiently fired to melt all the silica completely, but was regarded as, and worked as, glass by its manufacturers, notably in the production of beads where transparency was of little value.

Under the microscope such a material shows *anisotropic* quartz grains embedded in an *isotropic* base. The quartz grains are *pleiochroic*, that is, display different colours according to the angles at which they are viewed under a polariscope, in contrast to true glass, glaze or enamel, which are isotropic, that is, which do not change colour with light.

Identification of the material from which ancient beads were made is very ill-defined. Beads made of quartz, calcite or fluorite are often described as glass beads, even though these materials can be distinguished from glass. For example, quartz has a greater hardness and is twice as refractive; calcite though twice as refractive has a hardness of only three compared with glass of six; and fluorite has a hardness of four, but unlike quartz and calcite, it is isotropic. However, its specific gravity is 3.15 compared with 2.4–2.6 for ancient glasses. The natural glass obsidian, consisting of layers of different density, has a hardness of 6.5, and a specific gravity of 2.32–2.38. It is clear that such simple characteristics as hardness, specific gravity and refractive index are very sensitive to composition changes, and should therefore only be used as a rough guide; in fact it is impossible to determine the exact composition of a glass except by chemical analysis (Forbes, 1957). The chemical compositions of ancient glasses are extremely complex for, in addition to the essential ingredients, the sand usually contained impurities in the form of extraneous elements such as iron, magnesium and aluminium oxides. Chemical analysis is not usually easy or convenient (being destructive), and is always expensive. However, much progress has been made during the last 10 years in understanding the general compositional categories of vitreous materials, and how they may be recognized.

Chemical structure and composition

Glass is popularly regarded as a hard, brittle, transparent substance, with a fairly high softening temperature, and as being relatively insoluble in water and other common solvents. From a scientific standpoint however, glass may be defined as the product of the fusion of inorganic materials which has been cooled to a hard condition without crystallization taking place. A clear understanding of the structure of glass has only been achieved in the last 45 years. Zachariasen (1932) was the first to make a significant advance, and it is as a result of his work, and that of subsequent researchers, that it is now realized that the atoms in glass are linked together by strong forces, essentially the same as those in crystals. Thus it is misleading to describe glass as a *supercooled liquid* (as has formerly been the case), at least when it is below the *transition temperature* (T_g).

Silica melts at 1720°C at which temperature (silica) glass is formed. However, in order to make a workable glass it is necessary to add various oxides which act as network modifiers, stabilizers and colourants; and which also have a marked effect upon the structure of the resulting product.

Devitrification

When molten glass is cooled, the randomly distributed molecules will endeavour to adopt a less random configuration, more like those of crystals. However, an alternative three-dimensional structure forms because the process is hindered by the viscosity of the glass and the presence of network modifiers. The silica networks which form at high temperatures cause the melt to have a high viscosity so that the molecules do not have time to form themselves into crystal lattices before cooling. However, when network modifiers are added, they have the effect of considerably lowering the viscosity (see *Figure 1.10*), and thus there are opportunities for new types of crystals to form (which contain atoms from the modifiers) provided the melt is held at the *liquidus temperature* long enough. It can therefore be important to cool the glass reasonably quickly. Thus a glass with a molar composition of $16Na_2O$, $10CaO$, $74SiO_2$ can form crystals of *devitrite* ($Na_2O.3CaO.6SiO_2$) which grow at a rate of $17\,\mu m\,min^{-1}$ at a temperature of 995°C (the optimum for growth of devitrite in that composition of glass, *Figure 1.4*). Devitrite does not occur in nature as a mineral.

Devitrification products are of interest to conservators for a number of reasons. First, ancient glasses have such complex compositions that devitrification occurs less easily than in simpler (modern) glasses, so that their presence may be an aid to authentication. Second, the opalizing agent in some glasses is sometimes a devitrification product (i.e. areas of microcrystals), which forms only when suitable heat treatment has been given to the glass. Third, it is unlikely that devitrification would occur either during *glass-melting*, or as a result of a conflagration in a building containing glass vessels or with glass windows (since the glass would not have had the necessary long thermal treatment). Thus the presence

Figure 1.4 The strength of glass can be much reduced by devitrification, i.e. the formation of small local crystals. Glass contracts during the process of crystallization and frequently cracks as a result. The cracks often spread from the crystalline into the glassy area. In this photograph showing devitrification in silica glass, the central area is crystalline and much cracked; the black areas in the corners are glassy material into which the cracks are penetrating.

of true devitrification products of glass found *in situ* on an excavation site is an indication that *glass-making* operations have been undertaken there (as opposed to *glass-melting*). For example, the 8.8 tonne block of glass found in a cave at Beth She'arim, south-east of Haifa in Israel, was evidently made *in situ* since, apart from its enormous size, it was found to be heavily devitrified and to have unmelted batch materials at its base. The slab has been extensively investigated (Brill and Wosinski, 1965), a core drill being used to obtain samples of the glass through the thickness of the block. The slab was found to contain several ancient internal fractures which had weathered surfaces. Analysis of the glass showed variations with depth, but a surprising result of the research was the determination of a high lime content (15.9 per cent), higher than in any other analysed ancient soda glass. This had resulted in a failure to produce a well-melted glass, and thus it is concluded that the lime addition was not deliberate. The glass slab was found to be heavily devitrified. As a result of X-ray diffraction, the main devitrification product was identified as *wollastonite*, and calcite was present in the weathering crust. Experimental melts were carried out which showed that a softening point of 691°C, a liquidus temperature (above which devitrification does not occur) of 1130°C and a melting temperature of 1200–1300°C (above the liquidus temperature) would have been required to produce a well-melted glass. Thus at 1100°C (below the liquidus temperature) there was extensive devitrification due to the high lime content.

Here it should be noted that Kny and Nauer (1977) have claimed that devitrification might occur in cold glasses although thousands of years may be required for this to occur. They also claim to have found some microcrystallites of the order of 20 nm in size in ancient glasses.

In the true devitrification discussed above the total chemical composition remains unaltered. The composition will change locally as crystals separate from the base glass, but no atoms are added or subtracted which were not already in the glass. Archaeologists and art historians have, however, used the term devitrification in quite a different connection to mean *loss of vitreous nature* (see *Figure 4.18*). In those cases the glass has *weathered*, due first to loss of alkali followed by loss of other constituents and finally the creation of a silica gel. In this case the chemical composition has changed. This use of the term devitrification, therefore, is ambiguous, especially as some forms of weathering can take place without any apparent loss of vitreous nature. For example, the surfaces of all ancient glasses are de-alkalized and can be said to consist of a *hydrogen glass* instead of the usual *alkali glass* yet their surfaces can still remain shiny and vitreous although marked chemical changes have taken place. It is therefore recommended that the term devitrification should in future be restricted to the description of the formation of crystals from the melt (Newton and Werner, 1974).

Network formers

Much research has been undertaken on the properties which molecules must possess before they can combine to form the extensive three-dimensional network of glasses. The concept of network-forming oxides is illustrated in *Figures 1.5* and *1.6*. *Figure 1.5* shows the regular structure of an imaginary two-dimensional crystalline material; within the broken line there are sixteen black dots (representing atoms of type A) and twenty-four open circles (representing atoms of type O); hence the imaginary material has the composition (A_2O_3) and its regular structure shows that it is crystalline.

The network former in ancient glasses is silica (SiO_2). Silicon and oxygen in crystalline silica are

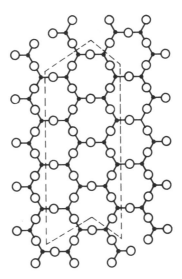

Figure 1.5 Schematic two-dimensional representation of the structure of an imaginary crystalline compound A_2O_3. After Zachariasen (1932).

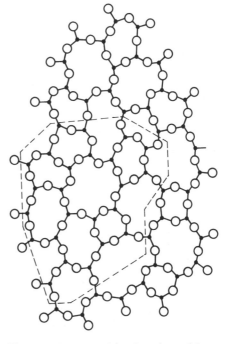

Figure 1.6 Structure of the glassy form of the compound in *Figure 1.5*. After Zachariasen (1932).

arranged in a definite pattern, the units of which are repeated at regular intervals forming a three-dimensional network consisting of tetrahedra with a silicon atom at the centre and an oxygen atom at each corner, two oxygen atoms being shared by each of the adjacent tetrahedra. Other network formers are the oxides of boron (B_2O_3), lead (PbO) and phosphorus (P_2O_5); the latter can be encountered in quantities up to about 5 per cent in medieval glasses made with potassium oxide. Thus the lattice structure is said not to have *long-range order* (Weyl and Marboe, 1967; Goodman, 1987).

If the imaginary crystalline material A_2O_3 shown in *Figure 1.5* is cooled quickly from the molten state the resultant solid might have the structure shown in *Figure 1.6*. Here the broken line encloses twenty-four black dots and thirty-six open circles and hence the composition is again A_2O_3 but the structure is irregular and non-crystalline, representing the amorphous, glassy or vitreous state of the same compound. The amorphous structure occupies a greater volume than the crystalline one, and hence the crystal is denser than the glass.

Network modifiers

Figure 1.7 shows a structure which is nearer to that of a silicate glass. It is again a simplified two-dimensional diagram, but the key mentions the term *ion*. Ions are simply atoms which have been given an electrical charge by adding or subtracting one or more electrons; *cations* have a positive charge because they have lost electrons and *anions* have a negative charge because they have gained electrons.

The network-forming atoms are represented by black dots within shaded triangles, and each is accompanied by three oxygen atoms, which can be of two kinds. There are *bridging oxygen ions* (shown by open circles) which are shared between two triangles thus joining them together and forming part of the network. There are also *non-bridging oxygen ions* (shown by circles with a central dot) which belong to only one triangle; each of these bears a negative charge which is neutralized by a positive charge on one of the cross-hatched circles (cations).

A small amount of crystalline material can be seen at (A) in *Figure 1.7* where four triangles are joined together, but at all other points the triangles form irregular chains enclosing relatively large spaces (and hence the density of the glass is less than that of the crystalline form). The spaces in the network have been created by the network modifiers (the cross-hatched circles). These modifying ions, which bear one or more positive electrical charges (because they have lost electrons to the non-bridging oxygen ions), can be considered as being held more or less loosely in these enlarged spaces by those electrical charges. First, consider the monovalent cations which bear single positive charges. They are the alkali metal ions such as sodium (Na^+) or potassium (K^+), two of which bring with them one extra oxygen ion when they are added to the glass as *soda* (sodium oxide, Na_2O) or *potash* (potassium oxide, K_2O). Because these cations bear only a single positive charge they can move from one space in the network to another. Thus, when an electric field is applied to the glass they carry the electric current, or when the glass is placed in water they can move right out of the glass into the water (being replaced by hydrogen ions, H^+, from the water). One disadvantage of this behaviour of the alkali ions is that the glass is made less durable, but the great advantage is that its melting point is lowered because the network is more open (less tightly bound). These monovalent cations are represented in *Figure 1.7* by the smaller cross-hatched circles.

The two larger cross-hatched circles are the *divalent alkaline earth* ions and they bear a double positive charge. Each of these brings one extra oxygen ion when they are added to the glass as *lime* (calcium oxide, CaO) or *magnesia* (magnesium oxide, MgO). The double electrical charge on these divalent ions makes it much harder for them to move from one space to the next one and thus they play little or no part in carrying an electric current through the glass under ordinary conditions. Similarly, they neutralize the negative charges on *two* non-bridging oxygen ions and thus tend to form a new link in the network. They can be regarded as offsetting the reduction in durability produced by the alkali ions.

At this point it should be remarked that *Figure 1.7* is slightly misleading because it makes no obvious distinction between the effects of monovalent and divalent ions; all the non-bridging oxygen ions seem

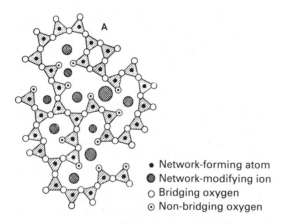

● Network-forming atom
◕ Network-modifying ion
○ Bridging oxygen
⊙ Non-bridging oxygen

Figure 1.7 Schematic two-dimensional representation of glass, according to Zachariasen's theory. Philips Technical Review.

to be similar whereas it is now known that, especially in poorly durable glasses, they are *not* equivalent.

Stevels (1948, 1960) devised a formula (expressed by a '*Y* factor'), calculated from the proportion of non-bridging oxygen ions in the glass, which was intended to represent the *total effect* of the modifying ions. It exhibits a close relationship with various physical properties of the glass, such as melting temperature, coefficient of thermal expansion etc., but these relationships seem to apply only to *durable* glasses. Taking *Figure 1.7* and considering only the addition of alkali ions, it can be shown that in a glass with equal numbers of network molecules and alkali molecules, such as the simple glass $Na_2O.SiO_2$, the network would disintegrate into short SiO_2 chains, and that *that* type of glass is actually soluble in water. Stevels (1960) points out that, as glasses are made more and more complex and modifier ions of different sizes and with different electrical charges on them are introduced, it is possible to tolerate a greater reduction in the proportion of silica without disintegration of the structure. A full appreciation of this situation can be obtained only when the compositions of the glasses are expressed on a molar basis and not on a weight basis, especially when very heavy materials such as lead are present in the glass.

Phase separation

It has become increasingly evident that, despite the essentially homogeneous nature of glasses, there may be minute areas, perhaps only 100 nm (0.1 μm) in diameter, where the glass is not homogeneous and *phase separation* has occurred. The regions which have separated possess a different chemical composition from that of the rest of the glass (the *continuous phase*) (Uhlmann and Kolbeck, 1976; Goodman, 1987).

It is now being realized that phase separation can occur in many ancient glasses, especially when magnesia is present. This can have a profound effect on the properties of the glasses, especially their durability, because the separated phase might be either more durable or less durable than the continuous phase. It must be emphasized that these phase-separated areas may be so small that they do not scatter visible light and hence the glass may be quite transparent. The amount of phase separation can be determined by using an *electron microscope*, and some of the perplexing behaviour encountered with historical glasses may be understood when more research has been carried out on them.

Colouring oxides

The coloured effects in ancient glasses were produced in three ways. First, by the presence of relatively small amounts of the oxides of transition metals such as cobalt (Co), copper (Cu), iron (Fe), nickel (Ni),

manganese (Mn) etc., which go into solution in the silicate network and form part of it in the way that other multivalent cations do. Second, by the development of colloidal dispersions of insoluble particles such as those in silver stains or in copper and gold ruby glasses. Third, opal and translucent effects were produced by the introduction of opalizing agents. There is much confusion about the production of colours in ancient glasses, since their compositions are so much more complex than modern glasses. The production of colours in glass depends not only upon the inclusion of a specific metal oxide (such as cobalt to produce blue glass), but also upon the presence of other oxides in the batch, and the temperature and state of oxidation or reduction in the kiln.

State of oxidation

In the traditional sense, a metal is *oxidized* when it combines with oxygen to form an oxide, and the oxide becomes *reduced* when it loses its oxygen (for example, when it is heated in charcoal) and the metal is reformed. The position is slightly more complicated when there is more than one *state of oxidation*. For example, iron (Fe) becomes oxidized when ferrous oxide (FeO) is formed and produces a blue colour in the glass (Fe^{2+} ions are present); but it becomes further oxidized when more oxygen is added to form ferric oxide (Fe_2O_3), which imparts a brown or yellow colour to the glass (due to the Fe^{3+} ions present). However, the situation is rarely simple; usually mixtures of FeO and Fe_2O_3 are present which produce glasses of varying shades of green.

When a chemical analysis of glass is undertaken it is customary to quote the amount of iron oxide as Fe_2O_3, but this does not imply that all of the iron present is in the fully oxidized state. (Older sources often reported the iron content as FeO, but, there again, there was no implication that the iron was all in its reduced form.) It *is* possible to determine the $FeO:Fe_2O_3$ ratio, but this is usually for purposes of research rather than as part of a routine analysis.

The example of FeO and Fe_2O_3 is a particularly striking one, but other colouring oxides can exist in more than one state of oxidation, and hence impart different colours to the glass. In addition, there can be complications due to the presence of other materials. For example, Fe_2O_3 can be colourless (instead of yellow) when fluorides and phosphates are also present; the colours produced by the addition of copper (blue, green or red) depend on other oxides present; and cobalt can produce red or green (instead of blue) in the presence of magnesium or zinc. Yet other complications can be caused by the basicity of the glass, and by the temperature of the melting operation.

The modern approach is to regard the *oxidation* process as one where an atom loses an electron; similarly *reduction* occurs when an atom gains an electron and the concept is thus widened to include some agents other than oxygen. The concept of adding or subtracting electrons helps, for example, in the understanding of the production of colours in the medieval forest glasses, all of which contain both manganese and iron, and which are predominantly green in colour.

Consider the two *reversible* reactions stated in equations 1.1 and 1.2, where e^- represents an electron. In equation 1.1 the forward arrow shows that an electron is lost when Fe^{2+} is converted to Fe^{3+}, and the reverse arrow shows that the addition of an electron to Fe^{3+} converts it to Fe^{2+}:

$$Fe^{2+} \rightleftharpoons Fe^{3+} + e^- \tag{1.1}$$

$$Mn^{3+} + e^- \rightleftharpoons Mn^{2+} \tag{1.2}$$

The combined effect of equations 1.1 and 1.2 is equation 1.3, which shows that there is an equilibrium between the different states of oxidation of the manganese and the iron:

$$Fe^{2+} + Mn^{3+} \rightleftharpoons Fe^{3+} + Mn^{2+} \tag{1.3}$$

But both Fe^{3+} and Mn^{2+} are the more stable states, and hence the equilibrium tends to move to the right. Thus when the conditions *during melting* of the glass are fully reducing (the equilibrium has been forced to the left, for example, by the conditions in the furnace atmosphere) the iron contributes a bright blue colour due to the Fe^{2+} ions (corresponding to FeO) and the manganese is in the colourless form so that a blue glass is obtained. When the conditions are fully oxidizing (the equilibrium has been moved towards the right by adding oxidizing agents or by prolonging the melting time) the iron contributes a brownish colour and the manganese contributes a purple colour, so that the glass appears brownish-violet. When conditions are intermediate all sorts of colours are obtainable, such as green, yellow, pink etc., *including a colourless* glass when the purple from the manganese just compensates for the yellow from the iron. In such a case, provided there is not too much manganese, it acts as a *decolorizer*.

These conditions have been studied by Sellner (1977) and Sellner *et al.* (1979) who produced a forest-type glass in which the colouring agents were only manganese (1.7 per cent MnO) and iron (0.7 per cent Fe_2O_3). A variety of colours was obtained from bright blue when the furnace atmosphere was fully reducing (for example, when there was unburnt fuel present, and only a very low partial pressure of oxygen in the waste gases) through green and yellow to brownish purple when the furnace atmosphere was fully oxidizing (fully burnt fuel, and plenty of oxygen in the waste gases).

Sellner (1977) and Sellner *et al.* (1979) also examined samples of glass excavated from two seventeenth-century glassworks sites, one at Glasborn/Spessart and the other at Hilsborn/Grünenplan. The compositions were similar but the former had produced predominantly green glass and the latter produced mainly yellowish or brownish-purple glass. Measurements of *electron spin resonance* showed that the green glass had been produced under reducing conditions whereas the melting process at Hilsborn had led to oxidizing conditions. Thus the colour of the glass had been controlled by the melting conditions and not by the deliberate additions of manganese or iron. Sayre (1963) claims that any manganese present in significant amounts was always added deliberately, but this concept has been challenged by Geilmann and Bruckbauer (1954), Brill (1970d) and Newton (1978a, 1985b), who, as the result of melting various mixtures of sand and beechwood ash, found that the resultant glass could vary from bluish-green through yellowish- to reddish-violet, depending on the furnace conditions. See also Schofield *et al.*, 1995.

At this point it should be mentioned that there has been much confusion in the literature when amber (or yellow) glasses have been discussed. These colours are often described as *carbon–sulphur ambers*, whereas nearly the same colour can be obtained, as described above, by using iron and manganese and having the correct state of oxidation. Both types of amber colour can be found in ancient glasses; an accurate method of distinguishing between them is to determine the *optical absorption spectra*; the iron–manganese ambers have absorption bands at 380 and 500 nm, whereas the carbon–sulphur ambers have absorption bands at 430 and 1050 nm. In the absence of such a test being undertaken it is better to describe the glasses simply as yellow or amber.

In addition, the occurrence of substantial amounts of both copper and tin in the glass strongly suggest that slag from bronze founding (or an oxidation product of bronze) has been added to the glass. Some of the green medieval glass at York Minster contains substantial amounts of copper and zinc which suggests that brass filings, rather than copper itself, might have been added to the glass to produce the green colour. However, the presence of noticeable amounts of certain elements need not necessarily indicate that some deliberate action had been taken to incorporate them in those amounts, although the circumstance should be investigated. For example, *Figure 1.8* shows remarkable differences in the potash and magnesia contents of Egyptian Islamic glass weights manufactured before, or after, AD 845. Brill (1970d) has suggested that there was no deliberate addition of these materials because the pre-AD 845 low-potash, low-magnesia glasses could have been made with alkali obtained from natron lakes whereas

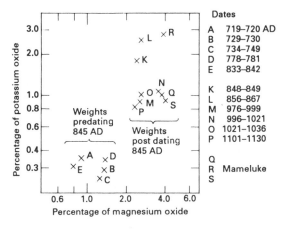

Figure 1.8 Chronological division of Egyptian Islamic glass weights into high- and low-magnesium types. From Sayre (1965).

the later higher potash, higher magnesia glasses could have been made with alkali obtained from the ashes of some maritime or desert plant. Thus there may have been a deliberate change from natron to plant ash but *not* a deliberate change in the potash and magnesia content. This problem is also discussed by Sayre (1965) and Newton (1985b). There are still many problems to be solved before a final understanding is gained about the sources of colouring agents for ancient glasses, and whether or not they were incorporated with conscious intent. The least ambiguous situation exists when contemporary references to glass-making are available and when ancient glasses can be analysed. The final stage of

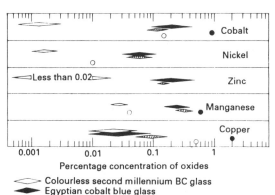

Figure 1.9 Colour element patterns in cobalt-blue glasses dating from the second millennium BC. From Sayre (1965).

research may be the melting of glasses according to the ancient instructions and obtaining the correct colour (Brill, 1963, 1965).

Despite the problems, discussed above, of characterizing the colours produced in the glass by various agents, there are a few cases where there are such differences in the colouring power of the oxides that some comment could be helpful. For example, as shown in *Figure 1.9*, cobalt is such a strong colouring oxide that only about 0.1 per cent is required to produce a blue glass and 0.025 per cent will produce a slight blue colour. On the other hand it requires some 2–3 per cent of the fully oxidized copper oxide (CuO) before a good copper-blue or copper-green colour is produced; whereas 0.5 to 1 per cent of the fully reduced iron oxide (FeO) can give a good iron-blue colour.

There seems to be a great deal of misunderstanding about the action of decolorizers in glass. If iron is the *only* colouring oxide present it will produce a blue colour when it is present in the reduced form, but a yellow colour of much lower intensity is produced when the iron is oxidized. As can be seen from equation 1.3, the addition of manganese oxide will oxidize the iron to the yellow ferric state, and if there is a very slight excess of manganese the pale purple colour which develops will tend to neutralize the yellow to produce grey. Thus, for at least the last few centuries, manganese has been deliberately employed as a decolorizer, *but it has its effect only on the iron* and not on the other colouring oxides which were used in ancient glasses. There are also other oxidizing agents, such as the pentoxides of arsenic (As_2O_5) and antimony (Sb_2O_5) which have an analogous effect on the iron except that they do not neutralize the yellow colour. It is on these grounds that the presence of manganese or antimony in a glass has been described as its deliberate addition as a decolorizer, but small amounts of these elements could have been added by choosing plant ash from particular sites (Newton, 1985b).

Dispersed metal colourants

The colouring effects of the metal oxides described above are produced because they *dissolve* in the glass and, in fact, the colours are not dissimilar to those produced when soluble compounds of those metals are dissolved in water; for example, copper sulphate produces a rich blue colour. Other colouring effects can be produced when a metal does not dissolve, but when it is dispersed as minute particles (i.e. as a *colloid*) in the glass, the colouring depending upon the size of the colloidal dispersion. Certain red, orange and yellow colours were produced in glass by dispersing silver, gold or copper metals. The

Lycurgus Cup, made in the fourth century AD, is a fine example of this technique (Brill, 1965; Chirnside and Proffitt, 1965). Viewed in reflected light it appears opaque green, and in transmitted light as transparent wine red. In general composition, the Cup is similar to modern soda-lime glasses, but the silver and gold content of the glass is responsible for the *dichroic* effect (though manganese may contribute partly to the reddish colour).

Dispersed metal colours are conveniently known as *silver stain yellow* or *gold* or *copper rubies*. Their technology is quite complicated because it is usually necessary to reheat the glass in order to cause the colour to appear, or *strike*. It is also often necessary to have other oxides present, such as those of lead or tin, for full development of the colour. A brief description of the composition of gold and copper ruby glasses is given below. The decorative technique of silver staining will be discussed in Chapter 3.

Gold ruby glasses

Gold ruby glasses have been discussed in detail by Weyl (1951). Gold has probably been employed to make ruby glass since the sixteenth century, but its use is certain from the seventeenth century when Johann Kunckel used *Purple of Cassius* (a purple pigment consisting of a mixture of colloidal gold and stannic acid) for making gold ruby glass. Kunckel evidently did not master all the difficulties involved in developing the full colour because only a small proportion of the melts seem to have been satisfactory. After Kunckel's death in 1705, the manufacture of ruby glass continued in Bohemia, certainly until the eighteenth century (Charleston, 1977b). There has recently been a resurgence of interest in Kunckel's work since the excavation of the site of his glassworks on Pfauen Island near Potsdam in East Germany (Schulze, 1977). Neutron activation tests on the glass samples recovered showed that the gold content was directly related to the depth of colour; the faintly coloured samples contained 0.025 to 0.03 per cent gold, and the more strongly coloured glass contained 0.06 to 0.07 per cent gold, which also confirmed the data in *Ars Vitrarii Experimentalis* (Kunckel, 1679). In passing it should be remarked that tales of the production of gold ruby glass by throwing gold coins into the batch have been investigated (Newton, 1970) and it seems that the practice certainly took place but it must have been for esoteric reasons (other than those of glass technology), because metallic gold does not produce the ruby colour and the manufacturers had already taken care to have introduced sufficient gold into the crucible in the form of a solution in *aqua regia* (a mixture of concentrated nitric and hydrochloric acids which will dissolve gold) (Frank, 1984).

Copper ruby glasses

Copper ruby glasses have also been described in detail by Weyl (1951), and have certainly been known since at least the twelfth century because copper is responsible for the red colour in the windows of that date. One problem in their use was that the colour was particularly intense, and a piece of glass only 3 mm thick (about the thinnest which could be used in a window) would have appeared black. In the twelfth and thirteenth centuries satisfactory ruby window glass was made because the colour was distributed in a multitude of very thin layers. It is not known how this effect was obtained, and many hypotheses have been advanced, but Cable (1979) believed that it was the accidental result of trying to obtain a very 'dilute' colour, and the inhomogeneities in its distribution influenced the 'striking' characteristics so that some layers became red and others did not.

From the fourteenth century onwards, quite a different technique was used for producing red window glass, that of *flashing* a thin red layer (0.5 mm or less) onto a colourless base glass.

Haematinum (or *haematinon*) is an opaque blood-red glass in which under magnification cuprous oxide crystals become visible against a colourless background. It was made in the early Egyptian period and in the Roman period, and was used in enamels and mosaics in addition to glass vessels. *Aventurine* is transparent glass flecked through with sparkling metal particles, similar in appearance to brownish aventurine quartz. The earliest form, of brownish colour flecked with copper (called gold aventurine), was first recorded in the seventeenth century and attributed to a glass-making family in Murano, Italy.

Before leaving the subject of transparent red glasses, some reference should be made to the patent taken out by a certain Oppenheim (Opnaim) in 1755, and for a second specification in 1770. The glass contained some 30 per cent of lead oxide and the chemically unspecified materials *braun stein* and *Dutch gold*. There are thus many technical difficulties in determining what type of red glass was manufactured by Oppenheim in what was in any case a relatively brief commercial enterprise (Engle, 1974b).

Opalizing agents

Opacity can be produced in glass by incorporating masses of tiny bubbles or other dispersed materials, but the majority of opal glasses are produced by the use of relatively few *opalizing agents* which form microcrystalline areas within the glass. These have been extensively studied by Turner (1957a,b, 1959), Rooksby (1959, 1962, 1964) and by Turner and Rooksby (1959, 1961). As a result of the research it

Table 1.1 Opacifying agents in glass, 1450 BC to AD 1961 (from Bimson and Werner, 1967)

Period	Type of glass	Opacifying agent	Number of specimens
1450 BC to fourth century AD	Opaque white and blue	$Ca_2Sb_2O_7$ (occasionally $CaSb_2O_6$)	15
	Opaque yellow	Cubic $Pb_2Sb_2O_7$	10
	Opaque red	Cu_2O	
		Cu_2O+Cu } or Cu	8
Fifth century AD to seventeenth century AD	Opaque white and blue	SnO_2 usually	10
		$3Ca_3(PO_4)_2 . CaF_3$ occasionally	4
	Opaque yellow and green	Cubic Pb_5SnO_4	17
	Opaque red	Cu	
		$Cu+Cu_2O$ rarely }	7
		$Cu+SnO_2$ sometimes	
Eighteenth century AD to present day	Opaque white	$3Pb_2(AsO_4)_2 . PbO$ (apatite-type structure)	4
		CaF or CaF_3+NaF	Many
		$(Na_2Ca)_2Sb_2O_6F$	1

was found that different opalizing agents were used in three distinct eras. *Table 1.1* shows that Roman and pre-Roman white opal glasses (blue if cobalt was present) contained calcium antimonate, whereas by the fifth century AD the opacifier in common use was tin oxide or, occasionally, calcium fluorphosphate. The use of tin oxide continued until the eighteenth century when it was replaced by calcium fluoride or lead arsenate.

A similar situation existed with yellow opaque glasses, which contained lead antimonate in the early period, and a lead–tin oxide later on. It should however be noted that Bimson and Werner (1967) have subsequently found cubic lead–tin oxide as the yellow opacifier in the first century AD gaming pieces from Welwyn Garden City, Hertfordshire. Thus the date for the use of this material should be regarded as being much earlier than at first supposed. The opaque red glasses (haematinum or aventurine) contain copper and cuprous oxide (Cu_2O, which is always red), and as stated by Weyl (1951) they also contain tin or lead.

Lead glasses

Although lead oxide seems to have been an unintentional ingredient of glass until Roman times, glasses containing lead were known in Mesopotamia, and probably existed as early as the second millennium BC, since lead was one of the ingredients mentioned in cuneiform glass recipes of that date. Analysis of a cake of red glass dating from the sixth century BC showed that it contained 22.8 per cent

PbO by weight. This figure gives the impression that one-quarter of the glass composition was lead oxide, but since lead is a very heavy element, the position is quite different when the glass composition is calculated on a molar percentage basis, the lead oxide content then being only 9.3 per cent. Thus 9.3 per cent of the molecules in the glass are lead oxide, and lead glasses can therefore be regarded as silicate glasses containing some 10 per cent of divalent network-modifying oxide.

A significant step in the production of lead glass was the publication in 1612 of Antonio Neri's *L'Arte Vetraria*, the fourth book of which was completely devoted to a discussion of various lead glasses and their use for counterfeiting precious stones, and for making high-quality glassware. *L'Arte Vetraria* was translated into English by Merrett in 1662 and would surely have been known to Ravenscroft who, in 1675–76, used lead as an ingredient in ordinary crystal glass. Ravenscroft attempted to obtain a more colourless glass firstly by using pure materials, but the vessels tended to crizzle and weep as a result of a deficiency of lime. However, Ravenscroft was eventually successful in producing glass which was aesthetically highly desirable by adding as much as 30 per cent lead oxide to the batch. The glass produced was free from seed because lead glass is about 100 times more fluid than soda–lime–silica glass at a given temperature; it was bright because of its high refractive index; it sparkled when decoratively cut because of its high optical dispersivity; and it had a clear ring when struck because alkali (potash) ions are bound more tightly in the lead–silicate network than in soda–lime glass and absorb less energy when in vibration.

Physical properties of glass

As explained at the beginning of this chapter, crystalline materials have a definable structure, whereas amorphous materials do not. It follows, therefore, that only somewhat general statements can be made about many of the physical properties of glass. When hot, it is ductile, plastic and malleable. In the molten state, glass can be blown, moulded, drawn, pressed and welded to itself. When cold, glass is transparent, translucent or opaque. It is brittle and breaks with a characteristic conchoidal fracture. It is liable to crack under a sudden change of temperature. When considering the physical properties of any particular piece of glass its *thermal history* has to be taken into account; in other words, glass which has been cooled suddenly has a built-in memory of what its structure was like at the moment before it was cooled (Hall and Leaver, 1961).

Consider a viscous glass melt which is cooled very slowly from a temperature T_1 to a lower temperature T_2. The energy available for molecular movements is gradually reduced but the network has enough time to readjust itself and become more compact. (In some cases actual crystals of various silicates may form and this process is then called *devitrification*.) In any event, the spaces in the network will tend to close up and the glass at temperature T_2 will be *denser* than at T_1; the glass has shrunk into a smaller volume by a process which is different from that of thermal expansion (contraction).

Now consider the same glass which is cooled *suddenly* from T_1 to T_2. The viscous glass does not have time for the network to become more compact and the glass at T_2 has the lower density which is characteristic of T_1; hence T_1 is known as its *fictive temperature*. This is the key to the slight uncertainty which must be expected when attempts are made to define precisely the properties of glass at a particular temperature.

Viscosity

Glass is generally regarded as being a rigid material, and as such it is in constant use in the form of windows and containers etc. However, whilst it is rigid at ordinary (low) temperatures, glass becomes plastic at high temperatures (about 900°C) when, as a viscous liquid, it can be worked in a variety of ways into a great many forms. The viscosity of a liquid is a measure of its resistance to flow. Glasses are much more viscous than other ordinary liquids, and a characteristic of its viscosity is the tremendous range of values it can have, depending on the composition of the glass and the temperature at which the viscosity is measured. *Figure 1.10* shows a plot of the logarithm of viscosity against temperature, where each division represents a 100-fold change in viscosity, and the full extent of the scale represents a change of 10^{20}, or one hundred, million, million, million times. Water is shown as having a value of $1 \times 10^{-3}\,\mathrm{N\,s\,m^{-2}}$ and treacle in a warm room as having a value of $1\,\mathrm{N\,s\,m^{-2}}$. An increase, compared with treacle, of ten times ($10\,\mathrm{N\,s\,m^{-2}}$) represents the most fluid glasses at their melting temperatures (e.g. *Figure 1.10*, point F, a high lead glass at 1200°C). In the manufacture of glass articles, glass is gathered at a viscosity of 40 to $100\,\mathrm{N\,s\,m^{-2}}$.

The viscosity changes so rapidly that a number of special terms are required to describe the various stages. For example, *Figure 1.10* shows the *working point* at $10^3\,\mathrm{N\,s\,m^{-2}}$; the *softening point* occurs at $6 \times 10^6\,\mathrm{N\,s\,m^{-2}}$; the *annealing point* is at 5×10^{12}; and the *strain point* is at 5×10^{13}. There is also a *transformation point* which is found between 10^{12} and $10^{16}\,\mathrm{N\,s\,m^{-2}}$. The working range is the difference in temperature between the working point and the softening point. From *Figure 1.10* it can be seen that glass C has a working range of 370°C, whereas glass F has only about 60 per cent of that working range

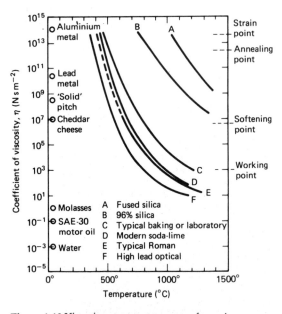

Figure 1.10 Viscosity–temperature curves for various types of glasses. After Brill (1962). The measurements in poise have not been converted to SI units (1 poise = $0.1\,\mathrm{N\,s\,m^{-2}}$), since it is generally felt that the poise will continue in common usage.

(220°C), but this is in the temperature range 580–800°C and glass F will cool more slowly than glass C, where the temperature range is 830–1220°C. Thus glass C has a wider temperature range in which it can be manipulated but it also loses heat more rapidly and it may have to be reheated in the furnace more frequently.

Glass C types could not have been in use before about AD 1850 since its working point (1200°C) could not have been attained in primitive furnaces. Modern technologists therefore describe it as a *hard* glass because it requires a higher temperature for working. At the other extreme, fused silica (line A), even at 1400°C, is more viscous than solid pitch at room temperature, and it is evident why fluxes (network modifiers) must be added to reduce the viscosity to a value of $1000\,\mathrm{N\,s\,m^{-2}}$ at 1000°C, the temperature attainable in furnaces of the second millennium BC.

It has recently been suggested (Toner, 1985) that the viscosity of glass can be explained by the theories of hydrodynamics; these are based on the interaction of thermally excited sound waves within fluids. Further information is awaited on this theory.

Plastic flow at room temperature

The annealing process (controlled cooling of glass to relieve stress) is actually an example of slow plastic flow of glass when its viscosity is in the range 10^{11} to $10^{13}\,\mathrm{N\,s\,m^{-2}}$, corresponding to temperatures in the region of 500°C (*Figure 1.10*). Because the viscosity increases continuously with decreasing temperature, without the discontinuity at the melting point which occurs in crystalline solids, it has been argued that cold glass should exhibit gradual plastic flow over very long periods of time. However, demonstrations to prove this have usually involved a misunderstanding of the actual mechanism involved, or misinterpretation of the evidence. Thus the various phenomena which have been claimed to demonstrate plastic flow in cold glass must be scrutinized carefully. For example, lengths of glass tubing which have been stored horizontally, supported by brackets for many years, are said to develop a curvature due to plastic flow. The more likely explanation is a statistical one since the first users of each new consignment of tubing would choose the straightest pieces, always leaving the most curved ones until last. It has also been claimed that medieval window glass is thicker at the bottom of the panes, again due to plastic flow, but there is no evidence for this and in fact medieval glass was often so irregular in thickness that there can be no reliable evidence that its thickness has changed. However, it can be demonstrated that plastic flow *can* occur in glass at room temperature, *provided* that the applied force is great enough. The Vickers' Diamond Pyramid Hardness Test produces indentations in a cold glass which cause the displaced glass to bulge upwards (Ainsworth, 1954). Douglas (1958) studied this phenomenon mathematically and has shown that irreversible flow can be expected to occur only when the applied force is at least 10 per cent of the *theoretical* breaking strength of the glass. As the *practical* breaking strength of commercial glasses is usually only about one-hundredth of the theoretical breaking strength it is evident that plastic flow can occur at room temperature only under rather exceptional circumstances (Peyches, 1952; Preston, 1973).

Frozen strains

When a sheet of glass is freshly made, the outside surfaces cool very rapidly and become stiff long before the inside cools and contracts. The thicker the glass, the greater the difference in cooling rate between the surfaces. The internal contraction places the surfaces in compression, and the interior in tension, thus resulting in an unstable condition. Therefore, unless glass is cooled gradually under controlled conditions (i.e. annealed), it will contain internal stress (strain) which may cause it to shatter spontaneously (Lillie, 1936; Hall and Leaver, 1961).

An extreme case of frozen strains in glass is that of the so-called *Prince Rupert's Drops* (*Lacrymae Batavicae*, *Larmes de Verre* or *Tears Glass*) (*Figure 1.11*). These tadpole-shaped pieces of glass are made by dropping a gather of molten glass into cold water. They were named after Prince Rupert, a nephew of Charles I of England, who produced the glass drops in 1661. The sudden chilling of the glass by the water freezes the outside while the fluid interior contracts so strongly that a hollow containing a vacuum

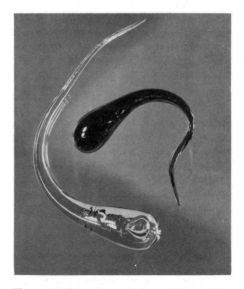

Figure 1.11 Prince Rupert's drops. Somerset County Museum.

appears in the centre. This internal contraction places the surface in great compression, so much so that the bulbous head can be struck with a hammer without causing rupture. However, if the thin tail is broken, its surface is scratched, or even if sand is dropped on it, the entire object disintegrates into fine particles because the neutral zone (between the compressive forces in the surface and the tension in the interior) is near the surface in the thin region of the tail. An account of the history of the drops is given by Moody (1980).

Thermal expansion

The majority of materials expand when they are heated and contract again when cooled. Over a wide range of temperatures the change in volume, termed the coefficient of volume expansion (CVE), is regular. However, for most practical purposes it is the *coefficient of linear expansion* which is important, that is the increase in length per unit length caused by a unit rise in temperature. Glasses have values of linear expansion coefficient in the range 5.0 to 10 $\times$ 10^{-6} per °C; the value for a particular glass can be measured by various techniques, or calculated from the chemical composition of the glass in question.

The fact that glasses have a rather lower linear expansion compared with other materials has been put to good use in the manufacture of decorative glassware. For example, one technique of decorating seventeenth-century Venetian *cristallo* was to plunge the hot vessel momentarily into cold water thus cracking the glass surface without causing the destruction of the vessel itself. Such a process would not have been possible if glass had a large coefficient of linear expansion. The majority of the constituents of a glass have a coefficient of less than 1.7×10^{-7} except those of the alkalis of sodium and potassium which are 4.32×10^{-7} and 3.90×10^{-7}, respectively. Thus the alkalis exert about three times the effect of the next most effective constituent. Silica with a coefficient of 0.05×10^{-7} has by far the lowest effect on linear expansion. Thus ancient glasses may be seen to have a higher expansion coefficient than modern ones. For example, the low-silica, high-potash, high-lime, medieval glasses will have about twice the expansion coefficient of a modern soda-lime glass. A forest-type glass might have the composition 40 per cent SiO_2, 30 per cent CaO, 30 per cent K_2O in which case its expansion coefficient would be about 17×10^{-6} compared with 8.5×10^{-6} for a modern glass with the composition 75 per cent SiO_2, 10 per cent CaO, 15 per cent Na_2O. Herein lies an apparently insuperable problem because the poorly durable glasses which are most in need of protection are exactly those which have particularly high expansion coefficients (low silica, high lime, high alkali).

Transition point (T_g)

It could be misleading to discuss the expansion of glasses without mentioning what happens when the full thermal expansion curve is measured, up to a temperature of the order of 700°C (depending on the composition of the glass). *Figure 1.12* shows a representative thermal expansion curve (curve B) for a well-annealed glass and it can be seen that the curve has a fairly constant slope until a temperature of about 580°C is reached; there is then a relatively sudden increase in the coefficient of expansion. The

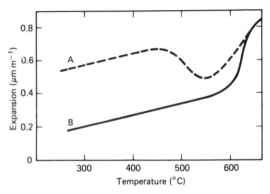

Figure 1.12 Thermal expansion of (A) a chilled sample and (B) an annealed sample of the same glass. After Holloway (1973).

explanation is that the temperature is now high enough (the molecules have enough energy) for the structure to become more random (disordered) in its distribution. It therefore assumes the higher coefficient of expansion that is associated with liquids, rather than solids.

Optical properties

Common glass *transmits visible light wavelengths* and also *ultraviolet* (u.v.) and *infrared* (i.r.) *radiation*; that is, it is *transparent*. It is *opaque* at u.v. and i.r. wavelengths where the frequencies of the incident radiation are in resonance with the frequencies of the molecular vibrations within the glass, and this results in its absorption by the glass. If impurities such as small quantities of iron oxide are present in the glass these may also result in absorption at visible wavelengths so that the glass appears tinted or almost opaque. However, glass is normally considered to be transparent even though it may be coloured. Apart from certain single crystals such as rock crystal (quartz), naturally occurring solids are not generally transparent; transparency is much more a characteristic of a liquid rather than the solid state. In a crystalline solid, which usually comprises many tiny crystals, light in its passage through the solid is reflected at each internal boundary. Some light is lost at each boundary with the result that the material is effectively opaque. A liquid, or glass, however, is structurally a large molecule, containing no internal surfaces or discontinuities having any dimensions approaching the wavelength of visible light. Consequently the light can pass through the glass virtually unhindered and the glass is transparent. This of course is the property which enables glass to be used as windows and, when polished, and silvered on the reverse, to be used as mirrors. Glass *reflects* light, that is, it causes light to rebound off its surface. When cut, ground and polished to form a *convex* surface, for example in the form of a convex lens, the refraction of light which occurs *enlarges* images viewed through the lens. Such lenses are therefore used in vision aids such as spectacles, magnifying glasses, binoculars and telescopes. The opposite effect is produced by a polished *concave* lens in which the same laws of refraction lead to a reduction of the size of images seen through the lens. Spectacles with concave lenses are used to improve short-sightedness. The fact that glass refracts or bends light is a

Table 1.2 Comparative refractive indices of some transparent materials

Material	Refractive index
Diamond	2.4173
Glass	1.5–1.7
Quartz (fused)	1.458
Ethanol (at 25°C)	1.359
Water (at 25°C)	1.332
Air (at 0°C and 760 mm)	1.000 293

consequence of the retardation of velocity which the light suffers as it passes from a medium of lower density, such as air, to one of higher density, for example glass. The *refractive index* (RI) of any material is calculated from the ratio of the sine of the angle of incidence to the sine of the angle of refraction when light is refracted from a vacuum (or, to a very close approximation, from air) into the medium. Some typical refractive index values are given in *Table 1.2*.

The *index of dispersion* of a transparent material is a measure of the extent to which the RI changes with the wavelength (colour) of the light: it determines the angular spread of the spectrum produced by a prism of the material in question. If the composition of the glass is known, the index of dispersion can be calculated. Dispersion tends to be correlated with the

RI; hence lead crystal glass with its attractive brilliance also has a high index of dispersion.

In theory, a knowledge of the refractive indices of ancient glasses would enable conservators to match them to the refractive indices of transparent adhesives, in order that joins made between glass fragments would be less visible than is normally the case. In practice this is not generally feasible since the refractive indices vary considerably with glass composition, it would be impracticable to analyse every glass to be restored, and (since adhesives eventually discolour with time) it may not be worth the time and expense involved in trying to match the refractive indices of adhesives and glasses. However, as will be discussed in Chapter 6, the study of RI values can be helpful in examining ancient glasses.

Density

The density (mass per unit volume) of glasses can fall within a wide range, from 2400 to 5900 kg m^{-3}, depending upon their composition (*Figure 1.13*). Certain glasses containing lead (and incidentally thallium glass for optical work) are of very high density. The specific gravity (relative density) of such glasses may vary from 3.0 to well over 4.0 (*Figure 1.14*). In soda-lime glasses, the density is considerably less, below 2.4 (Scholes, 1929). Ordinary crystal glass has a specific gravity of approximately 3.1.

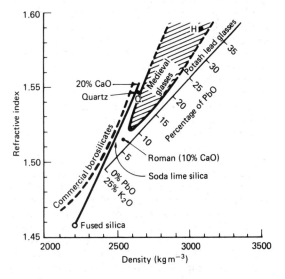

Figure 1.13 Graph showing the relationships between density and refractive index for various types of glass. Point H is the poorly durable glass H in *Figure 4.3*.

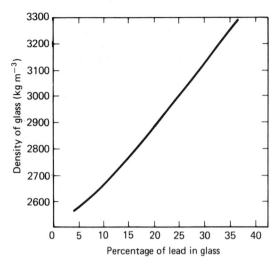

Figure 1.14 Graph relating the density of lead glass to its lead content. After Elville (1951).

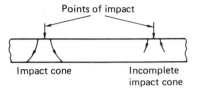

Figure 1.15 A section through impact cones on glass. After Moody (1977).

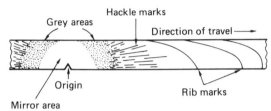

Figure 1.16 Diagnostic markings on the edges of fractured glass. After Moody (1977).

Hardness

The property of hardness cannot be defined as precisely as, for example, tensile strength or density, since it depends upon several other properties, according to the nature of the material being examined, for example whether it is brittle, elastic, plastic etc. The Mohs scale of hardness is based on the fact that each mineral listed is softer than (i.e. is scratched by) all those below it in the scale:

1. Talc
2. Gypsum
3. Calcite
4. Fluorite
5. Apatite
6. Orthoclase
7. Quartz
8. Topaz
9. Corundum
10. Diamond

Depending on their composition, glasses occupy positions between 4.5 and 6.5 on the Mohs scale. The term hardness is also frequently used to describe various properties in relation to glass. It is used by glass decorators to describe glasses which are difficult to wheel-cut, grind or engrave; high-lead glasses are thus said to be soft since they are easy to decorate by these techniques. Other qualities of glass also defined as hardness are a high softening point, durable glasses which are resistant to deterioration and glasses which fail to stain satisfactorily with silver (Willott, 1950).

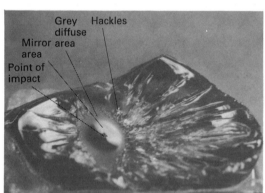

Figure 1.17 When glass fractures, ripples spread out from the point of impact or failure. This photograph shows markings on the edge of broken glass, known as the *mirror sequence*. The origin is a mirror-like surface which reflects easily. The surface is usually featureless, but sometimes there are faint ripples imposed on the mirror. The *mirror* develops first into a *grey* diffused area and then into long, irregular, jagged formations called *hackles*. The significance of the sequence is that the fracture always travels outwards from the mirror surface through the grey area into the hackle zone, and it represents an acceleration in the development of the fracture. The pointed appearance of the hackles is useful in tracing back towards the origin in those instances where the grey area and mirror surface have broken away and been lost. Courtesy of John Lomax, United Glass Ltd.

Brittleness

Glass is anelastic and absorbs energy when it is vibrated. For example, when a glass vessel is lightly struck the walls vibrate and emit a musical note. The vibrations die away because energy is absorbed when the alkali ions jump from one space to another in the network producing internal friction.

It is well known that glass is brittle and fractures easily. Glass, when newly formed with a perfect surface, is very strong, about five times as strong as steel, because of the nature of its interatomic bonds. In practice the presence of surface defects, such as those caused by chemical deterioration or mechanical abrasion, result in the concentration of any applied stress over only a few interatomic bonds at the apex of a crack or a point of pressure (*Figure 1.15*). Under stress, therefore, the strong bonds break and fracture occurs. Once started, the fracture has a high probability of spreading right across the glass because there are no internal grain boundaries to stop it (*Figures 1.16* and *1.17*). Thus a glass vessel or window will often shatter suddenly when subjected to stress. The ability of glass to fracture has been put to use since ancient times, because lumps of cold, solid glass can be chipped and flaked to produce artefacts.

2

Historical development of glass

Long before the invention of man-made glass, artefacts were being fashioned from the natural glasses described in Chapter 1. The first glass artefacts were knives and arrowheads of flaked obsidian made as early as Palaeolithic times. Obsidian is highly durable and there is at present no conservation problem associated with the tools. It has been possible to assign a provenance to many obsidian artefacts on the basis of the chemical analyses of the volcanic flows with which they are associated. As a result, the trade routes by which obsidian artefacts were disseminated to other parts of Asia Minor from Anatolia and the Aegean have been reconstructed (Cann and Renfrew, 1964; Renfrew *et al.*, 1965, 1966; Aspinall *et al.*, 1972a,b); and similar research has been carried out on artefacts in Canada (Huntley and Bailey, 1978).

Throughout historical time man-made glass has been regarded as a special material, and it is not difficult to see why this should have been so, since glass must have seemed to have had magical origins. To take sand and plant ashes and, by submitting them to the transmuting agencies of fire, to produce coloured liquids which, whilst cooling, could be shaped into an infinite variety of forms and textures, which would solidify into a transparent material with the appearance of 'solid water', and which was smooth and cool to the touch, was, and still is, the magic of the glassworker's art. Glass can be fashioned into shapes in ways which are not possible with any other material. It has unique optical properties: for example, glass can transmit images in an enlarged or diminished form, or invert them; a broken or cut glass surface can reflect light in the colours of the spectrum. Certain types of glass are especially appealing, particularly lead crystal glass by virtue of its weight, its great clarity, its ring when lightly struck, and when cut, the sparkle and colours which

arise as a result of its high refractive index and dispersion.

The aesthetic value of glassware has been interpreted in terms of its functionality for every aspect of human life, with a continuing identity across the millennia. For instance, glassware for drinking, eating, toiletry, lighting, and retaining the ashes of the dead fulfilled the entire gamut of requirements of the Romans, rich and poor. So it has been ever since, apart from a barren period after the fall of the Roman Empire in the West. In former times coloured or intricately decorated articles were destined only for the rich, but this is not generally the case nowadays, except for expensive collectors' items. Glass is essential to modern civilization, and has no substitute for use in car windscreens, television tubes, long-distance fibre-optic transmission systems and numerous other uses to which it is put.

In consequence of the supposed magical properties of glass and the technological secrets associated with its production, glassmakers were often granted a higher social status than was given to other craftsmen; and from time to time throughout history, special legislation was passed for their benefit. In ancient Egypt glass was regarded as being more precious than gemstones but, rather surprisingly, it seems that the Egyptians were initially unable to make glass from its raw ingredients. During the first phase of the Roman Empire, when the best glass was being made in Syria, the Syrian glassmakers were regarded as *Cives Romani* (Roman citizens) (Schenk, 1963). Once glass-making had been established throughout the Near East and the West, measures were being taken to safeguard the technological secrets of the trade. For instance, in medieval France glass-making methods could only be passed on through the male line, and then only between members of a few specific families such as Hennezal,

Thietry, Thisac and Bisseval (Ladaique, 1975). In 1369 Duke John I of Lorraine granted letters of privilege to glassmakers to encourage them to settle in Lorraine; and in 1448 Jean de Calabre granted a charter to the makers of glass in the Forest of Darney in the Vosges (Engle, 1975). The Italian city of Venice became an important glass centre in the middle of the eleventh century when glassmakers from Constantinople settled to make the mosaics for San Marco. The glassmakers of Venice eventually became so powerful that they were able to form a guild in 1220; emigration of guild members was forbidden on pain of death (Forbes, 1961). Another privilege, this time for glass vendors, existed in England in 1579 where laws were in force against rogues and vagabonds, but 'glass men of good behaviour' were exempt from prosecution if they possessed a licence from three justices of the peace (Charleston, 1967). It is interesting to note that this law was revoked in 1603. The restriction of the secrets of glass-making to certain specified families, or craft communities, has led to the perpetuation of glass terminology which has been handed down not merely over generations, but over centuries. Glassmakers along the Phoenician coast in the first to sixth centuries AD were using terms similar to those used in Babylonia in the seventh century BC, and following a study of sixteenth-century Italian glassmaking texts Engle (1973b) suggested that some of the early glass-making families of Europe may have originated in areas where Aramaic was spoken. In addition, family names in Hebrew, Flemish, French and English have been studied with a view to tracing the relationships between glassmaking families as they emigrated from Asia Minor through Sicily, Lombardy, the Rhineland and Lorraine to Britain (Engle, 1974a; Winbolt, 1933).

Origins of man-made glass

The date and place of origin of man-made glass may never be known precisely (Peltenburg, 1971). However, it is certain that the invention of glass was made somewhere in the eastern Mediterranean prior to 3000 BC. It is to the Roman historian Pliny (AD 23–79) that the classic association of the River Belus in Phoenicia (now the River Naaman in Israel) with glass-making is attributed. As generally known, Pliny drew much of his information from Greek sources. These were a rich mine of first-hand information (tinctured with legend), since Greek mercenaries, travellers and writers were visitors to the eastern Mediterranean from the seventh century BC. Pliny, however, has been so misquoted that it is worth giving his statement in full (Pliny, AD 77):

That part of Syria which is known as Phoenicia and borders on Judea contains a swamp called Candebia on the lower slopes of Mount Carmel. This is believed to be the source of the River Belus, which, after traversing a distance of 5 miles, flows into the sea near the colony of Ptolemais (Akko). Its current is sluggish and its waters unwholesome to drink, although they are regarded as holy for ritual purposes. The river is muddy and flows in a deep channel, revealing its sands only when the tide ebbs. For it is not until they have been tossed by the waves and cleansed of impurities that they glisten. Moreover, it is only at that moment, when they are thought to be affected by the sharp, astringent properties of the brine, that they become fit for use. The beach stretches for not more than half a mile, and yet for many centuries the production of glass depended on this area alone. There is a story that once a ship belonging to some traders in natural soda (natron, an Egyptian product) put in here and that they scattered along the shore to prepare a meal. Since, however, no stones suitable for supporting their cauldrons were forthcoming, they rested them on lumps of soda from their cargo. When these became heated and were completely mingled with the sand on the beach a strange translucent liquid flowed forth in streams; and this, it is said, was the origin of glass (Engle, 1973a; Newton, 1985b).

Engle examines the information available about the River Belus area, including a modern analysis of the sand available there which shows that the sand contains 8.7 per cent CaO. Turner (1956c) has published several analyses of the Belus sand which confirm its substantial lime content, and comments that it would make a good glass in the absence of any instruction to add lime, which was not specified as an ingredient in glass formulations until *circa* AD 1780, although it is essential for producing a durable glass. According to the Roman historian Josephus: '... numbers of ships are continually coming to take away cargoes of this sand, but it never grows less.' Similar statements were made about the sand at the mouth of the River Volturnus (north of Naples in Italy); and thus it seems that the ancient glassmakers went to great trouble to obtain a traditional raw material.

Most modern authorities claim Mesopotamia or Egypt as the birthplace of glass. Comparatively few glass objects have been excavated in Mesopotamia, but this may well be due to the relative humidity of the soil, and to the rise of the water-table in historic times, causing the destruction of much of the early glass which was inherently unstable in its chemical composition (and therefore water-soluble). However, it is known from glass objects which have survived burial, that coloured vitreous glazes were extensively used in the Badarian civilization of Egypt in the Jemdet Nasr phase of Mesopotamia and in the early Aegean in the fourth millennium BC for covering steatite and sintered quartz beads in imitation of semi-precious stones such as turquoise, lapiz lazuli and red jasper; and later glass beads were developed for the same purpose.

No hollow glass vessels of a date earlier than the second millennium BC have been found, and it may not be without significance that the ruling pharaohs at that time (the Eighteenth Dynasty) conquered Phoenicia and Syria and established contact with the Babylonian Empire in Mesopotamia. From 1480 BC the powerful Egyptian Pharaoh Thothmes (Tuthmosis III) is known to have made expeditions into Asia, and if glass-making was not known in Egypt he may have brought glassworkers back from Mesopotamia. Alternatively the making of glass in Egypt may simply have been the flowering of a civilization which had reached its apex. In any event, Thothmes established a glass vessel industry at Tell el Amarna in 1370 BC. Excavation of the site by Petrie in the nineteenth century showed that glass-making had been carried out on a large scale (see Chapter 3 Part 2). All that is known about the methods of making the first hollow glass containers, which often look more like stone or pottery than glass, has to be deduced from the vessels themselves, for no glass-making tools have yet been identified from an excavation, and the few surviving literary sources, while giving recipes for glass, do not mention methods of production.

The earliest glass vessels, produced before the invention of glass-blowing around 40 BC, were made using four different techniques: core-forming, mosaic, mould-casting and abrasion (of cold glass) (Harden, 1968).

In the process of *core-forming*, a core of clay or some other material was covered with glass either by dipping it into the melt, or by winding trails of softened glass over it. When the glass had hardened, the core was scraped out. Core-formed glass vessels have been excavated over a wide area of the Near East from Anatolia, Mesopotamia and Egypt (*Figure 2.1*).

The *mosaic* glass technique consisted of arranging sections of coloured glass rods on a hard mould. An outer mould was added to keep the sections together whilst they were heated and fused together. An important group of vessels from Mesopotamia and western Asia dating from the fifteenth and fourteenth centuries BC was made by the mosaic technique (*Figure 2.2*).

Casting in moulds was a process normally used for the production of small objects such as beads, inlays and figurines (*Figure 2.3*). But from the eighth century onwards mould-casting was used for producing larger vessels particularly bowls made of thick monochrome glass which was greenish, turquoise or

Figure 2.1 One-handled jug bearing the name of Tuthmosis III (*circa* 1504–1450 BC). Opaque light blue, with yellow, white and dark blue opaque trails, and white and yellow powdered glass fired on. Core-formed, with ground and polished surface, on rim and underneath the base. Intact and unweathered; some bubbles and sandy impurities in the glass. H 88 mm, GD 38 mm. Second quarter of the fifteenth century BC. Egypt. British Museum, London.

colourless. These mould-cast bowls were lathe-finished and sometimes decorated by wheel-engraving on both the interior and exterior surfaces (*Figure 2.4*).

The technique of *cutting and abrading* cold glass was used in Egypt, Mesopotamia and Phoenicia for producing vessels and for finishing cast artefacts (*Figure 2.5*).

It is important to realize that Egypt was more wooded in ancient times, that it had a plentiful supply of alkali in the natron lakes of the western deserts, and of course an unlimited supply of sand. The natural location of the glassworkers therefore tended to be in the delta of the River Nile near the natron deposit and fuel supplies. Egyptian glass is the most common known from this period, many

Figure 2.3 Figurine of Astarte, originally translucent greenish-colourless, now appearing opaque white. Plaque cast in a one-piece mould, the back flattened by pressure, and moulded in the front in the form of a standing figure of the goddess. L 85 mm, W 23 mm, T 16–18 mm. Fourteenth or thirteenth century BC. Atchana, Turkey. British Museum, London.

Figure 2.2 Fragments of mosaic beaker, composed of circular sections of white, red, yellow and dark brown opaque rods, set in horizontal zig-zags to form the whole vessel in a pattern which has the same aspect inside and outside. Built on a core, covered with an outer mould and fused; exterior ground and polished. The colours are often obscured by enamel-like weathering. L of largest fragment 77 mm, W of largest fragment 60 mm, average T 4 mm, average D of sections 2 mm. Fifteenth century BC. Tell al Rimah, Iraq. British Museum, London.

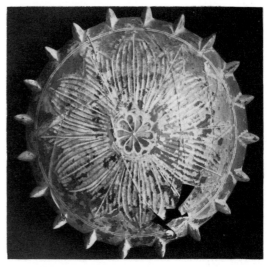

Figure 2.4 Deep bowl with band of bosses. Greenish-colourless glass now with an iridescent and flaking surface. Cast in a two-piece mould and finished by cutting and grinding; the bosses are in reliefs and the remainder of the design in intaglio. H 92 mm, D 205 mm. Late third century BC. Canosa, Apulia, Italy. British Museum, London.

examples having been found in the tombs of the eighteenth and nineteenth dynasties. The vessels are small and served mostly for holding perfumes and ointments or as tomb gifts and cult objects. They do not have the familiar forms (which appeared only with the invention of glass-blowing), but copy the shapes of contemporary vessels of pottery, stone and faience. These richly coloured vessels are almost opaque, due as much to the desire to imitate semi-precious stones in glass as to certain technological limitations.

Figure 2.5 Lidded ointment pot. Both lid and body are ground and polished from raw blocks of glass. Bands of thin gold plating on edge of lid and vessel rim and base. Surface dulled, some strain cracking. Total H 64 mm, H body 60 mm, D rim 63 mm, D base 52 mm, D tubular hole 18 mm, H tubular hole 45 mm. British Museum, London.

At roughly the same time, an independent glass industry was developing in Mesopotamia. Mesopotamian vessels were core-formed in much the same way as those made in Egypt.

Glass-making declined from the thirteenth until the ninth century BC, but did not die out altogether. For all practical purposes, however, glass-making came to an end in about 1200 BC when Egypt and Syria were invaded by the Philistines (Sandars, 1977). With the downfall of the various kingdoms under the impact of the invaders there was no longer a market for the fine and expensively produced glass articles. There is an almost total absence of glass finds from the end of the second and the beginning of the first millenia BC. This phase in ancient history is marked by the eclipse of the great empires and the emergence and migratory movements of new peoples and tribes in the Aegean and Near East. Not until the resurgence of the great empires in the eighth and seventh centuries BC was there again the necessary stability and concentration of wealth and resources for the renewed production of glass. Yet glass-making expertise must have continued somewhere because the re-emergence of the demand in the eighth century BC brought about the manufacture of articles by all four of the earlier techniques with increasing degrees of sophistication in Egypt, Mesopotamia and elsewhere. Core-forming persisted as an important glass technique for many centuries. Some vessels were carved, as if they were made of semi-precious stone. Other glass containers, particularly those from Mesopotamia, were cast in moulds and copied the shapes of contemporary metal vessels. Finely powdered glass was reheated in a clay mould until it melted; after cooling, the surface was ground and polished, probably by fast-turning wheels fed with abrasive. Other glass artefacts such as items intended for inlay were also made by the casting technique. Core-formed glass was usually opaque whereas Mesopotamian cast glass was often transparent pale green. The use of mosaic also continued as a glass-making technique reaching a peak of excellence in the second century BC. Examples of Egyptian and Mesopotamian glass have been found not only throughout the Mediterranean, but as far afield as Russia and France, no doubt distributed by Phoenician traders.

Hellenistic glass

During the Hellenistic Period (late fourth to second century BC), new shapes and decorations were introduced into core manufacture, although there was a falling off in aesthetic quality and a decline in the production of glass in Mesopotamia. Contemporaneously, there were major developments in glass-making, both from technical and artistic points of view. In this period there appear the hemispherical mould-cast bowls made of transparent, almost colourless glass, in the Assyrian tradition. These bowls were lathe-finished and mostly decorated with moulded and/or cut ribs and lines in imitation of their metal prototypes (*Figure 2.6*). Outstanding among this type of bowl are the sandwich-gold glass vessels dating from the late third century BC. These were formed of two glass bowls enclosing gold leaf decoration, which were ground and polished with such precision that the outer glass fitted so perfectly over the inner that no adhesive or fusion was required to hold them together (*Figure 2.7*). Only a few sandwich bowls have been found, and although distributed over a wide area, from the north Caucasus, central Anatolia and Italy, most scholars accept that they were made in Alexandria.

Figure 2.6 Greenish-colourless hemispherical mould-cast bowl, with moulded decoration in imitation of a metal prototype. Circa, fifth century BC. Probably Persia or Mesopotamia. Corning Museum of Glass, New York.

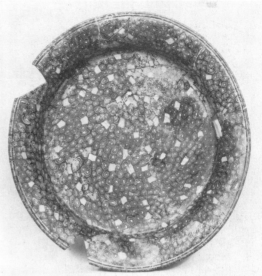

Figure 2.8 Shallow mosaic dish, composed mainly of sections of deep blue cane containing a white spiral surrounding a yellow centre, but with some monochrome and metallic sections. H 50 mm, D 308 mm. Late third century BC. Canosa, Apulia, Italy. British Museum, London.

Figure 2.7 Sandwich gold glass bowl. Colourless with gilding; glass dulled with some iridescence inside and out. Vessel formed in two layers, the outer one fitting over the inner one, but reaching only to a line 0.032 m below the rim. Between the two layers, applied to the surface of the inner one, is a floral design largely based upon the acanthus, in gold leaf. H 114 mm, D 193 mm. Late third century BC. Canosa, Apulia, Italy. British Museum, London.

One of the great achievements of late Hellenistic glass art was *mosaic glass (Figure 2.8)*. The fabrication process was difficult and complex: the required design was built up from canes of variously coloured glass into a slab of material. When heated and tugged at both ends the slab could be drawn out into a long rod which retained the original sectional design in miniaturized form along its whole length. The rod was then cut into small discs in which the design recurred each time. These discs were used as inlays for walls and furniture, or fashioned into beads and various kinds of jewellery. Also, as mentioned above, patterned sections were arranged in moulds and fused together. The resulting vessels, mostly small cups and bowls, transmit light with a polychrome brilliancy. Sometimes sections of coloured rods were fused together to create variegated patches in the body of the glass; or thin threads of glass were twisted into rods which were then fused together in moulds to form elaborate vessels of lace glass.

Another glass-making achievement of the Hellenistic period was the manufacture of *cameo glass*. Vessels and plaques made by this technique were composed of two or more layers of glass. The upper layers were then cut away to reveal the base colour which then formed a background to the relief design of mythological figures, vine leaves and other motifs of Hellenistic art (Cummings, 1980). It should be noted, however, that much of the celebrated cameo glass, for example, the Portland vase (*Figure 2.9*) and Auldjo jug, are early Imperial dating from the late first century BC/early first century AD).

Apparently all the techniques mentioned above were either invented or perfected in Alexandria, the cultural and industrial centre of Hellenistic civilization, which had been founded by Alexander the Great in 332 BC. Yet in this period there were other glass manufacturing centres, some with long traditions of glass-making, and in one of them the revolutionary invention of glass-blowing was made at

Figure 2.9 The Portland Vase, cobalt-blue glass amphora, cased with opaque white, in which a mythological scene is cut cameo-fashion in relief. H 245–248 mm, GD 177 mm, T (at bottom of broken edge of blue glass) 3 mm. Late first century BC or first century AD. British Museum, London.

Glass of the Roman Empire

The invention of glass-blowing

During the first century AD, the invention of glass-blowing, probably in Syria, turned glass into a cheap commodity which could be mass produced; and no doubt provided the stimulus for the proliferation of glasshouses throughout the Roman Empire. In contrast with the considerable amount of glass surviving from the Roman period, there is a dearth of information concerning the designs and workings of the glasshouses. Lang and Price (1975) excavated iron tubes at Badajoz, Spain, which may have been Roman glass-blowing pipes; see also Strong and Brown (1976).

At its height the Roman Empire included the countries which are now the United Kingdom (except Northern Ireland), France, Spain, Portugal, parts of the Netherlands, Germany, Belgium, Switzerland, Eastern Europe, Turkey, the Middle East and North Africa. Thus all the major glass-making centres came under the domination of Rome. In addition the art of glass-making was spread and important centres established throughout the Empire. However, the glass production remained essentially Roman with only minor regional variations until the collapse of the Roman Empire in the West soon after AD 400. Thus glass dating from the first to the fourth centuries AD may more accurately be described as Roman than, for instance, Spanish or Gallic (Harden *et al.*, 1968; Von Saldern, 1974). Glass ceased to be exclusively a luxury product, the styles became largely simple and functional, and in fact glass became more widely used for domestic purposes during the Roman period than at any subsequent time or place until the nineteenth century (Charlesworth, 1968). Glass containers were particularly valued as shipping and storage containers because they were light, transparent, reusable and did not impart a taste to their contents. They were packed in straw to survive long journeys by land and sea. Some containers were square-shaped for easier packing (*Figure 2.10*). Besides the utilitarian glassware, mould-blown bottles were widely made, in fanciful shapes such as animals, human heads, fruit, sea-shells and as souvenirs of gladitorial contests. Some glassmakers incorporated their names in their moulds. The most famous name is that of Ennion, a Sidonian who emigrated to Italy (*Figure 2.11*) (Harden, 1969). At the same time that utilitarian glassware was becoming commonplace, some of the most lavish glass ever made was being produced, for example, the gold-sandwich glasses. Many Roman glassworkers sought to imitate rock crystal with clear glass, and other semi-precious materials. Layered stones such as those used for *cameos* were imitated in glass and carved in high relief. Techniques of cold

some time just prior to the Christian era. Glass-making centres mentioned by the Roman historian Pliny the Elder include Sidon in Lebanon, Acre and the area around the mouth of the River Belus north of the Mount Carmel range in Israel, Campania in Italy, Gaul and Spain. Those mentioned by Strabo were Alexandria and Rome.

One of the interesting problems of glass history concerns the disparity between the considerable information about Alexandria as a glass centre and the small amount of glass found there. The scarcity of glass in places where glass must have been abundant is often due to the fact that broken glass was often collected and remelted as cullet to form new glass batches. A literary source of the first century AD (the poet Martial) mentions a hawker from across the River Tiber who bartered sulphur matches for broken glass.

Figure 2.10 Three green glass bottles, blown respectively into square, hexagonal and round moulds. Late first century AD. H tallest bottle 280 mm. Colchester and Essex Museum.

Figure 2.11 Green one-handled cup by Ennion, blown in a bipartite mould, handles added, and the rim cut and ground. Enamel-like flaking, iridescent. Inscribed ΕΝΝΙωΝ ΕΠΟΙΗCΕΝ AND MNH<C>OH O AΓOPAZωN. H 97 mm, D 135 mm. First quarter of the first century AD. From a tomb at Tremithus, Cyprus. British Museum, London.

painting, enamelling and gilding on glass were also highly developed. Other vessels were decorated with scratched or wheel-abraded designs.

Other products of the Roman glasshouses were jewellery, window panes, lamps, mirrors, mosaic *tesserae*, cast glass panels imitating jasper, porphyry and marble, and *opus sectile* (panels made up of flat glass pieces and set in mortar, *Figure 2.12*). A survey

Figure 2.12 *Opus sectile*. Mosaic panel of Roman glass. 160 mm. 100 BC–AD 100. Victoria and Albert Museum, London.

of glasses taken to be lenses has shown that their focal length was too short to have improved sight; their most probable use was as magnifying aids for engravers. Until the turn of the third century AD there is evidence of strong continuous links between glassmakers in the Middle East and the West, largely formed as a result of the migration of workers, mainly in the east to west direction. Contemporary literary sources mention Syrian glass manufacturers working in the Roman provinces; and glassmakers' quarters were established in every large city. During the first century AD glass-blowing was introduced to the glass-making district of Campania (the province around Naples); and many blown vessels have been found at Pompeii and Herculaneum, both of which were destroyed by the eruption of Vesuvius in AD 79. The accurate dating of ancient vessels is often made difficult by the fact that much of it does not have a recorded provenance and was not recovered from excavations. For this reason the wealth of glass objects found *in use* in Pompeii at the time of the eruption, is of the utmost importance, since it attests to the repertory of glass vessels current in the third quarter of the first century AD. (Much of the glass from these sites has been recovered from the cemeteries, and is therefore much older than that buried during the eruption of Vesuvius in AD 79.)

New glass-making centres arose in the north of Italy in the valley of the River Po, and at Aquileia on the Adriatic coast. From northern Italy, glass was exported as far as Britain.

Although glass was imported to Britain during the Roman occupation, there is archaeological evidence that it was also manufactured locally at London, Colchester, Wroxeter and Mancetter, on a modest scale. Production would mainly have been of simple vessels and bottles, and some window glass. The industry may not have survived the Roman departure, or it may have continued in isolated areas.

Fashion and innovations spread with the continuous traffic of glassmakers with the result that of the Gallic factories made cylindrical bottles which were stamped on the base with the name *Frontinius* or its abbreviated form FRON (*Figure 2.15*).

In the third century, glass-making reached a peak, both in quantity and quality of products. During the third and fourth centuries Egypt also had a considerable blown glass industry which had not existed there previously. A large number of blown glass vessels with local stylistic features such as the fashioning of the bases, was found in the excavations at Karanis (Harden, 1936). It is interesting to note that the Emperor Aurelian (AD 270–275) had imposed a duty on Egyptian glass imported to Rome, presumably to offset its cheapness. The success of the

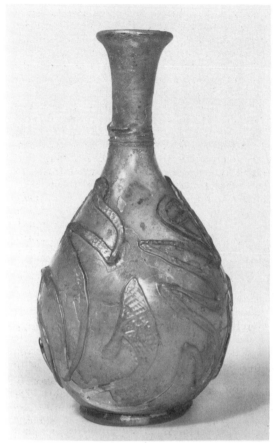

Figure 2.13 Flask of greenish glass with blue enamel-like weathering and flaking. On the body, three winding applied 'snake' coils, flattened and bearing a criss-cross design, ending in a triangular head. H 155 mm, D (rim) 30 mm, D (body) 81 mm. Late second century AD. Idalium, Cyprus. British Museum, London.

types of glass originally made in the East began to be produced in the West. Especially noteworthy are the two groups made from the second century onwards in the Rhenish centre of Cologne. One of these includes vessels with cut and engraved decoration. The other group bears the type of decoration known as *snake thread trailing* (*Figure 2.13*) which began to be made in Syria in the late second century and then, about 100 years later, appeared in a somewhat altered form in the Rhineland and in Britain (*Figure 2.14*); the western examples often bearing trailed decoration of a different colour from that of the body of the vessel (Harden, 1969).

Roman Gaul had a flourishing glass industry; some glass was already being made in Gaul before the influx of Sidonian and Alexandrian immigrants. One

Figure 2.14 Flask of colourless glass, similar to that shown in *Figure 2.13*, but found in the Rhineland. H 213 mm. Third century AD. Cologne. Römisch-Germanisches Museum, Cologne.

Figure 2.15 A two-handled barrel-jug. The body is mould-blown with corrugations at the top and bottom. On the base is the moulded inscription FRON, an abbreviated form of FRONTINIUS. H 191 mm. Last quarter of the third century AD. Amiens, France. Ashmolean Museum, Oxford.

Figure 2.16 Double unguent bottle. H 216 mm. Fourth or fifth century AD. Syria. Toledo Museum of Art, Ohio.

industry meant that it became subject to heavy taxation at various times. The Emperor Alexander Severus (AD 222–235) imposed taxes on all artisans. The following century, the Emperor Constantine (AD 337) eased the burden of taxation in order that the *vitrearii* could perfect their skills and bring up their sons in the family crafts.

By the middle of the fourth century, no doubt as a result of the division of the Roman Empire, East–West contact effectively ceased, and the different glass-making centres developed their own glass styles (Harden, 1958). Glass-making thus became less international, and more provincial, so that regional types of mould-blown, cut- and thread-decorated glasses are found within a limited range of distribution. For example, the Syrian double unguent bottle (*Figure 2.16*) is later than fourth century, and is not found in the West. In due course the regional styles developed into the glass types of the Teutonic north on the one hand, and the Syrian, Iranian and Egyptian styles of the Islamic period on the other.

Post-Roman glass in north-west Europe

There were marked cultural changes after the fifth century when barbarian incursions replaced central imperial power. The changes were reflected in glass-making by a general technical decline. The metal was inferior in quality and colour to Roman glass, and the vessel shapes were generally simpler. However, they were decorated with glass applied with considerable manipulative skill (Harden, 1956b, 1969, 1971, 1978).

In the northern European countries glass-making tended to move away from the centres of population into the forests which supplied fuel for the furnaces. It is possible that natron continued to be transported to these countries even after the collapse of the Roman Empire in the West, by overland routes through the Brenner Pass in Switzerland, by sea around the Iberian Peninsula, or up the Rivers Vistula and Danube (Besborodov and Abdurazakov, 1964; Besborodov and Zadneprovsky, 1963). However, at some time before the tenth century, the ash produced in glass furnaces was substituted for the ashes of marine plants which had been the almost universal fluxing agent used in Roman glass-making. This change to potash derived from the ashes of burnt trees, especially beech, resulted both in a change of alkali and lime contents of the glass, which is known as *forest glass* (Ger. *Waldglas*; Fr. *verre de fougère*— fern glass). The relationships of the northern glasshouses to the distribution of beech pollen in AD 1000 is discussed by Newton (1985b). The northern forest glass-makers conditioned by their raw materials, produced mainly green and brown glass, and

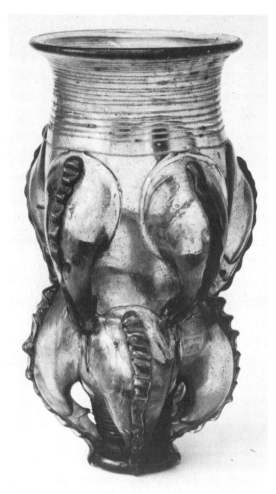

Figure 2.17 A Saxon claw beaker. H 158 mm. Late fifth or early sixth century AD. Found at Castle Eden, Co. Durham in 1775. British Museum, London.

decorated it with furnace-wrought embellishments of simple rib-moulding, applied trails and blobs, mostly in the same colour glass as the body of the vessel itself. The vessels fall into several categories: simple palm cups without handles, bag beakers, cone cups up to 265 mm in height and tapering to a pointed base, a variety of squat pots and bottles, and claw beakers (Ger. *Rüsselbecher*) (*Figure 2.17*).

The known glass-making centres at this time were Cologne, Liège, Namur, Amiens and Beauvais. It seems likely that glass was exported to Britain from northern Gaul and the Rhineland during the first seven centuries AD, but there was certainly some local production, at least from the seventh century.

Glassmakers seem to have been working in the Kentish kingdom in the seventh century because bag beakers and squat jars are more prolific there than on the continent; moreover, a glass furnace was found in the cloisters of Glastonbury Abbey near Bristol, beneath the medieval levels. With the spread of Christianity, the practice of burying grave goods with the dead slowly declined in Britain, northern France and the Rhineland. However, the custom continued in Scandinavia until the beginning of the eighth century so that the major source of glass from this period is from Scandinavian excavations.

In the course of the later Middle Ages glass was improved to produce a substantial material of beautiful quality and a variety of green tones, used in a characteristic range of shapes of great originality and charm.

Little is known of glass-making in the Rhineland from the eighth to the fifteenth centuries. A few specimens have been found which provide enough information to show that glass was made during this period, but it appears to have been confined to small, crudely made vessels of strictly utilitarian purpose. Two important pieces are reliquaries containing parchments dated 1282 and 1519. The former was discovered in a church at Michelfield near Hall, and is a small jar decorated with trailed threads reminiscent of the trailed-thread snake vases made in Cologne in the third century. The latter is a short parallel-sided beaker called an *igel* (Ger. hedgehog) the name being given because the applied decoration in the form of a series of spikes resembles the spikes of a hedgehog.

The general term for applied blobs of glass is *prunts* (Ger. *Nuppen*); and prunts are one of the most characteristic features of northern European glass from the late fourteenth century onwards (*Figure 2.18*). It is possible to draw a parallel between these prunts and the projections on late Roman glass vessels, and on Seine–Rhine claw beakers. Whereas in the earlier glasses the prunts were hollow blown and drawn out to form the distinctive long claws, the later prunts were restricted to solid lumps of glass which owed their appearance and decorative effect to the manner in which the surface was finished. They were drawn out in several styles. They were drawn out to produce thin spikes resembling thorns, drawn out and folded over to form loops from which small rings of glass were suspended, and drawn into curls and pressed back onto the surface of the vessel to resemble pigs' tails. They were also flattened and moulded to produce a beaded surface; these are commonly known as raspberry or strawberry prunts.

Gradually the squat *igel* became taller whilst retaining its parallel sides until glasses were made which were in excess of 300 mm high. This type of vessel became very popular and acquired different names according to their intended use and style of decoration. One version decorated with a row of

Figure 2.19 Excavations in 1932 at Lorsch Abbey in Germany unearthed fragments of painted glass which are thought to date from the ninth or tenth century. In spite of the dark gaps of missing glass, a head of Christ is suggested by this reconstruction of the ancient pieces, believed to be the earliest existing pictorial window glass. Darmstadt Museum, West Germany.

Figure 2.18 A *stangenglas*, a tall cylindrical vessel decorated externally with eight vertical rows each of nine prunts (and internally with eight rows of seven prunts). Dark blue-green glass. H 260 mm, D 81 mm. Early sixteenth century. Probably Rhineland. British Museum, London.

prunts which resembles broken-off leaf stalks was termed *krautstrunk* (Ger. cabbage stalk). Another version was a plain glass divided into zones by horizontal trailed rings, the *passglas* (Ger.) which each drinker in turn was expected to drain to the next division in one breath.

Origins of painted glass windows

The origins of decorated glass windows can only be speculated since no contemporary account of their use is known. Coloured window glass was known in Saxon times (Cramp, 1968, 1970, 1975); and a sixth-century fragment of window glass from Ravenna in northern Italy bears an outline drawing; but the earliest painted glass known is the ninth-century head of Christ from Lorsch in Hesse which is now in the Darmstadt Museum, Germany (*Figure 2.19*). The earliest surviving picture windows are the Augsburg Prophet Windows which date from *circa* AD 1130, and the Le Mans Ascension window of AD 1145. These examples are so fully developed that there must have been many precursors which have either perished or were destroyed in favour of a later replacement or, more likely, considering the major losses which would seem to have occurred, were lost by the deliberate destruction of the older (Byzantine) windows by the proponents of the Gothic era.

Glass-making in the medieval period was clearly dominated by the great demand for window glass for the cathedrals and churches being erected at the beginning of the Gothic era. Barrelet (1953) states that, for the cathedral of Chartres alone, at least 2000 m² of glass was required over a period of 30 years; this would correspond to about 8 m³ of glass or about 20 tonnes. It is therefore not surprising that there could have been a fuel crisis at the coastal glass-making sites; fuel must have been difficult to obtain at the best of times, and migration of the glassworkers to well-wooded sites would have been a natural consequence, especially north of the Alps where most of the new cathedrals were being constructed (von Witzleben, 1968; Harvey, 1968, 1972, 1975).

A succession of French glassmakers emigrated to Britain to carry on the glass trade; but there are no records of native Britons being engaged in glass manufacture at this time. Thus from the earliest times French glassworkers acquired a widespread reputation for the manufacture of glass, and in particular window glass; documents dating from the eighth century include requests for their assistance in supplying glazing for churches and monasteries in Britain. Of course, after the Norman invasion of Britain in AD 1066, when church building began to be carried out on a large scale, the trade would have increased.

The first recorded French glassmaker working in Britain was Lawrence Vitrearius of Normandy who obtained a grant of land at Dyers Cross in Sussex in AD 1220. In 1240 he was commissioned by Henry III to make plain and coloured glass for Westminster Abbey in London. Succeeding generations of the Vitrearius family were recorded until 1301. Then in *circa* 1343 a John Schurterre settled at Chiddingfold in Sussex and eventually became an important glassmaker in Britain. The Chiddingfold area of Sussex remained the centre of British glass-making for many years, having as it did an abundant supply of wood-fuel and alkali from beechwood and bracken-ash. A Venetian map of Britain dating from the sixteenth century shows two glass-making sites, both in Surrey, one at Chiddingfold, where a number of glasshouses have been excavated, and the other at Guildford (Brooks, 1973).

The fourteenth century saw a great increase in the production of decorated window glass as a result of the development of yellow (silver) stain. Many of the earliest painted glass windows in British churches date from this time and are of French origin (Drake, 1912; Woodforde, 1954; Wentzel, 1954, 1958). The early painted glass at Augsburg (1120–1140) near Munich, and at Wissembourg (eleventh century) near Karlsruhe, West Germany, were forerunners not only of the painted glass art, but also of the conversion of the glass industry to a major producer of manufactured material. The earliest reference to the principle of silver staining appears to be in a Hebrew manuscript dating from the eighth century, in which the use of pyragyrite, a natural sulphide of silver, is described. However, it was not until medieval times that the process was fully developed and exploited. It reached its peak on the Continent and in Britain during the fifteenth century when the perpendicular style of architecture, then in vogue,

required the use of enormous decorative glass windows. The great east window of York Minster for example measures 23.4 × 9.8 m.

In the sixteenth century the development of coloured enamels opened up the opportunity for easel painters to practice their art on glass. As a result many small panels and roundels were produced, painted in *grisaille* and with details added in yellow stain (*Figure 2.20*). Yellow stain was also used in combination with enamel paint during the following two centuries. A fundamental change in the history of painted glass occurred in the sixteenth century with the introduction of painting with translucent coloured enamels on clear glass; a technique which was closely related to a change in attitude to glass painting at the time of the Renaissance.

Following the increase of realism in fifteenth-century painted glass, the sixteenth-century glass painters increasingly tried to achieve the effects of easel painting until, in the seventeenth and eighteenth centuries, the leading, which had played so important a part in the design of a medieval window, was used merely to hold large squares or rectangles of white glass together, and the whole glass surface was painted like a canvas. By the late sixteenth century, translucent enamels were available in a wide range of colours, and their total adoption was perhaps

Figure 2.20 Glass roundel representing the month of September by a depiction of grape-picking. *Grisaille*, with details picked out in silver stain. Fifteenth century. Brandiston Hall, Norfolk, UK.

accelerated by the increasing difficulty of obtaining coloured glass, as wars and political unrest in Europe gradually brought the glass-making areas of Lorraine and elsewhere to ruin. On early medieval glass, coloured enamels were used in conjunction with coloured glass, but by the middle of the seventeenth century, enamel painting predominated and coloured glass was not fully used again until the revival of medieval-style stained glass in the first half of the nineteenth century (Lowe, 1975).

In Britain during the seventeenth and eighteenth centuries, the Calvinists, Fundamentalists and Cromwell's soldiery broke as many church windows as they could, since pictorial art was then regarded as being idolatrous. In France, the iconoclasm associated with the French Revolution was likewise responsible for the loss of much painted glass. Fortunately a considerable amount of French glass was bought by patrons of the arts in Britain so that many British churches benefited, for example those at Twycross in Leicestershire and Rivenhall in Essex. During the nineteenth and twentieth centuries there has been, first, a Gothic revival during which medieval methods of manufacture were investigated and reused, and, secondly, the development of new art forms such as glass-in-concrete, appliqué glass and fused glass windows in modern churches and cathedrals such as in Coventry Cathedral, Warwickshire. Lee *et al.* (1982) have published a comprehensive illustrated guide to the world's best painted glass windows.

Glass of the period is similar to that found throughout the Roman Empire, but during the Sassanian period (*circa* 100 BC to AD 600) leading up to the advent of Islam, a tradition of cut glass developed. For this purpose the glass needed to be thicker than for the earlier blown and moulded styles. Cutting generally took the form of facets or geometric patterns and was developed to a very high standard (*Figure 2.21*).

Glass vessels of the Byzantine period (fourth to seventh centuries AD) manifest daring imagination and great technical skill together with a somewhat heavy charm, yet in other respects they do not compare well with earlier glass. There is an absence of clear glass, and the coloured glass was not as vivid as previously, while the glass metal was generally impure. The vessels were irregular in shape and badly proportioned; the decoration is intricate and over-profuse. Cosmetic vessels in the form of two, sometimes three or even four tubes were widespread in the Near East (see *Figure 2.16*). The majority of these vessels were found in tombs, usually with the metal spatulas for applying the cosmetics still inside one of the tubes.

Another group of distinctive vessels appeared in the fourth century AD. These were the polygonal bottles (mainly hexagonal and octagonal), either without handles or with a single handle, and bearing moulded symbols on the sides. The most familiar and prominent of these symbols was the seven-branched candlestick (*menorah*) of the Jewish faith, while

Post-Roman glass in the East

The prominence of the Mesopotamian and Syrian glassmakers in the ancient world has already been discussed. Gradually they established themselves throughout the Roman Empire, and were again important in the development of Middle Eastern glass which culminated in the distinctive and sophisticated wares of Islam.

With the decline of Rome and the transfer of the seat of the Roman Empire to Constantinople (Istanbul) in AD 305, the capital of the Empire was right on the doorstep of the Syrian glasshouses which were established at Tyre and Sidon. It has been remarked upon by many authorities that despite its magnificence and importance, Constantinople appears never to have had a tradition of glass-making. This may be explained by the fact that since it was so close to Syria, whatever glass was made in the capital followed closely in the Syrian tradition; and it is also possible that there was never any great necessity to set up an independent manufacture when the best glass was so close at hand.

Figure 2.21 Sassanian bowl of thick colourless glass with heavy iridescence. Hemispherical. Base with central cut, on the wall five rows of round (lower portion) and polygonal facet-cuts. H 86 mm, D 105 mm. Sixth to seventh century. Probably Iran. Hans Cohn Collection, Los Angeles, California.

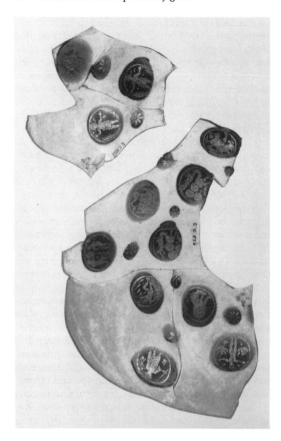

Figure 2.22 *Fondo d'oro* bowl fragments with emerald-green blobs, and with gold decoration between the inner faces of the blobs and the outer surface of the colourless glass bowl. Greatest dimensions: 10 mm (smaller portion), 168 mm (larger portion). Second half of fourth century AD. From St Severin's parish, Cologne. British Museum, London.

others were an arch supported by two columns (apparently symbolizing the Temple portals), palm trees and palm branches and other designs of uncertain significance. Although the exact provenance of the polygonal bottles is unknown, it is generally supposed that they were first produced in Palestine. A vessel of this type was reportedly found at Edrei (Daraa), a small town on the border of Syria and Palestine, which strengthens the theory of local manufacture. It is noteworthy that bottles almost identical in shape but with Christian symbols are also known. Apparently both types of vessel were made in one workshop but provided with different symbols according to the religion of the customer.

Other glass objects with religious symbols were the gold glass bases (Ital. *fondo d'oro*) in which a gold leaf etched or painted with a design was enclosed between two layers of glass (*Figure 2.22*). The technique was popular in Romano-Byzantine times (many gold glass vessels were embedded in the walls of the catacombs outside Rome). It was used almost exclusively for religious iconography, both Jewish and Christian. Religious symbols also appear on a category of objects of a personal character, such as bracelets and amulets, stamped with representations of *menorah*, lions, frogs, human masks, and also some more elaborate scenes and inscriptions.

Extremely common during this period are the conical cups which were used as lamps; these were filled with water and oil on which a wick was floated. The lamps were placed in holders or suspended by a chain from the ceiling. Other lamps were in the form of stemmed bowls or cups with a hollow projection in the centre to hold the wick. Similar types, placed in metal holders, were used for lighting in the Middle Ages. Glass was an important element in mosaics, a major art of the Byzantine period (Bovini, 1967). Itinerant mosaicists decorated Byzantine churches in Roman Ravenna (Bovini, 1964) and mosques in Damascus and Cordoba (Spain) with splendid wall mosaics. The synagogue mosaics in Israel included many glass *tesserae*, especially of colours not found in natural stone (Fiorentini-Roncuzzi, 1967).

Islamic glass

After the Arab conquest of the Middle East in AD 635, and the establishment of a capital at Damascus, there was a rapid move away from the Roman traditions of glass-making. The change in the balance of power affected glass production, which stagnated until the rise of the Abbasid dynasty, and the transfer of the capital to Baghdad in Mesopotamia (Iraq), in AD 750, which was outside the mainstream of an area which had been unsettled for many years. By this time the whole of the Middle East had become settled under the rule of Islam and new styles in glass slowly began to emerge to suit the tastes of a new society. In the early stages of their conquest, the Arabs adopted the art of the countries over which they ruled, and had their palaces built and decorated by local craftsmen. Only at the end of the first millennium AD did Islamic art begin to assume an individual character. As with Roman Imperial art, though to a lesser degree, the development of Islamic art was remarkably uniform, whether in Persia, Mesopotamia, Syria or Egypt; however, centres of influence moved from country to country in the wake of shifting centres of government.

Mesopotamia, important in the ancient glass-making world, again came to the fore; glass kilns were probably more common than pottery kilns in medieval Mesopotamia and southern Persia. Islamic glass-making centres developed on the Euphrates river east of Aleppo (Syria); at Samarra on the River

Tigris (Mesopotamia); at Siraf, an early Islamic port on the Persian Gulf; at Nishapur (Neyshabur), an important trading centre in northern Persia; and at Fustat south of Cairo (Egypt) which had taken over from the Roman glass-making centres such as Alexandria. There was much emphasis on mould-blown patterns and the cutting, engraving and polishing of glass, followed by pincering with tongs, lustre painting and gilding and enamelling (Brooks, 1973). The most striking was the cut glass. Surviving examples are either linear or facet cut.

A characteristic vessel of the Islamic period is the mould-blown flask with a globular body and long narrow neck. A fine group of such flasks dating from the eleventh- and twelfth-centuries AD and typical of the Gurgan district in north-eastern Iran is displayed in the Haaretz Collection, Tel Aviv (Israel), beside the clay moulds in which they were blown. The relationship between Islamic cut glass and similar glass of an earlier period is not clear. The technique of glass-cutting was already known in the Late Bronze Age and much practised in Roman times but did not reach its peak until the Islamic period. However, in Iran (and possibly also in Iraq) a tradition of cutting – from powerful relief work in the form of bosses, to delicate *intaglio* figural engraving – permitted the development, in the ninth and tenth centuries, of a brilliant Persian–Mesopotamian school of relief cutting on glass which was mainly colourless, the designs being outlined by deep notched lines. This engraving was occasionally executed on glass cased with an overlay of emerald green or blue glass. Parallel with this luxurious relief engraving went a simpler or rougher style of *intaglio* engraving.

Lustre painting was a characteristic form of decoration from the eighth century especially in Egypt where it may have originated (*Figure 2.23*). The earliest surviving example of lustre painting is on a bowl dated AD 773. This technique, which involved applying metallic pigments and firing them under reducing conditions in the kiln to produce golden or silver iridescence, probably developed simultaneously in Egypt and Mesopotamia. The surviving examples of this technique include fragments on which different hues were obtained by repeated firings in the kiln. Another interesting effect was lustre spots applied to the interior and exterior of glass vessels. Lustre painting was applied to glass *before* its use on pottery.

The art of gilding glass may also have originated in Egypt. Gilding formed the basic element in the technique of gilding and enamelling glass which developed in Syria, centred on Damascus, during the late twelfth and thirteenth centuries. The gilt and enamel glasses, largely beakers, bowls, flasks and mosque lamps, made mostly during the thirteenth and fourteenth centuries AD, are considered to be the

Figure 2.23 Bowl of colourless glass with a green tinge. Painted on the outside in brown lustre; horizontal band below lip; frieze of palmette scrolls between framing bands; between ribbings, vertical stripes and lanceolate leaves alternating. H 85 mm, D (rim) 109 mm. Egypt. British Museum, London.

Figure 2.24 Mosque lamp of colourless glass with a yellowish tinge and containing many bubbles and impurities. Six suspension rings trailed on body. Heavily decorated in *naskh* script in red, blue, black, white, green and yellow enamels (the last two badly fired). H 350 mm. Middle fourteenth century AD. Syria. British Museum, London.

Glass vessels were exported from Damascus to every part of the Islamic world, even as far as China. Under the influence of Far Eastern art, coming in the wake of the Seljuk and Mongol conquerors in 1258 the earlier heavier forms and styles of decoration became freer and more naturalistic, consisting of arabesque and floral designs. Enamel work declined at the end of the fourteenth century, and the manufacture of gilt and enamelled ware ceased almost entirely after the sack of Damascus by the Mongol chieftain Timur (Tamerlane) in 1402 during his conquest of the Middle East. The general decline in the production of Islamic glass which followed the conquest gave Venice the opportunity to expand and take over the markets which had previously been supplied by the East. The beauty of Islamic glass was already appreciated in medieval Europe. Vessels brought from Syria and Palestine by pilgrims and crusaders are now in many churches, monasteries, museums and private collections.

The Islamic wreck of the Serçe Liman which sank off the south-west coast of Turkey in AD 1025 has been excavated by Bass of the American Institute of Nautical Archaeology. The ship was carrying a cargo of approximately 1 tonne of raw and scrap glass; and from the ship's living quarters more than eighty intact engraved beakers and bottles of Arab manufacture have been recovered. These were perhaps used by the crew, or were intended for use as items of trade (Bass, 1980).

Post-Roman glass in south-east Europe

There may have been no real break in the southern glass-making tradition between late Roman times and the emergence of the Venetian glass industry in the thirteenth century, although there is as yet not much evidence of glass-making activity in south-east Europe between the fourth and the eighth centuries. In contrast with the northern forest glass-making sites, the manufacture of glass in southern Europe and the Mediterranean countries largely remained at sites near the coast such as Alexandria, Sidon, Damascus, Aleppo, Corinth, Aquilea, Murano, Florence and Barcelona. The towns offered many advantages: there were customers immediately at hand, especially the wealthy ones; there were churches and cathedrals with a demand for window glass; the towns provided communication and banking facilities; there was an impetus for innovation, such as the development of Venetian *cristallo*; and glassworkers' guilds could be formed to protect the interests of the industry. As a result of increasing demand, window glass was made more frequently, and many examples are now known of the early type of small *crown glass* window panes. The crown glass window panes in the church of San Vitale in Ravenna

chief glory of Islamic glass art. Two main styles of glass enamelling are discernible: one using enamel heavily laid on, usually in horizontal bands of intricate abstract patterns (the Koran forbids representational decoration) interspersed with quotations from the Koran, the other a fine linear style in red, both on a gold ground. On most of the vessels the gilt has been almost entirely abraded, much lessening their appearance (*Figure 2.24*).

The so-called mosque lamps are outstanding examples of gilded and enamelled glass. They are in fact not so much lamps as lamp-holders in which small glass lamps were placed. The usual shape of a mosque lamp (holder) was a large vase with a splayed neck. On the body were small glass lugs to which chains for suspending the lamp from the ceiling were fastened. Often the donor's name was included in the enamel decoration.

almost certainly came from the windows of the apse when the basilica was dedicated in AD 547. One bears an outline drawing of Christ nimbed and enthroned. Glass *tesserae* were used in wall mosaics; the mosaics at Ravenna were no doubt made locally as were those at Torcello.

Further evidence of the produce of the southern glasshouses is given in three papers describing the cargo of the Gnalić wreck. This vessel, probably the Gagiana, was on its way from Venice to the Levant, when it was sunk off the Yugoslavian coast in 1585. The cargo included 648 round window panes, 170 mm, 185 mm and 205 mm in diameter, and eighty-six types of glass objects. These included goblets, flasks, vases, pitchers, large square plates and two types of mirror, squared and round, which were obviously of Venetian origin. Some objects were of very thin transparent glass with greyish, greenish or purplish tints. A large number were decorated with vertical filaments or threads of white opaque glass. There were also several small bottles of cobalt-blue glass, and a group of glasses with delicate diamond-point engraving (Brill, 1973; Petricioli, 1973).

The glass-making of south-eastern Europe in the medieval period is as yet only imperfectly understood, but it is evident that good quality crystal glass had evolved by the thirteenth century at the latest. A considerable number of glasses, made of clear almost colourless glass have now been excavated in Italy and other parts of Europe, including England, and can be dated to the twelfth to fourteenth centuries. The forms made were long-stemmed wine glasses and prunted beakers often of considerable finesse and delicacy. Considerable use was made of opaque red glass, not only for whole vessels, but also for decoration. However, none of the glass can be attributed to the Venetian glasshouses with any confidence. Some of the clear glasses with prunts and trailed blue threads seem to have had their antecedents in the Byzantine glasshouses situated in Greece, one of which has been excavated in Corinth. (It has also been conjectured that after 1147 the Normans may have carried off Greek workmen and then established a glass-making centre in Sicily or southern Italy, which was responsible for producing the clear glasses.) It is however possible that a number of Italian glasshouses were involved in their production, but by the fifteenth century Venice had become the most important of these; and the eastern predominance in glass-making was usurped by Venice.

The technique of glass manufacture and its decoration had by this time largely developed, and therefore the historical development of glass-making tends to become a list of changes in style or decoration which occurred at various times in different countries.

The pre-eminence of Venice

As previously mentioned, glass-making in Venice may have had a continuous existence since Roman times, unless there was a migration of glassmakers from Aquilea, which is known to have had an established glass-making tradition. Certainly a glass-making industry was already established in Venice in the tenth century; and in records dating from 1090, mention is made of a *phiolarius*, which shows that vessel glass was being made there (Charleston, 1958). However, before the mid-fifteenth century, Venetian glassware was undistinguished and it is therefore difficult, if not impossible, to differentiate it from any other glass of the period. Whether or not there was some glass-making on a small scale since Roman times, the pre-eminence of Venice in the glass-making industry came about through a chain of circumstances: the accidents of geography, time, political power and the rebirth of the arts (the Renaissance) produced in Venice a standard of glass-making both of quality and imagination which had not been achieved previously. A lagoon of low-lying swampy islands was an unlikely place to create a city. The problems of construction, communication and health would make any site on firm ground seem more favourable, but the earliest settlers were probably refugees from the effects of the barbarian invasions which swept the area after the fall of the Roman Empire in the West, to whom the lagoons may have seemed to offer security. As at various times in other countries, turbulent and troubled times had an inhibiting effect on the practice of the domestic arts and crafts. If Venice was able to establish herself while the surrounding region was in a state of turmoil, she would have offered a refuge where artisans could practice their arts with the minimum of interference (Brooks, 1973).

In 1204 Constantinople fell to the Crusaders and the immediate beneficiary was Venice, whose fleets had carried them. The glassmakers surely then obtained all the glass-making information and assistance they required. At first, the Venetians may only have been glassmelters (i.e. not glassmakers), for masses of cullet are known to have been imported in the form of ships' ballast; and there was a law of the Marine Code, as late as 1255, which permitted *vitrum in massa et rudus* (crude lump glass) to be put on board ships as ballast.

That the glassmakers flourished, however, is certain, for by 1271 the first records of a glassmakers' guild appear; and shortly afterwards in 1291 the glass furnaces were moved to the island of Murano in the Venetian lagoon to avoid the risk of fire in a city comprised of small and densely populated islands. It may also have been that having become important and powerful enough to form a guild, it was felt that a tighter control could be maintained over the industry if the glassworkers were assembled in one locality. Glassmakers were highly regarded in Venice; the city records show that some became powerful and important men, ranking with nobility in a city which had a highly developed class system.

As communication and trade developed throughout Europe, Venice and Genoa became the natural focal points for the trade routes of the world. There was intense rivalry between the two cities, but Venice eventually emerged the victor. She then became the crossroads for land and sea traffic from east to west and from north to south. With this position secured, Venetian coffers swelled with the taxes and duties she levied in commercial traffic; Venice became the most powerful city in the Mediterranean. Venetian merchants travelled the trade routes of the world, and in the course of their dealings with the Middle East they would have encountered Syrian and Mesopotamian glassmakers so that the best of Middle Eastern glass would have found its way back to Venice. During this period the trade in glassware, which of course had been taking place for some three *millennia*, started to be documented. Trade routes were established, for example, between Genoa and Syria, the Mediterranean countries and Asia as far east as China, and between Murano and Dubrovnik.

With the overthrow of the Middle East by Tamerlaine in 1402, the decline of the glass trade in the Middle East left a vacuum in the supply of quality glass. Since Venice was in control of all the main commercial routes and had established a considerable glass trade of her own, it was natural that she should step in to fill the breach. In the face of the onslaught of the barbarian hordes the local inhabitants would flee wherever they could to find refuge, and what more natural than that the glassmakers would make for a place where, from contact with visiting merchants, they knew that there would be an opportunity to continue the practice of their skills? Thus, in addition to having new markets opened to it, Venice also had a second infusion of skills from the Middle East.

The last link in the chain of events which brought Venice to her peak was now about to be forged. As the world once again became a more settled place, prosperity increased and there came about a rebirth of artistic endeavour and achievement: the Italian Renaissance, during which talented artists, able to satisfy the aesthetic demands of a new society, were sponsored by wealthy patrons of the arts. Glass painters are recorded in Murano as early as 1280; and colourless glass was almost certainly made there in the thirteenth century. From the middle of the fifteenth century these two branches of the arts experienced an unparalleled expansion in what was by then a highly specialized industry.

Trade between Venice and the East declined after Constantinople was captured by the Turks in 1453;

and the Venetians then built up an active trade with the West based on the *façon de Venise* style which enabled them to continue to dominate the glass industry.

Venetian glass

The earliest Venetian glass vessels of any quality were goblets, usually flat-bottomed and with straight tapering sides mounted on a pedestal foot. They were made of coloured glass, usually blue or green, with enamelled decoration around the bowl (Gasparetto, 1973). Previously, stemmed glasses had been rare. At first the glass bowls were set on a plain ribbed pedestal in which stem and foot were one. Gradually the stems were made taller and were decorated with hollow blown bulbs (*knops*), until for the first time glasses with separate stems and feet were produced. Once the stem and foot were able to be made separately there was no limit to the ingenuity which could be used in fashioning the stem: hollow knops with moulded lion masks, stems with a central feature of glass threads drawn out in the shape of serpents or figures-of-eight, winged stems with

Figure 2.25 Tazza of *cristallo* (colourless) glass with a saucer-shaped bowl, and decorative stem incorporating a knop in the form of lion's heads, and a small foot. H 159 mm, D 159 mm. Late sixteenth century. Venice. British Museum, London.

pincered fringes, and many others (Tait, 1968, 1979). In a further development the Venetians improved their clear glass by the addition of lime to the soda–silica mixture to produce a fine clear glass (*cristallo*) which captured the popular taste of the fifteenth century (*Figure 2.25*). One of the great abilities of the Venetian glassmakers was their skill in the manipulation of the material. They acquired a dexterity in controlling the molten metal which enabled glasses of a delicacy, and with a degree of elaborate decoration which no one else could equal, to be produced. Such glassware was made for a wealthy and sophisticated market, and outside Venice that would mean principally the European nobility. Thus Venetian glass was for a long time the prerogative of the rich and educated. Later came plates, *tazzas*, flasks, chalices and a wide variety of other domestic vessels in blue, green or purple glass and later in *cristallo*. The glassware was enamelled and gilded and was the product with which Venice

first entered the world market. The decorative themes were of typical Renaissance inspiration: triumphs, allegories of love etc.

Inspired by classical Rome the Venetian glassmakers also produced mosaic, *millefiori* (*Figure 2.26*), aventurine (with copper particles), and *calcedonio* glasses, the latter in imitation of Roman agate glass produced 1500 years earlier, and which was itself an imitation of the natural stone. Enamelled glass gradually went out of favour, except for customers in northern Europe, and mould-blown or exquisite plain forms such as *aquamaniles* or *nefs* (decanters) succeeded (*Figure 2.27*). These were sometimes decorated with bands or cables of opaque white (*lattimo*) threads, that is, *filigrana*, and occasionally by gilding, diamond-point engraving (although the thin soda glass was generally unsuited to engraving), cold painting behind glass (Ger. *Hinterglasmalerei*) (*Figure 2.28a,b*), or a surface *craquelure* (ice-glass) (*Figure 2.29*). As the fifteenth

Figure 2.26 *Millefiori* miniature ewer of opaque blue glass, with canes of purple, green, brown and blue. H 127 mm. Early sixteenth century. Venice. British Museum, London.

Figure 2.27 *Nef* ewer of colourless glass, the bowl in the form of a boat with a spout forming a prow. H 343 mm. Sixteenth century. Venice. British Museum, London.

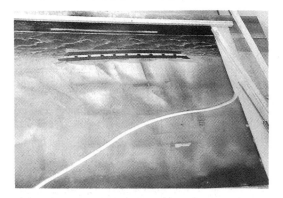

Figure 2.28 An example of reverse-painted glass (*Hinterglasmalerei*), (a) before and (b) after repair. English nineteenth century. Laing Art Gallery, Tyne and Wear, UK.

Figure 2.29 Large beaker of 'ice-glass', created by plunging the hot glass into water for a moment and immediately reheating. The roughened frozen surface appearance became popular in Venice in the sixteenth century and spread to Northern Europe, where it remained in vogue into the seventeenth century. H 209 mm. Late sixteenth century. Southern Netherlands. British Museum, London.

century progressed, furnace-wrought decorations of applied threads or bosses, often of fantastic forms, became more popular, and in the seventeenth century this tendency was sometimes carried to extravagant and not always attractive lengths.

Venice was jealous of her position in the world's markets, and to ensure that she kept it the Venetian Senate placed highly restrictive conditions on its craftsmen, especially the glassmakers. They were forbidden on pain of death to practice their skills anywhere outside Venice, or to impart their knowledge to anyone other than Venetians. However, the demand for Venetian glassware from the Courts of Europe was such that considerable inducements were offered to persuade Venetian glassmakers to risk the consequences and to set up their glass pots outside Venice. There are records of Venetian ambassadors using bribery and blackmail to persuade the unfortunate truants to return home. The tide could not be entirely stemmed, and slowly but surely at other glass centres throughout Europe the stylistic Venetian elements — the *façon de Venise* — were introduced by migrant workers from Venice itself, and from Altare near Genoa which was the traditional rival of Venice and where the glassmakers' corporation had a deliberate policy of disseminating workers and techniques. The Italian knowledge thus spread throughout Europe, reaching Vienna in 1428, Sweden in the 1550s and England by 1570 at the latest, so that Venice lost its supremacy in the glass-making industry. Each country showed just a little individuality of style which marked its product from the true Venetian glass.

Inevitably Venice made enemies who considered her power too great, or whose interests conflicted with her own. As a result there were many attempts to break her influence. When the Portuguese found a new route to the Far East via the Cape of Good Hope at the end of the sixteenth century, goods could be shipped to and from the Far East without the necessity of paying high duties to ship them through Venice. Her importance on the trade routes undermined, Venice started to decline, and the Republic finally collapsed in 1797. Long before this the glass trade in northern Europe had overtaken the Venetian manufacture, and from the end of the seventeenth century she had lost her important position to numerous rivals. Taste was beginning to change, looking more towards more solid, colourless crystal glass truly resembling natural rock crystal. Glass of this nature was successfully produced in Britain and Bohemia (Polak, 1969).

The rise of north European glasshouses

Bohemia

Records of glass-making in Bohemia date from the fourteenth century; and because of the abundant supplies of wood for fuel, and of raw materials for the glass, the craft soon established itself there. Glass-making became such an important part of the industrial life of Bohemia that, by the end of the nineteenth century, there were fifty-six glasshouses in operation. Several of the glass styles, the *roemer*, for example, were common to the whole of northern Europe, regional characteristics not developing until the eighteenth century. The *roemer (Figure 2.30)* originated as a large, cup-shaped bowl with a hollow stem which was blown in one piece, and mounted on a long narrow pedestal foot made from a thread of glass wound round a conical pattern. The stem connection was ornamented with prunts and milled collars at the top or bottom. As time passed, the foot assumed more importance and became taller, while the bowl tended to decrease in size. In later years, the pedestal was formed in one piece with a corrugated outer surface to represent the original thread of glass. (The name *rummer*, applied to the large beer glasses made in Britain in the 1780s, is said to be a corruption of the word *roemer*.)

During the sixteenth and seventeenth centuries, German glasses (*humpen*) became gradually taller and wider. They were usually decorated with coloured enamels, and are now classified according to the method of decoration. *Reichsadlerhumpen* bore the double-headed Imperial eagle, and on the outspread wings were painted the coats-of-arms of the fifty-six members of the Germanic Confederation. The thinly blown *kurfurstenhumpen* depicted the emperor and the seven electors. The *daumenglas* was a more robust, barrel-shaped vessel with a series of indentations in the sides to provide finger-grips.

Although the Venetians had supplied enamelled glass for the German market, this is usually easy to

Figure 2.30 Colourless glass *roemer* with a funnel-shaped bowl and a stem decorated with bosses of satyr-heads separated by groups of six prunts. H 107 mm. Sixteenth century. Venice or Southern Netherlands. British Museum, London.

distinguish from the German domestic products since these were more robust and the brighter colours more heavily laid on. Whatever it lacked in finesse, German enamelling succeeded by its sheer exuberance. *Schwarzlot* was another style of painting on glass which gained some popularity during the seventeenth century. This consisted of outlined pictures in black with the clear areas occasionally infilled with a brown wash. Fine examples of *schwartzlot* technique were produced by Johann Schaper (1621–1670) *(Figure 2.31)*.

Bohemian glass had begun to acquire its individual character in the late sixteenth century with the introduction of cutting and engraving. Glass made in the *façon de Venise* had spread northwards through Europe, and with it such techniques as the art of cutting glass as if it were rock crystal. This caught the imagination of the Bohemian glassmakers, and it was from this beginning that the great Bohemian tradition of cutting and engraving glass arose. In the early

Figure 2.31 Cylindrical-footed beaker decorated in *schwartzlot*: on the front a circular medallion frame inscribed, 'IONNES GEORGIUS: ELECTOR SAXONIAE', enclosing a portrait of John George II of Saxony, signed JS (in monogram); on the reverse, an enamelled black wreath, surrounding a small circular concave 'window' of wheel engraved, polished glass. H 82 mm. Probably decorated *c.* 1660-70 by Johann Schaper. Nurnberg, West Germany. British Museum, London.

Figure 2.32 Pokal with acanthus design executed in the *hochschnitt* technique by Friedrich Winter. H 167 mm. *Circa* 1687-91. Hirschberger Tal, Silesia. Kunstmuseum, Düsseldorf.

seventeenth century another innovation by the Bohemians was combined with their skill in engraving to produce some of the most remarkable examples of this technique ever seen. This was the development of a new glass metal which required the addition of lime to the potash–silica batch then in use, to produce a perfectly clear, solid crystal glass. The glass proved to be ideal for decorating by wheel-cutting and engraving; techniques which had been developed in Prague before 1600, and then transplanted to Nuremberg, where a school of engraving flourished throughout the second half of the seventeenth century. The elaborate goblets with multiknopped stems which were made in Nuremberg copied contemporary goldsmiths' work.

Political troubles eventually led to the dispersal of the engravers throughout Germany where engraving became a less popular method of decorating glass. Towards the end of the seventeenth century the taste for *façon de Venise* had declined and been replaced by the new style of wheel-engraving which made use of the qualities of the new glass metal, and which became highly developed in Bohemia and Silesia, a

speciality being imposing goblets engraved in high relief (Ger. *hochschnitt*), the ground of the design being cut back by means of a water-driven wheel (*Figure 2.32*). From Silesia the art of engraving was transplanted to Potsdam, one of the most accomplished workers being Gottfried Spiller.

Goblets with round funnel bowls had knopped stems cut with facets, well proportioned but less ornate than the Venetian equivalent. The glass was thicker and the bowls were often cut with vertical panels and had domed covers to match. The bowl, the cover and sometimes even the foot would be profusely covered with highly ornate baroque decoration interrupted by coats of arms or formal scenes in enamel. For special court commissions gold was often applied to the surface of the glass in relief. Constant handling of such glass would quickly spoil its glory and therefore the highly burnished fired gilding of the Potsdam glasshouses, patronized by the Electors of Brandenberg, was far more practical, and rather more spectacular. Frequently the wheel-engraved decoration on Potsdam glasses is heavily gilded and the overall effect is little short of ostentatious. In the course of the eighteenth century glass engraving spread throughout Germany and Central Europe, centres of special importance being Nuremberg, Kassel, Gotha, Weimar, Dresden and Brunswick, with Warmbrunn and others in Silesia.

Later in the eighteenth and nineteenth centuries more naturalistic themes were introduced, which included woodland scenes with deer. So highly was this combination of glass and engraving regarded that Bohemian artists were persuaded to go to Venice and Spain to introduce the technique there.

Some coloured glass was made in Bohemia, and the most important researcher connected with its development was Johann Kunckel, a chemist working in Potsdam. Kunckel (1679) produced a variety of colours varying from rose pink to purple using Purple of Cassius.

Although cutting and engraving were by far the most important of the decorative processes to be developed in Bohemia, several other techniques, well-known in antiquity, were revived and given a distinctive Bohemian quality: for example, about 1725, the art of enclosing a pattern of gold leaf and transparent enamel between two layers of glass (Ger. *zwischengoldglas*). The inner layer of glass had a lip on the outer surface onto which the outer layer joined, thus making a close-fitting joint which completely protected the delicate film of gold leaf inside. At about the same time Ignatius Preissler was establishing a reputation for painting on glass. Preissler's usual subjects were *chinoiserie* scenes enclosed in baroque scrolls painted in black enamel, and frequently highlighted with gold (*Figure 2.33*). In the early nineteenth century the black basalt wares of the Wedgwood factory in Britain were very popular, and this taste was reflected in black glass vessels: *Hyalith* glass made in Bohemia from 1822 onwards. One of the manufacturers of Hyalith was Frederick Egermann, who was responsible for a number of new varieties of glassware which imitated natural stones such as agate, jasper and marble, as well as transparent glass coloured with chemicals. In the early nineteenth century, transparent and opaque white glass were combined to produce the overlay glass whose popularity lasted throughout the century. It usually consisted of a layer of white over a base of transparent green, red or blue glass. The white glass was then cut through to form windows through which the coloured glass underneath could be seen. The whole was then decorated with gilding or coloured enamel. The idea was taken one step further later in the century when the overlay was reduced to one or two medallions. These were decorated in coloured enamel with portraits, or with bunches of flowers, while the body of the vessel was covered with a fine meandering pattern in gilt. This style of ware was usually made as ornamental ewers or vases.

A cheaper but effective method of producing coloured glass was to cover the outside of a clear vessel with a film of coloured glass. This was applied either as a stain or by dipping the gather in a pot of coloured glass. The commonest colours were fluorescent yellow — produced with uranium — and red, but green and amethyst examples are known. Some glasses cut with vertical panels had each panel coated with a different colour. If the vessel was embellished with engraved decoration the thin layer of colour was easily removed to show the clear glass underneath. Popular subjects were views of spa towns on beakers and tumblers which were sold as souvenirs. Although they were probably not very expensive when they were made, the engraving was always of a high standard.

In the late nineteenth century when the *Art Nouveau* movement began, a Viennese, Louis Lobmeyr, established a factory to produce glass of a

Figure 2.33 Conical bottle of colourless glass, painted in red with Chinese figures, floral scrolls, birds and a spider. Decoration attributed to Ignatz Preissler. H 133 mm. Second quarter of the eighteenth century. Silesia or Bohemia. British Museum, London.

high artistic and technical quality employing Bohemian craftsmen. This was a reaction against the vast quantities of cheaply made mass-produced glassware which was made everywhere during the second half of the nineteenth century. This effort to revive glass-making as an art was continued by the Loetz glassworks where beautifully coloured iridescent glass was made.

The Low Countries

The early history of glass-making in the Low Countries is as vague as that of the rest of northern Europe. Geographically the area comprises the country between the Rhine and the Mosel rivers (now forming part of Germany), the seven provinces of the Netherlands, and the general area of Belgium. It was rarely all under one rule at any one time, and was variously controlled by the Spanish and Austrians (Brooks, 1973).

Glass-making in the Low Countries first came to prominence with the introduction of Venetian glass in the fifteenth century. The Venetian *cristallo* which was such an improvement over its predecessors was displayed and advertised in all the courts of Europe, and seems to have attracted particular attention in the Low Countries. There are records of glasshouses being established to make the *façon de Venise* in Antwerp (1537), Liège (1569) and Amsterdam (1597). The trade flourished, and the area became the most important in Europe outside Venice to produce the Venetian style of glassware. Its distance from Venice, however, led to slight differences in the character of the glass but it is still difficult to distinguish the glass made in local glassworks from that imported from Venice.

While the *façon de Venise* flourished, other glassworks in the principal towns as well as many others in minor centres continued to turn out masses of utilitarian wares in the traditional styles of the region. The local tradition still made use of *waldglas*, but by the sixteenth and seventeenth centuries the greenish metal had been developed further, and a whole range of blue-greens produced. The *roemer* was one of the native styles which acquired great popularity, and several types, identified by the prunts applied to the stems, have been assigned a provenance in the Low Countries. One of these employed prunts which were flattened and smoothed to the point where they blended into the wall of the vessel. This produced different depths of colour according to the varying thickness of the glass. Two other prunt variations were those moulded on the surface with a face of Neptune, and those with beads of blue glass applied to the centres. During the seventeenth century *roemer* stands were made. They were tall pedestals in precious metals designed to have a *roemer* clamped into a mounting on the top.

Due to the proportions of the *roemers* then in use this had the effect of producing a tall metal goblet with a glass bowl. The total effect was reminiscent of the elaborate tall goblets made by the Nuremberg goldsmiths. Another style peculiar to the Low Countries was the tall, narrow flute. This was a very thinly blown glass up to 450 mm high and 50 mm wide. The funnel bowl was usually mounted on a single hollow knop and a spreading foot. Very few of these fragile glasses have survived (*Figure 2.34*).

Figure 2.34 Tall, colourless glass, conical flute. The bowl is engraved with a diamond point; on the one side a portrait of a young boy, on the other side, the coat-of-arms of the House of Orange. H 401 mm. Mid-seventeenth century. British Museum, London.

From the end of the seventeenth century the lead glass being produced in Bohemia and Britain became increasingly popular with Dutch glass engravers, by virtue of the clarity and denseness of the metal. The Bohemian glassmakers had an efficient marketing organization, and set up warehouses in the Netherlands to stock their products. The Newcastle light baluster style was particularly favoured; during the eighteenth century British lead glass was much imitated by local glasshouses. The traffic was not all one way however, elaborate baskets and dessert services made in Liège during the seventeenth and early eighteenth centuries were popular in Britain. These vessels were made of threads of glass built up in layers to produce an open-mesh design. They stood on plain glass plates decorated with a border executed in the same mesh style.

Engraving was the only applied method of decorating glass which achieved any degree of importance in the Low Countries, and throughout the seventeenth and eighteenth centuries there were a number of artists whose work was of the highest order. The technique as developed in the Netherlands was quite different from that practised in Bohemia. Dutch engraving was carried out on the surface of the vessel with the delicacy of painting, while Bohemian engraving depended on a good thickness of metal and was more closely allied to sculpture. One of the earliest recorded Dutch engravers, Anna Roemers Visscher (1583–1651), was one of a very few women known to have been engaged in this work. She specialized in a free-flowing style of calligraphic engraving, a method also favoured by Willem von Heemskerk (1615–1692) in the seventeenth century, and by Hendrik Scolting in the eighteenth. The finest seventeenth-century work was produced by artists such as Frans Greenwood, David Wolff and Jacob Sang. The first two specialized in stipple engraving, a method whereby the surface of the glass was marked by repeated light blows with a diamond-pointed tool. The density of the marks thus produced determined the variations in tone and shading of the completed picture. The resulting effect was rather similar to a thin photographic negative. It required a complete sureness of touch and considerable artistic ability for its success (*Figure 2.35*). Because of these demands on the artist, stipple engraving was never widely practised, but there are a few engravers at present working in Britain (1987) who can produce stippled decoration comparable in quality to that of the eighteenth-century Dutch masters. Jacob Sang specialized in wheel-engraving, and his work has a delicacy, precision and sureness of touch which few engravers have equalled. Foremost among his work are those glasses which he engraved with coats of arms.

Figure 2.35 Detail of a goblet of colourless glass, the bowl of which is almost entirely decorated with stipple engraving, and inscribed, 'F. Greenwood Ft'. H 242 mm. English, perhaps Newcastle-upon-Tyne, engraved in Dordrecht, Holland, by Francis Greenwood. *Circa* 1750. British Museum, London.

Britain AD 1500–1850

During the first half of the sixteenth century there was an influx of French glassworkers to Britain from Lorraine. It appears that they were not popular and eventually they left the Weald and settled in other parts of the country. The principal cause of their unpopularity was the rate at which the forests were destroyed by use of wood fuel in the glass furnaces. Glassworkers were in competition with ironworkers for wood fuel; the latter however were static, while the glassworkers with their much lighter glass pots could move on whenever the local supplies of fuel were exhausted. Crossley (1967, 1972) calculated that the furnace at Bagot's Park in Staffordshire (AD 1535) would use *circa* 130 tonnes of wood per month (i.e. 1.6 hectares of 15-year-old coppice) and that as a consequence the modern area of Bagot's Park would be denuded of trees in 15 to 20 years. The fuel consumption would correspond to about $60 \, \mathrm{W\,h\,g^{-1}}$

compared with 4 Whg^{-1} coal at the beginning of the twentieth century, and less than 1 Whg^{-1} in the best oil-fired present-day practices. With the consumption of forests at such a rate the British Government became alarmed about the loss of trees for naval building, and in 1615 James I banned the use of wood for making glass. Nevertheless the landowners welcomed the use for glass-making of otherwise unsaleable timber.

By the early seventeenth century coal was beginning to be used as an alternative source of fuel. This encouraged the dispersal of the French glass-makers from the south of Britain and led them to settle in districts where coal was readily available, such as Stourbridge and Newcastle, where their influence was to be felt for 200 years or more. One of the Lorraine glass-makers was Jean Carré who, in 1567, obtained a licence for 21 years to set up a glasshouse in London, where he undertook to produce glass in the *façon de Venise* since the Venetian product was still highly regarded in Britain. To this end Carré imported several Venetian glass-makers and was the first manufacturer in Britain to use soda instead of potash as a source of alkali, possibly as a result of his Venetian contacts. When Carré died in 1572 one of his Venetian craftsmen, Jacob Verzelini, took over the licence and in 1575 was himself granted a 21 year licence for the making of drinking glasses, '. . . suche as be accustomablie made in the towne of Morano' (Douglas and Frank, 1972), but in fact the Verzelini glass was much plainer and more functional than the continental examples of *façon de Venise*. Only a handful of glasses exist which can be attributed to the Verzelini glasshouse (*Figure 2.36*). They are all goblets in *façon de Venise*, engraved in diamond-point and bearing dates between 1577 and 1586. Verzelini ran the glasshouse for 17 years before retiring, and he finally died a rich and respected citizen of London in 1606.

With Verzelini's retirement the monopoly to make glass in Britain passed through several hands until Sir Robert Mansell gained control in 1618, having bought up existing monopolies. Mansell was successful as a result of the law of 1615 prohibiting the use of wood fuel for firing glass pots, since he had acquired the patents covering the use of coal as a fuel for that purpose. He established a number of glasshouses in England which made glass using Spanish *barilla* (containing soda and lime) as a source of alkali, coal fuel and employing workmen from Altare in Spain. Mansell maintained control of the glass industry for about 30 years. His enterprises do not seem to have survived the Civil War and the Commonwealth (1640–1660); and it was only on the restoration of King Charles II to the throne that glass-making began to flourish. In 1663 George Villiers, Duke of Buckingham, petitioned Charles II for what was probably a renewal of Mansell's monopoly. He

Figure 2.36 Goblet of soda glass by Verzelini, engraved probably by Anthony de Lysle; initials 'AT : RT' and date 1578. H 211 mm. Fitzwilliam Museum, Cambridge.

opened a glasshouse at Vauxhall in London with the aid of a Frenchman, Jean le Cam, to make looking glasses and imitations of rock crystal. However, Villiers never secured the totally monopolistic power of his predecessors.

In 1664 the Glass Sellers' Company was formed, and from that date onwards the glass trade was largely dictated by that company. Two factors illustrate this clearly. Firstly, in surviving correspondence between John Greene, a glass seller in London, and Allesio Morelli in Venice, from whom he bought glass, Greene states exactly how the orders are to be executed, often complaining of the quality and enclosing sketches of the shapes and styles to be supplied (Savage, 1965). The second factor concerns the backing of George Ravenscroft by the Glass Sellers' Company to pursue research into the development of a new type of glass. Thus the trade had changed in 100 years from an industry based on individual semi-itinerant glass-makers to a properly organized and commercial enterprise controlled by a regular trade association. This was to prove the springboard for the ascendancy of British glass over the next 150 years.

George Ravenscroft

Venetian glass was thinly blown and delicate, and fine pieces executed for wealthy families were undoubtedly treasured and carefully preserved, so that many of them still survive. However, little of the glass made for everyday use remains. Indirectly George Ravenscroft was to change this since his glass was more robust; and thus relatively large quantities of eighteenth-century domestic glass still exist (Davis, 1972).

Ravenscroft was not a glassmaker by trade, and reached the age of 55 years before setting up a glasshouse at the Savoy in London to carry out experiments to create a new type of glass. The late seventeenth century was a period of intense research and experiment by men of culture and education, to advance scientific knowledge for the benefit of their fellow men. The Royal Society was a product of this era. Ravenscroft's early experiments were unsuccessful, the glass crizzling as a result of the imbalance of constituents, but eventually showed such promise that in 1674 the Glass Sellers' Company established him in a glasshouse in Henley-on-Thames, Berkshire, to pursue his researches in seclusion. This was on the condition that when a successful formula was achieved, the vessels would be manufactured to the Company's own specifications. (However, Ravenscroft took the precaution of obtaining a 7 year patent on his new ideas) (Brooks, 1973; Rendel, 1975; Watts, 1975; Macleod, 1987; Moody, 1988).

Most early lead glass showed distinct tinges of colour, usually black, green or yellow, which were the result of impurities in the raw materials. Undoubtedly the glassmakers endeavoured to produce a metal that was colourless, and added various chemicals to counteract the impurities. However this was very much a case of trial and error, and success was achieved more by chance than chemical control. A more certain result could be achieved by using purer materials, for example, sand free from contaminants could be obtained from areas near King's Lynn in Norfolk, and near Newcastle-upon-Tyne; sand from these areas being shipped to all the British glass-making centres.

By 1676 such progress had been made that the Glass Sellers' Company issued a certificate expressing its satisfaction with the new *glass of flint* as it was called, and giving permission for the glassware to be identified by means of a seal bearing a raven's head. By this device a small number of glass vessels can be attributed to the Ravenscroft glasshouses. The secret of the glass production was the addition of lead oxide to the raw materials, which produced a soft and brilliant metal of great refractive quality. The Venetian *cristallo* had looked clear and transparent partly on account of its thinness, but the new lead glass remained clear and transparent when much thicker glass was blown. Lead glass did not lend itself to the extravagances of the Venetian style, but because of its lustre, plainer shapes made as effective a display (Charleston, 1960).

Ravenscroft terminated his agreement with the Glass Sellers' Company in 1679; and died in 1681 about the same time as his patent expired. The glasshouse was continued by Hawley Bishopp, who had worked with Ravenscroft at Henley on behalf of the Glass Sellers' Company, and who presumably knew the lead glass formula. However, before many years had passed lead glass was in common use in all the glass-making centres of Britain.

For the first few years after the introduction of lead glass, vessels continued to be made in the Venetian tradition. Indeed, Ravenscroft had imported two Venetian glassmakers to work in the Savoy glasshouse. As early as 1670 the designs which John Greene had sent to Venice had shown a tendency to simplify the Venetian styles, and as time went by several factors combined to create a particularly British style. As the demand for glass grew, and new glasshouses opened, there could never have been enough skilled Venetian workers to staff them all. Therefore increasing numbers of British glassworkers would have had to be trained and it is unlikely that they would have acquired and exactly imitated the abilities of their Venetian teachers.

Lead glass became so popular that, as previously mentioned, various attempts were made on the Continent to produce lead glass in the *façon de l'Angleterre*. This was not achieved until the late eighteenth century, largely due to the fact that in order to protect lead glass from the effects of smoke it was necessary to use covered pots, and this was not the practice in continental glasshouses. The British glass-making industry, however, was already using covered pots before the introduction of lead glass, as a direct result of the need to use coal as an alternative fuel to wood (Newton, 1988).

During the period under review the various changes of style and decoration followed each other in a regular sequence which has been catalogued by Barrington Haynes (1959). The transitional period from about 1680 to 1690 is usually referred to as the Anglo-Venetian, when such Venetian characteristics as spiked gadroons, trailed decoration and pincered stems still appeared on glassware. These gradually disappeared to give way to the first period which can be described as being peculiarly British: the period of heavy baluster stems, 1690–1725. The knop formations on the stems of the glasses derive from the hollow blown knopped stems of Venetian glasses, and were the last signs of Venetian influence on British glass. The stems of British glasses of the period were either solid or contained air bubbles (tears). The early baluster stems were notable for their size and weight. The bowls are usually solid at the base, and the knops appear in a variety of forms with such descriptive names as cylinder, egg, acorn and mushroom knop. As time passed the proportions of the glasses became more refined; the height increased, the weight decreased, and where the stem had previously been made with one knop, combinations of knops became fashionable. This style reached its peak with wine glasses made in the Newcastle-upon-Tyne glasshouses in the north of England. The Newcastle light baluster was tall with a multiknopped stem often containing rows of tiny air beads, and of clear colourless glass. One of the most famous glass-making families in Newcastle at this period was that of Dagnia. The family was of Italian origin and seem to have arrived in Newcastle from Bristol in about 1684. Until that time only sheet glass and bottles were made in Newcastle, and it is quite possible that the Dagnias brought with them the recipe for the new lead glass and began the quality glass trade which culminated in the fine wine glasses referred to above.

Contemporary with the baluster period was another group of glasses which owed their introduction to the accession of George I to the throne of England in 1714. To mark this event glasses with the so-called Silesian stems were produced. These glasses had tapering, four-sided moulded stems which the English glassmakers soon modified to six or eight sides. The glasses retained their popularity along with the baluster glasses until the introduction of the *Glass Excise Act* of 1745.

From the seventeenth century onwards the British Government had considered glassmakers to be a fruitful source of revenue. In 1695 William III had introduced a window tax which greatly reduced the output of glass and caused much unemployment in the trade. The duty was subsequently repealed, but was levied again in 1745 as a duty on raw materials. As a result glassware became plainer in shape and lighter in weight to minimize the effect of the tax; and plain-stemmed glasses containing less lead were introduced (Charleston, 1959a). From the mid-eighteenth century public taste changed, the more ornate *rococo* and *chinoiserie* styles becoming popular, and the glassmakers changed their styles to meet the demand. From 1750 onwards air-twist and opaque-twist stems made their appearance. Both these styles were suited to an art which put a premium on the amount of raw material used since they permitted decorative glass to be made without the large quantities of glass necessary for producing baluster stems. Air-twist and opaque-twist stems remained popular until 1777 when a further duty was imposed on the enamel rods used in the production of the opaque twist stems; these were then made in less quantity, and cutting began to re-emerge as the main form of decoration.

In the 1770s cutting again became popular (Bickerton, 1971), but this time as a method of decorating the glass stems with facets. The plain stems were cut with a series of scallops so that the intersecting edges formed diamonds or hexagons.

The art of glass-cutting spread rapidly and from 1780 onwards a wide range of glassware was being made with more and more elaborately cut designs. Cutting exploited the lustrous and refractive qualities of lead glass, and for the next 50 years British glass-making reached a peak of quality in both metal and decoration. After 1830 styles tended to become fussier and the art of cutting generally went into decline. Throughout the period many other domestic articles besides vessels were made in glass, for example chandeliers, candlesticks, jugs, bowls, decanters, bottles and sweetmeat dishes. Besides cutting, other forms of decoration were employed such as engraving, gilding and enamelling, but they rarely achieved either the degree of quality or popularity that they attained on the Continent. Engraving on glass is rare in the early eighteenth century, and when it began to make an appearance after 1730, wheel-engraving was the method of production generally preferred to hand-engraving (Brooks, 1973). In 1820 an annual licence was introduced which greatly disrupted glass manufacture. Its operation was very complicated; furnaces were locked by inspectors, and 12 hours' notice in writing had to be given before a glass pot was filled. Moreover, the regulations made it virtually impossible to introduce new types of glass, such as a type for lenses or for bottles which would be acid-resistant (Douglas and Frank, 1972). These restrictions were lifted in 1845, and the glass industry immediately entered a period of rapid growth.

Diamond-point engraving by British artists in the eighteenth century is virtually unknown. On the other hand, large quantities of the fine Newcastle light balusters were exported and most of those which survive bear Dutch engraving, both wheel-engraving and diamond-point, which is of an exceedingly high standard. Gilding occurs either as *oil gilding* which was not permanent and became barely distinguishable as a result of constant handling, or as gilding which was *fired* onto the glass to produce a permanent decoration. James Giles, a London engraver and decorator, executed a number of glasses decorated with fired gilding, and his style consisting of sprays of flowers and insects, is easily recognizable. In the last quarter of the eighteenth century the Jacobs family in Bristol also produced a great deal of gilded glassware; unusually, many of the pieces were signed. Enamelling was only carried out by a few artists. Most examples are attributed either to Michael Edkins or to the Beilby family, although there are a few enamelled glasses which do not conform to the style of either of these. The enamelled designs attributed to Edkins are nearly all executed on dense, opaque, white glass which was made in Stourbridge or Bristol to resemble porcelain. Edkins is recorded as having worked in both towns, and the decorations consist of birds, flowers and *chinoiserie* designs. The Beilby family, brother and sister, worked in Newcastle from 1762 to 1778. They painted small scenes of rural pursuits or classical ruins on sets of wine glasses, usually in white enamel. The family must have been widely known and highly regarded since a small number of surviving goblets carry coats of arms in polychrome decoration which had been executed to special orders for titled families (*Figure 2.37*). There was also a demand for coloured glass. While early eighteenth-century pieces do exist, they are rare, and the majority of surviving coloured glass dates from the late eighteenth and early nineteenth centuries. The principal colours used were green, blue and amethyst, while amber and red are rare.

Figure 2.37 Two clear glass goblets decorated with the crest, arms and motto of the Earls of Pembroke and of Montgomery, and signed Beilby 1765-1770. Newcastle-upon-Tyne, UK. Corning Museum of Glass, New York.

A method of dating glass of this period is by reference to the many pieces which were engraved to commemorate a person or event. Probably the best known British commemorative glasses are those relating to the Jacobite movement from the failure of the Rebellion of 1745 to the death of Prince Charles Edward in 1788. During this period several societies sympathetic to the Jacobite cause flourished, and it was fashionable though treasonable to drink a toast to Bonnie Prince Charles from glasses bearing his portrait or emblems representative of the movement.

Occasionally Latin mottoes expressing hope for his return from exile were added, such as *Fiat*, *Audentior Ibo* and *Revirescat*.

Britain after 1850

Towards the middle of the nineteenth century the orderly progression of one style to another which had occurred during the previous 150 years collapsed. Influences from abroad, notably Bohemia, had a marked effect on design in Britain, and the introduction of new production techniques such as press moulding from America led to cheaper glassware catering for a much wider market than ever before. National and international exhibitions culminating in the Great Exhibition of 1851 introduced many new styles to the British public. The purpose-built building in which the Great Exhibition was held, the Crystal Palace, was an enormous glass and cast iron construction. One of its principal features was a glass fountain weighing about 4 tonnes built by the firm of T & C Osler of Birmingham. At the exhibition the finest designs and the newest manufacturing methods from all parts of the world were displayed. When it was over glass-making in Britain changed radically: as the Industrial Revolution gathered momentum and manufacturing units became larger, small firms using traditional hand methods became uneconomic. This led to the concentration of the glass industry into fewer companies. Glass-making declined in areas such as Bristol and London, and became established principally in the Midlands, around Stourbridge and Birmingham, and along the rivers Tyne and Wear around Newcastle, where there was an abundance of fuel and raw materials. Whereas in earlier years every glassmaker had been content to produce what was in popular demand, after 1851 each manufacturer endeavoured to produce designs which were quite different from those of his competitors. To protect their interests designs were registered, and during the second half of the century literally thousands of patterns for glassware were registered. Changes in style and taste were so rapid that it becomes difficult to date glass made after 1850; but attribution to particular factories is often easier, since it was the practice of some factories to mark their products with the name of the company. The taste for continental glass was encouraged by the Great Exhibition, and Bohemian styles of coloured and overlay glass as well as the French style of opal and frosted glass decorated with coloured glass buttons became very popular.

Glass had to be manufactured to suit all pockets, and there was a demand for mass produced wares for the working classes, as well as for high-quality glass products for the wealthy. A good example of this dual production is the difference in quality that occurred in Bohemian-style ruby glass. Expensive glass was made by covering a clear glass vessel with a layer of red glass. Expert craftsmen would then cut through the outer layer to expose panels of clear glass. Vessels produced in this way were known as *Biedermeier* glasses. On the other hand, cheap glasses were produced by first cutting facets in the vessel after which the surrounding areas were filled in with a ruby stain. To produce the former foreign craftsmen were often brought to Britain to work in their own tradition while the cheaper versions could be made with almost any class of labour.

Among the immigrant workers who settled in the Stourbridge area were several decorators who established high reputations for their skill: Frederick Kny, William Fritsche and Paul Oppitz all executed the most beautiful engraving in the Bohemian tradition, and their work was shown at many exhibitions. Jules Barbe was a gilder in the French style whose work has never been bettered in Britain. All these craftsmen worked at one time or another for the firm of Thomas Webb & Son. Webb's which was founded in 1856 and which is still operating is one of several firms which established the high reputation of Stourbridge glass in the nineteenth century. Others were Richardsons, Stevens & Williams, and Boulton & Mills. In Birmingham, George Bacchus & Sons, Rice Harris & Sons, and T & C Osler were well-known glass-making firms.

The British glass-makers did not take their inspiration solely from European sources. For example, in 1885 Queen Victoria received a gift of Burmese glass (which had recently been invented at the Mount Washington Glass Factory in America); and in a short while Thomas Webb & Son had agreed to make Burmese glass under licence in Britain. This unusual glass was shaded from pink to yellow, an effect which was achieved by adding gold and uranium to the raw materials.

Cameo glass was redeveloped in the nineteenth century by John Northwood, a famous Stourbridge glassmaker, who was associated with the firm of Stevens & Williams. Cameo glass was always extremely expensive since it required great skill and patience on the part of the carver. One of the best known decorators in this field was George Woodall, who worked for Thomas Webb & Son. He specialized in carving classical figures in flowing robes; signed examples of Woodall's work command very high prices. Various methods were invented to produce glass which had the appearance of cameo glass but which could be mass produced.

Although glass-making largely died out in London, the oldest glass-making firm in Britain was a London company, J Powell & Sons, which was established about 1700. The firm made glass for William Morris and has been responsible for fine handmade glassware in the twentieth century. The other main centre of glass-making in the nineteenth century was in the north of England. The area around Newcastle-upon-Tyne produced much of the cheaper pressed glass for the mass market. The technique of press moulding was developed to a very high standard, and a wide variety of goods was made. The most sought after glassware was made from slag glass. This was an opaque glass in a variety of colours, the most typical of which had a purple and white marbled effect. The three most important companies which made slag glass, and which often added their trade mark to the moulds so that their products could be identified, were Sowerbys Ellsion Glass Works, G Davidson & Company, and H Greener & Company. In addition to moulded glass much coloured decorative glass was made in the north of Britain. It derived from the Venetian tradition with its liberal use of applied glass decoration. Coloured glass baskets, spill vases and candlesticks were popular.

In the twentieth century several attempts have been made to establish artist–craftsmen studios in order to break away from the mass production methods of the large factories. Among the better known of these are the names Greystan and Monart.

Ireland

There is documentary evidence for glass-making in Ireland from 1258 onwards, when French glassmakers began to operate there. They probably made their way to Ireland from the glass-making centres in Sussex. In 1586 a Captain Thomas Woodhouse acquired a patent giving him the sole right to make glass in Ireland for 8 years. However, the venture does not appear to have been very successful, for in 1589, George Longe, a trained British glassmaker with considerable interest in the British glass trade, bought the patent. Longe is the first recorded experienced British glassmaker; until this time the glassmakers had all been French or Italian. The Act of 1615 banning the use of wood for firing glass furnaces was not extended to Ireland until 1641, so that it is quite possible that there was a further influx of French glassworkers from the south of Britain after the Act was passed. After 1641 glass-making in Ireland seems to have declined.

The first glasshouse producing lead glass was set up in Dublin in 1690 by a Captain Roche, barely 10 years after Ravenscroft's patent had expired. Roche went into partnership with Richard Fitzsimmons, and the company continued in business until about 1760. At the same time as the *Excise Act* of 1745 imposed a duty on glass made in Britain, Irish glass was exempted, but its export to Britain was prohibited. This badly affected the Irish glass-making trade since the number of the island's inhabitants able to afford good quality glassware was too small to support any great manufacturing capacity. At the same time the effect on the Irish home trade was aggravated by the fact that imports from Britain were not banned. However, in 1780 the granting of free trade and the lifting of all restrictions on the industry put new life into the Irish glass trade. The art of glass-cutting was becoming fashionable in Britain at this time but, as mentioned previously, heavy duties had an inhibiting effect upon this type of decoration. The British manufacturers therefore saw the creation of free trade for Ireland as a golden opportunity to cater for the public demand without having to pay the heavy duties they would incur at home.

The reputation of Irish glass was made from 1780 to about 1830; and glasshouses were established in Cork, Waterford, Dublin and Belfast. Those amongst them which were financed by Irishmen, such as the Penrose brothers at Waterford, relied entirely, in the first instance at least, on imported British craftsmen to produce the glass. In 1825 the Irish free trade was ended, and the advantage of manufacturing in Ireland was lost. This, combined with an increasing floridity of style, caused a decline in the trade and the importance of Irish glass. Before the use of cut decoration, the product of the Irish glasshouses was indistinguishable from that of the British factories. After 1780 when cutting became fashionable the same patterns were produced in both countries, but there were certain characteristics which help to distinguish the Irish product. Most important among these was the occasional practice of impressing the factory name on the base of tableware, particularly decanters. Examples are the names of B Edwards, Belfast, Cork Glass Company, and Penrose Waterford. Certain styles of engraving are associated with particular factories, and some styles of cutting are peculiarly Irish (Warren, 1970; Brooks, 1973).

Irish glass is synonymous with the name Waterford (*Figure 2.38*). There is no doubt that the Waterford Glass Factory did acquire a very high reputation for its products, but there were other important factories also operating between 1780 and 1850: Cork Glass Company, Waterloo Glass House, Cork, Terrace Glass Works, Cork, B Edwards, Belfast, Belfast Glass Works, Richard Williams & Company, Dublin and Charles Mulvaney, Dublin. The history of the Waterford Glass House is well documented by advertisements, factory records and correspondence between members of the Penrose and Gatchell families. The factory was founded in 1783 by the brothers George and William Penrose; wealthy men who knew nothing of glass-making, but could see the opportunities which free trade offered. Initially the factory was staffed by British craftsmen under the leadership of John Hill of Stourbridge who was an experienced glass-maker. Hill stayed for 3 years and then left apparently in disgrace. Before leaving, Hill handed on his glass-making secrets for

Figure 2.38 Cut glass honey jar with raised diamond pattern. Eighteenth century. Waterford, Ireland. National Museum, Dublin.

mixing the raw materials to a clerk, Jonathan Gatchell. As the holder of such important information, Gatchell grew to be an important figure in the business, and in 1799 with two partners he bought out the then remaining Penrose brother. Thereafter the company remained in the hands of the Gatchell family until it closed in 1851.

North America

Glass-making in North America began in 1608, little more than a year after the first settlers had arrived. The glasshouse, owned by the Virginia Company, was situated at Jamestown (near Richmond, Virginia) and covered an area 15 m by 11 m. It was considerably larger than any of the contemporary medieval glasshouses in the Chiddingfold region of southern Britain. The furnace itself was rectangular and, like so many of the British examples, it was found to be devoid of useful fragments of the articles which had been made in it because the site would have been cleared of glass for cullet (Harrington, 1952). It seems that the Jamestown glasshouse had been set up to make use of the extensive forests available for fuel in the New World, and thus to provide cheap glass for use in Britain. This at a time when British glass-makers were discouraged and eventually prohibited from burning wood in their furnaces, and coal-firing was still in its infancy. There was not a large local demand for glass, either as tableware or as windows, in the pioneer Colonial houses, and the project was abandoned in 1624.

During the next 150 years there were desultory attempts to set up glasshouses, one of the longer lived being the glassworks built in 1738 by Caspar Wistar at Alloway, in Salem Co., New Jersey. This began the German domination of the American glass industry that was to continue until the nineteenth century. Wistar died in 1752 and his son, Richard, managed the modest business in an effective manner until 1767. Some of the glass made there has been found to contain about 17 per cent lead oxide, which probably got into the glass from the addition of English 30 per cent lead oxide cullet in an attempt to improve the glass. A more spectacular venture was started in 1763 by a 'Baron' Stiegel, first at Elizabethtown (near Lancaster, Pa.) and then at Manheim nearby. Stiegel ran the glassworks in a flamboyant manner, eventually becoming bankrupt and ceasing operations in 1774. The products of the Stiegel and Wistar glasshouses possess considerable artistic merit, but care needs to be exercised when using contemporary sources of information as evidence for the quality of the glass because, at that time, it was politically expedient to conceal from the British Colonial authorities the success which had been achieved by American glass-makers. Thus Benjamin Franklin instructed his son William, Governor of New Jersey, to report in 1768 that Wistar made only 'coarse window glass and bottles'. Stiegel imported glassworkers from Europe; and eighteenth-century American glassware was made in the German and British styles, making it difficult to distinguish from imported wares. Exceptions to this were the mould-blown flasks and bottles, on which the decoration was often of a commemorative nature, for example, those dating from after 1830, bearing the legend Union and Liberty.

After the War of Independence (1775–1783), the Amelung New Bremen Glassmanufactory was set up in 1784 at New Bremen on the Monocasey River in Frederick County, Maryland, by Johann Friedrich Amelung. He had previously worked at the famous Grünenplan glassworks in Germany (south of Hanover) where glass had been made since the fourteenth century. The British tried hard to prevent Amelung from going to America to set up the glasshouse, first by arranging for the Hanoverian Government to forbid emigration and secondly by trying to capture the vessel during its passage through

Figure 2.39 Aerial view of part of the Amelung glasshouse, USA, excavated in 1963, showing the west melting furnace with its four wings, which are believed to have housed small fritting ovens. Beyond these foundations, to the right, can be seen the remains of a pair of annealing ovens, while in the top left corner stands the east melting furnace. The modern metal roof in the background covers the pair of fritting ovens excavated in 1962. From Schwartz (1974).

the English Channel, but Amelung avoided both hazards. The Amelung New Bremen factory was burnt down in 1790 but some manufacture went on until 1795 (Lanmon and Palmer, 1976; Hume, 1976). The site was excavated in 1963 (*Figure 2.39*; Schwartz, 1974) and analyses were carried out on many samples of the glass. Their 'fine glass' (colourless, purple or blue) was found to be a high-potash glass with a moderate lime content (16 per cent K_2O and 9 per cent CaO), but the green, aqua and amber glasses had much less potash and much more lime (5.7 per cent K_2O and 19.6 per cent CaO). Brill and Hanson (1976) suggest that a constant batch composition had been employed but purified wood ash (pearl ash) had been used in the former and the unpurified ash had been used in the latter. Other interesting features were the presence of antimony and certain trace elements; and those glasses made before 1790 contain some lead oxide (0.11–0.64 per cent PbO) while those made after 1790 contain much less (0.0–0.04 per cent PbO).

Apart from the successful Amelung Glassmanufactory 'the intense demand for foreign commodities (following the War of Independence) operated as a strong deterrent to the construction of glassworks in the United States' (Davis, 1949). For this, and for other reasons, such as foreign competition and local taxes, glass manufacture in the United States of America did not make much progress, but between 1786 and 1800 glass-making was carried out in at least six New England states, and monopolies were soon granted; for example, in 1787 the Boston Glass Manufactory had a 15-year monopoly, its capital stock was exempted from all taxes, and its workmen were relieved of military duties.

The British blockade of the Napoleonic Empire brought prosperity to America, and this was reflected in an increase in the number of glasshouses, so much so that the first national survey of manufactures, in 1810, showed that twenty-two glassworks existed, again all on the eastern seaboard, with a total output of more than $1 million; window glass accounted for four-fifths of the total, the amount of lead glass being insignificant. The end of the war with Canada (1812–1814), however, 'not only put an end to rapid expansion of the glass industry but also brought distress to many of the glasshouses that had recently begun operations' (Davis, 1949).

In 1817 the New England Glass Company was formed. Under the ownership of E. D. Libbey, it was threatened in 1885 by a paralysing strike of workmen. Libbey, however, broke the strike and transferred his whole company across the Alleghenies to Toledo, Ohio, where he made a fresh start in 1888. The new company ultimately became the Owens–Illinois Glass Company, the largest and most influential maker of glass containers in the world (Meigh, 1972).

The Census of 1820 showed that deep industrial depression had returned to America, the total annual value of the glass output being only about $0.75 million, much less than in 1810, but 5.4 million ft^2 (5 × 10^5 m^2) of window glass was made, high-quality crown glass being produced in Boston, and cylinder glass elsewhere.

Manufacturing was again concentrated in the east-coast states, and an excellent source of sand was found at Milville (NJ), now the home of the Wheaton Glass Company and the Kimble Glass Company. Wood was generally used as the fuel, except at Pittsburgh where coal was used, and the furnace designs were based on those of Germany whence the migrant glass-makers had come. Some details are available about the consumption of wood in Canada, where the Ontario Glass Manufacturing Company leased 1500 acres of land in 1810. The area was richly covered in beech, hickory, oak and maple, but 14 years later the activities of the glass-makers had cleared 200 acres; however, the owners of the land sold this cleared area as valuable farmland (Polak, 1975).

There was a resurgence in the building of glasshouses between 1825 and 1831, and a higher proportion of lead glass was made. When the fourth Census was carried out in 1850 the annual value of the glass produced had increased to $4.6 million, and then to $8.5 million in 1860. The Civil War (1861–1865) brought about a considerable increase in production; in 1860 there were 1416 workers in thirteen factories but by 1870 these figures had risen to 2859 and 35, respectively.

In the early nineteenth century the even older technique of moulding glass in a closed mould was revived and improved by the process of *press moulding*. By this method flat or tapered vessels were formed in a two-piece mould; one half being used to compress the slug of molten glass into the shape of the other half so that at the point at which the two halves met the mould was full. With this method far more intricate patterns could be produced with much sharper definition, and perhaps even more importantly, articles could be produced at a faster rate. The earliest recorded patent for press moulding was taken out in 1829 when presses were manually operated. During the next 50 years a whole succession of patents was issued covering both improvements in power presses and in moulding processes whereby several articles could be moulded at one time. Press moulding enabled a wide variety of glassware to be made at prices which put cheap copies of cut and decorative glass into every home. Similar developments took place in France, Bohemia and Canada.

In the context of the exchange of ideas between Britain and America, it is interesting to note that Harry Northwood, son of one of the greatest of the Stourbridge glassmakers, John Northwood, emigrated to America in 1885, and 3 years later was running his own glassworks.

As well as the production of utilitarian wares, the continuing search for novelty culminated in a wide variety of flasks and bottles made to represent people, animals, birds, fruit, buildings and railway engines to name but a few. Towards the end of the nineteenth century American glass-makers became involved in the *Art Nouveau* movement, and much elegant and decorative glass was made in the *Art Nouveau* style. Tiffany and Carder were famous glassmakers in this style. Louis Comfort Tiffany (1848–1933) had a studio in New York where a whole variety of imaginative coloured glass was produced whose chief attraction was its iridescence (*Figure 2.40*). One of Tiffany's largest undertakings was a remarkable glass curtain for the stage of the National Theatre of Mexico, the Bellas Artes, in Mexico City. Frederick Carder (1863–1963) learnt his skills at Stourbridge. He emigrated to the USA and helped to found the Steuben Glassworks, Corning, New York State, where glass artists have created individual works which explore to the full the possibilities of shape and decoration.

The first use of natural gas in the industry (1881) gave another great impetus to glass manufacture

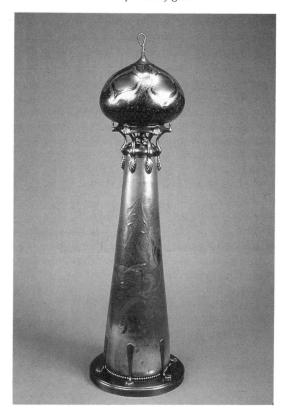

Figure 2.40 Tiffany-Massier lamp. L.C. Tiffany, Long Island/C. Massier, Golfe-Juan, France. *Circa* 1895-1910. H 815 mm. Corning Museum of Glass, New York.

(Davis, 1949), and there was an appreciable movement of glassworks to the gas fields of Pennsylvania, Indiana and Ohio; the total number of glassworks increased by 50 per cent between 1880 and 1890 and the first continuous-melting tank was installed at Jeannette (Pa) in 1888. Glassworkers' Unions and Manufacturers' Associations started to be formed around 1880.

After that time the story is one of growth and remarkable improvements in manufacturing machinery, the Arbogast press-and-blow machine being invented in 1882, the Owens Suction machine in 1904 etc. These developments and the many others in making window glass are recorded by Douglas and Frank (1972).

Summary of nineteenth- and twentieth-century glass-making

The second half of the nineteenth century was a period of enormous technical achievement with Britain and Bohemia leading the field in the middle of the century, but France coming very much to the fore in artistic glass-making towards the end of it, and the great industrial power of America gradually making itself felt, albeit mainly in styles imported from Europe (Newman, 1977). Apart from the traditional techniques of enamelling and gilding, wheel-engraving and wheel-cutting, this period saw the introduction of transfer printing and acid-etching; surface treatments such as revived ice-glass and acid-etched satin finishes; silver and gold leaf decoration, aventurine, and an electrolytic silver deposit process; bubbles of glass trapped within the glass; glass shading from one colour to another owing to heat treatment (Burmese, Peach Blow etc.); wrought decoration of every kind, with twisted and ribbed elements, opaque and coloured twists and threads; and applied drops, and threading (by mechanical process). All these methods were used in an infinite variety of combinations, reflecting the eclectic taste of the period. Of perhaps the greatest significance, however, was the perfection of press moulding in America about 1825, for this brought decorated glass within the means of the poorer classes of society. In France in the 1870s this multiplicity of available techniques was harnessed to the making of individual works of art by Eugène Rousseau and Emile Gallé. Rousseau was greatly inspired by Japanese art and his early glass pieces reflect this in their forms, their decorative composition and their themes. Later, however, Rousseau developed original shapes and decorative techniques of enclosed red, green and black markings, of *craquelure* and of deep wheel-cutting. Rousseau abandoned glass-making in 1885. Gallé had begun manufacturing glass in 1867, and after a period of experimentation with every available decorative technique in a variety of historic styles, he also came under the influence of Japanese art. About 1885 he developed a new lyrical style in which vases with mainly floral polychrome designs were made in complicated casing techniques, with much use of wheel-cutting and acid-etching. Such vases epitomize the *Art Nouveau* style in glass and were highly influential until the First World War (Arwas, 1977). Of equal complexity and sophistication were the glasses of the American Louis Comfort Tiffany, who used embedded drawn threads and other forms, combined with an iridescent surface treatment to produce glass objects equally characteristic of the period (Amaya, 1967).

After the disruption of war, a neutral country — Sweden — took the lead in glass fashion. Two artists, Simon Gate and Edvard Hald, employed by the Orrefors Factory, devised a varient of Gallé's cased glass, Graal glass, covering the cut and coloured layers with a colourless coating, thus embedding them and imparting a smooth surface to the glass. They also produced designs for wheel-engraving on crystal glass. The general Swedish ideal was to produce well-designed goods for everyday use, apart from the luxury wares; and in this their lead was followed by other countries in northern Europe. A more personal style of glass-making, however, was developed in France by Maurice Marinot, a Fauve painter who not only designed glass but made it himself, using techniques of trapped bubbles, powdered oxides, and deep acid-etching in glass objects which exemplified the forms and styles of the 1930s. This spontaneous approach to glass-making was reflected in the work of other French contemporaries: Henri Navarre, André Thuret and Jean Sala; and even the commercial firm of Daum abandoned the traditions of Gallé for glass made under Marinot's influence; while René Lalique applied a highly sophisticated taste to mechanical production by designing glasses with modelled decoration in high relief which could be enlivened by acid-etching and enamelling.

The northern European striving after functionalism was echoed in Murano in 1920, notably in the work of Paulo Venini, Ercole Barovier and Flavio Poli. After the decline of Venetian glass-making in the eighteenth century, the skills and traditions were kept alive through the nineteenth century mainly by the enterprise of Antonio Salviati, and were at the service of the new style when it came. The simple shapes of Venini were often decorated by the thread and mosaic techniques in the opaque white (*lattimo*) and coloured glasses traditional to Venice, while both Venini and Barovier invented new surface treatments to give their various glass products mottled, granulated or dewy effects. The work of these masters continued after the Second World War, but this period has been chiefly characterized by the emergence of the studio glassmaker, first in America — Harvey K Littleton, Dominick Labino and others — and then in Europe. Working single-handed, at small one-man furnaces, studio glassmakers have produced glassware in an infinite number of shapes, often non-functional and sculptural, decorated with bubbles, embedded coloured metallic powders, and other furnace-made ornaments, latterly supplemented by wheel-engraving (Charleston, 1977b).

3

Technology of glass production

Part 1 Methods and materials

The materials for making ancient glasses were naturally occurring rocks and minerals: a mixture of silica, alkali and lime. The silica was generally obtained from sand, but as this contained impurities, which in some areas were considerable, crushed quartz or flint was often preferred. To produce glass the mixture of ingredients had to be heated to about 1000°C, at which temperature the ingredients slowly became liquid and reacted. Fused silica is the parent glass (network former). It is the ideally durable glass but its melting point and its viscosity are so high (see *Figure 1.10*) that it is only in modern times that a satisfactory glass has been melted commercially from sand alone, and then only at considerable expense for special purposes. Since it was impossible for early glass-makers to reach and maintain such a high temperature long enough to melt glass in any quantity, all glasses which were melted in ancient times needed to have much lower melting temperatures (approximately 900°C) and this was achieved by adding alkali in the form of plant ashes, which had the property of lowering the melting point, and which also acted as fluxes or network modifiers. Roughly speaking the amount of modifier required depended on the state of development of furnace technology at any particular era. In antiquity, alkali (which was also used for medicinal purposes, embalming and soap manufacture) was obtained from dried lake deposits or from plant ashes. Ashes obtained by burning saltmarsh plants contain a great deal of soda; while those from forest plants have a high potash content (the latter were used chiefly in Europe during the Middle Ages). The addition of too much alkali to the glass batch had the unfortunate effect of decreasing its durability by increasing its solubility in water. However, there are other network modifiers such as calcium oxide which can act as stabilizers and thereby to a considerable extent balance the deleterious effect of the alkali, thus enabling quite durable glasses to be made. Since no reference is made to the deliberate use of lime in antiquity, its inclusion in the glass batch was probably as an impurity in the sand.

A second group of metallic oxides was used to colour glass. Included in this group are the oxides of copper, iron, cobalt and manganese. Glasses which had not been deliberately coloured tended to appear yellow or greenish owing to the presence of iron as a contaminant of the sand, but from Roman times the colour could be greatly diminished by incorporating a decolorizer such as manganese or antimony. The production of colours in ancient glasses (where this was deliberate) was more complicated than some authors have supposed, since the metal oxides used as colouring agents produced different colours depending upon the firing conditions in the furnace, that is, oxidizing or reducing atmospheres. Most of the early glasses were opaque or translucent as a result of low fusion temperatures which allowed microscopic air bubbles to remain in the viscous glass as it cooled. (High fusion temperatures reduce the viscosity of the molten glass thus allowing air bubbles to escape.) In the production of glass one other ingredient was commonly added to the basic ingredients, that is, scrap glass (*cullet*), which was normally of about the same composition as the batch to be melted. The function of the cullet was purely physical, it acted as a nucleus around which the new glass formed, and helped to eliminate unevenness such as cords and *striae* in the new batch. The use of scrap glass in this way probably accounts for the lack of waste glass products on many glass-making sites.

Apart from the raw materials the process of

making glass required a source of fuel (originally wood, later coal, and in modern production oil, gas or electricity), a furnace (kiln) and crucibles or pots made from refractory (heat-resisting) materials; in practice this material was clay free from fluxes.

The glass batch once molten is often termed *glass metal*. As the metal was cooled it congealed into a solid. The cooling had to proceed slowly in an annealing oven (later called a *lehr*) to relieve stresses set up during the manufacture otherwise the product would shatter.

Initially the methods of glass production were not founded on an understanding of the chemical processes but depended on trial and error, experiments with materials from different sites resulting in many jealously guarded secret recipes and glass-making traditions. There has been much speculation on the supposed technological expertise of ancient glass-makers, based on analyses of their wares and a knowledge of twentieth-century practices in modern glassworks with all their technological facilities. The following examples serve to illustrate how subjective, inconclusive and sometimes erroneous such hypotheses may be. Sayre and Smith (1961) analysed 194 glasses and found five main compositional categories of ancient glass (but ignoring coloured glass, and glass from the Far East). These categories were classified as: glass from the fifteenth century BC to about the seventh century BC — soda-lime glass with a high magnesium content (type A); an antimony-rich group (0.53–1.93 per cent Sb_2O_5) produced from the sixth to about the fourth centuries BC and characterized by low potassium (0.17–0.47 per cent K_2O) and low magnesium (0.60–1.24 per cent) contents (type B); a Roman type produced from the fourth century BC to the ninth century AD, which is similar to type B except that the antimony content is much lower (0.018–0.089 per cent Sb_2O_5) and 'in most cases the manganese content correspondingly higher' — this suggests the possibility that the distinction represents simply the use of one decolorant instead of another (type C); an early Islamic group (eighth to tenth centuries AD) 'is marked by a return to the higher magnesium (3.6–6.5 per cent MgO) and potassium contents' of type A 'but without showing the low manganese content of the early glass'; and six Islamic lead glasses containing 33–40 per cent PbO.

Despite this classification Sayre and Smith (1961) are careful to point out that 'No finality is claimed for these groups'; and Ankner (1965), using published data for 543 analyses of ancient glasses, concluded that Sayre and Smith's categories were not generally valid, the selection of glasses having been concentrated too heavily on material from Egypt, Syria, Greece, Iraq and Iran. Thus type A ignores glass beads from the Bronze Age and Urnfield cultures in Italy, Switzerland and South Germany. Similarly, type B does not include Carthaginian and Etruscan glass, nor glass from the Hallstatt period in Central Europe. Type C ignores the La Tène period, the Scandinavian Iron Age, and glass made by the Scythians, Huns and Awars. In fact Ankner (1965) calls for scepticism among archaeologists when using chemical analysis for determining the origin of ancient glass (Biek and Bayley, 1979).

Sayre (1963) examined about 330 glasses and found that the oxides of antimony and manganese had either a high value (around 1 per cent Sb_2O_5 or MnO) or a low value (say 0.05 per cent), with very few glasses having an intermediate content (about 0.1 per cent) of either oxide. Sayre thus concluded that the low value of the oxide had entered the glass as an impurity but that the high value must have been the result of a deliberate addition of the oxide to the glass batch as a decolorizer (the glasses were in fact colourless), but Newton (1985b) showed that the effect could be explained by the deliberate choice of suitable plant ash.

Sayre (1963) also discovered two other distinct groups of glasses in which magnesia or potash were either both high (e.g. 4 per cent MgO and more than 2 per cent K_2O) or both low (e.g. 1.9 per cent or less MgO and 0.1–2.0 per cent K_2O) which would imply that according to Sayre's earlier argument, the magnesia and potash had been deliberately added to the glass batch. However, Brill (1970d) has shown that the high MgO, high K_2O glasses could well have been made with plant ash as the source of alkali whereas the low MgO, low K_2O glasses were consistent with having been made from natron; thus a change to a high level of an ingredient need not necessarily indicate that a specific ingredient had been deliberately added to the melt, although it would suggest that there had been a change of a raw material. Hypotheses on ancient glass-making should therefore be viewed with extreme caution.

Cold, solid glass can be shaped and decorated by cold working, that is by *glyptic* techniques such as cutting and engraving. However, having the property of becoming molten (*plastic*) when heated to sufficiently high temperatures, practically all ancient and modern techniques of manufacture use glass in that condition and therefore can be described as *hyaloplastic*. Since glass can possess a remarkable wide range of viscosities (and thereby working ranges) depending on its composition and temperature (see *Figure 1.10*) glass artefacts can be made in an almost infinite variety of shapes. No other material has these properties or permits such a varied manufacture to be undertaken. In ancient times knowledge of the working ranges would have been part of the long-held secrets of the glass-making process.

With the invention of glass-blowing new techniques of producing glass artefacts were developed, and along with them the methods of decoloration. These techniques have thus been in use for about two millennia, usually with increasing sophistication, up to and including the present day, despite the introduction of industrial mass manufacturing methods in the nineteenth and twentieth centuries. Consequently, glass-making techniques will be described without attempting to deal with them in strict chronological order, although where possible some indication will be given of the date of their introduction. Tools for hand-working glass have remained essentially unaltered; but increased sophistication of glass designs led to changes in composition, that is choice of raw materials, and to furnace design. These will be discussed in the light of contemporary sources (in so far as these are available and reliable); excavation of land and marine sites; and modern melting trials and hypotheses on ancient glass production. Modern methods of glass-working will be mentioned only briefly, partly because information about it is more easily accessible, but also because on the whole the products pose few conservation problems, at least at present.

Network formers

Several inorganic oxides have the ability to form vitreous materials. Of these silicon dioxide (silica) is by far the most important although boric oxide (sodium borate, familiar as the borax bead of analytical chemistry) was also used in antiquity, although infrequently.

The main source of silica for ancient glass production was sand. In the Near and Middle East sands relatively pure and free from iron (Egyptian sands contain only 1–3 per cent iron) were widely obtainable and therefore the common source. The sands in many parts of Europe however were too impure to be of use in glass-making without prior treatment. In Italy, for example, suitable sand could be found at the mouth of the River Volturnus (mod. River Volturno); but that at the mouth of the River Tiber and on the Italian coast above Ostia was unsuitable since it contained large amounts of volcanic debris. Impure sands in northern Europe could be used for making dark glasses after they had been washed and then burned or brought to red heat to remove any organic matter present. As an alternative source of silica, crushed flint or quartz pebbles were often preferred. Pliny enumerates the following ingredients of the glassmaker: soda (*nitrum*), limestone (*magnes lapis*), shiny pebbles (*calculi*), shells (*conchae*), and excavated sands and sandstones (*fossiles harenae*). In 1645 the English diarist John Evelyn was in Venice and referred to white sand, flints from Pavia ground small, and the ashes of seaweed brought from Syria as the raw

materials used for glass-making (Forbes, 1957). In 1979, Brill filmed glass production in the ancient tradition in Herat, Afghanistan. The raw materials were quartz pebbles, plant ash and scrap copper. White quartz pebbles were collected from a dry river bed, one donkey load providing enough silica for one week's glass production. Plant ash (*ishgar*) was prepared by nomads: plant twigs being heaped together in a shallow pit and burned, after which the ashes were left to cool overnight. To test its quality the glass-makers tasted the *ishgar*, choosing that which had a sweet taste. Before being placed in the furnace to melt, the quartz pebbles were broken and ground and then mixed with the plant ash. To provide colour (the glass produced was bright turquoise), a lump of scrap copper was heated and the surface oxide scraped off and added to the batch. The furnace was fuelled with hardwood brought from the hills by donkey every two weeks; this was the most expensive commodity. A sawn-off rifle barrel was used as a blowpipe (Johnston, 1975).

Network modifiers

The principal network modifiers of which ancient glasses were composed were the oxides of sodium and potassium. Until about AD 1000 the oxide of sodium (*natrium* — *nitrum* in ancient times) was used universally and introduced to the glass batch either as sodium carbonate in the form of soda crystals (Na_2CO_3) or as sodium nitrate ($NaNO_3$). Sodium oxide could also be produced by burning saltmarsh plants, usually *salicornia kali*, or seaweed. Commoner sources of alkali included natural deposits resulting from drying and evaporation of land-locked seas and lakes; and salts obtained by deliberate evaporation of sea or river water in pans or pits. Undoubtedly natron, a natural sodium sesquicarbonate ($Na_2CO_3.NaHCO_3.2H_2O$) from the Wadi Natrûn, north-west of Cairo, would have been used in the glass-making activities there. The composition of natron is complex and variable: the sodium carbonate content varies from 22.4 to 75.0 per cent, sodium bicarbonate from 5.0 to 32.4 per cent, sodium chloride from 2.2 to 26.8 per cent, sodium sulphate from 2.3 to 29.9 per cent plus water and insoluble material. The use of sodium oxide as a modifier resulted in the production of *soda glass* which remained plastic over a wide temperature range, thus lending itself to elaborate manipulative techniques (Hodges, 1964; Toninato, 1984).

During the height of the Roman Empire, glass-making had, at least by AD 50, spread from Syria and Egypt to western areas, and then northwards so that, by about AD 100, glass-makers were operating in the Rhineland. The glasses made in Europe at the time contained low amounts of magnesia and potash, and since there do not seem to have been any sources of soda with the same characteristics available in Europe, it seems reasonable to assume that the glasses were made using natron rather than the ashes of maritime plants (which contain significant amounts of magnesia and potash). The deposits of sodium sulphate in Germany, even if they had been known at the time, would probably have been too difficult to exploit, given the primitive state of glass-making technology (Turner, 1956c). It is possible that natron continued to be transported to the Rhineland even after the collapse of the Roman Empire in the west, for although such a practice might seem to have been uneconomical, it must be remembered that the early glass-makers were extremely conservative about the use of tried and tested raw materials.

A dramatic change in glass-making practice began to occur around AD 1000, in that potash began to replace soda as the regular source of alkali. The exact reason for this change is unknown, but it may have been the result of a greater demand for glass (and therefore fuel). Only relatively small quantities of soda would have been required for the manufacture of glass vessels and ornaments, but, with the onset of the Middle Ages, and especially after the Gothic Revolution, there would have been a large demand for window glass, first for churches and cathedrals and later for palaces. Newton (1985b) has suggested that beechwood ash was used to make coloured glass, and this would have introduced much potash into the glass batch. Once it was realized that the use of beechwood ash would enable a variety of colours to be produced, the glassmakers would have moved into areas where beech forests existed, thus ensuring both a plentiful supply of fuel for their furnaces and of alkali for their glass. Newton (1985b) has shown that there was a scarcity of beechwood south of the Alps, and he has related the glass-making centres in Europe to the distribution of beechwood pollen in AD 1000. Nevertheless, care must be exercised before trying to draw a picture which is too simple. Geilmann and Bruckbauer (1954) showed that the manganese content of beech wood (and, in fact, any component of any plant) depended on the place where the tree had grown, the maturity of the wood, etc., and there must have been many difficulties and failures in trying to make the right colour glass.

The dependence of the physical properties of a glass on its composition is often complicated, although in certain cases the relationship is straightforward; a high content of lead provides a high refractive index and the glass will appear very bright and spectral colours will appear when it is suitably cut (cut crystal glass). Glasses made from beechwood ash contained potash instead of the soda which was characteristic of Roman glass, and they also contained much too much lime for satisfactory stability.

For these reasons medieval window glass decays in damp atmospheres, and all the problems which conservators encounter with medieval stained glass can be attributed to the use of beechwood ash in the manufacture of the glass.

Glass made from sand and modern soda is soluble in water and about 10 per cent of calcium oxide (lime) must be added to impart durability. Too much lime will have the reverse effect, as in the case of glass made with beechwood ash. Ancient soda, obtained by burning maritime or desert plants, was contaminated with enough lime to give a durable glass. Alternatively, if the source of ancient soda might have been reasonably pure, as was some natron, then it was necessary to use a calcareous sand, such as the sand from the mouth of the River Belus. Thus lime was not added in ancient times, but modern glassmakers must ensure that enough lime is present, usually by adding limestone, although many materials, such as felspars can also be used.

Lead oxide was also an unintentional ingredient of ancient glass until Roman times. It imparts a brilliance and density to glass, and was used with great success in the seventeenth century to produce *lead* ('flint') *glass* vessels suitable for facet cutting. Lead oxide was later introduced directly, as one of the two oxides, litharge (PbO) or red lead (Pb_3O_4), or indirectly as white lead or basic lead carbonate ($PbCO_3.Pb(OH)_2$), or as galena, the basic sulphide ore (PbS). The usual source of barium oxide, another unintentional ingredient, was barium sulphide ore ($BaSO_4$ — barytes or heavy spar). The inclusion of aluminium oxide (Al_2O_3 — alumina) which occurs naturally in clays or, in a fairly pure form, as emery or corundum, and in the hydrated form as bauxite ($Al_2O_3.xH_2O$), would improve the durability and also raise the melting point of the batch. Aluminium oxide was in fact an inevitable contaminant, being introduced from the fabric of the crucibles themselves.

Colourants

The common colourants for glass were precisely the same as those used in making glazes and enamels. Unlike the potters, however, who only had to alter the atmosphere of a kiln to produce oxidized or reduced colourings, the glassworkers needed the additional ability to achieve these effects within the batch. Normally the colourants would be in a reduced condition, but the glass modifiers such as the oxides of antimony and arsenic could produce oxidizing conditions within the molten glass, and thus oxidized colourings were produced. Doubtless ancient glassworkers learnt this fact empirically.

Coloured glass was generally *pot coloured*, but

certain colours, especially red, were *flashed*, that is, clear glass was covered with a layer of coloured glass. To produce pot-coloured glass, metallic oxide colouring agents were added to the molten batch in the crucible. Thus, when formed, the glass artefact would be uniformly coloured throughout its thickness. In the manufacture of flash-coloured glass, a gather of clear molten glass was covered by a second gather from a pot of molten coloured glass, so that when the coated gather was blown into a cylinder, cut and flattened out, it formed a sheet of glass which was coloured on one side only, the greater thickness of the glass being clear. Flashed ruby is by far the commonest colour after the fourteenth century, but in recent years examples of others, notably blue, have been found. The process of flashing glass was described by Theophilus in the twelfth century; and imperfectly flashed glasses are found in the earliest examples of glass windows. The flashed or coloured side of the sheet is generally found on the inner face of the windows where it would not be damaged by weathering.

Metals do not dissolve in glass, but exist as colloids in suspension. Gold and copper ruby glasses contain those metals dispersed on a submicroscopic scale, but other highly decorative glasses could be made to resemble the semi-precious stones agate, aventurine, chalcedony, onyx etc. by dispersing flakes of metal or metallic oxides in the glass before the artefact was formed from it. An alternative method of making onyx glass was to place two differently coloured opal glasses in the same crucible, and to make the gather before the mixing was complete. The cold glass could then be cut and polished so that the new surface displayed alternating layers of the colours.

On the whole, copper was used by the Egyptian and Mesopotamian glass-makers to produce bluish-green glass, and cobalt to produce blue or violet glass, although mixtures of copper, cobalt or manganese to produce blue glass were also common. Copper oxides may be introduced to the glass melt as any of the common copper ores, although the oxides and carbonates were the most usual. Under oxidizing conditions, copper oxide colours glass blue or green, depending partly upon which other glass modifiers are present. Thus, with lead oxide, copper oxide will produce greens; with sodium or potassium oxide the colour will be turquoise blue. Under reducing conditions copper oxide will produce a dull red colour. Copper oxide is usually present in the proportions of 2–5 per cent, above which it causes the colour to darken even to black. The Romans used copper and cobalt to produce blue glass, but were equally aware that this colour could be achieved by the use of ferrous iron, and that a reducing atmosphere in the furnace would deepen the blue colour by increasing the number of ferrous ions present. The making of blue glass continued from Roman through Islamic times and received a boost during the Renaissance when the Venetians began producing a rich blue glass. Blue glass was also made on a small scale in the northern Rhine area. It became very popular in Britain during the eighteenth and nineteenth centuries as illustrated by the blue glass being made at Nailsea near Bristol at that time (Chance, 1968).

Ancient red glass was generally made by using copper in a reducing furnace atmosphere. This resulted in a brilliant red opaque glass. A fine red glass from copper was made in Egypt from the time of the Eighteenth Dynasty. The Roman writer Pliny mentions an opaque red glass called haematinum implying it was of local manufacture. In medieval times red glass was still made with copper, but manganese was used to make a pale rose red or pink glass. Manganese oxide may be introduced to the batch either as the dioxide or carbonate of manganese, and will produce purple-brown or shades of violet depending upon which other modifiers are present. For example, with iron it produces black. Manganese is generally used as about 2.6 per cent of the glass metal; and its colour fades if fired above 1200°C. It was not until the end of the seventeenth century that a clear ruby or pink glass could be made consistently. Iron in its ferric state, that is, fired under oxidizing conditions, can colour glass yellow or amber. Any of the ores from which iron may be smelted may be ground and added to the glass metal. When the ore is poorly ground, or when a red clay contains small nodules of iron ores, these will produce local patches of excess iron oxide in the glaze appearing as dark brown or black spots in the surface. The Venetians made a particularly fine green glass in the Renaissance period. Copper or iron could be used to make the green colour under reducing conditions. The brownish-green colour of some English jugs made at the end of the eighteenth century is the result of iron impurities since the glass-maker, to avoid excess duty, had made the vessels from bottle glass. From at least the second century BC, black glass was made by using an excess of iron oxide, that is, 10 per cent or more of the glass batch. However, an excess of any colouring oxide will colour glass so deeply that it takes on a black appearance. The only instance of black glass being produced in Britain in the first half of the seventeenth century is a fragment found adhering to part of a crucible at Denton near Manchester. A combination of iron, manganese and sulphur in the glass, coupled with a smoky atmosphere in the furnace produced a black opacity. The next instance of black glass being produced is found in southern Bohemia, where Hyalith (a dense, opaque jet-black glass) was made from 1820.

The Venetians continually experimented with coloured glasses, and produced a rich purple probably by using manganese. Venetian opaline glass of the seventeenth century was made by using arsenic and calcined bones in the batch. When heated these materials struck an opalescent white colour. The Venetians also continued the ancient tradition of imitating semi-precious stones such as chalcedony, jasper, onyx and agate. From the late 1820s, Friedrich Egermann working in Bohemia, made Lithyalin glass in imitation of natural stones. This was a polished opaque glass marbled with red and other strong colours.

Opacifiers

Ancient glass-makers used antimony to produce a white opacity in glass. There was no great interest in opaque white glass, however, until its potential as an imitation of Chinese porcelain was seen by Italian glass-makers. Opaque white glass produced by adding tin oxide or arsenic to the batch was made at Venice before 1500 and continued thereafter, being especially popular in the eighteenth century. The products certainly had the appearance of porcelain, but feel different (cool) to the touch, and are generally considered to have none of the aesthetic qualities of either material. Tin oxide was normally added as cassiterite (SnO_2), although it could also have been added as an impurity in the raw material, for example, when calcined pewter was added to a batch to produce lead oxide. Tin oxide is not strictly speaking a colourant, but produced a white opacity in glass by existing as a colloid, that is, as a mass of minute crystals. In modern glass-making, fluorspar and zirconia are used to produce opaque white glass.

Modern chemistry has also added a new range of colours to glass-making, such as yellow-browns obtained from titanium, red from selenium, purple and blue from nickel and yellow-green from chromium. Chromium oxide is generally added directly as the oxide chromite which also contains iron, or as a chromate or bichromate. It is a difficult colour to use since the result so often depends not only on the other modifiers present but also on the temperature to which it is fired. Thus with lead, chromium oxide will produce reds at low temperatures and brown or green at higher temperatures. With tin it will produce reds or pinks. Nickel oxide may be introduced from a number of sources, chiefly the mineral millerite (NiS). Alone it produces drab greens, but with iron it produces browns, and if used in great concentrations, black.

Decolorizers

Ancient so-called colourless glasses had in fact always displayed a greenish tint due to the presence of iron from the sand which existed in the iron (II) state in the glass. Initially, care in the selection of proven materials, and their thorough washing, were probably the most common steps taken to avoid the inclusion of contaminants. It was then discovered that glass containing iron oxide could be decolorized by converting the blue colour of reduced iron to the yellow colour of the oxidized state, for example, by altering the melting conditions or by adding oxidizing agents such as the oxides of manganese or antimony to the glass batch. Traces of antimony have been found in glasses dating from at least 2000 BC probably present as an impurity in the raw materials. Depending upon the firing conditions and amount added, antimony can react as a decolorizer or, as mentioned above, an opacifier. During glass-melting with antimony present in the batch, a rise in temperature will convert opaque glass to crystal clear glass. It was therefore inevitable that ancient glass-makers should stumble upon the clarifying power of antimony. Its use reached a peak by Roman times in the second century AD. The development of colourless glass by the Romans was a gradual process, and utilitarian ware such as the typical square bottles (*Figure 2.10*) continued to be made in greenish glass. It was only after *circa* 150 that the real vogue for colourless glass began, and then it became so popular that it displaced strongly coloured glass from the market. Colourless glass also formed the medium favoured by glasscutters in the second and third centuries (Harden, 1969).

Manganese was used increasingly from the first century AD as a decolorizer. Added to the batch as manganese dioxide, it oxidized the greenish colour of the glass and the resultant yellow tinge was compensated for by the purple manganese. Nevertheless, the first author to mention manganese explicitly was Biringuccio (1540), translated by Smith and Gnudi (1942).

Colourless glasses could well have been made initially by using a raw material which (unknown to the glassmaker) contained antimony or manganese. Having obtained a desirable result the use of the material was encouraged (Newton, 1985b). For example, the ash from a certain type of plant (one *not* containing antimony or manganese) might have always produced a green-tinted glass (the iron was not decolorized) whereas the ash from a different type of plant (one which did contain enough antimony or manganese) might have produced a less green or even colourless glass. Brooks (1972) states that the brown marine alga *Fucus vesiculosus* can concentrate manganese to the extent of 90 000 ppm compared with 4800 ppm in vascular plants in general. Such a feature could well have been noticed by those who burnt the plants, or by the glassmakers. However, there is an additional technological complication because the amount of decolorization, and even the amount of opalization (in the case of excess antimony), depended upon the oxidation–reduction situation in the furnace. Geilmann and Bruckbauer (1954) studied samples of beechwood ash from different localities and from various parts of the trees, and found great differences in the manganese content of the samples.

As Sayre (1963) demonstrates, ancient white opaque glasses contain approximately the same amount of antimony as do the colourless high antimony glasses, but the opaque ones become colourless either when melted under reducing conditions or as previously mentioned at an elevated temperature. Thus another possible explanation of the high-antimony situation may be that the glass-makers sometimes obtained opaque glasses and sometimes clear ones depending on the type of flame in the furnace and the amount of organic matter in the batch.

Sayre (1963) also comments on two cases where parts of a glass article did not contain the decolorizer: in the first case a colourless high-antimony glass had a blue thread decoration with a low antimony content, and in the second the body of a bead was low in manganese whereas an outer layer was high in manganese. Sayre (1963) claims that these examples are 'another indication that the antimony was added for decoloration', but equally well, the outer parts of the article might have been made from imported glass (Newton, 1971b,c).

Bearing in mind the empirical and precarious procedures of glass-making used in ancient times it seems unlikely that the glassmakers were knowledge-able enough to be able to add about 1 per cent of an ingredient with any confidence and also disperse such a small amount uniformly throughout the batch (which is not an easy operation even with modern techniques). Moreover, there seems to be no reason to believe that antimony was known in Mesopota-mian times (Brill, 1970d), or that manganese was deliberately added to the glass batch earlier than AD 1540 (Turner, 1956a).

However, whether or not Sayre was correct about the deliberate use of antimony and manganese, his work has resulted in an invaluable wealth of analytical information about glasses from many different eras and geographical locations. Hahn-Weinheimer (1954) has also reported the results of spectrographic studies of many Roman glasses, and has drawn attention to differences in antimony contents.

A clear glass luxury ware was in production as early as the eighth century BC, the glassmakers probably being based in Gordion in Turkey and Nimrud in Mesopotamia. These glasses were mostly bowl-shaped and were ground, cut and polished with a high degree of technical skill. By the third century BC the same type of bowl was being produced in Alexandria in Egypt. However, it was the Romans who achieved the regular production of a transparent and nearly colourless glass. As Thorpe (1938) pointed out the ancient world made a careful distinction between ordinary glass (*vitrum*) and crystal glass (*crystallum* or *crystallina*). Strabo's (first century BC) various accounts (Thorpe, 1938) suggest that crystal glass may have been 'invented' between 20 BC and 7 BC, and by AD 77 it had become well enough known for Pliny to describe it as 'glass transparent in the white' (thus avoiding the ambiguity in the modern term, white glass). Pliny (AD 77) described the manufacture of colourless glass made from the fusion of ground sand and soda, followed by a second fusing with shells and stone referred to as *magnum lapis*, perhaps limestone or dolomite. Pliny (AD 77) called the product *vitrum purum* (pure glass) and remarked that the glass was colourless and transparent and as nearly like rock crystal as possible.

In the Dark Ages, glass of the soda-lime type had continued to be made as the glassmakers in western Europe were still able to obtain either natron from Alexandria or marine plant ash from the Mediterra-nean countries. Around the tenth century, however, European glassmakers switched to ashes from bracken and other woodland plants as a source of alkali thus producing green-tinted potash glass (forest glass). Elsewhere in Europe glassmakers producing soda-lime glasses produced vessels in the style of those from Venice (*façon de Venise*) but without the same degree of brilliance in the glass. Towards the end of the seventeenth century both Germany and Britain competed with Venice in producing glasses which were superior in quality to the original *cristallo*. By 1680 Germany had established a solid clear glass apparently first made in northern Bohemia by adding lime to stabilize the purified potash. In England the Glass Sellers' Company had, in 1673, commissioned George Ravenscroft to produce a substitute for the Venetian *cristallo*. Ravenscroft's first attempts using indigenous flint and potash to replace pebbles and soda produced from the Spanish sea plant *barilla* used by Venetian glassmakers was unsuccessful since the glass was inclined to crizzle. This crizzling took the form of a network of tiny cracks caused by the breakdown in the chemical structure within the glass due to an excess of alkali. (This phenomenon also occurs within *cristallo* itself.) To remedy this, oxide of lead was substituted for a proportion of the potash. Eventually this increased to as much as 30 per cent of the mix. A glass of high refractive index producing a brilliance was the result. Sand soon replaced the flints but the term *flint glass* continued to be used to designate Ravenscroft's glass. Lead glass was heavier and less fluid than Venetian *cristallo* but its lustrous appearance established it as the leader in the production of clear glass from the end of the seventeenth century.

Manufacture of glass

Since sustained high temperatures are required in order to melt the raw materials which produce glass, it seems likely that the art of glass-making originated somewhere where there was a closed furnace able to achieve these temperatures. A possible place for this to occur would have been in a pottery kiln (although metal-smelting furnaces have also been suggested) especially since the potter's craft was already long established by the time that glass made its first appearance, and potters already knew the art of glazing.

As previously mentioned, coloured vitreous glazes were used extensively in Egypt and Mesopotamia in the fourth millennium BC for covering objects in imitation of semi-precious stones. The first essential in making a good glaze was to reduce all the ingredients to a fine particle size by crushing. They were then mixed with water with or without the addition of an emulsifier to form a suspension. The glaze was applied by brushing or dipping the object after which it was heated in a furnace to melt the glaze with the object of distributing it evenly over the object, and to fuse the glaze particles. In antiquity the formulation of any glaze had to be arrived at by trial and error; and when one considers the cost of such experimentation to the potter it is hardly surprising that once a satisfactory glaze had been devised it remained in use, unaltered, over a long period of time. In theory it would have been possible to have produced a wide range of glazes with different melting points by altering the proportions of silica, lime and alkali (soda or potash), but in practice too much alkali resulted in a glaze prone to crazing, while too much silica resulted in a glaze with a melting point either too high for the primitive kiln or for the body to which it was to be applied; also, the coefficient of thermal expansion could become too high or too low. It was for this reason that soda-lime glazes were only used on objects of quartz, steatite or Egyptian faience (itself a soda-lime–quartz composite material) but not on pottery.

The transition from using glass for glazing to its being manufactured as a material in its own right was probably very slow. In any critical discussion of the production of ancient glasses it may be necessary to distinguish between three or four different activities; but the similarities between glaze and glass production are apparent.

Glass-making (fritting)

Glass-making is the preparation of molten glass from its basic raw materials, which in the case of most ancient glasses were solely sand and soda. Glass prepared by heating the raw materials could well possess a chemical composition characteristic of the local materials used.

In ancient times when furnaces could only reach temperatures of the order of about 1000°C there were considerable difficulties in producing glass from its raw materials. Attempts to make glass at such temperatures resulted in a viscous semi-glassy material full of air bubbles (*seed*) and unmelted batch materials (*stones*). At higher (modern furnace) temperatures the viscosity of the glass becomes low enough for the seed to escape, and all the batch material will react to produce a good quality glass. Therefore, whereas present day glasses are melted in one operation ancient glasses had to be made in at least two operations: the first was *fritting*, that is, reacting of the raw materials in the solid state by heating, after which the mass was cooled and ground to a powder (*frit*), a process which might be repeated several times to refine the frit; and the second was melting the frit at a higher temperature to form a homogeneous molten vitreous material (*glass melt*) which could be used to manufacture artefacts.

Thus in a furnace capable of reaching 1000°C good glass could be made by the process of fritting or allowing solid-state reactions to occur between the sodium carbonate in the plant ash or natron and the silica in the sand. This process was investigated by Howarth *et al.* (1934) and was found to occur slowly at 700°C, the reaction increasing rapidly with temperature until, at 850°C, there was a marked change in appearance, to that of partly melted sugar. This is no doubt associated with the melting of sodium carbonate (melting point 851°C; potassium carbonate melts at 891°C) (Turner, 1930, 1956c), and it indicates that the temperature was *too high*. If melting occurs, the viscous mass causes great difficulties in handling and it will be seen that all contemporary sources (for example, cuneiform tablets, Pliny, Theophilus and Neri) state that only moderate temperatures should be used and the frit should be kept well stirred so that it should not melt and lumps should not form. Nevertheless, nearly complete glass-making reactions can occur if heating is continued for long enough; at 750°C Howarth *et al.* (1934) obtained 98.5 per cent reaction in 15 hours, and 98.1 per cent reaction at 800°C in 10 hours, but much depends on the actual proportions of the raw materials, the reactions being more rapid when higher proportions of silica are present.

When completely reacted frit is ground and well mixed by hand, it can be *melted* to form a good quality, homogeneous glass at temperatures of the order of 1000–1100°C. Much of the first-quality Roman glass was no doubt made in this way, perhaps using more than one stage of quenching the melt in water, grinding and remixing by hand. This process of multiple-quenching was also used to purify the glass by removing undesirable inclusions. A good discussion of fritting is given by Turner (1956c). The subsequent melting was carried out in special kilns or crucibles, sometimes in several stages to permit the unfused elements to be drawn off from the molten mixture. After the mixture had turned to glass it was allowed to cool off in the crucibles, which later had to be smashed to release the glass ingots formed inside. The ingots were sold to the glass workshops, remelted and turned into finished objects.

Glass-melting

Glass-melting is the preparation of molten glass by melting down fragments of *cullet*. The term cullet also included specially made glass canes or cakes which were articles of trade, to be used by glassmelters in some other place. The term glass-melting also covers the melting of frit prepared elsewhere from sand and plant ash. Glass-melting is an easier process to carry out than glass-making, especially in a region which is less well-developed technologically, because no knowledge of (or access to) the basic raw materials is required (and herein may lie the reason why the Ancient Egyptians were not able to make their own glass, even though their glass-melting skill was highly developed) and because only one heating operation is required, that of melting (Turner, 1930). In some cases glass-making and glass-melting were combined, as they are in modern glass production when recycled glass bottles are added to the batch. It should be noted that the chemical characteristics of glass melt may not be as well defined as material made by the glass-making process if, for example, the cullet had been collected by itinerant glass-traders from a wide geographical area. On the other hand, a long continued reuse of cullet in one area could perpetuate a chemical characteristic of the glass long after one of the raw materials had ceased to be available. For example, such a practice might be one reason for the continual melting of soda glass in the Rhineland long after the Romans had left the area. A unique source of information regarding seventeenth century batch formulations and their use in Murano, Italy, has been published by Zecchin (1987). This contains a facsimile of the original notebook used by Giovanni Darduin (1584–1654), along with a transcription and modern commentary.

Glass-forming

Glass-forming is the heating and reshaping of a piece of glass without actually melting it. Many glass articles are said to have been *made* at certain sites whereas they were really only *formed* at the site. For example, a famous Romano-British purple and white glass bracelet from Traprain Law in Scotland was

formed by reheating a piece of a Roman pillar-moulded bowl (Stevenson, 1954; Newton 1971b). Since the glass was plastic rather than molten, the purple and white layers were deformed only, and did not merge into one another.

Sintering

Sintering was probably the technique used for producing the glassy material *faience*, which is not truly glass since it is not homogeneous on a macro-scale. A paste of ground quartz or sand was mixed with natron and sintered in an open pan. When soft the mixture was moulded into shape. A blue or greenish copper glaze was then fired on the surface. Apart from arrowheads fashioned from natural obsidian or glazed steatite objects, the first intentionally man-made vitreous artefacts seem to have been faience beads.

Faience beads

Faience beads are characteristic of the Bronze Age when bronze-smelting furnace temperatures were not high enough to fuse glass satisfactorily, but from which slags were readily available as a source of colourant. Truly fused glass could not be manufactured until furnace technology had developed to the extent where iron could be smelted, that is, higher temperatures could be reached (Lucas, 1962).

The vast majority of surviving faience objects are cylindrical beads (*Figure 3.1*) and in the Near East may have been made in millions since hundreds of thousands have been found in one site alone (the Grey Eye Temple at Brak in the Lebanon) (Mallowan, 1949); and a site at Nineveh in Iraq yielded a

Figure 3.1 Six Egyptian faience beads, which are typical of the segmented type found in Egypt, and other Mediterranean sites. Their occurrence on British sites is regarded as evidence of early trading contacts with the Mediterranean.

layer 2 m thick. The beads generally measure some 6 to 30 mm long, are 2 to 10 mm in diameter, have an axial hole and most are segmented. The earliest ones seem to have been made in Badarian contexts (fifth millennium BC) and good descriptions have been given by Beck and Stone (1936) and by Stone and Thomas (1956).

Relatively few faience beads (some thirty in all) are quite different in shape being either disc-shaped (quoit beads) or star-shaped (*Figure 3.2*), and much

Figure 3.2 Four Bronze Age star beads. Of the twenty-three examples of this type of bead known, sixteen have been found in Scotland, three in Ireland, two in England, one in the Isles of Scilly, and only one outside the British Isles. The beads would seem to have been made in Scotland. National Museum of Antiquities of Scotland, Edinburgh.

larger, about 30 mm in diameter. These are found almost solely in the British Isles (Stone and Thomas, 1956) and some authors (Newton and Renfrew, 1970; Aspinall *et al.*, 1972a,b) have argued that these two types were made locally, possibly at Glenuce and Culbin in Scotland in the British Isles. Doran and Hodson (1975) used the technique of cluster analysis to study the original data of Stone and Thomas and have also concluded that the star and quoit beads had an independent origin. Faience beads are quite durable, perhaps because most of the alkali seems to have been leached out during their long period of burial, and at present there seems to be no problem with their conservation. Various researchers have attempted to duplicate the manufacture of faience beads, for example, Binns *et al.* (1932), Lucas (1962), Wulff *et al.* (1968), Noble (1969) and Tite *et al.* (1983) carried out extensive research, first in Iran where modern *donkey beads* were being made at Qom, and subsequently in the laboratory. Briefly,

the core of the bead was composed of finely ground quartzite, made into a paste with gum tragacanth, and the glaze was made from the ash of *Salsola kali* and *S. soda*, mixed with slaked lime, powdered quartz, charcoal and copper oxide. After drying, the shaped beads were embedded in the glazing powder and the whole mass was fired at 1000°C. The beads were then removed from the glazing powder (which apparently had not melted at 1000°C) and were found to have a bright, glossy blue glaze. If the firing temperature was only 900°C, the glaze was coarse and pale, but if the temperature was 1100°C the glazing powder fused into a useless block. Thus the heating regime was fairly critical and it seems surprising that the plant ash did not fuse at a lower temperature.

Many laboratory investigations were carried out by Wulff *et al.* (1968) including chemical and petrographic analyses of the plant ash, the bead body and the glazing powder. It was concluded that the grains in the core had sintered together through the formation of cristobalite (a crystalline modification of silica) at their points of contact; and that the glazing action had been brought about in the vapour phase through the formation of soda (Na_2O) vapour, resulting from the interaction of the sodium carbonate (Na_2CO_3) with the slaked lime [$Ca(OH)_2$], which then reacted with copper chloride (CuCl) vapour formed by the interaction between sodium chloride (NaCl) in the plant ash and the copper oxide (CuO).

Noble (1969) adopted quite a different approach by mixing glazing material with core material *before* the beads were shaped. When the bead then dried out the sodium carbonate and bicarbonate ($NaHCO_3$), together with the copper oxide, had migrated to the surface as an efflorescence. Thus, when the bead was fired at 950°C, the alkali-rich efflorescence melted to form a glassy blue layer. If the copper was omitted, the resultant glaze was white but if iron oxide had been used the glaze was yellow. Manganese would give a purple glaze and Noble, in commenting on Wulff *et al.*, claimed that the above process for making faience articles was correct because ancient multicoloured articles exist and these could not have been made by the vapour process. However, the natron used in Noble's experiments may not have been representative, since the material seems to have much less Na_2CO_3 and $NaHCO_3$ than the fourteen analyses quoted by Douglas and Frank (1972).

Annealing

Annealing is a process which is applied to all glass artefacts in order to relieve stresses set up as a result of rapid cooling, or different rates of cooling of various components, for example, body, handle, foot. Failure to anneal glass in a suitable manner would leave it weak and brittle. Annealing is usually carried out immediately after the shaping process. The glass is reheated in a special furnace (*lehr*) to the required annealing temperature (which depends upon the composition of the glass), and is then allowed to cool at a controlled rate, whilst still in the furnace. The small amount of viscous flow which takes place during the annealing process leads to stress relaxation within the glass which is thus rendered relatively stress free (see Turner, 1949). It is thus unlikely that conservators will encounter badly annealed glasses since these would have fractured during their manufacture, or shortly afterwards during their functional life (Lillie, 1936).

The development of glass bead-making

The earliest vitreous material had been used in Egypt before *circa* 4000 BC, as a glaze to cover beads of stone and clay in imitation of coloured semi-precious stones. Later, *circa* 2500 BC, when furnaces were able to be maintained at temperatures high enough to soften glass, the same material was used in Egypt to make beads which were the first objects to be made entirely of glass. Glass beads are known from Mycenae from the sixteenth to the thirteenth centuries BC. Glass paste beads made at Mycenae *circa* 1300 BC are in the form of small thin tablets of which the ends are ribbed and perforated for threading. They were circular, rectangular or triangular, and usually of blue or pale yellow glass. The beads are decorated with relief Mycenean motifs, such as rosettes, ivy and spirals. They were formerly believed to have been used for necklaces and as decoration on garments, but a recent view is that the beads were also used to adorn diadems and the skulls of skeletons (Yalouris, 1968).

Glass beads can be made by at least six methods: winding threads of glass round a rod; drawing from a gob of glass which has been worked into a hollow; folding glass around a core, the join being visible on one side; pressing glass into a mould; perforating soft glass with a rod; and blowing (though cylindrical blown glass beads are rather exceptional). Bead-making by perforating glass with a rod is a technique still used in Africa as illustrated by Haevernick (1961). The same methods of decoration were applied to glass beads as to glass vessels, that is thread inlay, mosaic inlay, *millefiore* etc. An agate effect was produced by casing glass tubing with layers of differently coloured glass and then chamfering down the ends of cut lengths to expose the various layers. Examples of this type are the aggry (aggri) beads excavated in Africa (Hodges, 1964; Haevernick, 1961; Lamb, 1970).

The early decorative patterns on beads from *circa* 1500 BC are stripes and spots; later developments are eye beads and beads with zig-zags and chevrons. Egyptian beads were exported to many countries. These early beads were normally made of opaque glass, frequently blue with decoration in yellow and white. In the Roman era leech beads were sometimes used to cover the bow of fibulae. They were slightly curved, hollow cylinders with marvered combed decoration in a feather pattern. Some were made of Etruscan glass in the seventh century BC.

Since the manufacture of glass beads could only be carried out in furnaces hot enough to melt iron, their production in Britain is mainly associated with the Romano-British period; although on the Continent large annular beads and armlets were made in the La Tène I period (fifth century BC) (Ankner, 1965). Guido (1977) has published a comprehensive study of prehistoric and Romano-British beads found in Britain and Ireland. Many of the beads were imported but a map is included showing six local glass bead-making sites. There are also many distribution maps for different types of beads. In some cases the beads or bracelets were made by reshaping fragments of Roman glass articles, such as the bracelets from Traprain Law, and there is a strong suggestion that the highly coloured glass used for the applied decoration (spirals, eye spots etc.) was an article of trade imported from a glassworks which specialized in making coloured glass, perhaps in Gaul (Henderson, 1987).

Callmer (1977), discussing beads found in Scandinavia, described the same six manufacturing techniques mentioned above, plus that of producing beads by cold cutting blocks of glass. He has published a map showing probable areas of manufacture for beads of the period *circa* AD 800–1000, and discussed the part played by beads in developing trade routes (Callmer, 1977). Scandinavian bead-making is also discussed by Lundström (1976) who concludes that glass tesserae, glass sherds and glass rods were used as raw material for making glass beads, especially at Helgö. Some unperforated beads have been found at several sites, and it is not clear whether these were defective beads, whether they were awaiting perforation, or whether they represented glass weights or a kind of currency. The discovery of crucibles, with attached glass, at Helgö and Paviken seems conclusive proof that bead-making was carried out locally (Lundström, 1976).

Asahina and Oda (1954) conclude that Japanese glass beads were made in one of two ways: by drawing a tube, cutting it into short lengths and then manipulating it into a bead; or by drawing a glass thread and winding it on a metal thread coated with clay so that the rod could be easily withdrawn. Glass beads in Malaysia are discussed by Lamb (1966).

Dekówna (1967) has published a bibliography of selected publications on glass beads, together with chemical analyses of fourteen beads. She discusses the typology of beads and the advantages and disadvantages of different analytical techniques from the point of view of research. In another paper Dekówna and Szymanski (1970) discuss petrographic techniques for discovering how glass beads were made.

In Venice in the eleventh century and subsequently, glass beads were made for trade. Later they became popular in Bohemia and elsewhere, being made in many forms and styles including translucent, iridescent, facetted and enamelled in various colours. At present the principal sources of beads are Venice, Japan and the Gablonz region of Czechoslovakia. Some are of good quality and serve as costume jewellery, but vast quantities serve merely as tourist souvenirs. Coloured beads may be either inferior varieties coloured only on the surface, or be made entirely of coloured glass.

Most of the methods used in making glass beads can be applied to the manufacture of producing bangles. If not cut from a solid piece of glass, however, the commonest means of producing bangles are either by bending a glass rod round and fusing the two ends together; or by first blowing a hollow glass cylinder and then cutting it into short lengths. In the latter instance it is not uncommon to find that the glass gathering has been cased with several layers of differently coloured glass. All methods of decorating glassware can be applied to bangles (Hodges, 1964; Haevernick, 1960).

Fourteen hundred years before the invention of glass-blowing, four very different techniques were already in use for the production of glass artefacts:

core-forming; *moulding*; *cutting or abrading* (cold glass); and *mosaic*.

Core-formed vessels

The majority of pre-Roman glass vessels were made by the core-forming method. A core modelled on the end of a wooden rod to form the inside of the vessel would be dipped into the molten glass. When sufficient glass had been gathered the outer surface was rolled smooth (*marvered*) on a flat stone surface. Alternatively the glass was first drawn into rods (*canes*) which were then softened by reheating and wound round a core. The glass and the core were then repeatedly reheated, rotated and marvered to produce a smooth outer surface. A decoration of coloured glass blobs and trails could then be added and trailed (*combed*) into zig-zag patterns and embedded into the surface by reheating and marvering. Additional parts such as rudimentary handles, stems and footrings might be added; then on cooling the rod was removed and as much as possible of the core picked out, following which a rim could be trailed on and shaped.

The carrot and lentil shapes of the earlier vases and bottles were natural marver shapes and these vessels were usually about 80–120 mm in height, although a few larger examples exist. Core-formed vessels were mainly produced in Egypt but examples have been excavated in Mesopotamia, Cyprus, Syria, Crete, Rhodes and Greece.

Figure 3.3 Core-formed vessels of different periods, sixth to first centuries BC. These vessels illustrate the variety of shapes made on cores, in the Hellenic and Hellenistic periods. H 77-184 mm. British Museum, London.

Four distinctive types of core-formed vessels are known from the later Egyptian period (*Figure 3.3*): *alabastron* (cylindrical or cigar-shaped); *amphorisk* (pear-shaped); *aryballos* (globular); and *oinochoe* (jug with one handle and a flat base). These containers (*unguentaria*) seem to have been luxury articles and were used for ointments, perfumes and cosmetics. Core-formed vessels continued to be made throughout the Hellenic period, slowly retiring in the face of blown glass and *millefiore*-type vessels.

Small vessels formed over a core were formerly termed *sand-core* vessels after Petrie (1894) introduced the term, although he did not supply evidence that sand had been used to form the core. Schuler (1962) decided that sand could not have been used since it would have dried and run out of the orifice of the vessel. Schuler conducted experiments using a ceramic core on a metal rod and five different methods of applying the glass, including rolling on crushed glass, dipping into molten glass and trailing on a glass rod; but encountered difficulties because the glass adhered too strongly to the core and cracked as the ceramic shrank on cooling. Schuler therefore concluded (erroneously) that the glass might have been formed in an outer mould.

Labino (1966) carried out a series of experiments in the United States which showed that core-formed vessels could be made by trailing glass on to a suitable core. Labino did not disclose the composition of the core material in order to prevent its use in the production of fakes. However, he stated that the core material should be entirely inorganic and possess a coefficient of expansion greater than that of the glass so that the article would not crack on cooling.

In 1967, however, Bimson and Werner examined two core-formed vessels to find out whether any original core material still remained and discovered samples inside the shoulder of a Cypriot Bronze Age scent bottle and an Eighteenth Dynasty model coffin. Both samples of core material suggested that the original core had been made in two layers from a friable porous mass consisting of fragments of plants (probably as dung), and a highly ferruginous clay and ground limestone, the outer layer being largely ground limestone. Following the first paper on their discovery (Bimson and Werner, 1967), Bimson and Werner (1969) examined a further sixty-two samples of core material and found that early (Eighteenth Dynasty) material did not differ substantially from the two samples mentioned above, although later material (after 750 BC) consisted of sand grains cemented together with iron oxide. Wosinski and Brill (1969) examined ten examples of core material from three basic types of core-formed vessel and found that the core materials were mixtures of sand, clay and plant material (again possibly dung), but did not confirm the presence of a surface layer of ground limestone.

Casting in open or closed moulds

Casting glass into open moulds was a technique taken over from the pottery and faience industry. It was used for the production of open vessels such as bowls, dishes and wide-necked bottles, and plaques. Three techniques were probably used: direct pouring and manipulation of the glass in an open mould; fusing of powdered glass *in situ*; and the lost wax process. The figurine of Astarte from Atchana, Turkey (see *Figure 2.3*), dating from the early fifteenth century BC was cast in a one-piece mould, the back being flattened by pressure (Harden *et al.*, 1968). Bimson and Werner (1964b) suggest that a clay mould was used for making the glass stud on the Tara brooch; and an actual clay mould with the three-pointed star made from it is shown in *Figure 3.4*.

Figure 3.4 A three-pointed star, which was found in its clay mould, on the site of Phidias' workshop at Olympia in Greece. H of mould 60 mm. *Circa* 450 BC. Olympia Museum, Greece.

Numerous clay moulds which could have been used for moulding glazed quartz fritware have been found in Egypt. Harden (1968) shows that Phidias (*circa* 450 BC) cast small pieces of glass in clay moulds *in situ* at Olympia for the famous statue of Zeus.

Fusing of powdered glass *in situ*

Two parts of a mould might be made by shaping two pieces of wood to the desired shape and then lining them with clay. The mould pieces were designed to fit together leaving a space between them representing the thickness of the glass artefact. The mould would then be heated to 700°C (Schuler, 1959a) and the powdered glass (or even small fragments) would be dropped through an orifice in the top of the mould which formed the base of the vessel. In his experiments, Schuler gradually increased the temperature and, as the glass melted down, added more

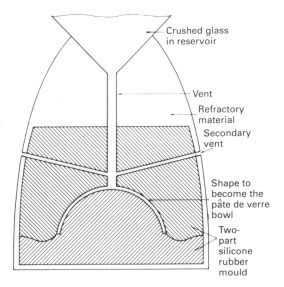

Figure labels:
- Crushed glass in reservoir
- Vent
- Refractory material
- Secondary vent
- Shape to become the *pâte de verre* bowl
- Two-part silicone rubber mould

Figure 3.5 Diagram of the cross-section of a modern mould for producing a *pâte de vere* bowl. The entire construction is heated until the crushed glass fuses. (Alternatively the glass could be layered into the bowl-shaped mould by hand.)

periodically. The glass eventually filled the mould (including the orifice which left a knob on the base of the bowl to be removed after the glass had hardened) when the temperature had reached 1000°C. The furnace was then cooled and the mould taken apart to release the glass vessel (*Figure 3.5*).

Artefacts could be produced by introducing *glass paste* (Fr. *pâte de verre* or *pâte de riz*) into a mould. Glass ground to a powder was mixed with a fluxing medium so that it would melt readily, and coloured. Alternatively coloured glass was used. The paste could be modelled like clay or pressed into a heated mould and fused *in situ* by firing. The varied colouring suggested by semi-precious stones was obtained by the positioning of different powdered ingredients in the mould. Some examples were built up into polychrome high relief or figures by successive layers added to the mould, and sometimes after refiring they were refined by being carved. This process was known in ancient Egypt; and was revived in France in the nineteenth century to form artificial jewels and other decorative articles, especially by the sculptor Henri Cros and his son Jean. Other exponents of the technique were Albert Dammouse *circa* 1898, Francois Decorchement *circa* 1900–1930, Emille Gallé and Gabriel Argy-Rousseau (Newman, 1977).

The moulding operation using a two-piece mould can be hastened by pressing on the upper (male) mould if the mould material is strong enough.

Pressure will also produce a sharper impression of any pattern on the inside of the external (female) mould. During the nineteenth century and subsequently a mechanical mould-pressing technique using metal moulds was used to provide cheap imitations of deep-cut glass. Glass made by this process bears the exact design and the contours of the two parts of the mould. Nineteenth century glassware which has external decoration (such as ribbing or deep impressions) and internal concavities which correspond with the raised portions on the exterior, will have been made by a mould-blown operation such as the blown three-mould process (Newman, 1977) or pattern moulding also known from the nineteenth century onwards as optic moulding (Newman, 1977).

The lost wax process

Glass artefacts such as figurines with a complicated shape with many undercuts could be made by the *lost wax process* (Fr. *cire perdue*; Ger. *wachsausschmelzfahren*). The desired object was modelled or carved in wax. The model was then encased in a mould of refractory material such as clay, incorporating air-holes and pour-holes at the base. The mould was heated so that the wax ran out and powdered glass was then introduced to the hot mould which was reheated, thus melting the glass to form a solid artefact. Alternatively, if a hollow glass object was required such as a pillar-moulded bowl an internal (female) mould was made of wood or refractory clay and covered with hot wax applied with a brush (Schuler, 1959a). The wax was shaped with a template or by building up and carving the wax to form the external shape of the object. Small metal bars incorporated into the female mould and protruding through the wax into the male mould kept the mould pieces apart during the casting process. A hole was left in the base of the male mould in order for the molten wax to run out when heated. Thus the space inside represented the form of the glass object to be cast. Powdered glass was then introduced into the mould and heated in order to melt it. On cooling, the moulds were removed and the result was a hollow glass object (*Figure 3.6*).

Abrading cold glass

Cutting or grinding glass is the only technique involving removal of glass from a cold mass which was used to produce a complete vessel. Techniques for stone- and gem-cutting were well established before glass-making, and it was natural that they should be extended to cutting glass once this material could be produced in massive form.

Cold glass has a scratch hardness between 4.5 and 6.5 (on Mohs' scale) depending on its composition,

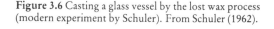

Figure 3.6 Casting a glass vessel by the lost wax process (modern experiment by Schuler). From Schuler (1962).

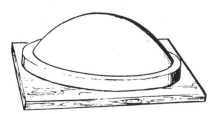

(a) The material used for the mould was one part plaster of Paris and one part very fine sand, mixed in water, then placed on a simple vertical lathe and shaped with a template while still plastic. When the core was formed it was dried in air.

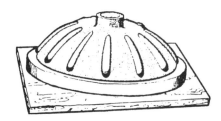

(b) Next, hot wax was applied with a brush and shaped with a template. Ribs of wax were shaped and applied, and a lump of wax was applied at the top to form a cavity for holding glass. (In a two-part mould clay can be used instead.)

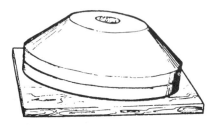

(c) The wax was covered with more of the plaster mixture and then dried. (If the mould is to be a two-part mould, the region at the base where the new plaster would be in contact with the old should be covered with a thin clay wash.) Now the wax was melted out with the mould inverted. (If, instead, a two-part mould is made, then the parts are separated, cleaned of clay and reassembled with a little fresh plaster mix to seal the joint.) The mould was wrapped with nichrome wire so that if by chance it cracked during the process, it would still retain the glass.

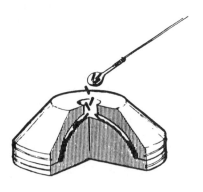

(d) A mould was placed in a furnace and heated slowly to 700° C. At this point small pieces of glass were placed, by means of a spoon at the end of an iron bar, in the hollow part of the top of the mould. The temperature was gradually increased, and as the glass melted down, more was added. (The temperature might have been held at 800° C if the process were to take longer.) The glass flowed down and filled the space in the mould; eventually there was excess glass in the hollow space at the top. When the temperature reached 1000° C and glass was observed at the top, the mould was assumed to be completely filled, and the furnace was cooled. When cold enough to handle, the mould was taken out and broken apart.

and it can readily be cut or ground by harder materials such as quartz or flint (scratch hardness 7.0). Cold-cutting or grinding were used at an early date for finishing glass objects or vessels which had been cast (Harden, 1968). The lidded ointment pot shown in *Figure 2.5* is an early example of glass abrasion. Brill (1968) published a cross-section of a cup which had been cut from a solid glass blank. The head-rest of the Pharaoh Tutankhamun (1352 BC) was cut from two blocks of glass, the join between them being covered by a gold band (*Figure 3.7*). A much later exmple of glass abrasion, an alabastron bearing the name of King Sargon of Assyria (772–705 BC), bears spiral grooves and an internal knob at the bottom, which are the result of cold-working (*Figures 3.8* and *3.9*).

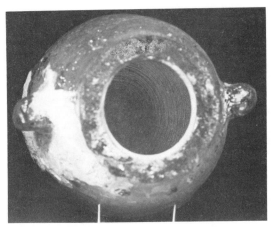

Figure 3.9 The interior grooves of the vase shown in *Figure 3.8* demonstrate that the vase was ground from a solid block of glass. British Museum, London.

Figure 3.7 A head-rest found in the tomb of Tutankhamun. Apparently cold-cut from the two blocks of glass, with a gold band bearing a hieroglyphic inscription to disguise the join. H 184 mm. 1352 BC. Cairo Museum, Egypt.

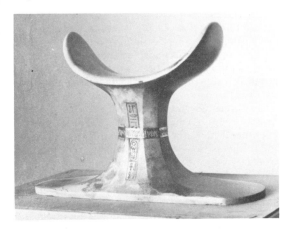

Figure 3.8 Glass vase engraved in cuneiform script with the name of King Sargon II of Assyria. Nimrud 722-705 BC. H c.150 mm. British Museum, London.

The techniques of casting glass into moulds and then the discovery of glass-blowing brought to an end the usefulness of abrading glass for producing vessels. However, it continued as a means of further embellishment as, for example, in the production of *diatreta*, as a means of surface decoration (cutting and engraving) or simply for finishing off cast glassware (Harden, 1968).

Diatreta (cage cups)

The process of cold-cutting glass was brought to an extremely fine art in making diatreta (cage cups). As the name suggests the cups bear a pattern which stands out from the (moulded) cup as an open network or cage. The majority of the pattern was completely undercut so that it stood free from the main vessel (the cup), being held to it by a small number of glass bridges (see *Figure 3.10*). There are two types of cage cup, the differences between the types have been discussed by Harden (1969).

For many years there was speculation as to how cage cups were made (Kämpfer and Beyer, 1966; Zecchin, 1968); in 1725 Winkelmann correctly suggested that they were cut from one piece of glass, but it was not until 1880 that a glasscutter, Zweisel, succeeded in reproducing an example, taking six months to complete the work. Other (incorrect) suggestions for method of manufacture were made by von Eiff — applied decoration — and by Wiedmann — a complicated system of prunts.

In 1930 Fremersdorf (1930) correctly described how the *diatretarius* had produced cage cups; and finally in 1964, Schäfer (1968, 1969), a glasscutter at the Akademie der Bildenkunste, Munich, West

Germany, made a perfect copy of the cage cup from Daruvar, Zagreb, Yugoslavia. Brill's illustration of a cage cup (Brill, 1968) also makes it quite clear that a cutting technique had been used in the example shown.

Two outstanding examples of cage cups are the virtually complete diatreta in the Romisch-Germanisches Museum, Cologne (see *Figure 3.10*); and the Lycurgus Cup in the British Museum, London. The glass of which the Lycurgus Cup is

Figure 3.10 Cage-cup (diatreta): pale greenish glass, circles green, bands amber, letters ruby. H 121 mm. Fourth century AD. Cologne. Römisch-Germanisches Museum, Cologne.

made displays a dichroic property, appearing opaque pea green by reflected light and translucent wine red by transmitted light. The cup was skilfully carved in high relief, the backs of the major figures being hollowed out in order to maintain an even translucency. At one point (behind the panther), the *diatretarius* accidentally pierced the wall, so that the vessel will not actually hold a liquid (Harden and Toynbee, 1959; Harden, 1963).

Surface decoration by cutting glass

Abrasive techniques for the decoration of glassware have as long a history as glass-making itself. Before glass was made, however, hieroglyphic inscriptions had been engraved on hardstone vessels, and there is evidence for glass engraving in Egypt as early as the sixteenth century BC. Engraving probably developed from the stone- and gem-cutting trade, being executed with the same pointed instruments. Harden (1968) drew attention to simple forms of incised decoration in three different eras. Cut or engraved patterns were rare in the pre-Roman period; during the Roman period good engraving declined in Egypt but excellent work was produced in Syria (Harden, 1969); and in the post-Roman era, engraved Christian motifs began to appear on glassware (Harden, 1971).

Diamond-point engraving is, as its name suggests, the technique of using a diamond-point to scratch the glass surface. Early examples are known from Roman times, although it has been argued that these were executed with worked flints. Diamond-point engraving was used to decorate Islamic glass. In the sixteenth century the technique was used by glass decorators in Venice; in Hall-in-Tyrol, Austria (Newman, 1977), where an important glasshouse under the patronage of the Archduke Ferdinand produced a great deal of diamond-engraved Venetian glass; and by German, Dutch and British engravers, firstly in the *façon de Venise* and subsequently in local styles. Diamond-point engraving was first used in Britain on glassware made in the glasshouse of Jacopo Verzelini (see *Figure 2.36*). In Holland it was mainly used by amateur decorators during the seventeenth century, especially for calligraphy (Tait, 1968). The technique was superseded in the eighteenth century by wheel-engraving and by enamelling. However, it continued to be used for stippling from the 1720s to the late eighteenth century, and also in Britain for producing Jacobite and other commemorative glassware. In the technique of *stippling*, grouped and graded dots were engraved with a diamond-point on the surface of the vessel. These represented the highlights of the design. The diamond-point was set in a handle which may have been gently struck with a small hammer to produce a single small dot on the glass. In the best examples of stippling the decoration can be compared to a delicate film breathed upon the glass (see *Figure 2.35*). Frans Greenwood, a native of Rotterdam, brought the art of stippling to its greatest height in the first half of the eighteenth century. In the last 40 years of the eighteenth century stippled engraving was practised by numerous artists, the most famous being David Wolff in Holland (Brooks, 1973). In passing, it should be noted that some weathered surface fractures give the impression that a human agency has been at work by developing into regular patterns on the glass surface as a result of weathering (Newton *et al.*, 1981).

Wheel-cutting and wheel-engraving

Wheel-cutting and wheel-engraving of glass are basically the same technique in which a rotating abrasive wheel is used to cut into the surface. In early times the same equipment would have been used for both methods: rotating wheels of various sizes propelled by a bow lathe. Gradually cutting came to be carried out with large wheels and was characterized by large-scale geometric designs, usually relatively deeply incised; whereas engraving was executed with small wheels and was usually the method used to produce fine or pictorial work since it was possible to achieve great detail.

Charleston (1964, 1965) has produced two summaries of the development of wheel-engraving. Rotary abrasion (using emery powder or perhaps powdered quartz sand) had been carried out as early as the Third Dynasty (*circa* 2100–1800 BC), and engraving tools of that date have been excavated, but firm evidence for the rotary wheel-cutting of narrow lines seems to be scarce. It is not known what type of abrading equipment was used to decorate glass in Roman times. There is a suggestion that an all-purpose tool could have been used which would be adapted as a lathe, drill or cutting or engraving wheel as required. The Romans used abrasives such as emery for cutting and pumice stone for polishing glass. With the decline of the Roman Empire in the West, glass engraving died out, principally because there was no fine quality glass made after this time which was suitable for engraving. In the East the technique never ceased, and glasses with cut decoration can be traced in continuity through Sassanian to Islamic times. In the ninth and tenth centuries a school of relief cutting flourished in Persia and probably also in Mesopotamia which was not rivalled until the end of the seventeenth century by European engravers.

A description of wheel-engraving dating from AD 1464 states that a diamond-point was used, 'and with wheels of lead and emery; and some do it with little bow (*archetto*)'. By the fifteenth century gem-cutting wheels of lead, pewter, copper, steel and limewood were being used to engrave and polish glass. By the sixteenth century the principle of continuous rotary movement had been established. A drawing dating from 1568 depicts a foot-operated treadle with a large flywheel. Wheel-engraving was to reach its greatest heights once Bohemia and Germany produced a potash–lime glass suitable for this technique in the early seventeenth century. Caspar Lehmann of Prague was the greatest exponent of the revival of glass engraving in Europe. He began his career as a hardstone engraver and presumably used the same equipment and skills for both crafts. This was a tradition which was to continue until relatively modern times. When Lehmann died in 1622, his patent to engrave glass was taken over by George Schwanhardt the Elder who founded a school of brilliant glass engraving in Nuremberg which flourished into the eighteenth century. Wheel-engraved glass was produced in Holland shortly after the middle of the seventeenth century and became popular by the eighteenth century. The most prominent engraver in Holland was Jacob Sang who worked in Amsterdam. English lead glass was also suitable for engraving, and in addition to an English tradition of glass engraving, blank vessels were exported in large quantities to be engraved in Holland (Brooks, 1973).

Intaglio decoration (Ital. *cave relievo*; Ger. *tiefschnitt*) was created by engraving or cutting below the surface of the glass so that the apparent elevations of the design were hollowed out, and an impression taken from the design produced an image in relief. The background was not cut away, but was left on the plane of the highest areas of the design. *Intaglio* work was carried out on rock crystal and other semi-precious stones and on glass by wheel-engraving in medieval Rome, but more particularly on glass in Germany and Silesia from the seventeenth century. For greater effectiveness the design was left matt or only partially polished.

The opposite decorative technique was *cameo* work (Ger. *hochschnitt*; Eng. high engraving) which involved the formation of a design in relief by cutting away the ground (*Figure 2.32*). The cameo technique, a combination of wheel-cutting and engraving, was used in Roman times, the two most famous Roman cameo work vessels being the Portland Vase in the British Museum in London and the Vendange Vase in the Museo Nazionale in Naples, Italy. Cameo carving of layered stones seems to have originated in Ptolomaic Alexandria; and since Alexandria was also one of the most important centres of ancient glass-making, it is reasonable to suppose that cameo glass was an Alexandrian invention in imitation of gem-stones. Cameo effects simulating agate and other similarly multicoloured stones were commonly produced by casing, for example, a coloured glass with a white one, followed by cutting away the white glass in low relief. The earliest known example of cameo glass design points to the same conclusion. This is a fragment of a plaque in the Department of Egyptian Antiquities of the British Museum, which shows a man's leg and part of a bull in a purely Egyptian style which cannot be later than the third century BC. The white-on-blue blank for the plaque must have been moulded, since glass-blowing had not been invented; but the relief was unquestionably carved. However, cameo glass which can be certainly ascribed to pre-Roman times is rare, and the bulk of that which has survived probably dates from the early Roman Imperial period. Two of the most notable specimens, the Blue Vase (National Museum, Naples) and the Auldjo Jug (British Museum, London — see *Figure 7.30l*), were found in Pompeii and must therefore pre-date the volcanic eruption of Mount Vesuvius which destroyed the city in AD 79.

The first step in the manufacture of a cameo glass vessel was to blow the blue glass body and then, in the case of the Portland Vase, to coat it with a layer of white glass reaching up to a level just above the shoulder of the vase. To achieve this the glassblower may have dipped a partially inflated *paraison* of blue glass into a crucible of molten white thus gathering a white layer over the blue; or a cup of white glass may have been formed and the blue glass blown into it. Having cased the blue glass with the white, the body was formed by further blowing and marvering. The average thickness of the blue glass is 3 mm. To blow a two-layered vessel as large as the Portland Vase required considerable manipulative skill, but the glassworker's chief difficulty was to prepare two differently coloured glasses with the same coefficient of thermal expansion (and therefore also contraction) as an essential condition if they were not to crack or split apart on cooling. The annealing process itself would have had to be carefully controlled. When the glass body was complete, the handles were formed from glass rods and attached, their lower ends to the white glass covering the shoulder, and the upper ends to the blue glass of the neck. The vessel was then handed to a glass engraver to carve the frieze, cut the ornament of the handles, and bring the whole to a finish. No doubt the frieze was copied from a model in wax or plaster, and the engraver would have begun by incising the outlines of the design on white glass, then all the white glass would have been removed from the background in order to expose the blue glass, and lastly the figures and features thereby left in block relief would have been modelled in detail. The grooved treatment of the drapery and rocks reveals the use of engraving wheels which were probably used for grinding away the background and other relatively coarse work; but for the more intricate and delicate details, small chisels, files and gravers would have been required (Haynes, 1975).

It was not until the nineteenth century that a glass cameo vessel such as the Portland Vase was produced again. The Portland Vase is such an exceptional work of art that considerable effort has been devoted to making a copy. In 1786 Josiah Wedgwood made a ceramic copy in Jasper ware; and in the early 1830s a prize of £1000 was offered for a copy in glass. This was achieved in 1876 by John Northwood Sen., but, even with the availability of modern techniques, there was an expansion mismatch and the vase

cracked after 3 years' work had been spent on it (Northwood, 1924). Other cased articles made by Northwood have also shown evidence of strain between the layers of glass. However, he popularized cameo glass to such an extent that its production became commercialized by the end of the century (Ryder, 1975). In order to increase production cameo workers worked as teams rather than as individuals; and the larger areas of unwanted overlay were removed by dipping the vessel into hydrofluoric acid having first covered the areas to be retained with a protective acid-resistant material such as wax. Cutting in high relief was used by the Chinese on scent and snuff bottles; and in the nineteenth century for the decoration of glass in the *Art Nouveau* style which arose in the 1930s, the name being derived from that of a Paris gallery devoted to interior decoration. Art Nouveau was adopted as a movement in Britain by William Morris (1834–1896) and his contemporaries. The style was adapted for glassware by Emile Gallé (1846–1904) in France and Louis Tiffany (1848–1933) in the United States, much of the decoration resulting from cameo-cutting.

Allied to cameo-cutting was the work of the *diatretarius* previously discussed, in which a glass blank was almost entirely undercut by lapidary means to produce the delicate decorative cage.

It is evident that ancient glasscutters knew how to exploit the refractive effects of glass by cutting facets in addition to engraved lines. Harden (1969) illustrates facet-cut bowls from the second century AD but states that by the fourth century the art of facet-cutting had degenerated to a mere abrasion of the surface both in the East and in the West. Some 200 years later, in the Sassanian area of eastern Iraq and western Iran, bowls were produced with regularly spaced deep circular or hexagonal facets. Another 600 years later in the twelfth century, the Hedwig glasses (Pinder-Wilson, 1968; Harden, 1971), possibly produced in Russia, portray animals most effectively with large sweeps of the cutting wheel. In contrast with the cutting of fine lines with a narrow wheel, the use of a large and wide wheel seems, not surprisingly, to have been established much earlier.

It is only towards the end of the seventeenth century that a genuine distinction between glass-cutting and glass-engraving can be made. For the first time it is obvious that different types of equipment for cutting and for engraving were being developed. The glass engravers' equipment was light enough at this period to be carried, and resulted in a number of travelling glass engravers who would engrave any design on the spot for customers. The most famous of these was Georg Franz Kreybich who travelled Europe at the end of the seventeenth century engraving glass. On the other hand the glasscutters' equipment used for facetting, *intaglio*, deep cutting, or roughing out for finer engraving was hardly portable. The large interchangeable wheels were rotated on a heavy, hand-turned cutting machine, a form of equipment which survived until the modern period.

By the end of the seventeenth century water power was in use for turning the wheels to cut glass. Water power was probably used to enable all-over facetting to be carried out as an obligatory prelude to the engraving of potash glasses in Bohemia and Silesia in the eighteenth century. The highest development of facet-cutting, to produce designs in colourless glass, occurred with the cutting of full lead crystal glass. Cut glass has become synonymous with the deep wheel-cutting used on Irish glass from the late eighteenth century onwards, and also on modern cut wine glasses and decanters (Hartshorne, 1897; Elville, 1951, 1953, 1961; Barrington Haynes, 1959). The popularity of present day cut glass products is a legacy of the great popularity this type of glass enjoyed in Britain in the later Victorian period. In this style of glassware angular cuts were made into the vessel which, when polished, act as prisms with adjacent cuts, producing a brilliant effect. The glass blank would first be marked with the pattern using a mixture such as white lead and gum water. Following the design, deep cuts would be roughed in against an iron wheel fed with abrasive such as sand. For coarse work overhand-cutting where the vessel was pressed down onto the wheel from above was usual, whilst underhand-cutting where the vessel was pressed up onto the wheel from below was used for more delicate work. After the initial design had been cut, fine-grained, water-cooled stones which required no abrasive were used to smooth the first cuts and to add finer lines. (Besides water power, steam-powered cutting mills were in existence by the beginning of the nineteenth century.) Finally the cuts could be polished with lead or wooden wheels or with rotary brushes charged with tripoli or putty powder. After the second half of the nineteenth century a method of plunging the glass vessels into a mixture of hydrofluoric and sulphuric acid was used to polish cut glassware. Two techniques related to engraving are sand-blasting and acid-etching.

Sand-blasting

In this process a stream of sand, crushed flint or powdered iron is directed onto the surface of the glass in a jet of compressed air. Parts of the glass to be left plain are covered with a stencil plate of steel or an elastic varnish or rubber solution painted on to form a protective shield. The type of finish is varied by altering the size of the nozzle directing the abrasive, the size of the abrasive, or the pressure of the air. Sand-blasting is normally carried out in a closed circuit in a cabinet which can be sealed. The technique has been in use since 1870 although it has rarely been applied to vessel glass except for lettering on mass produced items (Newman, 1977). The main use of sand-blasting has been on glass panels for decorative architectural use (Pollitzer, 1936).

In stained glasswork, thinly flashed glass, that is, colourless glass thinly coated on one side with a coloured glass, can be abraded (by wheel-cutting or sand-blasting) to form a design. The coloured glass can either be entirely abraded to expose the colourless glass in order for example to depict white pearls against a red dress, or abraded by degrees thus producing shades of the colour. By this process the subtle effects in painted glass windows were produced, often in conjunction with the use of silver stain.

Acid-etching

The effects of abrasion can be duplicated by etching with hydrofluoric acid (HF). A 90 per cent solution of HF possesses the unique property of dissolving silica:

$$SiO_2 + 4HF \rightarrow SiF_4 + 2H_2O$$

The effect depends greatly on the strength of the acid, and whether sulphuric acid is also present since some combinations of the acid mixtures polish the glass instead of producing a rough etched surface (Schweig, 1973). Hydrofluoric acid is both difficult to prepare and extremely dangerous to use from the health point of view. It seems that the earliest example of acid-etching was made by Schwanhardt at Nuremberg in 1670. This example has been the centre of much speculation in the past since it was not until 1771 that Scheele discovered hydrofluoric acid. However, it appears that the Nuremberg article was treated with a mixture of calcium fluoride and sulphuric acid which produced hydrofluoric acid.

The method of acid-etching generally employed was to coat the glass with wax after which the design was scratched through the protective layer onto the glass. The glass was then placed in a bath of hydrofluoric acid and was only etched in the areas from which the wax had been removed. In France, Gallé, Daum and Marinot used the technique to produce deep bold patterns on glass. Acid-etching is now used mainly to produce interesting surface textures and patterns on architectural glass.

Mosaic glass

Mosaic glass is composed of thin sections, cut from plain or coloured glass rods. The simplest way of producing a fine, short glass rod was to pour the molten *metal* very slowly from the crucible or ladle so that as it fell it cooled and solidified. In the same way a glass rod can be drawn from molten glass by dipping a *bait* into the surface and slowly raising it. The molten glass adheres to the bait and behaves rather like treacle, necking in rapidly to form a thin stream. Treacle will continue to run back from the bait but glass will soon freeze and stiffen (depending upon the rate at which the bait is raised, the temperature above the glass and the composition of the glass). A rod of surprisingly constant thickness can be made by this method; thicker rod being obtained with a slower rate of draw.

At a much later date longer and more even lengths of rod could be made by fixing a gathering of molten glass metal to an iron post or a plate on a wall and pulling out a length of rod with the aid of a punty by walking away from the gather. Much later again glass tubing was produced in the same way except that the glassworker drew out the gather with a blow iron, walking backwards and blowing gently down the iron at the same time in order to maintain the cavity in the tube. Needless to say this operation required considerable skill.

Monochrome rods of different coloured glass were then sliced into sections which could be placed adjacent to one another and fused to form a pattern by heating (*Figure 3.11*). An important group of vessels dating from the late fifteenth to the early thirteenth centuries BC from Tell al Rimah, 'Agar Quf and Marlik in north-west Iraq were made by this

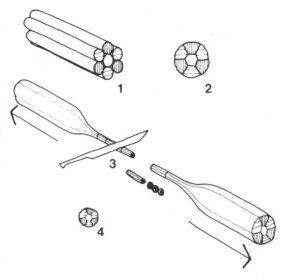

Figure 3.11 Mosaic glass: fusing, drawing, and cutting 'canes'. After Goldstein (1979).

method, the different coloured sections being arranged in patterns or in zig-zag bands (see *Figure 2.2*), probably on the outer surface of a circular mould having the interior shape of the vessel to be produced. The sections of rod may have been fixed to the mould with an adhesive which burnt out during firing or, in some cases, an outer mould may have

Figure 3.12 Roman cane-sectioned bowls. Victoria and Albert Museum, London.

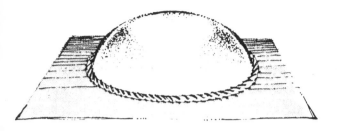

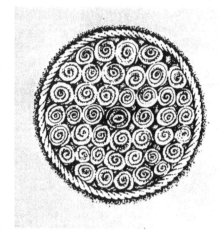

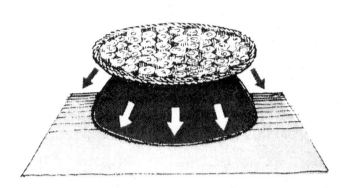

Figure 3.13 Stages in the production of a cane-sectioned bowl with a *reticelli* rim. (a) A *reticelli* (multicane) rod is lamp-formed to a similar diameter to that of a mould. (b) This cane is used as an accurate perimeter within which to fuse sawn cane sections to create a flat disc for sagging. (c) The disc is softened over a mould to create a bowl which is then finished by selective cutting and polishing. From Cummings (1980).

Figure 3.14 An Alexandrian *reticelli* bowl. The circles of twisted canes can be clearly seen, the rods having settled during fusing. The finished piece has been ground inside and out. British Museum, London.

been used to keep the sections in place. The mould was then heated sufficiently to soften the sections with the minimum amount of distortion required to fuse them together to form a mosaic vessel. In some cases the glass rods were multicoloured in concentric rings. When the mosaic was properly fused, and the article had cooled, it was removed from the mould, ground smooth and polished internally and externally. Mosaic bowls such as those mentioned above were the prototypes of the mosaic glassware of the late Hellenic and later periods. Further developments are shown in *Figures 3.12–3.15*. The mosaic technique was also used to form plaques such as shown in *Figure 3.16* in which the mosaic slices were adhered to a backing with bitumen. In the case of the theatrical mask, the face was formed as one half only, two slices from the same rod being placed side by side, one being turned over so that a completely

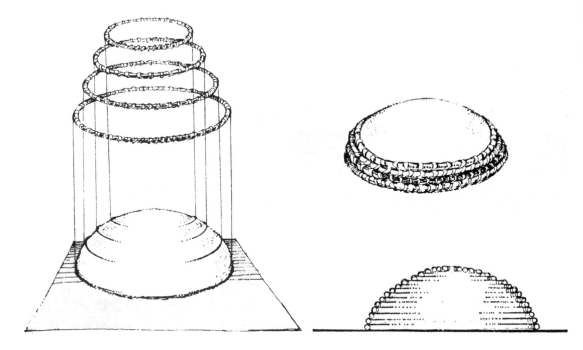

Figure 3.15 The stages in the production of a *reticelli* bowl. (a,b) Rings of *reticelli* canes are placed over a former.

(c) When the former has been completely covered the whole is heated until the canes fuse. From Cummings (1980).

Figure 3.16 A fused mosaic cane showing half the head of a satyr. Slices would be cut from the cane and two placed together side by side (one being reversed) to form the entire face. H 30 mm, W 21 mm, L 64 mm. First century BC–first century AD. Probably Egyptian. Freer Gallery of Art, Washington DC.

symmetrical face was produced. Schuler (1963) describes experiments carried out to duplicate Egyptian fused mosaics.

The distinction is not always made between *true mosaic* and *mosaic inlay* although the two are quite different. In true mosaic the coloured glass pieces formed the entire thickness of the article, whereas in mosaic inlay thin sections of glass rod were backed by a glass of uniform colour. In Venetian *millefiori* glass which sought to imitate true Roman mosaic, the glass sections were first embedded in clear glass and then blown to the final shape of the vessel. Modern glassworkers have often erroneously called any type of mosaic inlay *millefiori*.

The making of *millefiori* artefacts required great skill and patience, especially when complicated rod patterns were involved. The rods were produced by first casing a glass cane or tube with several layers of coloured glass on an appreciably larger scale than that which was finally required. Each layer could be reheated and shaped by marvering (round), pressing

Figure 3.17 Stages in the manufacture of a *millefiori* paperweight. The *millefiori* rods are drawn until very thin. Slices of the rods are then cut, laid in a mould, heated and covered with clear glass. Pilkington Glass Museum, St Helens, UK.

on the marver (square) or rolling on a corrugated surface (flower shape). (Later iron moulds were used to produce the same shapes.) When the design was complete, the glass rod was reheated to its softening point and drawn out so that its diameter decreased, the design decreasing proportionately until it was about 20–30 mm in diameter. The rod was then sectioned, the slices placed adjacent to one another (as in *Figure 3.17*) and fused by reheating. As a variation, sections of more than one *millefiori* rod or slices cut at an angle instead of transversely across the rod could be fused together, the latter producing elongated stripes of the design.

In AD 1495 the librarian of San Marco, Venice (Italy) — Marcantonio Sabellico — wrote of the inclusion of, 'all sorts of flowers, such as clothe the meadows in Spring, in a little ball' (of glass) which sounds remarkably like a description of *millefiori* paperweights made in the nineteenth century, when they became very fashionable. Paperweights often had thin designs such as flower petals (*millefiori*) incorporated in the body of coloured glass by picking up a thin section of glass on a gather and then taking another gather over the top. The numerous types of paperweight are described by Newman (1977), and many such as those made in Murano in Italy and Baccarat, St Louis and Clichy in France are now much-prized collectors' items (Hollister, 1964).

Glassblowing

It is remarkable that none of the contemporary Roman sources give any indication of a fundamentally important occurrence in the field of glass-making, namely, the invention of glass-blowing in about 40 BC; nor of the great increase in output of glass vessels which was brought about by its use. Later authors (Augustan and Tiberian) refer to the use of glass-blowing without saying when it was invented (Harden, 1969). Until comparatively recently literary sources have given the birthplace of glass-blowing as the Phoenician coast. However, on archaeological evidence it seems more likely that the invention took place in the Aleppo-Hama-Palmyra area of Syria, or in Israel. Grose (1977) has reviewed the evidence for the introduction of glass-blowing, and concludes that discoveries made in Israel in 1961 and 1970 point to glass-blowing having been invented there sometime in the period 50–40 BC.

The thinnest and most beautiful glass was produced at Tiberias and remains of glasshouses have been uncovered at Rishpon near Herzlia, Tiberias, Sussita (Hyppos) and in several places along the sea-shore in Israel. During the excavation of a first century AD cemetery at Acre a group of glasses (mainly piriform unguentaria) were found. These may have been the product of a local factory using the glass sand of the Belus district, which is known to have been shipped south even to Alexandria. At Beth She'arim (Sheikh Abreiq) near Nazareth a glasshouse was found which was working as late as the second and third centuries AD, and which produced very accurately shaped glass vessels. Many clay moulds were also found on the site. A contemporary glasshouse at Sussita on Lake Tiberias yielded a large quantity of glass vessels and wasters (Forbes, 1957).

The blown glass of this period is referred to as *Sidonian*, a term which is comparable to the much later *façon de Venise* since it was a tradition of blown glass shapes and techniques used by Syrians and Jews, which were handed from father to son, a training which was encouraged in the fourth century by exemption from taxes. The ancestors of the Jewish glassmakers must have learned a good deal about glass manufacture and glass painting during the Babylonian exile (seventh to fourth centuries BC).

From the very beginning many of the vessels have the air of being ripped off the blow iron as fast as they were produced. Handles and ornamentation also have the appearance of having been trailed on quickly. Speed of production gave early blown glass a pace and spontaneity which had previously been unknown. The operator could not think twice. The natural blown-up shapes and the play of volume and profile gave the so-called early Roman glass a classic place like that of T'ang and Sung in ceramic history. The shapes quickly grew more composite and within a few centuries glassware stood on the tables of ordinary citizens. At Karanis in Egypt a house dating from this period was excavated and yielded no less than eight oval glass dishes, sixteen bowls, five conical lamps, two drinking cups, two jars, two flasks and two jugs. At first blown-glass flasks were like their ancestors used for perfumes and other such luxury items and, like the earlier glass vessels, they were transported to southern Russia, Gaul or Germany packed in plaited straw covers like the modern chianti bottles. Such straw-protected bottles are shown in a mosaic at El Djem (Tunisia).

Sidonian (Syrian and Jewish) glassmakers exploited the glass-blowing technique, migrating west and northwards and establishing glasshouses abroad. Mould-blown glass was being made in Italy by the first century AD, and in the Alpine provinces and north-western Europe by AD 40–50. The famous glasshouses at Cologne were founded in the first century AD while the north Gallic and Belgic glasshouses were probably in full production by the second century. Their free- and mould-blown products were of a style directly related to the products of the central and eastern Roman Empire. The Egyptian workers based at Alexandria continued to specialize in cutting glass and in producing fine-coloured wares such as mosaic bowls, and did not adopt the glass-blowing technique until some time after the second century AD.

Exactly how the discovery of glass-blowing was made will probably never be known. For some time a picture of Egyptian metallurgists blowing a charcoal fire with tubes ending in clay nozzles was held to depict glassblowers and it took many years to dispel this legend despite the fact that there are no known examples of blown glass before the first century AD.

Harden (1969) suggests that solid metal rods had long been used for gathering molten glass from crucibles to introduce it into moulds (Lang and Price, 1975, describe iron blowpipes from a Roman glass-making site in Spain), and that it was but a short step to using a hollow tube to inflate the glass into a mould by blowing. Schuler (1959b) however, believes that *free (offhand) blowing* preceded *mould-blowing* since more skill was required to handle a blowpipe in the vertical position required for mould-blowing.

Glass-blowing techniques

The invention of glass-blowing brought about a complete revolution in the manufacture of glass artefacts. Glass ceased to be a luxury material since scores of vessels could be blown in a day in contrast with the use of the laborious core-forming process. Another great advantage was the possibility of making articles thinner and lighter and thus more acceptable for domestic purposes than was generally possible using the earlier glass-making processes. There was also a great increase in the variety, shape and number of small hollow articles, and for the first time larger containers and window panes could be produced.

The modern process of glass-blowing is described below but it is likely that the ancient process differed little from this, except that the blowpipe may have been simpler, and the furnace would have been far less sophisticated. The glassworker's blowpipe is a steel tube about 1.5 m long, tapered to a mouthpiece at one end. The gathering head is made by welding on a 100 mm length of thick-walled tube, made of wrought iron (or other alloy resistant to oxidation) having a diameter from 25 to 80 mm, the wider tubes being used for making the heavier ware. Several pipes are used by each *chair* or *shop* (a team of workers working from one pot, producing hand-blown glassware) so that a clean pipe at the right temperature will always be ready for the *gatherer* who starts the cycle of operations.

Molten glass will *wet* an iron rod which is hot enough to prevent the formation of a *skin* when it touches the glass, and hence the gatherer can collect from the pot a quantity of glass (the *gather*) whose size depends on the diameter of the pipe head, the temperature of the glass and the number of turns given to the pipe. Before blowing starts, it is necessary to form a skin of chilled glass (or the gather will perforate at the hottest point) and to make sure the glass is distributed evenly around the pipe. This is carried out by *marvering*, or rolling the glass on a hard, smooth surface, probably of stone (and in later times iron).

Large gathers, especially those made by double-gathering, are shaped by *blocking* or turning the gather in a shaped block of wet wood (usually pear wood); the steam produces an air-cushion which prevents the wood from burning. The gatherer will now puff or blow lightly down the pipe to form a small bubble of air and produce an internal viscous skin; the still molten glass between the two skins can now be manipulated to produce the desired distribution of glass needed in the final article. After puffing down the pipe, a thumb is immediately placed over the orifice and the air is allowed to expand until the correct size bubble (*paraison* or *parison*) is produced.

Many glass articles are produced *offhand*, that is, without the use of moulds. The blower (*gaffer*) sits at a glassworker's *chair*, a special seat invented in the mid-sixteenth century, which has long arms on which the blowpipe is rolled whilst the glass is being shaped (*Figure 3.18*). The term *chair* has been extended to describe the team for which the chair is the centre of operations (Charleston, 1962).

Manipulation of the glass was a natural development of glass-making once a bubble had been blown. By reheating and blowing alternately, and by holding the blowpipe above or below his head, the glassworker could control the shape and thickness of the blown vessel. If the glassblower was trying to make a vessel to a preconceived design it required a much greater degree of skill to achieve it by free blowing than by the use of a mould carved to the desired shape of the artefact. However, free blowing allowed spontaneity of design and it was perhaps for that reason that its use continued throughout the history of glass-making up to and including the present day. In the blowing of exceptionally large vessels a subterfuge could be used. Having blown a bulb, the worker took a mouthful of water and ejected it down the blowpipe quickly putting his thumb over the mouth-piece. The steam generated inside the glass bulb then continued the blowing process until it was released.

By successively reheating the article in a *glory hole* (a small furnace or an opening which leads to the hot interior of the furnace) a gaffer could manipulate the body of the vessel into a variety of shapes before the metal cooled; adding extra small gathers (brought to him by a *servitor*) to form stems, handles, bases etc.

The marvering surface itself could incorporate shaped hollows in order to produce definite patterns, or the glass could be shaped with the aid of a *battledore* (Fr. *palette*), a flat wooden board or even with a wad of wet newspaper. Tongs could be used to produce raised ridges and knobs by pinching out portions of the vessel's walls, or the pointed end of a reamer (a flat-bladed tool with a pointed end) could be used to produce ribs and furrows in the glass. It seems probable that the earliest decorative marks were made on glass at this stage, that is, before the molten glass had completely hardened (*Figure 3.19*).

When the main body of the article had been completed a solid iron rod, the *punty* (originally *pontil*) which had been heated and lightly coated with

Figure 3.18 A *gaffer* forming a glass object using a blow pipe and a mould. To the left another glassworker, seated at the *chair*, forms another glass object by rolling a blowpipe along the arms of the chair. Steuben factory at Corning, New York

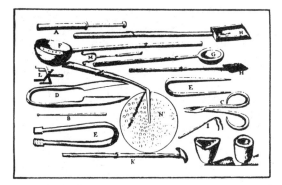

Figure 3.19 The tools of the glassmaker, taken from *De Arte Vitraria*, Neri-Merrett, 1st Latin edition, Amsterdam, 1668. The simple tools used by the glassmaker have changed little over the centuries and implements like those shown in this seventeenth-century illustration are still in use today. Amongst the tools seen in the picture are the blowpipe for blowing the initial shape, pincers, tongs and shears for finishing the piece, and a holder for carrying away the glassware.

glass, was attached to the centre of its base. The blower then wetted the glass near the end of the blowpipe or touched it with cold metal so that the glass vessel broke away from the blowpipe and was supported only on the punty iron. The open top was then softened in the glory hole, cut off at the desired height with shears and, if required, further opened or reduced with tongs (Ital. *pucella*). The vessel was then cracked off the punty iron and carried away for annealing. Subsequently, when cold, the scar from the punty (the punty or pontil mark) may be largely or even entirely ground away and polished. (Glass which has been made offhand has a fire-finished surface which is initially more durable than the surface formed against a mould because the surface becomes alkali-deficient when exposed to the flames of the glory hole, Bruce, 1979.)

Wine bottles were most commonly made by blowing a bulb, marvering it into shape and then pushing in the closed end to produce the characteristic dimple foot so carefully reproduced in the modern machine-made bottles. The bases of the bottles were substantially thicker than their necks. In blown glass generally there is a tendency for the material to be thicker at the furthest point from the blow iron.

Mould-blown techniques

The technique of blowing glass into moulds probably developed simultaneously with the discovery of glass-blowing. Once a gather of glass had been taken from the furnace on the end of a blow-iron, it was marvered, blown into a small elongated bulb and introduced into a two-piece mould, then blown to fill it. Until modern times the moulds would have been made of clay or wood (the latter was kept wet during use to prevent the wood from burning).

Casing and cupping

Cased glassware is made of two or more layers of differently coloured glass. To achieve this the glassblower either dipped a partially inflated mass of glass (*paraison*) into a crucible containing glass of a different colour, thus gathering it over the top (casing); or formed a cup of glass into which the second glass was blown (cupping). Having cased (or cupped), for example, a blue glass with a white glass, the body of the vessel would be brought to the required size and shape by further blowing and by rolling on a metal marver. (In making flashed window glass, the coloured glass is usually gathered first — termed the *post* — and then the colourless glass is gathered over the top of it; see page 96.) When the glass had been annealed, the outer layer of glass would be carefully abraded away to form a design in which the underlying glass was exposed or seen in varying degrees through the outer layer. An early example of cased glass dating from the first century AD is the Portland Vase (see *Figure 2.9*).

Technological features of the Portland Vase have attracted much attention since it was first discovered (probably in 1582). For instance, there is a complication in its supposed manufacture by blowing since the opal white glass casing only extends part way up the translucent blue glass vessel; and there are two substantial blue glass handles added over the white layer. The coefficients of expansion of the blue and white glasses apparently matched each other so perfectly that there is no evidence of strain in the vase. The results of recent investigations have been published by Bimson and Freestone (1983).

Pattern moulding

When glass was blown into a mould with a pattern carved on its interior surface, the pattern was impressed in reverse on the glass. Designs on a pattern-moulded vessel could be varied once the vessel had been removed from the mould by blowing or by twisting or swinging the viscous glass on the end of the blow-iron. For example, designs such as ribbing on the sides of a blown vessel were produced by blowing the glass into a ribbed mould. If the mould-blown vessel was removed from the mould and then gently reblown after reheating, the thicker glass between the ribs, being hotter than that forming the ribs, expanded so that the ribs were pushed to the interior surface of the vessel instead of remaining on the outer surface. Glass which has been mould-blown and then additionally blown to increase the size of the object or to soften or modify the lines of the pattern by blowing into a plain mould is sometimes referred to as having been *optic blown*.

The process of moulding glass lends itself to considerable variation, including the production of highly decorative effects such as the inclusion of rows of internal air bubbles in various patterns such as spirals, and the incorporation of white and coloured threads of glass.

Filigrana

Filigrana (Ital. *vetro filigranato*) is the Italian term which has been applied to glass artefacts, originally made in Murano *circa* 1527–1529, of clear glass with various styles of decoration produced by embedding threads of solid opaque white-glass (*lattimo*) forming *latticino* (or *latticinio*); or of coloured glass (or even occasionally a single white thread). It is now used to refer to all styles of decoration on clear glass made by a pattern formed by embedding threads of glass, including *vetro a fili* (threaded glass), *vetro a reticello* (glass with a small network formerly termed *a redexelo* and *a redexin* in Murano (Ger. *Netzglas*), and *vetro a retorti* (or *retortoli*), originally made in Murano but now termed *zanfirico* or *sanfirico* in Venice and Murano. *Vetro de trina* (lace-glass) is a term which has been used loosely to describe various types of *filigrana* glass, and is now considered to be superfluous and of no historical significance. Modern Venetian glassworkers find it hard to achieve the accuracy and lightness of design in *filigrana* of their predecessors.

In *vetro a fili* the opaque white and/or coloured glass threads are embedded in clear glass in continuous lines without any crossing of the threads, the lines being in a spiral or helix pattern (e.g. on plates) or in a spiral or volute pattern (e.g. on vases). In *vetro a reticello* the threads are embedded in clear glass in the form of criss-cross diagonal threads forming an overall diamond lattice network. There are three separate varieties, depending on whether the pattern is made with fine threads, coarse threads, or fine and coarse threads running in opposite directions. As the threads protrude slightly, tiny air bubbles (sometimes microscopic) are entrapped within each criss-cross diamond, the size depending on the process of production (*Figure 3.20*). On a few rare examples there are, instead of the air bubbles, thin wavy lines running in only one direction between the rows of white threads. The style has been used on vases, bowls, jugs etc. and also on plates (where the network often becomes distorted towards the centre or the edge of the plate). Several processes have been documented, and in Murano,

Figure 3.20 *Vetro a reticello.* Magnified detail showing crossed opaque white glass threads and entrapped air-bubbles. From *Venetian Glass at Rosenborg Castle* by Gudmund Boesen (1960).

according to local glassmakers, several methods have been used; the first two detailed below are the most authoritatively stated.

(1) A bulb (or cylinder) of blown glass in a mould, on which have been picked up on a gather parallel threads of glass (almost always *lattimo*) running diagonally in one direction (resulting from twisting the *paraison* after gathering the threads) and which is then blown into another similar bulb (or cylinder) with threads running in the opposite direction; the two bulbs (or cylinders) become fused together. The difficulty arises from the necessity of having the threads on each bulb exactly equidistant so that they will form equal and similar diamonds (except for distortions toward the extremities of the glass).

(2) A bulb of glass is made, as described above, with diagonal threads, and then half of the bulb is bent into the other half and fused, thus making the criss-cross threads. This method assures equal spacing, but is a difficult process.

(3) A bulb of glass is made, as described above, with diagonal threads, and then the glassblower sucks on the tube and collapses the further half of the bulb into the nearer half making a double wall with criss-cross threads.

(4) A bulb of glass is made, as described above, with diagonal threads, then it is cut and twirled to make, by centrifugal force, a flat open plate; another such plate is made with threads running in the opposite direction, and then the two plates are fused together by heating. This method also presents the difficulty of obtaining equal spacing of the threads on both plates.

In all these methods there develop, within the interstitial spaces made by the crossed threads, small (sometimes microscopic) bubbles, but occasionally they are elongated into thin wavy lines, and the enclosed areas sometimes have unequal sides. After the piece of glass with the crossed threads is made it is reheated, then blown and manipulated into various forms such as vases, plates and jugs.

Vetro a retorti is the Italian term applied to a style of decoration with parallel adjacent canes (vertical or spiral) of glass having embedded threads in various intricate patterns (as in the stems of some British wine glasses) and made by flattening the canes and fusing them together. It includes decoration made with opaque white or coloured glass threads or both embedded in the fused canes (*Figure 3.21*). The style has been used for plates, bowls, vases and, sometimes, for paperweights (Newman, 1977).

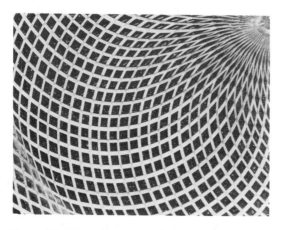

Figure 3.21 *Vetro a retorti*. Magnified detail showing parallel canes with twisted designs. From *Venetian Glass at Rosenborg Castle* by Gudmund Boeson (1960).

Air-bubbles and air-twists

A highly decorative effect was produced in the stems of British drinking glasses by twisting a rod of glass in which were embedded threads or tapes of opaque white or coloured glass (as described above), or air-bubbles and air-twists. The technique of deliberately incorporating air in glass stems dates from *circa* 1735, and was popular from the 1740s until the 1760s. It has been stated that there are over 150 varieties in different forms and combinations. Numerous examples are illustrated by Bickerton (1971). Air-twists were produced by two basic methods: by making a slot in a rod of glass, then drawing the rod until it became thin and twisting it to make the column of air spiral; or by moulding a pattern of circular holes or flat slits in the top of a glass rod, covering them with molten glass, and then

drawing and twisting the rod to make a spiral pattern of air (used to make multiple series twists). A quarter twist in a four-column stem would appear to produce a complete twist of 360°. In the early examples the twist was irregularly formed and spaced, but later the threading was uniform; it was sometimes carried down from the bowl of a two-piece glass. Another process involved placing several rods containing elongated tears into a cylindrical mould with grooves on its interior surface, then covering them with molten glass and, after withdrawing the mass on the punty, attaching another punty and twisting until the desired pattern was produced. In some examples one twist is concentrically within another (made by repeating the process with the mould, thus twice twisting the inner rod into a tighter twist); these are termed double series air-twist or even triple series air-twist. Occasionally an air-twist stem includes one or more knops, and the twist continues unbroken (but sometimes slightly distorted) through the knops.

Paperweights or other solid glass objects decorated with a pattern of regularly spaced air-bubbles, were made in a *spot-mould*. The mould was sectional with small spikes protruding in the interior. When the *paraison* (sometimes already having an interior decorative motif) was introduced, the sectional parts of the mould were tightened around it forcing the spikes into the glass. In this way small cavities were formed so that when the piece was cased, air-bubbles were trapped thus forming a pattern (Newman, 1977).

Sand-moulding

Sand-moulding invented in 1870 is a special form of moulding used to make glass liners for silver vessels. A wooden block is carved to fit exactly into the vessel, then removed and forced into a bed of damp sand, after which it is carefully withdrawn so that its exact impression remains in the sand. A gather of glass is then blown into the cavity to form the glass liner.

Good glassware was often (and still is) given a final polish using fine, hard abrasive, and where this was well carried out, much or all of the evidence that would suggest how the vessel had been made was removed, that is the casting flashes which remained on the glass at the junctions of the mould-pieces.

Lamp-working (at the lamp; at the flame)

Lamp-working is the technique of manipulating glass *at the lamp* by heating it with a small flame; and was probably discovered in the Roman era. Examples of pieces produced in this way range from small figures and objects to large composite three-dimensional scenic groups (Rule, 1967). The technique of *Verre de Nevers* is closely allied to lamp-work. Nevers figures were small figures made of opaque fusible glass in the late sixteenth and early seventeenth centuries at Nevers, and elsewhere, in France. Examples vary from 25 to 150 mm in height and are very detailed. Single figures often have stands of trailed glass threads; a figure without such a stand has usually been broken from a grotto (tableau). Some animals are mould-blown, with applied thin glass threads (Fr. *Verre frisé*). Occasionally large groups were made, such as a crucifixion scene or several figures with animals. They were made with portions of glass rods softened at the lamp and then manipulated with pincers or other instruments, and often fastened on an armature of copper wire. The names of some artists are known, including Jean Prestereau (1595) and his son Léon. Such ware, being made of white opaque material, might be mistaken for porcelain or faience. Most examples display coloured details. Similar figures were made in Venice, Germany, England and Spain in the seventeenth century and later; they are not readily distinguishable or dateable.

Decoration of glass artefacts

Since glass production began glassmakers and decorators have sought to improve simple glass shapes. The numerous techniques used can thus be divided broadly into two groups: those produced by the glassmaker whilst the glass was still hot; and those produced by the decorator on cold glass.

Glass-making techniques of decoration include colouring (and decolorizing), free blowing and shaping including special effects produced by tooling and marvering, and by pattern moulding. Embellishments produced by the glass decorator include cutting, engraving, cold painting, gilding and lustre and enamel painting. Lustre and enamel painting and some forms of gilding, however, require the use of a kiln to complete the process.

Glass-making techniques

Colouring, free blowing and blowing into patterned moulds have already been discussed under methods of glass vessel production.

Tooling the glass
Some early Islamic glass bowls and saucers bear patterns such as bull's eye circlets, rosettes etc. which were impressed on their sides by means of patterned tongs whilst the glass was still hot. Cylindrical bowls of the same period bear other designs such as lozenges and small birds impressed in the hot glass by shaped pincers (Harden, 1971). Pincering was a fairly general technique, some Venetian goblets have wings or flame-like protuberances formed by pincering the hot glass (Newman, 1977). It seems probable that tooling hot glass was one of the earliest forms of decoration.

Special effects produced by marvering
A variety of special effects can be produced by spreading various materials (such as chopped coloured glass rod, glass powder, chalk etc.) on the marver. The first gather is formed, marvered so that the powdered material is incorporated in the surface, and then a second gather is made. The chopped coloured rod spreads out like coloured worms, and the powdered chalk decomposes to produce particles of lime and copious bubbles of carbon dioxide. Shapes resembling petals can be produced by making several gathers, spreading chalk on the top of each, and pressing in a spike so that all the layers are depressed and trumpet-like shapes are produced (Newman, 1977). Harden (1968) refers to rare kinds of decoration of core-formed articles of the second millennium BC in which powdered glass was fired on to the surface, but not actually fused, after the article had been made (see *Figure 2.1*).

Ice-glass
Ice-glass (cracked glass), which has a rough irregular outer surface resembling cracked ice, was first produced in Venice in the sixteenth century, by two processes: plunging the partially blown gathering of hot glass momentarily into cold water and immediately reheating lightly so as not to close the cracks caused by the sudden cooling, and then fully blowing to enlarge the spaces in the labyrinth of small fissures; or rolling the hot glass on an iron marver covered with small glass splinters (sometimes covered) which adhered to the surface and became fused when lightly heated, a process which also removed the sharp edges (see *Figure 2.29*). Ice-glass was produced in Liège, Belgium, and in Spain in the seventeenth century. It was revived in England in about 1850 by Apsley Pellat who called it 'Anglo-Venetian glass'. In nineteenth-century France the first method described above produced a glass called *verre craquelé*, and the second method an effect called *broc à glaces*. A third method developed in modern times by Venini involves the use of hydrofluoric acid and produces *vetro corroso*. Ice-glass has been produced in the United States since the nineteenth century where it is termed overshot glass. The general Italian term is *vetro a ghiaccio* (Newman, 1977).

Davenport's Patent glass
This was decorated with the intention of imitating engraving or etching although it resembled neither.

The process was patented in 1806 by John Davenport of Longport, Stoke-on-Trent, an English potter and glassmaker. The process involved covering the outer surface of the glassware with a paste containing powdered glass, then removing the surface paste so as to leave the intended design and quickly firing at a low temperature to fuse the glass powder onto the surface without melting it. The designs were often heraldic insignia and sporting scenes. Such glassware was usually inscribed *Patent* on a label made and affixed by the same method (Newman, 1977).

Addition of glass blobs and trails

The addition of glass blobs and trails has been used since the late second millenium BC for decorating core-formed vessels with lines, dots, rings and hieroglyphic inscriptions (Harden, 1968). After trailing on the design of hot glass, probably from a metal rod, the trails were marvered flush with the surface, although in some areas which would be difficult to marver such as the foot or neck, the trails remained in relief (see *Figures 2.13, 2.14* and *2.17*). The Romans were particularly fond of trailing in relief. Threads marvered into the glass body could be combed by dragging a pointed tool across them before the trails cooled. Newman (1977) refers to a rare type of decoration (underglaze) where the coloured trails have themselves been covered with transparent glass, as in the case of the hollow fish-shaped container dating from the Eighteenth Dynasty (1567–1320 BC) and now in the Brooklyn Museum, New York (Riefstahl, 1972).

Trailing was especially popular in the sixteenth and seventeenth centuries AD and is still carried out in modern glass-making. Allied to trailing is the intricate stem work so popular with Venetian and *façon de Venise* glassmakers in the seventeenth century, though in these cases the trails are mostly free-standing.

Another relatively simple form of applied decoration is the use of blobs and prunts on glass vessels. Sometimes while still hot the blobs were stamped into designs such as raspberry or strawberry prunts with a metal die. The addition of prunts to a vessel besides being decorative also helped it to be held more easily in the absence of a handle. A further development was the application of hot blobs of glass to a vessel while it was still on the blowpipe (Newman, 1977). The vessel was then reblown so that the hot blobs blew out further than the cooler walls of the body. These were then drawn out with pincers, and blown at the same time to keep them hollow, then reattached lower down the vessel (Harden *et al.*, 1968). The earliest prunted beaker seems to be the dolphin beaker of the fourth century (Newman, 1977), but they became common in Saxon times (claw beakers) (Harden, 1971), and particularly so in the fifteenth century (Harden, 1971; Tait,

1968). In the *daumengläser* from Germany this technique has been put into reverse. After the blobs were applied to the heated body of the vessel, the glassmaker sucked through the blowing iron so that the blobs were made to extend into the interior of the vessel, forming hollow finger-grips on the outside (Newman, 1977).

Other forms of applied decoration owe more to the skill of the artist trained in other media than to the skill of the glassmaker.

Enamelling

Enamelling is the process of decorating the surface of glassware by the application of a vitreous material, coloured with metallic oxides, to the surface after which the enamel has been fixed by low temperature firing in a *muffle kiln*. Enamel decoration is in the form of scenes, figures, inscriptions and heraldry.

Enamel colours are metallic oxides mixed with a glass frit of finely powdered glass suspended in an oily medium (formerly honey) for ease of application with a brush. The colours are applied to the surface of the glass artefact and fixed by low temperature firing, in the range 700–900°C, in a muffle kiln, during which the medium burns out. A flux mixed with the enamel colours lowers the firing point to below that of the glass to which they have been applied. Enamel colours differ from cold colours in that they are fixed to the glass surface and are therefore not so readily affected by wear; the firing results in a smooth surface only slightly palpable to the fingers; and the final colours of the enamels are not often apparent upon application but only after firing.

The process of enamelling glass is a technique which can be dated back to the fifteenth century BC: a small Egyptian jug bearing the name of Tuthmosis III (*circa* 1504–1450 BC) was decorated with powdered glass fired to the body of the vessel (see *Figure 2.1*). Some Roman glassware was decorated with enamel painting which was carried out both in the East and in Italy in the first century AD (Harden, 1969). Vessels decorated in Egypt tended to bear human, animal and plant motifs; whereas those depicting wild beasts in the arena or in gladiatorial combat seem to have been made in the Rhineland. Italian glassware from the sixth to seventh centuries returned to trailed decoration (Harden, 1971) or had marvered splashes and blobs of white, yellow, or red glass all over their surfaces, but certain classes of articles, such as the Islamic enamelled mosque lamps and the 'Luck of Edenhall' deserve separate treatment.

The Luck of Edenhall (Charleston, 1959b; Newman, 1977) is a flared beaker of Islamic enamelled glass made and decorated in Syria (possibly at

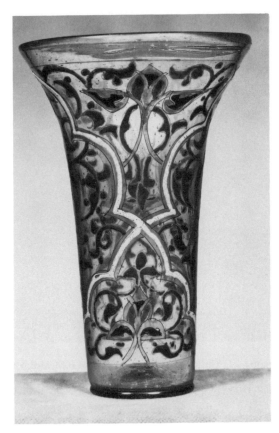

Figure 3.22 Luck of Edenhall. Enamelled beaker. Syrian (probably Aleppo). H 157 mm, *Circa* 1250. Victoria and Albert Museum, London.

Aleppo) in the thirteenth century, and now in the Victoria and Albert Museum, London (*Figure 3.22*). It is of clear glass with coloured enamelled decoration of finely drawn and stylized foliate and geometric forms in Islamic style in white, blue and red. The beaker was probably brought to Britain from Palestine by a Crusader towards the end of the fourteenth century. It was for a long time in the possession of the Musgrave family of Edenhall, near Penrith, Cumberland. A similarly shaped and enamelled beaker is in the Kunstgewerbemuseum, Cologne.

Enamelling was known in China in the eighteenth century; it was used extensively in Venice from the fifteenth century and elsewhere in Europe from the sixteenth century onwards. Opaque enamels were used generally but *transparent enamel* was developed in about 1810. The earliest mention of enamelling on glassware in England is a notice by a Mr Grillet in 1696, but no examples are extant. Early enamelling

was introduced by artists from Germany and the Low Countries, and was of the type known as *thin* or *wash enamel*, more suitable for the softer English *lead glass*, and was executed within outlines previously etched on the glass. Later *dense enamel* became the usual medium, first with designs of festoons and flowers, but later landscapes, figure subjects and coats of arms. It was in this period that the members of the Beilby family, William and his younger sister Mary, produced their remarkable enamelled ware. They always worked as a pair (in the period 1762–1778) and their association has been claimed as one of the greatest in the history of artistic glass (Rush, 1973), their fame bringing commissions from many noble families in England (Elville, 1951). William and Mary Beilby, and possibly Michael Edkins, were the leading enamellers of the eighteenth century; they decorated on clear glass and *opaque white glass*, respectively (see *Figure 2.37*). Some ware was enamelled by glasshouses in Stourbridge in the nineteenth century, and possibly by London jewellers and silversmiths doing work on glass boxes and scent bottles, as well as by artists who decorated porcelain in imitation of Sèvres porcelain and who did similar work on glassware in the mid-nineteenth century.

The earliest German enamelling on glass was in the second half of the sixteenth century, copying the Venetian enamelled armorial glasses that had previously been imported. The German enamelling is found on the typical German *Humpen* and *Stangenglas*, where the style evolved to cover almost the entire surface with painting subordinating the glass itself. Bright colours created the decorative effects, but the painting was not of superior quality. The early motifs were coats of arms, followed by a great variety of subjects, for example, painting of a religious, allegorical, historical or scenic nature, or showing artisan or guild activities, or satirical or family scenes, usually with dates or long datable inscriptions added. The place of production is usually unidentifiable, except in some special types such as the *Ochsenkopfglas* (Franconia), *Hallorenglas* (Halle), and *Hofkellereiglas* (Saxony or Thuringia). In the seventeenth century enamelling became more restrained and skilfully executed, with the artists usually signing the pieces. A new style of enamelled decoration, *Schwarzlot*, was introduced by Johann Schaper and his followers, Johann Ludwig Faber, Abraham Helmhack and Hermann Benckertt. The use of opaque enamel was superseded by transparent enamel, introduced in about 1810 by Samuel Mohn and also used by his son Gottlob Samuel Mohn and Franz Anton Siebel. In the 1750s some enamelling was carried out on opaque white glass.

Islamic enamelling, consisting of opaque vitreous enamelling (with gilding) as decoration on glassware was made between 1170 and 1402, when Tamerlane

(Timur) sacked Damascus and the local glass industry was moved to Samarkand, and some glassware associated with Fustat (Egypt) said to date from about 1270 to 1340. It is of five tentatively identifiable groups based on the criteria of style and date rather than any proven connection with the places of production identified with the groups, that is Raqqa, Syro-Frankish, Aleppo, Damascus, Chinese-Islamic and Syrian glassware (see *Figure 2.24*).

In the third quarter of the fifteenth century there was a phase in Venice when gorgeously decorated ware was made (Harden, 1971), such as the Barovier wedding cup (*circa* AD 1450–1475) (Gasparetto, 1958). The enamelling was executed at Murano on clear coloured glass and on opaque white glass. Although enamelling on glassware has recently been said to have been carried out in Venice at the end of the thirteenth century, no example is reported. From the late fifteenth century enamelling was carried out in a manner similar to that of Islamic glassware of the thirteenth and fourteenth centuries, the technique being said to have been reinvented by Anzolo Barovier. It was first used on sapphire blue glassware and other coloured transparent glassware, but towards the end of the fifteenth century coloured glass tended to be superseded for this purpose by colourless glass in Venice. By the end of the sixteenth century enamelling was little used there except on opaque white glass, which again became popular in the eighteenth century.

In gilt enamelling the decoration was first outlined with pen and brush and fixed in the kiln. Then the colours were spread on the outlying areas and the vessel fired a second time at a lower temperature. The vitreous colours are opaque and cover the surface in a thick coating. The numerous gilt designs were enclosed in red enamel lines for added emphasis. The colours used for enamelling modern glass tableware are usually based on glasses which contain substantial amounts of lead oxide, in order to reduce the fluxing temperature (e.g. 590°C) to below that of the softening point of the glass, and to produce a glossy finish on the fired enamel. Unless the enamel is formulated carefully so as to have adequate durability, it is possible to extract lead from the enamels, for example, during cooking or by leaving citrus drinks in contact with the enamel for a considerable time, and regulations have been introduced by the European Economic Commission to control the lead release (EEC, 1976).

Cold painting

Cold painting (Ger. *Kaltmalerei*; Ital. *di pinto freddo*) of glass dates back to the Roman period but, lacking the durability of fired enamels and therefore

Figure 3.23 The Daphne Ewer, cold-painted and gilded. H 222 mm, *Circa* late second, early third century. Roman Empire, possibly Syria. Corning Museum of Glass, New York.

rubbing off easily, it is a poorer form of coloured decoration (*Figure 3.23*). In this process lacquer colours or oil paint were applied to the surface of glassware. Such colours are effectively used when applied to the back of the surface to be viewed and protected by a layer of varnish, metal foil, or by another sheet of glass (Ger. *Hinterglasmalerei*). The process was sometimes used on *Humpen* and other large glasses of *Waldglas*. This was possibly because the glasses were too large to be enamelled and fired in a *muffle kiln*, and also because the glass was not sufficiently durable to withstand firing. Also the painting was carried out by peasants who had no furnace available. In the nineteenth century there was a great interest in the leisure-art of painting scenes in reverse on the backs of glass plates, sheets of glass, mirrors etc. so that the design was protected by the glass when viewed from the front. There was a bright luminosity in such paintings because there was no air gap between the paint and the glass (Newman, 1977; Stahl, 1915).

Lustre painting

Lustre painting is the term given to the process of applying metallic oxide pigments to the glass surface and firing under reducing conditions to produce a *metallic iridescent effect* (a *lustre*) (Newman, 1977). The process could be used to produce a ground completely covering the surface, or simply to produce a design (see *Figure 2.23*). Oxides of gold, copper or silver (and, in modern times, platinum and bismuth) were dissolved in acid and, after being mixed with an oily medium, were painted on the glass. Firing in a reduced atmosphere, smoky and rich in carbon monoxide, caused the metal to fuse into a thin film, producing a non-palpable, evenly distributed metallic flashing. Gold and copper yielded a ruby colour and silver a straw yellow colour. This style of decoration appears on Islamic glass from the ninth to the eleventh centuries; most specimens having been found in and attributed to Egypt, where the technique is thought to have originated.

Examples of lustre-painted ware in Egypt are dateable to the sixth if not the fifth century (Harden, 1971; Lamm, 1941), and continued until the late twelfth century (Pinder-Wilson, 1968). Modern opalescent glassware that has been treated with metallic oxides is heated in a controlled atmosphere to develop an iridescent effect. It was produced commercially in 1863 by J & L Lobmeyr and thereafter by many glasshouses under various patents.

Gilding

The technique of gilding is the process of decorating glassware on the surface, or on the back of the glass, by the use of gold leaf, gold paint, or gold dust. The history and technique of gilding have been comprehensively described by Charleston (1972). Harden (1968) drew attention to the appliqué gold sheet on Tutankhamun's head-rest (see *Figure 3.7*) and the plain gold bands on a lidded ointment jar in the British Museum (see *Figure 2.5*) as examples of the early application of gold (Harden *et al.*, 1968).

In the process of *fired gilding*, gold was applied to the outer surface of a glass by using gold leaf pulverized in honey, or powdered gold, and affixed by low temperature firing to assure reasonable permanency. The resulting appearance was dull with a rich and sumptuous effect but the gold could be burnished to brightness. Gold could be more permanently fixed to a glass surface by brushing on an *amalgam* of *gold* and *mercury*. Low-temperature firing caused the mercury to vaporize, leaving a gold deposit forming the design which could then be burnished to brightness. Mercuric gold has a thin, metallic, brassy appearance quite unlike the dull rich colour of honey gilding; it is much cheaper and easier to fix.

In some German diamond-point engraving the decoration is supplemented with gilding. By the seventeenth century decoration on the surface of glass was carried out by firing with gold leaf, using one of several methods (see above) or, especially in Venice, Hall-in-Tyrol, Austria, and the Netherlands by unfired gold painting. Such methods of decoration were for gold borders on engraved glassware, and in Germany on some Court glassware with gilt in relief. Gilding on the surface of English glassware in the eighteenth and nineteenth centuries was carried out by Lazarus Jacobs, the Beilbys, Michael Edkins and James Giles. In Spain gilding was applied to wheel-engraved glassware at La Granja de San Ildefonso in the eighteenth century, and similar work was produced in Germany.

The process of *unfired gilding* involved applying gold, in a medium, to the outer surface of glass resulting in a lack of permanency. It was a primitive method by which a preparation of linseed oil was applied to the glass with a brush after which the gold leaf was laid on and the oil allowed to dry. As it was unfired the gold readily rubbed off and, of course, it could not be burnished. This method was used in Britain on some *opaque white glass* and on *country-market glass* of the nineteenth century. It was also used on some German, Bohemian and Spanish glass, which has lasted better than that done in England, perhaps due to the fixative employed. Where such gilding has been rubbed off, the design may still be observed by the pattern on the glass left by the fixative. This method of gilding is also called *cold-*, *oil-*, *size-*, *lacquer-*, or *varnish*-gilding and is similar to applying cold colours.

Acid gilding has been used more recently, usually to produce decorative borders. A design, or ground, is etched on the glass with hydrofluoric acid, gold leaf is then applied overall. After being burnished, the polished raised areas contrast with the matt etched areas.

Sandwiched gold leaf

Gold leaf, with engraved designs, was sandwiched between layers of glass from ancient times. Some of the earliest sandwich gold glasses are the Hellenistic bowls found at Canosa in Apulia, Italy, dating to the third century BC, and now in the British Museum, London. Heraclius described the manufacture of gold-decorated glass bowls of the Canosa type (see *Figure 2.7*) (Forbes, 1957):

I obtained several bowls of high sparkling glass
These I painted with a brush dipped in a resin called gum
Then onto the golden bowls I
Began to put leaves of gold, and when I found them dried
I engraved little birds, and men, flowers and lions
According to my desire. Then I coated the bowls

With thin layers of glass for protection, blown at
the fire
And when this glass had enjoyed the even heat
It enclosed the bowls perfectly in a thin layer.

The outer bowl, which reaches just below the rim of
the inner one, has not been fused or glued to the
inner bowl but the two layers hold together simply
because they match each other perfectly. Sandwiching gold between two layers of glass protected
the gold leaf, but there was always the disadvantage
that air bubbles might get between the two layers and
disfigure the design. Later examples, where the gold
leaf lay under only parts of the surface, to which it
was fused with a layer of glass (*fondo d'oro*), were
found in the catacombs in Rome and in the Rhineland
in the fourth century AD (Painter, in Harden *et al.*,
1968). Examples of gold leaf protected between two
layers of glass are known from the Parthian or
Sassanian periods in Persia, perhaps the second to
fourth centuries AD, and from Egypt and Syria, when
a piece of glass was gilded and engraved on its reverse
and then fused to a layer of clear glass. A leaf of gold,
or silver, fixed to the back of a sheet of colourless
glass and formed into a pattern or scene, is known as
Verre Eglomisé. Highlights are produced by scraping
away the foil.

Some Roman glass gilding was done by applying
gold leaf to a hot bubble of glass which, when blown,
would break the leaf into speckles. Another method,
used on Roman glass and later on Venetian glass, was
sprinkling granular gold dust on to molten glass.
Islamic glass in the twelfth to fourteenth centuries
was very rarely decorated only with gilding, applied
by the use of colloidal gold and then fired; but mainly
such glass combined gilding with enamelling, for
example mosque lamps. Some Venetian glassware of
the sixteenth century has gilding as the sole
decoration, but normally enamelling was combined
with it.

The history and techniques of gilding glass have
been comprehensively described by Charleston
(1972); and the production of gold *tesserae* was
discussed earlier in this chapter.

Zwischengoldglas

In Bohemia a technique of sandwiching gold between
two layers of glass was developed in the 1730s to
decorate a type of drinking glass (Ger., literally
'between gold glass'). The vessels were decorated
with gold leaf by a process whereby the outer surface
of one glass was coated with gold leaf, the design
engraved through it, and then a bottomless glass was
sealed over the top (using a colourless resin) to
protect the design. The inner glass had been ground
down with great exactness for almost its whole height
so as to permit the outer glass to be fitted precisely
over it. On early rare Bohemian examples the joint

showed at the top of the rim, but on later ones the
rim of the inner glass was of double thickness for a
distance of about 10 mm, so that a projecting flange
fitted over the outer glass. The outer glass projected
slightly at the bottom, and the space below, in the
case of a beaker, was filled with a glass disc with
similar gold engraving and sealed by transparent
colourless resin. The outer surface of the double-
walled glass was sometimes further decorated by
cutting twelve to eighteen narrow vertical facets or
flutes. Silver leaf was sometimes used instead of gold.
A frequent form of this type of vessel was a small
straight-sided beaker, and popular decorations were
hunting scenes, views of monasteries, Bohemian
saints and armorial bearings, all very delicately

Figure 3.24 *Zwischengoldglas*. Beaker with faceted exterior,
Bohemian, second quarter of the eighteenth century. H
80 mm. Kunstgewerbemuseum, Cologne.

engraved (*Figure 3.24*). The best examples date from
the 1730s, but others were made until about 1755.
Such decoration was used not only on beakers but
also on goblets and other double-walled vessels,
sometimes with cold painting on coloured glass or
with enamelling. Such ware is sometimes termed
double glass. Johann Josef Mildner revived and
elaborated the technique in 1787 (Newman, 1977).

Other applications of metal

Ancient glasses may become iridescent as a result of the weathering process having produced layers of silica at their surfaces which are interspersed with air spaces within which light can cause optical interference phenomena; and as a result of deposition of metallic oxide ions on the surface. However, glass can be deliberately made iridescent by spraying on a solution of stannic chloride followed by firing in a reduced atmosphere to produce a transparent layer of stannic oxide which is thick enough to produce optical interference colours. Decorative yellow, orange or red effects can be produced on glass by firing on compounds of silver and copper and refiring.

Large distortion-free mirrors could not be made until the end of the seventeenth century when plate glass became available, but small mirrors were made from the twelfth century by backing glass with lead or tin (Newman, 1977). In the sixteenth century Venetian glassmakers made mirrors using cylinder glass and were sufficiently successful to form a Guild of Mirror-makers in 1569. Cylinder glass was also used in the manufacture of mirrors for the Hall of Mirrors in the Palace of Versailles in France. Large, good-quality mirrors were not made in Britain until 1773. A great deal has been written concerning the manufacture of mirrors, especially by Schweig (1973).

In passing, mention should be made here of the modern method of colouring float glass by discharging metal ions electrically into the glass surface as it is being formed.

Architectural glass

By far the most widespread use of glass in the architectural context was in the form of painted window glass, from medieval times onwards. However, in Roman times, glass in the form of mosaics and opus sectile had been used to decorate the interiors of buildings (see *Figure 2.12*); and glass with a greenish tint had been used for small window panes.

Mosaics

The architectural process of embedding small pieces of roughly squared glass (tesserae) in cement on walls or floors to form a picture was first developed by the Greeks, and then used extensively in the Roman and Byzantine periods. Roman mosaics were generally composed of stones, but there are early examples made of glass in Rome; and seventh century AD examples occur in Ravenna and Torcello, Italy. According to Theophilus (trans. Hawthorne and Stanley Smith, 1979), the Greeks made sheets of glass a finger (20 mm) thick and '. . . split them with a hot iron into tiny square pieces and cover them on one side with gold leaf, coating them with clear ground glass. . . ' as a 'solder glass' before firing in a kiln to fuse the gold leaf in place; 'Glass of this kind, interspersed in mosaic work, embellishes it very beautifully.'

Vasari (1511–1571) gives a description of the preparation of mosaic cubes. First, the glass is made opaque by the addition of tin oxide and/or coloured by the addition of metallic oxides. When the glass was sufficiently melted and fused it was ladled out in small quantities onto a metal table and pressed into circular cakes about 20 cm in diameter and from 1.0 to 1.25 cm thick. The solidified glass was then annealed, cooled and cracked into *tesserae*. The fractured surface was generally used to form the upper surface of the mosaic since it had a more pleasing surface and richness of colour. The thickness of the glass cake therefore regulated the texture. The use of the gold background in mosaic work was particularly associated with Byzantine architecture. The earlier mosaics at Rome and Ravenna generally have backgrounds of a dark blue colour, which is particularly fine at SS. Cosma and Damiano in Rome, and in the tomb of Galla Placidia in Ravenna. Fiorentino-Roncuzzi has published a study of the mosaics at Ravenna in the church of San Vitale (dedicated AD 547) and the Basilica of Sant Apollinare in Classe (*circa* AD 500). The mosaics at S. Sophia in Constantinople (sixth century) had gold backgrounds, as did all the later examples in Italy from the ninth and tenth centuries only. The finest examples are at St Sophia, St Marco in Venice, and the Cappella Palatina at Palermo.

Gilded *tesserae* were produced by hermetically sealing gold leaf between two sheets of glass. The technique of producing the *fondi d'oro* or glass vessels adorned with designs in gold and found in the Roman catacombs, was of the same nature. According to Vasari a glass disc was damped with gum-water and gold leaf applied to it. The gold-covered disc was then placed on an iron shovel in the mouth of the furnace. The glass covering was either made of a glass bubble or from broken glass bottles (cullet) so that one piece covered the entire disc. The disc was then held in the furnace until it almost reached red heat when it was quickly drawn out and cooled. In order to set the *tesserae* on walls or ceilings, a cartoon (drawing) was first pounced (pricked through) portion by portion on soft cement. Sometimes the resulting outline was coloured as a guide before the application of a thick cement and setting of the *tesserae*. The stucco cement remained soft for two to four days depending upon the weather. It was made of lime cement mixed with water, that is travertine, lime, pounded brick, gum-tragacanth and white of egg, and once made was kept moist with damp cloths while the *tesserae* were set (Maclehose, 1907).

Belcher mosaic – see Kreuger (1994).

Opus sectile

During the excavations at Kenchreai, the eastern port of Corinth (Greece), during the 1960s, over 100 panels of *opus sectile* worked in glass, were found, stacked on the floor of a building in the harbour area. The building and others associated with it, were in the process of being remodelled or redecorated, when they were submerged during a seismic disturbance in AD 375.

The panels can properly be regarded as a stage in the historic evolution of the use of richly coloured glasses fitted or fused together to form ornamental designs. The origins of this tradition lie in the early glass of Egypt, and develop through the Nimrud ivory inlays and the fused mosaic glass vessels like those from Hasanlu and Marlik. But the most immediate technological precursors of the Kenchreai panels are the whole array of objects from the world of ribbon glass and *millefiori*, including even the miniature fused mosaic plaques. The Kenchreai panels might be considered to be just a slightly different version of other *opus sectile* work, such as the examples at Ostia (Italy), except that they happen to have been executed in glass instead of stone. But the separate units in many of the details and highlights of the panels are themselves polychrome pieces of glass. These details were not formed by simply arranging separate, tiny units of differently coloured monochrome glasses. They were made by a series of intricate processes in which carefully shaped bits of monochrome glasses were fitted, fused together by heating, and while still softened, manipulated in various ways into complicated polychrome design components like the details of fish scales and bird feathers. This characteristic puts the work squarely into the *millefiori* tradition. It is a technique which could only have been executed in glass and should not be construed as purely an inlay or mosaic technique, which could have been executed, for example, with shaped, polished, coloured stones. The Kenchreai panels are a product of the pyrotechnological arts, and not simply the lapidary art (Scranton, 1967; Ibrahim *et al.*, 1976).

The panels may not only be a stage in this tradition, but could conceivably be regarded as its culmination; for it does not appear to continue. In the West a few inlays in caskets and jewellery occur later and eventually the *cloisonné* technique evolves. In the Byzantine world mosaics flourished on a grander scale than ever before, but still as a part of their own mosaic tradition: one colour for each cube, and only cube after cube, with few other geometrical shapes being utilized. With the decline of the Roman world, the centre of glass-making moved eastwards, and along with the other chemical arts, glass-making flowered in the Islamic world. But by then glass artists had become totally preoccupied with glass-blowing and three-dimensional forms and transparency.

There is a certain temptation to see in the panels distant forerunners of painted glass windows, but the separation in time is so great, and the difference in essential glass quality and its treatment so distinctly different, that this temptation is perhaps best resisted. The panels were of various sizes and shapes — squares and oblongs — among which the smallest dimension would be around 0.30 m, and the largest almost 2.00 m. According to one hypothesis, a surface of appropriate size and shape was prepared first — a table, or a tray with raised edges. On this was then laid a kind of pavement of large potsherds cut from coarse amphorae, approximately rectangular in shape. Over these potsherds, and impressed into the interstices, was laid a thick coat, perhaps 20 mm over the potsherds, of a kind of plaster of which the chief ingredients were pine resin and finely pulverized marble. This was brought to a smooth surface. On this surface were laid pieces of glass of various colours, cut to various shapes (about 2 mm thick), in order to create the desired pattern, and these were glued down with more resin. According to a second hypothesis, the pieces of glass would be laid face down on the tray, then covered with the coat of resin plaster into which the potsherds would be impressed.

When found, some of the glass was firm and hard, some had disintegrated to a powder, and some was preserved in one of a variety of states inbetween. Although the panels were colourful when found, the colours presented were apparently not the same as the original colours, in most cases at least. Thus the characteristics of the various kinds of glass at the time when they were applied to the panels can only be inferred. However, it would seem that some kinds, notably those used for human flesh and for the masonry of buildings, were cut from large thin sheets. Of other kinds, notably the neutral backgrounds, it has been suspected that they were troweled into place while in a more or less pasty state, though this is not certain. Some thin dividing lines, and especially the curved stems of flowers, may have been set in place as still-soft rods, or conceivably even as an extruded paste. More complex forms such as the seed-pods of lotus plants or the bodies of certain fish or birds give the appearance of having been made in a kind of *millefiori* and fused-glass mosaic techniques, externally moulded so that in cross-section the block would have the intended inner markings. Some particular shapes, such as the heads of birds or animals, may have been built up plastically in separate moulds, with certain details engraved or impressed on the face intended to be visible.

Manufacture of window glass

Mould-cast glass panes

In Roman times small panes of glass were produced by casting molten glass into shallow trays and spreading it out manually as it cooled. There is no contemporary reference to this process, but a number of mould-cast glass pane fragments have been excavated, for example, at Pompeii in Italy, and on several Romano-British villa sites. There is a fragment of Roman window glass from Caerleon in Wales (Boon, 1966) which seems to have been cast on wet wood judging from the impressions of wood grain on one side of it, although this has been disputed. Fragments of an almost complete pane of window glass dating from the second century AD were excavated in 1974 in a bath-house complex at the Romano-British iron-working settlement at Garden Hill, Hartfield in East Sussex (Money, 1976). The pane (*Figure 3.25*) measured 235 mm × 255 mm and is now in the British Museum. It has one flat side on which there are marks which suggest that it was cast on a bed of sand. Two edges are rounded while the others are grozed. The one remaining original rounded corner bears a mark made by pushing the molten glass into the mould with a pointed

Figure 3.25 Pane of moulded green window glass from a Roman villa at Garden Hill, Hartfield, East Sussex (after restoration). Upper and right hand sides grozed. H 255 mm, D 235 mm. British Museum, London.

instrument. There may have been other panes in the bath-complex; and they were certainly used elsewhere on the site since fragments representing several panes were unearthed in several locations. Fragments of window glass excavated at Stonea, Cambridgeshire in 1981 bear marks of wood grain on one side, and one bears evidence of having been manipulated to fill the mould.

Cylinder glass

The most prevalent and long-lived methods of producing early Roman window glass, however, were the *spinning process* which produced *crown glass*; and the *cylinder process* which produced *cylinder glass* (also known as *broad*, *sheet*, *spread* or *muff glass*, later *Lorraine glass* or *German sheet*). Cylinder glass tended to be irregular in thickness between the ninth and thirteenth centuries, and it lacked flatness, although it was glossy on both sides, unlike the Roman cylinder glass with one matt and one glossy side, probably because the kilns were not as hot as the Roman type. Chambon (1963) gives a very detailed account of the developments in making cylinder glass.

Cylinder glass-making seems to have been the earlier invention, but cylinder and crown glass-making repeatedly replaced each other during the fourth to the nineteenth centuries depending on the fashion; for example, Tudor leaded windows had crown glass, after which the methods were superseded by mechanical methods of sheet glass production. Cylinder glass was certainly used in Roman buildings in Britain, Italy and Greece (at Corinth) before crown glass became the fashion.

The cylinder process enabled larger and more even sheets of glass to be made than those which were produced by the mould-cast method. A gathering of glass was first blown into a broad bulb up to 1.5 m in length, and then given a cylindrical shape by swinging it back and forth (to lengthen it) and marvering (to keep it cylindrical). The ends were then cut off and the cylinder split longitudinally by a hot iron, and then reheated on the flat bed of a kiln. When it was hot enough, the glass could be flattened into a sheet with iron tongs and a smooth piece of iron or wood called a *rake*, *croppie* or *flattener* (*Figure 3.26*). This description is simplified in its essentials because the exact method of production varied from era to era. For example, Theophilus states (Dodwell, 1961; Hawthorne and Smith, 1963) that, after the bulb was blown, the end was pierced (by blowing it out after heating the end in a glory hole), the hole was widened to equal the bulb's widest diameter, and then pinched together so that the pontil could be attached. At other times the cylinder was cut with shears while still hot; there is evidence that this was the method used in Roman times (Harden, 1959). Cylinder-made glass can be

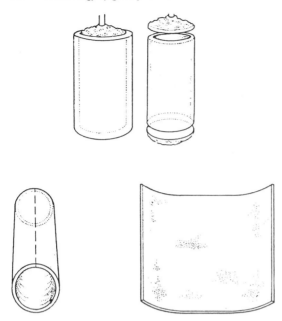

Figure 3.26 The technique of making cylinder glass. From Lee *et al.* (1982).

identified by the shape of the air-bubbles (*seed*) which it contains because they become elongated in straight parallel lines consistent with the elongated shape of the glass bulb. The edges of a sheet may also identify it as being made by the cylinder process since the top and bottom of the cylinder (the long sides of the resultant sheet) were rounded in the flame and hence become slightly thickened to produce a 'thumb' edge (Harden, 1961). The longitudinal split made in the cylinder (the edges of which are the short sides of the sheet) may show shear marks, or may be quite sharp. Much Roman cylinder glass is of the one matt/one glossy sided type because the cylinder was opened, and then pressed down by the croppie onto the sanded floor of the kiln. Green (1959) considered that the earliest type, which had a very flat and matt lower surface, and an undulating upper surface, was opened in a too-hot kiln. Later the glassmakers' increased skill resulted in the lower edge not being roughened, and eventually panes were produced which remained glossy on both sides. In 1973 Harden (1973) examined Romano-British glass excavated at Shakenoke Farm near Oxford and concluded that equal quantities of matt/glossy sided and double glossy sided window glass were used concurrently during the the third and fourth centuries. Harden (1961) describes some large panes of Roman glass, one measuring 395 mm × 260 mm, and another, an almost complete pane of cylinder glass measuring

535 mm × 305 mm. Two pieces, excavated in 1972 at Hartfield, Sussex, were 255 mm × 235 mm and 275 mm by more than 215 mm, and they varied in thickness from 2 to 5 mm (Harden, 1974). Other large pieces from Italy, also listed, were 330 mm × 270 mm and 267 mm × 267 mm (Harden, 1961).

It seems likely that northern Gaul and the Rhineland exported glass to Britain during the first seven centuries of the millenium, but there was certainly some local production at least from the late seventh century. In AD 675 Benedict Biscop imported workmen from Gaul to help in constructing the monastery at Monkwearmouth in Sunderland, 'in the Roman manner', and glaziers to glaze the windows of the church, porticus and refectory. That these glaziers melted glass on the site has been confirmed by Cramp's excavations; and the glass all seems to have been made by the cylinder process. The glass-making technique seems not to have become firmly established, for in AD 758 another appeal was made by Cuthbert for glassmakers to be sent to Britain. Glass with similar characteristics to that found at Monkwearmouth was excavated by Hunter (1977) at Escomb near Durham, Repton near Derby, Brixworth near Northampton and Hamwith (the Saxon settlement in Southampton). The fragments of Saxon glass were all quite small, the largest being only about 65 mm long.

In the fourteenth century there was a noticeable improvement in the quality of cylinder glass which probably first took place in Bohemia. The knowledge of its production was taken to Lorraine by four

Figure 3.27 The uneven surface of the cylinder glass, used for framing the picture on the left, has distorted the reflection of the rectangular leading of the window, compared with the smaller amount of distortion in the drawn sheet glass used for the smaller picture. P. Gibson.

known glass-making families and thus cylinder glass became known as *Lorraine glass* (Fr. *verre façon de Lorraine* or *verre en table*). Also in the fourteenth century, the Venetians used the cylinder process to make glass for mirrors *in lieu* of the wasteful crown glass method. In the eighteenth century a device was introduced to help maintain the shape of the cylinder during working. This was a wet wooden mould 'shaped like half a cannon'; and an improved surface finish was achieved by opening the cylinder out and flattening it out on a sheet of clean glass. The hand cylinder technique continued in use until the nineteenth century when it was replaced by machine drawn cylinder glass (Lubbers process). The distortions produced by cylinder glass can be seen in *Figure 3.27*.

Crown glass

The first examples of crown glass date from the fourth century AD, both in the East (from Jerash, Samaria, *Figure 3.28*) (Harden, 1959, 1961) and in the West (from Chichester, Sussex) (Charlesworth, 1977). These early crowns were quite small, being some 150–200 mm in diameter, and (at least in the East) they were mounted in pairs in plaster frames. It was not until a much later date that larger crowns were cut into panes (quarries). The flat panes of glass (*crowns*) were produced by blowing a gather of glass into a globular shape, transferring it from the blowing iron to the pontil, cutting it open and then after reheating in the glory hole, the pontil would be spun rapidly so that by centrifugal force the glass assumed the shape of a flat disc up to 1.20 m in

diameter (*Figure 3.29*). The glass was then annealed, either used whole or cut into rectangular- or diamond-shaped panes (*Figure 3.30*).

Pieces of crown glass can be identified by the curved lines in which the seed lie (with the pontil at the centre) and by the curved ripples in the surface (*Figure 3.31*). The complete crown has a much thicker centre, called a *boss*, *bullion* or *bull's eye* with the rough circular mark in the centre where it was broken from the pontil when cold; the pieces cut from near the boss are thicker than those cut from near the edge.

Harden (1971) drew attention to the sixth century crown glass window panes, 'found at the church of San Vitale in Ravenna in such a position that they almost certainly came from the windows of the apse'. They are mostly monochrome panes, 170 to 260 mm in diameter, although one fragmentary piece bears an outline drawing of Christ nimbed and enthroned and this may be a distant precursor of painted glass windows. Bovini (1964) and Harden (1971) suggest that these small crowns form a link between the fourth-century ones made in the East and the *Normandy mode* crowns of the fourteenth century. In Britain, however, cylinder blown glass continued to be used in the tenth century, as shown by a sample from Thetford, Essex (Harden, 1961).

The surfaces of crown glass were always bright and shiny because they had been heated in a glory hole and had not touched a sanded surface such as that which impaired the lower surface of cylinder glass. Thus a brighter and more transparent window glass could be made by the crown process than was

Figure 3.28 Early crown glass window panes: (a) from Jerash, Jordan; D 160 mm; sixth or seventh century; (b) part of a plaster window frame with rims of crown glass panes adhering, also from Jerash; modern crown pane from Hebron; D 168 mm. Ashmolean Museum, Oxford.

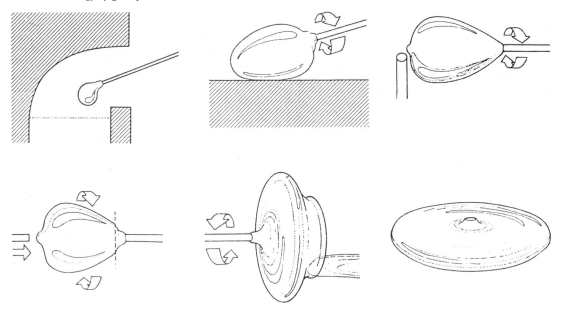

Figure 3.29 The technique of making crown glass. From Lee *et al.* (1982).

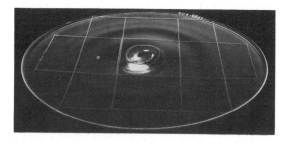

Figure 3.30 Crown glass. Glass marked for cutting into panes, model of sixteenth/eighteenth century method. Science Museum, London; Crown copyright.

Figure 3.31 Curved distortions produced by crown glass window panes. P. Gibson.

possible by the cylinder process (at least in antiquity), and the relative competition between the two processes depended on the fashion at the time. Thus a demand for large windows could be met only by the cylinder process whereas leaded light windows could be made better with crown glass.

The crown glass process was later termed the *Normandy method*, its invention having been uncertainly attributed to Philippe de Caqueray of Normandy who established a glassworks in Normandy in 1330 where crowns of 500–600 mm diameters were produced; despite the fact that crown glass had been in use for many centuries (Lafond, 1969).

In the sixteenth century Dutch crowns had an even better reputation than those from Normandy and the discs became larger so that, by 1700, the diameter was 800–850 mm. In 1724 an *Arrêt du Conseil d'Etat* obliged even the Normands to make discs which were 38 pouces (about 1010 mm) in diameter (Chambon, 1963) but this was evidently quite difficult to do because few were made that size, being generally only 30 to 36 pouces (800–960 mm) in diameter. The manufacture of large crowns was more complicated than shown in *Figure 3.29*; Chambon (1963, Plate II) illustrates sixteen different operations.

Chance Brothers continued to make crown glass at least until 1832. Chance (1919) commented that 'Crown glass excels in brilliance and transparency, but yields in other respects to plate and sheet. . . (the centre lump) and the circular form of the tables, prevent the cutting of large rectangular panes from them, and there is much waste... And, as the tables have a slight convexity the panes, unless flattened, show a distinct curvature and distortion of vision' (see *Figure 3.31*). 'Owing to... the British public (being) habituated to the small bright panes, it survived there for many years longer than on the Continent.'

Norman slabs

One simple technique for making window glass has not yet been mentioned. This involves blowing a square-sided glass bottle into a mould, much like a square Roman bottle, and then cutting it into the four side panels and the base panel (*Figure 3.32*). It is not known when this technique was first invented but it is used today if small areas of glass are required in a special colour, in quantities which would not justify the blowing of cylinders.

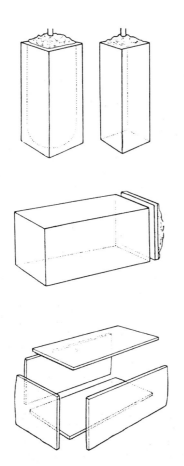

Figure 3.32 The technique of making Norman slab. From Lee *et al.* (1982).

It is not possible to make large areas of glass in this manner, and the largest square Roman bottles would have provided panels which were only some 200 mm × 100 mm, but the remarkably small pieces of glass found at Jarrow and Monkwearmouth could easily have been made from bottle panels.

The technique is now called *Norman slabs* but there is no suggestion that it was used by the Normans, nor that it originated in Normandy (Harden, 1961). When whole panels survive they can be recognized by their thin edges, because it is not easy to blow glass into the corners of a square mould and maintain the same thickness as in the rest of the bottle. The edges may also show some curvature if the cut does not run exactly down the edge of the bottle; but pieces cut from the panel may not be recognizable as such. Nevertheless, the bubbles will not be elongated in parallel rows as is often the case with cylinder glass, and Cramp's (1975) observations that some of the Jarrow glass had rounded bubbles could support a suggestion that the Norman slab technique might have been used.

Modern Norman slab has been used in the restoration of glass windows, for example the twentieth-century Rose Window in St Columba's Church of Scotland, London. (Modern Norman slab is only made in large quantities to special order.)

Painted window glass

A number of decorative techniques was used to embellish glass windows especially those in ecclesiastical buildings. During manufacture the glass could be coloured, or clear glass could be *flashed* with a thin coating of coloured glass on one side. The panes themselves could be painted, enamelled, stained, etched or engraved.

Throughout the Middle Ages decorative windows were composed of pieces of white and coloured glass, cut to fit the basic design (*cartoon*), and held together in a frame-work of leads. (A description of the modern technique which has changed little since medieval times is given in Chapter 7.) With the exception of black enamel painting and silver-yellow stain, the colour in medieval window glass came from the glass itself, the pot-metal having been coloured so that the colour ran through the entire thickness of the pane and was as permanent as the glass itself. Certain colours, however, particularly ruby, were so dense in tone that they would not transmit light sufficiently. In the twelfth and thirteenth centuries, therefore, the translucent red colour was produced by making multilayered glasses. It is not known exactly how such glasses came to be made but there are so many very thin layers, perhaps as many as fifty, which bend back on each other in the manner of hairpins, that it seems likely that they were not made by a process of repeated gathering alternatively from colourless and red glass pots. One suggestion regarding the method of manufacture of multilayered glasses was that red glass was stirred into a pot of colourless glass, and the gather for the cylinder was made before proper mixing of the glass had taken place. However, more recently (Cable, 1979) it has been realized that the conditions necessary for producing the ruby colour exist in a suitably non-homogeneous manner when the colour is prepared in a very dilute form, and thus the layering may at first have been an accidental consequence which was later deliberately exploited. Apparently it is much easier to produce a homogeneous red colour when enough copper has been incorporated to produce a red glass which would be too dense to use in the thickness of 5 mm required for a window.

There are, in addition, some twelfth century glasses which are multilayered in about half their thickness, the other half being of greenish glass. It is possible that the greenish part is a copper-containing glass which failed to strike during the essential reheating process, or it may be an early attempt at producing a flashed glass. The multilayered part is, however, so thick that glasses of this type should not, strictly speaking, be described as flashed glass. The detailed structure of multilayered glasses and the distribution of copper within them has been extensively studied by Spitzer-Aronson (1974, 1975a–c, 1976, 1977a,b).

The difficulty of producing transparent red glass was finally overcome in the fourteenth century by the production of flashed glass. The manufacturing process is relatively simple: a first small gather (called the 'post') was taken from the pot containing the glass batch which, although colourless in appearance, had been so formulated as to strike a red colour during an essential reheating process. A second, much heavier gather of colourless glass was then taken over the top of the first. The glass was blown to form a cylinder which was then cut, opened out and flattened. (Crown glass could also be flashed.) Finally the flashed glass pane was subjected to a controlled reheating process to strike the colour (*Plate 2*). The original necessity of flashing dense colours was frequently turned to advantage by the medieval glazier. By abrading the thin layer of coloured flashing, both white and colour could be obtained on one sheet of glass. For example, if a figure had a ruby tunic trimmed with white cuffs, the glazier abraded the area of the cuff from a piece of flashed ruby instead of having to cut and lead on extra pieces of white glass. In heraldry, with intricate charges on coloured grounds, this technique was particularly useful, especially as all the gold charges could also be obtained by painting the white abraded areas with yellow stain.

Glass painting

The craft of glass painting is relatively straightforward, and with one or two exceptions the methods have changed little since the eleventh century. Since that time two colouring agents have been used to decorate windows in association with clear and coloured glass panes. The first of these was the opaque black or dark brown enamel which was used for painting all the main outlines or trace lines, the washed tones and the shading on the glass; the second colouring agent was a silver-yellow stain. The enamel was originally made from a highly fusible green lead glass mixed with copper or iron oxide, a binding medium such as gum arabic (sugar, treacle or vegetable oil) and a flux. The use of copper and iron oxides varied at different periods, which explains the changes in colour from a full black to a somewhat reddish-brown. The ingredients were mixed together cold, as opposed to being mixed under heat, as were the later translucent enamels. The binding medium had the effect of enabling the enamel to flow and to adhere to the glass, and also hardened the paint, thus making it more resistant to accidental damage before firing. The addition of a flux was necessary to lower the softening point of the enamel below that of the substrate glass. After the painting was completed, the pieces of glass were fired, the flux of lead glass melting and fusing the enamel onto the substrate (Reyntiens, 1977; Lee *et al.*, 1982). The effect of coloured jewels in a painted glass window, for example, on the hem of a robe, can easily be produced by employing spots of different enamel colours; but at earlier periods four other processes were used (Newton, 1981b).

Theophilus (trans. Dodwell, 1961, Hawthorne and Smith, 1963), described a technique in which the jewels were cut from a piece of coloured glass, and fixed to the substrate glass with a thick ring of (black) enamel paint which was then fired. If the jewel subsequently fell off, the thick ring of paint remained to show where it had been. A Romanesque example of this type of jewel survives on the Jesse Tree window (1225–1230) at Regensburg Cathedral, West Germany; and fifteenth century examples are known from the St Cuthbert window in York Minster, and St Michael's Church, Spurriergate, York. A second technique for producing jewels is somewhat similar to that described above, and is known to art historians as 'annealing'. In this method, the two glasses (i.e. the jewel and the substrate glass) were sealed together by applying a layer of ground green glass (perhaps a lead glass) between them before refiring. The powdered glass melts and acts as a solder. Examples of such jewels do not seem to be known, despite the suggestion that they exist in York Minster (O'Connor and Haselock, 1977). The third technique was to insert circular jewels into the substrate glass. Holes were drilled, somewhat larger than the jewels to be inserted, and the jewels were then leaded into the holes. There are examples of this technique in St John's Church, Stamford, in Brown's Hospital, Stamford, in Canterbury Cathedral, and elsewhere. The fourth technique, occasionally confused with the third approach, was to lead-in small pieces of coloured glass using ordinary glazing techniques, as can be seen in York Minster, for example the northern-most window of the east wall of the North Transept.

During the sixteenth century a type of translucent enamel was developed. The enamels were made by mixing a flux of highly fusible lead glass with various metallic oxide colourants. With this type of enamel the oxide was dissolved in the flux by strong heat producing the required colour. The enamel was therefore merely a highly fusible coloured glass ground to a fine powder, which, mixed with a suitable medium, could be applied to the window pane as a paint. On being fired onto the pane of clear glass it regained the transparency it had partially lost through being powdered, and became a thin coat of transparent coloured glass upon the surface to which it had been applied.

Applying the trace line

In the initial stages of painting, the glass is laid over the drawing, the line work then being traced in glass paint on the surface of the glass. Using a sable-haired 'rigger' or tracing brush the painter gathers sufficient paint to produce a firm black line. Too little paint on the brush will produce a streaky or washy line, too much gives a blob which is difficult to control. Lee (1977) drew attention to the particular characteristics of painting on glass; the artist must have a full brush and paint the entire trace line in one continuous, confident sweep. Too much treacle or gum will cause the line to fry in the firing process, which in effect

produces a rough surface containing a mass of pinholes of light and a lack of adherence to the glass. Alternatively, a piece of glass may be coated overall with an opaque layer of paint, the design, be it lettering or diaper, then being scratched out of the black background by means of a sharp stick, needle or dart. Lettering on most twelfth- and thirteenth-century glass was carried out in this way.

Before application of any half-tone, the glass is fired, although in the days of virtual mass production of painted glass many techniques were evolved to economize on firing. To apply a wash of half-tone over an unfired line will cause the line to dissolve or at the very least to blur. A common method of overcoming this is to use acetic acid *in lieu* of water as the carrier for the paint which forms the linework. After 24 hours drying, a hard line is produced which remains undisturbed by subsequent overpainting.

Applying the matting

Whether line work is fired or not, on completion of the tracing the pieces of glass are laid flat in their relative positions on a large sheet of plate glass framed in timber, known simply as a *plate*, and spots of molten beeswax are dropped at the corner of each piece to hold it firmly in place (or beeswax is painted between the pieces). The plate is then lifted on to an easel where it can be seen against the light. To prevent the distraction of white light shining through the interstices between the pieces of glass, black lines are painted on the back of the plate to simulate the effect of lead (*Figure 3.33a–d*).

Plasticine may be used instead of wax for holding the glass on the plate. In very cold weather the wax can lose its adhesion, but the great advantage of Plasticine is that any individual piece of glass can be removed from the plate for repainting or restaining, and be immediately refixed by pressing it on the

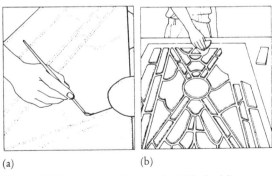
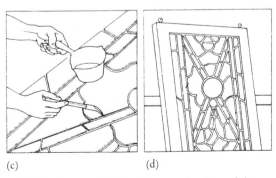

(a)   (b)   (c)   (d)

Figure 3.33 Preparing the glass panel. (a) The lead-lines, traced from the reverse of the cutting pattern on to plate, are painted to the same width as the flanges of the final leads. (b) The plate is turned over, and the pieces of glass are cleaned and placed in position, inside surface upwards.

(c) Molten beeswax is dripped between the pieces of glass. As the wax cools, it solidifies and attaches the pieces firmly to the plate. (d) The assembly is hoisted on to an easel, so that the effect against the light can be judged. From Lee *et al.* (1982).

Plasticine (which is still in place), whereas beeswax would need to be remelted. The Plasticine can be reused many times provided it is not allowed to become dry through too much contact with plaster scum adhering to recently fired glass.

In medieval times, in the absence of plate glass, painting had to be carried out with the glass in a horizontal position, or at best by holding pieces in the hand. The painting process, following the tracing, may be by the *direct* or indirect method, the former being frequently known as *smear shading*, in which a soft brush or mop is filled with paint which is applied directly to the areas of shadow. To avoid the paint running, and to brush the paint into areas where a greater density of tone is required, a long-haired brush of badger hair some three inches wide is used lightly to stroke the paint in alternate directions until an even layer or matt is obtained. In the twelfth and thirteenth centuries when the pattern of colour and the line work were the prime design factors, shading was carried out entirely in this manner and it was used to accentuate shadows such as those under the eyebrows, chin and in folds of the drapery. At times, as also in subsequent periods, simple tones were applied to the exterior side of the glass to accentuate tones still further.

By the fifteenth century much painting was done by the *indirect* method in which paint was applied evenly to the whole surface of each piece of glass, thus obscuring all light. This matt of paint was either left in a smooth state or lightly stippled with the tip of the badger brush before it was dry, to give a coarser texture. Therefore, even in the darkest tones, pinpoints of light are able to penetrate the glass. Once dry, the paint is carefully brushed away from the glass to form the highlights (this action can create a lead hazard, since the paint contained lead), while graduation of shadow is achieved by a combination of stippling, stroking and cross-hatching. Hog hair brushes, as supplied for oil painting, are normally used today, the bristles being cut down as desired. Paint with a generous portion of gum added is *hard* and requires short stiff bristles to remove it, while *soft paint* can be removed with the light touch of a softer brush (*Figure 3.34*). Everyday tools of the glass painter include needles, quills, darts and fingers which when rubbed lightly over the paint bring out the natural textures and irregularities of the glass to good effect. Paint textures have been subject to much experiment and development in recent years and its application is no longer bound by the disciplines which applied in previous generations of glass painting.

Whichever method of painting is used, the pieces of glass must be removed from the plate in order to be fired in the kiln, a process which causes a lightening of the density of the paint and thus usually demands that the whole process of painting be

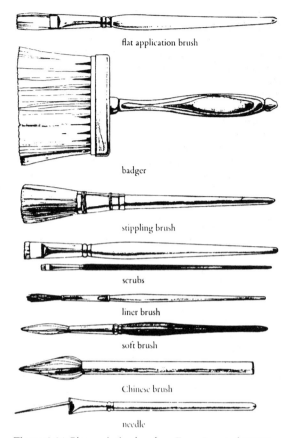

Figure 3.34 Glass-painting brushes. From Lee *et al.* (1982).

repeated to restore the original depth of paint. There have been many attempts to avoid this doubling of the work, from the medieval custom of applying tones to the back of the glass before firing, to complex Victorian techniques where the first matt of paint, after being worked, was overlaid by a second layer in which the paint was mixed not with water but with oil of spike (lavender oil). Thus alternate layers of oil-based and water-based paint could be laid on each other. Figures painted in this manner have a satin-smooth appearance which, once identified, is easily recognized. Today, such techniques are virtually obsolete, as are also many of the highly ingenious devices evolved to save time during the years of intensive competition in the nineteenth century; they are interesting to study but have little relevance to conservation problems, except for the practice of back-painting, carried out by the trade to avoid a second firing if the original painting seemed as though it might not be quite dark enough to produce the desired effect.

The use of paint is not to obliterate most of the light falling on the glass, but to enhance and enrich colour and to add texture and pattern. Skill in handling the brush is evident in the best glass of every age, and a flowing line produced by a fine brush stroke has a beauty of its own. Much exquisite line work, particularly on English glass of the fifteenth century, is so far away from the eye that it is difficult to see without binoculars, and hence is not appreciated. Incidentally, fine painting seems to be associated with care over the other aspects of the work, because a recent German study has concluded that the windows which have most resisted corrosion by the atmosphere are those on which the painting was the most skilful (Fitz *et al.*, 1984).

Firing the enamel

It is an anomaly that some of the earliest surviving window glass has perfectly preserved paint while, from the fifteenth century onwards, an irregular but steady decline in condition of the paint persisted until some of the worst is found in the first half of the nineteenth century. Although some of this is attributable to addition of borax to the paint, some is certainly due to inconsistency of firing, as testified by variations within the bounds of a single window. The firing was carried out in a muffle kiln (Fr. *petit feu*) at temperatures which did not cause the substrate to melt. While the temperature for fusing pigment into glass is between 600 and 620°C, much depends on the time that the glass is held at a given temperature. In the case of medieval firing, the temperature was gradually built up in the clay furnace, and the fire extinguished, or withdrawn, when the temperature was judged to be correct. The heat was thus retained by the clay walls and the resultant slow cooling gave a good period of annealing. The more customary method today is to use kilns in which several trays of glass are loaded into a warming chamber which brings the temperature gradually to approximately 350°C. One at a time, the trays are fed into a hotter chamber at some 620°C for approximately 10 or 15 min, at which point the paint fuses with the glass. When fired, it is returned to the warming chamber, or inserted for a time into an annealing chamber. Alternatively, a pottery type of kiln can be used, in which case several trays are inserted, the temperature being built up gradually to the desired point, the heat is then cut off, and the kiln allowed to cool slowly, usually overnight. Such glass is well annealed and the only drawback is a variation in temperature between the top and bottom of the kiln giving a slightly higher firing at the top. As some (soft) glasses start to soften at a lower temperature, these can be put on the bottom trays and the harder glasses at the top, thus counteracting the imbalance. Firing above the correct temperature will result in high gloss, burning away of the paint with subsequent need to repaint, and rounding of the edges of the glass. Underfiring will result in a rough surface, which will hold dirt, moisture and waterproofing cement, and will have a lower durability so that it is more likely to wear off in time.

As the glass at firing temperature is becoming tacky, it will adhere to the tray unless separated in some way. Traditionally, shallow trays of iron or steel are used, filled with a perfectly level layer of plaster of Paris into which the glass pieces are carefully laid. Alternatively, glass can be laid on sillimanite trays previously coated with a separator of whiting. Whichever method is used, the paint can be expected to lighten in the firing, and the higher the temperature the greater this effect will be. However, the temptation to underfire, to retain the tonal depth of the paint, must be rejected, this 'economy' (as well as the use of borax paint, discussed above) may have been responsible for some of the paint loss which disfigures much nineteenth-century glass and bedevils conservation.

Staining

The application of silver nitrate (or silver sulphide) to the back of the glass to produce a yellow colour when fired was introduced early in the fourteenth century and revolutionized painted glass design by providing the ability to incorporate more than one colour on a single piece of glass, for instance, golden hair or crown on the head of the Virgin. While at first confined to the yellow-on-white combination, it was extended within the next century to produce a green tint by applying the stain to blue. It was also realized that, by abrading away the coloured surface of flashed glass and staining the resulting white areas yellow, the interpretation of heraldry into glass became much simpler and enabled such charges as golden lions on a ruby ground to be carried out without complex leading. The process is still used extensively today although the flash of coloured glass is removed by the use of dilute hydrofluoric acid, a highly dangerous liquid which should not be used without professional advice and considerable precautions.

The effect of silver stain depends on the amount of stain applied and the number of applications, the temperature at which it is fired and the chemical composition of the glass. Of these the latter is the most restrictive and certain *hard* glasses such as modern soda glass are said resolutely to refuse to accept stain regardless of the other two factors, but makers of stains can guarantee success if they know the type of glass to be used. *Soft* glass will however produce a deep golden orange with a mere wash of stain and between the two are a host of different reactions which only experience can forecast. The finest staining glass is known as *kelp*, its alkali content being said to be derived from seaweed, although it probably contained additional oxides such as tin oxide. It was extensively used from the sixteenth to the twentieth centuries and could produce a stain which was almost a true red and, moreover, maintained a clarity equal to that of pot metal yellow or red glass; this kind of staining was used by Peckitt in York Minster (Brighton *et al.*, 1986; Newton *et al.*, 1989, 1990).

In modern glass painting and restoration work stain is obtained from silver chloride supplied as a powder in varying grades and suspended in a kaolin base. After grinding, it is mixed with water to a creamy consistency which is applied to the back of the glass where yellow is required. It is then brushed over lightly with a badger brush reserved solely for this purpose, to form an even layer; alternatively this 'badgering' technique is used to brush concentrations of stain into areas where a much deeper colour is desired. Firing is at a considerably lower temperature than that used for the paint, some 540–560°C being sufficient, and the temptation to fire both paint and stain at the same time should be resisted. Submitting to this temptation is the reason for the dense yellow-green metallic 'scum' found on the outside of much late nineteenth- and early twentieth-century glass, and is the result of overfiring the stain.

The medieval practice of preparing silver stain appears to have been to cut some silver metal into small pieces or to use it in thin sheets, and to burn it with sulphur in a crucible, which converted it into a sulphide. This was finely ground and mixed with an earthy vehicle such as pipe-clay which made the stain easier to apply. Yellow stain in medieval glass was usually painted on clear glass and was chiefly used to heighten details of figure or canopy work or grisaille ground patterns, but in later times it was painted on coloured glass in order to change the tint of the piece, or part of a piece. For instance, using blue glass and yellow stain, a green hill and the sky could be painted on one piece of glass. In figure painting, both hair and face could be painted on one piece of glass; and decorated borders to white robes were frequently stained yellow. Broadly speaking, fourteenth-century stain was golden in colour and some deepening came about until the red stain of the sixteenth century, and its associated lighter tints, brought about the high point of the stainer's art. It is no coincidence that this peak occurred at the time when availability and variety of pot metal colours was severely limited.

The first use of enamels had been on a small-scale for transferring complex heraldic charges on to glass, and for colouring the fruit and flowers of garlands, but subsequently it was used for the flesh tones of figures and ultimately it superseded most of the pot metal colours. However, at no time were the colours as transparent as those of silver-stained glass, or of coloured pot metal, nor did the enamels have a durability comparable to that of the coloured glass.

Modern glass paint is in the form of a dark powder comprising finely ground soft glass mixed with iron oxide. The latter gives it opacity while the former, when fired, forms an integral part of the surface of the glass.

Enamel colours are now rarely used in windows, although they are widely used for the decoration of tableware. When they are used for windows they require prolonged grinding before the water is added and then, like glass paint, they require mixing to the consistency of smooth, thick cream. They are applied with a sable rigger (a thin long-haired brush) and then swept evenly in alternate directions to produce a smooth, even layer. They are always applied to the inner surface of the glass and fired in the same manner as paint (although generally at a lower temperature), before any silver-staining is done but after the trace lines are applied. After firing, the enamel should have a dull shine although much Regency glass (for example, that in the Music Room at the Royal Pavilion, Brighton) has a matt finish which is little changed by time. In the second half of the nineteenth century the reliability of the enamels improved considerably and some virtuoso work was achieved by painters, particularly those of the Munich School.

Summary of nineteenth- and twentieth-century industrial glass-making

The nineteenth century was a period of great change (yet the rate of change was certainly eclipsed in the twentieth century), and only a few highlights can be recorded here. There are many publications on the subject of glass-making during these centuries, notably Dillon (1907), Hartsthorne (1897, reprint 1968), Barrington Haynes (1957), Powell (1923) and Thorpe (1929, 1935). Great improvements in melting efficiency became possible when the Siemens regenerative furnace was introduced in 1861 (Douglas and Frank, 1972), to be followed by the 'tank' furnace. There were 126 bottle-houses in Britain in 1833, but the number rose to its peak of 240 in 1874 (Meigh, 1972), thereafter declining as the tank furnaces became larger and more efficient. The first semi-automatic machinery for making jars (Arbogast) was introduced in America in 1882, and the first for making narrow-neck bottles was invented by Ashley in Britain in 1886 (Society of Glass Technology, 1951).

The construction of the Crystal Palace in 1851 was an extraordinary achievement for which nearly one million square feet of glass was required (Hollister, 1974). The first safety glass was invented in 1874

(Powell, 1875) and shown at the Motor Show of 1906 (Society of Glass Technology, 1951). The first electric lamp bulbs were made at Lemington (near Newcastle-upon-Tyne) for Sir Joseph Swan in 1860; to be followed by the Corning Glassworks in America who supplied Edison in 1881 (Douglas and Frank, 1972). Optical glasses were first studied seriously by Dollond in 1758, but the materials were of poor quality (Douglas and Frank, 1972). In 1798, Guinand discovered how to make glass homogeneous by stirring it during melting (the only effective means of obtaining homogeneity), but commercially satisfactory optical glass was not made until 1848, when Bontemps (1868) joined Chance Brothers in Birmingham. The firms' leadership in this field was not maintained, however, but passed to Germany when, in 1846, Carl Zeiss opened a workshop. He was later (1875) joined in the venture by a physicist, Abbe. Between them Zeiss and Abbe made a spectacular range of glasses during the 1880s. These had new optical properties which enabled great advances to be made in the design of lenses for cameras, microscopes and telescopes.

Even more remarkable advances were made in glass-making in the twentieth century. The first half of the century could be said to have been dominated by engineering-type developments whereas the post-1950 period has seen quite extraordinary changes in the compositions of glasses, especially in the fields of non-silicate glasses. The excellent *History of Glass-making* by Douglas and Frank (1972) deals particularly with the twentieth century.

In making flat glass, the first Lubbers cylinder machine was introduced in 1903, but the Fourcault machine for sheet glass was developed in 1913 and the mammoth machine for the continuous grinding and polishing of plate glass (it was about 400 m long) was invented by Pilkington Brothers in the 1930s (Douglas and Frank, 1972). This process was replacing all previous methods of making plate glass when, in 1959, the announcement of the float glass process, in which a perfectly smooth and brilliant fire-polished glass is floated from a bath of molten tin, secured for Pilkington Brothers the world lead in flat glass technology (Pilkington, 1971, 1976). The automatic machinery for making bottles and jars also developed greatly during the first half of the century. The Owens suction machine was first successful in 1903 and it rapidly dominated the glass container-making industry all over the world, partly because of its technical efficiency but partly because a cartel was set up regarding its use which excluded all others (Meigh, 1972). Gradually, however, between the wars, various types of *gob-fed* machine overtook the cumbersome Owens machines and displaced them (Meigh, 1972). The numbers of bottles and jars increased from 2.9 thousand million per annum in the United States in 1918 (and 0.5 in the United Kingdom) to 15.3 (3.1 in the United Kingdom) in 1950 to 44.3 (6.9 United Kingdom) in 1977; the 1977 total for the United Kingdom and the United States represented 14.3 million metric tons of glass.

The understanding of the chemical constitution of glasses, and the relationship between it and the physical properties has increased greatly in recent years: Pyrex glass was developed in 1915 (Society of Glass Technology, 1951); the delicate colouring produced by rare-earth oxides was discovered in 1927; top-of-the-stove ware was introduced in 1935; and *glass fibre* was first produced on a commercial basis in 1938. Remarkable improvements were made in optical glasses in which entirely new types of glass were made: the fluoroborates, phosphates, germanates, and all-fluoride glasses possess different combinations of refractive index and dispersion which had never been anticipated in the previous century (Douglas and Frank, 1972). Special ultra-pure high-transmission glasses have been developed for lasers and optical communication systems and a range of glass-ceramics has been produced which have a zero coefficient of expansion. The photosensitive silver-containing glasses, which were first introduced in 1950, have been developed for special purposes, such as sun-glasses which adjust their absorption coefficient according to the light intensity, and polychromatic glasses which can develop any colour in the spectrum according to the extent to which they are exposed to ultraviolet light and a subsequent heat treatment (Beall, 1978).

Enamels

True enamel is a vitreous coating fused to a metallic background, that is glass fused to gold, silver, copper or bronze or iron (Maryon, 1971). There is however a type of enamel ware where the base is glass, for example, Arab mosque lamps — glass vessels ornamented by patterns of a more fusible glass painted on and fused in a furnace, that is enamelled glass rather than true enamel.

Enamel is generally a comparatively soft glass; a compound of flint or sand, red lead and soda or potash, melted together to produce an almost clear glass with a bluish or greenish tinge known as flux or frit. It is made in different degrees of 'hardness', that is the more lead and potash it contains the more brilliant but softer it is. Soft enamels require less heat to fire them and are therefore more convenient to use, but they are not so durable. Because of this the hardest colours in a pattern should be applied first, and the softer ones kept for a later firing, at a lower temperature. A plaque may be fired a dozen or more times, depending upon the number of colours to be applied. To find out which colours require the most heat a little of each colour is arranged in a row on a clean plaque and put in the furnace. The order in which they melt as the plaque gets hot is carefully noted (or a 'gradient furnace' can be used). The clear flux or frit is the base from which coloured enamels are made — the colouring matter being metallic oxides. The inclusion of 2–3 per cent of an oxide to the molten flux is generally sufficient to produce a useful colour. The enamel, after being thoroughly stirred, is poured out onto a slab in cakes about 110 mm in diameter. For use it is broken up, ground in a mortar to a fine powder, thoroughly washed and spread on to a piece of metal. The work is placed in a furnace until the powdered enamel fuses and adheres to its metal base.

From early dynastic times (pre-2500 BC) in Sumeria and Egypt, craftsmen inlaid pieces of coloured stones in jewellery. The stones were set in cells formed from the upturned edges of the thin gold plates from which the jewel was made, or by the use of little cloisons — strips of sheet gold set on edge, and soldered to the backplate. The coloured stones seem always to be held in position by cement or the grip of the inturned edges of the cloisons. It does not seem to have occurred to the craftsmen that they might fill the cells with pieces of coloured glass and fuse them in position. It was not until about the thirteenth century BC that this discovery was made in Cyprus, and not until nearly 1000 years later that the use of enamel became fairly generally known.

As mentioned above, a true enamel is a vitreous substance fused to a metallic surface, it can be applied in a number of different ways, and thus be classified according to the structure of its metallic base and its relationship to it.

Cloisonné is the most primitive form of enamel. Each mass of powdered glass is placed in a separate compartment formed from strips of metal wire to which, and to the background if it has one, the enamel is fused by heating in a kiln (*Figure 3.35*).

On very thin metalwork the contraction of the enamel on cooling might be sufficient to cause the metal to warp, and to counteract this the reverse face of the object might also be enamelled, a process known as *counter-enamelling* or enamel backing.

Enamels could also be made without a backing, being held to the metal only at the edges. To do this type of work, *plique à jour*, the areas for the enamel were fretted and given a temporary backing of sheet mica or some similar material to which the enamel would not adhere. Once the enamel had been fixed by fusing, the backing was removed leaving a translucent enamel like a painted glass window, the lead lines of a window being replaced by the metal cloisons of the enamel. This type of work is fragile and not suitable for objects which are subject to rough handling.

In the second group the enamel is fused into cells, which are sunk with chasing tools, carved, stamped or cast into the metal base-plate. These enamels are known as *champlevé* (*Figure 3.36*). Beautiful examples of this work are known from Celtic and Anglo-Saxon Britain. Another centre from which great quantities of champlevé work came was the town of Limoges in central France where in the twelfth, thirteenth and later centuries thousands of

Figure 3.35 Detail of a cloisonne panel, in which the strips of metal defining the panels can be clearly seen. S. Dove.

Figure 3.36 Armlet with a central oval medallion decorated on one side in *champlevé* enamel with central flower and leaf sprays. L of jewelled ornament 93 mm. Eighteenth century AD. India. British Museum, London.

reliquaries, crosses, altar vessels and other works were sent to all parts of Europe. In most of the early work from Limoges each decorated space was filled with broken opaque colours, often blues and greens touched with creamy white. The ground is generally gilded, and the head of a figure is often made by *repoussé* work in fairly high relief from a separate piece of copper or bronze, gilt prior to the enamelling, and rivetted on. *Champlevé* enamels are rarely backed, but to ensure a good grip for the colours it was customary to leave the floor of the recesses rough.

A subdivision of this group is known as *bassetaille enamel*. In it, over a design in low relief, chased or engraved on a base-plate, a level-topped layer of enamel is fused. The modelled surface below is clearly visible and graduations in the height of the relief are reflected by variations in the depth of the colour in the enamels above it. One example of *bassetaille* enamel of outstanding merit is the Royal Gold Cup in the British Museum which, in its original condition, was one of the most sumptuous works of the goldsmith's art. It was made *circa* AD 1530, probably in Burgundy or Paris, and is decorated with scenes from the life of St Agnes. The whole of each figure, tree, scroll or piece of furniture represented is covered from side to side with enamels which extend as a level surface right across them. Each is thus shown in silhouette against the gold background. The enamels being translucent, all the detailed modelling of the faces, hands, the folds of the robes, and other objects are seen through the enamel, the deeper depressions appear richer in tone than their shallower neighbours. In this cup the different coloured enamels are not separated by metal cloisons; the different colours meet side by side (*Figure 3.37*).

In the production of *bassetaille* powdered enamels of different colours are laid down adjacent to each other and care must be taken that the boundary line between them does not become irregular. The most convenient way to prevent this is to add a little gum tragacanth to each batch of enamel, and to allow the first colours to dry before the next are laid alongside them. They will not then spread much on to their neighbours' territory.

In many medieval works executed by the *bassetaille* process, the enamel extends right across the panel, with no metal surface left exposed. In panels with figures even the flesh is covered with a layer of clear enamel which allows the modelling of the face and hands to show through.

Sometimes a panel produced primarily by chasing is sharpened by a certain amount of work done by engraving tools. Considerable traces of such work may be seen on the Royal Gold Cup, although the major portion of the relief was executed by chasing. It should be remembered that in *bassetaille*, because so much of its effect depends upon the modelling of the metal beneath it, the enamel itself must have a level and well-polished surface. All depressions in the enamel should be filled up and refired, and the surface ground level and polished. The metal background may be diapered and gilt.

Another subdivision of this group is formed by *encrusted enamels*. These are employed to decorate irregular surfaces, for example, the shoulders of finger rings, to ornament the mounts of cups or a figure in high relief formed by *repoussé* work and chasing. From the sixteenth century, goldsmiths have delighted in enriching their work with touches of coloured enamel.

One of the principal problems arising from the use of enamel in this way concerns the manner in which the object may be supported during firing. An elaborately constructed finger ring may have a number of soldered joints which must not be exposed to the heat of the furnace. Such joints must be protected by painting them with rouge or whiting before the enamel is fired. Likewise a pendant jewel built up from a number of separately formed members held together by solder may have enamelled decorations on surfaces inclined at many angles. The solder may be covered with plaster of Paris.

Enamels of the third group come under the general classification of *painted enamels*, although as with colours on a canvas, the material is sometimes applied with a palette knife. They have a plain foundation of a sheet of metal, generally slightly domed and as a rule the whole surface on both sides of the metal is covered with enamel (*Figure 3.38*).

Cloisonné and *champlevé* enamels had been made for many centuries before it was discovered that the metal outlines between the different colours were not essential to the permanence of the work, valuable

Figure 3.37 The Royal Gold Cup, detail of the *bassetaille* enamel, showing a scene from the story of St Agnes. H 236 mm. 1380-1. France. British Museum, London.

Figure 3.38 Detail of a Chinese painted enamel. Courtesy of Jacqueline McConnell.

though they were from the decorative point of view. Towards the end of the fifteenth century the craftsmen at Limoges in France began, in the enamelled pictures which they fitted into the work, to leave out the metal divisions altogether. The way in which they worked has been followed, with little variation, by enamellers ever since.

Wetted finely ground enamel was painted over a design scratched in a metal baseplate and each colour allowed to dry before the next was applied. All colours applied at one time had to be of the same hardness and thus were able to be fired together. The softer enamels had to be applied for subsequent firings. If a copper plaque were given a coat of flux before enamelling, the enamels would show much more brilliantly. Copper, with a coating of clear flux, appeared a bright golden or a pink coppery colour according to the composition of the flux used and to the temperature at which it was fired. Silver seen through clear flux resembled white satin; whereas the colour of gold hardly changed at all. Any drawing on the metal, whether scratched in with a steel point, or drawn with a lead pencil, showed clearly through the flux. The surface of the flux could, however, be roughened, then washed over with hydrofluoric acid to avoid milkiness in the colour, and the design transferred to it. The coloured enamels were then applied where required. The colours could be modified, shading if necessary, gold or silver foil added to make a more brilliant patch, parts of the design outlined, or touches of gold added.

Gold leaf or foil may be employed in various ways in enamel work: it may be used to cover part of the background, say, of a figure, as in some primitive Italian and other paintings. For such work a foundation of translucent yellow enamel was provided over which the gold may be laid. Before laying the gold, the surface was moistened and kept moist by breathing gently on the film of gold while it was applied. A temperature just high enough to fuse the

enamel was sufficient to fix the gold. If any defects appeared, the gold was brushed with a glass brush, another layer of gold placed over the first to cover the gaps, and refired. It was not necessary to put enamel over the gold.

Stars, *fleurs-de-lys*, rosettes or other devices could be stamped out in low relief in gold foil and laid on a foundation layer of enamel to form a diaper or other patterns. They were overlaid with a coating of translucent enamel, and the work fired. Translucent colours looked brighter when fired on a background of gold or silver than on copper or on the black or dark blue background employed by many medieval enamellers (Maryon, 1971).

Part 2 Furnaces and melting techniques

Pre-Roman glass-making

The first records of glass technology were found in Mesopotamia in the form of cuneiform tablets. The earliest text giving a recipe for glaze was found near Tell 'Umar (Seleucia) on the River Tigris. The tablet dates from the seventeenth century BC but presumes a well-established glass-making tradition. Amongst the many thousands of Assyrian cuneiform tablets excavated from the site of the library of Ashurbanipal (668–627 BC), a small number of broken tablets record information concerning the manufacture of coloured glass and glazes. These tablets were evidently copies of originals produced in the last centuries of the second millenium BC, showing that the essential principles of glass-making were understood in about 1700 BC. An important philological aspect of the cuneiform glass-making texts is that the seventh century copies contain the earlier Sumerian words and their later Akkadian translations; moreover, the former are related to words used in Ur III texts and the latter are related to words used by glassmakers on the Phoenician coast in Roman times. Thus the glass-making tradition seems to have been an extremely conservative one, the same term (and no doubt the same tried and tested formulae) being handed down for more than two millenia.

Comparatively few glass artefacts have been excavated in Mesopotamia, but this may well be due to the moisture content of the soil, and to the rise of the water-table in historic times, causing the destruction of much of the early glass which was inherently unstable in its chemical composition (and therefore 'water soluble') (Oppenheim, 1973).

The cuneiform texts with specific references to

glass have been translated at various times, notably by Thompson (1925) and Oppenheim *et al.* (1970). There are many difficulties about using the translations. First, the philologist needs the help of a technologist, and the glass technologist who advised Thompson was not aware of the composition of the plant ash used, and the profound effect it had on the composition of the glass. In a similar manner, Thompson referred to the use of human embryos in a glass-making connection, and this was quoted by Morey (1954, p. 6f) in such a way that other writers (for example, Gordon, 1975, p. 21) have assumed that 'human embryos, born before their time' were an actual constituent of Babylon glass. In Oppenheim's translation, however, the relevant word is *Kubu* (images) and they were set up as part of the ritual for building a furnace. Again, Thompson referred to the use of arsenic and antimony but Turner (1956a) pointed out that the arsenic is only a trace element in Babylonian or Assyrian glasses, and Brill (1970d), using Oppenheim's translation, concluded that there was no reason to believe that the Assyrians knew antimony, and that there was no proof that the clay tablets described ingredients which contain antimony. Similarly, it seems that Douglas and Frank (1972) were misled into believing that lime was specified as an ingredient of Assyrian glass. Secondly, Oppenheim pointed out that the texts were not technical instructions, despite their technical content, and that, 'They have to be considered, strange as it may seem, as literary creations within a complex literary tradition. . . (they were) subject to certain stylistic requirements; their wording and their literary forms were historically conditioned. . .'. Brill's recent investigations have shown that a coherent and useful interpretation is possible.

In Mesopotamia there were many words used for glass, glass intermediates, and glass-like substances (Oppenheim *et al.*, 1970). Three of these words investigated by Brill (1970c,d) were *zukû*; *immanakku* and *ahussu*, the ashes of the *naga* plant. As a result of the investigations it seems that the *naga* plant may well have been *Salsola kali* or a similar plant; that *ahussu* probably contained about 55 per cent Na_2CO_3, 8 per cent KCl, 8 per cent MgO, 4 per cent NaCl, 5 per cent $CaSO_4$ etc. (Brill, 1970c,d); that *immanakku* was ground quartzite pebbles from a river bed, probably containing 95 per cent SiO_2, 2.5 per cent Al_2O_3 etc.; and that *zukû* was an intermediate reaction product (a frit) obtained by heating the silica with plant ash at 'a heat which has the colour of the red of red grapes', that is, probably less than 850°C. After fritting was complete, the cold *zukû* was ground up and the colouring agents were added (see below); the mixture was then heated to 'a heat which is yellow' (probably about 1100°C) to produce the final glass.

Chief among the materials added at this second stage of glass melting were *urudu.hi.a* (slow copper) and *Sipparuarhu* (fast bronze). These materials have not yet been identified with any certainty but it is possible that *slow copper* was copper oxide (CuO) and that *fast bronze* was a (metallic) alloy of copper, tin and lead which would melt, form a layer below the glass, and confer a blue colour to it (Brill, 1970d).

Having established the probable nature of the ingredients of *zukû*, Brill (1970c) then heated them together for 10 hours at 920°C to obtain a frit which was cooled, pulverized and then heated for 16 hours at 1100°C to produce a well-melted homogeneous piece of pale bluish glass of very good quality. The resultant *zukû* glass contains 56.0 per cent SiO_2, 23.8 per cent Na_2O, 6.6 per cent CaO, 5.6 per cent MgO, 3.8 per cent K_2O, 2.2 per cent Al_2O_3 and various minor ingredients. Thus the glass was not unlike typical Mesopotamian glasses; and from its composition it would be expected to have a reasonable durability. Thus this trial was successful, but it must not be forgotten that there were earlier investigations which 'have followed the recipes and proved their validity (and thus the 'correctness of the translation') (Moore, 1944, 1948; Forbes, 1957) despite the fact that it is now known that those translations contained many errors.

Mesopotamian furnaces and melting procedures

The religio-magic preparations associated with the setting up of a furnace, described in translation by Oppenheim, reflect the limits of the Mesopotamian glassmakers' technical knowledge which was essentially empirical in nature. In view of such limited knowledge it would seem to be a mistake to believe that the glassmakers could make the slight deliberate additions of antimony or manganese which, it has been suggested, were required to decolorize the glass (Sayre, 1963). Such additions were probably accidental as impurities in the raw materials forming the glass batch (Newton, 1985b).

According to Thorpe (1938) it would seem as though there were three types of furnace described in the cuneiform texts. The glasshouse (the *bît kûri* or house of the furnaces) contained the *kûri ša abni* or furnace for the pot metal in which the glass batch was fritted. The *kûri ša siknat ênâtpel-ša* (furnace with a floor of eyes) was the founding furnace ('that where the workmen work'). A much later usage of the term 'eye' in this context is that of the Italian *occhio* or *lumella*, that is, the circular opening between the siege (middle or founding) storey of the three-storey furnace and the upper (annealing or tower) storey. The Mesopotamian furnace could probably achieve temperatures as high as 1000–1100°C. Finally the *kûri ša takkanni* (furnace of the arch) appears to have been a door (*bab kûri*) through which the finished articles were introduced. This corresponds to a lehr or annealing furnace.

The fire was made of Euphrates poplar logs and the duration of the found was, in certain cases, as long as 7 days during which it must have been difficult to maintain the high temperatures. However, there is no doubt that by the seventh century BC the glass furnace had developed considerably in Mesopotamia and that the battle for sustained heat had gone a long way. Although no proper description of the furnaces (specifically for glass) has yet appeared in any archaeological report, it is possible that the reverbatory furnace which would be a precondition for glass-blowing, may have originated in Mesopotamia (Forbes, 1957).

The texts make no distinction between the batch of unmelted materials and the frit, both *billu* and *abnu* (stone) being used to describe the mix. The glass pot or crucible (*taptu zakatu*) had to be clean and it was stilted (*nimedu*, stilt or support) so that it did not touch the furnace ceiling. Several types of mould appear to have been used (open and closed), the moulding processes possibly having been derived from bronze-working. The cuneiform texts also mention the hook or rake (*mutirru*, Syr. *mattara*, Lat. *rutabulum*), and a ladle (*su'lu*) for moving molten glass from large glass pots to smaller ones and for skimming the batch.

When producing the frit, the instructions were: 'When the glass assumes the colour of ripe (red) grapes, you keep it boiling (for a time)' [this is probably the evolution of carbon dioxide from the reaction between the sodium carbonate and the silica] '[Then] you pour it [the glass] on a kiln-fired brick... You put [it] into a kiln which has four fire openings and place it on a stand... You keep a good and smokeless fire burning [so that the flames come out of the openings] ... Not until the glass glows red do you close the door of the kiln and stir it once "towards you" [with a rake] until it becomes yellow [hot]. After it has become yellow [hot], you observe some drops [forming at the tip of the rake]. If the glass is homogeneous [without bubbles] you pour it [inside the kiln] into a new *dabtu*-pan...' (Oppenheim *et al.*, 1970). The constructional differences between the fritting furnace and the fusion furnace have been noted by Oppenheim *et al.* (1970). There are a number of technologically important observations to be made here: the use of a red heat (less than 850°C) for the first fritting and a yellow heat (1100°C) for the second firing, and also the use of a smokeless fire, so that reducing conditions were avoided. By experiment, these conditions can now be seen to be important for the success of the operation. Nevertheless, the variability in composition of the plant ash must have been a frequent source of failures; Brill's analyses of plant ash from bushes, bracken and seaweed (Brill, 1970d) show that the soda content could vary widely, from 14.2 to 42.5 per cent.

Mesopotamian transparent glasses

Analytical results for Mesopotamian transparent glasses are quoted by Turner (1954b) and by Brill (1970d). The glasses would be expected to be reasonably durable. Two samples quoted by Turner (1954b) showed weathering, equivalent to losses of substance of 0.18 mm per century (sample A) and 0.04 mm per century (sample B). However, all the non-red glasses from this era have much the same composition, and Turner (1954b) commented that it is a remarkable fact that glass from Nimrud, from Eighteenth Dynasty Egypt, and from Knossos in Crete have so much resemblance in composition despite the fact that they are spread over 700 years and a distance of 1700 km. This could be explained by the possibility that all the glass-making was carried out in Syria, and only glass-melting was performed in the other centres.

The possibility that the raw glass (cullet) was all made in Upper Syria, and that it was based on a traditional recipe, with manufacturing processes which were well-guarded secrets, may be a more feasible explanation of this uniformity in composition than the alternative hypothesis that different glassmakers tried to use all kinds of local raw materials, even though they might be following a traditional recipe. Again it has to be remembered that any glass having a distinctly different composition is likely to have had such a poor durability that it would have entirely perished during the intervening millennia.

Brill (1970d) also investigated the quantity of glass which might have been produced in an Assyrian furnace, and concluded that each complete operation might have produced about 3500 cm³ of *zukû* frit and 800 cm³ (about 2 kg) of the copper-containing red glass.

Mesopotamian opal glasses

There are two kinds of Mesopotamian glass which deserve special mention: the green and yellow opals which contain yellow lead antimonate ($Pb_2Sb_2O_7$) and the copper-containing sealing wax red glasses which had to be used in a special manner (in this early period they do not contain much lead, in contrast to the high-lead sealing wax red of the seventh century BC). The use of lead antimonate is particularly interesting because it seems that the Assyrians had no direct knowledge of antimony as such.

Brill (1970d) points out that the yellow $Pb_2Sb_2O_7$ was added to the blue transparent glass (*tersītu*) to form a greenish-coloured artificial lapis lazuli, and hence the lead antimonate is likely to be either *anzahhu* or *būsu*. It also seems that *anzahhu* was prepared by craftsmen other than the glassmakers and that it had been known over a period of fifteen centuries; it could therefore have been an article of trade and its use by the Assyrians need not imply a knowledge of the properties of antimony, either as an opacifier or as a decolorizer. The sealing wax red glasses are of even greater interest; their colour is due to the presence of colloidal cuprous oxide (Cu_2O) and its manufacture has its difficulties even today. It must be prepared under suitable *reducing* conditions, or the Cu_2O will be oxidized to give a transparent blue glass (Brill, 1970d), and the cuneiform texts specify that closed containers and long firing times should be used, and that the glass should be cooled within the kiln. Cable (1979) melted some of these glasses and points out that the cast slabs all have a black tarnished metallic lustre. If this surface film of metallic oxide is ground away, and the pieces reheated, the surface blackens again within 2 min at 550°C, at which temperature the glass is still quite solid, and thus such a glass could not have been hot-worked, as was the case with the other glasses. Brill (1970d) also remarks on the dark surface, and Turner (1954b) makes two comments which are of particular interest, stating that in 1952 Mallowan discovered traces of furnaces at Nimrud, and nearby cakes of sealing wax red glass had fragments of charcoal on them (which would have helped to maintain the necessary reducing conditions until the glass was cold). Secondly, that from such cakes of opaque glass Egyptian craftsmen cut thin plates which were ground and polished to use as inlays on funerary furniture. It thus seems likely that the sealing wax glasses were used only for lapidary purposes and not for hot-working.

One remarkable and rather important piece of glass is a dark blue ingot found at Eridu (about 175 km WNW of Basra) and dated (Brill, 1970d) to about 2000 BC. It seems to have been an ingot for remelting and this aspect of glass-working occurs repeatedly in the history of glass, that is that the secret of making good quality glass was by no means known to all glassworkers and many of them, perhaps even most, had to obtain their best glass from other sources (Forbes, 1957, 1961; Brill, 1970c) and this still applied almost 4000 years later (Moore, 1944, 1948; Charleston, 1963, 1967; Oppenheim *et al.*, 1970; Newton, 1971b,c).

Egyptian furnaces and melting procedures

There seems to have been no production of glass from its raw materials in ancient Egypt before the fifteenth century BC, and it is generally considered that the Egyptians had failed to learn the secret of glass-making (and this is borne out by the finds at Tell-el-Amarna), despite the fact that they were skilled makers of glass articles (i.e. glassmelters) from glass cullet which had been imported from Upper Syria.

Oppenheim (1973) gives evidence for stating that 'The craftsmen who produced the magnificent glass objects for the Egyptian Court depended for their basic raw materials, or for the essential ingredient thereof, on imports from Asia.' It is evident, from the urgency of the appeals from the Kings of Egypt for *ehlipakku* and *mekku* (both words for raw glass, the former of Hurrian origin and the latter West Semitic) that the Egyptians had failed to learn the secret of the Assyrian fritting technique. There do not seem to be any good *technological* reasons why the Egyptians should fail to discover the art of glass-making (fritting) when they knew how to melt cullet (Turner, 1954a). Various hypotheses have been put forward to explain this apparent failure, and the most reasonable one seems to be that they were unaware of the raw materials. Glass was a highly prized commodity at the time, some coloured glasses apparently being valued above gem stones; and it would no doubt have seemed inconceivable that glass could be made from such commonplace and unpromising materials as sand and burnt vegetation. Communication between Egypt and Mesopotamia would have been infrequent, and of course the Mesopotamians would have guarded their glass production recipes, thus maintaining the *status quo*.

In the light of the foregoing it is perhaps surprising that the earliest glass-working complex known to us is that at Tell-el-Amarna in Egypt (excavated by Flinders Petrie in 1891), dated *circa* 1370 BC, that is over 100 years after the discovery of glass-working in Egypt. Tell-el-Amarna, the new capital of Akhenaton, required a large amount of decorative work, and suitable factories sprang up to supply the materials. Glazes and glass were the two principal manufactures in which a variety and brilliancy was achieved, which was never reached in earlier or later times in Egypt. So far as the use of glazes is possible, this period shows the highest degree of success, and the greatest variety of application.

Fortunately the sites of three or four glass factories, and two large glazing works were discovered (*Figure 3.39*); and although the actual workrooms had almost vanished, the waste heaps were full of fragments which showed the types of product and their method of manufacture. Frits made in Egypt from the Twelfth Dynasty onward were composed of silica, lime, alkaline carbonates and copper carbonate varying from 3 per cent in delicate greenish blue, up to 20 per cent in rich purple blue. The green tints were always produced when iron was present, which

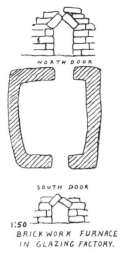

NORTH DOOR

SOUTH DOOR

1:50

BRICK WORK FURNACE
IN GLAZING FACTORY.

Figure 3.39 Brickwork furnace in glazing factory. *Circa* 1370 BC. Tell-el-Amarna, Egypt. From Flinders Petrie (1894).

was usually the case when sand was the source of silica. One of the first requisites therefore was to obtain raw materials free from iron. The question of how this was achieved was answered with the discovery of a piece of a pan of frit which had been broken in the furnace and rejected before the frit had completely combined. This contained chips of white silica throughout the mass which were clearly the result of using crushed quartz pebbles as a source of silica instead of sand. The lime, alkali and copper had already combined, and the silica was in the course of solution and combination with the alkali and lime. The carbonic acid in the alkali and lime had been partly liberated by the dissolved silica, and had raised the mass into a spongy paste. With longer continued heating the silica in other samples had entirely disappeared, and formed a mixture of more or less fusible silicates. These made a pasty mass when kept at the temperature required to produce the fine colours; and this mass was then moulded into pats,

and heated in the furnace until the desired tint was reached; a soft, crystalline, porous friable cake of colour was produced.

Among the furnace waste were many white quartz pebbles. These had been laid as a cobble floor in the furnace, and served as a clean space on which to roast the pats of colour, scraps of which were found adhering to the cobbles. The floor also served to lay objects on for glazing — superfluous glaze had spread over the pebbles in a thin green wash. Doubtless this use of the pebbles was two-fold; they provided a clean furnace floor, and they became disintegrated by the repeated heating so that they were the more readily crushed for mixture in the frits afterwards.

The half-pan of uncombined frit shows the size and form of the fritting pans: about 254 mm across and 76 mm deep (*Figure 3.40*). Among the furnace waste were also many pieces of cylindrical jars, about 178 mm across and 127 mm high. These jars almost always bore runs of glaze on the outside from the base to the rim; the glaze being of various colours, blue, green, white, black etc. evidently leaked from the pans, hence the jars must have stood mouth downward in the furnace to support the fritting pans and glass crucibles above the fire. Of the furnaces used for glass-melting there was no certain example; but a furnace discovered near the great mould and glaze factory contained a great quantity of charcoal, but no trace of pans, jars or glass. The furnace (see *Figure 3.39*) was an irregular square varying from 1092 mm to 1448 mm at the sides. It was originally about 889 mm high, but the roof had been destroyed. The northern door was 737 mm high and 381 mm wide, to admit the north wind and to serve for tending the furnace on the windward side. The south or exit door was 406 mm high and 330 mm wide to allow gases to escape. Probably the glazing furnaces were based on the same principle; and perhaps even the same furnace would be used for varying purposes.

Of the stages of production of the glass there is ample evidence. The crucibles in which it was melted were deeper than the fritting pans, being about 58

62 *Fritting Pans,*
supported in the
furnace on jars
inverted, down
which the glaze runs.
N.M.F.P.

PLATE XLII   Scale 1:6

Figure 3.40 Fritting pans supported in the furnace on inverted jars down which the glass has run. *Circa* 1370 BC.

Tell-el-Amarna, Egypt. From Flinders-Petrie (1894).

and 76 mm in depth and diameter. Their form was known from the shape of unused pieces of glass showing the section of the vessels in which they cooled. Many such pieces of glass were found retaining the rough surface, and even chips of crucible adhering to them, while the ancient top surface shows the smooth melted face, with edges drawn up by capillary action. The upper part of the glass was often frothy and useless. The presence of the froth (of carbonic acid expelled by the melting reaction) suggests that the glass was fused in the pans. The manner in which the crucible had been chipped off the lump of solidified glass in every case shows that the glass was left to cool in the crucible so as to allow the scum gradually to rise and the sediment to sink. If the glass had been poured out these features would not have been found, on the contrary masses of cast glass should have been in evidence. While the glass was being made samples were taken out by means of pincers, to test the colour and quality, and many of these samplings were found showing the impression of the round-tipped pincers.

Modern tests on the crucibles showed that they were not made of clay in the true sense but seemed to consist of mud and sand mixed together. Heating trials showed that the crucibles would have begun to vitrify at a temperature of 1100°C and that they fused to a black mass after 1 hour at 1150°C. It seems likely that the highest temperature for prolonged heating would be lower than 1100°C, and since no really high temperature could have been attained therefore, the glass was probably worked in a pasty state, mainly by drawing out threads and constantly marvering them on a flat slab. Indeed this supposition seems to be borne out by the excavated evidence (Petrie, 1894).

Roman furnaces

Although several glass-working sites are known from Roman times (Haberey, 1963), none offers any structure which can be interpreted to give an idea of what a glass-making furnace looked like. The only evidence on this point appears to be the representation on a clay lamp attributable to the first century AD of what may reasonably be taken to be two glassworkers at a furnace (*Figure 3.41*). The details are far from clear, but it seems that the furnace was in two tiers at least, presumably a stoke-hole below (represented by the filling hole in the lamp itself) and a chamber above. Unlike Roman pottery kilns, which were sunk in the ground, the Roman glass furnaces were built at ground level or even raised above it. The glass furnaces mentioned by Pliny were probably small beehive-shaped hearth furnaces with one or two compartments left empty to take the blown glass objects for cooling.

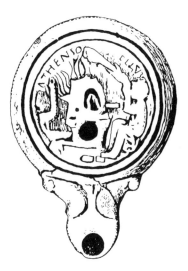

Figure 3.41 A scene on the discus of a lamp from Asseria, Dalmatia, showing two glassworkers at a glass furnace. First century AD. From Strong and Brown (1976).

The most revealing structural remains of identified Roman glass furnaces were those at Eigelstein near Cologne in the Rhineland (*Figure 3.42*), but unfortunately the excavation plans of the site were destroyed during the Second World War (Doppelfeld, 1965). However, it is known that the remains represented the lower courses of both circular and rectangular structures, somewhat separate from each other, but without any clear indication of their relationship. The excavations showed that the furnaces had been rebuilt, each rebuilding being carried out over the previous furnaces which had been razed to their foundations. Between the layers fragments of completely colourless glass were found. Remains of a Roman furnace site at Trier excavated in 1922 helped to identify the type of crucible used.

The evidence available for furnace structures in Gaul is no less sketchy. Again, little archaeological evidence has been found to indicate what British glass furnaces of the Roman period looked like, or how they operated. Excavations of putative Roman glass sites found at Wilderspool and Middlewich in Cheshire, Mancetter in Warwickshire, Wroxeter in Shropshire and Caistor St Edmund in Norfolk have revealed little structural detail. Five workshops were found at Wilderspool at the beginning of this century and the furnaces were described as small oval ovens with outlets and flues. More recent work (1964–5 and 1969–71) on a Roman glass site at Mancetter revealed a small, almost circular (880 mm × 770 mm) furnace, a description of which is given by Hurst-Vose (1980). It is presumed that the glass made in this furnace was melted from cullet.

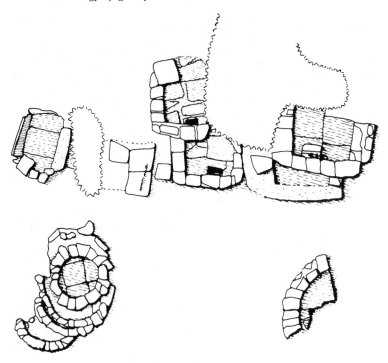

Figure 3.42 Plan of the glass furnaces excavated at Eigelstein near Cologne, showing successive rebuildings of the furnaces on the same site. Overall measurements c.4.9 m. From Strong and Brown (1976).

Brill (1963) carried out melting experiments using a gradient furnace, which is illustrated in the account, to conclude that a typical Roman glass would require a final melting temperature (i.e. when ground up and remixed after the fritting operation) of 1100°C, and that it would have to be at a temperature of at least 1080°C for satisfactory glass-blowing operations to be performed. (Reconstructions of Roman pottery kilns have achieved temperatures of 1100°C; Bryant, 1973.)

One of the most extraordinary glass artefacts ever discovered (Brill and Wosinski, 1965) is a massive slab measuring 3.40 m by 1.94 m, about 0.45 m thick, and weighing about 8.8 tonnes. It probably dates from the fourth century AD (Brill, 1967a; Engle, 1973a) and is in a cave at Beth She'arim, south-east of Haifa, Israel. It was evidently melted *in situ* since there are unmelted batch materials at the base. It was melted in what has been described as a *tank furnace*, although true tank furnaces, as they are now understood, are quite different and were not introduced until the middle of the nineteenth century. This ancient type of tank furnace has also been found elsewhere (Perrot, 1971). The reason for producing such an enormous slab is not known and it

has been suggested that it might have been intended as a massive source of cullet, because excavations at the extensive glass-working site at Jelemiye, a few kilometres to the south-west of Beth She'arim, have never revealed any evidence of glass-making.

Paradoxically, it is only with the Dark Ages that evidence becomes available to indicate what early glass-making furnaces were like. Under the unifying influence of the Roman Empire, the practices of glass-making in different parts of the Empire appear to have been much the same. With the collapse of the Empire, however, a cleavage developed between the practice in the north of Europe and in the south, and Newton (1985b) has suggested that the 'northern' furnaces (which had a good draught) were adapted for using beechwood ash to prepare coloured glasses whereas the southern ones (south of the Alps) were in areas deficient of beech forests.

The southern type of furnace

The first reasonably full description of a southern type of furnace is given in a Syrian manuscript in the

British Museum which apparently cannot be dated earlier than the ninth century AD:

> The furnace of the glassmakers should have six compartments, of which three are disposed in storeys one above the other ... the lower compartment should be deep, in it is the fire; that of the middle storey has an opening in front of the central chambers, these last should be equal, disposed on the sides and not in the centre(?), so that the fire from below may rise towards the central region where the glass is and heat and melt the materials. The upper compartment, which is vaulted, is arranged so as uniformly to roof over the middle storey; it is used to cool the vessels after their manufacture.

Not all the details of this account are clear, but the essentials are that the furnace was in three storeys, with a fire chamber at the bottom, a central chamber into which the heat rises to melt the glass, and a vaulted upper compartment in which the glass may cool. This arrangement may be seen in the earliest certain representation of a glass furnace (*Figure 3.43*)

Figure 3.43 The earliest illustration of a glass furnace, three tiers high. The craftsman on the three-legged stool is blowing a vessel, another vessel can be seen undergoing the annealing process in the top compartment of the kiln. Illustrated miniature from the manuscript of Hrabanus Maurus, *De Universo*, datable to 1023 AD. Abbey of Monte Cassino (Codex 132).

in a manuscript dating from 1023 in the library at Monte Cassino, a text of the work *De Universo* by Hrabanus Maurus (Archbishop of Mainz *c.*776–856). Again the details are not unequivocally clear, but the artist appears to have attempted to represent a cylindical structure, although the roof is shown as a simple tent shape. The manuscript may have been a copy of an earlier one dating from the fourth or fifth century AD. The main body of the furnace has been

interpreted as being rectangular in plan, but this seems unlikely from the elliptical rendering of the glory holes which would certainly not in any case be made at the corners of a rectangular structure; furthermore, the tent-like upper storey is carefully depicted as being adapted to the curved structure below. The essential features, however, are these: a single stoke-hole at the bottom, a middle chamber with multiple glory holes giving access to glass pots, and an upper compartment in which a glass may be seen annealing. If indeed the furnace represented was cylindrical or round in section, the illumination provides a most useful link, for on the one hand the later furnaces of this type were almost always circular, while on the other hand the remains of a seventh/eighth century glass-making complex on the Venetian island of Torcello, excavated in 1961/2 (Tabaczynska, 1968; Gasparetto, 1965, 1967), include the foundations of a circular structure which may have been a fritting furnace. However, it seems far more likely to have been the main (founding) furnace since it stood in the middle of the complex, as would be natural for the working furnace to which all surrounding structures are ancillary. A study of the site shows that temperatures of 1270°C had been reached in the melting furnace.

The glass mosaics used for decorating the Basilica of Santa Maria Assunta on *Torcello* started in AD 639 were probably made in the furnaces described above, but the glassworks was so close to the church (only about 35 m to the west of its walls) that it seems likely that it was dismantled when the basilica was completed. The spread of broken pots, glass waste etc. on the site was probably the result of clearance and disturbance at the time of demolition.

On a glass site at *Corinth* in Greece (Weinberg, 1975) (*Agora, South Center site*) however, dating from the eleventh/twelfth century, the foundations of a square furnace were unearthed which, from the absence of any ancillary furnace were reasonably taken by the excavators to have been the lowest storey of a three-tiered arrangement (Weinberg, 1975). The original conclusions have been modified by later finds, notably some limestone blocks covered with glass drippings which seem to suggest that either small rectangular tanks (320 mm × 270 mm) or square containers were used in the glass-making process. Finds of refractory pots with glass adhering, however, found in association with the Agora north-east glass-making complex (if such it is) suggest the more normal method of founding the metal. Fragments of glass found in the Agora South Center have been reinterpreted as pontil wads and suggest that (unless they were cullet, which seems somewhat unlikely) glass was actually worked in the vicinity of this furnace (i.e. that it was not merely a fritting or annealing furnace). The fact that there was so little space surrounding the furnace structure (barely 500 mm on three sides) is the strongest counter-indication.

A furnace excavated at *Monte Lecco* in the Apennines about 30 k from Genoa, and probably dating from the late fourteenth or early fifteenth century clearly revealed a circular structure with a central fire trench running between two roughly segmented solid *sieges* (banks on which the glass pots stood). The fire trench was dug down into an ash pit in the ground at the front, and had an outlet at the bank, presumably for the clearance of ashes. The furnace has been tentatively reconstructed as a three-tiered structure on the basis of a picture, perhaps dating from *circa* 1590, in the Oratorio of St Rocco at Altare. The absence of any structures in the immediate vicinity of the furnace suggests that all the processes were carried out in the one furnace, and that this was therefore likely to have been a three-tiered structure.

As the finds at Torcello suggest, the circular furnace (perhaps in three storeys) was probably from the first type used by the Venetian glassmakers who, from the mid-fifteenth century at the latest, began to dominate the world markets with their superior crystal glass. Two illuminations in manuscripts in the Vatican library portray glassmakers at work (*Figures 3.44* and *3.45*). The cruder of the two (*Figure 3.44*) shows two glassblowers sitting on three-legged stools, while another man attends to the stoke-hole. On the furnace is written unequivocally *fornax vitr* (glass furnace). It is represented clearly as three storeys, the upper two set slightly back, and this

detail is repeated in the second miniature (*Figure 3.45*). Here, however, four out of the six ribs are visible, rising from the broader ledge just below the level of the *bocca*. This ledge no doubt provided space for a marver. The *bocca* is shown as a round-topped arched opening, and the glassblower to the right holds his iron with his right hand in the circular *boccarella* (or little mouth). In front there is a circular aperture through which perhaps the *tiseur* could check the condition of the fire: alternatively, it may indicate in false perspective the central opening of the furnace. From the sixteenth century there survives an eyewitness account of an Italian furnace. In 1508, Peder Månsson, a Swedish priest living in Rome, interested himself closely in the glass industry, then unknown in Scandinavia, and compiled an account of it in *Glaskonst (Art of Glass)* (Månsson, 1520). Here he described the furnace as follows:

The second furnace, in which the glass is to be founded, is more difficult to build. It must be entirely built and walled up with damp clay capable of resisting the fiercest heat, and must be in the middle of a wide, roomy house. You lay the foundation wall round in a circle, with a diameter of 12½ ft [3.8 m]. At the point where the furnace mouth is to be beneath the ground, you lay no wall foundation. This furnace must have three arches, one above the other. The first and lowest arch must occupy the whole interior right up to the walls, and not be higher than 2½ ft [760 mm] from the floor and 1 ft 8 in [508 mm] in diameter. [This must

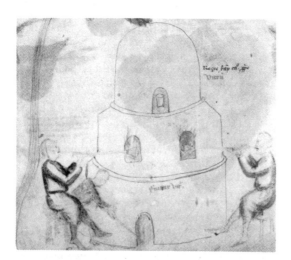

Figure 3.44 Drawing from a late fifteenth century manuscript depicting a three-tiered glass furnace. Vatican Library.

Figure 3.45 Drawing from a late fifteenth century manuscript also depicting a three-tiered glass furnace. Vatican Library.

mean 'in width'. Vault would perhaps give a clearer idea of the construction than arch.] On this arch must be set the pots in which the glass frit is put. Then you arrange the wall outside so that it has six thin ribs, and between each set of ribs you reserve an opening, through which the glass mass is drawn out, worked, inserted and handled. Directly in front of each opening a pot must be set in the furnace with the batch in such a way that the height exactly suits the opening. The second arch is made 4 ft 2 in [1.27 m] high above the first, extending over the whole furnace, except for a round opening, 10–15 in [250–380 mm] in diameter in the middle of the arch. Round the top of the opening there must be a ledge, so that the glasses, when put there to cool, may not fall down into the furnace. The third and top arch extends over the whole furnace, and there must be 3 ft 4 in [1.0 m] between it and the second arch, and three openings 10 in [250 mm] broad, through which the smoke discharges and the glasses are put in to cool. The furnace mouth below in the earth should be 1 ft 8 in [510 mm] broad. You stoke it with dry wood, the length of which corresponds to the inner breadth of the furnace; and for this purpose one digs out the earth in front of the furnace mouth. . . .

This suggests that there may have been a fire trench in the furnace, and this detail together with the mention of digging out the earth in front of the furnace, strongly recalls the furnace at Monte Lecco. A woodcut illustrating a glass furnace of this type appears in *De la Pirotechnia* (Biringuccio, 1540) (*Figure 3.46*). This shows a hive-shaped furnace with

Figure 3.46 Woodcut depicting glassworkers at a furnace, illustrating Vannoccio Biringuccio, *De la Pirotechnia*, Venice, 1540.

six external ribs, the stoke-hole to the front, the *tiseur* carrying an armful of faggots with which to replenish it. The glassblowers sit on either side on three-legged stools. In front of each (seen better on the right-hand side of the woodcut) is a screen to protect the blower from the glare of the glory hole, through which the glass pots are reached. Projecting

from the side of the furnace below is a marble shelf supported on an arch, the rudimentary form of the modern marver, on which the glass drawn from the pot is rolled to smooth it as a preliminary to blowing. Biringuccio describes the furnace as follows:

> Now in order to complete the purification, a round furnace is built of rough bricks from a clay that does not melt or calcine from the fire. Its vault has a diameter of about four *braccia* [550 mm] and a height of six *bracchia* [3.32 m]. It is arranged in this way. First a passage for the fire is made which leads the flames into the middle of the furnace; around the circle at the bottom a shelf ¾ *braccio* wide [100 mm] is made on which are to be placed the pots that hold the glass, and this must be about one *bracchio* [140 mm] above the ground. Around this five or six well-made little arches are built as supports for the vault, and under these are made the little openings which allow one to look inside and to take out the glass for working at will. Then the vault is continued to cover the glass, and only in the middle is a little opening of a *palmo* [280 mm] or less left. Above this vault another vault is made which seals up and covers the whole; this is two *braccia* [280 mm] high above the first so that it completes the reverbatory furnace. This is the cooling chamber for the works when they have been made, for if they did not receive a certain tempering of air in this, all the vessels would break as soon as they were finished when they felt the cold. . . .

By a curious convention, the illustrator of Biringuccio's work, in representing the top storey, or annealing chamber of the furnace, has shown the holes through which the glasses were inserted to anneal as seen from the outside, but has cut away the central panel of the furnace wall to reveal on the inside the hole through which the heat ascends from the founding chamber to the annealing chamber above. This cut is defective in many ways. It does not for example illustrate the arches made above the siege to accommodate the working openings. These arches were structurally necessary to support the vault above them when the glass pots were changed, as was necessary when an old pot cracked or otherwise became defective, and a new, preheated pot had to be substituted quickly with the minimum disturbance to the general working of the furnace. Biringuccio (1540) gave some indication of how this was achieved,

> After six or eight months from the time they were made, when you wish to put them [the glass pots] in the furnace in order to begin work, that place which you left open under the arches is a quarter closed with a wall and only enough space is left to allow one of the said vessels to enter. . . .

The aperture was then closed with clay,

> making two small holes from one large one so that
> the worker can take out the glass with his tube
> from whichever vessel he wishes in order to work
> it. In the other opening he keeps another iron tube
> so that it will be hot. Outside in front of these
> openings there is a support made of a marble shelf
> placed on an arch. Above this shelf and in front of
> the opening for the glass a screen is made to serve
> as a protection for the eyes of the workers and to
> carry an iron support which holds up the tube. . . .

These hooks (*halsinelle*) or supports for the blowing
iron and pontil are not shown in Biringuccio's
woodcut. Probably at a quite early date it was found
convenient to incorporate the working opening in a
slab of fire clay which could be removed and replaced

when the pots were changed. Fragments of such slabs
were found on the early seventeenth-century glass-
making site at Jamestown in Virginia, USA (Harrington, 1952) and have been reported from glass-making
sites in Denmark. The structure of these arched
openings, not shown in Biringuccio's woodcut, is
illustrated in the woodcuts to what is perhaps the
most systematic account of glass-making surviving
from the sixteenth century — the twelfth chapter of
Georgius Agricola's *De Re Metallica* (1556) (*Figures
3.47* and *3.48*).

Figure 3.48 Woodcut illustrating G. Agricola, *De Re
Metallica*, Basel, 1556, depicting a southern glass furnace of
the sixteenth century. The furnace has three sections, the
lower one for the fire, the middle one for the glass pots, and
the upper one for annealing the glass. The glass blowers are
working around the furnace and the vessels are packed in
the large box seen in the bottom right-hand corner. In the
background the sale of the glass is being discussed, and a
pedlar carries away the vessels. In the sixteenth century the
customer either ordered his glass direct from the maker or
bought it from the travelling hawker.

Figure 3.47 Woodcut illustrating G. Agricola, *De Re
Metallica*, Basel, 1556, showing the three-tier 'second glass
furnace', i.e. annealing furnace.

In many particulars Agricola was obviously dependent on Biringuccio as a source of information, but the situation on glass-making which he described was far more complex probably because in Agricola's time, in Saxony and elsewhere in Germany, the indigenous 'Northern' tradition was being penetrated by the Venetian tradition. The detailed woodcut in *De Re Metallica* shows a three-tiered furnace (*Figure 3.47*). In the lower picture the arched openings to the siege story of the furnace can be seen (but with a square *bocca* and no *boccarella*), and in the sectional rendering there is an indication of the vault supporting the siege itself, the central holes allowing the passage of the heat (the upper one square instead of circular), and the arched opening allowing access to the annealing chamber. In his text Agricola refers to 'six arched openings' but the illustration would suggest that there were at least eight. A similar discrepancy appears in his description of the two-storey 'second furnace' which is said to be strengthened on the outside with five ribs whereas 'in the wall of the upper chamber between the ribs there should be eight windows...'. The illustration suggests that there would have been at least eight ribs.

These illustrations were interpreted in a sixteenth-century wall-painting by G. M. Butteri which decorates the *studiolo* of Francesco I de' Medici in the Palazzo Vecchio in Florence (*Figure 3.49*). It shows the Grand Duke's glasshouse, which is known to have been of the Venetian type, and which seems to have begun operating about 1568/9. In the background of the wall-painting can be seen the great glowing furnace, the gaffers seated on their three-legged stools before the glory holes, from the glare of which they are protected by the fire-clay screen described by Biringuccio, whilst to one side and slightly lower down are the *boccarelle* accommodating three or more irons. The master to the left warms-in his glass at the glory hole, resting the iron on the lowest of the *halsinelle*. Above the masters' heads glow the apertures leading to the annealing chamber, through one of which a servitor (to the left of the picture) is placing a finished glass to cool. To the right of the seated gaffer with his back to the onlooker can be seen the stoke-hole, toward which the *tiseur*, apparently stripped to the waist, brings a fresh bundle of faggots. Above the furnace is a framework of beams on which the wood for fuel was set to dry, with a resultant very grave risk of fire.

When the *Crutched Friars glasshouse* in London burned down in 1575 it had 'within it neere fortie thousand billits of wood' (Thorpe, 1961). The furnace in Butteri's painting appears to be a developed form of that shown in Biringuccio's or Agricola's illustrations. The ribs of the furnace delineated as rather thin in Biringuccio and Agricola, here have become of considerable depth, at least at the base, thus providing a much wider working

Figure 3.49 Painting by G.M. Butteri inthe Studiolo of Francesco I de Medici, showing the Grand Duke's glassworks in the Palazzo Vecchio, Florence.

surface for the gaffer. This detail is seen again in seventeenth-century representations of Italian-type furnaces.

One curious feature of the Florence furnace is its asymmetrical form at the right-hand side, where the vault appears to project in an overhang. It seems possible that this may be the beginning of what later became the tunnel lehr. This development may be found in Biringuccio. His own Italian text is not easy to follow, but the French translation by Jacques Vincent offers a somewhat easier interpretation. Vincent (1556) writes, 'this cooling-off is effected by a certain opening made on the left-hand side [Biringuccio says "at the back"], and this channel is shaped like a trumpet; from it all the cooled vessels are skillfully drawn by means of a long iron, one after the other, in three or four goes, until they reach the mouth and are taken outside'. This 'trumpet-shaped opening' is perhaps the beginning of the lehr, and the man standing on the right of Biringuccio's woodcut is no doubt performing the office of moving the glasses along from hotter to cooler positions.

Merrett (1662) in a translation of Neri (1612) *Dell'Arte Vetraria — The Art of Glass* (see Turner, 1962, 1963) wrote:

The Leer (made by Agricola, the third furnace, to anneal and cool the vessels, made as the second was to melt the Metall, and to keep it in fusion) comprehends two parts, the tower and leer. The tower is that part which lies directly above the melting furnace with a partition betwixt them, a foot [300 mm] thick, in the midst whereof, and in the same perpendicular with that of the second furnace, there's a round hole [*Imperat.* and Agricola make it square and small] through which the flame and heat passeth into the tower; this hole is called *Occhio* or *Lumella*, having an Iron ring encircling it called the *Cavalet* or Crown; on the floor or bottom of this tower the vessels fashioned by the M^{rs} [masters] are set to anneal; it hath 2. Boccas or mouths, one opposite to the other, to put the Glasses in as soon as made, taken with a Fork by the Servitors, and set on the floor of the tower, & after some time these Glasses are put into Iron pans Agricola makes them of clay call'd Fraches, which by degrees are drawn by the Sarole man all along the Leer, which is five or six yards [4.5–5.5 m] long, that all the Glasses may cool Gradatim, for when they are drawn to the end of the Leer they become cold. This leer is continued to the tower, and arched all along about four foot [1.2 m] wide and high within. The mouth thereof enters into a room, where the Glasses are taken out and set. This room they call the Sarosel. . . .

This structure may be seen on the frontispiece of the 1669 Latin edition of Neri, published in Amsterdam (*Figure 3.50*), and a similar engraving illustrates the 1752 French edition of the same work (*Figure 3.51*). In these furnaces, however, the glasses appear to have been put directly into the lehr through small doors (N in *Figure 3.51*). The same feature appears in the great French *Encyclopédie* of Diderot and D'Alembert, in the volume of plates dated 1772 (*Figure 3.52*). The same volume also gives a vivid view of the interior of the lehr seen from the Sarosel room, with the fraches moving in two lines down the tunnel (*Figure 3.53*). An improved version of tunnel lehr was invented by George Ensell at Coalbrook, in the British Stourbridge glass-making district, about 1780, but it is not absolutely certain what the improvement was. It may well have been the provision of a separately heated lehr, perhaps one with two tunnels, for large and small objects respectively, such as became standard in British glasshouses in the nineteenth century. (By the mid-nineteenth century the pans were moved along the lehr mechanically and the double lehr had become a quadruple one.)

Figure 3.50 Frontispiece to the 1669 Latin translation of A. Neri's *L'Arte Vetraria.*

Figure 3.51 Plate IV from the French translation of A. Neri's *L'Arte Vetraria* (*Art de la Verrerie*, Paris, 1752) showing the 'Amsterdam' furnace.

Figure 3.52 Plate from Diderot's *Encyclopédie* showing 'Verrerie en Bois, Coupe et Plans d'une petite Verrerie a pivette: et Coupe de la Cave à braise' (pl. vol. X. pl. 3) showing the grille composed of very short bars to span the firing channel.

Figure 3.53 Plate from Diderot's *Encyclopédie* showing 'Verrerie en Bois, l'opération de retirer les Feraces et les transporter au Magasin (pl. vol. X, pl 22).

Figure 3.54 Frontispiece to G.L. Bianconi's *Due Lettere di Fisica*, Venice, 1746. Corning Museum of Glass.

Figure 3.55 Model of a glass furnace, tin-glazed earthenware (*maiolica*). Second half of the eighteenth century. H (max) 170 mm, W 135 mm, L 220 mm. Italy. Science Museum, London; Crown copyright.

It may be opportune at this point to cite two illustrations of Italian furnaces of the mid-eighteenth century. One of them (*Figure 3.54*) is the frontispiece of *Due Lettere di Fisica al Signor Marchese Scipione Maffei* by Gian-Lodovico Bianconi, published in Venice in 1746. Although it is difficult to envisage just how this furnace worked (it seems to have derived some of its features from Kunckel although its basic principles are different, and it seems to have one storey too many), the nature of its long lehr, with central archway, is unmistakable. The second piece of evidence is furnished by a tin-glazed pottery (*maiolica*) model of a furnace in the Science Museum, London (*Figure 3.55*). Here the long tunnel lehr is clearly in evidence, with the glass visible in the tower, apparently heated by the updraft from the founding furnace conveyed through a chimney which does not connect directly with the floor of the lehr. *Figure 3.66* shows the stoke-hole of the main furnace, and to the left that (presumably) of the fritting furnace, with the end of the lehr above it. *Figure 3.55* shows a second stoke-hole of the main furnace, and (presumably) the fritting platform incorporated into the same structure.

The Venetian-style glasshouse had one further subsidiary furnace. This was used for the preliminary roasting (fritting) of the silica and ash. Biringuccio described this process as follows:

> Then put all these things [that is, silica, soda, and manganese for decolorizing] mixed together into the reverbatory furnace made for this purpose, three braccia long, two wide, and one high, and

apply enough of the strong flames of a wood fire by means of the reverberator, so that the composition is melted well and is converted all into one mass.

Månsson confirms this general picture, adding the detail: 'The mixture is often stirred and turned around with an iron hook'. It is probably a fritting furnace of this type that is seen to the right of Butteri's wall-painting (see *Figure 3.49*). No really explicit representation, however, is available until the publication of the *Encyclopédie* (Diderot and D'Alembert, 1772) which contains an engraving showing the furnace in plan and section, and an illustration of the furnace-man at work raking the frit from the mouth of the furnace (*Figure 3.56*). Agricola's illustration of a fritting furnace also shows a round construction, although the text seems to indicate an oblong structure ('Their first furnace

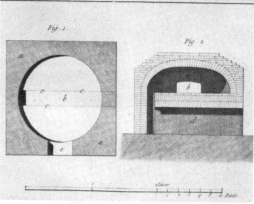

Figure 3.56 Plate from Diderot's *Encyclopédie* showing 'Verrerie en Bois, Plan et coupe de la Calcaisse, et l'Operation de retirer la fritte cuite' (pl. vol. X. pl. 15).

should be arched over and resemble an oven. In its upper compartment, six feet long, four broad, and two high, the frit is cooked...'). The *Encyclopédie* version is square on plan although the internal shape is circular. It has the advantage that it is fired at the side, for the greater convenience of the worker stirring the frit (Charleston, 1978).

The northern type of furnace

There is no evidence to throw light on the northern type of furnace as early as that available for the southern type. The earliest source is *Schedula Diversarum Artium (Treatise on Divers Arts)* by Theophilus Presbyter, in which a book is devoted to glass-making (Hawthorne and Smith, 1963). The date of Theophilus has been much disputed, but the most recent view is that Theophilus was the Benedictine monk Roger of Helmarshausen and that the manuscript was compiled between AD 1110 and 1140 (Dodwell, 1961). If the identification is correct, the author was a practising metalworker who was personally able to carry out most of the techniques he described and who would certainly have described the glass-making process with the insight of a craftsman:

> If you have the intention of making glass, first cut many beechwood logs and dry them out. Then burn them all together in a clean place and carefully collect the ashes, taking care that you do not mix any earth or stones with them. When the ashes have been well mixed for a long time, take them up with the iron shovel and put them in the smaller part of the kiln over the top of the hearth to roast [i.e. to frit]). When they begin to get hot, immediately stir them with the same shovel so they do not melt with the heat of the fire and run together. Continue this throughout a night and a day (Dodwell, 1961; Hawthorne and Smith, 1963).

Theophilus also gives precise instructions for making crucibles out of clay, and for making glass articles, but the important point to note here is that the frit must not be allowed to melt (and, by implication, the small part of the furnace must not be allowed to get too hot) so that the solid-state reactions can continue for a long time (a night and a day) without any molten glass being formed that would trap the released carbon dioxide as bubbles in the melt.

After this build a furnace of stones and clay fifteen feet [4.5 m] long and ten feet [3 m] wide in this way. First, lay down foundations on each long side one foot [300 mm] thick, and in between them make a firm, smooth, flat hearth with stones and clay. Mark off three equal parts and build a cross-wall separating one-third from the other two. Then make a hole in each of the short sides through which fire and wood can be put in, and building the encircling wall up to a height of almost four feet [1.2 m], again make a firm, smooth, flat hearth over the whole area, and let the dividing wall rise a little above it. After this, in the larger section, make four holes through the hearth along one of the long sides, and four along the other. The work pots are to be placed in these. Then make two openings in the center through which the flame can rise. Now, as you build the encircling wall, make two separate windows on each side, a span long and wide, one opposite [each] of the flame openings, through which the work pots and whatever is placed in them can be put in and taken out. In the smaller section also make an opening [for the flame] through the hearth close to the cross-wall, and a window, a span in size, near the short wall, through which whatever is necessary for the work can be put in and taken out.

When you have arranged everything like this, enclose the interior with an outer wall, so that the inside is the shape of an arched vault, rising a little more than half a foot [150 mm], and the top is made into a smooth, flat hearth, with a three-finger-high lip all around it, so that whatever work or instruments are laid on top cannot fall off. This furnace is called the work furnace [*Figure 3.57*].

Figure 3.57 Model of Theophilus' furnace. Science Museum, London; Crown copyright.

(Chapter 2) Now build another furnace ten feet [3 m] long, eight feet [2.5 m] wide, and four feet [1.2 m] high. Then make a hole in one of the faces for putting in and taking out whatever is necessary. Inside, make firm, smooth, flat hearth. This furnace is called the annealing furnace.

(Chapter 3) Now build a third furnace, six feet [1.8 m] long, four feet [1.2 m] wide, and three feet [900 mm] high, with a [fire] hole, a window and a hearth as above. This furnace is called the furnace for spreading out and flattening.

The implements needed for this work are an iron [blow] pipe, two cubits long and as thick as your thumb, two pairs of tongs each hammered out of a single piece of iron, two long-handled iron ladles, and such other wooden and iron tools as you want.

The illustration of the model of Theophilus' furnace made at the Science Museum, London is probably incorrect in showing four working holes per side instead of two. The feature of the holes made in the siege to take pots is unique, and one is tempted to wonder whether Theophilus was not misled by seeing in a furnace the ring of glass left on the siege when a broken pot was removed. The reconstructions (Theobald, 1933) have always been made very trim and square; the furnaces were probably always somewhat more rough and ready in practice. It should be noted that in this instance the small furnace was used for fritting, and a separate furnace for annealing. These procedures were often reversed, and sometimes the subsidiary furnace was used for both fritting and annealing. For the units of measurements used see Hawthorne and Smith (1963).

The treatise entitled *De Coloribus et Artibus Romanorum* (*On the Colours and Arts of the Romans*), attributed to a certain Eraclius (pre AD 1000), contains chapters on glass-making which have been added, probably in the twelfth or thirteenth century to an existing manuscript. These describe a tripartite furnace of which the largest section is in the centre and is the founding and working furnace. This has one glory hole on either side, apparently with two pots to each, perhaps in the same manner as the Theophilus furnace. To the left of this should be a smaller furnace used for fritting and pot arching, and to the right a still smaller compartment presumably for annealing. The actual ground plan of these furnaces is not prescribed, and they may not necessarily have been rectangular. For the text see Merrifield (1949). The fire trench down the middle of the whole furnace is clearly indicated, and it may be assumed that there were solid sieges to either side of it, rather than the improbably flimsy structure reproduced by Maurach.

That rectangularity was by no means the rule in practice seems to be shown by the evidence of a glass furnace at *Glastonbury* in Britain. This appears to date from late Saxon times (between the eighth and the eleventh centuries AD). Although not enough of the structure has survived to permit an exact reconstruction, the ground plan appears to have been oval. Similarly, four furnaces attributed to the ninth century AD excavated at *Nitra* in Slovakia had oval ground plans. This has been interpreted to suggest that the Bohemian furnace was of a type 'entirely different from the well-known description' in Theophilus (Hejdova, 1965). It may well be, however, that the essential element in the northern tradition was not so much the rectangularity of the ground plan as the fact that the main and subsidiary furnaces (or at least one of them) were on the same level and shared their heat either by having the same fire trench running the length of the composite furnace (as in Theophilus) or by transmitting the heat laterally from the main furnace to the subsidiary one, or by both. An arrangement of this kind can be seen in the famous illustration to Mandeville's *Travels* in a manuscript in the British Museum, London (*Plate 1*). This manuscript is considered to have been compiled in Bohemia in about 1420. There is no description accompanying the original manuscript, but that given by Kenyon (1967) seems to be the most interesting and the following is adapted from it.

All round there is forest, with a man carrying fuel in a basket, two others carrying ash in sacks, one man digging sand from a hill in a clearing in the forest with a stream at its foot, and another carrying the sand to the glasshouse in a shoulder hod. The glasshouse has a rough shingle-roofed open shed with its stoke-hole entrance sheltered by a roof made of wood billets drying on a heavy timber frame. The furnace appears to be rectangular, having rounded and domed corners with a circular flue on top. Part of the roof is missing, perhaps to allow the furnace gases to escape. The furnace may have had four crucibles, two each side, and the annealing furnace is built on at the end. Vessel glass is being made and the master, in a hat, inspects a jug with a handle; a workman is taking a vessel out to finish its annealing in a large storage jar. Two glassmakers, wearing sweat rags on their brows, are shown; one is gathering glass from a crucible with his blowing iron. The boy stoker is attending to the fire. The stream in the background suggests a need for water, for washing

the sand, mixing the ash, and perhaps preparing the crucible clay.

The whole lively scene, with its emphasis on the temporary woodland shack, rings true for a northern glasshouse. Some authors have misinterpreted the sand pit on the hill; Harden (1956a) stated that 'the figures in the background are engaged in the production of *rochetta*', and Engle (1978) suggested that 'potash is being worked loose from a large oval lump', but the brown colour in *Plate 1* suggests that a ferruginous sand is being dug out.

The artist's rendering of the crown of the furnace would suggest an oval ground plan. An actual furnace of about this period excavated at *Skenarice* (in the Semily district of present day Czechoslovakia) revealed an oval ground plan extended by two parallel lines of masonry, perhaps the original fire trench. Another structure close by and apparently of rectangular form has been interpreted as being the fritting furnace. Yet another furnace of this general type has been excavated in Czechoslovakia at *Ververi Bityska*. That the Bohemian furnace was not always oval, however, is suggested by further excavations in Czechoslovakia, this time at *Pocatky* (in the district of Pelhrimov). Here three walls of a furnace were preserved to a height of 400 mm and revealed a rectangular ground plan. This glassworks dated from the late fifteenth or early sixteenth century. A further furnace complex dating from some time later in the sixteenth century has been excavated at *Rejdice*. Here three rectangular furnaces were found, and the same pattern was confirmed by finds at the nearby contemporary glassworks at *Syriste* (founded 1558). Whether the variations between oval and rectangular furnaces in Bohemia is a question of date or of function, it is difficult to say in the light of the evidence available at present.

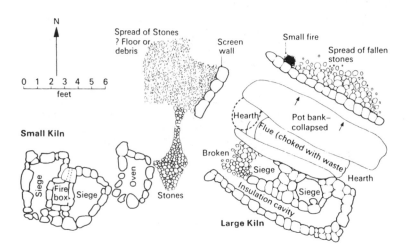

Figure 3.58 Plan of the medieval glasshouse at Blunden's Wood, Hambledon, Surrey. E.S. Wood.

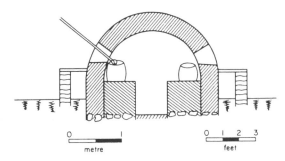

Figure 3.59 Reconstructed section of the glasshouse at Blunden's Wood, Hambledon, Surrey (see *Figure 3.58*). From Wood (1965).

In Britain, the rectangular furnace appears to have been the rule from, at the latest, the fourteenth century onward. At *Blunden's Wood*, Hambledon, Surrey, UK, a roughly rectangular furnace dating roughly from about 1330 (*Figure 3.58*) had a central fire trench roughly 3.2 m long by probably, originally, 610 mm wide, with a hearth at either end; to each side of this was a siege for two pots, 2.6 m long by 690 mm wide and 610 mm high (*Figure 3.59*). This showed the unusual feature of (apparently) a cavity between the siege and the outside wall, either for insulation purposes or possibly as a means of constructing the vaulted roof. This main furnace was accompanied by two subsidiary structures, presumably for the operations of the fritting, pot-arching and annealing (Wood, 1965) (*Figure 3.60*). A similar furnace, brick-built and almost 6.4 mm long and 770 mm wide, with clearly marked firing chambers at either end, was found well-preserved at *Fernfold*, Sussex, on a site connected with Jean Carré, founder of the 'modern' glass industry in Britain in 1567. A comparable furnace of early sixteenth century data, 3.7 m long, built of brick and stone and with sieges for three pots each side, was discovered at *Bagot's Park*, near Abbots Bromley in Staffordshire, and one

Figure 3.60 Reconstruction by James Gardner of a medieval glasshouse, based largely on Blunden's Wood. A = main working furnace with hearth at each end; B = apertures for pots; C = hearth; D = small furnaces for annealing and pre-heating pots; E = fuel (billets of beechwood); F = cullet (broken glass); G = raw material (sand etc.); H = new pots ready for furnace (pots not made at this site); I = marver on which glass was rolled and smoothed; J = water trough for cooling; L = bed of charcoal and sand on which to rest finished crown of glass; M = finished crowns of window glass; N = blowpipe and other tools.

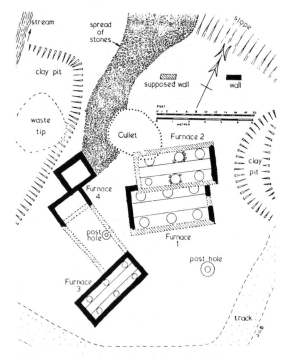

Figure 3.61 Plan of the glass furnace at Knightons, Alfold, Surrey. *Circa* 1550. Note the three six-pot furnaces, furnace 2 overlying furnace 1, and the two-chamber annealing furnace 4. E.S. Wood.

processes were carried out at this site (Pape, 1933). At the more or less contemporary site of *Vann*, near Chiddingfold in Sussex, however, the foundations of a larger, brick-built structure were excavated, the main furnace being an oblong (3.7 m × 1.7 m) at the corners of which were four diagonally projecting, fan-shaped wings (*Figure 3.62*). These were no doubt originally used for annealing, fritting and pot-arching (Winbolt, 1933). There was a great concentration of medieval glasshouses in the Chiddingfold area, at least thirty-six sites have been positively identified. (There are however by comparison 186 known medieval glass furnaces in France.) An interesting feature of the medieval forest glasshouses is that upon excavation they were found to contain very little broken glass; and it would seem that all the cullet was carefully collected when the glassmakers abandoned each site (perhaps because the furnace collapsed or because the supply of wood was exhausted in the vicinity) for use at the next.

The only excavated British glassfurnace which does not fall into the general pattern of a rectangular ground plan, with or without wings, is that at *Woodchester* in Gloucestershire, excavated around 1904. The circular structure was apparently 4.9 m in diameter with an internal diameter of 3 m, making the

ancillary furnace was excavated in the vicinity. Almost 300 kg of cullet was found on the site. A rectangular furnace site 3.7 m long by 1.2 m wide was found at *St Weonards* in Herefordshire in 1961. It was probably built of brick and stone, a square of large stones in the centre of a burned area probably representing the foundations of the founding chamber. Further rectangular furnaces, dating from the mid-sixteenth century, with three pots per siege, were excavated at *Knightons*, Alfold, Surrey in 1973 (*Figure 3.61*). Associated with these furnaces was a pair of smaller rectangular furnaces, perhaps for spreading window glass (Kenyon, 1967).

The picture at Blunden's Wood is repeated in essence at a late sixteenth- to early seventeenth-century glasshouse site at *Blore Park*, in Eccleshall in north-west Staffordshire. Here a fairly well-preserved stone furnace foundation was found and excavated, revealing a more or less square furnace with a long fire trench running east and west, and a siege on either side 300 mm high, 420 mm wide and 860 mm in length, accommodating two pots on each side. This furnace appeared to be complete in itself and no other structure was excavated, although traces were found in neighbouring mounds. There is therefore no means of knowing how the ancillary

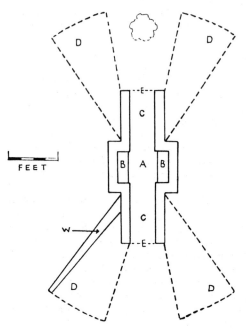

Figure 3.62 Plan of the Vann Copse furnace at Hambledon, Surrey, showing four 'wing' furnaces attached to the main furnace. A = fire chamber; B = sieges; C = hearth; D = ?annealing chambers; E = hearth lip (tease hole); W = taper wing wall. Based on S.E. Winbolt's rough sketch modified by A.D.R. Caroe.

walls 900 mm thick, a feature which must arouse some doubt. The firing hole was 1 m wide on the outside and 910 mm on the inside, exceptionally wide. A reexcavation, if any feature still remains, would be highly desirable. An adjacent rectangular structure 2.7 m by 2.1 m was interpreted as an annealing furnace. It has been suggested that the round furnace at Woodchester may be explained by the presence there of Flemish glassmakers. All these glasshouses made green 'forest glass' and their structure was described by Merrett in 1662:

> The Green Glass furnaces are made square ... having at each angle an arch to anneal their Glasses ... For green Glass on two opposite sides they work their Metall, and on the other sides they have their Calcars, into which linnet holes are made for the fire to come from the furnace, to bake and to prepare their Frit, and also for the discharge of the smoak. But they make fires in the arches, to anneal their vessels, so that they make all their processes in one furnace onely.

This general layout of furnace survived in Britain and France until at least the 1770s, although the adapted Venetian-type furnace was by now well established in both countries. (For comments on glass-making at this time, see Dossie, 1758.) Its characteristic of heating subsidiary furnaces through linnet holes recalls the two-chamber furnaces of Theophilus and the Mandeville illumination (*Figure 3.57 and Plate 1*). This plan appears to have survived in Germany until at least the end of the seventeenth century.

A four-pot bottle furnace with two (circular) wings was in operation from at least 1777 in *Gravel Lane*, Southwark, London (*Figures 3.63* and *3.64*). Here one wing was used for fritting, the other for heating bottle cullet before its transference to the pots. Annealing was carried out in seven independent subsidiary furnaces (uu and ww on the plan), and pot arching in another (t on plan). The origins of this type of furnace are at present uncertain. A furnace with a ground plan of this type excavated at Heindert (Canton d'Arlon, Luxembourg) is supposed to date from at least Carolingian times. In Britain, apart from Vann (see above), three-winged furnaces have been excavated in recent years at *Hutton* and *Rosedale* in Yorkshire (Crossley and Aberg, 1972) and at *Kimmeridge* in Dorset in 1980/81.

At *Hutton* (*Figure 3.65*) an earlier furnace of plain fire-trench type was overlaid by a second furnace with two fan-shaped wings to north-east and south-west, these being incorporated with a third overlying two-pot furnace. A second furnace, standing apart, may have been an annealing furnace for the first phase. The last phase of the furnace was dated to the late sixteenth century by thermoremanent magnetism. At *Rosedale* (*Figure 3.66*) a two-pot furnace of similar date had four fan-shaped wings.

Both furnaces were built of stone and clay. These furnaces are described in detail by Frank (1982). Excavations at Kimmeridge in 1980/81 revealed the foundations of an early seventeenth-century glasshouse having four fan-shaped wings (*Figure 3.67*). The sieges were badly eroded so that it was not possible to be certain how many crucibles had been set in the furnace, but there appeared to be ample space for four pots. Underground air passages were necessary to provide draught for the local oil-shale which was used as a source of fuel. The floors of the air passages were slabbed with stone and beneath them a drain channelled water towards the sea. Stone steps at the ends of the air passages farthest from the furnace gave access for raking out ash. The furnace was contained within a rectangular cover building with a shale-tile roof supported on timber on a stone foundation wall. This building protected the furnace and the working areas located on either side of it between the wings which were presumably used for ancillary processes. From a previous era of archaeology there is a record of a furnace excavated at *Buckholt* near Salisbury in Wiltshire which appears to have had a winged construction. The Buckholt glassmakers seem to have been, with one possible exception, French by origin; and the Vann glasshouse appears to have produced green glasses of the normal Wealden 'Lorraine' type.

The two Yorkshire glasshouses also produced characteristic green vessels of the same type, but it seems that higher temperatures had been employed than in the glasshouses of the Chiddingfold (Weald) area of southern Britain (Cable and Smedley, 1987). On the whole it seems likely that the winged furnace was of French origin. That it enjoyed a wider diffusion at a later date is shown by the British examples quoted above and by the following: a stone-built furnace in a glasshouse at *Karlova Hut*, in Czechoslovakia, founded in 1758; a furnace in the *Amelung* factory at *New Bremen*, Maryland, USA built after 1774 (and probably after 1784) (Hume, 1976). Both these furnaces appear to have had a plain firing trench, without a grill no doubt reflecting the use of wood rather than coal as a fuel. Amelung had begun his career at Grünenplan south of Hanover in Germany, and in Maryland took over a factory that had previously been run by Germans. Therefore it may reasonably be concluded that the winged furnace was also established in the German-speaking countries by, at the latest, the middle of the eighteenth century. It seems likely that the six-pot furnace with two annexed annealing furnaces was used at the *Notsjö* factory in Finland in 1799 (Seela, 1974).

Amongst the illustrations to Kunckel's *Ars Vitraria Experimentalis* (*Experiments in the Art of Glass*), first published in Amsterdam and Danzig in 1679, appear engravings showing the German furnace (*Figures 3.68 and 3.69*). Here the working furnace and the fritting

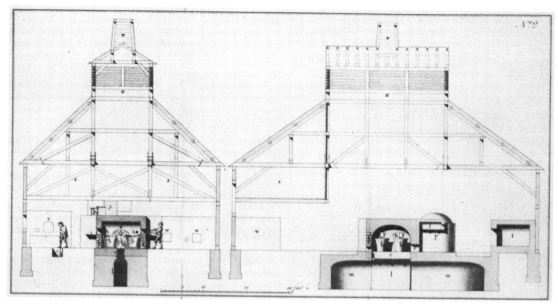

Figure 3.63 View of a bottlehouse in Gravel Lane, Southwark, London. *Circa* 1777. Drawing by C.W. Carlberg; c represents the grill.

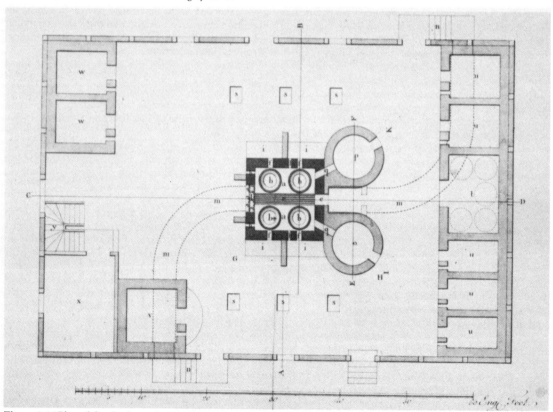

Figure 3.64 Plan of the glasshouse in Gravel Lane, Southwark (see *Figure 3.63*). qq are explained as 'openings into the vaults of these two furnaces, through which the heat is communicated from the founding-furnace'; uu are annealing furnaces, the largest accommodating 800 bottles; t is a pot-arching furnace; v is a furnace for chemical apparatus and other large pieces, the annealing furnace for which is at ww.

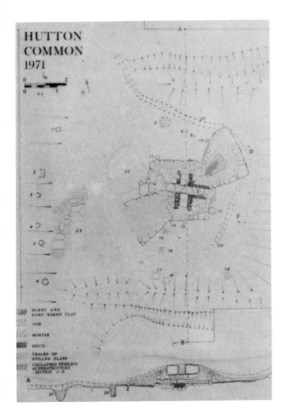

Figure 3.65 Plan of a green-glass furnace excavated at Hutton Common, Yorkshire. After D.W. Crossley and F. Aberg.

or annealing furnace are simply two chambers of the same structure, with the fire chamber running through their combined length (*Figure 3.69*). It is not clear from the engravings whether or not there was also a linnet-hole connecting the upper chamber (that is, the working storey of the main furnace and the actual annealing chamber of the subsidiary one), and Kunckel provided no explanatory text. Fortunately the illustrations were reproduced with explanatory text in the 1752 French edition of Neri.

It is important to note that the subsidiary furnace was used for annealing as well as for fritting; the opening marked X on the plan is described as an 'opening for placing the glass to anneal'. This type of furnace was clearly domesticated in France about as early as the winged furnace was established in Germany/Bohemia, for among the supplementary plates of Diderot's *Encyclopédie* is a series of engravings illustrating this double type of furnace, entitled interestingly enough, 'Round furnace or French furnace'. There are changes of detail, notably

a square plan for the subsidiary furnace and four ribs to the beehive founding furnace.

That the type of furnace represented in the French edition of Neri was continuously in use up to the date of Kunckel's book is indicated by the results of an excavation carried out on the site of a glasshouse at *Trestenhult*, in Sweden, dating from about 1630. That it was essentially a German-type furnace is confirmed by the fact that this factory was under the leadership of a certain Påvel Gaukunkel, probably one of a West German family of glassmakers, and that it made green glass of the German *waldglas* type. This furnace had an octagonal founding furnace with four pots, and a stoke-hole running throughout the length of the entire structure, which included an annealing furnace of circular plan, set slightly askew to the axis of the main furnace, with the result that the square hole permitting the passage of heat from the fire chamber to annealing chamber is off-centre (*Figure 3.70*). The two furnaces are interconnected at first floor level by a linnet-hole (K of the drawing, *Figure 3.70*) (Roosma, 1969). A furnace of the same basic type was already known to Agricola (*Figure 3.71*) in the sixteenth century, although in his illustration the annealing furnace is rectangular in plan, perhaps a throwback to the earlier traditions of Eraclius and Theophilus. Agricola described the furnace in the following terms:

The second furnace is rounded, ten feet [3 m] broad and eight [feet] [2.5 m] high, and strengthened on the outside with five ribs [460 mm] thick. This again consists of two chambers, the roof of the lower being [460 mm] thick. This lower chamber has in front a narrow opening for stoking the logs on the ground-level hearth; and in the middle of its roof is a big round aperture opening into the upper compartment so that the flames may penetrate into it. But in the wall of the upper chamber between the ribs there should be eight windows so large that through them the bellied pots may be put on the floor round the big aperture.... At the back of the furnace is a square opening, in height and breadth 1 palm, through which the heat may penetrate into the third furnace, adjoining. This is oblong eight feet [2.5 m] by six feet (1.8 m) broad, similarly consisting of two chambers, of which the lower has an opening in front for stoking the hearth .... (Winbolt, 1933).

This is in all essentials the Trestenhult furnace except for the ground plan and for the fact that apparently each furnace here has its own firebox, one set at right angles to the other. But the express mention of interconnection at the first floor level is a vital point and such a feature may have also existed in the furnace of Mandeville's illustration (*Plate 1*). Evidence for further furnaces of this type is to be found in the German-speaking areas of Central Europe:

ROSEDALE

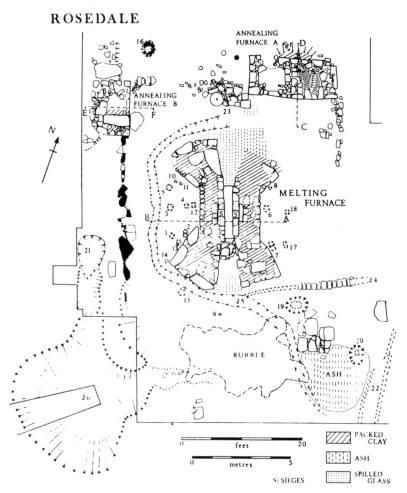

Figure 3.66 Plan of a green-glass furnace excavated at
Rosedale, Yorkshire. After D.W. Crossley and F. Aberg.

(1) The Preussler *Humpen* in the Museum of
Applied Arts in Prague (*Figure 3.72*) dated 1680.
(2) A second Preussler family *Humpen* of 1727,
showing a virtually identical furnace (*Figure 3.73*).
To the right may be seen the subsidiary furnace with
something stretched across the access door, as in the
case of the 1680 *Humpen*, which seems to show pot
arching in progress. To the left is a separate
secondary furnace (for fritting?).
(3) A glasshouse at *Reichenau* (probably that on the
Buquoy estates at Gratzen on the Austrian side of the
South Bohemian border), shown in *Figure 3.74*. The
house clearly made both window and vessel glass (the
latter by the muff process), with the circular furnace
for vessel, the structure to its left being designated by
the key as the annealing furnace, and that to the
extreme left as the *Taffel Offen*, presumably the

furnace for window glass. The structural connection,
if any, between these two last is unclear from the
engraving, but the lehr is clearly connected with the
circular vessel-glass furnace, although it seems to be
in use for annealing (and perhaps spreading?) muffs.
Probably this should be regarded as a bastardized
version of the German-type furnace.
(4) The illustration from the *Augsburg Bible* of 1730,
showing all the features of the Kunckel engraving,
and perhaps derived directly from it.
(5) Excavations of the *Junkernfelde* furnace.

Three sites excavated in Denmark seem to suggest
that the German-type furnace was also in use there:

(1) *Hyttekaer* in Tem Glarbo, in the general area of
Arhus, Jutland. Here six furnaces were discovered,
not all necessarily of the same period, of which two

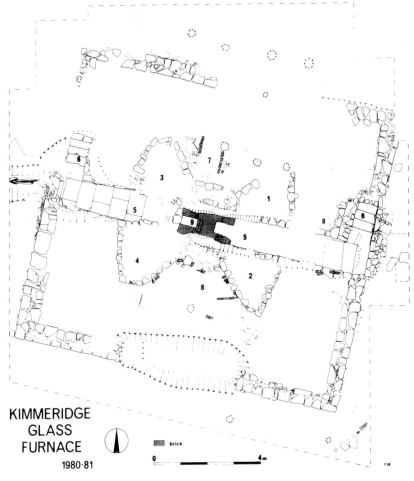

KIMMERIDGE
GLASS
FURNACE
1980·81

brick

0   4 m

Figure 3.67 Plan of the early seventeenth century glasshouse at Kimmeridge, Dorset, based on the 1980/81 excavations. Features: 1-4 wings; 5 air passages; 6 steps giving access to air passages; 7-8 working areas; 9 fire box; 10 robbing pit; 11 wall footing. Courtesy of D.W. Crossley.

appeared to have a common fire trench, one being circular, the other an oblong structure. Two further furnaces were apparently circular on plan, but although close to each other, their fire trenches were aligned roughly at right angles. Of the remaining furnaces apparently only the fire trenches survived, without any indication of their external shape.

(2) *Tinsholt*, south of Aalborg in Jutland. At least one furnace (or two contiguous furnaces) here apparently corresponds to the main Hyttekaer furnace, although the published details are somewhat unclear.

(3) *Stenhule* in Tem Glarbo (see above). Three furnaces were found (discounting an apparently earlier circular foundation), of which the founding furnace, probably for six pots, may have been almost square, 3.4 m × 2.7 m, with chamfered corners. Its very long firebox, projecting on the west side, may have heated a long, narrow subsidiary (annealing?) furnace which would have resembled that at Reichenau. The two remaining furnaces, apparently circular and oval on plan respectively, were possibly for fritting and spreading of window glass. However, the site at *Nejsum* in Vendsyssel north of Aalborg, the plan of which seems clearer than some of those mentioned, reveals a central fire trench projecting a long way out at either side of an almost circular furnace plan — very much as at *Fernfold* in the Weald, except that the furnace there was rectangular. The Stenhule furnace could well be reconstructed in

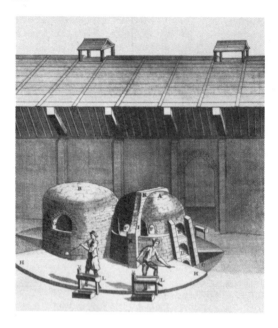

Figure 3.68 View of Kunckel's furnace (from the 1752 French translation of A. Neri, *L'Arte Vetraria*).

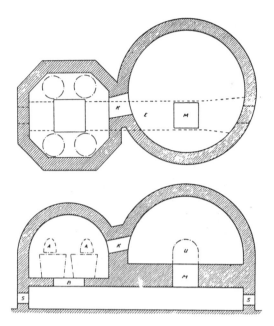

Figure 3.70 Reconstructed section of a green-glass furnace found at Trestenhult, Sweden. *Circa* 1630.

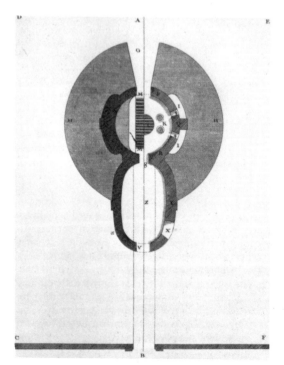

Figure 3.69 Plan of Kunckel's furnace, shown in *Figure 3.68*.

Figure 3.71 Woodcut illustrating G. Agricola, *De Re Metallica*, Basel, 1556, showing a 'second furnace' with conjoined annealing furnace. H shows the clay 'tunnels' in which the glasses were annealed.

Figure 3.72 Humpen of Christian Preussler with a view of the Zeilberg glasshouse, Bohemia, 1680. Museum of Applied Arts, Prague.

the same sense. It should be noted that all the glassmakers associated with these Jutland sites were Germans, some specifically from Hesse.

A glasshouse at *Henrikstorp* in Skane, Sweden, had a ground-plan suggesting an exceptionally long fire trench, and may have been a structure resembling that at Reichenau. Its reconstruction with four pots on one side of an offset fire channel, and with a circular annealing furnace, seems very improbable. Finally, a glasshouse dating from about 1530 excavated at *Junkersfelde*, in eastern Westphalia, revealed a four-pot furnace rectangular in plan, with chamfered angles (as at *Trestenhult* and *Stenhule*), apparently leading to an annexed annealing furnace.

Development of coal firing and the chimney furnace

With the exception of the glasshouse at Kimmeridge in Dorset, all the furnaces hitherto described were fired by wood. It fell to Britain in the sixteenth century, with the increasing competition among wood-using industries for the output of coppiced woodlands, to develop the use of coal for this purpose. The late sixteenth and early seventeenth centuries were filled with the clamour of rival patentees claiming monopolies for their particular systems of using coal for this and that industrial process. In glass-making, sufficient progress had been made by 1615 to enable the government of the day to issue a 'Proclamation touching Glass', forbidding the burning of wood in the glass industry. The essential feature of the coal-burning furnace was

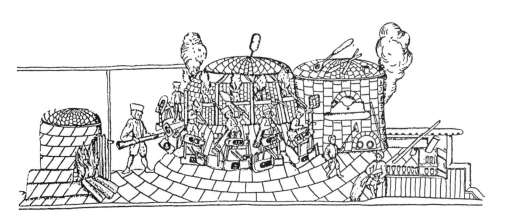

Figure 3.73 Humpen of the Preussler family; 1727. After Partsch, *Der Preusslerhumpen*, 1928.

Figure 3.74 Engraving showing the glasshouse at
Reichenau, from a drawing by Clemens Benttler. Middle
seventeenth century.

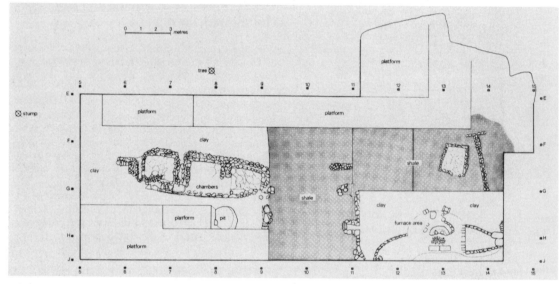

Figure 3.75 Plan of the seventeenth-century glasshouse at
Haughton Green, Denton, near Manchester (after the 1970
excavations). The main furnace lies to the bottom right, with
annealing chambers(?) to the left. From Hurst-Vose (1980).

the use of a grill of iron bars on which the coals could
be laid and raked periodically, the ashes falling into a
pit below. In general, the furnace at Kimmeridge,
operational between 1615 and 1623, resembled the
wood-burning furnaces which have been excavated
on both sides of the English Channel (see *Figure
3.67*). There was a central passage between sieges on
which the crucibles had been set. At each corner was
a triangular wing. The wings had formed the bases of
four subsidiary structures in which the preparation of
raw materials, and the working and annealing of the
glass, could be carried out. They may also have been
used for the prefiring of crucibles. Outside the sieges,
between each pair of wings, there were platforms on
which lay fragments of stone floors. The main

difference between Kimmeridge and the wood-
burning furnaces of the Lorraine tradition, were the
size of the firebox and the long vaulted passages used
to supply air. When burning wood, it was possible to
lay fires between the wings and to allow the flames to
travel into the arched structure in which the pots
were set. However, a coal fire gave a shorter flame,
and therefore had to be placed in the centre of a
furnace. At Kimmeridge a central block of brickwork
lay between the sieges in a stone-lined channel
approximately 1.4 m deep and 1.0 m wide. The 'coal'
(bituminous shale) was placed upon the central
block, or above it on fire-bars, of which no trace
survived at the time of excavation (1981). Another
example of an early seventeenth-century four-pot

Plate 1 An early fifteenth century glasshouse in the
forest-glass tradition. From Sir John Mandeville's *Travels*.
Reproduced by permission of the British Library.

Plate 2 Two fragments of red glass: that on the left is coloured throughout; that on the right is composed of clear glass which has a thin layer of red glass fused to one side (flashed glass).

Plate 3 A fragment of glass displaying an iridescent surface, the result of decomposition.

Plate 5 Cone vessel shown in Figure 7.31: completed restoration in polyester resin tinted with translucent polyester pigment. British Museum, London.

Plate 4 Squares of glass mosaic decorating an object of copper alloy, and partly obscured by copper corrosion products. Courtesy of J.M. Cronyn.

furnace with an ash-pit below the sieges, and an apparently vaulted firing chamber, was excavated by Hurst-Vose (1980) and Burke at Haughton Green, Denton near Manchester (*Figure 3.75*).

The development of air passages is to be expected at this time. Merrett's (1662) account of furnace procedure described air passages, and the use of fire-bars, 'Sleepers are the great Iron bars crossing smaller ones which hinder the passing of the coals, but give passage to the descent of the ashes'. This appears to be the earliest reference to this device, but it is clearly shown in the drawing of a London glasshouse made by a Swedish architect visiting England in 1777–8 (see *Figure 3.64*). The grill system seems to have been adopted on the Continent without much delay. It is shown in the illustration to Kunckel's *Ars Vitraria Experimentalis* of 1679 (see *Figures 3.68* and *3.69*) and is clearly seen in the illustrations to the *Encyclopédie*. The provision of an ash chamber added, as it were, an extra storey to the furnace.

Clearly the provision of an adequate draft was of critical importance in the firing of a coal furnace, and it was inevitably in this field that the British made a further important contribution to glass technology. The principle was to have a cone-shaped building to house the furnace, capable of having all its outlets closed. Underground flues, no doubt arranged with regard to the prevalent wind, led to the furnace itself. By closing the cone doors and opening the flues, a tremendous through-draft was created, the great cone acting as a chimney (*Figures 3.76* and *3.77*). Glassworks cones were built only in Britain and the Hanover region of Germany (which at that time had strong royal connections with Britain) but not in France or Belgium (correspondence between R.G. Newton and G. Schulze, 1985). Bontemps (1868) in his *Guide de Verrier* states, 'It is generally known that the English glasshouses are huge cones which surround the furnace. The English furnaces are thus situated under big chimneys which encourage energetic combustion in a way that is impossible in our

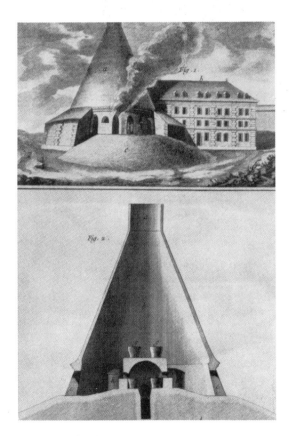

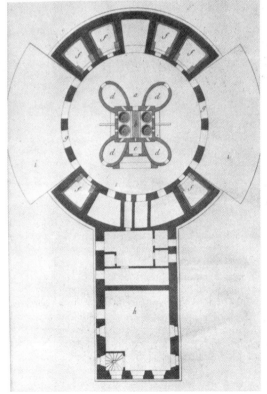

Figure 3.76 Plate from Diderot's *Encyclopédie* showing 'Verrerie Angloise, Vue et Coupe sur la Longueur de la Verrerie' (pl. vol. N. pl 2 of article 'Verrerie Angloise').

Figure 3.77 Plan of the glasshouse shown in *Figure 3.76* (pl. 1); b in Fig. 2 is the grill. The 'linnet-holes' to the 'wing' furnaces are visible in the engraving.

Figure 3.78 The interiors of glass cones were spacious and provided good working conditions for the glass blowers. Around the walls of the cone can be seen the mouths of the annealing ovens and the 'pot arches', or ovens for preheating the pots before subjecting them to the fierce heat of the furnace.

French furnaces, which have a louvered opening above the furnace for the combustion products' (*Figure 3.78*).

The advantages of this system are described in the *Encyclopédie* (Diderot and D'Alembert, 1772). The writer of the article *Verrerie* stressed the importance of the single upward movement of air facilitated by the cone superstructure, all the outward exits of which were shut during founding, allowing the air to enter the building only through three broad ducts laid in the foundations under the furnace. He calculated that this increased the efficiency of the British furnace enormously in comparison with that of the French type, the former being able to make in 12 days, other things being equal, the same number of bottles as a French factory made in 15 days. The same points are chosen for comment by a Danish visitor to London in 1727:

> It is known, that the English glass is of high quality, and this is ascribed to the intense heat of the coal which is used for this purpose; I therefore also visited two of their glass furnaces, which stand on an eminence, and in the ground there is an open passage from both sides to a very large iron grill, which is in the middle, and the coals on and about it; by means of this passage the coals receive the air they need and one can stir them with appropriate instruments.

Günther (1961b) pointed out that the cones served a dual purpose, being both a glass factory (i.e. a manufacturing area) and a waste gas extraction

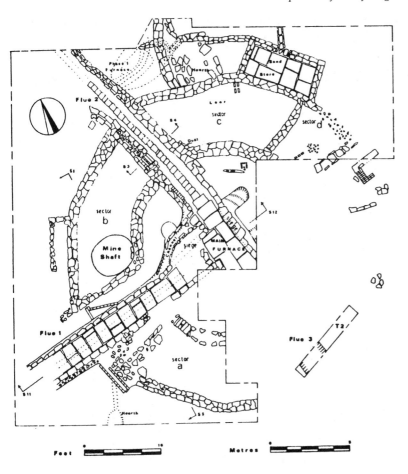

Figure 3.79 Plan of the cone glasshouse at Gawber, South Yorkshire, showing three flues or air intakes, feeding air from the exterior to the central furnace. S1-S12 refer to sections drawn during excavations. Site of the earlier (Phase 1) furnace is shown in the top left-hand area. T2 (Trench 2) confirmed that Flue 2 continued into Flue 3. Flue 1 was added at a later date. Sector 'a' seemed to be a smith's hearth for maintenance of glassworkers' equipment. Sector 'b' contained a mine shaft which antedates the main cone structure. Sector 'c' was probably the 'lehr' or annealing area, with a sand store adjoining the exterior wall. Denis Ashurst.

system. Günther was particularly interested in their technical performance and quotes the general height as being 15 to 25 m; the volume of masonry as being 1100 m^3 (the cone at Obernkirchen weighing 2800 tonne); the (diluted) waste gas temperature as 400°C; the exit velocity as 1 m s^{-1}; concluding that, at any time, the cones enable coal to be burnt more efficiently than in any other manner for achieving melting temperatures, and gave a more equable environment for the workmen. However, the cones no longer had this advantage in fuel efficiency once the Siemens regenerative furnace had been introduced (Günther, 1961a).

It is not certain exactly when the glass cone was first devised. Godfrey (1975) has an interesting discussion of the development of the cone furnace including some eyewitness descriptions of the *Winchester House* furnace, probably from as early as 1610. There is, however, some misunderstanding of the functions of the glass cone, which is quite different from a chimney leading from the furnace. The point is that the heat should be drawn over the glass pots and not out of the crown of the furnace. The cone and the underground passages simply augment the draft, which follows this course, emerging at the working holes of the furnace.

Captain Philip Roche was building a cone in Dublin as early as 1696 but this was probably preceded by a period of experiment. In 1702 *The London Gazette* reports the existence of a glass cone, '94 Foot high and 60 Foot broad' (28.7 m × 18.3 m). The 35 ft (10.7 m) building constructed in 1621 at Ballnegery was evidently a normal frame and shingle glasshouse with presumably no effect on the draft. The *Belfast News Letter* for 19 August 1785 referred to a new glasshouse 120 ft (31.1 m) high 'being the largest of any in Great Britain or Ireland'. In 1823 a cone 150 ft (32.0 m) high was recorded in the same city. In 1784, a prohibition was promulgated in Dublin against any glasshouse chimney less than 50 ft (15.2 m) in height.

Possibly the great heat reported by Merrett (above) was due to this device as early as 1662. More probably the cone was invented between this date and the end of the century. A few cones still survive although they are no longer in use (Lewis, 1973; Ashurst, 1970). In Britain they are now preserved as Ancient Monuments and can be seen at *Alloa* (Scotland), *Lemington* (near Newcastle-upon-Tyne), *Stourbridge* (near Birmingham) and at *Catcliffe* and *Gawber* in Yorkshire. The cone glasshouse at Gawber was probably constructed in the eighteenth century and is known to have been in ruins by 1823 (*Figure 3.79*). It illustrates the use of underground flues to induce the draft under the furnace. On the site of the main furnace were found lengths of fire bar, 2–3 ft (600–900 mm) long by 1¼ in (30 mm) square section, and a sandstone block carved with a slot into which a fire bar exactly fitted, to form the detachable fire grate. This seems to be the only archaeological record of the dimensions of fire bars. In Germany there are examples of glassworks cones at *Obernkirchen* and *Steinkrug* (near Hanover) and at *Gernheim* (near Minden).

The difference between the heat needed for making drinking glasses and that for window glass is made explicit in an entry in the diary of Sir James Hope in 1647 concerning the *Wemyss* (Scotland) glasshouse:

That window glasses and drinking glasses cannot be made in one fornace because those requyre a great deall stronger heatt than these: That the fornace for those is y^{r}fore long vaulted; and for these round bot however y^t could not make window glass, nather possiblie could find workmen who have skill of both. . . .

These observations were based on the experience of an Italian glassmaker, Christopher Visitella. The great heat reached in the green-glass furnaces is emphasized by Merrett: 'The heat of those furnaces, is the greatest that ever I felt . . . The workmen say tis twice as strong as that in the other Glass-furnaces ...'.

One further British invention resulted from the use of coal for firing. This was the covered glass pot. That open pots continued to be used in circumstances where the fumes of the coal made little difference (e.g. in bottle making) is proved by the details of the interiors of British bottle houses given by Carlberg in 1777–78 (see *Figure 3.63*) and by the illustrator of the *Encyclopédie* in 1772. Here the old type of pot is clearly visible. It seems more likely, therefore, that the development of the covered pot was associated with the evolution of lead crystal, for this is irreparably damaged by the sulphur compounds which result from the combustion of coal. Curiously enough the earliest mention of it appears to come from Norway. In 1756 at the *Nostetangen* factory there were prepared '16 English covered pots'. The earliest pictorial representation would appear to date from as late as 1802 (Newton, 1988).

The theory that there was a southern tradition of furnace building (in which the founding furnace was normally circular and incorporated a third storey for annealing); and a northern tradition in which the founding furnace was normally rectangular or oblong on plan and the annealing furnace often on a level with it and interconnecting by means of a common fore channel, and usually also by linnet holes, seems in general to have been borne out by recent archaeological discoveries. The differences are discussed by Newton (1985b) in terms of the availability of beech trees. The northern tradition clearly bifurcated at some point, probably in the sixteenth century, into those furnaces which were built with wings for subsidiary firing processes on the one hand and, on the other, two-chamber furnaces of the type represented in the Mandeville manuscript and Kunckel's engravings. These general developments must be viewed in the context of all the variables imposed in particular cases by site, available building materials etc. It is to be hoped that in all future excavations on glasshouse sites, proper measured drawings accompanied by photographs will illustrate the report, together with details of the refractories used (pots, *bocca* frames etc.) and of the glass items found on the site. All these are essential clues to the nature of the furnace used.

4

Deterioration of glass

Many ancient glass artefacts have survived exposure to the environment for much more than two millennia, but it is now realized that the specimens which have survived represent only the more durable of the glasses manufactured in the past, or those which have been buried or stored in conditions ideal for their preservation (Newton, 1980a). The main factors which affect the type and rate of glass decomposition are the *composition* of the glass and its *environment*; other factors are temperature, time, the pH of an aggressive solution, the surface area of the glass per unit volume of the liquid, and possibly also micro-organisms, traffic vibrations and earlier conservation treatments (Griffiths, 1980; Newton, 1985a).

Composition can be seen to be important because it is the reason for the difference between 'durable' Roman soda – lime – silica glass and the poorly durable medieval window glass, made from beechwood ash and containing too much potash and lime for good stability. But it should also be realized that Roman glass is only superficially durable, because a detailed study of the surface layers shows that the smooth, shiny surface is acually a 'hydrogen glass' which has replaced the original Roman glass.

Water is a primary agent of the environment which causes the deterioration of glass, its effect having been established by Lavoisier (1770), but the earliest scientific examination of weathered glass was that by Brewster (1863), who was mainly interested in lenses and prisms but who was also persuaded to study some iridescent glasses from Nineveh. He soon dismissed the legend that the rainbow colours on the surface were due to some lost secret of glass manufacture, by showing that the iridescence resulted from the interference between rays of light reflected from thin alternating layers of air and weathered glass crusts; if the gaps were injected with water the iridescence disappeared, to return again when the water dried out. He also showed that

corrosion proceeded *downwards* faster than sideways. Loubengager (1931) found similar crusts on glasses from a Cypriot burial vault.

It has long been supposed that air pollution, and in particular sulphur dioxide, has been responsible for much deterioration of stained glass, and a book has recently been devoted to this subject (Fitz *et al.*, 1984). Nevertheless, there seems to be no *direct* evidence that sulphur dioxide actually *attacks* the glass, although there is no doubt that it is responsible for the sulphates always found on the surface of medieval glass. It seems that a false conclusion has been drawn about an *attack on the glass by sulphur dioxide* because three stages are involved. First, an attack of the glass by water to produce hydroxides; then the subsequent conversion of these hydroxides to carbonates by the carbon dioxide in the atmosphere; and finally the conversion of those carbonates to sulphates (Newton, 1979, 1987b). The whole subject of the durability of medieval glass windows has been reviewed by Newton (1982b).

The European Economic Community has recently been much interested in the durability of enamelled tableware glass owing to the possibility that the enamelled decoration thereon may lead to the extraction of toxic levels of lead from the decoration (e.g. see EEC, 1976, and also later directives). Glasses are also being advocated for the encapsulation of high-level radioactive wastes, and bioglasses are being used for the replacement of human bones and teeth, the glasses being specially formulated to bond to living bone (Hench and Paschall, 1973). The development of glass fibre optical communication systems, which must have a long life when buried in suitable cables, has made it important to understand their environments. The introduction of returnable (US, one-trip) bottles has necessitated work to reduce the deterioration which occurs on the surface of household bottles (Moody, 1977). Yet another, rather specialized, durability problem concerns the acceleration of any fracture damage of the glass used in space-craft (Wiederhorn *et al.*, 1974a). All these, and in fact the whole subject of durability of glass, has been reviewed recently by Newton (1985a) and the International Commission on Glass (1972–1979).

Previous conservation treatments may have had a profound effect on the durability of medieval window glass and of glass objects. Apart from the obvious cause of damage, that is, careless work or injudicious choice or application of methods, it should be remembered that conservation techniques may be potentially harmful to glass. Discussions of their merits and disadvantages are to be found in the relevant sections of Chapter 7.

The corrosion of glass by water

When a glass reacts with water, or with an aqueous solution, chemical changes occur at the surface and may then spread to the whole of the glass, depending on which *type of surface* has been produced. Some surfaces are protective and others are not, and the type depends on a number of factors, especially the composition of the glass and the pH of the liquid. The initial stage of the chemical reactions has generally been regarded as that of ion exchange between the alkali ions in the glass and the hydrogen ions (protons) in the water (Charles, 1958), but Ernsberger (1980) showed that the explanation cannot be as simple as that because the field intensity of the bare proton is so intense that it cannot exist in a condensed phase, and the proton is probably accompanied by water molecules (Conradt and Scholze, 1984).

The concept of a simple exchange between monovalent cations seems therefore to require modification. It will probably be replaced by that of an inward diffusion of water molecules, which then react with non-bridging oxygen atoms to produce hydroxyl ions that migrate out with the alkali cations (causing the well-known alkali extraction) so that electrical neutrality can be maintained. Here it should be pointed out that this book does not contain many of the usual chemical or kinetic equations in the text, and these important features must be sought in the literature references; from the conservator's point of view, the details are not strictly relevant.

During the initial stage, the rate of alkali extraction is parabolic in character (Lyle, 1943; Douglas and Isard, 1949; Rana and Douglas, 1961; Tichane, 1966; Douglas and El Shamy, 1967; El Shamy *et al.*, 1972) but for various reasons, connected with the type of surface layer produced, this is succeeded by a reduction in the rate of leaching. To return to the simple concept of direct ion exchange, referred to above, alkali ions cannot leave the glass unless protons replace them to maintain electrical neutrality. The protons are smaller than the alkali ions (especially the potassium ion) and thus the alkali-depleted surface layer has a smaller volume; potash glasses have about half the durability of the corresponding soda glasses because the potassium ion took up so much space in the network before it was leached out. The reduction in volume of the leached layer causes shrinkage to occur, for example, as in crizzled glasses, and further shrinkage takes place if a hydrated alkali-deficient (hence silica-rich) layer loses water (see Newton, 1985a for references). Thus dehydration, often thought of as a cause of deterioration, merely demonstrates the deterioration that already exists. Scholze *et al.* (1975) have shown that the decrease in volume can lead to microporosity of the surface layer and this may be the cause of the many-layered effects found in the surface crusts of some medieval glasses.

The alkali-deficient surface layer then causes the alkali diffusion rate to decrease because there is now another layer through which the ions must diffuse in order to reach the unaltered glass, and the rate of extraction, which initially decreased with the square root of time, becomes slower, and linear with time. Thus a false impression can be given that the glass has become more durable as time goes on; and it can be dangerous to make generalizations which could be misleading in specific cases (Geffcken, 1939; Hench, 1975a,b; Hench and Sanders, 1974).

Conservators should note that this leached layer is often given alternative names which can be confusing; these include alkali-deficient, silica-rich, 'hydrogen glass' etc. The layer may be extremely thin, or thick enough to be seen easily under a microscope (Metcalfe *et al.*, 1971). Even when such a glass is stored in a desiccator, changes can continue to take place in the leached layer and it is becoming clear that the nature of the leached layer is of fundamental importance in understanding durability problems. Hench has identified six types of layer which will be described in detail below. Unless the leach solution is frequently renewed, the accumulation of alkali ions in the water leads to an increase in the pH value, (El-Shamy and Douglas, 1972) and a critical point is reached at pH 9.0 when the silica network is attacked. Both silica and the divalent network modifiers (calcium, magnesium, lead, etc.) can then be leached out and 'total dissolution' of the surface will occur. The speed at which the critical value of pH 9 is reached depends on many parameters, two important ones being the surface area (SA) and the volume (V) of water involved; thus the value SA/V can be very important (Ethridge *et al.*, 1979). This is why sheets of flat glass will be ruined rapidly if they are stacked face-to-face in a moist atmosphere (there is a very large SA and a very small V); this danger is discussed by Schröder (1953) and McGrath *et al.*

(1961), and it is interesting to note that the risk was appreciated as early as the sixteenth century. In a letter dated 1595, concerning glass imported from Venice, the instructions from the importer stated that the glass should be '... carefullij packt up and with thorou drij weeds, for if the weeds be not well drijed or doe take anij wett after theij be packt theij staijne and spoijle the glasses' (Charleston, 1967).

A variant of this type of attack occurs on those types of medieval painted glass that have an exceptionally high lime content, and less than 50 mol per cent silica, due to the use of beechwood ash in their manufacture. Breakdown of the silica network occurs readily and a surface crust develops which retains moisture and becomes highly alkaline. This type of weathering is characteristic of many church windows in Austria and, until recently, it was thought that the crust might be the result of some peculiarity of Austrian weather (Bacher, 1974a), but El-Shamy (1973a) has shown that this behaviour is to be expected when the silica content is less than about 62 mol per cent.

Accelerated durability tests

There is a vast body of literature concerned with the durability of glass. Necessarily, much of the research work has taken the form of accelerated aging tests on modern glass under laboratory conditions. Durability is critically dependent upon a number of surface state and environmental variables. These include the surface roughness, whether the glass is in bulk or in powder form (that is, surface area), whether internal or applied stress has been applied, phase separation or inhomogeneities in the glass, relative humidity, the ions in the corrosive solutions and their concentrations, time, temperature, pressure, attacking liquid volume etc. (Hench, 1975b, Paul, 1977). Obviously some of these parameters are interdependant, but the complexity of the situation is apparent. Some of the parameters tend to change in value during an experiment, and it is usually quite difficult to keep conditions constant because the reaction products from the glass modify the solutions. There is also the problem that most of the studies of chemical durability have naturally been carried out on glasses of fairly simple composition, whereas ancient glasses tend to be complex, probably by virtue of impurities in the raw materials used.

Many accelerated aging tests involve increasing the ratio of glass surface area to the attacking solution volume, often by using the glass in crushed form. This procedure may yield valid information on the properties of the bulk of the glass (Sykes, 1965), but these may be very different from the properties of the ancient glass surface, where protective layers of various types and other effects come into play.

One method of accelerating the deterioration of glass is to raise the temperature of its environment. An increase in temperature increases the rate of attack by aggressive agents; Paul (1977) states that, for most silicate glasses, the quantity leached in a given time is doubled for every 8 to 15°C rise in temperature, depending upon the composition of the glass and the type of alkali ion in question. Bacon (1968) gives the following formula:

$$\log t_1 = \log t_2 + (T_2 - T_1)/23.4$$

where t_1 and t_2 are the times for leaching at temperature T_1 and T_2 in °C. This produces a doubling in the rate of leaching for a rise of 7°C. The Chemical Durability Committee of the Society of Glass Technology have offered some comments on the factors which affect these temperature coefficients (Chemical Durability Committee, 1966); and there is the danger that reactions will occur at higher temperatures which hardly occur at all at ambient temperatures (Hench and Clark, 1978). In addition, the thickness of the protective high-silica surface layer formed on heating is far less than that formed at ambient temperatures. Another type of test which may yield results similar to those obtained in natural situations is the cyclic increase and decrease of humidity (Simpson, 1951, 1953). Suffice it to say, that before putting any conservation treatment which has been derived as a result of accelerated aging tests into practice, the conservator must carry out preliminary tests on ancient glass samples, to check its suitability.

The glass surface

The surface of a glass is highly influential in the effects of the weathering processes which occur on it. Weyl (1975) points out that a surface is a defect in itself, because all surface ions are in a state of incomplete coordination. This asymmetry of the surface produces abnormal interatomic distances and hence the space occupied by the surface ions is greater than usual, enabling replacement by ions of a larger or smaller radius to occur. Thus, as explained in the introductory pages to this chapter, the subsurface glass layer is porous. It is this microporosity that enables surface reaction with molecules of water, sulphur dioxide, oxygen and hydrochloric acid etc. to take place to a considerable depth.

Surface area

Surface area is an important factor in the corrosion of glass, as the amount of constituents released during decomposition is proportional to the exposed surface area. As the ratio of surface area to volume (SA/V) of the leaching solution increases, there is an increase in the extraction of silica. However, this can be attributed to the accompanying increase in pH of the solution on release of the alkali. In contrast, the quantity of alkali extracted does not vary with changing SA/V; it would be expected that the increase of pH would suppress further release of alkali from the glass, but this possibility is counteracted by the release of silica from the network as the pH increases but see Newton and Seddon, 1992. This dissolution of the silica network causes alkali to pass into solution, and reduces the thickness of the surface gel.

As the results of modern experiment, Hench (1977, 1982) and Hench and Clark (1978) have described six types of glass surface which are represented diagrammatically in *Figure 4.1.* Type I is an extremely thin

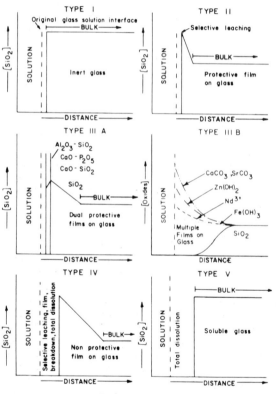

Figure 4.1 The six types of glass surface defined by Hench (1982).

hydrated surface with no significant change in surface composition; Type II is a silica-rich protective film with loss of alkali but no damage to the silica network; Type III is a double protective surface film of aluminium silicate or calcium phosphate, and can exist in two versions, IIIA and IIIB; Type IV is a silica-rich film, but the silica film is not thick enough to prevent loss of alkali or destruction of the silica network; Type V is soluble and may display

solution marks and a marked ability to form corrosion pits.

The Type I surface, with an extremely thin (less than 5 nm) hydrated layer and no significant change in surface composition, either by loss of alkali or of the silica network, represents an extremely durable glass (such as vitreous silica) exposed to a solution with a neutral pH. It is therefore unlikely that there are any ancient glasses with a Type I surface. A Type II surface possesses a silica-rich protective film, where the alkali has been lost but the silica network has not been damaged. The glass is very durable; it has a low alkali content and the pH of the leaching solution (for one reason or another) does not rise above 9.0.

Recent experiments have shown that exposure of a soda—lime–silica glass (such as a modern window glass or a container glass) to laboratory air for as little as 5 min results in a detectable change in the distribution of alkali at the surface. An extremely thin surface layer, only 5 nm thick, forms into which Na^+ and Ca^{2+} ions migrate, leaving a silica-rich layer 50 nm thick, and there is a corresponding increase in the H^+ ion concentration, thus confirming that ion-exchange had taken place. (When a container glass was exposed to pure water for 60 min at 37°C the resultant silica-rich layer was about 100 nm thick; Hench and Clark, 1978.) This silica-rich protective layer was of Type II; it clearly develops very quickly, and continued exposure to water increases its thickness.

Other procedures for reducing the alkali concentration in the surface layers, and thus improving the durability of commercial articles (at least until further ionic migration gradually nullifies the effect) have the same result of increasing the thickness of the silica-rich layer. They involve: heating the glass in a *glory hole* to produce a *fire-finished* surface; treatment with sulphur dioxide (Anderson *et al.,* 1975); treatment with sulphur, ammonium sulphate, ammonium chloride or aluminium chloride (Persson, 1962); treatment with fluorine (Brockway Glass Co., 1967); or simply *annealing* the glass (Brill, 1972).

A warning should be given here about the use of the autoclave tests to obtain an indication of the durability of a surface, since, for example, the Type II layer formed in the autoclave is much thinner than that formed at room temperature (Hench and Clark, 1978); in addition, the solubility of silica in water increases dramatically with temperature (Hench, 1977). The treatment of glass with sulphur dioxide (which depletes the sodium to a depth of 200 nm and produces a protective layer) can be removed by exposing the hot glass to water vapour (Bacon and Calcamuggio, 1967); and it seems inevitable that all such surface treatments, for example, flame-polishing (fire-finishing) will only be temporary because their effects will be destroyed by weathering, and by redistribution of alkali ions in the glass. There does not seem to be much experimental evidence on this point, although the brief study by El-Shamy (1973b) showed that a detectable redistribution of sodium ions occurred in 30 min at 100°C (or about 2.2 years at 15°C).

In cases such as the closely stacked window glass referred to on page 136, a durable Type II surface becomes poorly durable because the exposure conditions encourage the development of a highly alkaline solution. The key to this situation is the ratio of the surface of the glass (SA) to the volume of water (V) in contact with it; two sheets in contact had SA/V values greater than $100 \, cm^{-1}$ and the pH of the water rose to more than 9.0 in a few hours. For window glass an increase of SA/V from 100 to $1000 \, cm^{-1}$ increases the rate of attack on the glass by a factor of about 50 000 (Hench and Clark, 1978, see Figure 8). Therefore, it should not necessarily be considered that less harm is caused by a minute volume of water than by a large volume, since much more damage can be caused by a small volume of water trapped in prolonged contact with the glass.

A Type III surface (now called Type IIIA) has a double protective film on the surface. The addition of aluminium oxide or phosphorous oxide to the glass can add to the formation of an aluminium silicate- or a calcium phosphate-rich glass on top of a silica-rich layer. The glass is extremely durable both in acidic and alkaline solutions. These protective films can be produced by alkali extraction from a glass containing the oxides mentioned above, or by precipitating the alumina or phosphate from solution.

The addition of enough Al^{3+} ions to the water, for example, as aluminium chloride ($AlCl_3$) at a concentration of more than 25 ppm of Al^{3+}, can greatly reduce the deterioration of glass due to the formation of a Type III surface. The same formation can be brought about by adding alumina (Al_2O_3) when melting the glass. At first (for example, in the first few hours, depending on the Al_2O_3 content of the glass), the attack on such a glass can be relatively rapid, a Type V surface being formed, but within a day or two the situation becomes reversed due to the precipitation of an alumina–silicate complex on the surface (Hench and Clark, 1978).

There is thus a double layer (Type IIIA), an alumina-rich surface being formed on a silica-rich one, and the effects of both are to reduce greatly the leaching of alkali and the destruction of the network. In a similar manner the addition of 6 per cent of P_2O_5 to the glass produces a Type III surface, a layer rich in calcium phosphate being formed on top of a silica-rich layer. As the layer develops, the amorphous calcium phosphate film changes into a crystalline hydroxyapatite layer.

Many medieval window glasses contain substantial amounts of both Al_2O_3 and P_2O_5 and the formation of Type III surfaces must be considered as part of the general situation regarding their complex weathering behaviour.

Glasses with Type II or Type III surfaces appear quite glossy and unmarked, with any original surface blemishes easily visible, so that they may appear 'quite unweathered' to the uninitiated. Nevertheless, the surfaces would be largely free of alkali and would consist of a 'hydrogen glass'. Many Roman glasses are of this type and have led their owners to conclude that they are 'completely unweathered'. Cox and Pollard (1977), however, found that about 0.5 mm of the surface of Roman glasses must be removed before a satisfactory analysis can be obtained by X-ray fluorescence spectroscopy. The extremely durable blue twelfth-century stained glass also falls into this category (*CVMA News Letters*, 1976, 1977, 1978; Cox and Gillies, 1986). Oberlies (1956) described a case where an apparently unaltered 10 year old glass developed a roughened surface, visible under the electron microscope, when it was slightly heated, and she termed this 'invisible weathering'. Hydrated weathering layers, which look like unchanged glass, can be revealed by slow heating to 400–500°C and then show characteristic cracks (Geilmann, 1956, p. 146, col. 1 and Figures 3 and 4). A Type IIIB surface is the *sixth* type, added in 1982 (Hench, 1982), and it is characterized by the formation of *multiple* protective layers composed of oxides, hydroxides and hydrated silicates, but it is found on complex 'nuclear waste' glasses and need not trouble conservators.

A Type IV glass also has a silica-rich film but the silica concentration is insufficient to protect the glass from migration of alkali or destruction of the network. Many medieval window glasses fall into this category because they are rather low in silica.

A Type V glass is one which is soluble in the leaching solution, even if only slowly (e.g. 0.5 mm per century, as in much twelfth-century glass at York Minster: see Figure 6 of Newton, 1980a), and there is extensive loss of alkali accompanied by loss of silica. Because the attack is uniform, the surface composition is the same as that of the bulk glass, thus superficially resembling that of Type I, but Type I is extremely durable whereas Type V gradually dissolves in water and chemical analysis of the water would immediately disclose the difference. Type V glasses can also mislead the observer because at first sight they seem to be durable (Newton, 1969). Later Newton (1982a) realized that, far from being unweathered, the transparent samples showed much 'solution weathering' when viewed in oblique illumination. It is now suspected that much glass which had previously been considered to be 'durable' (for example, some Saxon vessel glass), may actually be of Type V, and they should therefore be re-examined in oblique illumination.

A Type V surface would be liable to form

corrosion pits because the *local* concentration of alkali in the pit can exceed pH 9.0 and then the local attack becomes progressive. This mechanism, and the manner in which it was investigated, is described in detail by Sanders and Hench (1973a).

In a similar manner, Type V surfaces are extremely susceptible to scratching and abrasion when the scratches are deeper than 0.2 µm. The scratch produces a small valley in which the extracted alkali can collect and progressive degradation of the network then occurs at that point (see *Figure 4.10*). This is well demonstrated by scanning electron micrographs (Sanders and Hench, 1973b) where the very fine scratches produced by 600-grit silicon carbide have developed into relatively deep (perhaps 0.4 µm) troughs by exposure to a small amount of water for 216 hours (this glass had a very low durability). When 120-grit silicon carbide was used as the abrasive, the resultant troughs are perhaps 1 µm deep (Sanders and Hench, 1973c). A striking example of this effect, in a fragment of Roman window glass from Great Casterton, Leicestershire, has been investigated by Newton *et al.* (1981). Here, as can be seen in *Figure 4.2*, the original scratches (of unknown

Factors affecting decomposition

Composition

Many experiments have been undertaken to study the durability phenomena of simple binary (silica and alkali) glasses, and these have been essential to understanding the fundamental behaviour of the durability of glass. However, binary glasses are not commercial glasses and they are not relevant to the problems of conservation; hence the discussion in this section will be restricted to glasses which have at least three components, silica, calcium oxide (lime) and an alkali metal oxide.

The majority of glasses are a network of silica and other metallic oxides in the roles of glass formers, intermediates and modifiers. Network formers are limited to those oxides which have high bond strengths, the most common being silicon oxide (silica). Modifiers break up the silica network, bonding ionically with the glassy network and altering properties such as viscosity, thermal expansion and durability. They have relatively low bond strengths and fall into two groups: *fluxes*, the oxides

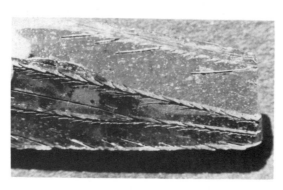

Figure 4.2 A fragment of Roman window glass from Great Casterton, Leicestershire, showing 'feather-type' cracking (oblique view).

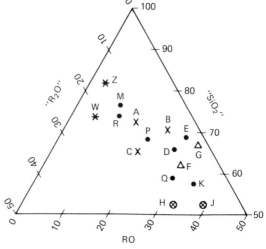

Figure 4.3 A triangular representation of glass compositions in which highly durable glasses (A, M, R) are placed near the centre, and the least durable glasses (H, J, K) fall at the bottom and to the right; glasses of the composition of W and Z may even decay in some museum atmospheres. A = Modern float glass; B = Gawber window glass of 1710; C = St Helens sheet glass of 1855; D = Bagots Park uncrusted glass; E = Rosedale glass; F = Bagots Park crusted glass; G = Hutton crusted glass; H = Austrian medieval glass; J = Ely Cathedral; M = Durable Saxon glass from Monkwearmouth; R = Roman glass; P,Q = 12th Century York Minster glasses; W = 'Weeping' glass; Z = crizzled glass. From Iliffe and Newton (1976).

depth) have produced the classical subsidiary branches and these must have been very shallow; yet after some 1700 years' burial the central cracks are some 1.5–2.5 mm deep and the side branches are 0.3–0.7 mm deep. The original surface is shiny, with some iridescent patches, and the glass would be regarded as being highly durable, yet the presence of a surface scratch has caused it to behave locally as if it were poorly durable, with a loss of substance of about 0.15 mm per century.

of sodium, potassium etc., which reduce the viscosity; and *stabilizers*, the oxides of calcium, magnesium etc., which improve the chemical durability and/or prevent crystallization. Oxides such as those of aluminium and iron are *intermediates*, and enter glass in either a forming or modifying position, having intermediate bond strengths. It is largely the presence, type and quantity of the modifiers which impair the highly durable nature of a pure silica network (*Figure 4.3*). In general the greater proportion of glass modifier such as calcium to sodium or potassium, the more stable the glass. However, if a glass containing large amounts of calcium oxide (lime) does deteriorate, the calcium will be leached out along with the sodium. The remaining silica may be so small a proportion as to be unable to maintain the bonds, thus the glass will disintegrate. The alkali/silica ratio is also important, the greater the percentage of silica, the less tendency for it to be extracted, the reverse being true in the case of the alkali. However, as previously explained in Chapters 1 and 3, additions to the glass network were (and still are) necessary for economic and technical reasons: pure silica melts at 1720°C, a temperature which could not be achieved in primitive furnaces. Even at lower temperatures the glass was too viscous to work. Therefore, to reduce the viscosity, fluxes such as soda or potash were added to the molten silica.

Silica content

The silica content of glasses is significant in the formation of a crusted layer typical of some corroded glasses. In attempting to resolve the problem of the Bagot's Park glasses and in using glasses in the potassium, calcium, magnesium and silicon oxide systems, El-Shamy (1973a) demonstrated that there was an increased tendency to form a crusted layer as the silica content of the glass decreased. This occurred critically when the silica content fell below 66.7 mol per cent. A rapid increase in leaching or corrosion occurs when the silica content drops below this percentage because it is at this composition that every silicon atom is associated with a modifier, calcium, sodium etc., atom as a second neighbour. Consequently there is always an interconnecting path of neighbouring silicon oxide ($Si-O^-$) groups which provide suitable sites for the movement of interchanging species between the solution and the glass. Above this percentage the $Si-O^-$ groups are isolated by $Si-O-Si$ groups which suppress the movement of ions involved in leaching.

The static fatigue strength changes little with the surface condition of the glass and varies inversely with the thermal expansion coefficient. Fused silica has the lowest coefficient of expansion, hence the highest stress resistance and durability.

Alkali content

Sick glass, that is, that which is *weeping* (*sweating*) or which has become crizzled, is the result of an excess of alkali and a deficiency of lime in the glass composition (Kämpfer, 1963; Brill, 1975). Weeping glass repeatedly generates a slippery surface or droplets of moisture if the glass is exposed to humid conditions, as the result of chemically uncombined alkali being leached out by the action of water vapour (*Figure 4.4*). Crizzled glass surfaces have diminished transparency owing to the formation of very fine surface crazing, and again suffer from the removal of alkali ions (*Figure 4.5*). Briefly, Brill's analyses of sick glasses reveal calcium oxide contents between 0.3 and 4.7 wt per cent, and potassium oxide contents sometimes as high as 24 wt per cent (17 mol per cent), although there is an early French glass (*circa* 1600) quoted which contains almost 18 per cent sodium

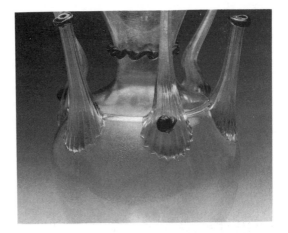

Figure 4.4 Close-up view of a weeping glass vessel, showing the drops of alkaline moisture which form on the surface. British Museum, London.

Figure 4.5 A crizzled posset pot. British Museum, London.

oxide; some late nineteenth-century American glasses which are based on soda; and two others which contain substantial amounts of lead. Maintaining a satisfactory environment for them seems to be the most suitable conservation procedure to prevent further deterioration.

Brill (1972, 1975) also drew attention to other glasses described as showing *incipient crizzling*, and it seems possible that these possess thick Type IV (thin silica-rich) surfaces since it is stated that they

> ... have taken up water over the centuries but ... do not exhibit very obvious signs of deterioration .... They have become hydrated and equilibrated over the centuries with humid environments. When brought into centrally heated galleries or apartments, they may be subjected abruptly to very dry conditions during the winter months .... Under such conditions these hydrated glasses become dehydrated, and the crizzling fissures ... open up ... this may happen in the course of only a few months (Brill, 1975).

Brill (1975) then showed that such glasses develop crizzles if stored in a relative humidity of 0–20 per cent, due to *dehydration* of the leached layer; it is thus possible that they really had a different type of surface, a Type IV surface, whereas the true sick glasses seem to have a Type V surface. It was concluded that storage in the range 40–60 per cent relative humidity is safe. (Formerly, Organ, 1957, had suggested that high-potash, low-lime glass should be kept at a relative humidity of less than 42 per cent, corresponding to the vapour pressure at which potassium carbonate deliquesces.) Sick glasses are also discussed by Bakardjiev (1977a,b,), Scholze (1978) and Werner (1958).

When the sixteenth-century glassworks at Bagot's Park, Staffordshire, was excavated in 1967, about 300 kg of glass was found in the cullet heap (Crossley, 1967). It was most remarkable that half of the material had a heavy, opaque weathering crust whereas the other half was quite uncrusted and transparent. Yet all the cullet had presumably been made on the same site and all had been subjected to the same weathering conditions. Chemical analyses of the two kinds of glass showed surprisingly little difference; the crusted glass contained 55.5 wt per cent SiO_2 and the uncrusted glass contained about 58 wt per cent SiO_2, but at the time this difference was regarded as unimportant and the difference in weathering behaviour was regarded as a mystery (Newton, 1969). The problem was solved in 1973 when El-Shamy (1973a) showed that the tendency of glass to form a crusted layer increases rapidly as the silica content of the glass falls below 66 mol per cent, the point at which every silicon atom in the glass becomes associated with a basic ion as its second neighbour. It is now well known, from the work of

Bettembourg (1976a), Collongues (1977), Cox *et al.* (1979), Perez-y-Jorba *et al.* (1975), Schreiner (1987) and Newton and Fuchs (1988), that crusting of the surface is likely to occur when the amount of network-forming oxides is less than about 62 mol per cent (see *Figure 4.3*).

A reduction in the corrosion rate of glass can be observed when a second alkali is added to a binary alkali system, that is, a *mixed alkali effect*. For example, when soda and potash are both present the durability of glass containing 3 mol per cent potassium oxide and 12 mol per cent sodium oxide is about twice that of a 15 per cent sodium oxide glass (Hench and Clark, 1978).

The maximum formation of the silica film depends on the type of alkali in the glass and there is a decrease in stability when there is a change from glasses with small cations to those with larger ones, provided the total alkali is less than 10 per cent. Results show that there is a decrease in resistance in the series: lithium, sodium, potassium, rubidium and caesium (the last two being similar) and that these differences are related to the stability of the surface film.

Small quantities of Al^{3+} or phosphorus, either in the glass or in the leaching solution, have also been observed to block the leaching reaction. Once again this is due to the increased stability of the surface film. The efficacy of aluminium in increasing the resistance to corrosion is in principle due to the reduced production of non-bridging oxygens, the fourfold coordination of the AlO_4^- requires alkali cations to maintain electrical neutrality.

However, the most significant reduction occurs in the 2–5 mol per cent aluminium oxide range, well below that required to eliminate all the non-bridging oxygens. This reduction is the consequence of the formation of an insoluble alumino-silicate which precipitates onto the silica-rich surface of the glass. In the case of phosphorus, there is a precipitation of calcium phosphate on to the surface of the glass, both hindering the diffusion of the alkali, and the breakdown of the silica network.

The change in durability on the addition of transition metal ions and others is complex. One Japanese study (Ohta and Suzuki, 1978) showed that the water resistance of the soda—lime–silica–R_mO_n glass is improved in the order: Ta_2O_5, La_2O_3, PbO, TiO_2, ZrO_2, MnO_2, $SnO_2 = Al_2O_3$. That resistance to alkaline conditions in the same series is improved with the oxides of zirconium, lanthanum, tin and chromium; unaffected by tantalum, titanium and manganese; and deteriorates with the oxides of aluminium, phosphorus, iron and lead. While this study suggests that aluminium causes a deterioration in resistance to alkaline conditions, others have shown it to improve durability even under basic conditions.

The mixed alkali effect described above is discernable when rapid ion-exchange is occurring but not when the reactions are very slow. Thus its occurrence during laboratory experiments is unlikely to help in explaining some of the unexpected weathering characteristics of ancient glasses.

Stabilizers

The addition of lime (CaO) to binary silicate glasses is known to increase the durability. If lime (CaO) is added to the glass in increasing amounts up to 10 mol per cent there is a rapid decline in soda extraction, owing to the increasing stability of the surface gel. The stability is due to the presence of CaO increasing the coupling of the vibrational modes of the silica non-bridging oxygen modifier bonds to the bridging of the $Si-O-Si$ network. It would be expected that the replacement of one Ca^{2+} ion by two protons (H^+) would have the same effect as replacing two K^+ ions from the network, but in the latter case a much more porous layer is formed.

If the lime content is increased above 15 mol per cent, the weathering resistance starts being drastically reduced, and it is hardly surprising that those medieval window glasses which contain 35 per cent CaO are now in rather poor condition. Lime was not specified as a constituent of ancient glasses and hence durable glasses were prepared more or less accidentally either from calcareous sands (in ancient times) or from high-lime wood ash (in medieval times); thus it is not surprising that there was a period when the addition of (extra) lime was regarded as being positively harmful (Turner, 1956a).

The effect of lime in terms of the amount present and its effect on the resistance of the glass to water or to acids is somewhat complicated, but a useful discussion (and guide to the literature before 1968) is given by Bacon (1968).

As mentioned above, the optimum lime content is about 10 mol per cent of CaO in the final glass, but some glasses were made in the middle of the seventeenth century by Ravenscroft (particularly in the period 1674–76), and in Venice at the beginning of the eighteenth century, which now have *crizzled* or *weeping* surfaces. Although these are the classical examples, other examples can be found in tableware from many countries; and nineteenth-century crizzled glasses are known. These glasses are characterized by lime contents which are usually less than 5 mol per cent CaO (and sometimes less than 1 per cent CaO) and their situation is frequently made worse because they contain potash as the alkali instead of soda. (Here it should be emphasized that modern lead crystal glass is made with potash, instead of soda, but it is a properly stabilized glass.) Additions of magnesium oxide and strontium oxide had a similar effect as calcium oxide, confirming the role of the alkaline earths as stabilizers in the silica network.

In 1975, when the concept of a triangular diagram was being developed as an aid to understanding the durability of glasses, it was realized that lime and magnesia had somewhat different effects on the durability of the glasses which contained them. It was thought that these differences would be largely removed if the proportions of these oxides were calculated on a molar basis, instead of on a weight basis, because the molecular weight of MgO is only 72 per cent that of CaO (Newton, 1975b; Brill in Newton, 1975b). However, the work of Cox *et al.* (1979) showed that the medieval window glasses which contained more than about 6 mol per cent MgO tended to behave differently from those which contained less than this amount, even when compared on a molar basis, and it was suspected that microphase separation was occurring at these levels of MgO. In addition, in these window glasses, the heavy crust of gypsum and syngenite which forms on the high-lime glasses seems likely to trap moisture in it, and hence accelerate the weathering, but such a crust would presumably not form on a glass which contained a comparable amount of MgO because magnesium carbonate and magnesium sulphate are so much more soluble than the corresponding calcium compounds (Perez-y-Jorba *et al.*, 1975).

Other modifiers

As previously mentioned, the presence of Al_2O_3 or P_2O_5 in the glass brings about a dramatic increase in durability, and it seems that these polyvalent ions have the power to immobilize the alkali ions, so that they are no longer free to move through the silicate network. Das and Douglas (1967) showed that zinc, lead, titanium and zirconium improved the durability, although only the first two, in addition to aluminium and phosphorus, are likely to be present in appreciable amounts in ancient glasses. The addition of these ions to the water which is in contact with the glass also depresses the extraction of alkali and the formation of the leached layer; copper, however, has a noticeable inhibiting effect (Bacon, 1968).

Metal oxide colourants

It has long been maintained that, because differently coloured glasses decay in different manners, the colour *per se* influenced the weathering. This seems to be false, and arises from the mistaken impression that all glass made for the same window (and hence made at the same time by the same glassmaker) will have essentially the same composition. For example,

Knowles (1935) wrote 'It is not surprising that in the Annunciation panel the *coloured* glasses are corroded and the rest not. In fact, that is what is to be expected', and Bauer (1967a) reported that bluish-green glass at Heiligenkreuz was particularly durable. In fact, there was little control over raw materials in medieval times, and the sources of colouring oxides might be highly contaminated by, for example, clay or lime, both of which would profoundly affect the weathering of glass made with it. In 1972 attention was drawn to a late twelfth-century border panel from the nave clerestory of York Minster in which all the pink glass had resisted weathering, and had shiny surfaces, whereas the green glass had rough crusted surfaces. Partial analyses of the glasses revealed that the green pieces contained relatively more lime, compared with potash, than did the pink pieces and it was this difference in composition, rather than the colour *per se*, which was responsible for the differences in weathering (Hedges and Newton, 1974). Brill (1975) drew attention to another common misunderstanding, that pink glasses are likely to crizzle; he pointed out that the pink colour is confined to the weathered layer and the glass is colourless when the crizzled layer is removed.

Nevertheless, there are some cases where the agent which affects the durability imparts a particular colour to the glass. Paul and Youssefi (1978a) have shown that the state of oxidation of the iron in the glass can affect the durability and also the colour. A green glass which contains FeO can be made more durable by oxidizing it to the corresponding yellow glass which contains Fe_2O_3, and they showed that the oxidized glasses had superior resistance to acids; Jantzen and Plodinec (1984) also discuss a similar case.

The paint, and/or the yellow stain, fired on to stained glass can have quite complicated effects on the durability of the underlying glass (Bauer, 1967b). The paint is generally more durable than the glass so that, after weathering, the painted linework may be raised above the rest of the surface of the glass (*Figure 4.6*) but less frequently it can have the reverse effect. The example in *Figure 4.7* is particularly striking because deep corrosion has occurred, but only where the glass had been painted.

In the case of the yellow stain, Knowles (1959) stated, incorrectly, that 'The yellow stain which is applied always to the back of the glass [i.e. facing the outside of the building] invariably protects it from corrosion'. An example where silver stain has been protective is shown in *Figure 4.8*, but there are plenty of examples where the reverse is the case and the stained areas have encouraged attack by the weather, as in *Figure 4.9*. Some linear attack may be the result of surface scratches, or of inhomogeneities in the glass, but the piece of glass in *Figure 4.10* with corroded lines on it shows no evidence of having

Figure 4.6 Fourteenth-century glass from York Minster, showing how the painted decoration has prevented the formation of the crust in the painted areas. Courtesy of the Dean and Chapter, York.

Figure 4.7 Glass from the church at Stanford-on-Avon, Northamptonshire. The deep pitted corrosion occurs only in areas where the glass has been painted. The smooth areas are the paint, and the mottled areas the unpainted glass. Courtesy of the Dean and Chapter, York.

Figure 4.8 An example of glass showing the protective action of silver stain against deterioration. Courtesy of the Dean and Chapter, York.

Figure 4.9 Fifteenth-century glass from York Minster, on which the corrosion has taken place along the lines of the silver-stained pattern. Courtesy of the Dean and Chapter, York.

Figure 4.10 Fourteenth-century glass from York Minster on which the corrosion has occurred along scratch-lines, or perhaps along lines of inhomogeneity. Courtesy of the Dean and Chapter, York.

been painted on either side (see also Maurer and Gratwohl, 1986).

It is possible to invent hypotheses in an attempt to explain some of the phenomena; for example, the paint could encourage corrosion if it had too high an alkali content, and it might protect the glass if it lost much of its alkali content to the atmosphere during firing. Similarly, the protective effect of silver stain could readily be explained on the grounds that the

sodium ions in the surface have been replaced by silver ions, and leaching of the silver would not make the solution alkaline in the way that sodium ions would. Also, the silver compounds were applied in a medium or 'mud' of various binders, and one of these might have caused the effect found in *Figure 4.9*. None of these plausible hypotheses has however yet been put to the test.

However, another earlier mystery, that of *back-matching corrosion*, has been solved. Knowles (1935) suggested that the enamel on the inside seemed to extract something out of the glass and render it more liable to corrosion on the *outside*; and in 1959 that 'the shading on the *inside* causes pitting to form on the *outside* which corresponds exactly in form and extent to the degree in which the enamel has been thickly or thinly applied on the other'. In 1972 it was widely believed that the paint on the inside could affect the corrosion on the outside, but it has now been shown (Newton, 1976d) that the corrosion on the outside is restricted to areas where the original artist, in a wish to strengthen the design on the inside, had applied *matting* (smeared or stippled paint) on the outside to supplement, and hence match, the paintwork on the inside. The matting was porous and could retain water, thus encouraging corrosion to take place (see *Figures 4.11a and b*).

Another case of weathering being affected by paintwork is the existence of ghost images. These have been shown (Newton, 1976d) to be caused by the volatilization of alkali from the paint on another piece of glass from the same panel when both were fired, one on top of the other, in the same kiln; the volatilized alkali rendered the glass less durable so that it lost 0.2 mm thickness in eight centuries (0.025 mm per century). All of the cases quoted above have recently been discussed by Newton (1982a, 1985b).

The leading on window glass has also been reported as having an effect on the durability of the glass. In some cases the corrosion appears to be enhanced along the sides of the leading, perhaps by virtue of moisture being retained under the lip of the leads if the cement had fallen out. Marchini (1972) drew attention to the many windows in Italy where loss of painted decoration had occurred along horizontal parts of the leading, and he attributed this to corrosion by condensed water which contained atmospheric pollutants; because the lead is a better conductor of heat than glass, there is greater tendency for dew to form along the leads. What are more difficult to understand are the many cases where the middle part of a piece of glass has corroded but the corrosion is absent in a band within about 20 mm of the leading.

If the leads have been cemented well, the original thickness of the glass can be estimated by measuring the part which had been protected, for example, as in

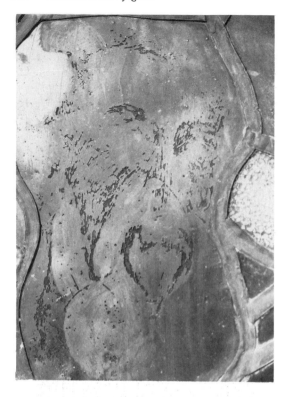

Figure 4.11 Mid-fourteenth-century glass from York Minster showing the phenomenon of 'back-matching' corrosion. (a) Exterior, (b) interior. Courtesy of Dean and Chapter, York.

Figure 4.12 Twelfth-century glass from York Minster showing protection against weathering around the leaded edges. The unprotected area is severely crusted, and deterioration has occurred preferentially in an oblique groove, presumably the site of an old scratch. Courtesy of the Dean and Chapter, York.

Figure 4.12, in any case, the original thickness would not have been greater than the width of the 'heart' of the leading. The surface of the weathered glass may also be influenced by the leading in other ways. Caviness (1971) states that the examination of some glass at Canterbury Cathedral, to which strap leads had been attached in 1850, shows that greater corrosion of the surface had taken place in the period 1850–90 than had occurred between 1180 and 1850, no doubt because water could be retained between the strap and the glass. The situation at Cothele Church in Cornwall (*Figures 4.13a,b*) seems to be an example of water being trapped at lead lines between two glazings which touched each other.

Much insight has been gained into the relative weathering behaviour of different glasses through the use of a *triangular diagram*, as in *Figure 4.3* (Newton, 1975b; Iliffe and Newton, 1976). The compositions of the glasses are first converted to molecular percentages of the constituent oxides and these are then combined into three categories, the network formers, the alkaline earth network modifiers and the *effective* alkali content.

The constituents of the glass exercise their effect on the weathering of that glass by virtue of the *numbers*

(a)

(b)

Figure 4.13 A fifteenth-century window from Cothele Church in Cornwall. After removal of the diamond-quarried external glazing in 1880, it was found that the medieval glass had deteriorated preferentially in areas which had been covered by the leading, the result of condensation. (a) Exterior view showing white, diamond-shaped patterns of corrosion; (b) interior view showing the (dark) diamond-shaped corrosion patterns. Courtesy of D.G. King.

of their molecules, in association with each other, and not by the *weight* of those molecules (which is the convention usually adopted, in reporting the results of analyses of glasses). The difference between the numbers of molecules and the weight of the molecules would not matter if all the molecules had similar weights, but this is by no means the case. The two main alkalis differ considerably, because the molecule of potash (K_2O) is 52 per cent heavier than the molecule of soda (Na_2O) [and more than three times that of lithia (Li_2O), which occurs occasionally in ancient glasses]. Similarly, a molecule of lime (CaO) is 39 per cent heavier than the molecule of magnesia (MgO) and lead oxide is 550 per cent heavier than MgO.

To obtain the relative numbers of molecules, the weight percentages are divided by the factors in *Table 4.1* (which are each one-hundredth of the corresponding molecular weight), and then the results are adjusted so that their total is 100 per cent. The method of calculation is easy to follow from the worked example given in *Table 4.2*. The first column is the composition of the glass in terms of its constituent oxides; the second column is the usual weight percentage distribution of these oxides; and the third column gives the factors, taken from *Table 4.1*, by which the weight percentages are divided. The fourth column gives the relative molar proportions, and their total is 162.4 so that each has to be divided by 1.624 in order to obtain the molar

Table 4.1 Factors for converting weight percentages into relative molar percentages, for frequently occurring glass-making oxides

Oxide	Factor	Oxide	Factor	Oxide	Factor
SiO_2	0.601	PbO	2.232	Al_2O_3	1.020
K_2O	0.942	CuO	0.796	Fe_2O_3	1.597
Na_2O	0.620	MnO	0.710	Sb_2O_3	2.915
Li_2O	0.299	ZnO	0.814	As_2O_3	1.979
CaO	0.561	CoO	0.749	B_2O_3	0.696
MgO	0.403	TiO_2	0.799	P_2O_5	1.420
BaO	1.534	SnO_2	0.507	SO_3	0.801

Table 4.2 Worked example, converting weight percentages to molar percentages

Oxide	Weight percentage	Factor	Relative molar proportions	Molar percentage
SiO_2	64.3	0.601	107.0	65.9
K_2O	16.7	0.942	17.7	10.9
Na_2O	0.7	0.620	1.1	0.7
CaO	10.0	0.561	17.8	11.0
MgO	7.1	0.403	17.6	10.8
Al_2O_3	1.2	1.019	1.2	0.7
	100.0		162.4	100.0

percentages given in the fifth column. It should be noted that the weight percentages of MgO, CaO and K_2O are quite different, but the molar percentages are almost the same.

These molar proportions of oxides (*Table 4.2*) are combined according to the following rules:

The alkaline earth component, RO, is obtained by adding together all the oxides with this formula, i.e. CaO + MgO + MnO + CuO + PbO etc. In this example it is CaO + MgO, or 11.0 + 10.8 = 21.8 per cent.

The network formers are almost entirely silica (SiO_2) but forest-type glasses often contain as much as 5 per cent P_2O_5 and this must be added to the SiO_2, as well as any TiO_2, ZrO_2, SnO_2 etc. In addition, it was shown in Chapter 1 that Al_2O_3 occupies a special place, each molecule being able to immobilize an alkali ion, and it can also be incorporated into the network. Thus the total of the network oxides has to be increased by *twice* the Al_2O_3 (and similar oxides, such as Fe_2O_2, Cr_2O_3 etc). In the example, the total of network-forming oxides (called 'SiO_2' because it is mainly SiO_2) is given by $SiO_2 + 2(Al_2O_3) = 65.9 + 1.4 = 67.3$ per cent.

The remaining component in the triangular diagram is the alkali oxide, called 'R_2O' because it represents only the *available* alkali, and not the total alkali, some of the alkali being immobilized by the alumina. Thus 'R_2O' = K_2O + Na_2O − Al_2O_3 = 10.9 + 0.7 − 0.7 = 10.9 per cent.

The total of RO + 'SiO_2' + 'R_2O' = 21.8 + 67.3 + 10.9 = 100 per cent. When the three values are plotted in the triangular diagram, shown in *Figure 4.3*, some care may be needed and it should be noted that in each case the coordinate lines run parallel to the side which becomes the base when the triangle is turned so that the numbers can be read in a horizontal manner.

In *Figure 4.3*, modern float glass is indicated by the cross at A and two examples of less-durable window glass at B (Gawber window glass of 1710; Ashurst, 1970) and C (St Helens sheet glass of 1855; Pilkington, 1855). The dots at M and R indicate the durable glass from Monkwearmouth (Cramp, 1970) and from Roman sites (Caley, 1962), thus this upper-central area indicates the range of durable glasses. The dots at D and E indicate four *uncrusted* samples (from Bagot's Park dated 1535; Crossley, 1967) and from Rosedale (Crossley and Aberg, 1972) and the corresponding *crusted* samples are indicated by the triangles F and G (F from Bagot's Park; Crossley, 1967; and G from Hutton; Crossley and Aberg, 1972). These four points confirm the fact that durability decreases when the silica content is less than 66.7 mol per cent, the line separating D and F being at 65 mol per cent of network formers. Points P and Q indicate the two types of twelfth-century stained glass from York Minster, one pink and one green (Hedges and Newton, 1974). The crosses within circles at H and J are medieval window glasses of a poorly durable nature with heavily crusted surfaces [H is from Austria (courtesy of Frodl-Kraft) and J is from the Lady Chapel of Ely Cathedral (courtesy of D. King)]. These glasses have decayed badly and represent a serious problem in conservation. The dot at K is the medieval glass from Weobley Castle, excavated in 1934 (Raw, 1955); in its decay it has lost thickness at the rate of 0.35 mm per century. Thus the glasses in the bottom right-hand corner of *Figure 4.3* decay so rapidly that they would lose 3–5 mm per millennium and any pre-Christian glass having such a poor durability would have had to have been more than 10 mm thick for any of it to have survived to the present century. The two remaining points, the stars at W and Z, indicate, respectively, weeping and crizzling glasses studied by Brill; thus the durability decreases very markedly as soon as the composition of the glass moves a little to the left of the group A, M, R. The importance of the RO (lime) content can now be seen by considering the glasses Z,M,A,P,D,F,J; they all have about 15 mol per cent of available alkali but the RO varies from less than 5 mol per cent in Z to nearly 40 mol per cent in J and the durable glasses lie in a narrow band between 10 and 20 per cent RO.

Thus the triangular diagram is of great advantage in helping to display the effects of these differences in composition, but its limitations should not be forgotten. For example, it does not discriminate between soda and potash, yet the soda glasses have about twice the durability of the potash glasses; nor does it discriminate between the effects of lime and magnesia; nor is it concerned with the type of surface and it is likely that those in the 'upper-central' area will have a Type III surface so that their apparent durability will be enhanced. It is even probable that there is a central plateau of very highly durable glass and the durability will fall off, suddenly and precipitously (rather like Figure 17 of Newton, 1985a), especially as the composition moves to the left but also as one moves towards the bottom right-hand corner; if so, it could have a bearing on the existence of highly durable pre-Christian glasses and complete absence (through deterioration) of glasses with less durable compositions.

The triangular diagram has clear advantages in displaying the effects of changes in the composition of the glass, but for its use it is necessary to have a complete analysis of the glass, and then to convert the results to molar compositions (although it is easy to program a computer to do this). However, the fact that most of the glasses lie on the line Z to J, discussed above, means that, in the majority of cases, it is necessary only to know the molar proportion of network formers in order to establish approximately where the glass will lie in the diagram. Thus, as a first approximation, the problems of analysis and calculation can be reduced by determining only the silica content. In fact Figure 1 of Cox *et al.* (1978) is dominated by the lines of equal SiO_2 content. El-Shamy and Ahmed (1977) discuss the basic rules for predicting the corrosion behaviour of glass from its composition. A method of predicting the durability of glasses on thermodynamic grounds has been published by Newton and Paul (1980).

Other factors associated with deterioration

In addition to the composition and environment of glass, there are a number of other factors which appear to be associated with its deterioration. Devitrification (in the chemical sense, *not* as used by archaeologists) may cause decomposition by virtue of the stress it creates in the surrounding glass. There has been a debate over whether a significant amount of devitrification occurs in glass over the centuries at ordinary temperatures. Claims have been made both for (Kny and Nauer, 1977) and against (Newton, 1982b) and further work needs to be carried out in order for any conclusion to be reached. The rate of devitrification will depend upon the composition of the glass in the region of devitrification and on the temperature.

Environment

Under the heading of environment, both general and local conditions will be considered. Environmental factors affecting decomposition are: (1) water in the atmosphere both inside and outside buildings (precipitation, humidity, condensation), or in the context of waterlogged or underwater burial sites; and (2) pollution of the atmosphere by gases which combine with water to produce acid solutions and/or form concretions. The effects of these agencies are linked to time and temperature. In the case of land or underwater burials the effects of impurities may also have to be considered (Weier, 1973). Other environmental factors to be considered in connection with glass decomposition are those of solarization, microorganisms, previous treatments and, more recently, vibrations caused by road, rail and air traffic.

Water

As previously mentioned, it has been shown that water and, above all, accumulated moisture are the most important factors initiating and sustaining forms of glass decomposition. Even damage caused by dehydration is the consequence of previous attack by water. Without water or moisture, glass can remain in excellent condition for centuries, little, if any, attack occurring in dry conditions. Water is essential for the replacement by protons of the diffusing alkali ions and the subsequent hydration of the silica network. It also removes the soluble salts formed from such reactions.

pH of the attacking solution

The water of the attacking solution will usually be either slightly acidic or alkaline depending on the soil or the atmospheric conditions. Many studies have investigated the role of changing pH on the corrosion of glass.

In general, the rate of alkali extraction in a buffered system at a pH of less than 9 is constant and independent of pH. There are exceptions to this, for example in a soda–lime–silica glass where the lime content is greater than 10 mol per cent there is a rapid increase in the rate of extraction when the pH drops below 3. The increased extraction is due to the increased solubility of lime, whose extraction was otherwise negligible. In contrast to alkali extraction, silica extraction is almost non-existent below pH 9, but increases noticeably above this.

Encrustations of carbonates, sulphates and silicates may form to obliterate the surface of buried glass in climates where there is sufficient precipitation to dissolve these compounds (which are nevertheless regarded as 'insoluble' since they are poorly soluble in water), but where there is also sufficient evaporation to permit them to be deposited again. Silicates are the least common since they are the least soluble but where they exist in the soil in great quantity, as in Egypt, a crust of them may form, although the rainfall there is so slight that it is not a usual phenomenon.

More recent research work seems to have been undertaken on the effect of alkalis on glasses than on the effects of acids, since commercial glasses are resistant to mineral acids on a relatively short time-scale (with the exception of hydrofluoric acid which readily attacks glass), whereas alkalis can cause great damage unless the glass has been specially formulated to be alkali resistant. However, there has been much work on the effect of dilute acetic acid (representing fruit juices) on the release of lead from enamelled ware. Many authors have shown that the attack by alkali becomes serious when the pH value reaches 9, and Scholze and Corbach (1971) showed that alkali attack will produce a surface which

contains very fine pores with sizes determined by the radius of the alkali ions being extracted (for soda-lime glasses the pore diameter is 0.3 to 0.4 nm). The presence of zinc and aluminium ions in the solution (or in the glass) can reduce the amount of alkaline attack (Geffcken, 1939, and many others). Tarnopol and Junge (1946) exposed samples of plate glass to various solutions, and comment that, even at 65°C the attack by mineral acids is about 15 μm per year (1.5 mm per century) whereas a 5 per cent solution of potassium hydroxide will attack the glass at a rate of 150 μm per year (15 mm per century). The quantity of alkali extracted in a given period of time increases with temperature. Approximately doubling with every 10–15°C depending on the composition of the glass and the type of alkali.

Many ancient glasses contain insufficient calcium to stabilize them and in any moist conditions, which inevitably obtain in an acid soil, the alkalis are replaced by hydrogen ions from the water and hence form a dilute solution of sodium or potassium hydroxide. The result is a surface layer richer in silica than the rest of the glass, and in time and in a variable humidity many silica layers may form due to cyclical phenomena (Newton, 1971a, footnote to p. 7). Carbonic acid may also help in the formation of alkali carbonates which, being hygroscopic, will attract more moisture to the glass.

El-Shamy et al. (1972) studied the effect of acids, down to pH 1.0, and showed that the pH was not important unless there was some 20 mol per cent of CaO in the glass, when the extraction of Na_2O and CaO increased greatly as the pH was reduced below about 4; and that such high-lime glasses are readily soluble in mineral acids (see also El-Shamy et al., 1975).

El-Shamy (1973a) gave special attention to medieval-type glasses and showed that the extraction of CaO by 0.5 M HCl (hydrochloric acid) was greatly increased when the CaO content of the glass was as much as 15 mol per cent, and the same applied to MgO when it was present at 15 mol per cent. When the CaO and the MgO were both present at 15 mol per cent, the extraction of both was more than doubled. Neither of these papers discusses what happens to medieval-type glasses exposed to weak acids, such as carbonic acid (a solution of CO_2 in water) or sulphurous acid (a solution of SO_2 in water), when the pH value is between 6 and 7, corresponding to rainwater or even polluted rainwater. This is a field which should be properly explored in the future. Ferrazzini (1976a) used 1 M HCl on a medieval glass and produced an ion-exchanged layer 1 mm thick in 1 hour.

Effect of complexing agents

In soils, particularly in peats and the humic horizons, there are numerous chelating or complexing agents, for example, amines, citrates, acetates. Many of these have a detrimental effect on the durability of buried glass. Paul and Youssefi (1978b) report that the presence of ethylene diaminetetraacetic acid (EDTA) and citrates are equally corrosive. EDTA favours rapid lead extraction in potash–lead–silicate glasses, and as a consequence increases the potash extraction.

If the complexes are water soluble, then there will be an increase in the rate of corrosion of the glass. In the absence of EDTA, the extraction of lead from the above glass at pH 9 is very small, but as the concentration of EDTA increases the K_2O/PbO extracted ratio decreases. This enhancement of potassium extraction is not due to the formation of complex K^+ salts, as potassium does not form a stable complex. It is due more to the removal of the blocking effect of the lead from the hydrated silica surface, hence an increase of diffusion.

Sugar forms a soluble complex with CaO, and although this oxide is normally expected to stabilize the network, it was observed that the presence of sugar almost doubled the extraction of Ca^{2+}. A slight increase in extraction of Na^+ and silica is probably due to the increase in surface area and reduction of the normal retarding effect of the CaO. Hence *all* chemical cleaning solutions should be examined for the presence of chelating agents.

Complexing agents can also decrease the rate of corrosion as in the case of ethanol which is adsorbed onto the surface of the hydrated silica and forms insoluble ethyl silicate which acts as a protective layer, retarding leaching. One of the worrying aspects of chemical cleaning of medieval window glass is that EDTA is recommended for use (Bettembourg, 1973; Bettembourg and Burck, 1974) and hence great care is needed to leave the preparations on the surface for the minimum time, and to monitor continuously the progress of cleaning.

Reaction with atmospheric gases and moisture ('acid rain')

This vexed, and highly political, subject deserves some mention, if only to remove some mis-apprehensions (Frey, 1973). The sulphur dioxide (SO_2) problem cannot be entirely divorced from that of carbon dioxide (CO_2) because it seems that sulphur dioxide may produce its effect *only after* there has been a reaction between the primary products of corrosion and the CO_2. The effects on glass of the oxides of nitrogen has not yet been established, and there does not seem to be any relevant information in the literature.

In 1962 the average CO_2 content of the air was 315 ppm and it was increasing at about 1.4 per cent per year (Stanford, 1968). It does not attack glass directly but converts the hydroxides, produced by the attack of water on glass, to carbonates and is responsible for the calcite frequently found in the weathering crust (e.g. Perez-y-Jorba *et al.*, 1975, 1978, 1980). The increase in level of 1.4 per cent per annum of CO_2 (Stanford, 1968) has however been so slow that it cannot have caused the increase in corrosion of medieval glass noticed since 1945.

Dry sulphur dioxide does not attack glass at room temperature (Douglas and Isard, 1949; Adlerborn, 1971). Ferrazzini (1976a) produced a marked attack on glass using a high concentration of the gas (5 per cent, or about one million times higher than in a polluted atmosphere; see Iliffe and Newton, 1976). This concentration would produce a pH of 2.4, so that it would be the *attack by the strong acid* rather than the polluted air which was being assessed! It is, in fact, rather difficult to carry out laboratory experiments on this problem, because (a) it is extremely difficult to produce a concentration of as little as $500 \mu g\, m^{-3}$ in a reliable manner and (b) such experiments as have been done with $9000 \mu g\, m^{-3}$ and 50 per cent relative humidity produced an attack which was difficult to distinguish from that of 50 per cent humidity alone (see *CVMA News Letter*, No. 15, June 1975). Painted glass corrodes inside buildings also, and there is little SO_2 there (Wilson, 1968; Thomson, 1978). The recent O.E.C.D. (1977) report does not give clear information about glass. There is no disputing that the surfaces of all crusted medieval glass contain sulphates, or that the sulphur has been derived from the SO_2 in the atmosphere; but many have assumed much too readily that the *only* conclusion is that the air pollution has *attacked* the glass (e.g. Frenzel, 1970a; Fitz *et al.*, 1984). Instead, it is noticeable that sulphur is not present in the reaction zone (see *Figure 4.22c*) and it seems that the formation of sulphates is merely the third step in the chain (Newton, 1979, 1987b):

$$\text{glass} + \text{water} \rightarrow \text{hydroxides} \rightarrow \text{carbonates} \rightarrow \text{sulphates}$$

Ray (1976) has suggested, however, that sulphites may play an important role in the chain of events.

Four electron microprobe analysis studies have now failed to demonstrate the presence of sulphur in the reaction zone (Perez *et al.*, 1978; Hreglich and Profilo, 1980; Bettembourg *et al.*, 1983; Perez and Dallas, 1984), and these studies must surely be convincing that SO_2 in polluted air does not attack medieval glass directly; it may even have a protective effect (Coward and Turner, 1938; *CVMA News Letter*, No. 15 June 1975). Nevertheless, the many comments in the literature that important windows have deteriorated since 1940, cannot be dismissed lightly. It would seem, however, that much potential damage was caused by bad storage during the war and would not have been immediately evident. The detailed arguments are set out in Newton (1982b, pp. xiii–xiv) and will not be repeated here.

It is possible that hydrogen fluoride may account for some damage, and there is a monitoring scheme at Cologne Cathedral for measuring the concentrations at various heights of hydrofluoric acid, hydrochloric acid and sulphur dioxide (Wolff and Luckatt, 1973). It seems certain, however, that water (and water vapour) is the most damaging constituent of the atmosphere towards medieval window glass.

Condensation

It has been suggested that cycles of condensation and drying may cause less damage to glass than does continuous exposure to high humidity (Newton and Bettembourg, 1976). Other extensive studies show that glasses corrode much more quickly when exposed to such cycling than when exposed to constant high humidity (Simpson, 1951, 1953). It seems that the apparent discrepancy may be connected with the extent to which 'run off' has occurred. If the condensation was so heavy in the former experiment that the droplets merged into a film which was thick enough to run off the surface, the alkaline corrosion products would be washed away. This is the case with the windows of houses and shops which are washed regularly, in contrast with the corroded surfaces of windows of the sheds in gardens and allotments, which are not washed regularly. If the condensation is such that it occurs in minute discrete droplets, which then dry out, any alkali extracted from the glass by the droplets remains as patches on the surface to form nuclei so that the droplets in the next phase of condensation occur at exactly the same spots. Solutions of high pH could then build up at each droplet site causing attack at those points. It seems, also, that corrosion is more rapid at a liquid/air/glass boundary (Weyl and Marboe, 1967) and these condensation points on the surface may be an explanation of the origin of pitting, especially as Adlerborn (1971) found such discrete spots with the scanning electron microscope. Condensation may occur on the inside of church windows, especially when heating is installed, and the inner surface of medieval stained glass is occasionally more corroded than the outside.

Humidity

It is well established that glass undergoes decay in contact with liquid water, but it also decays in the presence of water vapour (Stockdale and Tooley, 1950; Walters and Adams, 1975). A considerable number of molecular layers of water are adsorbed on glass surfaces at average relative humidities and it has been shown by infrared transmittance spectroscopy that the amount of water adsorbed on silica gel increases with time and with increasing relative humidity (r.h.). This would appear to apply to modern glass as well as to glass that is so decayed that its surface may be regarded as being a silica gel.

Attack by 100 per cent r.h. results in the same film formation as observed under attack by water but requires an incubation period, whereas 85 per cent r.h. attack does not result in the same stable film formation. It is not only the amount of water but the frequency with which it is replenished that determines the corrosion processes which prevail. Experiments by Paul (1977) indicated that there was a marked increase in the amount of silica extracted as the number of times the attacking solution is replenished is decreased. In conditions where the solution is frequently replaced there is no rise in pH accompanying the release of alkali and the silica network remains intact.

One of the more thorough investigations into the effects of different humidities on different glass compositions has been made by Walters and Adams (1975). A range of glass compositions was tested under constant conditions at 30, 50, 75, 90 and 98 per cent r.h. and 50°C. Experiments were also carried out by cycling the humidity in the range 77–98 per cent r.h. while avoiding any condensation. Some of the glasses showed the worst attack at 75 or 90 per cent r.h., rather than at 98 per cent r.h., but in all cases the r.h. at which the attack was worst was over 50 per cent r.h. [The considerable problems of exposing glass experimentally to a desired humidity are discussed by Price (1980) and Arnold and Price (1980).] It was found that regular washing greatly reduced the damage caused by high humidity. This implies that high humidity promotes the accumulation of corrosive substances on the surface of the glass or enables these substances to exert their corrosive action or both of these. It further implies that the corrosive substances may be removed by washing. The windows of the cathedrals in Vienna were regularly washed in the Middle Ages, and this probably retarded the onset of weathering (Korn, 1971). It would be desirable to reintroduce this practice and to wash ancient window glass regularly, but the cost would be considerable, even with 'Schnorkel'-type equipment.

Some medieval glass has deteriorated as a result of being stored in damp cellars during the war as a protection from damage by bomb blast. Exposure to 100 per cent r.h., and probably also surface moisture, for 5 years or more seems to have developed a hydrated surface layer which has subsequently been prone to rapid deterioration, probably due to the opening up of fissures in the hydrated layer as it dried out when the windows were reinstalled. Thus the glass could have seemed to be in good condition when it was removed from storage, but the seeds of its subsequent destruction would have been unnoticed on the surface.

This seems to have been the situation at Canterbury Cathedral. The glass was removed from the windows and placed in unlined wooden boxes on the (then) earthen floor of the partly underground St Gabriel's Chapel. The arcade to the crypt was walled up and earth was piled against the outside walls (and windows) as a protection against bomb blast. The walls of the crypt became so wet that the important ancient murals peeled from them and the glass is likely to have been permanently wet for 4 or 5 years. Many other examples of adverse war-time storage have been recorded (eleven reports in *CVMA Newsletters*, between 1972 and 1976); and there seems to be a correlation between damp storage and glass stored therein which is now in poor condition. Similarly, dry storage conditions are correlated with glass which is still in good condition, as at York Minster (*CVMA Newsletter* 22, 1976). The problem is also mentioned by Becksmann (1976), Schmidt (1976) and Grodecki (1978).

In the case of opaque glass objects having what appears to be a stable surface, any heterogeneity in the interior, which may be affected by humidity, will be concealed as long as the outer shell remains intact. Such an exceptional condition was illustrated by Plenderleith (1956) in the case of a large Egyptian scarab of the Eighteenth Dynasty, which had been formed by casting opaque blue glass into a mould. The scarab had remained intact for 3000 years; it had been on exhibition at the British Museum for a generation, and there had been no reason to regard it as being abnormal in any respect. Suddenly it was reported as having developed cracks, and was found to be so hygroscopic that it would not remain dry for 2 min at a time. Soon afterwards the glass scarab fell to pieces. From an examination of the interior of the scarab it was obvious that the condition of the inside was different from that of the exterior — a white

encrustation formed on parts of the fractured surface but no such crystallization occurred on the exterior. It had only required a microcrack to form in the outer shell for moisture to have access to the hygroscopic material inside, upon which disintegration occurred. A similar example is shown in *Figure 4.14*.

Solarization

Some originally colourless glasses have developed a marked tint when exposed to sunlight for a long time, a phenomenon known as *solarization*; similar changes can be produced in sensitive glasses by any kind of energetic radiation, from visible light to gamma rays. The effect is particularly noticeable in examples of nineteenth-century house windows which have assumed a marked purple hue in the course of time. Brill (1963) remarks that the change can be seen in the windows of old houses along Beacon Street in Boston, Massachusetts, USA. Examples can also be seen in Antwerp in Belgium, and most restorers of nineteenth century painted glass will have encountered it.

In 1825 Faraday produced a scientific report on the effect of solarization. Since then the phenomenon has been much studied and it has been shown that the darkening of glass by *radiation damage* (or *X-ray burns*) is part of a general effect of electron trapping. The colour can be removed (if necessary and if the glass will withstand it) by heating to 350°C.

The effect is discussed at length by Weyl (1951) who states that the first satisfactory explanation of the development of the purple colour was given by Pelouze (in 1867), showing that it was produced by the interaction of Fe_2O_3 and MnO, leading to the formation of Mn_2O_3 and FeO (compare equation 1.3 in Chapter 1). This reaction may well be the explanation for the claims that modern technologists cannot reproduce the exact shades of medieval glasses even though they have analysed the old glass, the implication being that the medieval craftsmen had secret formulae which had been lost; instead, it may just have been an effect produced by centuries of sunshine. Far from possessing the secrets of producing coloured glasses, it seems more likely that the medieval glassmakers were at the mercy of their raw materials and furnace atmosphere. A brown solarization colour, instead of purple, can be produced when as much as ten parts of arsenic and selenium per thousand parts of sand is present in the glass.

Vibration

It has been claimed that the shock wave set up when a supersonic aircraft exceeds a speed of Mach 1 (the sound barrier), can damage painted glass windows. One article (Neuen Glaszeitung, 1954) states that jet fighters broke 500 panes of glass at a small-holding in Bishop's Waltham, Hampshire, in 1954. An enquiry

Figure 4.14 Egyptian faience scarab, which had split due to the action of moisture on the hygroscopic interior, after repair and showing storage with silica gel. British Museum, London.

with the Royal Aircraft Establishment, Farnborough, established that the incident had been caused by a supersonic aircraft, accelerating at a lowish altitude, in a turn. Such a manoeuvre was permitted in 1954 but is now forbidden. The resulting sonic bang had been focussed so that only a small area had been affected and the overpressure was about ten times greater than would be expected from civil supersonic aircraft operating commercially.

Since that time, two studies of the problem have been published. The first was to expose specially constructed stained glass windows to artificial sonic bangs and the other was to monitor the normal window movements in two cathedrals over a 2-year period, both near the flight path of Concorde during its acceptance trials over the Irish Sea. The cathedrals were those of Truro, in Cornwall, and St David's in Wales. It was found that considerable movements of cathedral windows occur under normal conditions and that the fluctuations caused by sonic bangs are less dangerous than those caused by strong winds and gales. If damage were to be caused to a leaded window (and hence a flexible one) the bang would have to be twenty times greater than that caused by a cruising supersonic transport aircraft, but unleaded (inflexible) windows could be damaged twice as easily as leaded ones (Pallant, 1973; Webb, n.d.). Similarly, road traffic vibration might be expected to cause damage to window glass *in situ*.

Micro-organisms

Organic growths may be associated with glass deterioration. Micro-organisms such as mosses, lichens, liverworts and algae do not attack clean glass. While they do not require any nutrients since they obtain food by photosynthesis, they require dirt, grease or pitting as a substrate to provide a foothold on the glass. Lichenous growths probably do not attack glass directly but promote corrosion by trapping moisture next to the glass and thus help to accelerate decomposition. Bettembourg (1976a) and King (1971) have each published illustrations of lichens growing on wet windows. Obviously the most difficult problems associated with organic growths on glass are found in hot humid countries, but they occur in neglected churches in the United Kingdom and elsewhere. Mellor (1924) has described twenty-four different types of lichen found on church windows, the most common being *Diploica lanescens Ach.*, *Pertusaria leucosora Nyl.* and *Lepraria flava Ach.*, all frequently being found on smooth glass. Most of the lichens found on church windows have crust-like growth and are best adapted to an exposed substratum because the whole of their under-surface is attached to the support. Most lichens are found on the outer side, particularly on north, west and east facing windows, where there is

good air circulation, a certain intensity of light and some humidity; but wind and hot sun-rays are inhibiting. It seems that water is retained between the glass and the lichen by capillary action. The water contains CO_2 from respiration of the lichen. As the hyphae become more or less turgid due to growth and water availability, so the glass is subjected to pressure and chemical attack.

Fungi are also found on glass (Tennent, 1981) even though they require an organic source of nutrient which seems to be available from CO_2 in the atmosphere (Tribe and Mabadeje, 1972). It has been suggested that 'silicophage' bacteria may attack buried glass, but no details appear to have been published (Winter, 1965; see also the discussion in Newton, 1982b, p. xviii). Recent examination of a batch of blackened water-logged glass from the marine underwater archaeological site HMS Sapphire (1696) at Bay Bulls, Newfoundland, by Florian (1979), showed that the blackening was due to the deposition of ferrous sulphide, and that much of the deterioration of such glass is associated with microbiological organisms — bacteria being present on all surfaces examined (the samples had been stored in fresh water for nearly a year prior to examination).

Weathering of buried glass

Durable glass such as Roman, a soda–lime–silica glass, varies little on burial. Medieval glasses which form a crust in the atmosphere also form one in the soil. However, the nature of the crust differs. In the soil it has a lamellar nature and is dark in colour in contrast with the featureless fissured and pale colour of the atmospheric corrosion product. The darker colour is usually the result of precipitation in the crusts of compounds of iron and manganese. These appear to enter with the attacking solution through the cracks and channels of the weathered crust.

Buried glasses have been studied in a long and detailed paper by Geilmann (1956), and a typical example is the sample glass No. 4/1 — tenth to eleventh century window glass from the Royal Palace at Werla, near Schladen (Lower Saxony). It was black in colour but still completely smooth with a shiny glass surface (emphasizing that a hydrogen glass is present on the surface). Some samples were completely decomposed throughout, a cross-section showing that the lamellar structures which started from each surface had met in the middle. The weathered product loses 50–75 per cent of its mass, despite having the same volume, and hence it must be extremely porous.

In another paper, Geilmann (1960) described some excavated glass from a Roman villa at Konz, West Germany, and as a result of its examination, showed that old cracks in the glass formed the starting point for a special deep form of corrosion which, he

Table 4.3 Comparative analyses of glass and weathering products

Oxide	Glass	Weathering product on the glass of Sample 4/1		Sample 4/2 completely destroyed
		Inner layers	*Outer layers*	
SiO_2	56.81	73.45	73.60	81.58
Al_2O_3	3.30	8.45	6.79	3.25
Fe_2O_3	0.62	1.40	0.83	1.67
TiO_2	0.11	0.73	0.59	0.43
MnO	1.29	0.80	1.06 ⎱	1.30
MnO_2	–	1.77	4.35 ⎰	
CaO	19.82	8.77	8.55	5.35
MgO	3.01	1.26	0.75	0.85
K_2O	10.11	1.70	0.89	0.53
Na_2O	2.06	0.32	0.16	0.23
P_2O_5	2.70	1.40	2.77	3.21
SO_3^-	0.51	Trace	0.05	0.27
Cl^{2-}	0.31	–	–	0.10
CO_2^{2-}	–	–	–	0.95
Total	100.65	100.05	100.39	99.72
H_2O	–	20.88	20.64	19.37

Adapted from Geilmann (1956).

believed, cannot occur on undamaged glass. The effects on the durability of scratches in the surface have been discussed by Newton *et al.* (1981).

Table 4.3 has been adapted from Geilmann's (1956) Table A to indicate the kind of results obtained. The noteworthy points are that in the crust the silica content has increased greatly, and the lime, magnesia, potash and soda contents have decreased; also, the sample is hydrated to the extent of about 20 per cent. This water content may pose a conservation problem because the crust may become friable when the water dries out, and any cleaning of the surface may have to be done before it is fully dry. Even when the glass has been completely decomposed, some soda and potash are still present. Geilmann also discussed the problem of how to compare the analysis of the glass with that of the weathered product. One method is to recalculate the composition on a water-free basis, as shown in *Table 4.3*, but another approach is to find an oxide which is neither extracted nor absorbed from the surrounding soil, and to use it as a reference point. Titanium dioxide (TiO_2) is such a material because it is claimed to be rare in ground waters and is not extracted from glass within the pH range 3.5 to 12. The compositions were recalculated on the assumption that the TiO_2 did not change but the results fluctuate so widely that they fail to be convincing; no doubt part of the difficulty is that the

TiO_2 content is generally much less than 1 per cent and the multiplying errors are therefore correspondingly large (Geilmann, 1956).

Further discussions of excavated glass are given by Raw (1955) and Winter (1965). In 1972 Fletcher (1972) began a burial experiment using modern glass at Ballidon in Derbyshire. Glasses of known compositions have been buried in soils of known pH, and will be excavated and examined at various times over a number of years. The experiment has been continued by Newton (1981a).

The most lucid description of the visual appearance of different types of weathering found on excavated vessel glass in museum collections was given by Harden (1936) more than 40 years ago, yet it requires little updating except in the case of recently excavated glass from land and underwater sites and for a redefinition of the term *devitrification*. Harden states that 'The term *weathering* is applied to any change for the worse on the surface … of glass that is caused, during the passage of time, by contact with outside influences … the term covers, therefore, a wide range of phenomena'. The main visual varieties of glass surface weathering were defined by Harden as follows: dulling, strain cracking, frosting, iridescence, milky or enamel-like weathering. There is also the phenomenon of sick glass to be considered.

Dulling is the simplest type of weathering in which

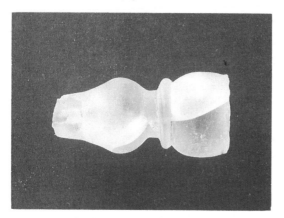

Figure 4.15 Dulling, the simplest type of weathering, in which glass loses its original clarity and transparency. Courtesy of J.M. Cronyn.

the glass loses its original clarity and transparency and becomes merely translucent (*Figure 4.15*). This is easy to distinguish from dulling that is due to scratches or stains.

The term *strain cracking* describes an infinite number of small cracks running right through the glass in all directions which finally give it a sugary appearance and cause the vessel to disintegrate. Harden attributes this to 'a devitrification' caused by 'too speedy annealing' but these are probably examples of dehydration of a hydrogen glass, rather than the strain-cracking discussed by Newton *et al.* (1981).

Spontaneous fracturing of painted glass has presented an occasional conservation problem (yet considerable when encountered). Because it happens so rarely, the phenomenon appears mysterious, and it has been baffling to know how to combat the effects; Newton *et al.* (1981) have recently attempted to rationalize the situation. One difficulty has arisen from the tendency to describe several different phenomena under the one name, when at least three separate effects seem to be involved. Firstly, the formation of a thick hydrated surface layer which later undergoes a decrease in volume; the resultant strain in the surface is relieved by fractures which may remain in the surface or which may penetrate right through the glass so that the article falls into several pieces, each of which contains other cracks. Only very few glasses appear to show this behaviour (see below). Second, a relatively slight scratch in the surface of the glass may subsequently lead to the formation of a shell fracture on one side of the crack. These characteristic fractures grow in a curved manner and reach the surface of the glass again so that a small lenticular fragment can leave the surface. A pit remains which may at first sight resemble a corrosion

pit, but it does not have the usual circular shape with straight sides; instead it is usually elliptical in shape, except where it abuts the scratch which initiated it, and is shallow, the sides bearing conchoidal fracture marks. This also is a rare phenomenon (see below). Third, a scratch in the surface may penetrate a Type V (soluble) surface layer and thus lead to greatly accelerated corrosion beneath the scratch. Thus, what had been relatively slight surface damage develops onto a deep groove which can penetrate the glass *as if the surface had been fractured* (see *Figure 4.2*); this again seems to be a rare phenomenon, but it has been duplicated experimentally.

Examples of a thick hydrated surface layer which has undergone a decrease in volume have occurred in a glass vessel which was placed in the foundations of the Chapel-in-the-Fields Congregational Church, Norwich (Norfolk) for 120 years (Newton, 1982a); in the case of the 'sugared' Sandringham glass (Norfolk) (*Figure 4.16*); and perhaps also in the

Figure 4.16 Fragments of window glass with a sugar-like surface, from Sandringham Church, Norfolk. Courtesy of D.G. King.

Roman vessels excavated by Ypey (1965) and which were held together only by the earth which had filled them before they fractured into quite small pieces. This type of spontaneous cracking is discussed by Adams (1974) who showed that the behaviour was due to the effect of water in causing the surface layer to hydrate. Freiman (1974) found that some alcohols caused less cracking than did others, and that it was the water content of the alcohol which was important. Tummala (1976) showed that the resistance of glasses to stress corrosion is related to the coefficient of thermal expansion which in turn is related to the alkali content; thus high-alkali medieval glasses which show the phenomenon may be inherently incurable by any means.

Wiederhorn (1967) showed that water vapour had a profound effect on crack growth, 100 per cent r.h. producing about 10 000 times the growth at 0.017 per cent r.h. Wiederhorn *et al.* (1974a,b) found that the susceptibility to crack growth in a vacuum depended on the composition of the glass. Thus the situation is complicated and there is little that can be done by a conservator who has a susceptible glass in his or her care except perhaps to keep it in dry air.

Slight scratching of the surface leading to spontaneous cracking also occurs rarely but it is found in some ancient glasses. The phenomenon is also rare in medieval painted glass, but when it does occur, the evidence is considerable. For example, it is a characteristic of the glass from St Michael's Cathedral, Coventry, West Midlands; of certain windows at Thornhill Church, near Dewsbury, West Yorkshire; and in a few other medieval windows. Only one case has yet been found at York Minster, and only a few examples are known at Canterbury Cathedral. Scratching leading to spontaneous cracking has been described by Newton (1974b), but the description given on pages 11–33 is incorrect since the holes in the glass do not have sloping sides which meet at a point at the base. Glasses described by Homer and Crawford (1970) may exhibit spontaneous cracking.

Spontaneous cracking resulting from scratching of a Type V surface layer has been reported by Harden (1959) on glass from Great Casterton (see *Figure 4.2*) and by Cramp (1975) who incorrectly described it as 'a feather pattern incised on the surface'. The linear mark in *Figure 4.23* is probably an example of the same phenomenon, as is also that discussed by Geilmann (1960). There is even the possibility that the scratches which develop when glasses are experimentally corroded may have arisen by an accelerated corrosion of this kind (Ernsberger, 1959; Olsen *et al.*, 1970; Ferrazzini, 1975).

The term *frosting* describes a network of small cracks on the surface of the glass 'resembling the patterns made by frost on a window pane...'. Harden (1936) also attributes this phenomenon to 'devitrification', that is, loss of glassy substance (but see page 4 for the modern usage of this term). However, it is more likely to be the result of further dehydration of a hydrated layer which formed on a Type IV surface with extensive loss of silica. The water which caused the hydration may have derived from the humidity of the atmosphere, from its condensation on the glass, or from a chemical autocondensation reaction of the type described by Paul (1977). Dehydration could occur at ordinary levels of relative humidity without the air having to be particularly dry. In such cases the moisture in the cracks may be all that holds the glass together, so that it could disintegrate on drying (see *Figure 4.5*) *Crizzled* surfaces (not described specifically by Harden since they are usually associated with glass

from the sixteenth to eighteenth centuries) have diminished transparency and a lustreless appearance owing to the presence of very fine surface crazing. Under the microscope, a close network of small cracks can be seen, and if the glass is seriously affected small pieces may have spalled away. Weeping (sweating) glasses repeatedly generate droplets of water on the surface if exposed to humid conditions, owing to leaching of alkali by atmospheric moisture (see *Figure 4.4*). Crizzled and weeping glasses are often referred to as *sick* glass. They have been thoroughly investigated by Brill (1975).

Iridescence is a variegated coloration of the surface of glass, giving a rainbow-like effect, sometimes occurring alone, sometimes as a concomitant of other types of weathering (*Plate 3*). When found alone it is first visible in filmy patches. In a more advanced state it begins to flake off. Finally, in its most virulent form, it causes a powdery disintegration of the vessel owing to continual flaking of the surface. On Roman glass from Egypt it rarely reaches this advanced state. All of these effects would be produced by a progressive breakdown of a highly siliceous layer in a Type IV surface. From the conservation point of view, these glasses are often valued for the beauty of their iridescence, and they need to be handled carefully or the silica flakes may be detached, and their appearance spoiled. In particular, any adhesive could penetrate the air gaps (as found by Brewster; see the introduction to this chapter) and destroy the iridescence.

Milky or enamel-like weathering is patches or streaks, usually opaque white, appearing on the surface, gradually eating more and more deeply into the walls of the vessel. In its more virulent forms it may be black or brown in colour, or may even have a mottled, polychrome appearance. In its incipient stage, when visible merely as small spots or streaks of white, it is termed *milky weathering*, and may sometimes be confused with *stone*. The chief difference between the two is that patches of weathering always start on the surface, whereas blobs of stone may occur both internally and externally. After a patch of milky weathering has eaten some distance into the wall of a vessel it begins to flake away in small crystals, leaving pits in the glass. The most extreme form, *enamel-like weathering*, appears as a thick coating varying in colour from white to brownish-black, over a large part of the entire surface of an object (*Figure 4.17*). This too has a tendency to chip off exposing highly iridescent pits and thin *lamellae*; and when highly deteriorated can crumble in a mosaic-like manner (*Figure 4.18*).

From the point of view of loss of substance it might seem that Roman vessels, even under the most virulent attack, might have lost about 0.5 mm in two millennia, or about 0.025 mm per century. Thus, compared with some medieval glass, this is fairly

Figure 4.17 Torso of Aphrodite. The surface is covered by a thick milky-white weathering surface, which in some areas has flaked away to reveal an iridescent layer beneath. H 95 mm. *Circa* first to second century AD. Near East or Italy. Corning Museum of Glass, New York.

Figure 4.18 A fragment of glass with a thick blackened enamel-like surface. The glass has become so weakened through deterioration that pieces are falling away. Courtesy of J.M. Cronyn.

even a very slight change in environment may produce a markedly different kind or degree of weathering on two parts of the same vessel.... No strict rules can therefore be formulated. The causes and effects of weathering are as manifold as they are elusive.' It has since been realized (Cox *et al.*, 1979; Newton and Fuchs, 1988) that the weathering is closely related to the chemical composition of the glass in question.

The surfaces of many pieces of excavated glass have a thin opaque blackened layer on the surface (*Figure 4.19*). In section, a brown-black dendritic invasion of the interior of the glass may also be observed, apparently following the lines of cracks into the glass (*Figures 4.20 and 4.21*). The staining appears to have diffused into the glass on either side of the cracks. The main branches of the dendritic staining appear to have side branches along their length, often amounting to little more than knobs. These may be the result of diffusion out of very small side cracks along the sides of the main cracks. The staining may be due to

Figure 4.19 A restored, excavated dish displaying a thin opaque blackened weathering surface. Courtesy of S. Smith.

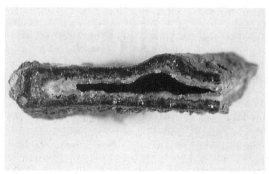

Figure 4.20 Section through a fragment of deteriorated glass, showing the invasion of the interior. Courtesy of J.M. Cronyn.

durable. The brown or black discoloration may well have been due to contamination by iron or manganese compounds.

Harden (1936) continues, '... it is quite impossible to foresee what type or degree of weathering will be produced on a piece of glass after preservation for a fixed time under seemingly fixed circumstances...

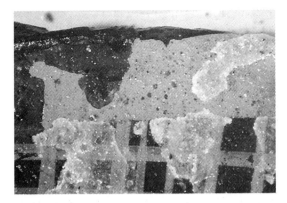

Figure 4.21 Magnified section through a fragment of glass, showing deterioration proceeding from the surface to the interior, presumably following the lines of cracks. Courtesy of J.M. Cronyn.

lead sulphide (Smithsonian, 1969), ferric ions or manganese dioxide, the latter being implicated in some staining at least (Shaw, 1965).

Damage to archaeological glass by soluble salts is discussed in Chapter 7.

Weathering crusts on painted glass windows

It seems likely that the weathering crusts found on some examples of medieval window glass are an extreme form of the *enamel-like weathering* described above. The crust may be more than 1 mm thick, and the window rendered quite opaque, thus no longer fulfilling its original function of allowing light into a building. The crust may be white, brownish or even blackish, and a great deal of gypsum is usually present. The crust may be very soft and powdery, or extremely hard and flinty. Scott (1932) seems to have been the first to demonstrate that the weathering products on painted window glass consist largely of sulphates. A scraping was taken from the inside surface of the fourteenth-century glass at Wells Cathedral, Somerset, and when analysed it was found to consist largely of calcium sulphate. Scott was at a loss to explain its presence and eventually attributed the sulphur content to sulphur dioxide from the gas flames used for lighting the cathedral, and the calcium content to dust rising from the limestone floor. It seems more likely, however, that the calcium had been extracted from the glass itself (Cox *et al.*, 1979). In Austria until quite recently it was thought that crusting might be the result of some peculiarity of the Austrian weather (Bacher, 1974a). However, it is now realized that glasses which contain less than 62 mol per cent SiO_2 will form a crust; and that Austrian window glass contains an unusually high proportion of lime

(*CVMA News Letters* No. 11, Nov. 1974; No. 18, Feb. 1976; No. 24, Feb. 1977).

In 1960, Geilmann (1960) carried out a study of eleven weathered windows and as a result found that the weathering crusts consisted of silica, together with various sulphates, such as gypsum ($CaSO_4.2H_2O$), syngenite ($K_2SO_4.CaSO_4.H_2O$), gorgeyite ($K_2SO_4.5CaSO_4.H_2O$) and polyhalite ($K_2SO_4.2CaSO_4.MgSO_4.H_2O$). It was remarked that the chemical composition of the weathering products, produced on church windows in widely spaced and climatically different areas (Cologne, Nuremberg, Oppenheim, Ulm and some Frankish glass), had a high degree of similarity, and this argues against the suggestion that local air pollution played a major part in the formation of the sulphates. Moreover there has always been sufficient SO_2 in the

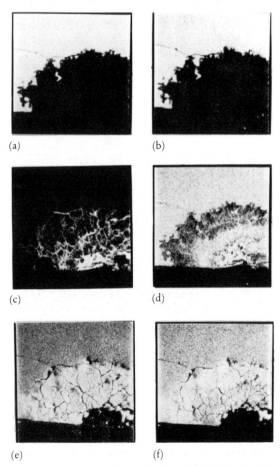

(a)   (b)

(c)   (d)

(e)   (f)

Figure 4.22 Electron microprobe photographs showing the presence or absence of particular chemical elements in glass weathering crusts. (a) Potassium, (b) magnesium, (c) sulphur, (d) calcium, (e) aluminium, (f) silicon. From Perez-y-Jorba *et al.* (1978).

air, arising from natural sources, to account for all the sulphates found in the surface of crusted glasses (Newton, 1982b).

The most informative studies of weathering crusts have been carried out by Collongues and Perez-y-Jorba in several publications (Collongues, 1974, 1977; Collongues *et al.*, 1976; Collongues and Perez-y-Jorba, 1973; Perez-y-Jorba *et al.*, 1975, 1978, 1980). *Figure 4.22* (Perez-y-Jorba *et al.*, 1978) shows how revealing the studies have been. In the illustrations, all of which are 300 μm square, the pit is at the bottom and towards the right. The pictures were obtained with an electron microprobe, and each shows whether a particular chemical element is present or absent and, roughly, the amount of each element present. In illustrations (a) and (b), the pit looks empty (black) because there is no potassium or magnesium in it due to the fact that their compounds are generally readily soluble in water; but both elements are present in the glass, which appears whitish. Illustration (d) shows that calcium is present in the glass, and in much of the contents of the pit, *except* in the vicinity of the glass. In (e) and (f) aluminium and silicon are present in the glass, and in the contents of the pit, *except* at the top of the pit which is in contact with the air; both (e) and (f) show that the contents of the pit are much fissured (see also *Figure 4.29*). In (c) it can be seen that there is no sulphur in the glass, but that it is present in fissures in the contents of the pit, and that it is especially concentrated at the top of the pit where aluminium and silica are absent, but where there is a great deal of calcium. In fact, only calcium and sulphur are present at the top of the pit which therefore consists of *gypsum*. It is particularly interesting to note that there is practically no sulphur in contact with the glass. Thus as stated earlier in this chapter, sulphur dioxide is not a primary agent in the attack of glass, but it has a third-order effect by converting the calcium carbonate (which arises from the attack on the glass by water, and its conversion by carbon dioxide in the atmosphere) into gypsum, and then only at the top of the pit or in the fissures. Returning to illustration (d), one interpretation placed on the various bands, and particularly the dark zone (at the base of the pit and next to the glass), is that calcium hydroxide, although only slightly soluble in water, is much more soluble than calcium carbonate (more than 100 times). Thus the dark band could correspond to calcium hydroxide which has diffused away from the glass surface, the middle bright band could represent the insoluble calcium carbonate, and the top of the pit is calcium sulphate where sulphur dioxide has reacted with the carbonate. Another hypothesis proposed by Ray (1976) is that *acid sulphites* are formed near the glass; these compounds, $Ca(HSO_3)_2$ and $Mg(HSO_3)_2$, are extremely soluble and could account for the dark band in illustration

(d). As the acid sulphites migrate towards the surface and into the fissures, they could be transformed into *neutral sulphites*; $CaSO_3.2H_2O$ is only somewhat more soluble than $CaCO_3$, but $MgSO_3.6H_2O$ is very soluble, and would be readily washed out of the pit. The calcium sulphite would eventually be converted at the top of the pit into much more soluble calcium sulphate. (Phosphorus also plays a role in the reactions which take place in the pit.) Further work is required to establish whether the two kinds of sulphites play a part in the reactions or not. The crusts were also shown to contain quartz and calcium carbonate in addition to the various sulphates and double sulphates mentioned above.

Hypotheses of pit formation

Until recently, the deterioration of glass by pitting and crusting was regarded as being essentially two different phenomena. Bimson and Werner (1971) suggested that the former occurred only in potash glasses, and the latter only in soda glasses, but this is not the case. It now seems likely that crusting is preceded by pitting. Cox *et al.* (1979) showed that unweathered glass from York Minster generally had a SiO_2 content greater than 60 mol per cent; that crusted glasses usually contained less than 60 mol per cent SiO_2; and that pitted glasses generally lay in the range 57 to 63 mol per cent SiO_2. In classifying 200 samples into different categories of weathering, Cox *et al.* (1979) found difficulty in allocating nine of the samples which could be described as either pitted or crusted. It seems probable that there may have been a statistical probability situation. For example, if a piece of glass has only slightly less network former than would correspond to the *boundary* between weathered and unweathered glass, only a slight amount of attack might occur, for example at a few centres, which would then develop into pits. If, however, there was somewhat less network former, then the statistical probability of forming a pit, or of a pit growing, could be greater, and many (or larger) pits might form. At very low levels of network former the pits might coalesce and form a crusted surface (Moser, 1961; Newton, 1976a).

The presence of pits in glass presents several intriguing problems; namely, the mechanism of their formation, the reasons for their distinctive straight-sided (cylindrical) shape, and for the uniformity in the size of pits in any one piece of glass. In addition the size of pits varies from one piece of glass to another, and strangely, pits form in some glasses but not in others. One of the first researchers to attempt to clarify these points on a scientific basis was Heaton (1907), who put forward the hypothesis that pit formation was based upon devitrification: '... what happens [the development of devitrification crystals] in a few hours when the glass is hot tends to take place on prolonged exposure to the atmosphere ... molecules tend to separate out from the homogenous mixture and collect round a point, forming a centre of decomposition'. However, it is now realized (Douglas, 1966) that cold glass is so rigid that such crystal growth would not occur. Heaton (1907) went on to argue that a pit is formed (apparently at more or less its full depth) when '... the whole mass comes away...', and correctly deduced that pits tend to develop along the line of cracks, but did not link that observation with an hypothesis (for example, by showing why weathering would form preferentially along the scratches). Also that pits, once formed, are '... a resting place in fact for the water, until eventually the whole fabric of the glass is destroyed.'

In a discussion of the paper, Reid (in Heaton, 1907) suggested that sections should be cut through a number of pits in order to make microscopic studies of their nature, but it was about 70 years before anyone seems to have adopted this idea; the sections prepared for the microscope by Geilmann (1956) and by Brill and Moll (1961) were of the plugs formed in the weathering crust of buried glass, which seem to exhibit quite a different phenomenon.

Also in the discussion of the above paper, Newman (in Heaton, 1907) remarked that pitting occurred on the outside surface of glass (that facing to the exterior of the building) and not on the inside, and that this seemed to contradict Heaton's hypothesis; this important point had been ignored by Heaton who merely stated that '... the action was going on underneath a surface which was perfectly bright and free from corrosion ...' This 'under-surface' effect has since been reported by Holloway (1984). Winter (1965) considered that pock-marking of the glass may have had an organic origin, but also considered that the thick deposits on the outside of the windows (? crust) were formed by the agglomeration of particles held in place by an electrostatic charge.

Frenzel (1970a) suggested that foci for attack are formed by inclusions in the glass, such as impurities, unmelted sand grains, air bubbles etc., however, pits also form in glasses which are free of inclusions; though admittedly if pits formed around inclusions their development would presumably destroy the evidence and the remainder of the glass would have to be studied for the indication of inclusions. Werner (1966) pointed out that adhesive labels can accentuate the deterioration of glass, presumably by holding moisture in contact with the glass. Examples of this have been reported at the Museum of London and the Turner Museum, Sheffield. It is also possible that specks of dust sticking to a fragile glass might also attract and hold water at various points which would then become alkaline in nature and promote the formation of pits. Marschner (1977) regarded pitting

as being characteristic of the early and middle stages of corrosion of medieval window glass; which as it continued to develop, turned into surface corrosion with precipitation of secondary reaction products on the corroded area. It was claimed that pitting is preceded by the formation of defect zones 0.1–0.2 mm in diameter *underneath* the glass surface (c.f. Heaton, 1907, and Holloway, 1984, above), and that the defect zones are surrounded by spiral cracks, perpendicular to the surface, perhaps formed as a result of tensile stresses in the leached and hydrated layer. The defect zones were thought to be linked to mechanical damage of the glass surface, which would explain the fact that the defects seemed to be beneath the surface; mechanical damage to a Type V layer would form a penetrating crack which would encourage an alkaline reaction to occur at the point of damage, and this would therefore appear to be beneath the surface. *Figure 4.23* (Perez-y-Jorba *et*

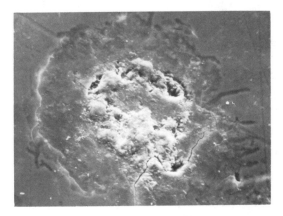

Figure 4.23 The early stages of pit formation (×400). The chemical attack seems to be taking place below the surface, but there is an extensively damaged area on the surface, and also the suggestion of a surface crack (running from the top left corner to just below the middle of the right edge) which might have initiated the weathering. Courtesy of *Verres et Réfractaires*.

al., 1978) shows the early stages of formation of such a pit. Another possible explanation concerns the microporosity of the alkali-depleted layer; that is, water could penetrate the pores and this would lead to subsurface deterioration. Thus the problem is only partially solved. Pitting occurs only in a certain compositional range (at least as far as the glass from York Minster is concerned), and it can certainly be associated with surface damage, although it would be surprising if this were *always* the case, as in micropitting. One hypothesis could be that random point-type damage occurs on the surface of the glass, and each point becomes a focus for pit growth (by destroying the Type V surface). Thus a large number of damage points could produce many pits, for example, micropitting (*Figure 4.24*), or a low frequency of damage points could lead to fewer pits (*Figures 4.25 and 4.26*). But then there is the problem as to why a few pits may grow large, and a multitude of pits may remain small and do not merge (as seems to happen when the glass has a lower SiO_2 content). Another feature is that very large pits grow deep whereas micropits do not, the pit depth being

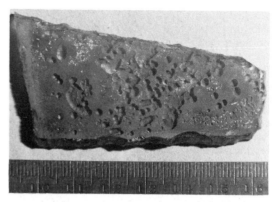

Figure 4.26 Small empty pits which have become joined together, but which do not contain decomposition products, and therefore the glass surface does not appear to be crusted. Courtesy of the Dean and Chapter, York.

Figure 4.24 Micropitting: isolated pits (0.1–0.2 mm diameter) containing no deterioration products. The unweathered edges were originally covered by lead cames. Courtesy of the Dean and Chapter, York.

Figure 4.25 Small pits (about 1 mm diameter) mostly containing white decomposition products (appearing white in the photograph); or brownish contents (appearing speckled). Some pits have become joined, producing crusted surface areas. Courtesy of the Dean and Chapter, York.

somehow proportional to the pit diameter, as if there is a kind of protective barrier between such pits.

Another hypothesis not yet discussed, is that the pitted glasses are phase separated, a phenomenon brought about by changing composition. There are two main types of phase separation: *droplet structure*, where one phase forms discrete droplets or regions inside the other matrix phase, and the *twophase framework* where both phases are continuous. Each phase having a different composition renders itself open to different rates of attack. (Borosilicate glasses often exhibit this phenomenon, but the tendency towards phase separation is reduced with the addition of alumina.)

The size, depth and distribution of the pits would be related to the size and distribution of the droplets and it would be an interesting project to examine these glasses with an electron microscope to discover whether phase separation is present and, if so, the size of the droplets. On the other hand, such glasses would, presumably, also form pits on the side facing the interior of a building.

Pit sizes

As mentioned above, a striking and as yet unexplained feature of pitted glass surfaces is the remarkable constancy of pit sizes on any one piece, so much so that four categories are easily discernible:

Micropitting, where the pits are very small (perhaps only 0.2 mm in diameter) and very crowded (as many as $100+\ cm^{-2}$) as shown in *Figure 4.24*.

Small pits in the range 0.5–2.0 mm. They may be quite empty of deterioration products (*Figure 4.26*), or contain white or brownish material as shown in *Figure 4.25* in which case some of the pits have become linked and form crusted areas. Thus, in the

Figure 4.27 Very large pits (5 mm diameter) in an otherwise glossy and apparently unweathered surface. The white contents of the pits, as they eventually join together, will produce a crusted surface. This should not be confused with traces of cement from the leading, which is present on the bottom and right-hand edges. Courtesy of the Dean and Chapter, York.

Figure 4.28 Old very large pits (4 mm diameter) in an inhomogeneous glass. The remains of a few isolated pits can be seen, but the majority have linked up to form linear grooves. (The grooves are not associated with the enamel paintwork on the other surface.) The surface visible is much striated as a result of inhomogeneities in the glass weathering differentially. Courtesy of the Dean and Chapter, York.

sample shown in *Figure 4.27*, there could be some ambiguity as to whether the glass should be described as being pitted or crusted. In *Figure 4.26* small empty pits have joined together, but the absence of any contents in the pits results in the glass not appearing crusted, and eventually it may develop solution marks.

Large pits in the size range 2.0–4.0 mm, and *very large pits*, larger than 4.0 mm in diameter (*Figures 4.27 and 4.28*). In *Figure 4.27* the surface of the glass between the pits is quite glossy and apparently unweathered; and this would seem to be an example of a damaged Type IV surface, which is durable unless cavities form in which alkali can accumulate. In *Figure 4.28*, the pits have become linked to form linear grooves; these do not correspond with any part of the painted design on the other face of the glass, and hence are not an example of 'back-matching' corrosion but there may have been a scratch on the original surface which led to the formation of the groove. The corroded surface is much striated where inhomogeneities in the glass have weathered differentially.

When the glass has a low durability, the pits may penetrate right through the glass. Cole (1972) has pointed out that some of the genealogical panels at Canterbury Cathedral have pits which penetrate the glass, and it was the opinion of some experts from the Corpus Vitrearum Medii Aevi, who met in 1972, that these pieces of glass would disintegrate in 10 to 20 years unless some action were taken to preserve them. Newton (1975b) drew attention to an extraordinary type of weathering in which deep narrow pits are surrounded by a wide shallow circle of corrosion, superficially reminiscent of the cathodic corrosion of stainless steel (an electrochemical phenomenon).

Microclimates in the pits or in the crust

There has been much discussion in the literature as to whether the crust on crusted glass (or in the pits which contain white deposits, e.g. *Figure 4.25*) has a protective action by preventing aggressive agents from reaching the glass (Frodl-Kraft, 1967a, 1970, 1971) or whether it has an accelerating action on deterioration by retaining water, and hence alkali, in contact with the glass (Winter, 1965). It is important to try to answer this question because it has a bearing on whether conservation of such glass is, respectively, less or more urgent.

It seems to be a difficult question to answer, but some observations seem pertinent. *Figure 4.29* (Perez-y-Jorba *et al.*, 1978) shows a scanning electron microscope view (× 1000) of the interior of a pit. The many fissures would suggest that water could easily enter them and the pit could harbour much moisture and hence accelerate the attack on the

Figure 4.29 Scanning electron micrograph of the contents of a pit, showing the highly fissured nature of the white deposit present. The fissures would be likely to retain water and thus promote pit-growth. Courtesy of *Verres et Réfractaires.*

glass; this may, in fact, be the reason why the pits develop 'downwards' (i.e. inwards into the glass) if any moisture is held preferentially by surface tension at the bottom of the growing pit.

The second observation concerns an experiment carried out on a small piece of poorly durable twelfth-century glass from York Minster; the piece was chosen to be as similar as possible to the green, poorly durable piece described on page 144 *and* to have a crust on both faces and all four edges. This piece was weighed, washed for 30 min at 60°C to remove any alkali (some potash was washed out) and then exposed to renewed distilled water for 50 hours and 85°C, when further potash was extracted, thus showing that the crust had not protected the glass against such attack (*CVMA Newsletter*, 12, 13, 14, 1975).

Thus both observations suggest that the crust does *not* protect the glass against further weathering, but there is an urgent need for some really exhaustive experiments to be carried out under laboratory conditions.

From the foregoing, it may be seen that although the mechanisms of glass deterioration are still not well understood, progress has been rapid during the past 20 years (Hench *et al.*, 1979; Cox and Cooper, 1995). There is every prospect that further progress can readily be made as the result of careful observation during the course of excavation examination and treatment, and through experimentation. Deterioration is an extremely important field of research, since efficient development of improved conservation methods for glass depends on a thorough understanding of its modes of decay.

5

Materials used for glass conservation

Cleaning

The materials chosen to clean a particular piece of glass will depend on the substances to be removed. Extraneous matter can range from calcareous deposits found on buried glass, to moss and lichens growing on stained glass windows. In addition, products formed during the decomposition of glass may have to be removed. A wide range of materials is therefore required for cleaning glass: water, detergents, chelating (sequestering) agents, acids, organic solvents and biocides. It must be remembered that these materials, especially those which are formulated commercially, may have deleterious effects on glass if used injudiciously. Their uses are described in Chapter 7, but their important properties in relation to use on glass, and dangers to the conservator, will be discussed below.

Water

Water, the most common cleaning agent, *when present in small amounts* (see the discussion of surface area/volume values on page 139), can be quite damaging to glass surfaces; and washing water may remove poorly adhering paint or other decoration (Frodl-Kraft, 1976).

Tap-water often contains calcium and magnesium hydrogen carbonates, chlorides and sulphates. The amounts vary with the district; in hard-water areas the amount of salts can be more than $170 \, mg \, l^{-1}$. The hydrogen carbonates which cause *temporary hardness* are stable in solution only when the water is acidified with dissolved carbon dioxide. These salts can therefore be precipitated from ground or atmospheric water by boiling. The sulphates and chlorides cannot be removed by boiling and cause *permanent hardness* (Furon, 1967).

When calcium and magnesium salts are in contact with alkaline glass surfaces, they may be precipitated.

Visible deposits of calcium carbonate can sometimes be formed in flower vases when the water has stood for considerable lengths of time. Deposits of salts are sometimes visible as 'water stains' when droplets of water have dried on glass leaving the salts in place. In order to prevent further deposition therefore, purified water (which has had the salts removed) should be used when treating glass objects. Impurities in water can be removed by two methods: distillation (to produce *distilled* water); and treatment by ion-exchange resins (producing *deionized* water).

Washing of glass with water should be kept to a minimum; glass should not be left to soak, if possible (obviously this cannot apply to glass from wet environments, stored in water).

Detergents

The term detergent is applied both to the chemical compounds (*surfactants*), and the commercial products (*formulae*) which act in a solvent to aid the removal of soiling and contaminants. Surface active materials for use in water can be divided into three groups: *anionic*, *cationic* and *non-ionic*. The terms refer to the nature of the polar, hydrophilic, group in the molecular structure of the surfactant. Surface-active compounds have a twofold nature, since each molecule has a polar and a non-polar end. One end is compatible with the solvent used and the other will interact with the soiling substances.

The solvent most commonly used for detergents is water, although detergents have been developed with the increased use of non-aqueous (i.e. dry-cleaning) solvents.

A commercial detergent formula is a mixture of chemicals each of which plays a role in the cleaning operation. A typical formulation for washing powder contains alkali, surface-active chemicals, chelating agents, suspension and thickening agents. Many of these ingredients can damage glass or other surfaces (even sugar and alcohol can damage glass; Paul and Youssefi, 1978b). The use of commercial products cannot be recommended because their ingredients are unknown in detail and thus the effects of their ingredients on ancient glasses cannot be foreseen.

It is unlikely that the commonly used detergents have any serious toxicity if used sensibly. However, long immersion of the hands in detergent solutions will extract the oily protective chemicals from the skin and leave it open to invasion by infection; conservators with a sensitive skin should wear protective gloves because barrier creams may contaminate the glass. See also Davidsohn and Milwidsky (1978), Durham (1961) and Rado (1976).

Chelating (sequestering) agents

Many metal ions are stable in water solutions only when the pH is in the correct range, or when appropriate anions are present. Chelating agents can stabilize metal ions over a wide range of solvent conditions. A chelating agent has a strong reaction with the metal ion, enclosing it in a protective complex (Richey, 1975), for example, ethylenediaminetetraacetic acid (EDTA):

$$(\text{HOOC} \bullet \text{CH}_2)_2 \text{N} \bullet \text{CH}_2 - \text{N} \rightarrow \text{Ca} \begin{array}{c} \text{CH}_2 - \text{C} \overset{\displaystyle O}{\underset{\displaystyle O}{\diagup}} \\[2ex] \text{CH}_2 - \text{C} \overset{\displaystyle O}{\underset{\displaystyle O}{\diagup}} \end{array} \tag{5.1}$$

The characteristic of chelating agents is the formation of stable multiple bonds between the chelating agent and the metal ion.

The materials which usually have to be removed from glass with chelating agents are weathering crusts which consist of calcium carbonates and sulphates in combination with silica. The metal ions which have to be removed are the same as those that make up the glass, and it is therefore difficult to apply any solution to the weathering crust that will not soak through and also react with the glass under it, or react with the glass as soon as the crust has been removed. For this reason the use of chelating agents must be assumed to affect the underlying glass and it is the conservator's job to minimize the contact of these reagents with the glass surface (Ferrazzini, 1977a). The use of pastes made up with a thickening agent such as Sepiolite (magnesium trisilicate) or carboxymethylcellulose sodium salt may confine the action of the solution to the surface to which it is applied. However, these chelating agents will extract the more accessible atoms first and it is therefore possible that

the weathering crust may be weakened before any significant attack on the underlying glass takes place. The weakened crust may then be removed by gentle mechanical means (Bauer, 1976), but the removal of crusts from glass is a drastic treatment which needs careful consideration.

Chelating agents can conveniently be divided into three groups: polyphosphates, aminocarboxylic acids and hydroxycarboxylic acids.

Polyphosphates

Polyphosphates were introduced as water softeners in the 1930s to chelate and keep in solution calcium and magnesium ions. They are still widely used in commercial detergents; Calgon, for instance, is a polyphosphate where the value of n (below) is about 12 (Albright and Wilson, 1978). They can therefore be used to dissolve calcium and magnesium salts from hard crusts.

$$O = \overset{\displaystyle O}{\underset{\displaystyle O^-}{\overset{\|}{P}}} - \left(O - \overset{\displaystyle O}{\underset{\displaystyle O^-}{\overset{\|}{P}}} - \right)_n O - \overset{\displaystyle O}{\underset{\displaystyle O^-}{\overset{\|}{P}}} - O^- \tag{5.2}$$

$n = 0 \ (\text{P}_2\text{O}_7)^{4-}$ pyrophosphate
$n = 1 \ (\text{P}_3\text{O}_{10})^{5-}$ tripolyphosphate

Other phosphates are:

PO_4^{3-} orthophosphate
$(\text{PO}_3^-)_n$ metaphosphate (a ring structure)

Bettembourg's (1972a, 1973) solution A consists of an aqueous solution of 10 per cent sodium thiosulphate ($\text{Na}_2\text{S}_2\text{O}_3.5\text{H}_2\text{O}$) and 5 per cent sodium pyrophosphate ($\text{Na}_4\text{P}_2\text{O}_7.10\text{H}_2\text{O}$). The reported effects of these polyphosphates on glass seem contradictory, and it is possible that much may depend on the nature of the actual piece of medieval glass being cleaned; for example, Frenzel (1970b) recommends the use of Calgon, but Frodl-Kraft (1967a) used it only with caution, provided the solution process was halted *before* the actual surface of the glass was reached, and provided it was not allowed to touch the painted line-work. Four years later, however, Frodl-Kraft discontinued the use of Calgon because it was found to creep along the glass surface, under the painted decoration, and loosen it (Frodl-Kraft, 1970, 1971). Ferrazzini (1977a, Figures 2 and 3) has published illustrations showing how Calgon produced cracks and other types of damage on glass surfaces, which become apparent on drying or aging.

Polyphosphates tend to hydrolyse in solution to the orthophosphate anion, which forms insoluble salts with alkaline earths. They should therefore not be used on glass as there are better materials available.

Aminocarboxylic acids

The most commonly used chelating agent of this class is EDTA:

$$\text{HOOC} \bullet \text{CH}_2 \diagdown \\ \hspace{3cm} \text{N}-\text{CH}_2-\text{CH}_2-\text{N} \hspace{1cm} \diagup \text{CH}_2 \bullet \text{COOH} \\ \text{HOOC} \bullet \text{CH}_2 \diagup \hspace{3cm} \diagdown \text{CH}_2 \bullet \text{COOH}$$

(5.3)

The tetra acid can be partly or totally neutralized with sodium hydroxide, and various EDTA products with different proportions of sodium are available (Richey, 1975, Table 1, p. 230).

EDTA can be used to hold calcium and magnesium ions over a wide range of pH values between pH 7 and pH 11, and it will chelate lead from a lead-containing glass (Paul and Youssefi, 1978b; Olsen *et al.*, 1969). There is a large number of other aminocarboxylic acids which are similar to EDTA but provide a range of potentially useful properties. An example is N,N-*bis*(2-hydroxyethyl)glycine, $\text{HOOC-CH}_2\text{N(CH}_2 \text{ CH}_2 \text{ OH})_2$. This does not chelate calcium and magnesium ions but does hold other metal ions in solution (Davidsohn and Milwidsky, 1978, p. 76).

Bettembourg's (1972a, 1973) solution B is an aqueous solution of the sodium salt of EDTA, 30 g l^{-1} buffered with 30 g l^{-1} ammonium hydrogen carbonate ($\text{NH}_4.\text{HCO}_3$). At first Bettembourg (1972a, 1973) would seem to have used it without any other caution, soaking entire glass panels (still in their leading) in baths of EDTA solution for two to three hours, or until the required degree of cleaning had been achieved. However, in 1975, Bettembourg and Perrot (1976) changed the procedure to three successive applications of the solution on cotton wool swabs. Bauer (1976) claimed that EDTA does not harm the surface of glass, whereas Ferrazzini (1977a) has illustrated damage caused by EDTA to poorly durable glass surfaces. No doubt, like the experience with Calgon, much depends upon the type of glass which is being treated, but there is sufficient evidence of the deleterious effects of EDTA on glass to show that great caution must be exercised in its use.

Hydroxycarboxylic acids

Hydroxycarboxylic acids act in two different ways at different pH values. Below pH 11 these acids form only weak complexes with alkaline earths, and a large excess of the chelating agent is necessary to ensure the dissolution of calcium ions. Above pH 11 they are more effective than EDTA or polyphosphates as chelating agents for calcium. Hydroxycarboxylic acids chelate iron and other multivalent ions over the whole pH range.

COOH	H	H
H—C—OH	H—C—COOH	HO—C—COOH
H—C—OH	HO—C—COOH	HO—C—COOH
H—C—OH	H—C—COOH	H
H—C—OH	H	
H—C—OH		
H		
Gluconic acid	Citric acid	Tartaric acid

(5.4)

At pH 7, therefore, gluconic acid might be used to extract copper or iron staining from glass with relatively little effect on the alkaline modifiers of the glass. Citric acid is well known for the damaging effect which it can have on glass surfaces (Bacon and Raggon, 1959).

As previously discussed chelating agents are non-specific in their action and will attack glass, especially at high pH values, causing damage by complete removal of the surface (Bacon and Raggon, 1959; Ernsberger, 1959) or by selective leaching of the alkaline earth modifiers (Paul, 1978). Glass surfaces which have been subjected to chelating agents are therefore made more liable to deterioration (Ferrazzini, 1977a). The conservator must therefore apply any solutions as specifically as he or she would mechanical methods, that is, treating only local areas, although Paul (personal communication, 1979) is experimenting with a system which may deposit a protective film as soon as the weathered crust has been removed. As yet there is no treatment for safely removing the iron staining from glass surfaces; improvements to chelating agents may however produce reagents which are more ion-specific. A review of chelating agents by Richey (1975) outlines the toxic hazards and main points of interest in the use of chelating agents.

Hydrogen peroxide

Hydrogen peroxide solutions are used to bleach out organic stains on glass surfaces (Moncrieff, 1975). Hydrogen peroxide breaks down in solution to evoke an active form of oxygen $\text{H}_2\text{O}_2 \rightarrow \text{H}_2\text{O} + [\text{O}]$ which can react with and decolorize organic material. A preservative, typically parts per million of phosphates, is added to solutions to slow down the spontaneous production of oxygen, and alkali can be added to increase the rate of oxidation.

Hydrogen peroxide is purchased as a solution in water. The concentration of the solution is normally indicated by the volume of oxygen gas which one unit volume of solution will produce, for example, 100 vol. hydrogen peroxide is a 30 per cent solution. The solution should be diluted to a 10 vol. solution for use on glass.

As oxygen can be evolved in large amounts which rise as bubbles to the surface, hydrogen peroxide should not be used or stored near highly inflammable substances such as solvents. Hydrogen peroxide can oxidize organic material such as skin or clothing and it should be used with care especially when in concentrated solution.

Mineral acids

The acids used on glass in the past were hydrochloric, nitric and hydrofluoric acids. All of these can attack poorly durable ancient glasses, especially when the lime content is high, as in medieval painted glass, and should not normally be used on glass because alternative treatments are now available.

Mineral acids are supplied in the form of concentrated solutions: hydrochloric acid (HCl) 30 per cent; nitric acid (HNO_3) 75 or 90 per cent; sulphuric acid (H_2SO_4) 98 per cent; hydrofluoric acid (HF) 40 per cent. All of these, but especially sulphuric acid, become very hot when added to water. For this reason acid should *always* be added to water, *never* the other way around. This will reduce the danger of concentrated acid boiling and spitting when it comes into contact with water.

Mineral acids can cause burns on the skin, and hence protective clothing (gloves, eyeshields and aprons) is needed, and scrupulous cleanliness is important. If dilute solutions are splashed on clothing, or on the bench, they will evaporate, become more concentrated, and be likely to cause burns hours after the acid bottles have been put away in a safe place.

Hydrofluoric acid is particularly dangerous because it differs from other acids in the way it attacks living tissue. The concentrated acid can attack the surface of the skin, as do other acids, *but* the fluoride ion diffuses through healthy skin and fingernails to precipitate calcium in the tissues beneath, thus causing intense pain which can occur some hours after contact with dilute fluoride solutions has ceased (Browne, 1974). Although still used commercially for etching glass, hydrofluoric acid should not normally be used for conservation work. However, should its use ever become necessary, it is of the utmost importance that advice be sought upon the stringent safety precautions to be taken and the specific First Aid treatment required in the event of an accident occurring. Antidotes for poisoning with hydrofluoric acid are calcium gluconate gel (Browne, 1974) in the United Kingdom and zephiran chloride (a benzalkonium chloride) in the United States (Nixon, 1981).

Organic solvents

Organic solvents are used for three purposes in conservation: for removing greasy dirt, for applying or diluting polymers in solution, and for removing polymers. The term solvent is usually assumed, as here, to mean a mobile organic liquid, but it can be extended to cover solids, such as those polymers which can dissolve dyes, etc., by absorption. Polymer – solvent interactions are important, and it is therefore necessary to understand those properties. Several guides are available for this (Burrell, 1955, 1970, 1975; Crowley *et al.*, 1966; Duve *et al.*, 1975; Durrans, 1971; Feller *et al.*, 1971; Fuchs and Seihr, 1975; Hansen, 1967, 1968; Horie, 1987; Marsden, 1963; Mellan, 1970; Shell, n.d.; Stolow, 1971; Teas, 1971; Torraca, 1975; Ueberreiter, 1968). The dangers inherent in swelling certain polymers in some solvents are discussed by Alfrey *et al.*, 1966.

All solvents are dangerous, and care is required whenever they are used. Fume extraction facilities should be used wherever possible. Sometimes, however, it is possible to exchange a dangerous solvent for a less hazardous one, yet still retain suitable solvent properties and this should always be done. The hazards of solvents fall into two categories, flammability and toxicity.

Flammability

All organic solvents, except the highly halogenated ones, are flammable. Any fire must start in an air/vapour mixture, and hence the more volatile the solvent, the more readily it is ignited. A good indication is the *closed cup flash point*, which is the lowest temperature at which a spark above the liquid will cause the vapour to ignite. The lower the flash point, the greater the hazard, and the vapours can travel some distance from an open vessel containing the solvent. Hence naked flames, cigarettes, electric switches and other sources of sparks must not be used when solvents are employed. Even the non-flammable chlorinated solvents such as trichloroethylene can be dangerous when exposed to naked flames or cigarettes because they can be converted to the poisonous gas phosgene.

Toxicity

All solvents are toxic to some extent (Browning, 1965; Sax, 1975). Perhaps the most common and insidious damage is caused by breathing the solvent vapours over extended periods of time; for this reason the effects and relative dangers of solvent vapours have been extensively studied (see below). However, liquid solvents can be absorbed through the skin and they dissolve the protective chemicals from the skin, thereby allowing ease of entry for infection.

There are two different kinds of vapour toxicity, both of which may occur with the same solvent: *narcotic effects* causing drunkenness or poisoning which wear off as the solvent is eliminated from the body (e.g. ethanol); and *chronic effects* which persist long after the solvent was initially absorbed (e.g. methanol). The cancers induced by some solvents fall into the category of chronic damage.

The type of toxicity caused by two chemically similar solvents, such as ethanol and methanol, is not necessarily the same. Ethanol in moderate doses causes drunkenness and even unconsciousness, but the effects wear off as the ethanol is eliminated from the body. Methanol, on the other hand, is metabolized into products which cause permanent damage to the nervous system and may lead to blindness.

The relative danger of different solvents is given in the United Kingdom by *Occupational Exposure Limits* (OEL), and in the United States by *Threshold Limit Values* (TLV), which are the maximum concentrations of vapour in the air which can be tolerated by a worker without a significant *known* risk. Two values are commonly listed: one for exposure during the whole of the standard working week, the *Time Weighted Average* (TLV–TWA); the other for short-term exposure up to 15 minutes (TLV–STEL) (Baer, 1984). The OEL and TLV values are listed by British (Health and Safety Executive, 1984) and American (American Conference of Governmental Industrial Hygienists, 1983) institutions. These and other publications should be consulted for further details of values and methods.

The measurement of the concentration of a solvent vapour has been made much easier in recent years by the development of simple and relatively inexpensive instruments. For example, the Draeger system works by drawing a known amount of air through a tube of chemicals which indicate the concentration of vapour in the air by changing colour.

Biocides

Micro-organisms can cause difficulties during the conservation of glass. Archaeological glass excavated from waterlogged conditions is frequently dirty and hence can support fungal and bacterial growths; stained glass can act as a support for the growth of mosses and lichens (see Mellor, 1924; Tribe and Mabadeje, 1972; Upsher, 1976; Tennent, 1981).

When archaeological glass from wet sites is stored, biocides should be added to prevent spoilage of the excavated material. Alkaline sodium salts should not be used because it is likely that they will cause corrosion during storage, and the quaternary ammonium compounds can form a hydrophobic layer (see above). 2-Hydroxybiphenyl is the only appropriate material that seems to have been investigated for conservation use (Baynes-Cope, 1975). A saturated

stock solution in water (0.07 per cent) can be added to packaged material awaiting stabilization. The weight of solution should be approximately equal to the weight of preserved material, thus producing a 0.035 per cent solution, which is sufficient to kill fungi. Too low a concentration of 2-hydroxybiphenyl should not be used because it may not immediately kill the organisms and they may become resistant to the biocide.

Algae may be more troublesome to control, but they rely on light for photosynthesis to occur and hence the treated packages should be stored in cool dark locations. Any package which has been treated with a biocide should be marked with the name of the material used, the amount added and the date.

The growth of mosses, and especially lichens, on buildings is frequently considered to be attractive and hence they may be encouraged to grow. However, mosses and lichens do harm stonework and painted glass windows, and methods for their removal are well established (Building Research Establishment, 1977).

A lichen is a symbiotic association between an alga and a fungus, and either an algicide or a fungicide will be effective against it. Mosses are usually controlled by treatments with compounds of heavy metals. Phenol derivatives are frequently used for control of fungi, but no evidence has yet been produced for fungal *attack* on glass (despite an appeal for information; see *CVMA News Letter*, No. 19, April 1976), although there is plenty of evidence that glass may act as a *support* for fungi (for example, Mellor, 1924; Tennent, 1981). 2-Hydroxybiphenyl, pentachlorphenol and their sodium salts are frequently used; these salts are alkaline (pH 10) and hence treated glass must be carefully washed. The phenols themselves are only sparingly soluble in water, but are soluble in many organic solvents. Chlorinated phenols should be avoided because they are so toxic to many animals and birds.

A new class of algicides and fungicides is the quaternary amine type, which is also effective against mosses when combined with organo-tin compounds, and they are less toxic to mammals. The ammonium compounds, Tego 51B and Thaltox Q, form strong bonds to glass, and this may be an advantage for *in situ* applications. An experiment to compare Santobrite, Tego 51B and Thaltox Q was started in Nettlestead Church, Kent, in 1979 (see Abstract No. 417 in Newton, 1982b). The windows were inspected by Peter Gibson in March, 1985. He reported verbally that there had been no reinfestation of the windows on which Santobrite and Thaltox Q had been used, but that there was some indication of algal growth where Tego 51B had been applied. In no instance was there any sign that the original painted line-work had been loosened by the treatment.

Formaldehyde is an active pesticide and has no

adverse effect on glass when applied as a 5 per cent solution in water, but its vapour is toxic with an OEL or TLV of only 2. Algal infections may occur on the inside surfaces of church windows when the buildings are damp, and then additional care is required as some toxic materials are subject to control by public authorities. In any event it is important to follow the manufacturer's instructions, and to use masks, gloves and protective clothing when these are advised.

Laser beams

Laser beams have been advocated for cleaning glass (Asmus, 1975) but they have not been adopted owing to the expense of the equipment.

Adhesives, consolidants and lacquers

Before the advent of synthetic polymers, the materials used for the consolidation, repair and restoration of ancient glasses were animal glues (Harding amd Macnulty, 1961), natural waxes and resins (Mills and White, 1977; Koob, 1979; Horie, 1987), and plaster of Paris. Their only advantage was that they held the fragments together, at least for a limited period. All had serious disadvantages compared with modern materials: glue shrinks, wax flows and attracts dirt, natural resins are brittle and plaster of Paris is opaque. These traditional materials are still used in some countries, and may be found on ancient glasses from collections.

After the Second World War there were considerable advances in commercial and industrial polymer chemistry, one result of which was to make available many new materials, and further developments have tended to create a particular product for the intended end-use. But it is also necessary to evaluate the materials for permanence of their properties. In practice, however, it is usually necessary to make a compromise by selecting the material which has the least number of *disadvantages* with regard to the particular conservation task in hand. It has often been the case that, once a polymer has been found that satisfies enough of the requirements, it tends to be widely recommended until it is superseded by a new material (Feller, 1967). However, the formulation may be changed by the manufacturer without notice and this may affect the result when it is used in conservation. The desirable qualities of adhesives are set out in a questionnaire by Notman (1973a). At present the materials used in conservation, and discussed in this chapter, are: cellulose derivatives, epoxy polyester and acrylic resins (including cyanoacrylates and photoactivated or ultraviolet curing adhesives), vinyl polymers, polyurethanes, and silicones. Where possible the chemical composition of materials should be known; also their toxicity

before and during curing, or their potential as a cause of skin ailments such as dermatitis. The use of a fume-cupboard, extraction fan, goggles or protective gloves may be necessary. In general, products should be easily available at a reasonable cost, and preferably in small amounts, to reduce wastage due to expiry of shelf-life. The shelf-life of unmixed components should be known. Polymers are discussed by Billmeyer (1971), Brandrup and Immergut (1975), Brydson (1989), Feller (1971a,b), Mandelkern (1972), Mark *et al.* (1964), Saunders (1977) and Shields (1984). Adhesion and adhesives are discussed by Cassidy and Yager (1972), Lee (1975), Johnston (1974), Skeist (1977), Wake (1976), Zisman (1975, 1977) and Brommelle *et al.* (1984). A comprehensive, if technical, review of the mechanisms of adhesion has been published by Wake (1978), and an important review of the use of polymers in conservation is that by Horie (1987).

Adhesion

In order for materials to fulfil their roles as adhesives, consolidants or gapfillers, it is obvious that they must have a reasonable adhesion to glass. In order for this to be so, materials used to conserve and restore glass must have a strong attraction for glass surfaces; thus, when applied, they will flow and cover the glass so wetting it. They must then set (cure) to prevent movement of the fragments or vessels being treated. They must be able to adjust to strains set up during and after setting, should not put undue strain on the glass, and be as unobtrusive as possible (De Bruyne, 1956, quoted in Wake, 1976). It is also desirable that adhesives, consolidants and gapfillers should remain soluble over considerable periods of time.

Glass has a high energy surface and, when clean and dry, will be readily wetted by any adhesive or contaminant. It is therefore essential that the surfaces to be adhered should be thoroughly cleaned to remove grease and dirt. However, the surface of glass is very hygroscopic and in normal humidities has many molecular thicknesses of water lying on it. The non-hydrogen bonding organic liquids do not spread spontaneously on the water-bearing glass surfaces (Zisman, 1975). The area of contact between organic liquids and glass can be increased by lowering the level of relative humidity. It is therefore likely that poor initial wetting of the glass surface by the adhesive will result from the use of adhesives that cannot displace the water from the glass surface. Having once formed the adhesive bond, an adhesive (or gapfiller) may gradually be displaced from the surface by the attraction of glass for water. This displacement may be further induced by the deterioration reactions that occur at glass surfaces exposed to water; alkali ions in the glass migrate to the surface to produce their soluble hydroxides.

All polymers are permeable to water to a greater or lesser extent. All adhesives therefore allow the penetration of water through their films, and on to the glass surface. The water molecules can react in the pores of the glass surface which have not been coated with polymer and also at the interface of the glass under the coating. The alkaline solution formed in the pores and at the interface will absorb more water by osmosis which will gradually generate a hydrostatic pressure confined by the adhesive (Bascom, 1974). This pressure will put a stress on the polymer–glass adhesion and promote further loss of adhesion (De Lollis and Montoya, 1967). The hydrolysis reactions take place faster on highly alkaline glasses than on the more stable modern glasses (Delmonte, 1965).

Silane treatment

It has been suggested that the problem of adhesion might be solved by pretreating the glass surface with a coupling agent before application of an adhesive (Bettembourg, 1972b, 1973; Bettembourg and Perrot, 1976; Albright and Wilson, 1978; Cameron and Marsden, 1972; ERDE, 1973; Gledhill and Kinloch, 1975; Kinloch *et al.*, 1975; Errett *et al.*, 1984). There are various families of coupling agents, including phosphate and chromate, but the silane family has the most widespread use, and has already shown promising results in the field of stone-restoration. Silicone adhesives in general are discussed by Beers (1977).

Silane coupling agents are a class of monomers in which both the silicon group and the organic radicals contain reactive groups. They are of the general form $R-Si(Y)_3$, Y being commonly $-OCH_3$ methoxy or $-OC_2H_5$ ethoxy, and R is a reactive organic group. The Y groups hydrolyse with water to form reactive silanol $R-Si(OH)_3$ groups which can then react with themselves and with the surfaces to which they are applied. The R group can be chosen to react with a polymer which is subsequently applied to the surface; for example, unsaturated R groups are chosen to improve adhesion of vinyl-reacting polymers such as polyesters, and amine-containing R groups can be chosen for epoxies.

A typical silane coupling agent is aminopropyltrimethoxysilane, $H_2N-CH_2-CH_2-CH_2-Si(OCH_3)_3$. This is used to promote glass–epoxy adhesion, but many other silanes, with different organo-functional groups, are available (Marsden and Sterman, 1977).

The silane, applied in a dilute solution, reacts with water, on the glass surface and in the air, to form silantriols by eliminating the hydrolysable groups:

$$R-Si(OC_2H_5)_3 + 3H_2O$$
$$\rightarrow R-Si(OH)_3 + 3C_2H_5OH \text{ (ethanol)}$$
$$(5.5)$$

These silantriols react with hydroxyl groups on the surface, and with themselves, to form a tightly cross-linked three-dimensional layer attached to the surface (Norman, 1973; Norman *et al.*, 1970) with strong covalent bonds.

Coupling agent (5.6)

Glass

A polymer system that will react with the organo functional groups can then be applied, the amino groups on the silane reacting with epoxy groups and bonding chemically to the adhesive. Coupling agents considerably improve the adhesion of polymers to glass, both initially and on prolonged exposure to water. The silane groups immobilize the silicon atoms to which they are attached and reduce the adsorption and reaction of water thus delaying failure of an adhesive bond. However, coupling agents will not be able to prevent the diffusion of water molecules into the pores and onto the surface completely (Johannson *et al.*, 1967; Ritter, 1973a,b). The use of coupling agents can therefore increase the initial strength and life expectancy of an adhesive join considerably, but the bond will eventually fail due to water penetration and glass decay. However, their use on glass artefacts in the relatively dry atmosphere of museums, may ensure that adhesive bonds will be effectively non-reversible.

Strain

Stress and strain on glass can result during and after curing of polymers which invariably shrink on gelation due to loss of solvent, or to a polymerization reaction. This shrinkage sets up stresses at the interface between the polymer and the glass surface which makes the bond susceptible to both mechanical and chemical attack, for example, by the absorption of water, and the glass may deteriorate in special ways (Ritter, 1973a,b; Newton *et al.* 1981). The effects of such stress will depend upon the force (*elastic modulus*) necessary to maintain the adhesive stretched over the non-yielding surface of the glass. A large shrinkage of the adhesive will cause only slight stress when the elastic modulus of the polymer is low. If, however, the elastic modulus is high, such as in the case of epoxy resins, then large stresses are created even though there is only a small shrinkage of the resin during curing.

Table 5.1 Coefficients of expansion of polymers and glasses

Material	Coefficient of linear expansion (cm °C^{-1} × 10^{-6})	Tensile modulus (10^8 Pa)
Epoxy resins	45–90	24
Polystyrene	60–80	28–41
Silicones	200–400	0.6
Medieval window glass	8–15	–
Modern window glass	8	–

Strains may also arise from the mismatch of thermal expansion coefficient between the glass and the polymer (*Table 5.1*). The amount of strain produced at the interface will depend on the temperature change and the force necessary to compress the polymer when it tends to expand more than the glass.

Strain may remain locked in the polymer system and thus remain a potential source of weakness in the bond; or cause cracking of the glass, in the polymer, or along the adhesive interface. Alternatively the polymer may slowly flow to relieve the strain.

Refractive index

Reflections result from light striking an interface between two materials with different refractive indices, for example air and glass, or polymer and glass. The larger the difference in refractive indices, the greater the degree of reflectance. Theoretically, the refractive index of an adhesive should match that of the glass exactly in order to avoid reflections from the surfaces of breaks, etc. For purposes such as joining the glass elements in an optical instrument, the refractive index of the adhesive need only match that of the glass to ±0.02. In optical elements, however, the light strikes the glass/adhesive interface nearly at right angles, but as the angle becomes more glancing the reflection increases. Light strikes a repaired glass object from all angles and hence cracks and joins will be rendered visible by glancing reflections from the crack surfaces, unless the refractive indices match by ±0.01 (Tennent and Townsend, 1984a).

Unfortunately, the refractive index of a material varies with the wavelength, that is, the colour of the light. The value usually stated for a material is the refractive index found using sodium (yellow) light (this is the n_D value). A slight mismatch of refractive index may lead to the formation of colours in the cracks (Ogden, 1975; Tennent and Townsend, 1984a,b). An added difficulty in matching the indices is the change of refractive index which occurs at a glass surface when weathering takes place.

However, there are other sources of reflection; when glass vessels break, they tend to spring out of shape, releasing the stresses in the glass, and a reconstruction is likely to leave slight misalignment between fragments which create thin lines of reflective surfaces across the vessel. Excess adhesive is frequently removed from a join before it hardens, by using solvents, or mechanically after setting. If too much adhesive is removed, reflections will arise from the dry edges left uncovered.

Deterioration of polymers

The polymers used for glass conservation are to a large extent derived from organic molecules and, therefore, like other organic materials, they are susceptible to oxidation and deterioration. The main environmental influences acting on polymers used in conservation are light (Kinmouth and Norton, 1977; Horie, 1987), oxygen and water; heat only rarely causes problems.

The mechanisms of deterioration are characteristic for each polymer and they are frequently difficult to unravel, but some general remarks can be made.

Any or all of the following reactions can be caused by light, oxygen, water, or other impurities in the polymer film: cross-linking of chains; breaking of the chains (chain scission); formation of chromophores (groups which absorb light) leading to yellowing of the polymer. The cross-linking reaction in thermoplastics will convert a soluble film into an insoluble one.

Chain-breaking reactions cut the polymer chain, thus reducing the molecular weight. (It is this reaction which causes shortening of the cellulose chains in paper, thus weakening it rapidly when exposed to light and/or air.) Those polymers containing ester groups along the chain, such as polyester resins and polyurethanes, can be hydrolysed. They can, therefore, be slowly weakened by chain scission when exposed to water.

Yellowing of resins is caused by the absorption of blue or ultraviolet light by the chromophores. In most of the cases studied, the chromophores arise from loss or alteration of side groups to form conjugated double bonds and carbonyl groups along the chain. These chromophores are reactive and will absorb more energy from the light, causing further deterioration. The energy contained in light, especially ultraviolet radiation, is sufficiently powerful to break chemical bonds in polymers; it frequently initiates deterioration (Rånby and Rabek, 1975), and is a common cause of failure in polymers.

All the forms of deterioration described above are caused by chemical changes in the molecular structure, but the physical state of the polymer can change in response to the environment. If the temperature rises above its glass transition temperature (T_g) a polymer has sufficient mobility in its molecules to be able to flow. For this reason even very tough thermoplastics, such as nylon, cannot be used where a constant force is applied. Creep under stress (cold flow) results in the stretching of joins made with poly(vinyl acetate). Movement of the polymer chains can also occur on a smaller scale and a particle of dust or dirt lying on the surface of a polymer above its T_g can be slowly incorporated and become fixed in the polymer film; this effect can be seen in emulsion paints where the T_g is less than 4°C, and in polyethylene bags ($T_g = -20$°C) both of which attract and hold dirt, even after washing. In addition, water will dissolve in a polymer film, causing slight swelling which may create stresses between the glass and the polymer.

The majority of polymer properties can be altered by adding another material. For example, poly(vinyl chloride) has mechanical properties which are similar to poly(methyl methacrylate) but the addition of softening agents (plasticizers) makes the PVC polymer flexible. The plasticizers are liquids which act as non-volatile solvents, but they can slowly migrate or evaporate, causing the polymer to become brittle.

Reversibility

The deterioration of polymers may or may not make their removal convenient. In any event, products used for conservation should have clearly established methods of reversibility (US – redissolubility) which avoids damage to the glass at any time in the future.

The concept of reversibility, that is, that of taking the object back to its state before treatment, is basic to the whole of conservation, nevertheless it must be honestly stated that many conservation processes are not reversible. Everything, from drying the article to removal of weathering crusts, transforms the object in some way, and hence some information about the original state of the object may be lost during its treatment. However, the condition of some objects is so poor that action must be urgently taken to stop them disintegrating.

Reversibility must be seen on two levels: whether the gross treatment of an object, coating, adhesive, etc., can be removed without harm to the object; and whether the treatment, even after it has been reversed, distorted the information that could have been obtained from the original state of the object, for example by chemical analysis. Studies of the traces of adhesive left after self-adhesive tapes were stripped from glass plates, have shown that minute quantities of adhesive remain, and can be detected, on an apparently clean, smooth surface (Gul' *et al.*, 1974). The same may well be true of the polymers alleged to have been completely extracted from the pitted and porous surfaces encountered in conservation. Therefore the treatment of an object with any polymer cannot be considered completely reversible because of the likelihood of traces remaining, but the treatment used must be recorded for future reference.

In practice, however, reversibility must be considered on a less rigorous basis, and polymers have been placed in two categories: permanently soluble polymers; and polymers that form cross-links.

It must always be borne in mind that it is the particular use of the polymer (the process) that determines whether the treatment is reversible, not the potential solubility of the polymer. For example, the majority of cross-linking resins will swell considerably when soaked in solvents, and this swelling will usually disrupt any edge-to-edge join, or surface coating, sufficiently to permit mechanical removal of the bulk of the resin. This use of cross-linking resins is therefore reversible when the surfaces of the object are smooth and non-porous, even though the polymer is not soluble.

Swelling of a polymer, whether cross-linked or not, will put stress on the object to which it is attached. Therefore, it is better to remove as much adhesive or coating as possible by mechanical means before swelling, in order to reduce the final stress on the object. The stress is likely to be low when the polymer is free to expand in at least one direction, for example, when used as a coating. However, when the polymer has penetrated into pores or between fragments of an object, the swelling of the polymer will tend to push the fragments of the object apart.

The process of consolidation uses the polymer to penetrate, harden and thereby bind fragments of an object together. It is in such a situation that removal of the consolidant will do most harm because the swelling will tend to disrupt the consolidated part of the object. Unfortunately the swelling of the polymer will tend to put the object into tension, the kind of force that most friable structures are least able to withstand. Thus any process involving the partial or complete consolidation of a porous object with any polymer should be considered to be irreversible.

As conservation methods improve, treatments which were considered to be irreversible *may* be able to be reversed. For example, the possibility of removing organic materials by the use of oxidizing plasmas has recently been demonstrated (Daniels *et al.*, 1978). This technique may permit the removal of so-called insoluble coatings.

The polymer selected to fulfill a particular role will depend upon the influences that the bond is expected to resist. A glass vessel standing in a museum case has less need for a water-stable adhesive than glass in a window which is frequently wetted, and which is inaccessible to further conservation work. Although it would be undesirable, the vessel could be restored every few years, but painted glass in a window must be expected to remain in place for more than 100 years.

It is unlikely that an adhesive joint can combine reversibility with durability. The achievement of durability in the glass–polymer bond seems to require chemical reaction between the polymer and the glass surface. The durable bond will degrade in time, with the loss of some part of the glass surface. The reversible glass–polymer bond will operate by physical attraction and so it can be displaced physically by water in the environment; thus it is less durable.

For durable chemical bonds between most polymers and glass a coupling agent should be used. The improvement in adhesion will be gained only when both the polymer and the glass react with the coupling agent. This implies the use of one of the reactive, cross-linking, polymers as adhesives, consolidants or lacquers.

Types of polymer

Cellulose derivatives
Cellulose derivatives have been used for the adhesion and consolidation of antiquities for many years, and their properties are well understood. The use of cellulose nitrate on decayed glass was advocated by Pazaurak (1903) in the early part of this century, using a material called Zapon. In the form of H.M.G., Durofix and Duco Cement (US) cellulose nitrate is still in common use (Koob, 1982). In the form of Frigiline it has been suggested for use as a consolidant for decayed enamels (Mills, 1964). However, cellulose nitrate is known to have poor aging qualities (Hedvall *et al.*, 1951; Miles, 1955), and its use is causing some concern (Koob, 1982).

Dextrins
Adhesives based on dextrin have been used both to repair glass and as gum on labels to mark glass (Werner, 1964). Dextrins are polysaccharides produced by breaking down starches to form more soluble products; and they suffer the same form of degradation as cellulose. Moreover, the low molecular weight of dextrin makes the product hygroscopic and therefore unsuitable for the conservation of glass.

Synthetic polymers
Soluble nylon, usually made into a 3 per cent w/v solution in industrial methylated spirits, has been advocated for wide use in conservation (de Witte *et al.*, 1978) for fixing flaking surfaces on light-weight materials (BASF, 1969). Its use on flaking glass has been mentioned by Dowman (1970), and Melucco (1971) who added that soluble nylon acted as a holding treatment, not prejudicing future treatments of the glass. However, doubts have now been expressed concerning its resolubility, especially after prolonged immersion in water when used as a consolidant prior to desalting (de Witte, 1975), but also after lengthy exposure to the atmosphere (Bockhoff *et al.*, 1984). The problem of cross-linking together with the fact that soluble nylon attracts dust onto the surface of objects on which it has been used, and that there are now more suitable materials available (e.g. Paraloid B-72) should result in discontinuation of its use. Undeteriorated glass is almost impermeable to solvent vapours, and hence resins which require solvents to evaporate in order to effect their cure are inconvenient for use in repair, consolidation or restoration. For this reason, resins which polymerize *in situ*, and which do not require access to the air for evaporation of solvent, are more suitable. In addition, the shrinkage of a polymerizing polymer is considerably less than a solvent-deposited polymer and hence strains are less likely to be exerted upon the glass. Resins commonly in use at present for repairing glass are epoxies, polyester, silicones, ultraviolet light curing acrylics and cyanoacrylates.

Epoxy resins used in conservation are typically composed of two parts, a diepoxy component and a polyamine cross-linking agent, both of which are compounded with diluents and catalysts.

$$\text{Amine group} \quad H-N-R'$$

$$
R-CH-CH_2 \ (\text{Epoxy group}) \ + \ H-N-R' \longrightarrow R-CH-CH_2-N-R' \quad (5.7)
$$

The hydroxyl groups formed in this reaction can take part in and contribute to further reaction with epoxy groups.

The epoxy resin shown in (5.8) on page 176 (Brydson, 1989) is commonly used, and is a bisphenol A and epichlorohydrin condensate. The value of n usually should be less than two (Salva, 1977) in order to maintain the epoxy as an easily worked liquid.

There is a wide range of amines available for use; many of the low viscosity amines are skin sensitizers and have a dangerously high volatility. For domestic use less unpleasant liquid polyamides are used with a catalyst (Wake, 1976). The polyfunctional epoxies and amines ensure a cross-linked polymer of high strength. The advantages of epoxy adhesives and gapfillers are their relatively high adhesion and low shrinkage on curing. However, there is always some shrinkage in the polymerization of monomers. The shrinkage of an epoxy resin occurs at two stages: the first during the liquid state, the second during the gel state. A room-temperature curing adhesive underwent 3.5 per cent volumetric shrinkage within a few hours, rising to 5 per cent in a week (Lee and Neville, 1967). About a half to a third of the shrinkage of epoxy resins occurs after gelation (Danneberg and May, 1969) and is reduced by lowering the temperature of curing. Igarashi *et al.* (1979) found that a volume contraction of 3.55 per cent could occur when the resin set, leading to a stress of $45\,kg\,cm^{-2}$. A disadvantage of the bisphenol A/amine adhesives is their tendency to yellow with time and light exposure, owing to the formation of chromophores arising from the benzine rings which react with amine breakdown products. Bisphenol A epoxies, when cured with anhydride cross-linking agents at 80°C, form stable, non-yellowing polymers. Slight discoloration of the resin is noticeable when it is used on water-white glass, but is not usually a problem on archaeological glass.

Non-aromatic epoxy resins can be made which have a lower viscosity in the uncured state and an increased flexibility when cured. The low-viscosity epoxies developed for the impregnation of wood are claimed to have no shrinkage and to be non-yellowing (Munnikendam, 1978, in discussion). These and similar products may have a use in glass conservation in the future. A disadvantage, however, of aliphatic epoxies is their greater sensitivity to moisture. Terwen (1981) has suggested that epoxy resins could be used on church windows if they were protected by external glazing.

The use of epoxy resin has been suggested for consolidation of glass on site (Wihr, 1977), but the resin yellows, is difficult to remove from the glass surface, and is irremovable from porous materials such as decayed glass. In general epoxy resins should not be considered for use as glass consolidants, particularly as there are more suitable products available, such as Paraloid B-72 (US Acryloid B-72, an ethyl methacrylate/methyl acrylate copolymer).

Araldite AY103/HY956 was used for many years with considerable success as a glass adhesive. However, the original water-white formula was changed so that the product appeared slightly yellow, and a more recent formula under the trade-name Araldite 2003 is actually straw coloured and highly viscous. At present excellent results in the repair of vessel glass are being obtained by the use of Ablebond 342-1 and HXTAL-NyL-1. Epoxy resin has also been suggested for fixing loose *grisaille* decoration on windows and Cole (1975) found that the resin could be removed with water-miscible Green Label Nitromors (active agent dichloromethane) (Wilcott) without disturbing the *grisaille*.

From the description of the method of application, it seems that the epoxy resin did not penetrate beneath the paintwork. However, doubts have been raised about the wisdom of using epoxy resins for this purpose by the restorers of the Frank-Mayer studio (Becksmann, 1976). Bettembourg (1972a, 1976b, 1977) and Bettembourg and Burck (1974) used accelerated aging to test many of the possible adhesives for stained glass and came to the conclusion that epoxy resins were not sufficiently stable for exposure to the weather. Fiorentino and Borrelli (1975) tested many different epoxy resins and other adhesives by accelerated aging, and recommended Araldite GY292/XD537 as having the best resistance to light, but subsequently abandoned it in favour of Araldite BY155/HY2696 and a polyester casting resin. Likewise, Notman and Tennent (1980) tested a range of epoxy resins and found that Ablebond 342-1 was the most resistant to discoloration on aging. See also Outwater and Murphy (1970); Tennent (1979) and van der Merwe (1979).

Polyester resins

Polyester casting resins are widely used for joining glass elements in optical instruments, but there are few recommendations for their use as adhesives in the conservation of glass antiquities. However, those incorporating an ultraviolet light absorbant are extremely useful as gapfillers, and will be discussed in more detail in the section on casting materials. Casting and laminating polyesters (Brydson, 1989) are solutions of unsaturated polyesters in an unsaturated reactive monomer. Typical polyesters are made from propylene glycol, maleic anhydride and phthalic anhydride, and have a short molecule (molecular weight 2000) of general formula shown in (5.9). This represents a highly unsaturated polymer. Styrene is usually chosen as the reactive monomer because of its low cost and ease of use. Methyl methacrylate can replace some of the styrene when resistance to light is required. The cross-linking between the chains is achieved by copolymerizing the styrene with the unsaturated bonds in the chain by using a peroxide initiator. This results in a cross-linked polymer which is both hard and rigid. The properties of the cross-linked, cured resin can be varied by altering any of the several components that make up the formulation. All polymerization reactions result in shrinkage, and polyester formulation is no exception. A typical value for the shrinkage is 8 per cent by volume, most of which occurs after gelation. Heat generated during polymerization can lead to charring and cracking when large masses of polyester resins are being cast. (Large amounts of resin are not commonly used in the conservation of glass.) The refractive index of stabilized polyester resins is typically 1.54–1.56 (Siconolfi, 1968).

Epoxy resin: condensate of bisphenol A and epichlorhydrin (5.8)

Propylene glycol   Maleic anhydride   Phthalic anhydride (5.9)

Components of a typical polyester resin, n 4

Acrylic polymers

The monomers from which acrylic polymers are made, fall into two groups, acrylates and methacrylates. The methacrylates were one of the first synthetic resins used to coat glass (Hedvall *et al.*, 1951), and as consolidants they are still amongst the most popular (Röhm and Haas, 1974; Wihr, 1977; Philipott and Mora, 1968). Acrylates and methacrylates are nominally derived from acrylic and methacrylic acids, respectively. These acids can be esterified with alcohol to produce a wide range of monomers:

(5.10)

Poly (alkyl acrylate)   Poly (alkyl methacrylate)

Acrylic polymers, monomer units. The alkyl (—R) group can be chosen to produce a range of polymers

The polymers made from the acrylates tend to have lower T_g points than the equivalent methacrylates. For example, poly(methyl methacrylate) such as Perspex has a T_g of 105°C, whereas poly(methyl acrylate) has a T_g of 3°C. Poly(methyl methacrylate)

sheet does not yellow on aging, and typifies the major advantage of acrylics; that is, their lack of colour change and resistance to oxidation. The T_g and refractive index values of acrylic polymers are given by Luskin and Myers (1964). However, both the polyacrylates and the higher polymethacrylates will cross-link under the influence of ultraviolet light and will eventually become insoluble. Poly(methyl methacrylate) is the most stable of the acrylic polymers reacting only very slowly to ultraviolet light. The presence of methyl methacrylate in copolymers increases the resistance to deterioration by light disproportionately to its concentration in the polymer (Siconolfi, 1968). For this reason methyl methacrylate is much used in both acrylic and other polymers.

As poly(methyl methacrylate) has too high a T_g for many adhesive and coating uses, softer acrylic polymers, which still retain colour stability, are prepared. Poly(butyl methacrylate), which has frequently been used in the past (McGrath *et al.*, 1961; Misra and Senguptal, 1970), has been shown to cross-link in ultraviolet light (Feller, 1972), and hence suggestions for its use, often under the trade-name of Bedacryl 122X (now Synocryl 9122X) should be reconsidered. Wihr (1977) used a solution of Plexigum 24 [a poly(butyl methacrylate)] and stated that it did not yellow and adhered well to the glass. However, this material could be expected to cross-link in time. Paraloid B-72 is now being widely used in conservation as a consolidant both on vessels and painted window glass. Paraloid B-72 is a very stable resin with a T_g of 40°C and a refractive index of 1.49. However, in 1978 de Witte *et al.* (1978) warned that the ratio of the resin's components had been changed by the manufacturer, and that as a result its long-term durability should be examined.

Poly(alkyl methacrylates) with longer side chains have lower T_g values and may be useful for conservation purposes. Copolymers of the methacrylates with acrylates such as ethyl- or 2-ethylhexylacrylate are used to achieve softer products with good colour stability. The relatively good stability of acrylic polymers over other polymers has resulted in a large number of speciality adhesives and coatings designed for use where degradation is a problem (Martin, F. R., 1977).

Cyanoacrylates

Cyanoacrylate resins have been widely recommended for use in repairing glass (Ferrazzini, 1976c,d; André, 1976; Moncrieff, 1975) because of their ease of application. Cyanoacrylates polymerize *in situ* in a few seconds at room temperature without the addition of a catalyst, the reaction being promoted by the presence of moisture or weak bases present on the glass surface:

$$\text{(5.11)}$$

R can be methyl, ethyl or butyl

$R =$ $-CH_3$ $-C_2H_5$ $-C_4H_9$
Approx T_g 165°C 120°C 100°C

Poly (alkyl cyanoacrylate)

Cyanacrylate monomer unit. The alkyl (—R) group can be varied to modify the polymer properties

The cured products are high molecular weight polymers which can be dissolved in organic solvents. The dilute alkali solutions on the glass surface cause deterioration of the polymer; thus cyanoacrylate adhesives are generally unsuitable for glass restoration except for effecting temporary repairs, for example when pressure-sensitive tape cannot be used on a delicate surface. Care should be taken in their use since cyanoacrylate resins bond very readily with skin tissue. In order to prolong their shelf-life the resins should be stored at a temperature of -20°C. See also Leonard *et al.* (1966), Horie (1981) and Coover and Wicker (1984).

Ultraviolet curing (photosensitive) acrylates

Acrylic resin formulations which cure on exposure to ultraviolet (u.v.) light, have been specially developed

for joining glass to glass and other substrates. The curing reaction results in a highly cross-linked polymer:

$$A\text{---}(HN\text{---}CO\text{---}O\text{---}R_2\text{---}CO\text{---}CH\text{==}CH_2)n$$
$$|$$
$$R_1$$
$$\text{(5.12)}$$

$R_1 = HCH_3$

$R_2 = -C_2H_4-, -C_2H_4 (CH_3)-$

A = poly(isocyanate), e.g. diphenylmethane 4,4-diisocyanate

The only brand of u.v. curing acrylate which has been tested for use in conservation and published (Madsen, 1972) is the American product Opticon UV57 which was found by Moncrieff (1975) to have poor physical properties both in the uncured and cured states. A second American u.v. curing adhesive, Norland Optical Adhesive 61, is currently (Robson, 1986) in use for tacking small fragments of glass which are difficult to tape. The use of u.v. curing adhesives should normally be considered to be non-reversible especially on porous glass surfaces where it is likely that mechanical keying will hold the polymer in the pores of the glass thereby making the bond virtually impossible to separate. The bond may only be considered to be reversible if it has been made between two smooth surfaces which can be cleaned mechanically after the join has been disrupted by soaking in solvents such as acetone or dichloromethane. Alternatively prolonged soaking in water can destroy the adhesive bond (but not dissolve the adhesive) if no coupling agent has been used (Davison, 1978).

An unexpected danger has been noticed when exposing glass to u.v. light. A test piece which was joined with a u.v. curing adhesive crizzled during the exposure to u.v. radiation. It is likely that improved u.v. curing products will become available, which will merit testing for conservation purposes.

Polyurethanes

Polyurethanes adhere well to polar surfaces because the isocyanate groups react with adsorbed water and hydroxyl groups; the tightly cross-linked network is fairly resistant to swelling by solvents.

Polyurethane foams are formed by mixing an isocyanate (generally toluene diisocyanate) and a polyhydroxyl component (a polyester or a polyether), and the foaming itself is frequently achieved by adding small amounts of water which react with the isocyanate to produce carbon dioxide. The adhesion of foamed polyurethanes is similar to that of the polyurethanes used for coatings; their resistance to solvents is greater, but they are less stable on aging (Moncrieff, 1971; Watkinson and

Leigh, 1978). Polyurethane foams are also referred to under lifting materials (page 184).

Bettembourg (1976b) tested a wide range of polymers for use as coating materials intended to protect medieval painted glass against attack by rain and atmospheric humidity. It has since been believed that these materials, being permeable to water vapour, will not only permit the attack to occur but will make matters worse by trapping the products of corrosion at the interface (Fitz *et al.*, 1984). In 1976, however, the most promising polymer seemed to be a polyurethane formed by the cross-linking reaction between a polyhydroxy acrylic resin (Viacryl) and an aliphatic polyisocyanate (Desmodur N). Viacryl has great stability to light and weathering and the permanence of the resin gave a false impression that the treatment was satisfactory but, as pointed out by Ferrazzini (1977a,b), damage could still occur beneath the resin. Further discussion of these problems, and of attempts to solve them, can be found in European Science Foundation (1976), ISC (1982, 1983, 1985) and Newton (1982b, 1987a). In addition, Viacryl has a T_g of 14°C and treated stained glass windows are likely to incorporate dirt into their surfaces during the summer months. Although Viacryl becomes insoluble, the film can be swelled and softened by one of the dichloromethane-based paint strippers, and then be removed mechanically (Ferrazzini, 1977a; Bacher, 1978).

Silicones and silanes

The term silicone is used as a loose description for the many compounds formed from silicon and organic radicals, and it therefore covers a series of compounds analogous to carbon compounds, but containing silicon in the main chain.

Silicon materials used in conservation (Horie, 1987) may be divided between the silanes and the silicones. The silanes are fairly simple molecules that are formulated to react strongly and irreversibly. These alkoxysilanes penetrate well and are used primarily (as coupling agents) to increase adhesion between a surface and a polymer (Moncrieff, 1976; Arnold, 1978), though they may also add to consolidation and reinforcement (Errett *et al.*, 1984). Silicone rubbers (USA: silastomers) are used where a flexible, stable rubber is required for joining fragments, as a mastic, or as a moulding material, and are of the room temperature vulcanizing (RTV) type (Noll, 1968; Beers, 1977). They have the general formula:

$$R\!-\!\underset{\underset{CH_3}{|}}{\overset{\overset{CH_3}{|}}{Si}}\!-\!O\!-\!\underset{\underset{Y}{|}}{\overset{\overset{Y}{|}}{Si}}\!-\!R \qquad (5.13)$$

where Y is either methoxy ($-OCH_3$), ethoxy ($-OC_2H_5$), acetoxy ($-O-(C=O)CH_3$), or dimethylketoxime ($-O-N=C(CH_3)_2$).

The rubbers start as viscous liquids (composed of large silicone molecules plus fillers etc.) which then react to form a cross-linked rubbery solid, more or less rigid depending on the formulation. The large molecules have reactive end groups which cross-link through small reactive molecules (silanes). Traces of water and metal catalysts are normally required. The liquid pre-polymers are available as two-part formulations where the catalyst is added, or as one-part formulations where water is excluded until they are used. All the formulations contain a proportion of unreacted silicone oil which, because it has a low surface tension, can migrate away from the rubber to cause staining of porous materials, and may act as a release agent.

The rubbers made from silanes are inherently water white and have exceptional weathering stability. They change hardly at all with exposure to u.v. light and water, but they have little strength compared with other elastomers. The two-part (RTV) silicones do not have much adhesion to surfaces such as metal, but have sufficient adhesion to glass to need a separating agent when silicone rubber moulds are made. The one-part curing silicones can have appreciable adhesion, depending on their cross-linking functional groups, although they may require coupling agents for maximum adhesion. Silicones are insoluble in solvents but they will swell considerably in aliphatic, aromatic and chlorinated hydrocarbons (Noll, 1968, p. 512).

Clear silicone rubbers with a refractive index of 1.43 are used commercially to repair damaged plate glass windows. However, since they have a very low T_g of -123°C they attract dirt and within a few weeks the lines of silicone rubber become grey and then blackened as a result of dirt held on, and eventually in, the polymer (Billmeyer, 1971).

Obviously the moisture-curing silicones cannot be exposed to the air without starting to cure. It is therefore difficult to add dyes to the rubber before it is applied. The use of these rubber adhesives will therefore leave a clear (uncoloured) line between the fragments, and this is especially noticeable when dark glasses, such as ruby glass, are joined. If, however, anhydrous solvents are used (Bettembourg, 1975), the silicones can be diluted, and this procedure makes it easier to incorporate pigments into the silicone rubber.

Moisture-curing silicone rubbers are very stable to light, and during curing probably form bonds with the silanol groups on the surface of the glass to create a strong and stable joint. They have the added advantage of being flexible and they can therefore adapt to movements of the glass with temperature. One important aspect, not investigated by Bettembourg, is the reversibility of silicones. As it will be virtually impossible to remove silicone rubbers from rough glass surfaces it may be unwise (but perhaps impossible to avoid in practice) to allow the diluted silicone to touch an exposed glass surface. It is likely that swelling of the rubbery silicone mass in a solvent would cause less disruption of the polymer film than would similar swelling of an epoxy resin, and thus make the separation of joined fragments of glass and removal of the adhesive extremely difficult if not impossible.

Silane coupling agents were discussed in the section on adhesion and silicone moulding materials will be discussed under moulding materials.

Vinyl polymers

Poly(vinyl acetate) (PVAC) has been used in conservation for many years, but only recently for the consolidation of glass on a wide scale (Brill, 1971a; Davison, 1978; Dowman, 1970; Garlake, 1969; Hutchinson, 1981; Majewski, 1973; Unwin, 1951). PVAC is stable, has a refractive index of 1.46 (similar to that of glass), a good resistance to yellowing (Geuskens *et al.*, 1972), and it is available in a wide range of molecular weights (Moore and Murphy, 1962). The molecular weight is related to the viscosity of the solution and is important for achieving adequate penetration, for example, a PVAC molecule with a molecular weight (MW) of 51 000, equivalent to 600 monomer units per chain (the degree of polymerization, DP), would have a minimum diameter of 13 nm, and thus it could not penetrate pores as small as that (Kurata *et al.*, 1975). However, it has a low T_g (28°C) and is therefore prone to cold flow, and to attracting and absorbing dirt, when the MW is low (<57 000), (Torraca, 1968). In order to inhibit this tendency to attract dirt, a top coat of a compatible polymer with a higher T_g should be applied. PVAC appears to be a useful consolidant for dehydrated glass, as a 25 per cent solution in toluene, or as more dilute solutions in alcohol.

Poly(vinyl chloride) (PVC) solutions (Derm-O-Plast SG, ArcheoDerm) have been recommended for consolidating degraded glass (Wihr, 1977). Unfortunately, PVC is one of the most unstable polymers in commercial production and should therefore not be used in direct contact with antiquities (Matheson and Boyer, 1952); it will degrade, discolour, release hydrochloric acid, and probably become insoluble with time.

Poly(vinyl butyral) (PVB) has a refractive index of 1.49 (and is used as the interlayer of laminated windscreens for motor vehicles); it has good adhesion to glass and a fairly satisfactory T_g of 62–68°C, but it cross-links on prolonged exposure to light and should therefore be considered to be insoluble in the long term. Of the grades of PVB which have been recommended for glass conservation are those with lower MWs, for example, Butvar B-98 (Monsanto) and Mowital B20H (Hoechst). PVB has been used by Vos-Davidse (1969).

Vinyl polymers which are polymerized in emulsion can be significantly different from those polymerized by other techniques because surfactants and other emulsifiers become inextricably incorporated in the polymer. The advantage of emulsions is that water (inexpensive and non-toxic) is used as the diluent, and the absence of hazardous solvents has encouraged the use of emulsions where large open areas of liquid are required, such as in the conservation of textiles and paper.

A polymer emulsion has a very high solids content with a low viscosity. Frequently the viscosity of the emulsion is deliberately increased by the manufacturer to make handling easier. The high content of solids permits thicker films to be deposited, with less shrinkage than is the case with films applied from solvents. Up to 10 per cent of the solids content of an emulsion consists of the emulsifiers and stabilizers. When the emulsion dries to form a film, the emulsifiers in the polymer film are known to cause sensitivity to water and a lowering of clarity. Many of the emulsifiers cause yellowing of the film, for example, films of PVAC cast from emulsions turn yellow far more rapidly than those cast from solution. Further problems arise when polymeric emulsifiers such as poly(vinyl alcohol) (PVAL) or poly(acrylic acid) have been incorporated into the film. Both can undergo cross-linking reactions and thus reduce the solubility of the polymer to which they are attached.

Emulsifiers usually work best with a proper balance of ionic materials in the solution. There are three categories of emulsifiers: anionic, non-ionic and cationic. The cationic emulsifiers are rarely used. Anionic emulsifiers require acid conditions, while non-ionic emulsifiers can withstand a wider pH range. Before using any emulsion on glass, conservators should ensure that it has a pH at which that glass is stable.

The films formed from emulsions are frequently soft, with T_g points below room temperature. As the water evaporates from an emulsion, the polymer particles are forced closer together. These particles must coalesce if a coherent film is to form and therefore the particles must be soft enough to flow into one another. In general the polymer particles must be above their T_g for coalescence to occur and thus the polymer film is usually above its T_g when set. Films formed at room temperature will therefore have a T_g below room temperature and will absorb dirt.

Volatile solvents may be added to the emulsion in order to soften the polymer temporarily. Only small quantities can be added before the solvents destabilize the emulsion.

Emulsions are usually formulated by manufacturers to fill a particular need, and many of the detrimental effects of the present emulsions available commercially could be reduced by changes in formulating the product. Investigations should be made to determine the optimum combination of properties for a particular conservation use.

Mastics

Painted glass windows are constructed by fixing the pieces of glass into lead strips and sealing the edges of the lead with a mastic. The traditional mastic (the *cement*) which consisted of linseed oil, whiting, red lead etc. is still widely used but modern polymeric materials (Damusis, 1967; Panek, 1977) are also being tried. The role of the mastic is to hold the glass firmly in place and yet absorb the movements of the window under the forces of wind pressure etc. The mastic must therefore maintain flexibility for the period between releadings (say 150 years). The method of application of the various mastics depends on the type of material being used.

Oil-based putties

Linseed oil putties start as viscous liquids and set by oxidative cross-linking to form flexible solids; these then gradually degrade to brittle solids that crack and eventually fall out of the flanges of the leads (Bettembourg *et al.*, 1984). The newer oil mastics, based on soya bean oil (Bieneman, 1967), set more slowly but take much longer to become brittle. See also Wexler (1964).

Butyl rubber

Butyl rubber is one of the more stable of the hydrocarbon elastomers (Stucker and Higgins, 1977) and it would be expected to have a reasonable durability, although not as long as that of silicones. The material used in the painted glass workshops in Canterbury and York is Arboflex 500. It is like Plasticine in consistency and is pushed into the gap between the glass and the lead. The material does not set but eventually, after many years, will become brittle due to oxidation.

Silicone rubber

Bettembourg (1975) tested a range of silicone, mercaptan, rubber and traditional materials for use as adhesives and fillers for the leading on painted glass, and concluded that the one-part moisture-curing silicone rubber adhesives were the most suitable.

Many of the silicone sealants on the market liberate acetic acid on curing and it might therefore be thought that they should be avoided for use on lead, owing to the danger that the acetic acid may cause corrosion of the lead. In fact, a case has been reported (*CVMA News Letter*, no. 18, Feb. 1976) where such corrosion has occurred in a sealed enclosure (a 'plated' glass) but no cases have yet come to light where corrosion has occurred in a freely ventilated situation.

Other types of silicone rubber, for example the oxime-curing silicones such as Type 3144 (Dow Corning) or the alkoxy-curing silicones such as Type 1200 (Vallance), would not cause corrosion of lead but they cure much more slowly (in hours, rather than minutes) and this disadvantage seems from most glaziers' viewpoints to outweigh the rare possibility of corrosion in an unventilated situation.

The layer of lead oxide which normally occurs on metallic lead weakens the adhesive bond between lead and polymer. Thus, in order to obtain the best adhesion, the lead should be abraded to remove at least some of the oxide film, then degreased and be treated with a primer such as SCP 3153 (Vallance) before the silicone adhesive is used (*CVMA News Letter*, No. 22, Oct. 1976).

Modelling materials

Missing areas of glass may be modelled up *in situ* prior to moulding, using one of several commercially produced modelling materials. Those most commonly used are potters' clay and Plasticine. Plasticine is a putty composed of petroleum jelly, fatty acids and whiting. These oily substances enable the Plasticine to be worked to a smooth surface; however, it does not adhere very well to glass, and will contaminate the surface. Plasticine residues should be removed with cotton wool swabs moistened with a degreasing solvent such as acetone or toluene before adhesives are applied to the glass.

Aloplast is a modelling material similar to Plasticine in texture, but formulated especially for use against polyester resins. However, being dark blue in colour it has a tendency to discolour the resin.

Damp clay adheres very well to glass and is easily worked to a smooth surface with a spatula dipped in water. In addition any fragments of glass which can be positioned accurately but which do not actually join to the body of a vessel (i.e. floating fragments) may be held in position by placing them *in situ* on a clay former. The disadvantage of using clay is that moisture contained within it separates any adhesive used in the repair from the glass. Backing joins with tape, rubber latex or thin sheets of wax does not prevent this from occurring. In fact adhesive on Sellotape and masking tape breaks down with moisture to form a messy substance, removal of the wax sometimes causes the joins to fail, and latex flows into tiny cracks and chips and is difficult to remove without dismantling the glass.

Moulding materials

Materials used for taking moulds from glass artefacts should have the following properties: They should not harm the object physically by adhering too strongly to the surface, by pulling off glass projections, or by heat generation. They should not harm the glass chemically by contaminating or reacting with it. Moulding materials should reproduce all the fine details of the original without distortion. The viscosity and thixotropic properties should be sufficiently variable by the manufacturer or conservator to allow the materials to be adapted to meet different requirements. They should preferably be available at reasonable cost and have an adequate shelf-life. Moulds must be able to withstand heat of polymerization of the proposed casting material and must not react with that material.

For moulding glass the most suitable material is usually silicone rubber (USA, silastomer) which is available in several grades of thixotropicity. However, the cheaper materials, plaster of Paris and dental wax, are frequently used.

The majority of silicone rubber products used for moulding cure by catalytic elimination of alcohol to form cross-links between the chains. When the alcohol evaporates, the rubber shrinks but the amount of shrinkage is small (less than 1 per cent) and occurs over a period of a few days. However, shrinkage of 2.2 per cent has been observed to occur over a number of years. Silicones are insoluble in solvents but can be swelled considerably by the use of aliphatic, aromatic and chlorinated hydrocarbons (Noll, 1968). Wihr (1977) has suggested swelling silicone rubber back to size by exposing it to organic solvents, but this would seem to be an unreliable method.

In the majority of cases silicone rubber requires no release agent between it and the glass surface, although instances of silicone rubber adhering to glass and porcelain have been known (Morgós *et al.*, 1984), and therefore preliminary tests must be undertaken. A release agent such as petroleum jelly or an organic lacquer must be used if silicone rubber is to be cast against a cured section of silicone rubber, or the two will adhere. Thin layers of silicone rubber may tear when peeled off an object, but thick layers are hard-wearing and the moulds are reusable. If necessary, it may be overcatalysed to shorten its setting time, for instance, when silicone rubber is being used to reattach a silicone rubber mould to glass.

Inert fillers such as kaolin, talc or aerosol silica may be added to thicken mobile grades of silicone rubber. Unfortunately many cured silicone rubbers are prone to tearing and must be applied in thick section and often with a rigid case mould for support.

Rubber latex shrinks too much to be of use in moulding such a precise material as glass; a small shrinkage will mean that details such as trailed threads on the glass will not match up with those on the cast. A mould must remain stable for several days or weeks whilst restoration is in progress.

Hot-melt preparations

Hot-melt preparations such as gelatine, Formalose and Vinamold (PVC) should be avoided for direct use on glass since the heat may cause damage. However, Formalose, a gelatine material containing glycerine to keep it flexible (Wihr, 1977), is useful for reproducing the interior shape of an object with a narrow neck where plaster or rubber cannot be introduced. The Formalose can be poured hot into a plaster mould and, on cooling, it sets and begins to shrink uniformly. A watch must be kept and when there is a gap between the Formalose and the plaster, representing the thickness of the glass vessel to be reproduced, resin can be cast into the gap. The Formalose core must be supported away from the plaster walls. The method is described by Petermann (1969).

Dental waxes are composed of a number of different waxes and are often supplied as sheets measuring 180 mm × 82 mm × 1.5 mm. Dental waxes are available in various grades of hardness, in sheet sizes up to 305 mm × 203 mm, and in thicknesses of 0.4 to 3 mm. For making moulds the sheets or parts of them can be softened by gentle heating in water or warm air before shaping them over the glass object. Before casting, the wax mould must be coated with poly(vinyl alcohol) (PVAL) (which is difficult because it tends to run into pools) as a release agent between the wax and the resin to be cast against it. The PVAL must be brushed continuously until it has almost set, and it may be necessary to apply a second coat when the first has dried.

Plaster of Paris

Plaster of Paris (calcium sulphate) is prepared by heating gypsum ($CaSO_4.2H_2O$) to drive off some of the combined water, forming $2CaSO_4.H_2O$. On adding more water, the calcium sulphate rehydrates, forming interlocking crystals which set to a rock-like mass with very slight expansion, typically 0.5 per cent. Various grades of plaster are available with different setting times, expansions and particle fineness. Dental plasters are available which set to form very hard solids with minimal expansion. The material is cheap and is a useful product for the construction of case-moulds over silicone rubber. However, it requires release agents between plaster-to-plaster surfaces and plaster-to-resin ones. It is rigid and hence any undercuts on the glass must be moulded separately, preferably in silicone rubber. If incorrectly placed it is difficult to remove without causing damage.

Release agents

Release agents must prevent adhesion between objects, moulds and casts; the agent chosen will depend upon the materials being used. As previously mentioned, silicone rubber only requires the use of a release agent such as petroleum jelly or organic lacquer when it is being cast against a section of cured silicone rubber. The surface of plaster of Paris mould pieces, however, must be sealed as each is made to prevent it adhering to the adjacent pieces; and release agents must be applied to facilitate removal of resin if it is cast directly into a plaster mould.

Shellac in a solution of industrial methylated spirit (IMS) (US, grain alcohol), or a solution of PVAL, can be used to seal the surface of dry plaster of Paris mould-pieces, after which the surface is coated with soft soap, Vaseline, detergent, petroleum jelly or a wax emulsion (Koob, 1979). If the resin is to be cast directly into plaster moulds, a specially formulated release agent must be applied to the plaster surface, such as Scopas (PVAL). This is frequently coloured so that it can be seen when all the surfaces have been covered adequately, but will be a disadvantage if PVAL remains on the cast.

Silicone release agents can be used as liquids or in spray cans. Traces of silicone oils will remain on the cast, and if they are not removed completely they can prevent paint or adhesives bonding properly to the surface.

Polytetrafluoroethane (PTFE) dispersions in aerosol cans are also used as release agents.

Casting materials

The requirements for casting materials for use with glass are very severe. It should be possible to pour the material into moulds; it should set with minimal shrinkage to form a hard solid; and it should be crystal clear and remain colourless indefinitely. No materials meet this specification completely, although some come close to it.

Polyester resins

Many clear polyester embedding resins are available, but it is obviously outside the scope of this book to discuss them all. Suffice it to say that before restoration work begins, the resin to be used should be tested by mixing and casting it into a mould of the same material to be used in the final reconstruction. This will ensure that the resin's shelf-life has not expired and its behaviour is as expected (i.e. the formula of the product has not been altered by the manufacturer since it was last ordered).

Polyester resins are normally cast into closed moulds; as they are generally used in small quantities steps should be taken to minimize wastage. It is not usually practical to work on several objects at one time, but small quantities of resins may be accurately weighed on a digital balance, or dispensed from a disposable syringe (minus the needle).

Where polyester resin is applied as a flat surface against a one-sided mould, it must be applied in thin layers, each layer being allowed to cure in turn. If only one layer is required in order to correspond with the thickness of the glass, it may be possible to incorporate glass fibre surfacing tissue to impart strength. However, the fibre filaments will remain slightly visible within the resin (see *Figures 7.22* and *7.29d*). Clear polyester resins may be coloured without noticeably altering their transparency by the addition of minute quantities of translucent polyester pigments.

Disadvantages in the use of polyester resins are the shrinkage of 8 per cent during curing (though this can partly be compensated for by topping up the mould as the resin polymerizes); the emission of styrene for some considerable time after curing; and the fact that the resin surface often remains tacky for some time. Reasons for this latter phenomenon are interference from atmospheric moisture, aging of the hardener, or, if they are stored under refrigeration, using the resin and hardener before they have reached room temperature, thus preventing the complete chemical reaction.

Hardening of the surface is aided by polymerizing the cast in a dry atmosphere, for example, in a sealed cabinet containing trays of silica gel. Warming the cast in an oven is not recommended since it may cause premature discoloration of the resin. Polyester embedding resins abrade and polish easily.

Poly(methacrylate) resins

Plastogen G with Lumopal hardener, used by Wihr (1963) and Errett (1972) is transparent and mobile and is therefore normally cast into closed moulds (see above). The liquid resin is mixed with 0.25–0.5 per cent hardener (powder) which is difficult to assess in small quantities, and the addition of too much hardener may cause premature discoloration of the resin. Plastogen G has a 15 min pot-life but cannot be worked during that time because a skin quickly forms over the surface; it also has an extremely powerful, unpleasant smell. After mixing, and if necessary colouring, the resin should be covered and left to stand whilst air-bubbles escape. Notman (1973b) used a coloured acrylic resin to build up grozed edges in stained glass so that the pieces could be edge-joined.

Technovit

The grade most suited to glass restoration is 4004A, which is translucent and therefore can only be used as a gapfiller on opaque glass. The polymer (powder) is mixed with the liquid monomer in the ratio of 5 parts to 3, but the proportions are not critical and the setting time may be varied by changing the amount of powder. When mixed in the recommended proportions Technovit 4004A sets at room temperature in 10 to 15 min, but can be worked with a spatula during this time. This product is guaranteed by the manufacturer not to shrink or expand on curing. It emits heat if cast in large amounts. Technovit adheres well to glass, is relatively hard and can be abraded and polished.

Epoxy resins
Araldite AY103/HY956 and similar types of epoxy resins available in other countries may be used as gapfillers. However, all epoxy resins are slightly yellow and can further discolour in time and thus are generally unsuitable unless the resin is to be pigmented. In general, epoxy resins do not respond well to polishing after abrasion.

Colouring materials

Materials used for colouring fall into two categories: those used for mixing in with resin and those applied to the resin after it has cured. Colours for mixing in with the resin may be transparent or opaque depending upon the desired effect.

When incorporating colour with a resin, enough coloured resin must be produced to complete the restoration and allowance must be made for areas which may have to be cast more than once, or may have to be made good. This is important since a colour can rarely be exactly matched a second or third time. Hardener is then added to small amounts of the coloured resin as required for use and the resin is allowed to stand before use to enable air-bubbles to escape.

Most glass on display in museum cases is exposed to high levels of illumination and hence light-resistant pigments are needed in any restored portions. Improvements in pigment technology have provided the conservator with a fairly wide palette of colours, and a list of light-resistant pigments has been given by Thomson (1978). Other pigments are used by Wihr (1963), Davison (1981), Errett (1972) and Staude (1972).

Occasionally, pigments can produce adverse effects with some reactive polymers and hence it is then more satisfactory to purchase ready-mixed colours. There are colours for polyesters, silicones, and for epoxies; their light stability must be checked before use.

Unfortunately, the transparent epoxy and polyester adhesive and casting materials often require the use of dyes rather than pigments to colour them, in order to retain their transparency, and there is a much smaller range of light-stable dyes available for use in polymers.

Retouching lacquers
The lacquers usually employed for retouching the restored portions of glass objects are frequently those used in the restoration of ceramics, porcelain in particular. Transparency and retention of colour are important, but unfortunately the widely used moisture-curing polyurethane PU-11 has been discontinued, and its suggested replacement, PU-16, is unlikely to be suitable because it is an alkyd resin which will discolour much faster than the polyurethane. The two-part polyurethanes, such as the Viacryl System, have better retention of colour than the one-part polyurethanes, but they are more difficult to use. Chinaglaze, a urea-formaldehyde/melamine-formaldehyde mixture, forms a hard clear coating when catalysed, and has good colour retention. However, this type of polymer is almost unaffected by solvents and it would be most difficult to remove from a glass surface. For this reason it should be used only on the restored parts, and not on any original material.

Enamelled decoration may be copied on resin casts using any pigments and media used for ceramic restoration, provided that they adhere to the cast and the solvent does not damage it. Gold decoration may be copied in leaf gold applied on a size, or as liquid metallic paints, though the latter will probably discolour on aging.

Lifting materials

Poly(ethylene glycol)
Poly(ethylene glycol)s (PEG) are widely recommended for providing reinforcement and bulking during removal of objects from the ground. Various grades are available (Blackshaw; 1975), but it is the harder, higher molecular weight polymers (4000 and 6000) that are used for this purpose. PEG will shrink slightly on freezing, and also on cooling to room temperature. PEG can be removed by remelting, or washing in solvents such as water, alcohols, trichloroethane or toluene (Union Carbide, 1976).

Poly(vinyl chloride)
Vinyl polymers have already been discussed, but the use of poly(vinyl chloride) in the field should be mentioned here.

A poly(vinyl chloride) solution, Derm-O-Plast SG, has been recommended for consolidating both the soil and fragile objects (Wihr, 1977). This product has now been discontinued but a new product (Archaeo-Derm), presumably of the same type, has been substituted (Filoform). PVC is one of the most unstable polymers in commercial production and should not be used in contact with artefacts. Small traces remaining after cleaning will degrade, discolour, release hydrochloric acid, and probably become insoluble.

Flexible polyurethane foams

Polyurethane foams are expensive but may be convenient materials, owing to their lightness, for lifting and for packaging excavated artefacts and fragile structural remains (e.g. glass kilns). Polyurethanes are made by mixing two components (isocyanate and polyol) each of which is available in a range of formulations. This in turn creates a range of products of varying properties, for example, flexibility and stability. The greatest variability is the polyol component which may be polyester or polyether. Various catalysts such as amines and tin compounds are incorporated which may increase the degradation of the foam and its effects on objects. The isocyanate used to produce flexible foams is generally toluene diisocyanate:

$$\text{(5.14)}$$

On mixing, the components expand forming a foam within 3 min, the exact time being dependent on the temperature.

All the isocyanates are very toxic but the smaller and more volatile compounds are the most dangerous because of the ease of breathing in the vapour. For example, toxic fumes (TLV, 0.02 ppm) are given off by the isocyanate component in polyurethane foam and this can survive unchanged in the completed foam. Thus extreme care must be taken when using products based on polyurethane.

The flexible foams are resilient open cell structures. In general, the polyether derived foam is preferred for packaging, having better cushioning properties and being less likely to degrade. However, both polyester and polyether foams will gradually deteriorate on aging, especially when exposed to light; polyester foams in particular can disintegrate forming a sticky powder.

Packaging materials

Flexible food-wrapping films are often suggested for keeping objects wet during storage. Such products as Clingfilm or Saranwrap are poly(vinyl chloride) films heavily plasticized with a material such as dioctyladipate, and are prone to degradation especially if exposed to light. Poly(vinyl chloride) films will retain water to a certain extent, but the rate of water diffusion through them is greater than through poly(ethylene) sheeting of the same thickness. For storage periods longer than a few days therefore, heavy gauge poly(ethylene) sheeting, heat-sealed around the edges, would provide better protection for objects.

Self-adhesive (pressure-sensitive) tapes are widely used in conservation for packaging purposes and do not present any problems. Where greater strength is required, plastic tape or string may be used. However, certain difficulties may be encountered in the use of self-adhesive tapes for holding fragments of glass in place during setting of adhesives. Liquid adhesives can flow into the pores of an object and may increase the adhesion of the tape to the surface of objects if the tapes are left in position for longer than necessary. Thus on removal the tapes may lift fragments of glass with it. Tape alone should never be used for supporting fragments of glass during storage since it will degrade to a brittle or sticky mass with some resulting damage to objects.

If there is any risk of endangering the object, solvents should be used to soften the adhesive before attempting to remove the tape. The tapes use a natural rubber, or similar, contact adhesive, which can degrade more or less rapidly to form an intractable brown mass. This seems to have been the cause of the yellow staining in some of the windows when traces of 'Tesa' film were left on the stained glass windows in the St Lorenzkirche at Nuremburg (Frenzel, 1969) and in Cologne (Moncrieff, 1974). As it may well be impossible to remove the last traces of the adhesive from this type of self-adhesive tape, it would be wise to use only those tapes which use a more stable adhesive, such as an acrylic, which have been introduced in recent years.

Nevertheless, efforts should always be made, by using solvents, to remove the last traces of any adhesive which remains after stripping the tape from the object. A useful mixture for removing self-adhesive tape from antiquities is made up as follows: 5 ml toluene, 5 ml 1,1,1-trichloroethane, 1 ml concentrated ammonia and 10 ml industrial methylated spirits.

Fragile objects will need to be packed in *acid-free tissue* (never cotton wool) and/or an inert foam inside strong cardboard boxes. Paper used for storage must be long lasting, and as such will normally consist of highly purified cellulose, perhaps buffered to ensure that the paper is acid-free. The term acid-free means only that the paper is currently non-acidic, and is no guarantee that deterioration will not produce acids or other harmful emissions. However, for the majority of chemically insensitive materials higher specification than acid-free is unnecessary.

Poly(ethylene) foam is composed of poly(ethylene) (sometimes copolymerized with vinyl acetate) which has been blown into foamed sheets. The foam is made of closed cells which result in increased stiffness and resistance to compression. It is available in a range of thicknesses, split or laminated from the standard sheet size; and is easily cut with a sharp knife. *Cardboard boxes* are made of compressed paper pulp (usually recycled) which is made into board of various thicknesses by building up layers of thinner plies, and frequently faced with brown paper. The boards commonly used range from 1.0 to 2.2 mm thick. The board is bent to shape and fixed by staples (stitches), brass being preferable to stainless steel. On aging, fibreboard oxidizes and becomes weaker, a process which is accelerated in damp conditions since it is permeable to and absorbs water vapour. The life-span of a good fibreboard box in good storage conditions seems to be in excess of 20 years. In poorer conditions and over longer periods there is increased danger of the box collapsing.

For further information on materials used in conservation, see Horie (1987).

6

Technical examination of glass

A conservator can obtain a great deal of information about a glass fragment or artefact from simple observation and tests. By examination through a hand lens or through a binocular microscope the following details may be seen: evidence of the methods of manufacture and decoration, scratches and imperfections, wear and weathering, colour, transparency or opacity, and any physical impurities contained in the body of the glass (Smith, 1963a,b).

The chemical analyses of glasses by traditional methods are falling into disuse for conservation purposes. The reasons for this are that chemical analyses are extremely time consuming, require highly trained analysts, need substantial amounts of glass as samples, and require preliminary dissolution of the glass with hydrofluoric acid, or by fusion with sodium carbonate. Nevertheless, in competent hands, excellent results can be obtained by chemical analysis of very small glass samples (Besborodov, 1957), using instrumental techniques such as atomic absorption spectrometry (AAS) (Howden *et al.*, 1977). For example, Cowell and Werner (1973) used samples only 10 mg in weight, and determined twelve oxides (all the significant ones except SiO_2 and P_2O_5).

In addition to physical and chemical methods of examination, a wide range of instrumental methods of analysis is used in other areas of scientific research, and may sometimes be of use in the examination of glasses (Vassas, 1971a,b). Very few conservation laboratories will contain the specialized equipment for scientific examination and analysis, but it is often possible to work in collaboration with a research laboratory, should detailed information be required. This introduction to the examination of glass is, therefore, largely advisory in nature, stating the purposes which many of the more sophisticated tests serve, rather than describing how to carry them out. Brill (1968) and Hench (1975a) provide further information on the application of scientific techniques to glasses, and references for further reading; many of the details of the techniques themselves are given by Tite (1972). Before scientific methods of analysis can be used with confidence, it must be certain that the results of analyses in one laboratory will be essentially the same as those from the same glass from another laboratory (Brill, 1971c). Otherwise, observed differences in composition etc. could be due either to true compositional differences, or to those inherent in the particular analytical procedures of the laboratories concerned, the accuracy of which will depend very much upon the expertise of the scientist. The establishment of standard reference glasses is therefore important in order to achieve any meaningful results (particularly as glasses have such a complex nature). It is for this reason that analyses of glasses have not been included in this volume.

Visual examination and simple tests

Use of a hand lens

A good hand lens of reasonable diameter is a good investment, and it is worth obtaining an aplanat which gives a flat field of vision. Opinions differ as to the most useful power of lens, but personal convenience is important (Organ, 1968). It is useful to have a magnifier with two lenses (e.g. ×4 and ×10), but lenses which are stronger than ×15 are not easy to use. It may be advantageous to examine glass by transmitted light, for example, by placing it on a photographic light box.

Use of microscopes

The maximum magnification which can conveniently be obtained with a hand lens is about ×20. To obtain higher magnifications, a microscope is used. The most useful type of microscope is the binocular type which provides a stereoscopic three-dimensional image (Brill, 1968), that is, one with two objective lenses. These microscopes are also designed with a long working distance (say about 100 mm between the object and the bottom of the objective lens) so that an object can be manipulated, pits can be cleaned, weathering crusts can be examined etc., while an enlarged stereoscopic view is still obtained. They may also have a variable magnification obtained by a *zoom* lens in the system, sometimes from ×7 to ×50, but more often the magnification is only doubled or trebled. There are many cases when much higher magnifications (up to ×1000) are needed, but higher magnification microscopes are considerably more expensive because other attachments will become necessary, for example polarizers for examining crystals etc.; surface illumination (metallurgical microscope) for looking at opaque materials etc.; and equipment for phase-contrast studies. Instructions for the use of sophisticated microscopes can be found in Martin and Johnson (1962), Richardson (1971) and McCrone and Delly (1973).

Recording information

The results of observations must be *dated* and noted *at the time of examination*. Notes and sketches made from memory are unreliable, particularly as they may incorporate preconceived ideas about the glass, for example its method of manufacture. Observations must be separated from conclusions; for instance, an observation of painted medieval window glass may reveal a yellow colour which might be concluded to be yellow stain. Measurements should be given in Système International (SI) units, metres (m), millimetres (mm), and micrometres (μm) etc. An exception to this rule is the use of cm^2, because there is such a large gap between mm^2 and m^2; but millilitres (ml) should be used instead of cm^3.

Sketches should be made at a consistent scale, such as 1:1. If the object being studied is large, reduced size sketches will be required such as 1:2, 1:4, 1:10 etc. Small fragments of glass may need to be enlarged and here it is even more important to indicate the scale, for example 2:1, 4:1 etc., preferably with the addition of a drawn scale.

Photography

It is essential that a photographic record be kept of the evidence discovered by examination of glasses. This record may be in the form of black and white prints or 35 mm transparencies, depending on the features being recorded. With the aid of a camera attachment, it is possible to take photographs through a microscope. A camera which provides instant prints may also prove useful, especially for recording transient phenomena. Such cameras can be used for all types of photography, in monochrome or in colour, and their potential should not be overlooked for recording stages of excavation or cleaning on site or in the laboratory, which cannot be repeated. When photographing successive stages in the conservation of an artefact, it is important to give early consideration to the lighting, which will have a profound effect on the appearance of the result. The eye is accustomed to shadows falling to the right, and at the bottom, to represent relief. Thus the light should fall from a point at the upper left. But the position of the light should be constant for each stage in the process. The light source, filter, colour film, and magnification should also be the same for each stage so that the prints (or colour slides) should all be comparable. A scale of millimetres should appear in each photograph, and preferably also the reference number of the sample. Some samples will need to be photographed by transmitted light in addition to reflected light.

In taking macrophotographs (an enlargement of more than 1:1) when using long extension tubes with the normal lens (instead of using a macro lens), a better image will be obtained by reversing the lens, using a reversing ring (which enables the large end of the lens to be fitted to the extension tube, with the small end, normally inside the camera, pointing towards the object) because the lens has been designed so that the small end accepts rays at acute angles and the large end accepts rays which are more nearly parallel. When the camera is so close to the object that the light from it reaches the lens at an acute angle, then a better image is obtained by reversing the lens.

Examination of the surface

Firstly the condition of the surface of the glass in question should be examined. Note should be taken as to whether the surface is shiny, dull or iridescent, if it is noticeably weathered or pitted, and if so, the size and frequency of the pits should be recorded. Alternatively, the surface may be crusted or scratched and fractured, or crizzled. If the glass has been in a fire the damage caused to it can be extremely variable, depending on the circumstances: prolonged exposure to a hot (1000°C) fire will melt the glass into lumps, whereas an intact window exposed to a blaze on one side may develop characteristic wavy, oblique cracks.

If the sample is a piece of window glass, and if it has a reasonably shiny and reflective surface, the following procedure should be used (Cable, 1979): the reflection from the surface should be examined carefully, especially if black lines can be viewed in the reflection. First, one can distinguish between optical distortion produced by waviness of the surface, and that produced (in glass with a flat surface) by the presence of internal cords and striae. Secondly, the reflection of ruled black lines is a sensitive indicator of the way the glass was made; crown glass shows the presence of circular lines; cylinder glass shows unevenness produced by flattening with a *rake*; and Fourcault glass displays parallel lines (*piano lines*) on the surface.

If the glass surface bears flaking or enamel weathering, it should be examined for signs of forgery, which may take the form of flakes of glass applied with adhesive, and masked with mud. Weathering of the surface in parallel ridges (*Figure 4.10*) may indicate the presence of inhomogeneities in the glass. The surface may show signs of wear especially on the base of an object; abrasion should be examined to determine whether it is the result of usage or burial (e.g. it is fairly uniform around the vessel, and has rounded edges), or whether a forger may have abraded it artificially.

If the glass surface is merely translucent, this will usually be the result of abrasion or weathering; but the glass may also have been sand-blasted or etched with acid, and here again, it may be necessary to consider whether a forger has been at work (von Saldern, 1970; Goldstein, 1977). Finally, if there are drops of moisture on the glass surface, these should be tested with pH paper. If they are strongly alkaline, and reappear a short time after the surface has been wiped, the glass may be weeping and require special treatment as discussed in Chapter 7, Part 1.

Examination of the body

If the glass is coloured, the colour should be noted along with the way it is distributed on or through the glass. It is usually sufficient to describe colour in plain terms (that is, blue, green etc.) which is more accurate and therefore less misleading than descriptions of particular shades. Greater objectivity can be obtained by the use of standard colour charts, such as the Munsell system (Munsell, n.d.) or, if the matter is sufficiently important, the colour can be measured on a scientific basis (Thomson, 1978). When the colour is distributed uniformly through the glass, the latter is described as *pot metal* because the colouring oxides were added to the melting crucible, or pot. In some cases, especially *copper rubies*, the colour is very dense and it can be used only as a thin layer, called a *flashing*, on a thicker colourless base glass. Flashed glasses appear uniformly coloured when viewed at right angles to the surface but seem largely colourless or greenish when viewed through the edge. In some modern flashed rubies the flashing may be very thin (e.g. 0.1 mm thick) and quite difficult to see in an edge view. Colours other than red may have been flashed if the artist wished to produce special effects, for example, in the case of cameo cutting. Non-uniform colourings may be present in the form of *enamels* and *stains*. Enamelling was applied to the outer surface of vessel glass and to the front of window glass (i.e. facing inside the building). Quite a different technique, that of *silver staining*, was applied to the exterior face of window glass. It is frequently stated that silver (or yellow) staining protects the glass against the effects of weathering (see *Figure 4.8*), but there are many examples on record where the contrary is the case (see *Figure 4.9*). Therefore the description of stained glass should state whether the stained area is weathered or not, and whether it displays an iridescence (i.e. has *metallized*) due to overfiring. Another coloured effect, which may be seen in some glass which has been exposed to sunlight for a considerable period of time, is that of solarization. For example, some nineteenth-century window glass has developed a purplish tinge, but the original colour can be seen where the edges have been shielded from the light by leads.

A rare colour phenomena is that of dichroism, that is, the glass appears to be one colour when viewed by reflected light, and another when viewed by transmitted light. The Lycurgus Cup (British Museum) is the most famous example, but a few others have been recorded (Brill, 1968). Some glasses may bear water-soluble paints, perhaps the most notable examples being Chinese snuff boxes, where the water-soluble paint is on the interior surface, the design being viewed through the glass.

Transparency or opacity

By viewing glass by transmitted light, it will be seen to be either translucent or opaque. If the glass is opaque, it should be determined whether this was the original condition, or whether it is the result of deterioration. If the glass is transparent, it may be clear and homogeneous, or it may contain inhomogeneities of some kind, such as air-bubbles (*seed*), or *striae* and *cords* (streaks in the glass which have a different refractive index from the body of the glass).

Striae are fine and hair-like, whereas *cords* are thicker and more fibre-like. The third type of inhomogeneity is opaque inclusions (*stones*). If seed are present, they may be spherical (showing that the glass was undisturbed as it cooled), or elongated (showing that they were stretched as the glass flowed while it was being manipulated when hot to form the artefact). The size and distribution of the seed (e.g. per ml) can be measured and recorded. If the glass is from a window, the seed may be elongated in parallel rows as a result of the cylinder process; or lie in arcs of a large circle as a result of the crown process.

If the air-bubbles are large and lie at the surface, or very near it, they are called *blisters*; if any blisters are broken, weathering of the glass may have taken place inside them. Flat bubbles can also occur between the layers of successive gathers.

Striae and cords can be observed by holding the glass against a brightly lit area with a dark edge (a window frame will do) and moving it back and forth across the edge (there is no need to be close to the window), or by using a cord-detector. The presence of seed and striae can give information about the quality of the glass (optical glass contains neither) and about the method used for making the article.

Stones in the glass are generally opaque inclusions (although some stones may be transparent devitrification products) and they can have four quite different origins: batch stones consist of undissolved batch materials, usually grains of sand; refractory stones are portions of the melting crucible which have broken away; products of devitrification where special compounds have crystallized from the glass because it has been held in a molten state near the *liquidus temperature* for too long; and accidental inclusions such as earth, stone, metal etc. Taylor and Hill (1952) and Clark-Monks and Parker (1980) discuss in great detail the many possible kinds of stones, and techniques for identifying them.

Even if the glass looks homogeneous it may contain annealing strains, which can be detected with a strain viewer; and it may be coloured in an inhomogeneous manner (flashed or stained). A hardness test can be helpful in distinguishing between glass and hard gemstones; the latter will scratch modern window glass.

Indications of fabrication techniques

Close examination of a glass artefact will often reveal details of its manufacture. The types of information which may be revealed are endless and the conservator must be continually aware of the possibilities. Examples of the evidence to look for are: order of manufacture, for example, handles etc. added after blowing, flash lines (seam marks) resulting from mould blowing or pressing; jagged broken marks on the bases of vessels, left by a punty iron (i.e. punty mark); and circular grinding marks on vessels ground from a casting or from a solid block of glass, especially on the interior, where less trouble would be taken to grind the marks away. Brill (1968) shows an interesting section of such a vessel, where the inhomogeneities in a thick-walled blank had been cut through during the grinding process.

If the article was cast, or pressed into a mould, there will be flow lines where the glass flowed into projections of the mould (such as a rimmed base) or into a corner. These flow lines can be identified by the lines of seed, or the elongated shape of the air-bubbles, or lines of *striae*, which follow them (Bimson and Werner, 1964b). If several gathers of glass have been used for making a thick or heavy article, there will be changes of refractive index at the junctions of the gathers because volatilization of alkali will have occurred at the hot surface of the two

gathers. The resultant small changes in chemical composition at the interface are too slight to be revealed by any chemical technique but the change of refractive index is easily seen by eye, especially if a cord-detector is used.

In addition to details of the glass itself, examination may reveal the presence of other materials in association with it. For example, in the case of glass beads, there may be traces of fibres from the cords on which they were threaded, or of metal rods on which they may have been wound during manufacture. The presence of metal corrosion products on glass may indicate that it had been buried adjacent to metal artefacts; that the glass had been set into a metal base, or even that enamelled metals have been revealed.

Simple physical tests

At one time it was thought that the chemical composition of a glass could be deduced by making sufficient well chosen measurements of physical properties but that is now considered to be unlikely (Isard, 1963).

Measurement of density

A simple test for identifying lead-containing glasses is to measure the density. Lead oxide has a pronounced effect on the density of glass (see *Figure 1.14* which shows how the density is related to the lead content). Ravencroft's lead glasses have a density of about 3150 kg m^{-3}, compared with 2460 kg m^{-3} for soda–lime–silica glass and 3580 kg m^{-3} for opaque Bristol-blue glass (Day, 1953); but some lead glass beads can have a density of 6000 kg m^{-3}. Elville (1951) discusses the determination of the density of an object by weighing it first in air and then in water. The loss of weight of the glass in water (weight in air − weight in water) is approximately equal to the volume of the glass in ml and hence the density = weight in air (g) divided by the volume (ml). Further accuracy can be maintained by making corrections for the density of the air and the temperature of the water, but this is rarely worth while for ancient glasses. The presence of an air-twist stem, a tear stem, a hollow stem, or even many seed in the glass, will invalidate the result (the apparent density will be less than the true one owing to the presence of the air inside the glass). If the glass is in small pieces, or if a fragment can be obtained, the most accurate determinations are made by the *sink-float* method (Knight, 1945; Scholze, 1977).

Some Chinese glasses may contain substantial amounts of barium, which can have about three-quarters of the effect which PbO has on the density. Thus caution may sometimes have to be exercised to ensure that these Chinese (or Japanese) glasses are not confused with lead glasses.

The refractive index (R.I.) and the density of glass are closely correlated, but different relationships apply to different types of glass (Bannister, 1929); nevertheless, the relationships provide another way of estimating the R.I. of a glass because it is sometimes easier to measure the density (d) than the R.I. (depending on the equipment available in the conservation laboratory). The R.I. and d can be calculated from the composition of the glass (where this is known by analysis), and there are various empirical formulae (Weyl, 1951) for estimating the R.I. from d (or vice versa), a simple one being $(n-1)/d = C$, where n = R.I. and C is a constant depending upon the type of glass (Huggins and Sun, 1946). However, the simplest procedure is to use the graphs in *Figure 1.13*.

In the diagram it will be seen that the lead glasses fall on a line at the right-hand side of the graph, the average value of C being 0.19; these are actually *lead crystal* glasses, with potash as the alkali, and the weight percentage of PbO is indicated on the line.

The *soda–lime–silica* (SLS) glasses fall on a much steeper line to the left of the diagram; this has an average value of $C = 0.21$ and it connects the point for fused silica (at the bottom) with a glass containing 60 per cent SiO_2, 20 per cent CaO and 10 per cent Na_2O (at the top), intermediate values of CaO being spaced, more or less equidistantly, on the line.

Ancient glasses fall between the two lines; Roman glass falls at the point R (70 per cent SiO_2, 10 per cent CaO, 20 per cent Na_2O) but the medieval glasses fall within the shaded area because the MgO, Al_2O_3 and P_2O_5 which they contain have more effect on the density than on the R.I.

Borosilicate glasses were not made in ancient times (they are used for laboratory and oven glassware) and fall on the broken line at the left. It is interesting to note that quartz, which has the same chemical composition as fused silica, falls in quite a different position on the graph (at Q) because the crystalline material is more dense, and has a much higher R.I. than the amorphous (fused) silica. The R.I. of a glass is of importance when choosing adhesives etc. as explained by Tennent and Townsend (1984a,b).

Examination by immersion in liquids

It is often difficult to see details inside a piece of glass, even when the glass is transparent, because the surface may be scratched, abraded, etched or sand-blasted, or it may be curved so that it acts as a lens and distorts the detail, or there may be reflections from surface features such as the design on cut-glass objects. All of these interfering surface features can be effectively visually removed by immersing the object in a liquid which has the same R.I. (or similar) as the glass. If the R.I. match is exact, the surface of the glass seems to disappear and

all the internal features, such as seed, striae and stones become easily visible.

The R.I. of soda–lime–silica glasses lies in the range 1.51–1.52, whereas full-lead crystal glass has an R.I. of 1.565 (see *Figure 1.13*). The R.I. of a glass of known composition can be calculated (Gilard and Dubrul, 1937) and it can be seen that high-lime glasses will also have a high R.I. The poorly durable medieval glasses at the bottom of the triangle in *Figure 4.3* are glasses of that type, and one with the composition: 50 per cent SiO_2, 15 per cent K_2O and 35 per cent CaO would have an R.I. of 1.59 and a density of 3.1, that is, at point H in *Figure 1.13*.

Convenient immersion liquids, and their R.I. values, are: xylene (1.490), chlorbenzene (1.525), nitrobenzene (1.553), aniline (NB a carcinogen) (1.586) and quinoline (1.624) (Taylor and Hill, 1952; Clark-Monks and Parker, 1980; Rawson, 1984). An interesting example of the use of the immersion technique is given by Bimson and Werner (1964b); one of the minute heads on the Tara Brooch was so small that it was thought to have been a carved gemstone, and not glass, but immersion in toluene (R.I. = 1.496) revealed the presence of air-bubbles. Thus it could not be a precious stone, and characteristic markings showed that the heads had been made by casting into moulds. Dabbs and Pearson (1970, 1972) have studied variations in specific gravity and in refractive index of window glass.

Detection of striae and cords

Simple methods of detecting striae and cords are discussed by Day (1953) and by Elville (1951). The latter studied the striae in Ravenscroft glasses; immersion of the glasses in monochlorobenzene easily revealed the method of manufacture.

The detection of striae is greatly affected by the orientation of the sample. For example, none may be seen when looking through a piece of window glass, yet they are quite obvious when looking through the edge of the glass.

Detection of strain

If glass contains numerous cords and striae, or has been badly annealed, it will exhibit signs of strain which can be detected by means of a strain-viewer (Werner *et al.*, 1975; Clark-Monks and Parker, 1980). Badly annealed ancient glass will not usually be encountered since it is unlikely to have survived, but there may be occasion to look for the presence of strain-producing inhomogeneities (Elville, 1951). Glass which is subjected to strain (bending or stretching) becomes birefringent, that is, it acquires two different refractive indices. Thus a single ray of light which enters the glass will emerge as two separate rays. This phenomenon can be used to detect, and to measure, the frozen strains resulting from unsatisfactory annealing. Briefly, when plane-polarized light passes through a material of a birefringent nature, it becomes elliptically polarized, and hence strain-viewers make use of polarized light produced either by reflection from a polished metal surface, or by the use of Polaroid filters. There are various commercial instruments available; or a strain-viewer can be made (Day, 1953), in which the polarization of light is produced by two pieces of black plate glass, placed at Brewster's angle (56.5°). Alternatively, a smaller polariscope can be made by using pieces of Polaroid film.

Fracture analysis

Fracture analysis is a well-developed technique which enables the origin of a fracture in glass to be identified by showing the directions in which the fracture propagated itself. Fractures which occur at a speed of about $2\,km\,s^{-1}$ are easy to study, but those which occur perhaps as slowly as a few millimetres per century are more difficult to understand. In the great majority of cases the break starts at a single point and the fractures spread out from this point of origin. If the glass is broken into a number of fragments the smallest ones are closest to the point of origin. A fracture arises from a tensile stress in the glass and hence it starts at right angles to the stress which produced it. However, if the stress is great the crack, once started, may fork so that there is an acute angle between the two new branches. Cracks rarely join up and hence these acute-angled forks point towards the origin of the cracks.

At the actual origin of the crack the broken edge bears a characteristic *mirror area* which (see *Figure 1.16*) is surrounded by *grey areas*, *hackle marks* and, finally, *rib marks* which may extend a long distance from the origin and indicate the direction in which the fracture travelled. The rib marks are places where the fracture has hesitated briefly before continuing its start–stop advance, and they represent the leading edge of the fracture at successive moments. Murgatroyd (1942) observed that these rib marks are always curved and they present their convex faces to the direction in which they are moving. They are thus important for determining the direction in which the crack was growing. The investigator simply follows the reverse direction until he meets rib marks which point the other way. Murgatroyd (1942) also showed that, when glass breaks due to excessive local heating, the rib marks are spaced well apart on the cold side and they crowd together on the hot side.

The origin of the fracture is always at the surface of the glass and the rib marks generally face the same side as the origin of the fracture. If the outside of a vessel has been given a sharp blow, the area which receives the blow may be crushed (causing a bruise

consisting of powdered glass) with a surrounding stressed ring from which a family of cracks start. This ring of cracks forms an *impact cone* which may separate from the glass in the form of a plug (*Figure 1.15*; see also McKenna, 1961).

Another feature of the fractured surface which is useful to bear in mind is the size of the mirror area. Kerper and Scuderi (1964, 1966) showed that the energy of a fracture is directly related to the diameter of the mirror area; for example, a mirror diameter of 0.1 mm corresponds to a stress of about $200\,MN\,m^{-2}$ (30 000 psi), whereas one of 2.5 mm corresponds to only some $40\,MN\,m^{-2}$ (6000 psi).

Discussions of fracture analysis can also be found in Holloway (1973), Ernsberger (1977), Scholze (1977) and Rawson (1984).

Simple tests

Universal indicator papers

Strongly alkaline solutions (those with a pH value of 9.0 or greater) will cause breakdown of most glasses and certainly all ancient glasses. Similarly, acid solutions (those with a pH value of 5.0 or less) will attack the high-lime medieval glasses such as H and J in *Figure 4.3*. It is therefore useful to measure the pH value of a solution which might be used for conservation purposes (Wihr, 1977). For example, some fungicides are highly alkaline and it is also useful to make routine pH tests on the soil from which glass is excavated. If glass is found to be in a sweating or weeping condition, the liquid on the surface should be tested for alkalinity.

Electrically operated pH meters are available, but the simplest method, and one adequate for conservation purposes, is to use universal indicator papers. They are available in three types: the full-range paper, where pH1 shows as a red colour, through shades of orange to pH7 (a greenish yellow) to a deep blue colour at pH14; the narrow-range paper for acid solutions, where pH4.0 is yellow and pH5.5 is blue; and the narrow-range paper for alkaline solutions, where pH7.0 is green and pH9.0 is dark blue. A small piece of the paper is torn off, moistened with the liquid and laid on a white tile; after 30 seconds the colour is compared with the colour chart supplied with the indicator paper.

Determination of the chloride ion

Glass which has been excavated from marine environments must be desalinated by soaking in many changes of sea, fresh and distilled water, until the wash water is free from chloride ions (i.e. salt). Wihr (1977) recommended that the amount of chloride ions present should be determined by titration with N/10 silver nitrate solution. However, all that is really necessary is to determine the point at which the wash water is salt-free, that is, when white precipitate no longer forms after a drop of silver nitrate solution is added following a drop of nitric acid (to remove carbonates which may be present). (It should of course be remembered that tap water contains chloride ions.)

Spot test for determining lead

Lead glass is usually detectable by its physical properties. However, a simple method of identifying lead in glass is to apply a drop of hydrofluoric acid, mixed with a drop of ammonium sulphide solution, to a small area of the glass in an inconspicuous spot. If lead is present, a black colour will develop in the solution due to the formation of lead sulphide. Soda–lime–silica glasses, and high-density glasses containing barium, do not produce the black colour. However, the test results in a permanent dulling of the surface at the test point, and must therefore be regarded as being destructive. (Hydrofluoric acid is extremely harmful to skin tissue and its use should be avoided.)

Instrumental methods of analysing glass

Fluorescence in ultraviolet light

Fluorescent radiation from glass subjected to an ultraviolet light source can often be used to identify its type (Elville, 1951). For example, lead glasses have a characteristic blue fluorescence (especially when only a small amount of lead is present – it changes to green with larger amounts) and some glasses containing manganese can give either a greenish-yellow fluorescence, or an orange-red one, depending on the state of oxidation of the manganese (Linwood and Weyl, 1942). According to Weyl (1951) the fluorescence which occurs in commercial soda–lime glasses depends on the presence of elements in minor concentrations, such as iron, titanium, antimony and arsenic. Hence the colour of the fluorescence is not so much a characteristic of the type of glass as of the refining agents, the furnace atmosphere during melting, and the melting temperature. This last point does, in fact, provide the most important use of fluorescence for the conservator, since two pieces of glass rarely exhibit the same tint of fluorescence. Thus it will help to determine whether a glass article was made from one piece of glass alone, or whether two or more pieces were used (Grant, 1936; Radley and Grant, 1954). It is also a likely indicator as to whether an artefact is a multicomponent fake, that is, a conglomerate (Goldstein, 1977). Fluorescence has been used to distinguish between paperweights made by Baccarat, Clichy and St Louis (Newman, 1977).

Radiation monitoring of potash glasses

It is sometimes necessary to be able to decide whether a piece of painted glass in a cathedral is an original medieval piece or whether it is a clever later replacement. The former will contain potash, derived from the beechwood ash from which it was made, whereas later replacements (certainly after the sixteenth century) will have been made from an alkali which was predominantly soda. Potassium contains a naturally occurring, weakly radioactive isotope (^{40}K), and hence medieval glass will slowly cause darkening of a radiation monitoring badge over a period of about two months (Hudson and Newton, 1976).

Use of a profilometer

A profilometer can be used to define the nature of a glass surface in terms of its smoothness, and this has been of value in considering how any roughness affects the strength of glass (Semenov *et al.*, 1972). The British version of the profilometer, called the Talysurf, can measure the roughness in 25 nm, and it has been used to show how the roughness, produced when paint (enamel) is fired on to glass, is less than one wavelength of visible light, yet restoration of a lost image is quite feasible (Newton, 1974d). There are also optical methods of studying surfaces, such as the *Schmaltz light cut* (Vickers Projection Microscope Handbook).

Specialist techniques

It is useful for conservators to be aware of various highly sophisticated techniques which they are unlikely to use themselves because they require very expensive equipment. Such techniques may be useful for authentification and may well be available in the nearest University or Polytechnic. They are listed briefly below, and useful accounts are given in Dekowna (1967, 1980), Hench (1975a), Clark *et al.* (1979), Frank (1982) and Schreiner (1987). As these make use of various physical properties of glass, discussion of those properties will be found in Day (1953), Doremus (1973), Holloway (1973), Morey (1954), Rawson (1984), Shand (1958), Stanworth (1950), Scholze (1977) and Tooley (1953).

Electron microscopy

The electron microscope can be used in various ways, such as examining surface replicas or direct viewing of very thin sections. Its great advantage is the tremendous magnification which can be achieved (for example, ×100 000), and Ferrazzini (1974) used it as a sensitive method for recognizing the earliest stages of corrosion.

Scanning electron microscopy (SEM)

The SEM is an extraordinary versatile instrument, and is a modification of the electron microscope which can retain the enormous magnification of that instrument but is generally used at much lower magnifications. Its main characteristic is an extraordinarily great depth of field, so that quasi three-dimensional effects can be obtained (and also real stereo pairs, for a full three-dimensional effect). Its only (slight) drawback is the need to apply a thin and invisible conducting coating to the glass sample. *Figure 6.1* is an SEM photograph of weathering layers

Figure 6.1 Scanning electron micrograph of weathering layers (×700).

(Newton, 1972). The SEM can be used in conjunction with electron microprobe analysis to provide a micro chemical analysis of the area in the field of view of the SEM. Werner *et al.* (1975) used the SEM to study faked weathering surfaces on glass. In cases where a glass surface had been etched with acid (Gairola, 1960; Tavas, 1975), no weathering crusts remained.

Electron microprobe analysis (EMPA)

The electron microprobe can either be used with the SEM (as above) or separately. It can be used on broken surfaces, or cut sections, of glass in order to obtain a chemical analysis from a very small area, using a principle like that of X-ray fluorescence (XRF) except that electrons are used as the exciting radiation instead of X-rays. It has been used by Brill (1968), and many others. Its great value in interpreting complex chemical situations can be seen from *Figure 4.22c*, where it is revealed that air pollution does not *attack* painted glass because sulphur-containing compounds are found only at the surface of a pit, and not at the bottom where corrosion reactions are occurring. The disadvantages are that it analyses the surface layer only; lighter elements are harder to measure than the heavier ones, and alkali elements can be forced deeper into the glass by the charge on the electron beam.

Radiography

This can be useful if a glass object is suspected of having been repaired, especially if the repair has been

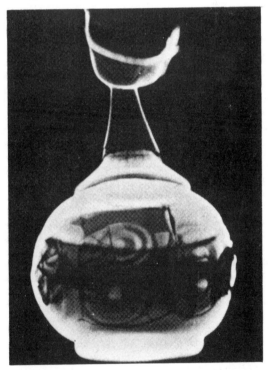

Figure 6.2 Radiograph of an ewer in which can be seen the addition of a ribbed ewer spout and neck to the body of a pincer-decorated bottle. (The addition of a snake-like handle of plastic, seen as a faint shadow on the right of the radiograph, is not visible in the illustration.) Note that there are several non-joining pincer-decorated rosettes and concentric circles 'floating' in the body of the vessel. H 146 mm. Islamic fragments. Corning Museum of Glass, New York.

obliterated by the application of weathering products from elsewhere (*Figure 6.2*). Goldstein (1977) illustrated two examples of repairs detected by X-rays; a large amphora with a tip reconstructed from a modern dropper tube, and an ewer to which a plastics handle had been added. The possibility of darkening of lead glass by the use of X-rays must be considered (see below).

X-ray diffraction (XRD)

When a beam of suitable X-rays is passed through powdered crystalline material, diffraction patterns are formed which can be detected photographically as a series of curved lines that can be interpreted as having come from the particular material. It is in this way that we can identify (for example) gypsum as one of the many weathering products on the surface of old glass (Perez-y-Jorba *et al.*, 1975, 1978, 1980, 1984).

X-ray fluorescence (XRF)

XRF is a 'non-destructive' technique which is now widely used for the chemical analysis of materials because it is rapid and accurate, and can be carried out on equipment that is available commercially (Brill and Moll, 1961). A suitably prepared test piece (hence not truly non-destructive) is irradiated with suitable primary X-rays, and the sample then emits secondary X-rays that are characteristic of the elements that make up the sample. These secondary X-rays can be detected in two ways: the earlier technique measured their wavelengths (Hall *et al.*, 1964; Hall and Schweizer, 1973); modern techniques measure their energies and are hence called 'energy-dispersive' XRF tests. The energies appear as peaks on a video monitor; the positions of the peaks indicate the chemical elements, and the heights of the peaks measure their concentrations. A computer program assists in the interpretations and makes allowance for the mutual interferences of certain elements. The sample can be affected by the test; Brill (1968) mentions damage by radiation burns, and lead-containing glasses can be darkened unless suitable precautions are taken. Cox and Pollard (1977) showed that older weathered glasses possessed an ion-exchanged layer from which alkali ions had been removed so that the surface layer (even though it looked quite unaltered) had a composition different from that of the interior; they found it necessary to grind part of the surface away to a depth of 0.5 mm and then polish it smooth. Pollard (1979) used the technique extensively in his thesis, and many other workers have found it invaluable.

Atomic absorption spectroscopy (AAS)

This is a simple and accurate technique, yet still requiring relatively expensive equipment. Its method of operation can be visualized by recalling that the composition of the 'surface' of the sun was determined from the presence of many dark lines when its light was viewed in a spectrometer (the Fraunhofer lines); in fact, helium was first discovered from its Fraunhofer lines. The sample is made up into a dilute solution which is sprayed into a burner in front of a hollow cathode discharge lamp that emits light characteristic of a particular element, and the same element in the solution will produce some darkening of the light emitted from the lamp. (A different lamp is needed for each element it is desired to analyse.) Hughes *et al.* (1976) give a detailed description of the application of AAS to archaeology. Brill and Hanson (1976) used AAS to analyse fragments of glass excavated from the site at New Bremen; Lambert and McLaughlin (1978) used it for Egyptian glass.

Electron spectroscopy for chemical analysis (ESCA)

This method analyses the surface of glass by means of photoelectrons emitted from the surface when it is bombarded by suitable X-rays, and it can be of value in following the early stages of weathering (Hench, 1975a). Budd (1975) has used the technique for studying bottle surfaces which were given lubricious coatings.

Secondary ion mass spectroscopy (SIMS)

This is highly specialized, but it has the advantage that any element or isotope (including hydrogen) can be analysed, and the alkali ions are not driven further into the glass, which is the case with EMPA (Hench, 1975a).

Infrared reflection spectroscopy (IRRS)

This again is restricted to the study of glass surfaces, and it has been used by Hench *et al.* (1979) to characterize the weathering of medieval glasses, and for predicting the weathering behaviour of others.

Ion beam spectrochemical analysis (IBSCA)

This has also been used by Hench *et al.* (1979), Rauch (1985) and Lanford (1986), an it is so sensitive that studies can be made of the relative durabilities of different areas of any piece of glass.

Emission spectroscopy (spectrography)

This is a well-known destructive technique in which the whole of a tiny fragment of glass is completely volatilized in an electric arc discharge and the resultant radiation is studied for the elements which it contained. It will analyse for almost any element in a semi-quantitative manner and was the classical technique used from the early part of the twentieth century. It can be used over a wide range of concentrations and this is why Sayre and Smith (1974) used it for their study of glass from the New Kingdom to early Islam. Newton and Renfrew (1970) made use of results, taken a generation before, to study the origins of British faience beads. It is now largely replaced by XRF.

Neutron activation analysis (NAA)

This is a valuable technique for determining the bulk chemical composition of a glass, and it is particularly suitable for detecting minor and trace elements, but it has two disadvantages; it is restricted to the availability of a nuclear reactor and, although it is described as being 'non-destructive', some samples, for example, those which contain much antimony or cobalt, are rendered so radioactive that it may be many years before they are safe to return to the owner. It has been used by Brill (1968) to determine minute amounts of gold and silver in dichroic glasses, and it has proved useful in the characterization of medieval window glass (*CVMA News Letters*, No.22, September 1976; No.25, April 1977; No.27, June 1978). Olin *et al.* (1972, 1976) showed that valid information can be obtained from samples as small as 10 mg. Because NAA is capable of high accuracy it has been useful as a discriminating tool in studies of faience beads; Aspinall *et al.* (1972a,b) used it to characterize obsidians.

Auger emission spectroscopy (AES)

AES is a relatively new non-destructive technique for the chemical analysis of surfaces. The surface is bombarded with primary electrons in such a way as to cause the emission of an electron, known as an Auger electron, from the surface. It has been used by Dawson *et al.* (1978) and Pollard (1979) in their investigations of the durability of medieval window glass because the results are limited to the first few atomic layers of the surface, rather than the 10–100 μm commonly analysed by XRD. It was also used by Chappell and Stoddart (1974) to study the surfaces of float glass.

Beta-ray backscattering

This has been used to determine the lead content of glasses by irradiating the surface with electrons and then measuring those which are scattered back again by the atoms of lead. Emeleus (1960) used it on many samples of Ravenscroft's early glasses, and Asahina *et al.* (1973) used it to study a Japanese blue bowl.

Isotopic ratios

Brill (1968, 1970b) has shown how certain elements, notably lead and oxygen, have different proportions of their isotopes present according to the geographical source from which they were obtained, and their isotopic ratios can be used for tracking down the source of the material. Lead has four stable isotopes: ^{204}Pb, ^{206}Pb, ^{207}Pb and ^{208}Pb, and it is easy to separate these in a mass spectrometer. Lead from Derbyshire has $^{206}Pb/^{204}Pb = 18.6$ and $^{208}Pb/^{207}Pb = 2.46$, whereas lead of Italian origin has values of 18.8 and 2.48, respectively. Although these pairs differ only by about 1 per cent they are nevertheless statistically different. Rather surprisingly, Brill was able to show that yellow and red lead-containing glasses from the Kenchreai panels described in Chapter 7, Part 1, were each made from lead compounds of different origin. The explanation may be that the glassworkers of Alexandria did not realize that both colours were lead compounds, or the colours may have arrived in coloured cullet of different origins. Brill (1970b) and Brill *et al.* (1970) discuss the origins of different lead compounds of ancient origin, and advice on how to get samples tested is given by Brill (1968, p.63). Brill *et al.* (1970, 1974), discuss the origins of opacifiers in Egyptian glasses, and Barnes *et al.* (1978) point out that this is one of the few techniques that supply geographical information about the origins of the glass-making materials. In a similar manner, the proportion of the isotope ^{18}O can be characteristic of glasses made in different places (Brill, 1968, Figures 13 and 14, 1970b).

Electron spin resonance (ESR)

This technique can be used to determine the state of oxidation of elements present in the glass; for example, Sellner (1977) and Sellner *et al.* (1979) used it to measure the states of oxidation of iron and manganese in medieval glasses from two sites, and thus show that a wide range of colours could be obtained by using beechwood ash as the source of alkali and varying the state of oxidation of the glass.

Inductively coupled plasma source spectrometry (ICP)

The ICP technique has developed comparatively rapidly in recent years as a technique for elemental analysis. It is possible to measure both major and trace constituents in silicates by ICP spectrometry with acceptable precision and accuracy, down to 1–10 ppm levels for most trace elements. ICP is not entirely free from interference, but those encountered are almost certainly less than with other analytical methods, and in most cases they are well understood and easily corrected (Greenfield *et al.* 1964). The sample, about 0.5 g of material (though as little as 0.1 g will produce meaningful results), is ground and put into solution, either by hydrofluoric acid and perchloric acid digestion techniques or by fluxing with lithium metaborate and dissolving in dilute nitric acid. The sample solution is then fed via a peristaltic pump to the nebulizer which emits a fine spray of the solution into the argon plasma at a temperature of 6000 K. This high temperature causes electron transitions which give rise to spectral lines characteristic of the elements present. The emitted light passes through a diffraction grating which consists of a series of channels corresponding to characteristic wavelengths of a range of elements. Standard solutions of rocks or glass are run at regular intervals for comparison. The results are printed out either as spectral intensity or as the concentration of the elements in the sample (in terms of standard geological oxides). From this, information can be gained about the physical and chemical properties of the glass such as composition, viscosity and an estimate of the working temperature range of the glass.

ICP may help to identify glasses from a particular glasshouse and provide information regarding the technology behind its production. ICP produces similar results to AAS but is quicker and is as accurate. ICP can analyse fifty or more elements at once whereas AAS requires the use of larger samples and must be run fifty times over to produce the same results. In addition, since AAS is carried out at lower temperatures, it is liable to more interference.

Dating glasses

It has often been supposed that it should be possible to date ancient glasses from a knowledge of their composition. However, this is not the case since composition was so varied and complex, although there are, in general terms, some correspondences, such as the high-potash and high-lime contents of glasses made with beechwood ash in the medieval period. Nevertheless, the techniques described below can be applied to glass in particular circumstances, and may occasionally serve to distinguish between ancient and modern specimens even if they cannot determine actual dates.

Radiocarbon (^{14}C) dating

^{14}C dating is very useful for wood and other organic materials and it would seem to be unlikely to be

useful for dating glass. There have, however, been two cases reported where enough carbon was present to make dating possible. Glass from the great slab at Beth She'arim, Israel, described on page 110, was found to contain 3 per cent dissolved carbon dioxide and ^{14}C dating was stated to have been undertaken (Brill, 1968), but no result seems ever to have been published. Fiorentini-Roncuzzi (1970) dated the Byzantine mosaics in Ravenna from the pieces of straw etc., present in the mortar, as 1450± 175 years before the present, that is, AD 345–695.

Fission track dating

This technique depends on assessing the damage done to glass by the tracks from nuclear fission, over a long period of time, by the spontaneous disintegration of any uranium atoms that it happens to contain. Thus it is rarely likely to be useful because man-made glasses rarely contain uranium, nor have they been made long enough for sufficient fission tracks to have formed (Brill *et al.*, 1964). It has, however, been used to date obsidians (Wagner, 1978), and Yabuki *et al.* (1973) used it with some vessel fragments from the Karbala desert, Iraq, obtaining ages of 2900 ± 1200 years and 3000 ± 800 years. Nishimura (1971) used it with some glass containing uranium. The applications have been reviewed by Green (1979). Huang and Walker (1967) made use of the analogous technique of alpha-particle recoil track dating.

Thermoluminescence (TL)

This technique is useful for dating pottery because the material is opaque, and exposure of a transparent material to sunlight will invalidate the results. There is a modification of the technique, called radioactively induced TL, which has been used for characterizing obsidian (Huntley and Bailey, 1978).

Counting the weathering layers

Some glasses, which have weathered in certain conditions, may develop crusts on the surface where the alkali has leached out in an exceptional manner, a thick crust having formed on the surface. Sometimes these crusts can even be 4 mm thick and, when a section is examined under a microscope, the crust is seen to consist of a multitude of very thin layers (see *Figure 6.1*). Brewster (1855) found 'twenty or thirty [layers] crowded into the fiftieth of an inch', and they were noticed by Fowler (1881), Raw (1955) and Geilmann (1960). Brill and Hood (1961) noticed that, in eleven samples out of about 200, the number of layers in the crust was approximately the same number of years that the piece had been buried, or immersed in seawater or in a river, and they suggested that the layers were an annual phenomenon which could be used for dating the time that weathering started. However, eleven out of 200 samples cannot be considered to be substantive. The matter has been investigated by Newton (1966, 1969, 1971a) who concluded that there were too many uncertainties present to make the technique reliable, such as the effect of temperature (producing ten layers in an autoclave in 4 hours) and the evidence that layers could merge into each other (Newton, 1972). Douglas (on p.7 of Newton, 1971a) suggested that the layers were the result of the alternation of two weathering processes which accidentally took about a year to complete a cycle. Shaw (1965) used EMPA to show that the silicon and calcium contents of the crust alternately rose and fell with a periodicity of 6 to 8 µm, the same as that of the visible layers in the crust. Newton and Shaw (1988) have illustrated a case in which the weathering layers are at an angle to each other.

Hydration rind dating

Lanford (1977) noticed that the alkali-deficient layer on the surface of weathered glass became thicker with age, and he suggested that measurement of the thickness could be used for dating the sample, but he discovered many difficulties which can now be seen to have resulted from the presence of Hench's Type IIIa protective layers, etc. The much greater age, and the more stable weathering environment, of obsidian made a similar technique useful for Friedman *et al.* (1963), and Barrera and Kirch (1973) used it for the dating of basaltic glass artefacts from the Hawaiian Islands.

7

Conservation of glass

Part 1 Archaeological and decorative glass

This part of the chapter concentrates on the conservation and restoration of archaeological and decorative vessels, which usually form the major portion of glass collections. Other decorative items such as chandeliers, mirrors, and reverse paintings on glass (Davison and Jackson, 1985), jewellery and historic enamels will not be covered in detail, since many of the processes described may also be applied to them, though modifications may be required. (Remirroring is considered to be too specialized to be included; see Schweig, 1973.) The techniques involved in conservation and restoration include excavation, cleaning and examination, consolidation, repair, and possibly restoration with synthetic resins or glass replacements (Fisher and Norman, 1987). The case histories illustrated are not intended to be taken as model treatments, but as methods which have been devised to meet specific problems *at the time*.

Painted window glass (commonly referred to as stained glass), glass mosaic and *opus sectile* panels may also be found in collections, and examples of treatment are given. However, a substantial amount of painted glass has remained in the buildings for which it was designed. It may at some time require treatment either *in situ* or in a studio. The techniques employed differ considerably from those employed on decorative glass vessels etc. and are described in Part 2 of the chapter. The lifting of glass mosaics and *opus sectile* requires specialist techniques (Novis, 1975) which are considered to be outside the scope of this volume.

Excavated glass

Glass may be excavated in the form of fragmented vessels, windows, industrial waste or as objects such as bracelets and beads. It is usually found in the form of broken or shattered artefacts where the pieces are either more or less in their original positions, or else scattered over the site. Glass can also form a minor part of an object such as inlay in jewellery, or *tesserae* in a mosaic of diverse materials (Bimson, 1975; Cronyn, Foley and Hunter, in Bacon and Knight, 1987). The greatest quantity of excavated glass, however, consists of individual fragments from any of these sources. Nevertheless, even from such fragmentary evidence, profiles and other details of the original artefact and of the site are often retrievable. As archaeology and its associated techniques continue to develop, new questions will be asked of the evidence and therefore all excavated glass fragments should be retained wherever possible.

However, for economic or other reasons, full conservation of all material may not be possible, and a selection process may have to be adopted. This must result from discussions between the archaeologist, conservator and museum curator to ensure that all relevant criteria are considered. One of the most important is the archaeological significance of the glass, not only in relation to the discipline as a whole, but also to its own particular context. Selected glass may be stabilized, repaired, or even restored for display; other glass may be cleaned for study and publication only, whilst some may simply be recorded.

However, long-term storage of all glass should be such that even untreated glass will be protected from further damage as far as possible. A small proportion of excavated glass from every site should, where possible, be conserved simply by correct packaging, without the intervention of cleaning and the addition of any synthetic materials, in order to provide the possibility of future analysis of uncontaminated material should this be required.

Stages of conservation

The first stage of conservation must take place even before the excavation begins; in theory there should be no excavation without prior consideration being given to conservation of the finds. Liaison must take place between the excavator, the conservator and the curator of the museum or store in which the finds will ultimately be deposited, to ensure that there is adequate time, money, space and administrative machinery to accept any glass which may be found on site. It should be possible to give the glass first-aid treatment in the field, and to follow this with the relevant conservation techniques in a laboratory. On-site conservation consists of the correct lifting, labelling and packaging of the glass. In the laboratory, conservation starts with examination, which itself must continue through the subsequent processes of cleaning and, where necessary, consolidation of the glass. The assembly of fragments usually follows, but it may not always be considered essential. Subsequently full reconstruction may be restricted to those objects required for display. Finally there is the long-term storage of the glass which must be considered as a conservation technique. In choosing treatments for individual conservation problems, the conservator must be aware of the condition of the glass, and understand the effects of the processes and materials used.

Labelling

Marking glass itself on site is extremely difficult and, if present in large quantities, time-consuming. If the glass is wet or damp, the data should be recorded on a waterproof label (with a waterproof pen) placed in the polythene bag containing the glass, and again on the exterior of the bag. Dry glass which is neither crumbling nor flaking, but which has a porous surface, can be marked by first creating a writing surface on a small area of the artefact. This is achieved by applying a coat of lacquer or consolidant to the area to receive the marking. When dry, the data is applied using black waterproof ink and using a fine-pointed wooden stick as an applicator in order not to scratch the glass. A second layer of lacquer may be applied over the ink. It is probable that most excavated glass will be unsuitable for direct marking without such surface treatment. (Glass with a sound surface, particularly historical vessels etc. which have not been buried, may be marked as described above,

but without the application of a lacquer to the surface.)

Initial examination

As with all excavated material, glass will normally be found covered in a layer of obscuring deposits. Much of this is usually dispersable in water but some superficial white or buff deposits may not be so because they are only sparingly soluble; they are termed insoluble salt deposits (*Figure 7.1*). The most

Figure 7.1 A deposit of insoluble salts, blending with the weathering crusts and obscuring the surface of the glass.

common of such concretions are calcium salts such as carbonates and sulphates, and silicates which form deposits on porous material, such as decayed glass, mainly in semi-arid environments (Dowman, 1970). These concretions can in fact be fused to the decayed glass or, together with the soil, may be holding a broken object together (Wihr, 1977). If the glass is part of a metal artefact, it may be totally obscured by the corrosion products of the metal, as often happens with enamels on copper alloys (*Plate 4*). Below these superficial deposits the glass may appear to be unweathered but it is probable that the surface of the buried glass has been altered in some way and close examination may well show solution marks, indicating that some decay of the surface has occurred. Some weathered glass surfaces powder readily and can resemble patches of soil on a reasonably preserved piece of glass, but closer inspection reveals that the surface of the glass has been lost.

A common visual sign of decay in partially dried glass is dulling (see *Figure 4.15*) or iridescent patination (*Plate 3*) of the surface, the causes of which were discussed in Chapter 4. This condition may not be immediately visible on glass from damp or saturated deposits or when the glass is wetted. Further deterioration may cause *lamellae* to fall off, and eventually the total disintegration of the glass may occur.

Weathering crusts which do not present an iridescent surface are described as enamel-like or opaque (see *Figure 4.17*). They can chip off to reveal iridescent pits or *lamellae* or, when extreme, can crumble in a mosaic- or sugar-like manner (see *Figure 4.16*). If the glass is totally weathered through, the sample can be mistaken for pottery or a piece of soft rock.

The apparent absence of any glass at a site may even be a result of its total destruction, and not a reflection of the technology at the time. It is doubtful if sick glass would survive burial in any except the most arid of environments. There is a variety of factors which cause the colour of glass to alter during burial. The original colouring agents of the glass may be leached out of the weathering crust, which, if thick, appears milky. However, it can then become blackened, often superficially, which may be due to the oxidation of iron and manganese in the weathering glass.

The blackening of high-lead content glass from wet, anaerobic deposits has been noted, and in one case was shown to be due to the formation of lead sulphide (Smithsonian, 1969). However, much glass which does not contain lead also blackens in waterlogged deposits. Recent work by Florian (1979) on a batch of waterlogged glass from the marine underwater archaeological site HMS Sapphire (1696) at Bay Bulls, Newfoundland, showed that the cause was deposition of ferrous sulphide. In addition, much of the deterioration of waterlogged glass was associated with microbiological organisms, bacteria being present on all surfaces examined. The glass of excavated enamels is rarely blackened. It often weathers to form an opaque but coherent surface, the colour of which may differ considerably from that of the original glass. Thus red copper/cuprous oxide glass normally weathers to a green, a colour which may also be induced by the uptake of corrosion products from a copper alloy substrate. More extensive deterioration causes the coherent weathered layer to crack, break up into splinters and finally powder (Cronyn, in Bacon and Knight, 1987).

Water content

When excavated, glass is suddenly exposed to a new set of environmental conditions, perhaps after hundreds of years' burial; thus it cannot be considered surprising if the glass reacts to such change. Glass which may seem to be in good condition upon excavation may form iridescent layers within a few minutes or hours. Therefore, if a photographic record is required, preliminary photographs must be taken as soon as the glass is exposed to the atmosphere. (If a large amount of glass is involved, it may be advisable to lift the glass and place it immediately into a controlled environment pending photography.) The change in appearance is not a result of a rapid increase in the rate of deterioration of the glass, but is simply a revelation, as a result of dehydration, of the deterioration which has already taken place. (It may also be due in part to oxidation reactions, Geilmann, 1956.) The free water which is present in newly excavated glass maintains the transparency and also holds weathered layers together by virtue of surface tension. Hence drying may cause the glass to crumble or flake. Once the free water has evaporated, allowing air to enter the weathering crust, it is extremely difficult (if not impossible) to make the glass appear translucent again. The free water will also contain dissolved salts, derived either from the environment or from the decaying glass itself. On drying, these salts will crystallize out, disrupting the weathering crust and (if allowed to remain) ultimately destroying it by the oscillation of their volumes as the ambient humidity changes. Deposits are often much easier to clean off the glass when they are damp as they will be softer; if they are allowed to dry out, the soil or other deposit may contract and damage the delicate glass surface. An important aspect of on-site conservation, therefore, is the provision of first aid treatment, with adequate packaging incorporating humidity control, in order to preserve glass in the condition in which it was found. Correct treatment and regular monitoring can delay the further deterioration of glass after excavation for a considerable period of time. Treatment should begin *immediately* the glass is exposed, *not* after it has been lying in a finds tray for several hours or days. Ideally, packaging should be devised to cover the short period between excavation and laboratory conservation. In practice, however, this period of non-treatment often becomes permanent due to lack of funds, and this fact must be taken into consideration when planning the work.

The water content of deteriorated buried glass can vary from *saturation* in material excavated from marine or waterlogged environments, though to *damp* in glass from the majority of sites in cool, temperate climates, to *dry* from sites in warmer seasons or climates. In hot seasons or semi-arid climates, the glass may be *partially desiccated* (free from surface water). In arid environments such as some desert tombs or caves, the glass can be *totally desiccated* although, in a physical sense, there will always be some free water.

Glass from marine or freshwater sites

When glass objects are retrieved from marine or other waterlogged sites it is advisable to determine the state of preservation, and to group the objects accordingly. This will aid in packaging, and in alerting the laboratory conservator to the conditions of the objects before they are unpacked. There should be no attempt to clean the glass on site since evidence of manufacture, original design and shape preserved in the weathering crust may be removed. If glass from a marine site is allowed to dry immediately upon recovery, salts will crystallize in the weathering crust and disrupt it (Pearson, 1975) (see *Figure 7.2*). The

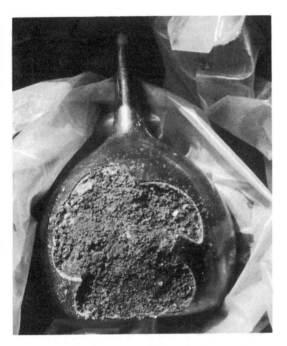

Figure 7.2 Chloride salts crystallizing out of concretion filling a glass flask recovered from a marine excavation.

salts must therefore be removed as quickly as practical. As a precaution the glass should not be placed directly into fresh (tap or distilled) water in case an osmotic pressure develops between the salt-laden glass and the wash water, causing the water to force entry into the decayed weathering crust and disrupt it. Desalination is accomplished by slowly reducing the salt content of the water in which the glass was found, followed by immersion in changes of fresh water (either by changing the wash water daily or maintaining a continuous gentle stream of water through the container).

The pressure or movement of the water should not be allowed to disrupt the weathering crust from the glass surface and if possible the object should not be lifted in and out of the bath as spontaneous drying will affect the deteriorating surface. The progress of the treatment can be monitored simply by carrying out silver nitrate tests on the wash water to check for the presence of chloride ions. Provided that the glass will withstand continuous washing, treatment should continue until such chloride tests prove negative.

Once the desalination is complete, the glass should not be allowed to dry out since the apparent state of preservation in the wet state is no real indication of what the object may look like once it has dehydrated. The glass should be kept in water for *temporary* storage (remembering that prolonged contact with water promotes its deterioration).

If samples of the objects are to be taken for biological or analytical study either in the field or at some later date, the glass should be stored in 70 per cent ethanol (which will prevent further biological attack from solutions not experienced by the object during burial, and will preserve the micro-organisms present on the glass). If possible, soil and water samples from the region of retrieval should be taken for study purposes. The glass, stored in ethanol or fresh water and fungicide, should be packed in heat-sealed polythene bags and the fragments separated from each other by wads of polyester foam or bubble packing. The objects should be coded so that the more fragile glass is placed near the top of the container and thus more easily retrieved for conservation.

Glass from waterlogged land sites

Glass found in waterlogged land sites should be kept wet before lifting by covering with saturated plastic sponge and sheets of polythene (Reisman and Lucas, 1978). After lifting, glass need not be kept immersed in water unless the presence of large quantities of salts is suspected. For a short period it can be placed in sealed, water-tight polythene bags together with a few ml of distilled water. Since such bags are virtually never totally water-tight, they should be placed in seal-tight polyethylene boxes where they can be carefully laid on top of one another with suitable padding of shredded polyethylene sheeting or plastic sponge. To prevent the growth of fungus or bacteria, no tissue or other organic packing or labelling materials may be included, unless they have been rot-proofed, and the glass should be kept cool or refrigerated. Where this is not possible a solution of a neutral biocide should be included.

In such waterlogged conditions hydrolytic breakdown of the glass can continue, especially when the pH within the bags rises. Thus this type of storage must on no account be needlessly prolonged. For longer periods of storage the possibility of deep-freezing glass at a temperature of −20°C has been suggested (Nylen, 1975; Arrhenius, 1973). However, further work on freeze-drying excavated glass is essential before such a method can be recommended unreservedly. Another method for prolonged periods of storage is to start the process of consolidation by replacing the water by an inert solvent which allows the glass to be dehydrated, but prevents air entering the weathering crust. The wet glass should be immersed in a 50 per cent mixture of ethanol and water and, after approximately an hour, moved into increasingly solvent-rich mixtures until the glass can be stored in a pure solvent. The experiences of the Corning Museum of Glass, when rescuing material from their disastrous flood, have been documented by J.H. Martin (1977).

Glass from damp deposits

Depending on its state of preservation, and its degree of saturation with water, the total extent of decay of glass may or may not be visible. Glass from damp deposits must therefore be treated with extreme care, and initially kept damp after exposure. After recording, it may be convenient to allow a small, representative sherd to dry out slowly away from direct heat. If no appreciable deterioration occurs, the glass may be allowed to dry out. If deterioration occurs, then the glass must be packed damp and sent for treatment to a laboratory.

Glass from dry deposits

Glass from dry deposits should be maintained in dry conditions. The fragments should be placed in self-seal polythene bags and laid *horizontally* in strong cardboard boxes padded with polyester foam or pads of tissue paper. Cotton wool (US, surgical cotton or cotton batting) must be avoided in direct contact with the glass as its threads can be difficult to remove from delicate artefacts. Entire vessels should be well padded with acid-free tissue and polyethylene foam and placed in strong boxes with well-fitting lids (*Figure 7.3*). Excavated glass should never be stored

in less than 42 per cent relative humidity (Organ, 1957) to avoid further dehydration of the weathering layers, even if the glass appears to be well preserved. It is conceivable that glass may be recovered from conditions of low humidity which has caused it to have crizzled, that is, become permeated with a network of fine cracks; however, none has been recorded at the time of excavation. Such cracks may also result from stresses set up by the weight of soil. In some cases it may well be that all that holds the glass together is a small amount of chemically combined water or surrounding soil, so that the glass may disintegrate on lifting.

Glass lifted in soil blocks

Glass which can only be removed by using the lifting methods described below will already show considerable signs of deterioration in the ground. If it has been lifted simply in a block of soil, the moisture content of the burial environment should be maintained as far as possible in packaging. Thus, blocks of soil and glass should be placed in well-sealed polythene bags or boxes, stored in cool surroundings, and treated *as soon as possible*. Any drying will cause the glass to deteriorate, and the soil block to crumble within its casing, causing further damage to the glass within.

Glass in association with other materials

Problems of storage may arise when glass is found in association with some other materials, such as metals, as in enamels where the glass is bonded to the metal, usually a copper alloy. One method of preventing the rapid deterioration of copper on excavation is to keep it in a relative humidity of less than 50 per cent (Werner, 1966); usually this is achieved by placing it in a polythene bag with a suitable amount of silica gel (approximately an equal volume to that of the space to be desiccated). However, where copper alloys are in association with glass as in enamels, the relative humidity must not be allowed to fall too low; here the gel must be equilibrated to between 40 and 50 per cent relative humidity. Whilst these conditions may be satisfactory for enamels from very dry deposits, they could be detrimental for those from damp or wet ones. Since copper alloys cannot be stored in water, storage of enamels from these types of deposits must follow the solvent or freezing techniques in which the corrosion of metals is also inhibited.

Removal of glass from the ground

Glass sherds which have some strength can simply be taken straight out of the deposit individually. However, if there are any signs of flaking or of gilding or painting on the surface, a layer of soil must be allowed to remain attached to the glass to prevent

Figure 7.3 Stem of an excavated wine glass packed in polyethylene foam and a strong cardboard box. Courtesy of O. Theofanopolou.

the surface layer becoming detached. Complete vessels must be totally uncovered before removal to prevent damage from occurring.

In the case of a fragmented vessel or window pane, the spatial relationship of the sherds may well be essential for later reconstruction, or interpretation of the iconography. Thus, before these are removed individually, they must be adequately plotted, drawn and photographed.

More complex methods must be used where the glass is either too frail to support its own weight or where the related fragments are too small to be removed individually. Conservation time (and therefore money) can be saved if the glass can be correctly lifted by the excavator. On the other hand, when a conservator is available on site he or she should work as quickly as practicable without unduly disrupting the progress of the excavation. Conservators should check that the area in which they are working has been recorded if the earth has to be removed to any depth in order to recover important artefacts.

Lifting methods will vary with the state of the glass and the nature of the surrounding soil. The aim of the lifting technique is (a) to render the glass itself immobile or (b) to render the soil around the glass immobile so that it will support the glass on excavation. No method which will prejudice future conservation treatments may be used, and all methods should follow the conservation ethic of minimal intervention.

Immobilization of the glass alone

It is difficult to immobilize glass by consolidation when it is still in the ground, and it may be premature to do so for several reasons. Firstly, because the glass cannot be thoroughly cleaned first, dirt inevitably becomes consolidated on the surface. It is not always possible to remove either the dirt or consolidant at a later stage without damage to a flaking glass surface. Secondly, the consolidant is unlikely to penetrate throughout the weathering crust, so that spalling may occur at a later date. Thirdly, glass in the ground may well be damp or wet and therefore must be dried before consolidation (which may cause damage), or a water-miscible consolidation system must be used. In order to overcome the problem of dampness, Bimson and Werner (1971) suggested adapting a technique using Carbowax 6000, poly(ethylene glycol), for use in the field. An extremely dilute solution would have to be used in order to ensure good penetration, but the consolidant would be resoluble in water, and therefore relatively easy to remove from the surface at a later date. However, hygroscopicity of the wax may cause difficulties in moist storage conditions. Wihr (1977) and Ypey (1960–61, 1965) advocated the use of Dermoplast SG Normaal [poly(vinyl chloride) in a ketone hydrocarbon solution] for consolidating glass *in situ*. However poly(vinyl chloride) is unstable and will cause future conservation problems. Emulsions such as those of poly(vinyl acetate) may be useful in damp conditions, but they may not penetrate fully, and are difficult to remove later. Silanes are not resoluble and cannot be recommended for consolidating glass except in extreme circumstances.

Another approach would be to dehydrate the glass first and then to apply a resin. Wihr (1977) described such a method in which Araldite AY103/HY956 (epoxy) was applied to a glass vessel in the ground after the vessel had been dehydrated by filling it with two changes of acetone. Apart from causing damage to the glass, grinding and abrading techniques had to be used to remove excess resin. More suitable methods of lifting glass are available, these are described below.

Immobilization of a soil block

The simplest and quickest method of providing support is to isolate the glass on a platform of soil, and then to push a thin metal sheet or spade into the soil well below the glass. The soil platform may be strengthened by covering it with aluminium foil and wrapping gauze bandages dipped in plaster of Paris around it (*Figure 7.4a–e*). Such a system should only be considered as a temporary measure in order to remove the glass from an excavation, it is not strong enough to support the glass during transport to a museum. Another temporary support of this kind was used by Garlake (1969) in the dry climate of South Africa: poly(vinyl acetate) was painted around the edges of the soil platform. Consolidating the soil in this way, with a moisture-curing resin such as Quentglaze (polyurethane), has also been suggested (Dowman, 1970), but as such a resin is not resoluble it must not be allowed to come into contact with the glass itself. Another method for immobilizing the soil block is to freeze it with *dry ice* (solid carbon dioxide). This method has been used in Sweden (Arrhenius, 1973) for lifting archaeological materials on site; and it is possible that it might occasionally be of use in temperate climates.

A sophisticated method for immobilizing a soil block is the construction of a protective casing with plaster of Paris or polyurethane foam. In this method, both the glass and the surrounding soil are rendered immobile by enclosing them in a rigid casing. Great care must be taken to prevent the materials of which the casing is constructed from coming into contact with the glass itself. Thus the block is isolated with damp paper tissue in the case of plaster, and aluminium foil or thin vinyl plastic film in the case of foam. Whilst plaster of Paris is cheap, it is heavy so that for the construction of large casings it may be preferable to use polyurethane foam which, although expensive, is light, rigid and easily cut with a knife for removal at a later date. The foam is formed

(a)

(b)

(c)

(d)

(e)

when two components are mixed together, setting hard in about 5 to 10 min. However, the foam may not cure in cold or damp conditions; and there is a potential health hazard in its use, since one of the components is isocyanate-based and can thus cause severe irritation of mucous membranes and of the skin. Great care must therefore be taken not to allow it to come into contact with the skin or be inhaled when it is being mixed, or when the foam is cut at a later date (Escritt and Greenacre, 1972; ICI, 1977; Moncrieff, 1971; Watkinson and Leigh, 1978). Protective gloves and a face mask must be worn (and some form of fume or dust extraction utilized if the foam is mixed or cut indoors). The foaming reaction is exothermic and if there is any risk of the heat affecting the decayed glass, a layer of tightly packed sand could be placed over the isolating film before the foam is applied; or the foam can be applied in several thin layers.

The procedure for making a casing around a small glass object is shown in *Figure 7.5a–d*, and described below. The measurements quoted can be adjusted according to the size of the object to be lifted.

The object is isolated on a platform of soil some 25 mm larger than itself. This platform is then undercut as far as possible leaving the object on a pedestal about 50 mm high. A collar of corrugated cardboard is placed around the pedestal, allowing a gap of 20–30 mm between it and the collar and allowing the collar to stand 20 mm proud of the uppermost surface of the object. Soil is heaped around the outside of the collar, blocking any gaps and weighing it down. Any fragile undercuts in the object are filled with soft soil or tissue. To prevent the foam coming into contact with the glass, the object and pedestal are then covered with a piece of clear vinyl plastic film (e.g. Clingfilm or Saranwrap), thin polythene sheeting or aluminium foil. A small quantity of foam is applied from an aerosol can or is prepared as directed by the manufacturer, and poured into the collar, ensuring that it runs beneath the pedestal. This process is repeated until the foam nears the top of the collar when a piece of wood is placed over it and pressure exerted to produce a flat surface. The surface should be marked with the site

Figure 7.4 Removing archaeological glass from the site by isolating the soil in which it lies, with a plaster of Paris casing. (a) Glass in a block of earth, protected by aluminium foil, over which the plaster case is applied. (b) Sides wrapped with gauze bandage dipped in plaster of Paris. Metal sheet slid beneath to facilitate its removal. (c) Block inverted and the base protected by foil prior to applying plaster of Paris. (d) Completed case secured with plaster bandage and removed from site. (e) Removal of the case at a later date.

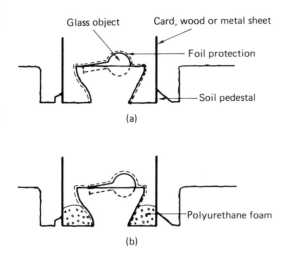

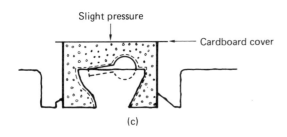

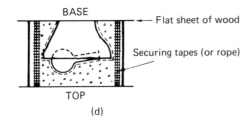

Figure 7.5 Removing archaeological glass from site by isolating the surrounding soil in a foamed polyurethane casing. (a) Glass on a pedestal of earth and protected by foil or vinyl wrapping, and surrounded by a collar of corrugated cardboard. (b) Commencement of application of foaming polyurethane. (c) Flat sheet of wood placed on the foam to produce a flat surface. (d) Inverted block after inversion and application of more foam to complete the casing. Courtesy of J.M. Cronyn.

name, year, orientation and details of its position on site, also with the word TOP. The pedestal and collar are then undercut by a thin metal sheet, and the whole case is inverted. The surface thus exposed is isolated as described above and a layer of foam applied. The complete case is then reinverted so that it stands on its original base. The case is then ready for transport to a laboratory.

Cleaning on site
Cleaning of glass finds in the field should normally be kept to the minimum required to define them, since they should be thoroughly examined both before and during cleaning and of course this is difficult and too time-consuming to achieve during an excavation. Exceptions to this rule may be the cleaning of large quantities of glass waste or cullet from glass-making sites or shipwrecks; and cleaning of important glass finds prior to marking. Where cleaning has to be carried out on site, laboratory methods should be used, adapting them to suit conditions where necessary.

Laboratory treatments

Examination
Visual examination is one of the fundamental principles of archaeological conservation (Biek, 1963; Dimbleby, 1978; Nylen, 1975). Before and during cleaning, the conservator should look for clues as to the technology, decoration, use, type of burial deposit and associated material as well as the actual shape and state of deterioration of the artefact. Records must be kept at the time of any features noted. A good light source and the aid of a ×4 magnifying lens or a binocular reflecting-light microscope are essential. The first thing to examine is the material adhering to the glass because it may contain, for example, fragments of metal corrosion from a missing part of the artefact, signs of the thread used to string beads together, or the remains of the adhesive used to stick a bead to a brooch. A search must be made for any applied decoration, such as gilding or painting, to avoid any risk of their being destroyed. As the deposit is cleaned away, more will be revealed of the decoration and state of deterioration of the glass and finally the shape of the object, and details of its method of manufacture can be sought. If, at any stage, an item of interest is uncovered which may be removed during further treatment, it must be photographed. The dimensions of sherds and thicknesses of vessel walls should be measured immediately in case the glass flakes or crumbles without warning. If the object is a vessel, any contents must be kept for close examination (Wihr, 1977; Biek, 1963) and possible analysis. Further information on examination can be found in Chapter 6.

Cleaning
As previously mentioned, cleaning of excavated glass involves the removal of obscuring soluble and insoluble deposits to reveal the shape, decoration and original surface of the glass. Routine cleaning of glass in collections may also be necessary, or the removal of old restoration materials prior to treatment. The

parameters governing these cleaning methods are relatively clear compared with those concerning the removal or non-removal of a decayed weathering crust.

Weathering crusts

When glass deteriorates in the ground, it seems that it does not increase in volume and thus the original surface and dimensions of the glass will be represented by the outside of the weathering crust. It follows therefore that if the whole crust is removed, or if part of a thick crust is removed in order to create a smooth patina, the dimensions of the artefact are irretrievably altered. Furthermore, it has been shown recently (Hughes, in Bacon and Knight, 1987) that useful archaeometric data can be retrieved from the weathering crusts of enamels. Finally, even though it may not be immediately apparent, the weathering may have proceeded right through the glass and removal of the crust in such a case could lead to complete destruction of the object.

Plenderleith and Werner (1974) recommended that the discoloured crust on enamels should be removed in the case of cuprous red glass which has become superficially green. Such treatment was carried out on escutcheons on Anglo-Saxon hanging bowls from Sutton Hoo in Suffolk (Bruce-Mitford, 1975). It is possible that a green crust need not be removed completely, since the last traces could be rendered transparent by consolidation with a resin, a test first being made with toluene to ascertain if enough crust has been removed. However, removal of any or all of the crust will destroy the flush finish of the glass in its setting and this discrepancy in level may have to be made up with a suitable resin to maintain the coherency of the design. Thus removal of weathering crusts on enamels is not to be recommended in general. In the case of a hanging bowl from Lincoln where a similar problem of discoloration was encountered, the original surface was retained (Foley and Hunter, in Bacon and Knight, 1987).

Nevertheless, since the weathering crusts on glass are often iridescent, opaque or black, and hence the original colour and transparency cannot be seen, removal of crusts has often been advocated on aesthetic grounds. Although this cannot necessarily be condoned, it may be that the removal of light opaque powdery deposits which do not form a substantial surface of the original glass, may be justified. Should removal of weathering crusts become necessary it is probably best carried out mechanically, as this treatment can be confined to small areas, by using scalpels, wooden picks and soft paint brushes.

Dilute mineral acids have been used to remove weathering crusts *in toto*; however, even dilute acids may affect the remaining glass and will penetrate deep into the glass through cracks and flaws endangering the whole object. Dilute concentrations of acids have been used in attempts to remove carbonate deposits, and even iron and manganese, from *within* the weathering crusts, in order to produce brightened silica surfaces. However, the resulting effervescence tended to disrupt the fragile weathering crusts, and the blackening seemed little improved.

It is possible that sequestering agents in the form of pastes could be used either to remove weathering crusts or selective ions within them. For example catechol $[C_6H_4(OH)_2]$ sequesters silica, and tetra-sodium ethylenediaminetetraacetic acid (EDTA), $,-[CH_2N(CH_2COOH)_2]_2$, sequesters calcium and magnesium, but these have both been shown to attack glass at high pH values, even though the damage may not be visible at first. It should be remembered that sequestering agents will also affect enamelling and gilding, and hence if employed, they must be used with the greatest of caution.

The very strong reducing agent hydrazine (N_2H_4) has been used to brighten coloured medieval window glass which has discoloured brown (Fitz, 1981; Müller *et al.*, 1987). However, because of its high pH (11 at 24 per cent concentration) and toxicity it should be used with great care.

Removal of lead sulphide blackening

The only method attested for the removal of lead sulphide (PbS) was carried out at the Conservation Analytical Laboratory of the Smithsonian Institution (Smithsonian, 1969). Here a blackened, nineteenth-century goblet was lightened by immersion in dilute hydrochloric acid for 1 min; this was said to convert the PbS to yellow sulphur, much of which could be removed with a soft brush. Any sulphur caught within the weathered layer was dissolved by immersion in carbon disulphide (CS_2) for 24 hours, leaving the glass colourless but hazy because the weathering had been made visible (note that CS_2 is very toxic, with a TLV of 20 ppm).

Removal of insoluble deposits

On strong, barely decayed glass, insoluble deposits can be removed mechanically using scalpels; or possibly an ultrasonic dental descaling unit; or an air-abrasive unit (Newton, 1976c). It may be virtually impossible to remove disfiguring deposits from fragile glass even if the glass is consolidated prior to or during the cleaning process.

Removal of superficial deposits from consolidated or block-lifted glass

If glass has been lifted from an excavation inside a protective casing, its micro-excavation is carried out in the laboratory. If the glass is particularly badly deteriorated, then only small areas at a time are exposed. These are cleaned and consolidated before the next is uncovered. Where it has been necessary to consolidate glass prior to cleaning, the overlying deposits may be softened by placing the artefact in a solvent vapour for a short period of time, and then removed mechanically with a scalpel and solvent swabs.

Removal of soluble or dispersable deposits

The removal of soluble salts from glass from wet sites or marine excavations was described earlier as a treatment which could be undertaken during a period of temporary storage. However, if salt removal has not already been achieved in the field, it must be carried out in the laboratory as soon as possible. Artefacts from muddy deposits, especially urban excavations, are often covered in a film of grease, which should be removed from the glass using water or other solvents before it is dried, consolidated or repaired.

By careful cleaning of a small area it should be ascertained whether or not decayed glass is actually being held together by dirt or calcium concretions. These may fall off unaided, but may be encouraged to do so by using small wooden toothpicks and soft brushes. Barely damp swabs of distilled water, propan-2-ol, or industrial methylated spirits (IMS) can be used to remove the last of the dirt but care must then be taken not to use excess amounts of IMS or blanching of the glass may occur (Dowman, 1970).

Lal (1962–63) suggests binding flaking glass with cotton thread before it is cleaned in order to keep any loose fragments in place. However, this is likely to cause physical damage to the glass. In general dirt should be left on the glass rather than risk the removal of a flaking surface. Sound archaeological glass may be washed in water, preferably distilled or deionized. If really necessary, a 25 per cent aqueous solution of hydrogen peroxide may be used to loosen stains and dirt held in cracks on this type of glass.

It is sometimes possible to remove mud trapped inside a hollow rim or foot of a broken vessel by flushing it out with jets of water from a pipette. If the glass surface and any decoration appears to be sound, that is, not disintegrating, and very adherent, the object *may* be immersed in water in an ultrasonic tank for a few minutes. Ultrasonic transducers generate high-frequency (non-audible) sound waves, typically 20–50 kHz, which interact in a liquid to produce minute bubbles. These bubbles expand and contract violently and it is the shock waves produced by this action which speed up the loosening of dirt. This effect, combined with the vibration induced by the ultrasonic waves in friable materials, can cause rapid disintegration of the structure of the material. For this reason it is most useful for removing mud and porous encrustations, but can also cause severe damage to friable substrates. It is essential that the progress of cleaning should be constantly monitored.

The use of ultrasonic methods for cleaning fragile glass is fraught with difficulties because of the possibility of causing or promoting cracking of the glass. Ultrasonic cleaning has been successfully and safely used on glass in good condition (Gibson and Newton, 1974), but damage has been shown to be severe on other painted glass (Frenzel, 1975a). The state of preservation of objects varies considerably, and preliminary experiments should always be made on valueless materials before a new treatment is introduced.

The aqueous cleaning solutions recommended by suppliers of ultrasonic equipment are frequently harmful to glass. Only mild cleaning agents should be used, especially when such a powerful cleaning method is employed.

Glass bearing unfired pigments, or flaking paint or gilding must be treated with the greatest of care (Moncrieff, 1975). If glass is found to have water-soluble pigments on its surface, such as Chinese snuff bottles (Newman, 1977), it must not be washed. It would be possible to consolidate it, and it may be possible to re-affix flaking paint or gilding, with a consolidant.

Removal of previous restoration materials

In the case of glass artefacts which have been in a collection for a number of years, there may be evidence of attempts at partial repair (*Figure 7.6*). This often consists of the use of adhesives ranging from animal glues to epoxy- and rubber-based compositions; with wax or plaster of Paris as the replacement for missing areas of glass, coloured with a variety of paints (Wihr, 1963), as shown in *Figure 7.7*. It may not always be possible for the conservator to decide which materials have been used, or even be necessary for him to know, provided they can be removed without damage to the glass (Moncrieff, 1975). Where safe removal is not possible, a sample of the material may be tested in order that the correct solvent may be chosen. In general, the usual practice is to begin removal of previous restorations with the least toxic solvent, that is, cold water, and if this has no effect to try warm water, followed by acetone, IMS, white spirit, xylene and dichloromethane. Once softened, the material may be completely removed using a sable paint-brush and with the use of a scalpel. Force should never be applied since fragile glass may break before a strong adhesive is dislodged.

Washing non-excavated glass

Non-excavated vessels, prior to washing, should be examined for any signs of previous restoration because this may not be immediately apparent. Glass can then be washed in tepid water (never hot) in a polythene bowl (to prevent breakages should the vessel slip). A small amount of a non-ionic detergent, e.g. Synperonic N, may be added to the water (if too much is used the glass will not be visible through the

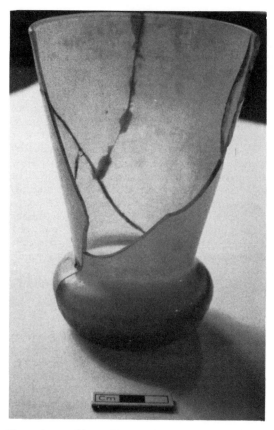

Figure 7.6 An old, unsightly repair in which an excess of animal glue has been used.

Figure 7.7 An old, unsightly restoration of a glass vessel, which has been gapfilled with plaster of Paris painted silver. British Museum, London.

suds) and only one object should be placed in the bowl at a time. Care must be taken not to exert pressure on the glass during cleaning, especially on fragile areas such as a rim or stem of a drinking vessel. When clean, the glass should be laid on paper towelling to drain. The towelling will prevent the glass from sliding on a wet surface and also absorb the excess water. Breakages may occur on the slightest impact and therefore the working surfaces should not be overcrowded, especially as it is sometimes difficult to judge how much space there is between transparent objects. Drinking glasses should not be held by the stem in case they snap under pressure, but they should be supported by cupping the hand under the bowl. A soft cloth, or paper towelling, is used to dry the glass, again taking care not to exert any pressure. Drying should be carried out over a bench spread with a thick layer of towelling, in case the glass should slip. The glass should be free from surface moisture before being stored.

Washing weeping glass

The immediate treatment for weeping glass (a phenomenon described in Chapter 4) is as follows:

Figure 7.8 Storage of weeping and crizzling glass and enamels in an 'air-tight' case incorporating a dehumidifier which maintains the atmosphere inside at a constant relative humidity. British Museum, London.

after washing the glass thoroughly in distilled water, it is passed through two baths of IMS and allowed to dry. This treatment will retard the disintegration of the glass for a short time and also improve its appearance because dirt, which tends to adhere to the sticky surface of weeping glass, will be removed. However, washing does not offer any long-term protection against recurrence of weeping if the objects are again exposed to a moist atmosphere. The safest way of dealing with potentially unstable weeping glass objects is to ensure that they are kept under conditions of controlled atmospheric humidity (42 per cent relative humidity) (*Figure 7.8*; see also page 240).

Consolidation

Consolidation of weathered glass or fragile surface decoration with a resin may be undertaken when the glass is liable to crumble or flake upon drying or handling. It has also been used to reintroduce transparency to *thin* weathering crusts. The treatment should be considered to be irreversible, even when resins which are normally resoluble are used, because they swell during solvation and the glass is unlikely to survive both this swelling and the prolonged immersion required to remove a consolidant. Even if the glass could survive, it is unlikely that all traces of a resin could be removed. Consolidation therefore should only be carried out where absolutely necessary for the survival of an artefact. The question of whether to consolidate before or after cleaning presents a difficult problem. Pre-consolidation may make cleaning more difficult if consolidated dirt has to be removed from a fragile glass surface. On the other hand, it may not be possible to clean a fragile glass before it is consolidated. Therefore each case must be judged on its own merit. In this chapter the term *consolidant* is used to define a resin used for the purposes of consolidation, and *consolidation system* to define the liquid phase in which the consolidant is applied whether it be molten, in solution, or as a polymer pretreatment. When choosing a consolidant, the conservator must bear in mind the nature and properties of the resins and solvents to be used (see Chapter 5), and the condition of the decayed glass to be treated.

In the case of weathered glass, it is not only necessary to consider the glass crust as the substrate; there may also be a solid glass core to which the consolidant must adhere. Not only is the surface of this core normally associated with water molecules, but (the amorphous silica of the weathering crust being hydrophilic) it is usually highly hydrated. Thus to obtain enhanced penetration and adhesion, a consolidation system which displaces or incorporates this water must be employed. Preliminary drying out

of a crust by heat or high vacuum must be avoided since this would lead to shrinkage and disruption. However, it is likely that further research into pretreatments using coupling agents (Errett *et al.*, 1984) may lead to increased wetting of the substrates by subsequent consolidation systems. In general the approach to the consolidation of extensively weathered glass has been either that of preliminary dehydration with solvents, or that of using a water-miscible consolidation system, and of choosing a consolidation system which combines low viscosity with a high deposition of solids on setting (Bimson and Werner, 1971; Brill, 1971b). Systems which are too viscous fail to penetrate the glass, resulting in the formation of skins which spall off, whilst those with too low a solids content fail to fill the interstices. Viscosity varies with consolidant; thus, for example, Paraloid B72 in a 20 per cent solution of toluene at 21°C has a viscosity of only 29×10^{-3} N s m^{-2}, whilst poly(vinyl acetate) (of approximately 520 degrees of polymerization) in a 20 per cent solution has a viscosity of 40×10^{-3} N s m^{-2}. Reduction of viscosity can be achieved by a number of means, most commonly by altering the concentrations of the consolidation system. Another method is the application of heat, but temperatures in excess of 60°C must be stringently avoided in order to safeguard the glass; and consideration must be given to the vapour pressure and flash points of the solvent. Penetration of an air-filled weathering crust can also be improved by removing the air by reducing the atmospheric pressure around the artefact during consolidation, as described below.

Preliminary dehydration
Preliminary dehydration of damp or waterlogged glass by replacement of the water by air usually results in loss of transparency and often in flaking of the surface. Therefore the bulk and surface-layer water must be displaced by a solvent, which in its turn will be replaced by the consolidation system or be incorporated into the consolidation system. Hydrophylic solvents such as ethanol, propan-2-ol, acetone or butanone are suitable. Without allowing the glass to dry, it is first placed in a 50:50 mixture of water and solvent. After an hour or so the glass is passed through a succession of baths of increasing solvent concentrations, and finally into the solvent in which the consolidant is to be dissolved. The glass can then be transferred to the consolidation system itself.

Application of consolidant
Spraying, dripping or painting the consolidant solution on the glass are far less efficacious than the methods decribed above but they might have to be

Figure 7.9 Application of a consolidant (10 per cent Paraloid B-72 in toluene) to flaking glass by brush.

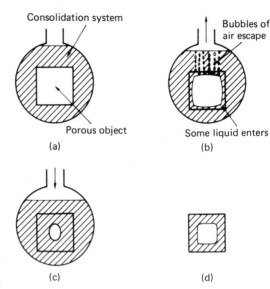

Figure 7.10 Impregnation of a porous object under reduced pressure; (a) atmospheric pressure, (b) reduction of pressure, (c) return to atmospheric pressure, (d) evaporation of solvent carrying resin towards the surface of the object. Courtesy of J.M. Cronyn.

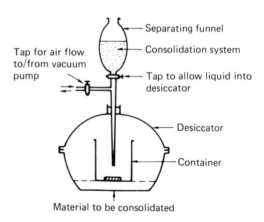

Figure 7.11 Equipment for the impregnation of porous objects under reduced pressure. After Wihr (1977).

used on individual fragments or objects on site; or in the case of large or very delicate objects (*Figure 7.9*). In these cases, the first applications must have especially low viscosities in order to achieve penetration right into the crust and hence several dilute coats are much more helpful than one thick one. A syringe may be useful for impregnating areas of an object which are difficult to reach with a brush.

If the glass in question is not completely waterlogged, that is, the weathering layers contain air, then the consolidation system may be best applied under conditions of reduced pressure. The glass can either be immersed in a consolidant and the pressure reduced, or the pressure can be reduced and the solution dripped onto the glass. The former method may give better support to a whole, fragile vessel but greater disruption is likely when the pressure is reduced. If the dripping method is used, for example, in cases where the glass is liable to lose flakes in solution, sufficient consolidant to cover the fragment should be dripped into the consolidation chamber before the vacuum is released.

Reduced pressure is used primarily to remove air from the pores and capillaries of decayed glass which would otherwise impede the penetration of the consolidation system, and secondly to introduce a low pressure into the pores so that, when the assembly is returned to atmospheric pressure, more of the consolidation system is forced into them due to the pressure differential (Biek *et al.*, 1955; Rees-Jones, 1963); this principle is illustrated in *Figure 7.10a–d*. This lowest practical pressure will depend in part on the apparatus and pump available (*Figure 7.11*) and in part on the vapour pressure of the liquid at the given temperature (because a liquid boils when the ambient pressure reaches its vapour pressure); solvents with high vapour pressures will evaporate even when the pressure is only slightly reduced. However, it should be remembered that the vapour pressure of a solution is lower than that of a pure solvent. Reduced pressure will therefore tend to concentrate the solution and, if taken to excess, it

could cause the consolidant to solidify. A reduction in the pressure also increases the rate of setting of epoxy resins, probably by the removal of water vapour and oxygen. An excessively low pressure should, however, be avoided because there is a danger that any sealed bubbles (seed) which are very close to the surface of the solid glass might burst. The atmospheric pressure should be reduced only slowly in order to prevent air rushing from the glass and causing it to disintegrate (Wihr, 1977) and to allow time for the pressure in partially sealed pores to come to equilibrium. This is especially true when the glass is immersed in a liquid before the pressure is reduced, because the viscosity of the liquid retards the process. Again, the reduced pressure should only be slowly increased in order to avoid air rushing into cavities where the solution has not fully penetrated.

The use of silanes in pretreatment as coupling agents for the bond between hydrated glass/weathering crusts and the acrylic consolidant Paraloid B72 has been used successfully on extensively weathered glass by Errett *et al.* (1984). Whilst the long-term stability of the technique is still unknown, the approach is one which *might* have a wide application on archaeological glass.

Drying after consolidation
After consolidation by immersion, the glass is placed on silicone (US, Glassine) paper and excess consolidant allowed to drain off the surface. This process may be aided by the use of cotton swabs soaked in solvent or simply by mopping with tissue. It is then advisable to replace the object in a solvent atmosphere whilst it dries out, either in a glass receptacle or, if in the ground, by covering the glass with a polythene bag (Garlake, 1969). Drying the glass in this way will slow the rate of evaporation so that the resin remaining on the surface will be more thinly dispersed and therefore appear matt. Covering the glass also prevents dust from adhering to the consolidant. Generally speaking, a matt surface will render surface details, such as engraving or paint, more readily visible on an uneven weathered surface. Hedvall *et al.* (1951) achieved such a finish by gently heating the consolidant bath. Other methods of revealing surface detail have been the application of a thick layer of poly(vinyl acetate) to the surface of the blackened sherds of medieval window glass to reveal paint (Hutchinson, 1978; Newton, 1982b entry No. 416), and the application of a glossy resin (Plexigum P24) over the primary treatment, a fluoro-silicate, Durol-Polier-Fluat SD (Karl, 1970). However, none of these methods can be recommended for reasons previously discussed.

Surface treatments
In order to adhere flaking glass surfaces and cracked enamels, solutions of various resins, such as poly(vinyl acetate) or the methacrylate copolymer Paraloid B72, have been applied as a surface treatment (Wihr, 1977; Dove, 1981). Whilst such treatment may reduce the visual effect of iridescence, neither it nor the consolidation systems previously discussed can restore transparency to a thin weathering crust completely. Improved transparency of weathering crusts on small glass objects has been variously achieved by surface treatment with Paraloid B72 after solvent dehydration, or with an epoxy resin such as HXTAL NYL 1 after air drying. Naturally, the success of such an operation depends upon the condition of the glass undergoing treatment.

The use of organic lacquers has been suggested as a protective film for weeping glass; and Hedvall *et al.* (1951) have described a technique in which such a glass was impregnated with a poly(methylmethacrylate) under vacuum. Laquering may appear to delay further deterioration, but all organic lacquers are permeable to water vapour, and the chemical reaction of disintegration will continue. Thus the reaction products will be trapped at the interface, and their build-up may eventually cause the total collapse of the glass object. At present, the only method of dealing with weeping glass is the provision of suitable storage conditions as described on page 000.

A method of consolidating fully decayed glass was developed by Bimson and Werner (1971) for a fragile potash glass alembic head dating from the fourteenth or fifteenth century AD. The alembic head had been successfully excavated, along with several other fragments of medieval distilling apparatus, but had been subsequently severely damaged by poor storage. More than half the object had been crushed to tiny flakes and the remainder was in an extremely fragile condition and could not be safely handled.

The problem was not only to consolidate those fragments so that they could be safely handled but also to use a consolidant that would serve as a gapfiller, because most of the fragments were joined only at one or two points. Glass and amorphous silica are hydrophilic, and it was decided to use a poly(ethylene glycol) wax which is also hydrophilic, the actual material used being Carbowax 6000. (Care had to be taken to ensure that the treated glass was not subject to a moist atmosphere.) The procedure used was as follows: each fragment of glass was supported on a raft of aluminium foil and laid on the surface of the molten Carbowax 6000 in a dish which was placed in an oven at a temperature of about 80°C. It was feared that the Carbowax 6000, having a relatively high viscosity, might disintegrate the glass further, but this did not happen. After 2 hours the raft with its fragment of glass had sunk to the bottom of the molten wax and all the bubbles of displaced air had separated from the surface. The fragment was then gently removed from the wax bath by lifting the corners of the raft, and replaced in the oven on a pile of absorbent tissues. When the excess molten wax had run off, the aluminium raft was carefully removed, and any remaining wax mopped off with the hot tissues. The fragments were then allowed to cool to room temperature when it was found that they had sufficient mechanical strength to be handled safely, and their appearance showed remarkably little change. In order to join the treated fragments together, the wax on the edges was melted using a special Microweld torch which restricted the heating area to a few square millimetres. This enabled the wax to be melted in any given small area without softening joints already made, and small lumps of the wax could be melted to fill gaps and strengthen the joints. It would be wrong to suggest that the glass is now in a robust physical condition, but several years later it was possible to handle it in order to fit mounts for display.

Reisman and Lucas (preliminary report, undated) carried out experimental research into retrieval and consolidation of glass from underwater environments in 1978. The method of consolidation was as follows. The object was weighed on removal from its last water bath, and then immersed in a bath of ethanol (anhydrous ethanol). The ethanol bath was changed every few days to ensure that the water was being replaced. After a few changes, the specific gravity of the ethanol bath was tested to ensure that it was water-free. When the ethanol exchange was complete, the glass object was reweighed. It was then submerged in the consolidating material, PVA-AYAA 5 per cent in 95 per cent ethanol. The object was left in the consolidant for 15 min after which a vacuum was drawn to 5 in Hg and held for 15 to 20 min. The percentage concentration of the solution was increased to 7 per cent by adding more PVA-AYAA, the vacuum drawn to 5 in Hg, and after 15 min to 7 in. After 15 min the percentage of PVA-AYAA was increased to 10 per cent, the vacuum applied and if possible the percentage of the PVA-AYAA further increased. The highest concentration of consolidant possible consistent with impregnation should be achieved especially if the glass surface is insecure. The object was then removed from the vacuum and placed in a chamber over ethanol vapour for several hours to force the PVA-AYAA into the surface of the crust even further and to prevent the surface from drying with a glossy appearance. During this time the object was observed to note any shrinkage, delamination or spalling. The object was then removed from the desiccator and allowed to dry at ambient temperature.

Experiments are continuing into the preservation of glass from waterlogged environments; it seems that consolidation with acrylic emulsion, or with Paraloid B72 after dehydration through solvents, will produce the most satisfactory results.

The following method for temporary storage and consolidation of wet excavated medieval window glass was developed by Hutchinson (abstract No. 416 in Newton, 1982b) in the conservation laboratory of The Historic Buildings and Monuments Commission for England (London).

On excavation, the glass was kept wet and packed in single layers between sheets of polyester foam of a grade which retained water well. The glass was then placed inside two self-seal polythene bags and labelled both on the outside and on a waterproof label inside the outer bag. The glass was kept in a cool place. (If a refrigerator is used to store the wet glass there must be no possibility of the water freezing.) During temporary wet storage the water surrounding the glass should not be changed. Experience has shown that the pH of the solution does not rise above 8.0.

Once in the laboratory, the glass was unpacked and whilst being kept wet, as much mud and loose encrustation as possible was removed mechanically. The fragments were then consolidated with a mixture of PEG 4000, poly(ethylene glycol) and Vinamul 6815, a poly(vinyl acetate) emulsion. This acted as a bulk filler and consolidant. The mixture was prepared as follows: the required amount of Vinamul 6815 was diluted with an equal amount of distilled water and the required amount of PEG 4000 was dissolved in water in the proportion 500 g to 1 litre of water. The consolidation mixture itself is composed of 4 parts diluted poly(vinyl acetate) emulsion, 2 parts distilled water, and 2 parts poly(ethylene glycol) solution, all parts being measured by volume. The glass fragments were then laid flat on coarse nylon netting in a shallow container, the netting ensured that the consolidant completely surrounded the glass. If it was allowed to overhang the sides of the container it could be used as a support when removing very delicate fragments. Several layers of net and glass could be placed in one container; if necessary extra pieces of mesh could be used as separators or to spread the load. The consolidant was then slowly added to the dish, ensuring that the fragments did not float (they did not if waterlogged), until there was at least 10 mm of liquid above the glass. The top of the container was then covered with plastic film to prevent evaporation, the vessel was clearly labelled with its contents, and was then left for approximately two months. After this time, the fragments were removed from the consolidant, and any excess mixture and loose encrustation removed. The glass was then placed on silicone paper and allowed to dry. Repairs were carried out at this stage, using a cellulose nitrate adhesive (HMG). Finally all the surfaces of the glass (including the edges) were painted with a 30 per cent solution of poly(vinyl acetate) in toluene. Since toluene is less volatile than, for example, acetone, the solution did not form into brush lines on the surface while drying. Lacquering the glass in this way alters the optical appearance of the surfaces, thus enabling the painted design to be seen through the thin layers of dirt and decayed glass remaining. Glass treated by this method has been found to be in good condition several years later; favourable storage conditions will be a major contributing factor to this. Experiments with the method are continuing; however, it may be that the use of Paraloid B72 and aqueous solutions of acrylic emulsions described below will prove to be more widely accepted.

Koob (1981) began experimenting with acrylic colloidal dispersions as a consolidant for newly excavated archaeological bone. Since the smaller particle size and low viscosity of the colloidal dispersion system permitted better penetration at higher concentrations, it was concluded that they were the most suitable consolidant in a water-based system for the consolidation of fragile materials, especially bone and other organic materials because of their near neutral pH. Furthermore, resistance to high temperatures and characteristically good working properties are assured by the glass transition temperature and the minimum film temperature respectively. In addition, the relatively high moisture barrier, due to an acrylic film's low water permeability and absorption, protected objects against climatic fluctuation. After drying, the acrylic resin film was hard and durable.

(a)

In 1983 an aqueous solution of Primal WS-24 acrylic emulsion was used to consolidate fragments of excavated glass beads and painted window glass in Denmark (Roberts, 1984). The glass beads, dated to between AD 400 and 700, arrived for treatment packed in a closed polythene bag. Since condensation had formed on the inside of the bag, it was at first difficult to determine their exact quantity and condition (*Figure 7.12a*). However, it could be seen that the fragments were in an extremely friable condition (due in part to improper lifting and packaging), and that they would require consolidation before being cleaned. To this end, a number of tests were carried out using 20, 50 and 100 per cent solutions of Primal WS-12, WS-24 and WS-50 acrylic emulsions on silica gel lying on damp soil to represent the beads, before a 50 per cent aqueous solution of Primal WS-24 was chosen as the solution with which to consolidate the glass under moist conditions. The bag containing the bead fragments was then placed on a glass plate for support and cut open to reveal the contents as one glass bead and one bead fragment. The exposed surfaces of the beads were consolidated with a few drops of Primal WS-24, 100 per cent, that is, as supplied. While the earth was still moist from the condensation and the Primal solution, the glass bead that was intact was removed from the surrounding soil with soft brushes and distilled water. Cleaning in this manner was terminated when the glass began to split. Consolidation was renewed with a 50 per cent aqueous solution of Primal WS-24. The consolidation medium was applied drop by drop, until saturated, and excess was removed with a cotton swab. In order to slow down the evaporation rate, the bead was placed in an open plastic bag under a slightly raised glass beaker. After an hour the bead was transferred to silicon release paper and was further consolidated with Primal WS-24, 50 per cent aqueous solution. When an excess was apparent, consolidation was terminated. The glass bead was allowed to dry overnight (*Figure 7.12b*). Final cleaning was accomplished by dissolving the consolidant on the surface with toluene, and cleaning the bead with a soft brush. The cleaned surface was then reconsolidated with an 8 per cent solution of Paraloid B-72 in toluene. After treatment it could be seen that the glass bead was turquoise in colour, with a marvered design on bands of white and red-orange glass (*Figure 7.12c*).

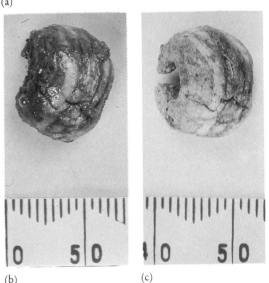

(b)   (c)

Figure 7.12 (a) Excavated wet glass bead fragments in a polythene bag, obscured by gravel. Light cleaning being undertaken with a sable brush. (b) Glass bead after consolidation with 50 per cent Primal WS-24. (c) Glass bead after removal of excess solvent. National Museum, Copenhagen.

(a)

(b)

A method of consolidating excavated glass with Primal WS-24 and Paraloid B-72 was also used to conserve a fragment of a painted glass roundel or *kabinettscheibe* from Slagelse in Denmark (Roberts, 1984). The rondel had a diameter of 72 mm and was decorated with a high-fired design layer and script on the front, with evidence of a silver stain on the reverse. The fragment was received for treatment in a waterlogged condition, but had subsequently been allowed to dry out. Upon drying, the glass surface and consequently the paint layer began flaking and cupping on both sides of the fragment (*Figure 7.13a*). It is thought that the force of contraction of the paint layer during evaporation of the water contributed to the damage to the glass itself, thus creating an extremely fragile artefact. Treatment was begun using a 3 per cent solution of Paraloid B-72 in toluene applied to selected areas and allowed to penetrate the surface layers by capillary action. Since it was observed that moisture relaxed the flaking surfaces of both the glass and the paint layer, a water-soluble acrylic consolidant, Primal WS-24 (as a 20 per cent solution in water), was introduced with a brush. Again, capillary action distributed the consolidant. After drying, the surface of the glass was brushed with a solution of 8 per cent Paraloid B-72 in toluene. In areas of heavy flaking, such as the painted script, the surfaces of both the glass and paint were gently warmed with a heated spatula (temperature controlled at 25°C), in order to aid the flattening and relaying of the paint. The results can be seen in *Figure 7.13b*.

The use of an electrically heated spatula in this way, applied to the glass and/or paint usually over a small piece of Melinex sheet, and in conjunction with small amounts of solvent and/or consolidant to relax the surfaces, is often successful in relaxing and relaying flaking painted designs on (painted) glass.

Reinforcing

It is possible that crumbling glass may not be strong enough to handle even after consolidation, and that a support in the form of a backing material will be required. Working on very decayed glass from Sardis in Turkey, Majewski (1973) used Japanese mulberry tissue with poly(vinyl acetate) (PVAC), the resin which had already been used for consolidating the glass. It would have been preferable to have chosen a resin which would not dissolve in the same solvent as the consolidant in case the backing material needed to be removed at a later date.

Figure 7.13 (a) Flaking and cupping of a fragment of a painted glass roundel. (b) The same fragment after consolidation with a 20 per cent aqueous solution of Primal WS-24, and surface treatment with 8 per cent Paraloid B-72 in toluene. National Museum, Copenhagen.

Another, unusual approach to reinforcing fragile glass is illustrated by the following example. It demonstrates the way in which normal laboratory methods may be adapted for use in the field, where conditions and the supply of materials are usually restricted. If the conservator had had access to a museum laboratory (and time), an attempt may have been made to remove from the last vestiges of mud from the case bottle. In some instances, however, marine concretion which had hardened inside glass vessels, which had then become partially or totally destroyed, may represent the original shape and form of the artefacts.

A case bottle retrieved from a wreck off Mombasa was found to be virtually complete but the glass had begun to exfoliate, was badly cracked and only held together by the compacted clay inside. Since removal of the clay would cause disintegration of the bottle it was decided to trim down the mud to leave a 5 mm lining, by excavating it through a hole in one side of the bottle from which glass had been lost during burial. It was then proposed to reinforce the mud lining with netting and resin. To support the glass while the mud was being removed, the bottle was faced with netting held in place with PVAC but because of the fragile condition of the glass the facing could only be applied while the bottle was still supported in water. The level of the water was reduced to expose the upper face only which was dried thoroughly by swabbing with IMS and acetone. The surface was consolidated with PVAC and a synthetic net facing applied. The facing was secure enough to withstand soaking in water while the other sides were faced. The mud was then removed to leave a thin layer on the inside of the bottle. At this stage the bottle could be taken out of the water and dried, after which a netting support was applied to the inside layer of mud with 5 per cent Paraloid B-72 (in acetone) an acrylic resin which is not soluble in IMS. The PVAC and net outer facing could be safely removed with this solvent with no risk of weakening the lining. Finally the surfaces were cleaned and given a final consolidating coat of PVAC (Turner in Piercy, 1978).

Glass opus sectile panels from Kenchreai

As a case study of an important, if rather atypical, group of materials, the conservation and restoration of some of the panels of *opus sectile* from Kenchreai in Greece will be described. The treatments, undertaken at the Corning Museum of Glass, include drying, cleaning, reinforcing and restoration of the glass fragments.

In AD 365 and 375 the Greek Peloponnesus suffered catastrophic seismic disturbances with overwhelming tidal waves. During one of these disturbances, there were over 100 panels of *opus sectile*

(a)

(b)

(c)

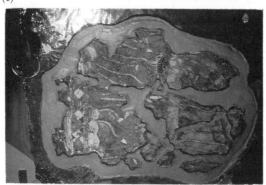

(d)

worked in glass, resting on the floor of a building in the harbour area at Kenchreai (Ibrahim *et al.*, 1976). The panels had not long been delivered from abroad (possibly from Egypt or Italy) and were in temporary storage still in their shipping crates, leaning against the walls at an angle fairly close to the vertical with one long side resting on the floor. There were four to ten crates in each of nine stacks (*Figure 7.14a*). As a result of the catastrophe the entire building was tilted, so that the floors sloped downward towards the south. It must be assumed that the panels themselves were disturbed by the shock. Most important, they were drenched with water, so that the plaster slab on which the glass was affixed lost its cohesion and the panels were no longer solid or rigid – they could not be moved without crumbling to pieces. Presumably other damage was caused by the fact that the edges of the crates resting on the floor would have been dislodged so that they slid away from the wall, allowing the panels to sag and warp. The building and its contents were subsequently abandoned, filled in with debris and built over. During the period of submerged burial, continuous reaction to the chemicals of the sea water and decaying animal and vegetable life resulting in extensive decomposition of much of the glass; the parts of most crates highest above the floor were eroded by wave action, or by subsequent despoiling of the walls to obtain building material.

(e)

Figure 7.14 (a) Stacks containing panels of *opus sectile* with preserved end-pieces of the crates *in situ*, after preliminary cleaning. Kenchreai, Greece. (b) Fragment of an *opus sectile* panel from Kenchreai, wrapped in yellow flannel cloth and supported on a sheet of Masonite. (c) Cleaned and consolidated fragment of *opus sectile* (panel number 2 layer B), fixed to a sheet of fibreglass screening. (d) Part of a glass panel from Kenchreai surrounded with a supporting fill of Vel-mix. (e) Restored section of a panel, similar to that shown in (a) to (d), on display in Nauplion, Greece. Part (e): Keith Lord.

Clearance of the site began in 1965. In the summer of 1968 tanks were built of masonry on shore in order to store the *opus sectile* panels. On excavation, each stack was immediately placed in the tanks which contained fresh water. The water was replaced daily over a period of one month, and readings of the salinity of the water taken at the end of each day. The results (unpublished) seemed to show that by the end of the period of immersion, the salts had been removed. The crates were then taken to Nauplion (Greece) for dissection and conservation. The fact that the panels had to be dried out before conservation could begin, presented further problems.

The condition of the glass when discovered, however it might have altered from its original condition, was in a state of precarious balance of saturation by water. In the sea it had reached equilibrium with its surroundings, but if dried out, much of it would disintegrate immediately. In the process of dissecting each crate and conservation of the glass within, therefore, there were two conflicting problems: to clean and treat for preservation each panel as carefully and effectively as possible; and to finish each panel and get through the stack before it dried out. To keep part of the stack in its accustomed state of saturation with water, while spending an indefinite amount of time on the exposed panel, was impractical under any method discovered, because the moisture from the wet part of the stack would move continuously toward the dry part. Therefore, the glass of the several panels could not, excepting in two or three instances, be fully cleaned and really meticulously treated for preservation.

Through all these vicissitudes the panels suffered, and there was extensive loss, though what has survived is of such a nature that it has preserved a disproportionately large amount of evidence.

In 1971, seven fragments of the *opus sectile* panels were sent to the Corning Museum of Glass (USA) for research on conservation techniques. It was hoped to be able to devise a method of conservation which would stabilize the fragments; and which could be used at a later date on the remaining panels in Greece. As previously mentioned, the panels had received some treatment both at the site of excavation and at the workshop in Nauplion. However, the exact details of the procedures and the materials used were not recorded. It was only known that some form of poly(vinyl acetate) and gauze backings had been applied to the panels for support; and that the panels had been thoroughly washed so that no salt remained to complicate the conservation treatments.

The fragments were wrapped in yellow flannel cloth for protection and supported on sheets of Masonite (*Figure 7.14b*). Upon arrival at Corning, the panel fragments were examined visually and by radiography before being stored in their original packing until conservation experiments could begin.

Unfortunately, the Museum was inundated by flood during 1972, and it was nearly three weeks before the panels were retrieved. As a result of this, the glass was covered with mud, a layer of mould-growth developed on the flannel, and the Masonite supports warped. The flood waters had softened the background material of the panels and the consolidant, so that the gauze and the flannel cloth adhered to and in some areas had become partially embedded in the panel surfaces. The panels were cleaned superficially and set aside to be worked on when time permitted. Conservation experiments began in 1974. A new set of X-radiographs was made in order to achieve a better understanding of exactly which areas of each panel were glass and which were matrix material. With a few exceptions the glasses were heavily weathered and had little resemblance to their original colours. The shapes which stood out most clearly in the radiographs were the areas of red, yellow and green glass, owing to the lead, tin and copper in their compositions (known from chemical analysis of similar glass in other panels).

The materials used in making the panels were the glasses themselves, the plaster (an adhesive mix of resin and crushed marble), the pottery backing tiles which provided support and the wooden slats of the crates in which the panels had been shipped in antiquity.

Preliminary experiments were carried out on the fragments, as a result of which a treatment for the cleaning, consolidation and mounting of the panels was devised and applied to one of the smaller panels. The treatment consisted of removing the gauze backing from the surfaces of the panel with ethanol, and then covering the surfaces with polyester gauze. The fragment and its polyester support was then placed on a wooden stretcher and further cleaning by soaking it in ethanol baths, which removed any foreign matter and any resinous deposits on the surface of the glass. After these baths, cotton wool swabs moistened with ethanol were used to remove the final traces of dirt. The fragment was then placed on a fibre glass support and immersed in dilute baths of ethanol and 15 per cent AYAF, poly(vinyl acetate), in order to consolidate the weakened panel. On removal from the final bath, excess consolidant was removed with ethanol, and a second frame was placed over the panel to complete the consolidating and mounting procedures.

From this and a number of other experiments, it was clear that care would have to be taken not to saturate the panels with water, alcohol, acetone or any other solvent, since after prolonged contact the fragments became weak and sticky.

The specific aims of the conservation procedures were defined as follows: to clean the panels as thoroughly as possible; to consolidate the panels and to give them sufficient rigidity to allow them to be exhibited; to protect the glass from further deterioration; and where possible, to clean individual glass pieces so as to expose the original colour and shape of the unweathered glass.

Initially it was necessary to decide if an attempt should be made to separate each pair of panels (they had been crated two panels to a crate, placed face to face). Over the centuries, the complex of materials supporting the panels had coalesced so that each pair had in effect become one. Thus when they had been excavated only the reverse or exterior of each panel was visible. It soon became evident that it would be virtually impossible to separate the pairs of panels since such an operation would completely destroy the integrity of both faces. Thus it was decided to expose and treat one (reverse) face only, and as far as possible, to leave the (reverse) face of the second panel visible for examination.

Previous attempts at removing weathering crusts from the glasses had consisted of mechanically scraping the surfaces with various small tools. However, this was not only tedious and time-consuming, but scraping was detrimental to the glass, leaving a scratched surface. It was therefore decided to clean the glass fragments with the aid of an Airbrasive unit, using microscopic glass beads and crushed glass as the abrasives.

In general, the Airbrasive unit proved to be an excellent method for cleaning the Kenchreai *opus sectile* fragments, with few disadvantages. The principal disadvantage was the possibility of working right through the glass if the abrasive was concentrated on one spot for too long. However, within a few seconds of beginning the cleaning of a corner or edge, it became apparent as to whether or not there was any glass remaining beneath the weathered layer. If there was no glass present the treatment was stopped immediately. Another problem was the tendency of the abrasive powder to adhere to the background material from which it was difficult to remove. Some of the powder was removed with compressed air after which the remainder was removed with cotton wool swabs moistened with alcohol taking care that a minimum amount of solvent came into contact with the glass.

Once the panels had been superficially cleaned, they were fumigated in order to kill any micro-organisms which might have been present. This was carried out by placing the panels in a sealed fumigation chamber containing two dishes of water to cultivate the micro-organisms under a vacuum of 28 psi. Oxyfume 12, a fumigant-sterilant gas, was then introduced for a period of 15 hours. Following this treatment, the panels were removed from the chamber, their Masonite supports taken off and the panels placed on sheets of cardboard. They were then ready to undergo the cleaning techniques which had been formulated.

Firstly the flannel wrapping was lightly moistened with water and cut away from the top surface of the panel. Alcohol and acetone were applied on cotton wool swabs to loosen the layers of gauze which had become fixed to the upper side of the glass fragments. The gauze was then cut away with scissors and scalpels. The sticky resinous substance which coated many surface areas was removed with acetone. The panel was turned over and the cleaning procedures repeated. A sheet of fibre glass screening was laid on the glass and adhered with a 12 per cent solution of AYAF, poly(vinyl acetate), in alcohol; the solution also acted as a consolidant to some extent (*Figure 7.14c*). The panel was left overnight so that the alcohol could evaporate. The panel was turned over in order that the other side could be cleaned mechanically and with acetone to remove gauze and other foreign matter from the surface. The surface was then carefully cleaned in the Airbrasive unit using crushed glass as the abrasive, using a pressure of approximately 60 psi with a powder flow of 2.5–3.0. For stubborn areas the pressure was increased to 80 psi with a powder flow of 3.0–4.0. Residual powder was blown off the glass by attaching a quick release 3 mm high pressure air nozzle to the air compressor, followed by further cleaning with alcohol on swabs where necessary. When the cleaning had been completed, a more thorough consolidation process was carried out.

A wall of potters' clay was laid around the edge of the fragment a few centimetres from it, and also around the edges of any voids in the interior. The wall was of the same height as the fragments so that the material used to gapfill missing areas would not have to be filed down. The panel, still on its layer of fibre glass screening, was then placed on a sheet of aluminium foil. Kerr® Vel-Mix stone coloured with Liquitex acrylic pigments and textured with sand was used to fill the missing areas and to form a surrounding support. Vel-Mix is similar to dental plaster but is harder and much more durable. The mixing proportions are 22–25 ml water to 100 g of powder (approximately 1 part water to 4 parts powder by volume). The powder was added to the water and mixed for about 1 min. It was then poured into the areas to be filled where it settled out forming a smooth surface, and set in approximately 10 min. On setting, the texture was improved by working the Vel-Mix with wooden tools (*Figure 7.14d*).

When necessary, the filler was reduced with sanding discs attached to a flexible drill. The fibre glass screening which extended beyond the newly formed border was then trimmed. The panel was then turned over and a layer of filling material poured around the edges and into the voids to raise the level to that of the fragments. The majority of this side was left exposed so that future study of the glass is still possible. The Vel-Mix was then coloured with

Liquitex pigments and a thin layer of Liquitex Matte Varnish applied to the restored areas in order to reduce the glossy appearance of the paint.

To protect the edges of the panel which were vulnerable to chipping, it was edged with lead came secured with a layer of Dow Corning Clear Seal (mastic). Where necessary the lead cames were cut and soldered to fit the panel, soldered areas being smoothed with steel wool. To restore a glassy appearance to the surfaces of the cleaned glass, each piece was coated with Paraloid B-72 in acetone; Paraloid B-72 was not, however, applied to the opaque weathering crusts.

Upon their return to Greece in 1976, the *opus sectile* panels from Kenchreai were in a stable condition. The panels had been cleaned as thoroughly as possible, so that either the original colours were visible, or a clear understanding of the form and design of the fragments were apparent. Any extraneous foreign material had been removed, either mechanically or chemically, and the panels had been treated so that any further deterioration would be retarded. Mounting the panels on fibre glass screening enabled them to be framed for display (*Figure 7.14e*), or more readily handled for study purposes (Corning, 1976).

Repair

In considering the repair and/or reconstruction of broken glass artefacts, that is, the physical joining together of fragments, there are three important factors to be borne in mind: the condition of the glass itself; the type of adhesive to be used; and the method of supporting the vessel whilst the adhesive sets.

Condition of the glass

In the case of excavated material, reconstruction work should normally be carried out only when necessary, since a constructed or half-constructed artefact is more difficult to store, and may be more likely to become further damaged than a properly stored group of sherds. However, repairs may be justified for the purposes of study, drawing for publication, display purposes, or to maintain the continuity of several sherds which do join together. Filling gaps in iridescent or consolidated glass is extremely difficult and should be attempted only where this is *absolutely necessary*, for the safety of the object. Flaking, painted and gilded glass should not be moulded for fear of damaging the surface (Davison, 1978).

Decorative glass, and more specifically glass vessels, form one of the most difficult groups of antiquities to repair for a number of reasons: the edges of unweathered glass are normally smooth and therefore do not provide a key for good adhesion; the surfaces of glass objects are covered with many molecular layers of adsorbed water, thus reducing the bond strengths of adhesives; and since most glasses are transparent it is normally not possible to disguise the repair or restoration completely.

In comparison with other materials therefore, relatively little work has been published in the field of glass conservation, the majority of recent work having been in the area of painted glass windows *in situ*. However, this situation is improving because adhesives and resins have more recently become available which are more suitable for repairing and restoring glass and which have enabled more complicated work to be undertaken (Hussong and Wihr, 1954; Rathousky, 1957). In the last decade articles on vessel glass restoration have been published (Wihr, 1963, 1968, 1977; Staude, 1972; Martin, J.H., 1977; Davison, 1978, 1981; Jackson, 1982a, 1983). Some have described new materials available to conservators (Davison, 1981; Jackson, 1982b); and others have illustrated successful projects without giving the finer working details or emphasizing the fact that glass restoration can be a complicated and time-consuming operation which may not always produce satisfactory results. The materials available influence the aesthetic quality of restoration work but the work can only be as good as the skill of the conservator who uses them.

Some of the most detailed and useful publications are in German, using materials which may not be readily available in other countries at a reasonable cost, or which may differ in composition from those which are available, thus producing different results. In the latest publications, cited above, the materials used for glass vessel restoration are epoxy, polyester, and polymethacrylate resins whose trade names, compositions and properties will to some extent vary with the country of origin.

Choice of materials

In attempting to join weathered glass, penetration of the deteriorated layer along the faces to be joined, and strong bonding with the remaining glass core by the adhesive, are essential; otherwise the weathered layer will simply pull away from the glass at a later date. Thus the chosen resin must act both as an adhesive and as a consolidant. The choice of adhesives for sound glass is discussed in Chapter 5, with the cross-linked, epoxy resins appearing the most suitable. However, once such resins penetrate and consolidate the weathering layers they must be considered as irreversible. Fiorentino and Borrelli (1975) suggest that this irreversibility can be circumvented by the use of a stable soluble resin such as Paraloid B-72 as a primer underneath the epoxy, but several hours of immersion in a solvent are still required to break down a joint even on copper test pieces. However, in the absence of satisfactory alternatives to provide strong joints for vessels or display pieces such a system might be useful.

For much archaeological glass, strong adhesives are neither necessary nor advisable. Glass which is badly weathered can lose up to 75 per cent of its weight (Geilmann, 1956), and glass which has lost its weathering crust through time or misadventure can be very thin and delicate; neither of these will require an adhesive as strong as modern glass requires. Added to this is the fact that badly weathered glass may be joined by adhesives which set by loss of solvent because the solvent can to some extent evaporate through decayed glass whereas it does not do so through undeteriorated glass. Furthermore, adhesion of weathered glass will be facilitated by the keying of adhesive into the surface of microcracks. If the glass has been consolidated, the characteristics of the adhesive must match those of the consolidant, remembering that the solvent used to apply the adhesive will probably cause the consolidant to swell. A similar problem is encountered when attempts are made to remove the adhesive. Such difficulties might be used as an argument for consolidating a reconstructable artefact with a cross-linked resin.

Cellulose nitrate, marketed in Britain as HMG and Durofix (and in the US as Duco cement), has been used successfully for joining weathered glass and it is convenient to use. Its long-term instability has been mentioned (Koob, 1982) and this should be taken into account. No long-term tests have been carried out on the stability of the joint when cellulose nitrate has been used on consolidated glass. Poly(vinyl acetate) has also been used as an adhesive but it has a tendency to plastic flow if kept in a warm environment. Paraloid B-72 could be used as an adhesive but has not been studied as such (Taylor, 1984).

The major disadvantage of weaker adhesives is that a restored object may eventually fall apart causing further damage, not only to the object itself but possibly to others nearby.

Supporting the fragments

While the adhesive is setting, glass which has a sound surface may be supported by taping the joint, making sure that the tape is of a type which can easily be peeled from the glass without damaging it, and/or partially immersing it in a sand-tray or a tray of glass beads, with a paper tissue barrier between the glass and the sand, adding small clamps if necessary (see *Figure 7.18*). In many cases the objects are self-supporting, provided that the fragments to be joined are correctly balanced, and the adhesive in one crack is allowed to set before the next fragment is added. However, it may be necessary to use blobs of faster

setting adhesives such as cyanoacrylate on surfaces which are delicate and therefore difficult to tape without causing damage to the glass.

Procedure

Firstly, the glass fragments should be sorted, for example rim fragments from pieces of the body and base, and laid out as nearly as possible in their correct positions, rather like a three-dimensional jigsaw puzzle (see *Figure 7.15*). Second, the broken surfaces

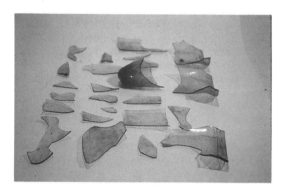

Figure 7.15 Glass fragments laid out in preparation for reconstruction. British Museum, London.

should be cleaned with acetone on tight cottonwool swabs (US cotton buds) to remove grease from handling. (Uniform wetting by the acetone often indicates that the adhesive will disperse uniformly.) If the glass is to be repaired with a cellulose nitrate adhesive such as HMG restoration should begin by working from the heaviest section, normally the base or rim, and allowing the adhesive on each piece to set before applying the next.

Adhesives which are not available in tube form may be conveniently applied with syringe, cocktail stick or fine paint brush (see *Figure 7.18*). Tiny fragments of glass can be manipulated with hand-held or vacuum tweezers. André (1976) suggests manipulating fragments by attaching them to a small ball of clay on the end of a stick, but this cannot be recommended since the clay may adhere to flakes and detach them. Any fragments which cannot be placed should be put in labelled containers and kept with the object. They may be of use for analysis at a later date. Care must be taken not to apply an excessive amount of adhesive to weathered or flaking glass since it will be difficult to remove from the surface. On sound glass adhesive may be removed with cotton swabs moistened with acetone.

If the glass is sound, and the vessel does not bear vulnerable decoration such as gilding or unfired painting, epoxy resins may be used for its reconstruction. Glass which can be repaired in this way will also withstand removal of the resins by softening with solvents such as Nitromors or Desolv 292 (which contain dichloromethane). If the glass is to be reconstructed with an epoxy resin, such as Ablebond 342-1, work again proceeds from the heaviest section, that is the base or rim, using narrow strips of self-adhesive tape placed on alternate sides of the glass to support the fragments as in *Figure 7.16* (assuming that the interior of the vessel is accessible). Spots of cyanoacrylate resin placed at each end of every break (*Figure 7.17*) is a useful method of applying a temporary support, especially where the interior of the vessel cannot be reached after repair, or when the humidity of the surrounding air is such that it causes tape to peel away from the surface of the glass.

Tape strips alternating on both sides of the glass

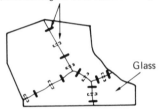

Glass

Figure 7.16 Diagram showing positioning of pressure-sensitive tape before application of epoxy resin.

Tape strips alternating on both sides of the glass

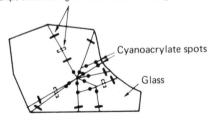

Cyanoacrylate spots

Glass

Figure 7.17 Diagram showing spots of cyanoacrylate resin used to hold glass fragments in their correct positions prior to application of epoxy resin.

No epoxy resin is applied at this stage and it can thus be ensured that all the fragments fit together accurately, there being no build-up of adhesive to distort the shape. The adhesive to be used, Ablebond 342-1, is mixed in the ratio of 100:32 using a wooden stick (a metal spatula may affect the hardening or the colour of the adhesive), and allowed to stand in the mixing beaker for 15 to 20 min. The beaker should be covered because the hardener is hygroscopic, and it is

therefore an advantage to ensure that the resin-hardening reaction is well under way when the mixture is used (Ciba-Geigy, 1970, 1978). The adhesive is then applied along the joins in the assembly with the wooden stick (*Figure 7.18*). It is so mobile that it seeps into the cracks and is drawn along, by capillary action, behind the strips of tape, completely filling the voids.

Figure 7.18 Close-up of a glass vessel taped whilst epoxy resin is applied to the breaks. British Museum, London.

In some cases, such as cone-shaped or narrow-necked vessels, where both sides of the vessel are not available, it may be necessary, for ease of working, to reconstruct the vessel in two halves with tape on both sides. The two halves can then be married together to ensure that they will fit, then separated and epoxy resin applied to the cracks in each half; when this has set the tape can be removed from the inside and the two halves joined with tape on the outside and secured with adhesive.

After about 10 min any excess resin, which may have run down the surface of the glass, may be quickly removed with a cotton wool swab (US cotton bud) moistened with acetone. However, overcleaning at this stage will weaken the adhesive or even prevent it from setting. It is therefore better to leave the resin to set overnight and then to remove small excesses with a scalpel. Epoxy resins may exert enough force on the glass to pull flakes from the surface when they age (Moncrieff, 1975; Bimson and Werner, 1971; Hahnloser, 1972).

For several reasons, notably dehydration of the glass which may lead to visible crizzling (Brill, 1975, 1978), or even surface damage (Bimson and Werner, 1964b), any repair using direct heat from a desk lamp or infrared lamp is not to be recommended. This warning about the possible danger of heating glass antiquities is of some importance, because several techniques for the treatment of glass which involve heating at some stage have been described (Schröder and Kaufman, 1959; Smith, 1963b; Staude, 1972; Wihr, 1968, 1977). It would be possible to warm an adhesive before applying it to the glass but this might cause premature discoloration of the adhesive.

Springing

Springing may occur when a glass is broken due to the release of tension created either when the glass was made (particularly in the area of a bowl where the glass has been stretched by blowing and the tension not removed by annealing) or by hydration of the surface. The result is that the glass fragments do not fit together correctly when reconstructed. Because glass is fragile it may not be possible to make a successful repair using strips of tape, or a *tourniquet*, to close the gap after the adhesive has been applied, as with ceramics. However, this is the only technique which can at present be recommended in cases where the glass is sufficiently thick to withstand such treatment.

Cracking

Broken glass may be found in a cracked condition in which the cracks do not run right through the glass. Although cracks may have no effect upon the mating of fragments, unless the glass has sprung, their presence in a glass artefact is potentially dangerous. As breaks in the glass surface, cracks are points of weakness from which damage may propagate if the article is subjected to mechanical or thermal stress or even further weathering (Newton *et al.*, 1981). As they contain glass/air/glass interfaces, they present a plane for reflection of light which is a distraction to the eye and thus detracts from the aesthetic qualities of the object.

The suggestion that a crack can sometimes be arrested by rivetting or drilling is not recommended because it produces an unsightly repair and may result in further cracking (*Figure 7.19*).

In order to prevent cracks from lengthening, it is sometimes possible to introduce a thin epoxy resin into them by applying the resin along the cracks with a cocktail stick. The resin is drawn into the cracks by capillary action (*Figure 7.20*). On *modern* glass, this

Figure 7.19 An unsightly repair on a heavy cut glass bowl, in which lead ties have been used to secure a fragment.

Figure 7.20 A thick glass vessel repaired with Ablebond 342-1 (epoxy) resin. The two parallel lines across the centre represent each glass surface, the area in between having been filled with resin, whose refractive index closely matches that of the glass itself.

action can be made more effective if the object is alternately gently heated with a warm air blower and then allowed to cool several times. Of course if cracks can be gently eased open it will be easier to introduce the resin. However, it must be remembered that this action may cause cracks to lengthen su ldenly and dramatically. Glass which has broken as a result of overheating, such as candlesticks and lampshades, will almost certainly retain residual strains which may cause it to shatter when pressure is put on the object in order to join the fragments.

For the repair of a cracked clear glass a close match of refractive indices (R.I.) is desirable (Tennent and Townsend, 1984a), but this might be difficult to obtain for the following reasons: the R.I. of glass changes with composition; the surface R.I. of glass changes on weathering and the R.I. value for a recent crack could be different from that of an old one in the same article. It may be possible to formulate a range of adhesives of different R.I. values so that the adhesives could be matched to the glass. However, since adhesives are expected to yellow with age, thus disclosing the area of repair, exact matching may not be important, except in special cases, although Tennent and Townsend (1984a) point out that yellowing of a crack may not be important when the crack is to be viewed endwise. There is also the ethical consideration of whether cracks should be concealed.

Dowelling
In the case of broken wine glasses or glass figures, it may be necessary to insert an acrylic or glass dowel to strengthen a repair (*Figure 7.21a*). This is a potentially dangerous operation since it necessitates the drilling of small holes in the glass, which may cause more damage. Dowelling cannot therefore be recommended as a general procedure.

Larney (1975) refers to a dowelling technique which involves drilling a hole free-hand into each half of the wine glass stem, and inserting a piece of glass rod ground down to fit. A problem encountered in using this technique is the difficulty of locating the exact centre of the glass stem, particularly on an uneven surface. It is also difficult to ensure that the holes are drilled vertically into the stem. Unless the centre point of each half of the broken stem is accurately determined, the dowel cannot be inserted. Alternatively, oversized holes would have to be drilled into the glass to allow some leeway in inserting the dowel, with the risk of cracking the stem. Success with this method is more likely if one hole is drilled into one half of the stem, the edges marked with ink, and the other half of the stem pressed against it in order to mark the correct position for the second hole. Furthermore, the minimum thickness of glass rod available is 3.0 mm and in practice this would have to be considerably ground down to be used as a dowel, unless the rod is drawn thinner in a blowpipe.

The problems associated with Larney's (1975) technique were overcome by producing a metal collar on a lathe, which fitted over the stem of the wine glass and through which a central dowel hole could

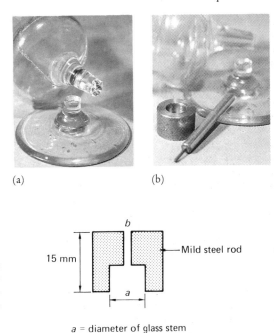

(a)   (b)

b

15 mm   — Mild steel rod

a

a = diameter of glass stem

(c)

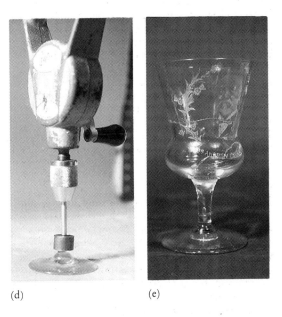

(d)   (e)

Figure 7.21 (a) The broken stem of a wine glass, which will require the insertion of a dowel to strengthen the repair. (b) A metal collar used to centre the drill on the break edges of the wine glass stem. (c) Section through the metal collar. (d) The use of a diamond-tipped drill to form a dowel-hole in each section of the wine-glass stem. (e) The repaired wine-glass stem incorporating a Perspex dowel secured with epoxy resin. Courtesy of P.R. Jackson.

be drilled into the glass (*Figure 7.21b*). The size of the dowel hole was reduced by using a 1.0mm Perspex rod, poly(methacrylate).

Having measured the diameter of the wine glass (*a*) (the greatest diameter if the stem is not truly round) with a micrometer, a short length of mild steel rod, with a diameter sufficient to enable it to fit over the glass stem to form a sleeve with an adequate radial thickness (*Figure 7.21c*), was placed in a lathe and faced. The centre point was marked, with a centre bit, and a hole, of a diameter accommodating a 1.0mm glass drill bit (*b*), drilled to a depth in excess of 15mm. This was followed by a drill with the same diameter as the stem (*a*) and drilled to a depth of 10mm. The rod was cut to a length of 15mm, reversed in the lathe and faced.

The metal collar was placed over the section of broken stem attached to the foot of the glass. Using a 1.0mm MM Glazemaster glass drill, a hole was drilled into the stem (*Figure 7.21d*). The broken stem attached to the bowl was drilled in the same way. A Perspex rod was cut to the correct length to form a dowel and, with Ablebond 342-1 (epoxy resin), was secured in the holes thus bringing the base and bowl of the wine glass together.

Once the resin on the stem has set (approximately 24 hours) the adhesive used in the previous restoration of the bowl was removed with acetone on cotton wool swabs. The bowl was then reassembled using Ablebond 342-1 (*Figure 7.21e*).

The use of a metal collar as a jig to hold the drill bit in place produced very accurate results. The dowel holes were only 1.0mm in diameter and were correctly centred, aligned and vertical. In this way very fine glass stems can be repaired with less danger of cracking the glass (Jackson, 1982a).

Restoration

In the case of incomplete glass artefacts which are being considered for full *restoration*, that is, replacement of missing areas with a synthetic resin, the most important factor is to decide whether such a procedure is desirable on ethical grounds, after which the feasibility of the operation must be assessed. Restoration may be undertaken to improve the stability of an object such as a glass vessel or simply to improve its appearance for display purposes. If a great deal of the vessel is missing it may not be worth restoring in terms of the time taken to carry out the work, unless the glass is historically important or is of particular value to a collection. (However, glass which is of less importance to one collection may be valuable to another.)

Feasibility is usually determined by the percentage of the object remaining, the shape and thickness of the glass, and the condition and type of any applied decoration present. Restoration, as opposed to reconstruction from existing fragments, is essentially a moulding and casting operation. Moulds may be taken from the glass itself or from a modelled clay or Plasticine (US, Plastilina) former representing the missing glass. The moulds are then secured over the area to be replaced, and a clear resin is cast into them. The choice of materials is governed by the effect desired from the restoration, cost, availability and properties in relation to the job in hand (Davison, 1984; Jackson, 1984).

It is part of a conservator's task to adapt restoration techniques as required, since each restoration is an individual understanding; however, restoration processes may be conveniently classified as follows:

Partial restoration
Gapfilling with casts from moulds taken from the glass itself
Replacements with casts from a mould taken from a modelled section or a previous restoration
Gapfilling where the interior of the vessel is inaccessible for working
Gapfilling where the vessel is too thin to be moulded

These methods of restoration will be discussed below and illustrated with actual case histories.

Partial restoration

Where a glass vessel has large areas missing but does not warrant total reconstruction, for example because it is of a complicated construction and is destined for storage or occasional study, it may be partially restored for safe handling, as in the case of some Anglo-Saxon claw beakers. Strips of glass fibre surfacing tissue cut to size and impregnated with cellulose nitrate adhesive or epoxy or polyester resins, are used to bridge gaps in the glass and to hold floating fragments in their correct positions. Total reconstruction of small vessels is also possible by this method, with the results shown in *Figure 7.22*. It is not aesthetically pleasing but may be useful as a temporary measure for study or drawing purposes.

Gapfilling with casts from moulds taken from the glass itself

Where small fragments of glass are missing from a vessel, for example part of a rim or edge of a foot, their shape may be copied by taking a mould from a similar area of glass and then repositioning the mould behind the area to be filled with resin. Resin may then be applied in thin layers, each one being allowed to set in turn; when hardened, it can be sanded and polished as necessary. The moulding material may be either silicone rubber (which is convenient to use and

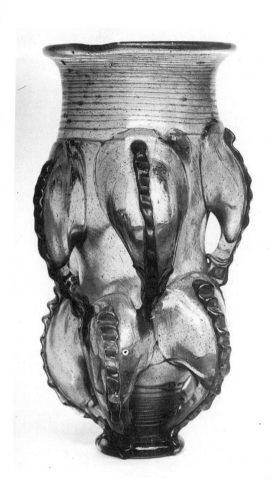

Figure 7.22 Anglo-Saxon claw beaker totally restored with polyester resin and glass-fibre surfacing tissue. British Museum, London.

(a)　　　　　　　　　　(b)

(c)　　　　　　　　　　(d)

Figure 7.23 (a) Silicone rubber used to form a mould over an area of glass similar to that to be replaced. (b) A thin strip of silicone rubber trailed close to the broken edge, on both sides of the glass, in order to secure the silicone rubber mould. (c) The silicone rubber mould secured over the area to be filled. Note the slit in the rim, through which the mould will be filled with resin, and through which air will escape. (d) The polyester resin cast after finishing and polishing.

gives the best results) or sheets of dental wax (which are cheaper but which do not take fine detail and may have to be coated with a release agent). For replacing larger areas of glass, far superior results are obtainable by casting the resin into a closed silicone rubber or wax mould. Silicone rubber is applied around the edge, to both sides, of an intact section of the glass vessel to cover an area slightly larger than that which is to be replaced (*Figure 7.23a*). After curing, it is peeled off the glass, moved to cover the missing area and fixed in position with uncured silicone rubber (*Figures 7.23b,c*). The glass vessel is positioned so that the edge of the mould is uppermost and a slit is made in the mould with a scalpel (see *Figure 7.23c*). When widening the slit, care must be taken to ensure that no pieces of silicone rubber fall into the cavity. Resin is then poured into the mould which is gently squeezed to expel the air. The process

is repeated until the mould is full and it will be necessary to top-up the mould with resin, just before it gels, to compensate for a small amount of shrinkage. The resin is then allowed to set, after which the mould is removed and any necessary sanding and polishing of the resin carried out, to achieve the finish shown in *Figure 7.23d*.

Where a missing area is a hole in the main body of the glass vessel, a comparable area of the vessel will have to be moulded both inside and out with silicone rubber. The moulds are then peeled off and attached over the missing area, using uncured silicone rubber. A hole is made with a scalpel through the silicone rubber on one side of the vessel, normally that on the outside for ease of working, and resin is introduced as described above.

Another method is to construct a wax-mould (Staude, 1972); this is a slightly more complicated procedure but is useful in special cases.

Replacement by casts from a mould taken from a modelled section or a previous restoration

In the case of glass vessels having extensive, or more complex, missing areas, or where a raised design must be copied, a former is constructed of modelling clay on to which the remaining fragments are placed. The design may be modelled and the whole is then moulded in order that resin may be cast into the areas of missing glass.

The first step is to make any joins in the original glass. For this a cellulose nitrate adhesive such as HMG will suffice because the various processes which follow will cause the fragments to part and the adhesive will be easy to remove. The fragments are then placed over a former of clay which may be turned or modelled up by hand, on a sheet of plate glass. It is usually better to invert the glass vessel so that the even rim rests on the plate glass and the vessel does not bear the weight of the clay. Where fragments are missing, the clay is built up to the outer surface of the glass and any modelling of the design is carried out, loose fragments being floated into the design. At the highest point of the clay, two clay stumps are placed. These will create a pour-hold and an air-hold through the mould.

A mould of the entire structure is then made (*Figure 7.24a*). First, a 30 mm clay wall is constructed around the glass, about 20 mm from it. Silicone rubber is then poured over the whole, to form a thin layer, ensuring that it covers the glass and clay entirely. When this has set a second layer of silicone rubber, mixed to a putty-like consistency with an inert filler such as silicone matting agent (e.g. Santocel), is applied over the first layer to strengthen it and to prevent the rubber from tearing when it is eventually removed. However, the silicone rubber layer should not be so thick as to prevent it from being peeled back slightly. (If the object being restored is relatively small, with no great curve, then the silicone rubber layer may be made thicker and a plaster of Paris or resin mother-mould can be dispensed with; see case history below.) When the silicone rubber has set, the clay wall is removed and the 20 mm silicone rubber flange around the glass is loosened to release the suction between it and the glass sheet and thus make its eventual removal easier. The silicone rubber is then supported by the addition of a plaster of Paris mother-mould, about 40 mm thick, which should be constructed with a flat top. It

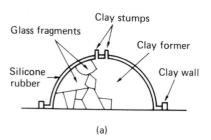

(a)

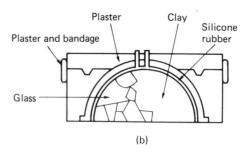

(b)

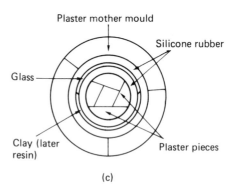

(c)

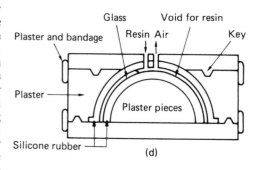

(d)

Figure 7.24 (a) A diagram showing the silicone rubber mould over a missing area of glass which has been modelled in clay. (b) A diagram showing the construction of a plaster of Paris mother-mould over the silicone rubber mould. (c) A diagram showing the construction of a plaster of Paris piece-mould over the silicone rubber inside the vessel. (d) A diagram showing the completed plaster of Paris mother-mould.

must be remembered that a spherical shape cannot be moulded in plaster of Paris in fewer than three pieces since the curve would prevent its removal. No release agents are required either between the glass and the silicone rubber or between the silicone rubber and the plaster, but a release agent such as Vaseline or liquid soap is required between the plaster pieces and between them and the plate-glass. The plaster pieces should be numbered in order of manufacture since they will be removed in reverse order, and, on completion, the plaster pieces are secured to one another with cotton bandage or scrim dipped in plaster of a creamy consistency (*Figure 7.24b*).

When the plaster has set, the whole assemblage is inverted on to its flat top, the silicone rubber flange trimmed back to the inner edge of the plaster, and the bulk of the clay former removed with a spatula, taking care not to dislodge any of the glass fragments now supported in the silicone rubber mould. If any fragments are loosened, they should be reattached with silicone rubber (see below). Clay is left in the areas of missing glass and smoothed with a spatula until it is level with the inner surface of the vessel, that is, it represents the missing glass. Vaseline is applied to the top edge of the silicone rubber mould and a thin layer of silicone rubber poured over the interior. When this has set, a second thickened layer is applied as before, and a 10 mm wide flange modelled up at the rim.

The interior of the vessel must now be filled with a plaster piece-mould in order to support the silicone rubber, and on which to key a plaster lid on which the mould will stand during casting. *Figure 7.24c* demonstrates the way in which the plaster pieces should be constructed, taking care to chamfer the edges of each piece. To ensure that these plaster pieces can eventually be removed easily, each one should be removed after it has set, sealed with shellac, and Vaseline applied as a release agent before casting the next piece against it. The tops of the pieces must be flush with the top edge of the rubber and the outer mother-mould, except for the centre piece which should project for ease of removal (this, being the last piece made, will be the first to be removed). The top edges of the interior plaster piece-mould, and the mother-mould, are given a coat of shellac and Vaseline. Plaster of a creamy consistency is then applied over the top area in order to form the lid about 40 mm thick.

When the plaster has set, the lid is removed, followed by the inner piece-mould, the inner rubber mould (which may have to be slit with a scalpel and later resealed with silicone rubber), and the clay. On no account should the mother-mould be disturbed. Every trace of clay must be removed with moist swabs of cotton wool, and any loose fragments of glass rejoined with HMG. It is very likely that floating fragments of glass may become loose at this

stage, and the only satisfactory method of replacing them is to use silicone rubber as an adhesive (for this purpose it may be overcatalysed to save time) and to wait for this to set before proceeding with the restoration.

When all the fragments are secure in the mould, a 5 mm wide, normal mixture of silicone rubber is painted around the areas of the missing glass, leaving a 25 mm gap between the silicone rubber and the edges. The inner silicone rubber mould is then replaced before the silicone rubber sets and the strip of silicone rubber seals it to the glass surface (the 25 mm gap from the edge of the break is to allow for the liquid rubber to spread out during replacement of the mould) Thus preventing resin seeping into the gap created by removing the mould and breaking the suction between it and the glass. This is extremely important since the resin finds its way into the most minute gap.

Next, the upper edges of the silicone rubber moulds are degreased with a tissue and sealed together with a normal mixture of silicone rubber; this again is to prevent resin seepage. When the silicone rubber has set the plaster pieces are replaced, followed by the lid, which is sealed to the mother-mould with plaster and bandage as previously described. The whole assemblage is then inverted and the resin (mixed according to instructions) poured into the mould through one hole until it appears in the other indicating that the mould is full (*Figure 7.24d*). When this occurs, the resin is left to set. When it is certain that the resin is cured, the mould can be dismantled and the glass and cast removed together. Any joins which break down are remade with HMG or, if required, the entire glass may be reconstructed using epoxy resin.

Excesses of resin can be removed by the careful use of a dental drill, and the resin can, if necessary, be filed and sanded to some extent, though care must be taken not to crack the cast by applying too great a pressure. After sanding with progressively finer grades of sandpaper the surface may be finished using Solvol Autosol as a fine abrasive on a tiny buffing wheel held in the drill-head, and finally polished with an even softer buff. (However, care must be taken in the use of Solvol Autosol since the white paste may become irremovably trapped in small deficiencies in the cast such as air-bubbles, or at the junction between the cast and original glass.) During any operation involving the use of a dental drill, it is wise to step down the current with a rheostat in order to prevent friction from spoiling (melting) the surface of the resin; and to prevent the restored object from being accidentally spun out of the conservator's hands.

A case history illustrating a simpler adaptation of the method described above, that is, using a thick silicone rubber mould and dispensing with the use of

(a)

(b)

Figure 7.25 (a) Silicone rubber mould over a section of an Anglo-Saxon cone vessel. (b) The missing area of glass modelled in clay. (c) The completed restoration in polyester embedding resin tinted with translucent pigment. British Museum, London.

(c)

a plaster of Paris mother-mould, is shown in *Figure 7.25*. Fragments of the Anglo-Saxon brown glass cone were assembled with cellulose nitrate adhesive. Next, a silicone rubber mould was made over the inner surface to cover most of the unbroken area, including the glass rim (*Figure 7.25a*). When the silicone rubber had set, it was peeled off the glass and then reattached to the glass behind the missing area with silicone rubber (see above). When this had set, the missing area of glass in front of the mould was filled with clay and the surface modelled to reproduce the glass trails (*Figure 7.25b*). The clay was then covered with silicone rubber thickened with kaolin and joined to the inner mould at the rim, thus producing a mould which covered both sides of the clay. When the silicone rubber had set it was carefully pulled away from the front of the clay, the clay removed, and the mould carefully readhered with silicone rubber. When this had cured, a sharp scalpel blade was used to cut an opening in the mould at the top of the rim, through which to pour the resin and through which air could escape. A clear polyester

Figure 7.26 (a) Glass oinochoe with missing neck, spout and handle. (b) The missing areas modelled in clay prior to moulding. (c) Neck and spout cast in Technovit 4004a. The cast was produced in a silicone rubber mould taken of the model shown in (b). (d) Glass tubes and plastic drinking straws used to produce rods of Technovit 4004a, one of which was used to form a handle for the oinochoe. (e) Technovit casts, after reshaping in boiling water, attached to the oinochoe. (f) Restoration coloured to tone with the original glass. Corning Museum of Glass, New York.

embedding resin was mixed and coloured with transparent pigment paste and poured into the mould. After the resin had been allowed to settle, it was topped up and left to set. Once the resin had hardened, the mould was peeled off and the surface polished with Solvol Autosol, using a buff held in a dental drill (*Figure 7.25c*).

The thermosoftening property of Technovit 4004a [poly(methyl methacrylate)] has been exploited by Errett (1972) to reshape small casts and thus dispense with the need to make complicated moulds. An example of this technique is described below (Jackson, 1983). The vessel to be restored was a blue glass, core-formed Italic *oinochoe* (jug) with prunts which dated from the sixth or fifth century BC. The *oinochoe* was about 80 mm in height and the glass itself was in fairly good condition (*Figure 7.26a*). There was some surface weathering but no actual flaking occurring. The neck, spout and handle were missing but the foot and prunts had previously been restored with wax. It was decided to leave the previous restorations intact since they were dimensionally and aesthetically stable, and to reconstruct the neck, spout and handle, which could be copied from a photograph of a similar *oinochoe*. From the photograph it can be seen that in order to produce a one-piece cast, the mould required would be both difficult and time-consuming to produce. In particular the thin, curved flange forming the spout would present problems in the moulding process. An alternative approach was therefore adopted which made use of the fact that methacrylates are thermoplastic, softening at temperatures around 60°C. Once cured, they can be softened by heat and reshaped by hand.

Experiments were undertaken in heating and reshaping simple resin casts to form complicated shapes. As a preliminary to the project several discs of a size and thickness similar to those of the spout were cast in Vosschemie (polyester) resin and Technovit 4004a. When cured, the discs were heated in various ways (i.e. warm air, warm water and boiling water) until they became pliable enough to fold into shape. The folded discs were then held in cold water until they hardened. It was found that the polyester resin disc softened at a much lower temperature than the methacrylate disc which had in fact to be placed in boiling water for a few minutes until it could be shaped easily. The polyester resin disc softened easily in warm air, but in warm water it became opaque. The discs of resin were left overnight under a desk lamp (approximately 27°C) to determine whether they would distort under display conditions. The polyester discs flattened considerably whereas the shape of the methacrylate disc did not alter at all.

The use of Technovit 4004a as a casting material in the restoration of glass is well established, due to its ease of availability and minimal shrinkage on curing.

However, since the cured resin is opaque, the use of clear polyester resins is generally preferred. Nevertheless, when the glass to be restored is not transparent (for example, as a result of weathering), or, as in this case, heavily coloured, the opacity of Technovit 4004a does not matter and therefore use can be made of the material's thermoplastic property.

The neck and spout of the *oinochoe* were modelled *in situ* in fine-quality potter's clay (*Figure 7.26b*). The curved flange of the spout was not actually modelled to shape but was left as a flat disc and the neck was modelled without a hole through the middle. Once the clay was leather hard (after 4 hours) the model was removed from the *oinochoe* and moulded with Dow Corning Silastic E RTV (silicone rubber). After curing, the rubber mould was removed from the clay and the mould cleaned with water. The mould was filled from the top with Technovit 4004a which was allowed to cure. The rubber was then cut away revealing the cast (*Figure 7.26c*). Using the appropriate sized drill bit, a vertical hole was drilled through the centre of the resin cast. Holding the piece by the neck with tongs, the flat resin cast was placed in boiling water until it had softened, removed and the edges of the disc bent up by hand to form the flange shown in *Figure 7.26e*. When the required shape had been achieved the resin was immediately held in cold water until it hardened. The surface was then finished with fine glass paper. The moulded neck and spout were then attached to the broken neck of the *oinochoe* with Araldite AY103/HY956 (epoxy resin) and gaps between the glass and the cast filled with Technovit 4004a.

The handle was produced by a similar although more direct method (*Figure 7.26d*). A rod of Technovit 4004a was cast using a glass tube as a mould. The tube was filled with resin; when this was hard (approximately 30 min) the glass was broken away. As shown in the photograph, plastic straws could have been used as moulds, but in this particular case the glass tube happened to be of exactly the right diameter. The resin rod was subsequently cut to the length of the original handle, heating in boiling water, bent to shape and hardened in cold water. The handle was attached to the *oinochoe* with Araldite AY103/HY956 (*Figure 7.26e*). Deka glass colours (textile colourants therefore possibly a dye) were used to colour the reconstruction to match the glass (*Figure 7.26f*).

For this particular object the method used proved to be very successful. The working time was substantially reduced, firstly because it was not necessary to make a complicated piece-mould from a clay model; and second because the methacrylate resin used cured in 30 min whereas polyester resin would have taken 24 hours. Furthermore, there were no problems with mould relocation on the *oinochoe* or removal of flash-lines left on the cast by use of a

(a)

(b)

(c)

(d)

(e)

Figure 7.27 (a) Small blue glass jar with lid, previously restored by filling with plaster of Paris, now in need of removal. (b) Jar with the plaster removed, dental wax representing the missing areas of glass, and covered by a silicone rubber mould. The Perspex rods attached to the wax will form pour- and air-holes through the mould. (c) Completed inner and outer silicone rubber moulds. (d) The polyester resin cast *in situ*, revealed by removal of the inner silicone rubber mould. (e) Completed restoration after the resin cast has been abraded and polished. British Museum, London.

piece-mould. As the Technovit 4004a could be softened and reshaped after it had been cast into a basic form it was very easy to make minor adjustments to the curves of the spout and handle. Thus the method proved to be both much more flexible and less time-consuming than casting alone and should be considered whenever a complicated shape is to be copied and water white clarity of the restoration is not a priority.

If a previous restoration needs replacement for aesthetic reasons, but is dimensionally sound, a mould may be taken from it before it is removed. This will dispense with the need to model-up the missing area in clay or Plasticine. *Figure 7.27* illustrates such a case. Only the base, and half the circumference, had remained of the blue glass jar shown in *Figure 7.27a*. The earlier restoration had consisted of filling the remains with plaster of Paris, shaping it to the original dimensions, and colouring it blue to match the glass. The restoration was heavy and obscured the interior of the jar, and therefore it was felt necessary to remove the plaster and to replace it with the more suitable polyester resin. However, the restoration was dimensionally correct and hence a mould was taken from the plaster prior to its removal by inverting the jar on a sheet of glass and pouring thickened silicone rubber over it to a thickness of 15 mm. Once the silicone rubber had set it was slit from the rim, using a sharp scalpel, to allow the glass to be released. The cut was made behind the original glass so that it would not leave a seam on the new restoration, and the slit was sealed with uncured silicone rubber. Meanwhile, the plaster of Paris was removed from the glass by soaking in water, followed by gentle scraping with a scalpel. Once the glass fragments were clean and dry, joins were made with HMG. The glass was then replaced in the mould in its correct position and the missing area of glass filled with pieces of toughened dental wax, cut to shape and welded together where necessary using a heated spatula. (The wax happened to be exactly the same thickness as the walls of the vessel.) As shown in *Figure 7.27b* a short length of acrylic rod (e.g. Perspex) was fixed at each end of the wax (by softening the wax) to form holes through to the interior mould which was to be constructed. The top edge of the silicone rubber was greased with Vaseline and thickened silicone rubber applied to the interior to a thickness of 15 mm (see *Figure 7.27c*). The relative positions of the two mould pieces were marked by drawing lines across the joint with a felt-tip pen. Once the silicone rubber had set, it was removed, followed by the acrylic rods and dental wax. At this stage several of the joints in the original glass broke down and had to be remade with HMG. The glass was again inserted in the outer mould and the inner mould placed in position. The two moulds were sealed with uncured silicone rubber around

their junction to prevent resin escaping. Tiranti's clear embedding resin, coloured with blue translucent pigment, was then poured into the mould through one hole until it began to appear at the other, thus indicating that the mould was full. After a few minutes the resin had settled in the mould and it was topped up. When the resin had set, the joint between the two moulds was slit with a scalpel (see *Figure 7.27d*) and the inner mould was released. The two resin stumps, left in the pour- and air-holes, were abraded away with a dental drill and the resin polished, using Solvol Autosol and a soft buff held in the dental drill. By leaving the glass and cast in the outer mould during these operations it was hoped to prevent vibration causing damage, but, once the outer mould was slit open, the glass and cast separated from one another as they were removed. This was turned to advantage because some resin had seeped behind the glass in the mould and, although it was easily released from the glass using a scalpel, it could be detached from the cast and the exterior of the cast polished before joining it to the original with epoxy resin (Araldite AY103/HY956). The final result (*Figure 7.27e*) was pleasing, although it was realized that too much colour had been mixed with the resin and thus in future it would seem more satisfactory to tint the resin rather than to try to aim at a colour-match in the solid resin.

Gapfilling where the interior of the vessel is inaccessible for working

If the vessel to be restored has a narrow neck, so that the interior cannot be reached, it will be necessary to adopt special methods (see *Figure 7.28a*) of restoration. If the vessel is damaged only in the body, that is, the neck has not become detached, the fragments must be taped in position and epoxy resin introduced to all the cracks except those around the perimeter of the damaged area. Once the resin has set, the damaged area can be removed as one piece, missing areas within it backed with tape, wax or silicone rubber, depending upon their size, and filled with resin (*Figure 7.28b*). When the resin has hardened and any necessary cleaning and polishing carried out, the repaired section may be taped in position on the vessel, and the perimeter cracks sealed (*Figure 7.28c*).

If, however, the vessel is much damaged, and has a large area of glass missing from the body, it may still be possible to reconstruct it with epoxy resin as described above, leaving a large area unglued around the edges so that it can be removed. This allows access to the interior of the vessel for ease of working. When gapfilling of the missing glass is complete, the glass can be replaced and the perimeter cracks sealed. In the case of the glass amphora shown in *Figure 7.29a*, a sheet of dental wax was shaped over

(a)

(b)

(c)

Figure 7.28 (a) Broken Roman glass flask with a narrow neck, which makes the interior inaccessible for working purposes. (b) Completed restoration of the vessel. (c) Closer view of the restored area of the vessel.

the outside of the glass, coated with poly(vinyl alcohol), and then transferred to cover the missing area and fixed there by running a warm spatula around its edges (*Figure 7.29b*). A large area of glass was removed from the opposite side of the vessel to enable work to continue in the interior (*Figure 7.29c*). A piece of glass fibre surfacing tissue was cut to the shape of the gap to be filled, laid in it and covered with a thin layer of polyester resin (*Figure 7.29d*). When this had set a second layer of resin was introduced and, when this had hardened, the wax

mould was cut away, the poly(vinyl alcohol) removed with water, and the resin cleaned and polished (*Figure 7.29e*).

A more complicated version of the silicone rubber moulding technique had to be devised in order to restore the Auldjo jug, a cameo glass on display in the British Museum. This vessel has a narrow neck and therefore access to the interior for moulding purposes was severely restricted (Jackson, 1985).

The jug had been broken at some time in its past and a considerable amount of the body was missing.

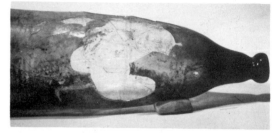

(a)

(b)

(c)

(d)

It had previously been repaired, probably with animal glue, and gapfilled with plaster of Paris coloured dark blue to match the remaining glass. The plaster restoration had become damaged and unsightly and it was therefore decided to remove the plaster in order to effect a more accurate, light-weight and aesthetically pleasing restoration. In order to achieve this it was necessary to produce two silicone rubber moulds which conformed to the inner and outer profiles of the jug. Since the previous plaster restoration was dimensionally correct, it was possible to take a silicone rubber mould from it after some repair had been effected. The positions of funnels through which to introduce resin into the area at present occupied by the plaster was decided upon, and to form them, plastic drinking straws were attached to the plaster with small lumps of Aloplast (a modelling compound similar to Plasticine but especially formulated for use with polyester resin).

The globular shape of the Auldjo jug determined that the outer silicone rubber mould would have to be made in two sections in order to facilitate its removal from the vessel. To contain the uncured rubber, a wall of Aloplast was laid over the glass surface so that it divided the jug into two sections. A thin strip of lead wire was embedded in one side of the wall to form a key in order to reposition the mould pieces accurately prior to casting the resin (*Figure 7.30a*). The jug was then laid on its side and a thin layer of silicone rubber was brushed over the uppermost side thus covering the previous restoration and remaining glass fragments. When the silicone rubber had cured it was reinforced with glass fibre woven matting and a second layer of rubber. The jug was then turned over and supported with the opposite side uppermost. The Aloplast wall was removed and poly(vinyl alcohol) painted along the exposed silicone rubber to act as a separating agent between it and the second part of the mould which was made as previously described (*Figure 7.30b*). A two-piece mother-mould was then made over the silicone rubber using rigid polyester laminating resin strengthened with heavy grade glass fibre matting. Small holes were made through the mould pieces where they joined each other in order to incorporate

(e)

Figure 7.29 (a) Missing area of glass near the base of a tall, narrow-necked amphora where the interior is inaccessible for working purposes. (b) Wax mould in position on the outer surface of the amphora. (c) The wax mould as seen from the inside of the amphora, after removal of a section of glass on the opposite side. (d) Glass fibre surfacing tissue and polyester resin filling the missing area of glass. (e) Completed restoration, after removal of the wax mould. British Museum, London.

235

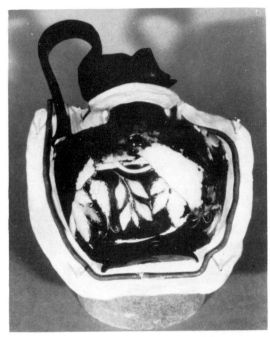

(a)

(b)

(c)

(d)

(e)

(f)

236

(g)

(h)

(i)

(j)

(k)

(l)

nuts and bolts which would secure the mould during the casting process (*Figure 7.30c*). This completed the construction of the outer mould, which was then carefully dismantled and removed from the jug. The adhesive and plaster used in the previous restoration was easily removed from the glass fragments by soaking the jug in warm water (*Figure 7.30d*).

Since access to the interior of the Auldjo jug was restricted it was not possible to make or to remove a mould of its interior profile in the same manner as the outer moulds. Therefore a different method had to be devised bearing in mind that the completed mould would have to be thin and flexible enough to be pulled out through the narrow neck after the restoration was complete; firm enough to support the weight of the glass neck and handle of the jug during restoration; and capable of adhering to the inner surface of the glass fragments in order to prevent resin from flowing behind them. In order to choose a moulding material which would fulfil these criteria, a number of experiments were carried out using a narrow-necked laboratory jug to represent the Auldjo jug. After several attempts at filling a toy balloon with air, sand or water, it was found to be impossible to fit the balloon closely against the sides of the bottle. A method was then devised to produce a rubber skin similar to the balloon, but which conformed closely to the inner surface of the bottle. For this purpose several different grades of silicone rubber and rubber latex were tested. Each rubber moulding material was poured into a bottle which was then slowly rotated so that a thin skin formed over the interior, before the excess rubber was poured out through the neck. The rubber was then

left to cure and the resulting mould pulled out of the bottle, thus testing the tear strength of the rubber. Other observations made were the extent to which the material had coated the inside of the bottle, and the ease with which the rubber could be removed. As a result of these tests, two brands of silicone rubber were selected for further testing: Silcoset 105 and Rhodorsil 11504A, although neither product possessed all the required qualities (*Figure 7.30e*).

Silcoset 105 was extremely fluid, coated the glass surface well and was self-supporting. However, when cured it was rather rigid and thus proved difficult to remove from the bottle. The addition of silicone oil as a thinner produced a less rigid mould but considerably reduced the tear strength of the Silcoset 105. Rhodorsil 11504A produced a very thin, flexible mould which was easily removed from the bottle but which was not self-supporting. Various attempts were made to support the mould *in situ* by filling the bottle with sand, water or vermiculite granules, of which the latter proved to be the most successful. Vermiculite had the advantages of being dry, extremely light, easy to use, and, although the granules tended to compress slightly, of being easy to remove. Rhodorsil 11504A supported by vermiculite granules were therefore chosen as the materials from which to make the interior mould of the Auldjo jug.

The fragments of the Auldjo jug were coated with poly(vinyl alcohol) to prevent excess resin from the casting from adhering to them and were reconstructed using Ablebond 342-1 and laid in one half of the outer mould (*Figure 7.30f*). Areas of the jug from which the glass was missing were then filled with Aloplast which was modelled and smoothed to represent the thickness of the original glass (*Figure 7.30g*). Fragments of glass which overlapped the edge of the mould (i.e. which overlapped into the other half of the mould) were carefully removed without disturbing the Aloplast model. These and other remaining fragments were laid in the second half of the outer mould and the areas of missing glass filled with Aloplast as previously described. The two sections of the silicone rubber mould and the glass fibre outer mould were then brought together and located in their correct positions by means of the keys incorporated in their adjoining edges, and secured with small nuts and bolts. The interior of the jug was then inspected with the aid of a small dental mirror to ensure that the glass fragments and Aloplast had remained undisturbed. The seam-line between the modelling compound in the two halves of the mould was smoothed down on the inside using a Perspex tool made especially for the purpose.

Rhodorsil 11504A was then poured into the jug through the neck opening and the vessel slowly rotated so that the rubber flowed over the interior completely covering the glass and Aloplast (*Figure 7.30h*). Excess rubber was then allowed to drain out

Figure 7.30 (a) A wall of Aloplast dividing the previously restored Auldjo jug into two sections; and incorporating a thin lead strip to form a key. The thin wooden sticks will form holes through the mould into which small nuts and bolts will be inserted to secure the mould pieces during the casting process. (b) The completed silicone rubber mould. (c) Completed glass fibre mother-mould secured by nuts and bolts; and incorporating plastic straws to form pour- and air-holes. (d) Fragments of the Auldjo jug after removal of the old restoration. (e) Comparison of different types of silicone rubber to form an inner mould. Left: Silcoset 105. Right: Rhodorsil 11504A. (f) Fragments of the Auldjo jug repositioned in one half of the outer mould, showing the extent of the missing areas of glass. (g) Missing areas of glass filled with Aloplast. (h) Forming the inner mould with silicone rubber. (i) Coloured polyester rigid laminating resin coating the inner silicone rubber mould to prevent the next layer of resin from seeping between the mould and the glass. (j) Introducing the coloured polyester embedding resin from a syringe. (k) Removal of the silicone rubber mould. (l) Completed restoration of the Auldjo jug after polishing the resin cast. British Museum, London.

by inverting the mould. When the Rhodorsil 11504A had cured the interior of the vessel was again inspected to ensure that the rubber had completely covered it, after which the jug was packed with vermiculite granules to support the mould during the casting process.

At this stage the Auldjo jug with its missing sections temporarily replaced with Aloplast was totally enclosed between two moulds. The next step was to remove the Aloplast and to replace it with Trylon polyester resin. In order for this to be achieved, one half of the outer mould was carefully dismantled so that the Aloplast could be removed carefully with a spatula thus exposing the inner rubber mould surface. This was cleaned with acetone, and a thin layer of polyester gel coat (a thixotropic paste) which had been coloured with blue polyester pigment paste was brushed over the mould and over the broken edges of the glass (*Figure 7.30i*). The outer mould was then replaced and the process repeated on the other half of the jug. The two sections of the mould were then again bolted together. This procedure ensured that the gel coat resin was in close contact with the inner mould and the edges of the glass fragments, and that the casting resin would be less able to flow behind the remaining glass.

A batch of clear polyester resin was coloured with blue opaque polyester pigment to match the glass. The bulk of the resin was catalysed and introduced to the mould from a syringe through the plastic straws incorporated in the outer mould to form funnels for this purpose (*Figure 7.30j*). A small amount of the coloured resin was kept uncatalysed in order to effect any necessary repairs to the cast. Air-bubbles in the resin were encouraged to rise and to escape through other straws forming air-holes by gently tapping the mould. The resin was then allowed to cure for three days before removing the mould.

After this had been carried out, the vermiculite granules were poured out of the jug and the inner rubber mould successfully removed in one piece (*Figure 7.30k*). Excess resin on the outer surface of the cast in the form of seam-lines and stumps which had formed in the pour- and air-holes was removed with a small metal grinding wheel attached to a flexible drive drill. Tiny faults in the cast in the form of holes caused by trapped air-bubbles were filled using coloured resin applied with a syringe. When the resin had fully cured the restored areas were polished to a glossy finish using a felt polishing buff attached to the dental drill, and Solvol Autosol (*Figure 7.30l*).

Gapfilling where the glass is too thin to be moulded

In cases where the glass vessel to be restored is too thin (or the repair is too extensive) to withstand a silicone rubber being pulled off its surface, it is possible to enclose the area to be filled with sheets of dental wax, and introduce the resin through a hole made in one of them. Without touching the glossy side of the wax sheets and thus marking them, they are softened in warm water or with a hot air blower

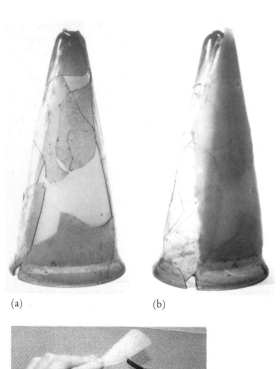

(a)   (b)

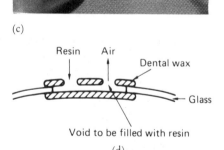

(c)

Resin   Air
           Dental wax

Void to be filled with resin

Glass

(d)

Figure 7.31 (a) Internal wax mould in position on a thin, fragmented cone beaker. (b) External wax mould in position, and showing the holes through which resin will be poured (left) and air will escape (right). (c) Melting the edge of the wax onto the glass, with a heated spatula. (d) Diagram of a section through the wax mould. British Museum, London.

and gently moulded over an existing area of glass – one on the inside and one on the outside of the vessel – which conforms to the same shape as the missing area (i.e. on the same horizontal plane). The sides of the wax which will be in contact with the resin are coated with a solution of poly(vinyl alcohol) to which have been added a few drops of detergent to break the surface tension. When this has dried, the wax piece forming the inside of the mould is fixed in position by running a warm spatula around its edges (*Figure 7.31a*). At the highest point in the curve of the outer mould, small air-holes and a larger pour-hole are made through the wax from the concave side, using a metal prong (*Figure 7.31b*). This ensures that any excess wax from the holes is on the outside of the mould. The pour-hole is then carefully enlarged with a scalpel, and the wax forming the outside of the mould is fixed in position with a warm spatula (*Figures 7.31c and d*). It is difficult but important to ensure that the wax fits tightly against the glass, or the resin will seep out over the glass leaving a large amount to be cleaned off after the mould is removed; this is both time-consuming and a risk to the glass. A small funnel made of aluminium foil is secured in the pour-hold with a warm spatula, the glass is supported with the funnel uppermost in the sand-tray, and the resin poured into the mould until it begins to seep out of the air-holes. At this point the funnel may be broken off so that excess resin does not continue to flow out over the surface of the glass; or a syringe may be used to introduce the resin instead of a funnel. Once the resin has set, the wax is removed, the poly(vinyl alcohol) is washed off, and the resin is trimmed, smoothed and polished with Solvol Autosol (*Plate 5*). A similar restoration, using the opaque resin Technovit 4004A, on glass which had become semi-opaque as a result of weathering, is shown in *Figure 7.32* (for comparison, see also *Figure 7.7*).

Figure 7.32 Completed restoration with methyl methacrylate of the opaque glass cup shown in *Figure 7.7*. British Museum, London.

Gapfilling with preformed acrylic sheet

An alternative method of replacing missing areas of glass which has been suggested (Gedye, 1968) is to cut the shapes from preformed acrylic sheets, for example, Perspex (US, Plexiglas), bend them to the required curve after softening with a hot air blower, and attach them to the glass with adhesive. However, this is a lengthy process requiring accuracy in cutting and filing, and the finished result is in no way as aesthetically pleasing as casting in the missing fragments with a clear resin; it is therefore not recommended for general use.

Replicas and fakes

From the foregoing section it will be realized that the conservator is not only able to carry out repairs with great precision but may also be able to make replicas of glass objects. Wihr (1963, 1968) has made copies of a whole series of Roman glass vessels, and illustrates three of them: a dish engraved with a design of Abraham and Isaac, an extremely delicate *diatreta* glass, and a Portland vase (Wihr, 1963). Methods of glass reproduction are also given by Petermann (1969).

Replicas of glass vessels may be produced for loan to institutions and/or for study purposes where the original is too valuable or fragile to be handled (Goldstein, 1977). With the synthetic materials now available, the transparency and colouring of the replica can be so good that, visually, it can be very difficult to distinguish between the original and the copy (Mehlman, 1982). However, differences both in the weight and feel of the synthetic material, compared with the glass, will usually enable one to distinguish between the two. The ability to produce copies of glass vessels raises the possibility of replicas being passed off as original, that is, fakes, but this would be unusual for the reasons mentioned above. However, it would be easier for a broken vessel with a heavy weathering crust to be heavily restored and presented as being complete. Examination under a hand lens or binocular microscope will usually enable resins, wax, plaster and paint to be detected; the use of an ultraviolet light source, which will produce different fluorescent effects on some materials used for restoration, is of great use in this respect.

It is also possible to copy glass vessels in modern glass and, if necessary, create a patina by chemical treatment. A more serious possibility of faking would be that of modern decoration of an ancient glass vessel, for instance by engraving a design on the surface; or by artificial aging (perhaps by etching with hydrofluoric acid) to increase its monetary value. It may be possible to detect such attempts by the use of a binocular microscope or a scanning electron microscope, beneath which it may be seen that engraving continues unbroken over a damaged surface, or the 'engraving' is really etched so that the edges of the lines are polished, not cut (Werner *et al.*, 1975).

Storage

The environment for storage and display of artefacts is discussed in detail by Thomson (1986). Treated excavated glass, although robust, should never be stored in either excessively dry or wet conditions because further dehydration (or hydrolysis) can occur through a layer of consolidant. The glass should be kept cool because consolidants and adhesives may begin to creep as the temperature rises, or become tacky and pick up dirt, or adhere to packing materials. To circumvent this last problem, consolidated glass could be covered with acid-free tissue or silicone paper. Sherds should be stored horizontally in perforated polythene bags. Vessels must be stored in dust-free cases or boxes with adequate padding of inert foam or acid-free tissue paper (never newspaper or cotton wool). Where glass is patinated or iridescent, handling must be kept to a minimum to prevent further damage to the surface.

The humidity should be regularly monitored by the installation of a thermometer and a hygrometer. It is sufficient to note the readings of these instruments at regular intervals, perhaps twice a day, but where a continuous record is required a thermohygrograph, which records both temperature and relative humidity on a paper chart, may be used. Such instruments require recalibrating every month (Thomson, 1986).

Display

Display cases and the shelves within them should be stable and level so that glass exhibits cannot move due to vibrations in a gallery caused by visitors' movements, passing vehicles, trains, underground railways or aeroplanes etc. If necessary, glass objects may be supported by acrylic mounts; and mirrors may be used to reflect light upwards on to details of decoration so that the objects need not be placed immediately over the light bulbs. Ideally, lighting should be external and properly situated so as not to cause a heat build-up, and infrared absorbing filters should be used. The deleterious effects of spot-lighting glass vessels for dramatic exhibition are appreciated by conservators but not by all curators or collectors. The effects of heat build-up can be very serious on certain types of glass, for example, glass

with incipient crizzling, painted surfaces or weathering products (Brill, 1975, 1978), because it lowers the relative humidity of the air.

Enamels must be kept in a constant temperature so that the differential expansion between the glass and the metal does not lead to disruption of the object. Those enamels in which it has not been possible to stabilize the metal must be kept in an atmosphere which is neither too damp to allow the metal to corrode nor too dry to desiccate the glass; in the case of copper alloys this would be about 35 per cent relative humidity. Brill (1978) has discussed a method of controlling humidity in museum cases.

Ideally, glass should be stored in glass-fronted cabinets so that the contents are readily visible. The shelves should not be overcrowded and the glass vessels should not be allowed to touch one another. Vessels which have more than one component need special care; lids and stoppers should either be stored separately (and identified), or bound in place with cotton so that they cannot fall when the vessel is lifted. Smaller items of glass should be placed at the fronts of the shelves so that they are easily seen (Rottenberg, 1980). If mould growth is noticed, for instance, on animal glue restoration, it must be removed with a dilute solution of a disinfectant such as Panacide on swabs. It may sometimes be necessary to dismantle and restore such a vessel, using a more suitable adhesive.

Special storage conditions are required for sick glass, that is, glass which weeps (sweats) (see *Figure 4.4*), or which has become crizzled (Brill, 1978). Such glass is best stored at a R.H. of 42–55 per cent (Brill, 1975) or 40–55 per cent (Brill, 1978). The R.H. may be achieved by the inclusion, in a well-fitting display case, of trays of silica gel which have been *previously equilibrated* to the target R.H. (Brill, 1978; Thomson, 1986); or by the use of a dehumidifier. Such an arrangement exists in storage cases at the British Museum, London (Organ, 1957) as shown in *Figure 7.8* and at the Corning Museum of Glass, Corning (NY) (Brill, 1975, 1978). The temperature and R.H. of the cases should be regularly monitored by the installation of a thermometer and a hygrometer, or a recording thermohygrograph.

Resetting excavated window glass

The resetting of fragile, excavated window glass has only recently been attempted, and ideas are still undeveloped. Much excavated material, even after consolidation, is not robust enough to be releaded, nor stable or transparent enough to be placed in a window opening. Nor is it aesthetically attractive due to the presence of opaque weathering crusts. However, some of the glass excavated at Kirdford in Sussex has been leaded into a church window; there is a similar window at Chiddingfold Church (Sussex)

(Winbolt, 1934), and sixteenth-century painted glass fragments from Rycote Chapel have been joined using an epoxy resin (Musty and Nevinson, 1974). Fragments of Anglo-Saxon glass excavated from Jarrow Monastery have been releaded for display in Jarrow Museum. Fragile glass would not withstand incorporation in heavy leading, even for museum display, and, therefore, fine leads or other materials or devices may have to be explored. For example, a light-weight, rigid synthetic could be used for cames and the window suspended vertically; or the glass could be laid flat, or at a slight angle, and mirrors used to produce a vertical effect. Before resetting, it is essential that all details which will be hidden by the new cames, such as grozed edges, or which will be too distant for examination in the new position, are thoroughly recorded.

Handling

Glass, being light, is easy to knock over. When items have to be moved out of the way in order to reach an object, they should be placed on another adjacent surface and not merely pushed to one side, especially if the shelf if crowded. On no account should one reach over glass vessels to move others at the back of a shelf. Before moving a glass, a check should be made that it does not consist of more than one piece, or that any previous restoration is not failing, so that removal may cause a breakage. Glasses should never be picked up by the rim, but the bowl should be cupped in one hand and the base supported in the other in order to cradle the glass against knocks. Vessels should be carried one at a time unless a carrying basket or tray is being used, in which case the trays should be lined with cotton wool covered with neutral tissue paper, and the objects separated from one another by twists of tissue paper. One should never turn to talk to anyone while setting a piece of glass down since the distance between the base of the object and the tabletop will almost certainly be misjudged and the glass may be broken. The base of a glass should be set down flat and not heavily at an angle.

Glass objects should never be left near the edge of a table as they could easily be brushed against and knocked over, particularly as they are sometimes difficult to see.

Adherence to these simple rules will prevent accidents.

Packing

Temporary packing of glass vessels for transit within a building has been dealt with above. For transport to other institutions at home or abroad, glass vessels should be extremely well packed in sturdy wooden boxes filled with sheets of solid polyester or polyethylene foam such as Plastazote (see *Figure 7.3*). The packing operation should be planned so that, if possible, glass is separated from other materials, and that in any event heavier objects are placed at the bottom of the container. Enough squares of 50 mm thick foam should be cut to fill the box being used to transport the glass. (Other materials which can be used are Kempac, bubble-pack and tissue paper twisted into toroids; Wakefield, 1963.) The vessels should be placed on a sheet of foam (on their sides if they are tall), their shapes being first marked on the sheet and then cut out using a sharp knife, through enough layers of foam to encompass their depth. There should be at least 50 mm of solid foam between two objects. The vessels should then be wrapped in neutral tissue paper and the foam cut-outs trimmed down and fitted inside the glass. They are thus fully supported inside and out and cushioned from shock. Should an accident occur, or a repair break down in transit, all the fragments will be retained in the tissue paper in their relevant positions.

The lids of boxes are best secured with a 'hook-lock' which can be easily opened for Customs inspection if necessary, and which will enable the box to be reused. If boxes with screwed-on lids are reused the screw-holes eventually become enlarged and there is a possibility of the lid becoming loose during transit (Organ, 1968). Securing the box with string is not to be recommended since string can easily become chafed or cut. Metal handles may be screwed on to the box. The box should be clearly labelled 'fragile' (using the international glass symbol) and with its origin and destination. Loans should always be accompanied by a member of the staff from the lending institution, preferably by a museum assistant or whoever has packed the objects and will place them on exhibition at their destination. This will ensure that the glass does not undergo rough handling.

Part 2 Architectural glass

This part of the chapter describes the practical aspects of the conservation of medieval window glass, and offers solutions to the problems encountered. General discussions are also to be found in Frodl-Kraft (1963), Frenzel (1970a), King (1971), Newton (1974a, 1982b), Bettembourg (1978), Newton (1987c) and Kerr (1988).

Medieval window glass requiring conservation usually comes from an ecclesiastical building and it is therefore helpful if the initial enquiries come via the architect responsible for the building, since he or she will be able to define the problem in relation to the other important aspects, such as the condition of the stonework, any need for ventilation of a church, etc. In order to be complete, the enquiry should include any relevant information from architectural surveys during the past 20 years; include references to art-historical reports; and should note the existence or otherwise of any previous restoration reports. Facilities for on-site conservation works may have to be sought; and it must be ensured that the relevant church authorities are aware that a conservation survey is to be undertaken.

Preparing for a visit of inspection to a church

Visits to a church to inspect the glass are time-consuming and expensive, and the conservator should state that an inspection fee will be incurred which will cover the costs of the time taken during the visit, travelling and accommodation, and preparing the proposals for conservation. The incumbent should also be informed that this fee may be recoverable in advance from any grant-giving body which may be involved with the restoration. Further expense can be avoided if arrangements are made to ensure that all the interested parties, including the architect, are represented on the day of inspection, and other administrative arrangements have been made in advance, such as the provision of ladders which are long enough to reach the window.

The architect should be able to supply historical information about the windows and the building, and this can be supplemented in Britain from Pevsner (1950 etc.), county histories, Nelson (1913) or the Royal Commission for Historical Monuments reports. The York Glaziers Trust is in a fortunate position in having an Academic Consultant who provides background information about the ancient windows, as well as advising on any rearrangement of the glass which may be required on iconographic or stylistic grounds when the window is restored. It is possible that the nearest university or polytechnic School of Art may have on the staff an art-historian who has an interest in the particular medieval window; and the local Historical or Antiquarian Society may also have an interest.

Equipment needed for the visit of inspection

A surveyor's ladder (consisting of four sections each about 0.75 m which will interlock to form a ladder about 2.5 m long) may be useful and can easily be carried in the luggage compartment of a car. An extending ladder will have to be requested, but wooden strainers or various lengths (up to 2 m long) should be taken, with ropes to tie one securely to the top of the ladder in order to bridge the window openings, across the mullions. A dusting brush with long (70–80 mm) soft hairs, for dusting the glass, cills, *ferramenta* (metal framework) etc., is important, as is a stonemason's hammer and chisel (25 mm) for testing the hardness of the mortar in the glazing groove. Some emergency repair work may be needed, especially if vandalism has been involved, and glazing tools, spare leads, butyl mastic etc., should be carried, as well as hardboard and a saw.

The actual survey is likely to take some 2 to 3 hours at the site, including taking photographs (daylight in preference to flashlight) to illustrate the report. A single lens reflex camera is particularly useful, as is a 200 mm interchangeable lens for tripod photography from floor level, and a long (200 mm) cable release to help in avoiding camera shake. A black cloth (or paper) will help in eliminating reflections from other bright windows. Photographs should be taken at an early stage, or when the light is good, and not at the last moment when the light is fading. A considerable number should be taken; the cost of film is small compared with the total cost of the visit. Photographs supplement the written description and they are invaluable when preparing the report. Photographs taken should include the church from outside and inside to show the window position; the complete window both internally and externally; the separate lights and individual panels, again internally and externally; particular attention should be given to any key panels and close-ups taken (perhaps with an extension tube or a macro lens) of any special corrosion, damage, or growth of moss etc.

General measurements (as distinct from the precise measurements required when taking sizes and templates) should be made using a 10 m tape, and a 2 m folding surveyor's rule unless the tape is rigid enough to support itself when held against the window at any angle. The height and width of the window and of each light, the height to the *spring-line* (the point where the arch starts), the dimensions of the panels, the width of the mullions and the approximate sizes of tracery openings should all be measured.

Finally the telephone numbers of all persons involved should be noted, in case an emergency arises during the journey to the site; and in order to be able to answer queries arising from the survey.

Inspecting the glass

During the visit to inspect the glass, notes should be taken continually. Features to be examined first are the windows, both internally and externally, to check the condition of the leading. This might be buckled or broken especially along the soldered joints, and partially corroded on the interior by the action of *acetic acid* arising from wet oakwood. The windows may have lead-covered cills which protect the stonework and help to channel condensation away from the glass. Second, the state of the glass itself should be examined. It may be dull, pitted or crusted and there may be evidence of moss growth or algae. Third, the state of the painted line-work should be noted; it may be firm or loose, there may be areas of paint missing, evidence of overpainting or of misordering the design during a previous attempt at restoration. Fourth, the condition of the *ferramenta* should be noted; this may be good, broken or rusted, and the rust may have split the surrounding stonework due to the increase in volume during corrosion.

It must be considered whether the restoration work can be carried out *in situ* or involves the removal of the window. *In situ* work can be accomplished from ladders, portable scaffolding or specialist scaffolding. If the latter is required, photographs should be supplied to the scaffolding firm with notes of any pews, monuments etc. which may need to be removed. The other windows in the church should be examined in case fragments from the window in question may have been displaced into them, and may need to be recovered for the restoration in hand, or at a later date. In addition, the incumbent will usually appreciate any comments which may be made about the condition of the other windows. This is also the time to obtain background information; for example, if the glass must be removed for conservation, will hardboard (painted dark grey) be acceptable as a temporary filling of the window space or will plain glazing have to be provided? Is vandalism known to be a possibility and will wire guards or other external protection need to be considered? Keyholders to the church should be notified of the arrangements made. Water should be available on site (for mixing mortar), also an electricity supply (which may be on a time switch), and a safe storage space for tools and glass. The times of religious services should be noted so that the work can be planned around them if this should be necessary. The provision of parking space on or near the site, and the possibilities of accommodation for the glazing team must be noted; also parties requiring copies of the restoration report (together with any courtesy copies required for fund-raising purposes). Finally, if available, a copy of the church guide book should be purchased since it will provide valuable information about the church and its history.

Preparing the proposals for restoration
The conservator should prepare a preliminary scheme in consultation with any other specialists involved, for example an architect or art-historian, as soon as possible after the inspection. The document should include: the way in which the enquiry originated; the names and titles of the persons present on the day of the inspection (even though they may not all have been present all the time); the details, and positions in the church, of all the windows which were examined, together with the relevant photographs; a brief note of the contents of the panels (the full iconographic account would be in the restoration report) together with their sizes, the technical condition of the glass and leading; the recommendations made by the restorer (perhaps with alternative proposals); the estimated cost of the work involved, itemized according to the main items, and for each window separately, so that the incumbent and his advisers can decide whether and how, the finances, which might be limited, may be allocated; the time the work will take and some indication of the earliest date on which it might be carried out. There should also be a statement of any additional charges, such as hire of transport, supply of long ladders locally, scaffolding etc., and any fixing charges involved. The report should be dated, and the date quoted for the period in which the estimate for the work will be valid. The architect and any governing body will need copies of the report, as will the Council for the Care of Churches (in Britain), and any charitable trust which might be requested to give Grand Aid.

Removing the window

The workshop briefing
The glaziers who will remove the window must be made fully aware of the details; they should have seen all the photographs and have read the proposals so that they can make additional suggestions about the tactics in removing the window, and should understand the administrative details, such as arrangements for parking vehicles, unloading etc. They should have a complete list of names, addresses and telephone numbers of all persons who may need to be contacted: incumbent, architect, churchwardens or other keyholders, local garage, etc. A medium-sized job may require several days at the site by two or three craftsmen, and a van will be needed to carry ladders, for example 3.65 m double-extension, 2.4 m triple-extension, step ladder, hardboard (painted dark grey), brown paper and white card (for taking templates), dust sheets for furniture, polythene sheeting to put on floors, emergency lighting (e.g. Calor gas cylinders and floodlights on tripods), a trolley (especially if access to the church is not easy), crates for the glass, sand and cement for pointing (which may be surprisingly difficult to obtain locally if the church is remote). A list should be made of the tools, which should be checked at the end of each working day. The following lists give an indication of the types of tools, and other equipment, which may be required for work carried out *in situ*.

• For taking sizes: rulers, wooden laths, spirit level, pencils, rubbers, scissors, brown paper, white card, self-adhesive tape (Sellotape, Scotch tape or masking tape), plumb line, heel ball and detail paper.

● For removal and reinsertion of the glass: dust sheets (linen and polythene), hardboard, ladders, strainers, elasticated hooks (*spiders*), packing cases, saws (for metal and wood) and spare blades, snips (for cutting sheet metal and wire), copper wire, paint brushes, turpentine substitute, putty, wooden wedges, buckets, electric torch, sand and cement mixture, ropes, Galvafroid (a protective paint comprised of zinc powder, polystyrene and xylene), wire brushes, emergency lighting (e.g. Calor gas), electrical extension cables, transformer (if required for the power tools, e.g. 110 V equipment), grinder and spare cutting discs, jigsaw, electric drill (with hammer attachment or a hammer drill), spare *ferramenta*, a bank of old – generally nineteenth century – glass of various colours (for emergency repairs), Rawlplugs, assorted screws and nails, industrial-type vacuum cleaner.

● Protective clothing: heavy-duty gloves, goggles, safety helmets, overalls, waterproof jackets, first-aid kit.

● Supplementary tools and equipment: trestles and bench-top, portable vice, sash brushes, mortar pointing board, lampblack, spare copper ties, gas soldering iron, tallow, solder, strap leads, window leads (mixed sizes), cleaning cloths, brush and shovel, multipurpose truck.

● Personal tool kit: each conservator should have a personal tool kit consisting of a portable tool box, cutting knives, stopping knives, 3 m extending tape, assorted screwdrivers, hammers (light-weight and heavy duty), spirit level, assorted stone-cutting chisels, lathekin, side cutters, hand brush, pricker, note book, pliers (small for grozing edges, and heavy duty), glass cutter (with spare wheels) and a sharpening stone.

Preparations for removing the window

The window(s) may have been fixed into the stonework in various ways. The panels may be supported on T-bars and intermediate saddle bars or in some narrow lights, the panels may not rest on T-bars but be secured to each other *and to the saddle bar* by lead or copper ties. The panels may be fixed into metal armatures. When preparing to remove a window it is first necessary to ensure that none of the glass is so loose in its leading that it might fall out, and that none of the *ferramenta* are loose. Having followed the scheme for numbering the panels, in the window plan, the numbers should be scratched on a wide part of the leading, and also added to the working plan of the windows on which the measurements and other details are written. When

panels have to be handled in a window opening it is preferable, when possible, for a conservator to be working on each side of the panel, one inside and one outside the building.

Removing a window secured on T-bars

Firstly, most of the ties which secure the panel to the saddle-bars should be loosened. Next, all but two of the copper pins (spaced every 150 mm, 6 in, or so along the T-bars) are removed. Third, all the putty at the tops and bottoms of the exterior of the panels is chipped away so that the panel can be gently loosened on the T-bar and saddle-bars (still keeping the two T-bar pins in place); the panel will then also be held in the mullions by the pointing. Fourth, the mortar is carefully chipped away, using a stonemason's hammer and chisel and working from back to front, that is, starting with the mortar which is furthest from the glass and working close to the glass only when most of the mortar is loosened; work should also be started at a point where there is a leaded joint. These four operations must be repeated for each panel. When the glass is free of all mortar, templates can be taken of any shaped stonework so that the exact (and mortar-free) shape of the stonework is known, and it is convenient to start taking templates at the top (the head) of the window.

When templates have been taken, and the panels have been checked to see that they are quite free of mortar and hardened putty, and all ties (to the saddle-bars) are undone, the panels can be removed, one at a time, starting from the bottom and working upwards so that nothing might fall from an upper position on to a lower position. The remaining T-bar pins are removed from the panel in question, the panel is gradually lifted from its position (at all times taking care to support it from below), lowered to the ground and stored in a safe place. The vacated glazing groove, and the T-bars, are then cleared of any debris.

Tracery panels usually fit directly into the stonework and thus the template should be taken as soon as the pointing has been removed (unless the panel is buckled) and before the panel is taken out.

If required, temporary panels of glass with appropriate light values (i.e. with surface matting if the church is normally dark) should be inserted; otherwise hardboard may be used as a temporary filling. The temporary filling should be inserted as soon as the glass has been removed, so that birds cannot fly into the building. If the filling is hardboard, once in position it should be secured to the saddle-bars by copper ties, and repointed on the T-bar with putty or with butyl mastic (the butyl mastic may be used only temporarily in such a position because it is essentially a glazing material and not a pointing material). The pins should be reinserted in the T-bars and *working sizes* of the window openings should be taken. Finally, the temporary filling should be pointed at the glazing groove using a weak lime–mortar mixture (6 parts of sand, 1 of cement and 1 of lime).

If scaffolding has been used to remove the panels, the glass must not be left standing unsupported on the staging. Instead, the window should immediately be lowered to the ground in the *carrying frame*; this consists essentially of a bottom shelf, for example 1.1 m long and 100 mm wide, with a 25 mm lip at the front, on which the panel rests, and four back supports (say 0.9 m high, 75 mm wide and 20 mm thick) which themselves bear cross-struts (100 mm wide and 75 mm thick) with spaces of about 25 mm between them. There must also be an attachment for the rope to raise and lower the panel and other thinner ropes are used to tie the panels firmly against the cross-struts at the back. If the panels are not lowered to the ground immediately, the carrying frame should be tied to a scaffold pole for safety. When the panel is at ground level it should at once be put into one of the wooden crates.

Removing a panel from a narrow light in which it is secured by division leads

Narrow windows may not have T-bars and the panels are then joined by interlocking leads (called *division leads*), a wide (12 mm) division lead being soldered to the base of a panel, into which fits a narrower one soldered to the top of the panel below. Copper ties, soldered to each of the division leads, are then tied around a saddle-bar installed at the junction of the panels. Sometimes, as in quarry glazing, the division leads may be on one of the diagonals. It is breakage of these ties which cause the panels to buckle and separate.

When removing such panels, work should begin at the top of the light, or unsupported panels may be at risk; this is the reverse of the procedure for removing a window secured on T-bars and hence special care must be taken not to dislodge anything (such as loose pointing) which may fall on to lower panels. A sheet of hardboard resting against the mullions is usually enough protection.

The normal procedure (if the glass is not in a desperate condition) is first to loosen most of the ties on the saddle-bars to permit the panels to be slightly more flexible when chipping out the mortar. Check that all the saddle-bars are secure in the mullions. Loosen the mortar using a stonemason's chisel, again starting at a leaded joint and working from back to front. When each panel is free in the glazing groove the remaining ties are loosened and the interlocking panels gradually separated at the division leads. This may be difficult if the panels have been in place for 100 years or more but persistent easing at the division lead will gradually separate them and the upper one

can be removed before chipping the mortar from the one below.

Removing panels from armature fixings

Twelfth- and early thirteenth-century windows often consisted of panels glazed not into stonework but into wrought iron armatures some 30 mm × 20 mm in section. The individual shapes of these armatures formed attractive geometric patterns (medallion windows). The complete armature fitted into a rebated wooden strip (100 mm × 20 mm) which itself fitted into the stone rebate of the window. The armature bears metal lugs at 150–200 mm intervals which are pierced so that tapering metal wedges can be driven into the holes. The panels are held in position by saddle-bars which are often shaped in interesting ways so that they harmonize with the artistic designs on the glass; they may be hooked or fastened on to the lugs, or even nailed into the wooden rebate.

The painted glass panels are shaped so as to fit snugly into the various openings in the armature and are bedded on to putty; thus it is a relatively easy matter to remove only one panel from the window without disturbing the others. The steps to be taken in removing a panel are: removal of the wedges and saddle-bars followed by removal of the putty from around the panel and unfastening any ties. *From the outside*, the panel is eased from the armature into the hands of a conservator positioned on the inside of the building.

Taking templates

Information about the sizes and shapes of the panels and the stonework is needed to prepare the working drawings.

A *template* is taken of the *shape of the stonework* at the head of a light, or in a tracery opening, as marked on a piece of brown paper and then on light-weight white card. Panels are usually fixed into the openings from the outside, and hence templates also should usually be taken from the outside, after all debris has been cleared from the glazing groove. If hardboard is to be used as a temporary replacement for the windows, it is convenient to take the templates after the hardboard is in position, because there is then a firm surface against which to press.

The brown paper should first be cut roughly (slightly oversize) to the shape of the opening and then pressed against the glazing groove using a stout pencil, such as a carpenter's pencil. When an accurate shape has been obtained on the brown paper, it is transferred to the light-weight card and the shape is cut with scissors or a sharp knife. The shaped piece of white card can then be checked for accuracy by placing it into the opening and, using a spirit level (or a plumb-line from the top of the arch), a horizontal (or vertical) line is marked on the card so that the restored panel can be arranged with the figures vertical, even though the stonework may be out-of-true. TOP should be marked on each template (even though it may be obvious) because in complicated tracery openings the orientation becomes less obvious when the template is in the workshop.

Numbering of panels in lights and tracery openings

Panels are usually fixed from the outside, but the lights at York Minster are numbered from the inside starting on the left, and the panels from top to bottom. Thus 1 L 1 P means the top panel in the left-hand light (from the inside), 3 L 4 P is the fourth panel from the top in the third lancet from the left. Tracery panels are numbered from the top and working from left to right (again from the inside). The Corpus Vitrearum system for the numbering of panels is different, again being taken from the inside, for the purposes of art history. The horizontal rows have Arabic numerals (starting at the bottom) and the lancets have lower case letters (starting at the left) as viewed from inside the building; thus the bottom left panel is 1a. A medallion between the verticals b and c, in the fourth row up, is called 4 b/c. Tracery panels have capital letters. Rose windows are divided into radial sectors, distinguished by capital letters etc. (CVMA, 1958).

Window sizes

When measuring the sizes of window openings two types of measurements must be borne in mind. The *sight size* (or *daylight size*) which is the minimum width of the stonework opening and corresponds to the dimensions of the template. The measurement is required to ensure that none of the design in the panel will be hidden by the stonework. The *full size* is the overall measurement of the panel, including the leads, which must fit into the glazing groove, and it is larger than the sight size by the depth of the rebate used for glazing the window. The working drawing of the window should also bear an indication of any irregularities in the stonework, or whether any stone requires replacing.

Treatment in the workshop

Examination

After unpacking each window panel from its crate, it should be confirmed that no glass has been dislodged during transit. Each panel is then examined on an illuminated glass table.

If photographs are available from a previous inspection or restoration, notes should be made of any differences in weathering, or in the arrangement of the pieces. Any lead or copper ties should be unsoldered so that they do not damage an adjacent panel during storage. Areas of loose paint are noted

as these will have to be refixed. After removing dust with a soft brush, and any adhesive labels present, each panel is photographed in monochrome and in colour transparencies, on a light-box. A record of each exposure should be kept, not only the lens aperture and exposure time, but also the name of the church, the position of the window and the panel number.

This is a convenient point at which the church architect can be consulted, together with the art-historian who will advise on any rearrangement of the glass which may be required, if a previous restoration has led to a jumbling of the design. Notes must be kept of any discussions which take place during these inspections. If the window is so important that a committee has been constituted to oversee the restoration, the members should be called to view the panels at this stage.

Here it must be emphasized that the rearranging of a medieval panel which has become jumbled is a task which may be carried out only by an experienced conservator in conjunction with an iconographer. In fact, at York Minster, during the period 1920–39 the policy was to relead panels *exactly* as they were found even though the head of a figure might be upside-down, because at that time it was wisely considered that insufficient research had been carried out on the proper interpretation of the panels. The wisdom of that policy has been vindicated because the *main lead-lines* were undisturbed, and these provided clues to the proper understanding of the panel. If, in any future window restoration, a grave problem is encountered in interpretation, then the same procedure should be followed. Even when the iconographer feels justified in recommending a rearrangement, the final decision must remain in the hands of the owner of the glass, and it is particularly important that the restoration report should contain a record of all the discussions which take place.

Refixing loose paintwork

It has been stated that loose paintwork should be reattached before the panel is removed from a building, to prevent further losses (Becksmann, 1976; Weintraub and Greenland, 1984). In theory this is probably correct; however, in practice it will usually prove impossible to achieve owing to the vertical position of the glass, difficulty of working and interference from the weather. The principle involved in refixing loose paintwork is that of introducing a reversible adhesive, having a low viscosity and a low surface tension, between the paint and the glass. In practice there are many difficulties; the following paragraphs draw attention to articles discussing the refixing of paintwork. Frodl-Kraft (1967b) gave a brief discussion of the situation as it existed in 1967, and Jacobi (1971) described the use of silicone lacquers in 1971. There seems to be a gap in the literature at this point until Frenzel (1975b) used Viacryl, and King (*CVMA News Letter* No.17, Nov. 1975) showed how the efficacy of use of Viacryl resin to reattach loose paint can be carried out using his resurfacing procedure in which it is possible to view the undersurface of the painted line. From that point onwards, there have been many proposals; Bettembourg (1976b) stated that the first operation, before any cleaning is carried out, is to introduce a solution of Viacryl VC 363, diluted with ethyl acetate, beneath the loose paint, using a capillary tube.

Bacher (1976b) expressed doubts about the validity of using a reversible process for reattaching loose paint because the paint fragments could become lost when a solvent was applied to the glass (see also the discussion reported by Becksmann, 1976), and this caused Ferrazzini (1976a) to suggest that a small amount of epoxy resin should be added to the adhesive in order to introduce some controllable reversibility.

Elsewhere, Ferrazzini (1976c) has tested twenty different adhesives and recommended a cyanoacrylate monomer (Cyanolite 201), giving full details of the technique for applying the diluted adhesive (depending on the thickness of the surrounding weathering crust), and discussing the sources of error and methods of overcoming them. The hardened adhesive can be removed with dimethyl formamide.

Two other approaches, used in East Germany for reattaching loose paint, were described in 1975; Drachenberg (Abstract No.119 in Newton, 1982b) used a solution of a metal soap in oil and turpentine, applied with a paint brush and fired or burnt-in at 250°C in an oxidizing atmosphere; Schmidt (1976) used a solution of Piaflex but the nature of this material is not known. Recently beeswax has come into favour (Möller, 1980); Cole (abstract No.412 in Newton, 1982b) used a heated spatula to introduce a mixture of paraffin wax and microcrystalline wax beneath the loose linework. King (1989) has suggested the use of a laser beam to attach the linework. The SZA paint layer consolidant developed at Würzburg is proving effective (Fuchs and Leissner, 1992).

Dismantling the panel

The first step is to take a *rubbing* of the panel as received for conservation; an essential preliminary because it is important to have an exact full-size record of the lead-lines. The panel is laid flat on a bench (preferably illuminated) and covered with white detail paper which is secured at the corners; an overall overlap of 100 mm should be allowed so that the details of the panel can be recorded, and the top of the panel should be indicated. The panel is then rubbed through the paper with brown or black cobbler's heel ball in order to mark the position of every lead in the panel. It is important that none should be missed or problems will arise later. At the outer edge of the panel, small pieces of lead should be detached (50 to 80 mm long) so that the exact glass size will be recorded on the rubbing, and used when the working *cutline* is prepared. (Note: cutline is used here to describe the rubbing (or a new drawing) adjusted for the sight sizes. A cutline is also used to indicate the size and shape of the individual pieces of glass.) All the additional information should be added in a different colour, such as blue. Care must be taken not to exert too much pressure on the glass when making the rubbing; it is better to feel the edges of the lead with the fingers before marking it with heel ball.

When the rubbing has been completed, partial dismantling of the panel can start. The rubbing is laid on a wooden bench and covered with a sheet of glass larger than the panel; this can be 3 mm glass in the case of smaller panels (say 0.75 m^2), but 6 mm glass should be used for the larger panels. After each piece has been dismantled, it is placed on the sheet of glass, to correspond with its shape on the rubbing beneath.

Using a *cutting knife* and a small pair of *side-cutters* the panel should be dismantled a few pieces of glass at a time (not more than a dozen) by cutting through the lead. Sometimes medieval lead is encountered and this should be preserved.

When some pieces of glass have been removed from the panel, old leaded-light cement which still adheres to the *edges* of the glass should be cleared away; at this stage cleaning of the glass surfaces should not be attempted.

Reuse of leads

At the York Glaziers Trust, old lead is never recycled but is sold for scrap. In 1945, when lead was in short supply, some old window-leads were melted and reformed but the resultant leads were brittle and hard to cut, presumably owing to the addition of tin from the soldered joints. There would seem to be some ambiguities here because Cole and Taralon (*CVMA News Letter* No.17, p.6, Nov. 1975) report that original lead (made in AD 1200) contained 13 to 30 per cent tin; it was much stronger than modern lead but had a smaller extension before breaking, that is, 16 per cent instead of 60 per cent stretch at the breaking point. It has been suggested (Taralon, 1962; Frodl-Kraft, 1975) that modern painted glass windows bulge more readily than did medieval ones, partly because the profiles of the older leads were more rounded and partly because the tin-rich older leads were stiffer. The confusion has been increased because Taralon (1962) states that the older leads contained 30 per cent of tin whereas Brown (1928) has stated that the thirteenth-century leads contained 18 per cent tin, and were therefore likely to decay. Some modern leads have an addition of antimony to make them stiffer. Newton (unpublished), as a result of experience during the restoration of the windows at St Ann and the Holy Trinity, Brooklyn, NY, noticed that many of the leads had cracked near soldered joints, thus weakening the network. This was eventually attributed to the use of lead which was too pure, having had all the silver removed from it; in consequence it was subject to fatigue crystallization which was hastened by the 'heat treatment' of soldering. (The modern approach is to use lead that resists fatigue crystallization, by adding a small amount of copper and perhaps tellurium, as in BS 334: 1982, Appendix D. American conservators will find the equivalent 'copper-bearing lead' in ASTM B29-84.)

Cleaning

It should be noted that the resurgence of scientific activity which occurred in the 1970s on the subject of cleaning medieval glass arose from a plea made in plenary session on the occasion of the 9th International Congress on Glass, held at Versailles in September 1971 (Brill, 1971a). This paper lists the procedures which were then being carried out and recommends changes in cleaning techniques. Brill had also carried out several preparatory studies on the composition of painted glass (Brill, 1970a, 1971b).

The question about whether medieval glass should be cleaned, or not, is a controversial one which is discussed by Newton (1982b). There has also been much discussion as to whether a patina, or the opaque weathering crust, has a protective action, and should therefore be left in place. Studies carried out in 1975 (*CVMA News Letter*, No.12, Jan., 1975) suggested that the weathering crust could retain alkaline corrosion products that might enhance further weathering. It has also been claimed that the original 'fire-finished' surface should be left untouched because it possesses enhanced durability, but there is plenty of evidence that the original protection of a fire-finished surface may last for only a few months in a damp atmosphere before ion-exchange has rendered it ineffective (Bishop and Mowrey, 1952; Simpson, 1953). Moreover, as can be seen from photographs of the panel from Chartres Cathedral, in France (Bettembourg and Perrot, 1976), the opaque crusts which form on certain glasses prevent the window from fulfilling its proper function of admitting light.

It is therefore assumed, in this book, that the windows *will be cleaned*, despite the objections from some artists who claim that ancient glass is more beautiful when left uncleaned (Piper, 1968; Oberberger, as reported on p.xx of Newton, 1982b). The cleaning of the three windows on the West Front at Chartres Cathedral, which removed the crust from the colours other than blue (the blue glass was one of those which did not form a crust) evoked an outburst

that the 'heavenly blue radiance of Chartres' (Johnson, 1965) had been 'destroyed' by diluting it with the colours which had originally been put there by the medieval artist! Many French persons rallied to petition the President to stop further cleaning (ADVF, 1976; Bazaine and Manessier, 1976).

There is a problem, however, as to what method of cleaning should be proposed. First, it must be made clear that *all methods of cleaning medieval painted glass* have, at some time and by some person, been shown to be potentially harmful to the glass (despite the claims of those who have advocated the method).

Use of water

Water is the method usually regarded as being the safest (during the period 1945–76 warm water was the only method used for cleaning the glass at York Minster), but it has been shown to be potentially damaging if any paintwork is weak (Frodl-Kraft, 1974). Hence the real key to the cleaning of delicate and poorly durable glass lies in the care which is exercised by a skilful and conscientious conservator. If a prior inspection had shown that any of the painted line-work at York Minster was loose, then not even water was used. Frodl-Kraft (1971) also recommends the use of water only, soaking the panels for 24 to 48 hours in order to soften any crust. Although gypsum is slightly soluble in water, hard crusts on glass would take a very long time to dissolve away in a stream of fresh water.

Frodl-Kraft (1971) also found that the addition of any chelating agent such as Calgon, a sodium (polyphosphate) complex, could creep under the painted line-work and loosen it. Lowe (1975) recommends a solution of Lissapol N in water.

Ultrasonic bath

The mechanism of ultrasonic cleaning has been described in the first part of this chapter, and it has been recommended for use with medieval glass by several authors (Brill, 1971a; Bettembourg, 1972a; King, 1972; Gibson and Newton, 1974).

The separate pieces of glass are placed in a wire basket (120 mm × 140 mm × 280 mm) which is immersed in a stainless steel bath, containing dilute ammonia and energized by a piezo-electric ultrasonic generator for a period of 3 min (*Figure 7.33*). Glass which has any loose or flaking paintwork, or overpainting, should not be cleaned in this way. (Frodl-Kraft, 1967b) has shown that overpainting can be detected by the use of ultraviolet light.) It may also be risky to clean enamelled glass ultrasonically. The experiments showed that half a minute in the ultrasonic bath was not sufficient for cleaning (there seems to be an induction period) but periods longer than 3 min did not seem to increase the effectiveness of the cleaning. Another form of ultrasonic cleaning

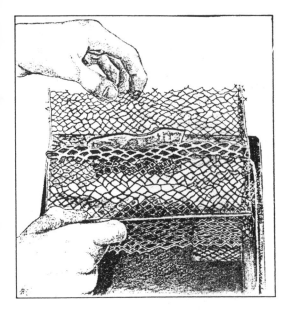

Figure 7.33 Ultrasonic cleaning dislodges loose dirt. The glass is suspended in a wire basket in a small tank containing a dilute solution of 10 per cent ammonia and water. An electrical discharge sends intense vibrations, about 600 per second, through the solution. After 3 minutes all loose dirt falls away. From Lee *et al.* (1982).

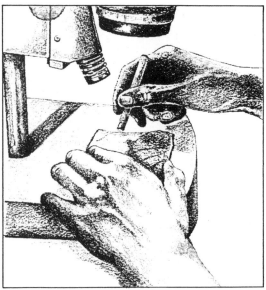

Figure 7.34 Cleaning the surface of the glass using a glass fibre brush, and with the aid of a binocular microscope. From Lee *et al.* (1982).

is effected by the use of a dental ultrasonic descaler, for example, the Cavitron model, which has been used by King (1972) for removing very hard weathering crusts and filled pits. The Cavitron can also be used to clean around the edge of a painted design, but this technique does not remove iron stains produced by rusty *ferramenta*. After cleaning, the glass must be thoroughly rinsed in distilled (or de-ionized) water (Stafford, n.d.).

Mechanical methods

Glass fibre brushes consist of a bundle of long glass fibres held in a small chuck (or by tape), for example 10 mm diameter, so that the length which protrudes beyond the face of the chuck can be adjusted (Frenzel, 1975a). They are effective in removing hard weathering crusts in a small area at a time. The work must be undertaken using a binocular microscope, and care should be taken not to scratch the glass (*Figure 7.34*).

The use of an air abrasive machine, for example the Airbrasive model, has proved to be an extremely effective method of removing the very hard crusts which form on some glasses and it has been widely used (Bettembourg, 1972a; Brill, 1971a; King, 1972; Newton, 1976c) with a variety of abrasives (grits) ranging from very hard silicon carbide to very soft sodium bicarbonate, according to the hardness of the

deposit to be removed, and the nature of the substrate. The machine produces a jet of compressed air (or cylinder gas) in which the grits are held, and the work is carried out in an enclosed compartment.

A detailed study has been made of the relative cutting power of the different grits (Newton, 1976c) but the effects are more complicated than seemed to be the case at first. For example, the silicon carbide will quickly damage microscope slides, but *ballotini* (microscopic glass beads) produced only a negligible effect. The *ballotini* will easily cut away weathering crusts, and it was falsely concluded that *ballotini* could be used to clean away weathering crusts, and their cutting action would cease as soon as unweathered glass was revealed. Subsequent trials, however, showed that medieval glass could be damaged by the *ballotini*, even though modern glass was not damaged. Moreover, different sizes of *ballotini* had different effects, the 20 μm diameter material used at the Canterbury Glass Restoration Studio causing less damage than the 60 μm material which had been used in experiments at York (*CVMA News Letter*, No. 27, June 1978).

The effectiveness of the cleaning depends on the skill of the conservator, although it is possible to use coatings such as rubber latex to protect painted decoration from damage. King has demonstrated that a skilled operator can use the Airbrasive jet to remove a hard crust within 0.3 mm of a painted line (*CVMA News Letter*, No. 17, Nov. 1975). Bauer (1976) showed that air abrasion can damage glass, and this is

(b)

(a)

Figure 7.35 (a) Top half of the twelfth-century panel of Adam Delving, from Canterbury Cathedral, before restoration. (b) The panel after restoration. The name ADAM was rendered legible by painting the word on a backing plate, following the outline of the original. Courtesy of the Dean and Chapter, Canterbury.

agreed; the conservator must keep a continuous watch on the progress of the cleaning operation.

There are various ways of controlling the cleaning action, in addition to starting and stopping the machine. For example, the size and type of the nozzle can be changed; the air pressure (and hence the rate of air flow) can be altered; the distance between the nozzle and the workpiece can be varied; and the jet can be operated in short bursts, which can have a different effect from that of the normal operation. The jet can also be moved with a sweeping motion, which enables the operator to judge when the crust has been removed.

Air abrasion can also be used to clean out the pits in the glass, and the work is normally carried out on individual pieces of glass in a glass fronted cabinet (the enclosed compartment, mentioned above) which has an internal strip light. At Canterbury, a movable dome has been devised, with an extraction hose leading to the dust collector. Working under this dome it is possible to remove the crust from panels without deleading them. The twelfth-century panel of 'Adam Delving' was cleaned in this way (*Figures 7.35a and b*).

At York, air abrasion is used only when the glass is so heavily crusted as to be opaque, and the coating cannot be removed in the ultrasonic bath.

Before the Airbrasive machine was introduced, the only satisfactory method of removing the contents of the pits was to use dental drills (Lowe, 1960), but Frodl-Kraft comments in King (1971) that this was justified only because the fragments being treated were museum pieces.

Scrapers and wire brushes should not be used because the glass can certainly be damaged.

Chemical cleaning methods

Chemical cleaning methods such as the use of EDTA advocated by Bettembourg and Burck (1974), must be carefully monitored and arrested as soon as the last traces of weathering crust have been removed as the solution becomes more alkaline as the cleaning proceeds, rising from pH 7.2 to 7.6 in 30 min and continuing to pH 8.0 after approximately 1.5 hours (Bettembourg, 1977). Ernsberger (1959) was able to produce a marked attack by EDTA on durable glass in the pH range 8–14, and Olsen *et al.* (1969, 1970) in the pH range 9.0–12.3. Paul and Youssefi (1977a) found that EDTA would attack glass even in neutral solutions.

Calgon and other proprietary detergents and sequestrants (chelating agents) will remove ions from the glass. The use of strong alkalis (and to a lesser extent acids) will affect the silica lattice. Cleaning can be speeded up by immersion of the glass in a chemical and subjecting it to ultrasonic vibrations (Gibson and Newton, 1974; Bettembourg, 1972a). This, however, should only ever be undertaken on glass with a sound surface, and in the case of enamelled glass, where the paint is firmly adhered. Ultrasonic cleaning requires careful monitoring. McGrath *et al.* (1961) recommended the use of hydrofluoric acid as a cleaning agent for glass. However, this acid is extremely dangerous to use (*CVMA News Letter*, No. 16, 1975), is not easy to control, and leaves a glass surface which is susceptible to attack (*CVMA News Letter*, No. 19, 1976). Dark, crusted glass has been rendered translucent with hydrazine (Fitz, 1981; Müller *et al.*, 1986).

Resurfacing

One process used for removing hard opaque crusts which form on the outer surfaces of high-lime medieval glasses was that of *resurfacing* (King, 1971). If medieval glass is reasonably flat and sufficiently thick, the opaque crust can be ground away using a horizontal carborundum wheel, or a metal wheel to which an aqueous slurry of carborundum powder is fed, first with coarse grit, and then with a fine one. When all the opaque areas have been removed, the matt ground surface is polished, using Cerirouge (cerium oxide) on a felt buffing wheel.

Polishing imparts a new shiny exterior surface to the glass and its transparency is restored. However, the exposed glass, having the same composition as that which has decayed to form the opaque crust, will deteriorate unless it is protected from attack by rain and condensed moisture. Microscopic evidence of this deterioration has been confirmed on a piece of resurfaced glass after a lapse of 20 years (*Figure 7.36*),

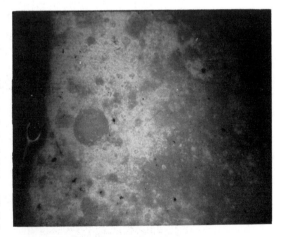

Figure 7.36 Enlarged view of incipient corrosion spots on resurfaced glass from Winchester College Chapel after storage for 20 years. The large corrosion spot to the left of the photograph is 40 µm in diameter. Courtesy of D.G. King.

where the large corrosion spot is 40μm in diameter.

It has also been argued that the mechanically polished surface will have a lower durability than the original fire-finished surface (*CVMA News Letters*, 1975); this is not necessarily true but it seems clear that the enhanced durability of any of these surfaces is unlikely to persist for more than a few months. An argument advanced against resurfacing is that the process destroys the original thickness of the glass, and that any external painting or silver stain will be lost. Glass (especially British glass) does not have much external decoration, although the technique of backpainting seems to have been used more frequently than had previously been thought (Caviness, 1972).

It is extremely unlikely that any future process will succeed in restoring any paintwork on the *outside* of crusted glass, since the glass immediately beneath the paint will have perished. In such cases the best measure at present would seem to be to make a careful copy of what can still be seen (e.g. by photography) before the crust is removed. Resurfacing cannot be recommended for use on medieval glass because of its destructive nature and non-reversibility.

Repair

The repair of a window may imply the making of some modifications to it, and the ethics of restoring painted glass windows have been discussed by Sloan (1987).

In cases where there are areas of glass missing, it may be necessary to insert new pieces of glass. After the coloured replacement glass has been chosen, it is cut to shape. This process requires a great deal of skill and experience in order to cut correctly and economically. The medieval glassworker used a hot iron. Theophilus (translation by Dodwell, 1961) wrote, 'Heat in the fire the dividing iron, which should be thicker at the end. When it glows, apply it to the edge of the glass which you wish to divide, and

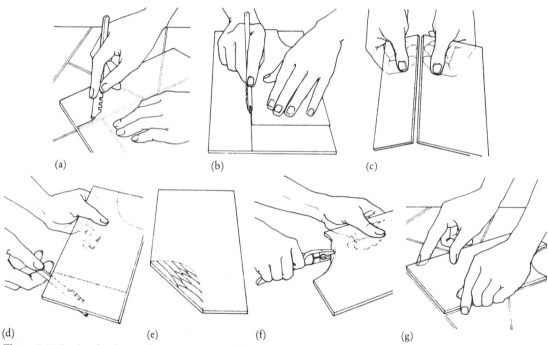

Figure 7.37 Cutting the glass to shape either on top of the cutline or around templates. Glass is a material that has to be cut in two stages. First a line is incised, which starts a fracture. This line, or trail, is then deepened either by hand pressure or by tapping, and the glass divides. As glass cannot easily be cut into sharp angles or curves, these are grozed, that is the edges are slowly nibbled away to produce the required shape, which must be accurate. The final piece of glass must match the pattern exactly. (a) In the cutline method, a steel wheel-cutter is run over the glass on top of the cutline, leaving a thin incised trail. (b) In the template method, the template is placed on the glass and the steel wheel-cutter is run along one side of the pattern. (c) To divide the glass, the thumbs are placed parallel to the trail and pressure is applied. Usually the glass splits. (d) If the glass does not come apart under hand pressure it is tapped with a glass cutter and then separates easily. (e) To cut deep curves, first the full curve is outlined with the cutter, and then a series of small incisions is made. (f) The segments within the curve are either tapped out or are grozed away little by little with special grozing pliers. (g) After cutting, the piece is put on the cut line or template. If it is too large, it is grozed; if it is too small, the piece is recut. From Lee *et al.* (1982).

presently the commencement of a small fissure will appear... Being cracked, draw the iron along where you wish to divide the glass and the fissure will follow'. For shaping the cut pieces more precisely, a grozing iron was used. This was an iron bar with a slot or hook at either end which was used to nibble away at the glass until the required outline was made. At present, the main tool for cutting glass is a steel wheel-cutter (*Figure 7.37*). The glass is cut to shape either on top of the cutline or around templates. First a line is incised which starts a fracture. This line or trail is then deepened either by hand pressure or by tapping, and the glass divides. As glass cannot be easily cut into sharp angles or curves, these are cut in tiny sections (*grozed*), that is, the edges are nibbled away to produce the required shape. The final piece of glass must match the pattern exactly.

Five courses of action are open to the conservator for the repair of broken window glass: the traditional use of mending leads; the use of a copper foil technique; edge-bonding with adhesives; plating; or laminating (i.e. the Jacobi process).

Mending leads

In the past, the traditional method of repairing cracks in pieces of glass was to insert mending leads (string leads). These had a narrow leaf or face (1.5 mm), but often had a heart as thick as normal glazing leads. Therefore, the edges of the fragments to be joined had to be grozed (chipped away) in order to make a gap between them and thus accommodate the leads. Mending leads were disfiguring to the design especially when inserted in faces or inscriptions.

Copper foil

A less visually disturbing effect for painted glass which is displayed in museums is produced by the use of copper foil instead of mending leads (Husband, 1972). The self-adhesive copper foil technique (originally used by the Tiffany glassworks) is valuable wherever edge bonding with adhesives cannot be used, and even in those cases where, on aesthetic grounds, the adhesive bond is more visually disturbing than a thin copper line. The edges, whether grozed or not, must be perfectly clean before the copper foil is applied. A length of self-adhesive copper foil (available in widths of 4.7 or 6.4 mm) is cut slightly longer than the length of the edge to be covered (*Figure 7.38a*). Care must be taken not to touch the adhesive side of the copper foil as the backing strip is peeled off. The edge of the glass to be bonded is laid on the copper foil as the protection strip is peeled back, centring the glass as nearly as possible on the strip. The edges of the foil are then folded back over each side of the glass and rubbed down well with a bone or wooden tool, taking care to smooth out any small creases (*Figure 7.38b*). The ends of the copper foil which project beyond the

(a)

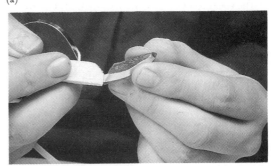

(b)

(c)

(d)

Figure 7.38 (a) The materials used in the copper foil technique. (b) A strip of copper foil being rubbed down onto the glass edge, with a wooden tool. (c) Soldering the copper-foiled glass edges together. (d) The completed repair using the copper foil technique. National Museum, Copenhagen.

glass are trimmed back. When both pieces of glass have been treated in this way they should be held together against a light to ensure that a perfect fit has been made. Any slight projections in the foil can be smoothed down with fine emery paper.

The next stage is to trim the width of the copper foil back, along all four edges, as finely as possible and parallel to the edge of the glass, using a small-bladed sharp knife; it is essential to keep the blade very sharp to ensure the foil is cut through cleanly. The surplus can be peeled away to leave the fine edge of copper foil on the glass.

The two pieces of glass are then placed together on a soft board ready for soldering (*Figures 7.38c and d*), and held in position by tapping pins into the board around the edge of the glass, padding the glass underneath if necessary to keep it level. A blob of solder is placed on each end of the copper foil to hold the pieces steady while soldering is carried out. It is essential that all copper foil is clean and, hence, it should be soldered as soon as possible after the copper foiling has been completed. A multicore solder is the most efficient one to use with an electric iron having a small bit. Care must be taken not to flex the repaired piece of glass before it is leaded up.

Adhesives

Edge joining with adhesives can be used to repair glass where there are clean breaks in the fragments and where the edges have not been grozed. It is a useful method where the broken piece is part of a significant feature, such as a face or inscription where legibility is important; if the glass has become extremely thin due to deterioration; or if there are several breaks radiating from one point (Kuchel, 1987). Chips and small holes can also be filled with adhesive if the glass forms part of a museum collection, but this is unsuitable for window glass *in situ*. In the first half of this century, joiners' glue (animal glue) was used at York Minster and Canterbury Cathedral (Caviness, 1971). However, such glue can damage fragile glass, and tends to fail in time, either by dissolving in condensed moisture or because micro-organisms consume it. Gaps which result from the removal of the glue enable soot and dirt to enter and form linear deposits (see *Figure 3*, p.4, *CVMA News Letter*, No. 14, Apr. 1975) on nearby surfaces such as the plating glass. In 1947 the use of joiners' glue was superseded by Seccotine (animal glue) and Durofix (cellulose nitrate); and from 1967 Araldite (epoxy resin) was used for repairing glass (Frenzel, 1969). Research carried out by Bettembourg (1975) has shown that silicone mastics have many advantages for repairing glass windows, notably because they remain flexible for a considerable period of time. Refixing of paint is discussed extensively by Femenella (1994).

Plating

Edge joining can be used in church windows when silicone adhesives are used, especially if there is an external protective window, but glass which is very thin, or which has any cracks, should be plated externally, or double plated (a plating placed on both sides).

In the plating operation, the ancient glass is supported against a thin (2mm) piece of sheet glass which has been cut to exactly the same size and shape. If the medieval glass is not flat, the plating glass (after being cut to size) can be shaped by heating it on a plaster of Paris mould which itself has been shaped to fit against the repaired medieval glass. (This shaping operation is also called *contouring* the plate glass(es) because the thin modern glass softens and collapses into the mould to take up the latter's contour.)

The two (or three) pieces of glass, that is, the edge-joined medieval glass and its one (or two) shaped plating glass(es), are sealed at the edge with a mastic strip or with silicone rubber, and held together in an extra-wide lead. If the plating glass is required solely as a support for newly painted areas of glass, as in *Figures 7.35a and b*, the modern piece is termed a *backing glass*. Considerable amounts of plating were required for the restoration of York Minster windows after damage caused by a fire in 1829. This can be seen by an external examination of the western choir clerestory windows. It is claimed that the internal reflections, which may result from the use of plating glass, can be reduced by the use of non-reflecting glass, but such glass is only effective when the light falls at particular angles. Plating is discussed in further detail later in the chapter, under the heading of protection of restored windows. An extreme form of double plating, known as the lamination process or the Jacobi process, is discussed below. Double plating was used in the conservation of the York Minster Rose Window after the fire of 9 July 1984. Mills (1987) advocated the use of 'gel-plating' in which the air inside the plating is replaced by a thixotropic gel. This is intended to exclude all the water and water vapour from the surface of the painted glass.

Repainting missing details

When an important piece of a design is missing, it is possible to improve the visual impact by various means; and the all-important decision must be made as to whether to conserve the window in its present form; to restore the window in the spirit of the original style; to restore it either directly on the medieval glass or on a backing plate; or to take some other action. The different approaches can be illustrated by discussing actual examples, one in

Figure 7.39 A late fifteenth-century window from the Salvator church in Munich, West Germany, showing three different styles of restoration. Left: the head of Mary restored in the original style. Centre: the head of Christ repainted in a modern style. Right: the head of St John replaced with a piece of toned antique glass (this head has now been repainted). Franz Meyer & Co., Munich.

Germany and two in England. *Figure 7.39* shows a late fifteenth century window from the Salvator church in Munich, and now in the 'Bavarian Duke's' window of Munich Cathedral, West Germany. The panels were damaged by bombing in 1944, the heads of all the figures being lost. In 1950 the window was reconstructed and inserted in the Cathedral. Mary, on the left, was given a new head based on the original in a pre-war photograph, that is, restored in the spirit of the original style; the Christ figure had a completely new head, that is, a modern restoration; and that of John the Evangelist, on the right, had a piece of toned antique glass inserted, that is, was

virtually untouched. That arrangement can, however, no longer be seen. A new head was painted, based on that of another saint in the Salvator church; and the head of Christ was repainted more strongly, in order that the appearance of the design was more uniform.

Figure 7.40a shows a panel from one of the twelfth-century clerestory windows in the nave of York Minster, where the head on the left had been replaced by plain glass, the shape of which resembles an inflated balloon, and that on the right is so damaged as to be virtually worthless. The heads of the three humans and two devils, however, were

(a)

(b)

Figure 7.40 (a) A twelfth-century clerestory panel from York Minster showing the heads of three humans and two devils repainted in the twelfth century style. (b) Close view of the human head on the right side of the panel. The date of the repainting (1975) can be seen alongside the neck. Courtesy of the Dean and Chapter, York.

skilfully painted in the twelfth-century style. *Figure 7.40b* shows a closer view of the head of the human at the right of the picture and its date (1975) can be seen at the side of the neck, thus ensuring that the restoration cannot be mistaken for the original.

An interesting example of restoration, used in the 1945–52 restoration of the Great East Window at Gloucester Cathedral (the Crécy Window) in Britain, is the smudging of a piece of antique glass so as to *resemble a face*. The result is successful because the figure looks complete when viewed with the unaided eye from the floor of the chancel, but when viewed with binoculars or with a telephoto lens it is immediately evident that no attempt has been made to imitate any particular style.

If the original glass is still usable, and bears enough trace of the paintwork, it is possible to repaint the head on a plating or *backing glass*. The backing glass is positioned behind the medieval piece so that the image appears to be complete when seen from the floor of the building. The missing design can be identified in various ways: sometimes an old photograph or a drawing is available, which can be copied; sometimes traces of the image can be seen in the weathered surface; and sometimes seemingly invisible marks on the surface can be rendered visible either by improving the reflectivity of the surface (Newton, 1974e), or by using graphite (Marchini, 1976).

It is important to point out that some art-historians strongly disapprove of the use of backing glasses, because it is no longer possible to see the damaged medieval image in its entirety; no such work has been permitted at Canterbury Cathedral since 1977.

It is possible to repaint designs using cold setting (or unfired), and therefore soluble, paints. This may be undesirable because, should it ever become necessary to remove the paint at a later date, the act of redissolving it might weaken or remove the remaining original paintwork. The removal of a painted backing glass is less likely to disturb the original work, but each case must be considered on its merits and, for example, the repainting of a small area of linear work may well be justified.

Refiring

It has sometimes been the case that restoration has been carried out by firing modern paint on to the original medieval glass. This is termed refiring. Refired work will not be reversible, and hence the technique should be rejected on ethical grounds. The argument that it is dangerous from the point of view of the glass is probably only rarely valid, since much refiring of medieval glass was successfully carried out during the first quarter of this century, when the Zettler process was extensively used. In the Zettler process a fusible glassy powder was sprinkled on to individual quarries and fired. It is an early example of protecting painted glass, but the process is irreversible and, furthermore, any dirt and weathering products are sealed in (Frodl-Kraft, 1963a; Frenzel, 1968).

Releading

No substantial alteration of the scene
Before releading takes place, any re-ordering of the design which may be required should be discussed with the art-historian and the architect involved with the project. In addition, consideration should be given to the replacement of any misplaced glass (from the same window into another window) or intruded glass (from another window). The presence of a large amount of displaced glass could increase the cost of the restoration, *if* all the glass were to be rearranged at the same time. It may therefore be necessary to plan the work over many years, removing any intruded glass for safe storage and substituting suitably toned modern glass for the misplaced glass until the latter becomes available, when it may well be a simple matter to substitute a few pieces with the panel *in situ*.

After the pieces of glass have been cleaned and repaired, they are releaded following the lines of the rubbing taken before the panel was dismantled, and which is adjusted for the sight-size measured when the panel was removed from the stonework.

Substantial alteration of the scene
Occasionally it becomes possible to reconstruct a jumbled panel entirely, as in the case of the twelfth-century panel depicting the Supper at Emmaus, shown in *Figure 7.41a and b. Figure 7.41a* shows the panel in its jumbled state, and the *main lead lines* have been picked out in white. These suggest that there were three figures seated at a table, the central figure being nimbed, and that vessels were present on the table. Careful consideration of all the information, in consultation with an art-historian, led to the reconstruction of the panel as shown in *Figure 7.41b*, the new heads being painted in twelfth-century style and dated.

When such extensive rearrangements are envisaged, enough time must be allowed for full discussions to take place with all those who can contribute information, and all other representations of the scene can be considered. Another notable reconstruction is that of the Nine Orders of Angels, in the third window from the east in the South Aisle of the Church of All Saints, North Street, York (Gee, 1979; Stacpole, 1972). This window was last seen in good condition in 1730, after which the component pieces somehow became jumbled.

Leads
In general, two types of lead came are available for releading, the convex or round section and the flat lead (although many other types can be obtained as special orders) (*Figure 7.42*). Both round and flat leads were used by medieval glaziers although the lead was sometimes rather narrow (3.0mm). Convex leads can be bent round sharp corners more easily than the flat section which has a tendency to wrinkle on the inside of the curve, but the rigidity of the curved flange makes it difficult to carry out repairs *in situ*. The depth of the heart of the lead came can vary between 4.0 and 20.0mm, and the width of the leaf from 2.0 to 20.0mm. Early methods of fabricating leads are discussed by Knowles (1929).

At the York Glaziers Trust, 6.0mm lead is used for the main lead lines, with narrower leads being used for the subsidiary leading, even down to 2.0mm in some enamelled medallions. In the early part of the twentieth century, only 11.0mm flat lead was used for reglazing work at York Minster and hence the essential distinction between main and subsidiary lead lines tended to be lost.

This is a suitable point at which to point out the *hazards of working with lead*. There is a real risk of absorbing enough lead to have a deleterious effect on the health through enhaling dust from filing and soldering lead and through contaminating the hands with cementing compounds containing lead and failing to wash the hands before handling food. The symptoms and treatments of lead poisoning are discussed by Frohbieter-Mueller (1979a,b) and Guffey *et al.* (1979).

At York, releading is carried out on illuminated, acrylic-topped, benches in the glazing workshop, but the matching of any replacement glass must be carried out against daylight, for example using a diffusing screen. After releading each joint is soldered, the task being one which requires much skill if the lead is not to be *burnt* nor the glass cracked. Other restorers may prefer to relead on a wooden bench, directly on the cutline.

It is first necessary to stretch the lead to remove any kinks or irregularities which may have occurred during or following its manufacture, and to trim off any surplus material from the edges. Smoothing is done by means of a shaped wooden tool (a *lathekin*), or with the blade of a *stopping knife*. The cutline is pinned to the bench and glazing normally starts at one corner where laths have been nailed down to represent two of the edges of the window. The outer leads of the window are laid against these and the first corner-piece of glass inserted. The lead is then shaped around each piece in turn and cut where it comes into contact with adjacent leads. At this point, the lead must be cut exactly at the correct angle to form a neat joint. The knife used for cutting may be a cut-down putty knife or palette knife which is held vertically,

(b)

(a)

Figure 7.41 (a) Twelfth-century panel depicting the Supper at Emmaus at York Minster. The glass fragments are shown in their jumbled state. The main lead lines, picked out in white, suggest three figures seated at a table. (b) The panel after rearrangement of the components and repainting of the heads in the twelfth-century style. Courtesy of the Dean and Chapter, York.

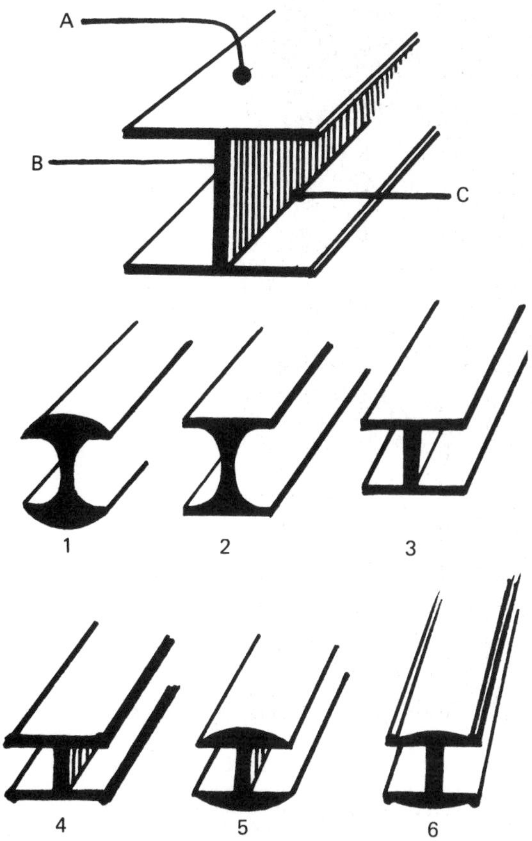

Figure 7.42 Lead profiles. A, the leaf; B, the heart or core; C, milling on the heart; 1 and 2, medieval lead; 3, eighteenth-century flat lead; 4, modern flat lead; 5, modern round lead; 6, modern beaded lead.

giving the maximum pressure on the blade, or a special, curved bladed knife held horizontally. Joints may be butted (as is usual in Britain) or one lead may be tucked under the leaf of that on which it abuts (as in much continental work). At the top and bottom of the panels, that is, where adjoining the next panel, special leads are used, that at the top of the lower panel being of a narrow heart, that in the bottom of the upper panel being of the standard, or broad heart, which straddles the panel beneath, giving a weather-proof joint. As each piece of glass is inserted in place, it is held temporarily by nails, such as horseshoe nails which have flat edges less likely to damage the glass, and broad heads to hold the glass in place, along each edge (see *Figure 7.43*).

When a complete panel has been assembled, battens are fixed around the remaining two sides, after ensuring that the corners are strictly square. The lead is thoroughly cleaned at every joint with *scratch-card*, and flux in the form of tallow or resin is applied to each joint. Whichever flux is used, all surplus must be thoroughly cleaned off after the soldered joint is made. Gas soldering irons are the most adaptable and the most commonly used, as the intensity of heat can be varied accurately in relation to the speed of work (*Figure 7.44*). An experienced conservator will require the full heat for making twenty joints per minute, but the beginner, at three or four joints a minute, will need to reduce the gas supply in order not to burn a hole in the lead or crack the glass. Sophisticated electric irons have thermostatic controls but there is a noticeable time-lag in temperature change compared with the immediate response of a gas iron. In either case, the copper bit must first be filed and then tinned (coated with a layer of solder) by rubbing it in flux and solder when

Figure 7.43 Glazing—using a stopping knife with a weighted end to insert flat-edged nails.

Figure 7.44 Glazing—
soldering the joints.

hot. When the iron is at the required temperature, a small spot of solder is applied to its tip which is then held on the joint for a few seconds, during which the solder will spread evenly. The amount of solder applied is critical; too little will produce a weakness which will break in time; too much, in the form of blobs or buttons, will eventually produce a crack around the joint due to the different coefficients of expansion of lead and solder.

When soldering has been completed on one side, the panel should be carefully examined against daylight because, at this stage, any mischoice of glass can easily be rectified. The panel is then turned over and, on a wooden or illuminated bench, soldered on the other side.

It should be noted that the conservator will occasionally encounter panels which have been soldered on the inside only, to cut costs; this must be rectified as rainwater can enter the leading on the unsoldered side and hasten the decay of the window. Panels soldered on one side only are more flexible and hence easier to install, but the practice cannot be condoned.

As the depth of the heart of the lead is fairly constant, usually about 6 mm, and the thickness of the glass is variable, it follows that the thicker glass will fit tightly while the thinner glass will be slack. The application of waterproof cement both keeps the weather out and solves this problem. Following this, the complete panels are returned to the glazier for fixing the copper ties which, on installation, will be attached to the horizontal bars. These ties, of strong copper wire, some 100 mm long, have to be firmly soldered to the panels at specified points which have been marked on the cutlines at the intersection of leads. At divisions between panels, both the top and bottom panels will have shorter ties fixed at corresponding points where they can be wrapped around the bar and joined.

Glazing for restoration requires little more than additional care in shaping the lead around the pieces due to the vulnerable nature of much old glass. In the case of reglazing much eighteenth- and nineteenth-century glass, problems can arise from the fact that much lead of that period had an extremely thin heart; when using contemporary lead, with the standard heart, the completed panel may be substantially larger than that which was dismantled. In such cases, a panel of the correct size can be achieved by slightly grozing the edges of the glass as it is reassembled. However, strictly speaking, this practice is unethical and should be avoided.

The handling and storage of panels is a matter for great care, particularly before they are cemented. When lifting a panel, to turn it over after soldering one side, it is essential to lift or lower it on a board, or at least to support it with hands underneath while raising or lowering. Panels should always be carried vertically, with support at the lower edge, and never held by the top edge (because the top lead may be pulled away). Panels which have been cemented should be untouched for about two weeks; some workshops keep them in a vertical position, and others in a horizontal postion, apparently depending on the stiffness of the cement. Vulnerable glass awaiting restoration should be stored on boards, with a lip along one edge to enable it to be carried safely. It can then be slid on to the glazing bench without any flexing of the panel.

Cementing

The properties of a good cement are that it should be liquid enough to apply relatively easily, that it should dry out relatively quickly, and yet for many years remain flexible enough to accommodate slight movement of the panel without falling out. Of windows made approximately 100 years ago, many have no cement remaining and leak profusely. A good composition for this material is (by weight) 40 parts whiting, 20 parts plaster of Paris, 4 parts vegetable black, 1 part red lead, to which is added, in equal proportions, boiled linseed oil and turpentine. This produces a black treacly mixture which is liberally applied to the glass (*Figure 7.45a*) and rubbed thoroughly underneath the leaf of the lead with a stiff brush (*Figure 7.45b*). The panel is then coated with whiting to absorb excess oil before being turned over for the same treatment on the other side. The surplus cement is then brushed off (*Figure 7.45c*) and finally (usually the next day) picked out from around the lead with a small-pointed stick (such as a butcher's wooden skewer) or a knitting needle (*Figure 7.45d*), the panel being polished with whiting or sawdust to give a shine to the lead and remove any trace of cement from the glass. In the case of wide lead (flat lead), of 10 mm face or more, the leaf is lifted up before application of the cement to allow better penetration, and subsequently flattened into place. The excess cement is then scraped off and the glass cleaned with a soft bristle brush.

Good cementing determines the life of a window; it is not possible to re-cement a window properly without releading. The whole process is rather vigorous and is therefore unsuitable for ancient glass; in addition, the cement would fill any pits and craters previously cleaned out. Instead it is necessary to apply butyl mastic under the lead by hand, a time-consuming but unavoidable process. An easier

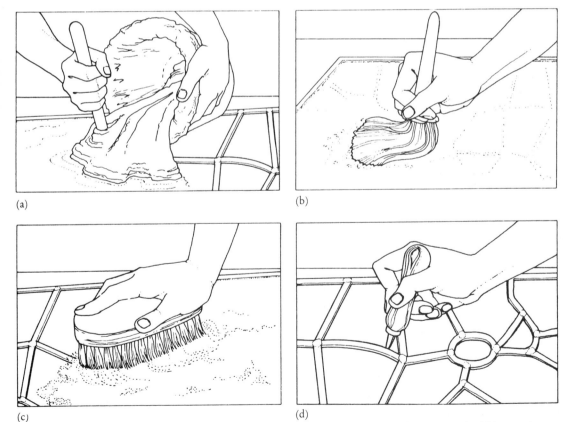

(a) (b) (c) (d)

Figure 7.45 Glazing—cementing the panel. (a) Pouring the cement onto the panel. (b) Brushing cement under the leads. (c) Scrubbing away surplus cement. (d) Picking out the remnants of cement near the leads. From Lee *et al.* (1982)

and less messy alternative would be to use a butyl rubber sealing strip such as Scotchseal 5313 (3M). The rubber, wetted with water to reduce its tackiness, is stretched into a thin strip and applied dry to the edge of the glass, which is then inserted into the leads in the usual way. The strip will stick to both the glass and the lead, and it absorbs any movement between them, and remains flexible for a considerable number of years.

The panels should preferably be stored for at least a month before being reinstalled *in situ*. (There are two schools of thought regarding the storage of cemented panels; that is, whether to store them vertically or horizontally. The difference of opinion relates to the viscosity of the cementing material used by different restorers.)

Preparation of the restoration diagram

After the restoration of medieval glass panels has been completed, an essential step is the preparation of a proper restoration diagram, so that the owner and any future restorer, and any art-historian who is interested in the window, can know exactly what has been done. The rubbing taken of the panel can be used as the basis of the diagram, unless substantial rearrangement of the panel has taken place. The symbols adopted by the *Corpus Vitrearum* are shown in *Figure 7.46a* (CVMA, 1958); those adopted by the Council for the Care of Churches are shown in *Figure 7.46b*.

The diagram thus records *all* the lead lines (including any mending leads), if necessary prepared from a new rubbing, and each piece of glass is shaded according to the schemes shown. In addition, the Council for the Care of Churches recommends the use of the following abbreviations on glass conservation diagrams:

C   Cleaned — written record will specify methods used.
Ea Edge joined by adhesive — specify in written record.
Eb Edge joined by copper foil.
Es Edge joined using strap lead.
F   Artificial filling.
Lc New linework in cold colour.
Lf New linework in fired colour.
Ac Newly painted area in cold colour.
Af Newly painted area in fired colour.
Mg Modern clear glass newly inserted.
Mt Modern coloured or tinted glass newly inserted.

Lc, Lf, Ac or Af may be used in conjunction with Mg or Mt to denote new painted colour on newly inserted glass.

Pi Plated on the front (inside).
Po Plated on the back (outside).
Ps Plated on both sides.

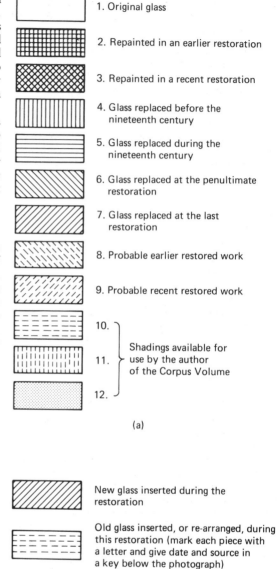

1. Original glass
2. Repainted in an earlier restoration
3. Repainted in a recent restoration
4. Glass replaced before the nineteenth century
5. Glass replaced during the nineteenth century
6. Glass replaced at the penultimate restoration
7. Glass replaced at the last restoration
8. Probable earlier restored work
9. Probable recent restored work
10. ⎫
11. ⎬ Shadings available for use by the author of the Corpus Volume
12. ⎭

(a)

New glass inserted during the restoration

Old glass inserted, or re-arranged, during this restoration (mark each piece with a letter and give date and source in a key below the photograph)

Glass plated during the restoration. Indicate within the frame if the plate is:

Painted

Silver stained
or
Original glass glued edge to edge

(b)

Figure 7.46 Shadings for use in restoration diagrams. (a) Shadings used by the Corpus Vitrearum. (b) Shadings used by the Council for Care of Churches. (These are liable to be modified; the CCC should be consulted.)

If plating is tinted 't' may be added. Lc, Lf, Ac or Af may be used in addition to denote new painted colour or plating glass.

n   May be used with abbreviations for plating or modern glass to indicate stippling.

S   Sheet lead placed over modern glass — use after above symbols where appropriate.

Other symbols may be added if necessary for individual projects. The purpose of the diagram is to provide factual information on work included in the current programme of conservation, rather than an assessment of the date of every piece of glass in the window.

Refixing panels *in situ*

Preparation

T-bars should be cut to the required length in the workshop, and the holes for the copper pins drilled. Saddle bars can, however, usually be cut to size on site. The basic field working kit will again be required. Temporary hardboard (or plain glass) fixed in the window openings should be removed by scraping out the weak lime-mortar used for pointing, and replaced with a restored panel, one at a time.

The opening to be filled may vary from 0.23 m wide, in a small thirteenth-century Gothic lancet, to 2.44 m wide in a Romanesque or Renaissance window. For widths from 0.23 to 0.76 m, the only structural provision is for horizontal saddle bars to be provided at intervals of between 300 and 480 mm to which the panels of painted glass are attached by means of ties made of 16 SWG (standard wire gauge) copper wire, 1.62 mm in diameter and 130 mm long (in early windows the ties may be of lead). Saddle bars of steel or, preferably, manganese bronze (architectural bronze) are fixed into holes in the stonework forming the window aperture, and thus carry most of the weight of the glass. Manganese bronze is expensive but resists corrosion and, being dark brown in colour, is aesthetically pleasing. Economy in the use of saddle bars by spacing them too far apart gives rise to large unsupported areas of glass, and this is a frequent cause of bulging in much second-rate Victorian glass panels. Some saddle bars are bent, or otherwise specially shaped, in order to avoid obscuring detail in the panel, and in these cases the positions at which the ties are soldered will have to be adjusted. If the panels are of the type which use division leads, additional ties will be required at the top and the bottom; such ties are usually 75 mm long, and are soldered in pairs opposite one another so that they can be tied around the intervening saddle bar.

In spite of the saddle bars, a substantial amount of the weight of a panel is carried by the panel beneath and to prevent this weight causing too much pressure

(a)

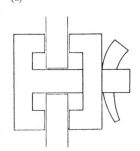

(b)

Figure 7.47 (a) In France T-bar armatures are used between panels. On the outside of the Loire window, they appear as metal frames between the panels. (b) In the French T-bar armature, panels rest on the centre of the sideways T, and are held firm by another frame and a key. From Lee *et al.* (1982).

it is necessary, in tall windows, to insert special bars at intervals of approximately 2 m which come between panels, and on which they rest. These bars are of 'H' or 'T' section and, having a face width of at least 25 mm, are noticeable in the overall effect of the window, and must be incorporated in the design (*Figure 7.47*).

Wide openings require more complex provision of *ferramenta*, and such windows will contain two or more panels in the width, thus producing a vertical joint between them in addition to the horizontal ones. This, in turn, requires a vertical metal bar to which the copper ties of the joint can be attached. A grid pattern is thus necessary, which in the case of Romanesque and early Gothic work could be very complex. At that period copper ties were not used, panels being held in position against flat ironwork which carried projecting lugs into which wedges were inserted after the glass had been put in place. With narrow Gothic lights, the problem disappeared, only to recur with the large window apertures of the Renaissance period. In many eighteenth-century examples a framework of small T-section cast iron completely superseded leading, the painted glass being puttied directly into the frame.

If the glass is to be fixed to T-bars, they should all be inserted into the stonework to a depth of 20 mm, using sheet lead as packing for the holes, and replacing the temporary infill as each bar is fixed. In York Minster the T-bars are sometimes fixed with the horizontal flange (on which the panel rests) facing inwards, instead of outwards as is usually the case, because the window has external protective glazing and the panel has been replaced without wishing to disturb the external window. If ventilated external glazing is to be used, special slotted T-bars may be required. Care should be taken to fix all T-bars exactly horizontal (using a spirit level). The holes for the saddle bars should be drilled in the masonry at the same time, slightly oversize and deeper on one side than on the other, to allow the bar to be inserted into the deep side and then slid back into place.

Fixing the panels to the T-bars involves filling the two rear edges of its flange with butyl mastic and then, having inserted the saddle bars into their position, lifting the panel on to the flange of the bar. Depending on the depth of the groove in the mullion, it may be necessary to turn back the leaf of the outermost leads so that the panel can be fitted snugly into the opening. When the panel is in position the leaf can (eventually) be turned back to its original position by means of a *persuader*, a tool about 250 mm long and 40–50 mm wide, with a curved, tapering point; this will be done after all the panels have been correctly aligned.

Once the panel is resting on the flange of the bar, it is advisable to hold it in place by loosely wrapping a few of the ties around a saddle bar. The panel can then be secured in the groove by means of small wooden wedges while other panels are inserted in the same way. When all the panels of one light are in position they may need to be adjusted slightly so that there is a better alignment of the design features from one panel to the next. When this has been done, any leaves of the leads which have been folded back can be repositioned. The tops and bottoms of the panels are then firmly pressed against the butyl mastic.

The ties can now be fastened permanently to the saddle bars. In the case of copper ties, the practice is to twist the wires together until the panel is tight against the saddle bar and then to cut off the ends, leaving enough to be turned neatly under the saddle bar (*Figure 7.48*). If lead ties are used, they also are twisted together (but not too tightly or the lead will

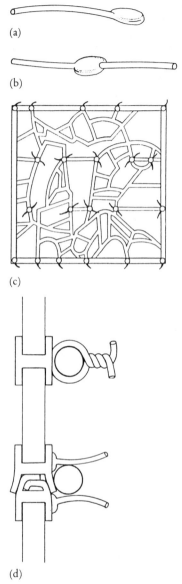

Figure 7.48 (a) Copper division ties. (b) Ties soldered to the panel at the edges and on lead joints at places where bars will cross. (c) Ties twisted around the bars; where panels meet, the lower lead may be folded and overlapped. From Lee *et al.* (1982).

tear), and the ends are cut off, leaving about 25 mm which is laid against the front face of the bar.

The panel is pointed in position, both in the groove and on the T-bar, using a permanent mortar such as 6 parts sand (or stonedust, as appropriate to the building), 1 part Portland cement and 2 parts lime (to give a smoother consistency). A sash brush is then drawn across the surface to improve the appearance and to give better resistance to weathering. Any excess mortar should be wiped away from the surface of the glass and leads, and the flange of the T-bar can receive additional pointing, using a waterproof pointing compound such as metal casement putty (not butyl mastic because it cracks on exposure to the weather). Copper pins should then be inserted through the holes already drilled in the T-bar, and the metal casement putty then reshaped if it has been disturbed by the insertion of the pins.

When tracery panels are fixed, the leaf of the outer lead of the panel needs to be turned back to facilitate fixing. Once installed in the groove, it is essential to wedge the panel safely in position using small tapered wooden wedges. If wire guards are to be installed, the chamfer of the mullion must be drilled to take the plugs which are used to hold the galvanized (and Galvafroid coated) screw eyes used for securing the wire guards with copper wire.

Sometimes lead sills (4 mm thick) may be placed at the base of individual lights, and turned upwards on the inside to form a lip 25 mm high to drain condensation; on the outside of the window the sheet lead follows the contours of the stonework but is rarely longer than 300 mm. It is essential for the conservator to know whether the architect wishes to use such a sill because it must be allowed for in the preparation of the working drawings.

If the panels are to be fixed with *division leads* (T-bars are not used), the stonework should be marked with the sizes of the panels and the positions of the saddle bars. This can be achieved by means of a length of brown paper gummed tape on which all the positions of the bars have been marked. Then, starting at the bottom of the light, holes are drilled for the saddle bars which support the panel and for the one which divides the panel from the next one above it. The bottom panel is then wedged in the groove, and loosely tied to the saddle bars, and the one above is similarly fixed in a temporary manner, and so on to the top of the light (*Figure 7.49*). The same procedure is used for the other lights in the window until all the panels are loosely fixed; the panels are then carefully aligned and particular attention is paid to the saddle bars, to ensure that they are all aligned and level (the aesthetic effect of the window can be spoiled by crooked *ferramenta*). The panels are then wedged into the glazing groove, using small wooden wedges, and pointed with mortar; butyl mastic is placed between the flanges of the division leads.

The final operations

In the final cleaning-up operations, an industrial-type vacuum cleaner is useful because it will pick up all dust, dirt, rust, cement, leaves etc., both inside and outside the church. A final check should be made on-site of all the equipment and tools. Arrangements should be made with the architect or incumbent to inspect the restoration work.

The restoration report

A report must be prepared in which the details of the restoration work undertaken are recorded. This is a valuable document particularly when further restoration becomes necessary. The report should include a copy of the restoration diagram, which may be based on the original rubbing, unless substantial rearrangement of the glass pieces has been necessary. Thus, *all* the lead lines are recorded (including any mending leads), and each piece of glass is shaded according to the schemes shown in *Figure 7.46a and b*. The restored panel should be photographed in both colour and black and white. For colour, 35 mm film is usually sufficient but particularly important or detailed panels should be photographed in a larger format, for example 125 mm × 100 mm, to obtain better quality prints. A small area photographed at a scale of 1:1, for example, may be difficult to relocate and it may therefore be useful to make a file-mark on an adjacent lead, or two marks, one on the lead at one end and the other at the side to locate the co-ordinates (Ferrazzini, 1974). Significant details should be photographed in close-up. If the glass has corroded badly it probably has a poor durability, and macrophotographs should be taken of the worst parts, so that a future restorer can know whether the corrosion has become worse; remember that it may be 100 years or so before the panel is easily accessible

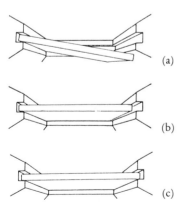

(a)

(b)

(c)

Figure 7.49 Replacing the window. The first panel is eased into place once the aperture and the grooves have been cleared of old glass and cement. The panel having been pushed deep into the groove on one side of the aperture (a), the other side is fitted into place (b); is then centred (c). From Lee *et al.* (1982).

again (this is particularly important at present, when experiments are being carried out on the effects of protective treatments).

A comprehensive report form has been prepared by the Stained Glass Sub-Committee of the Conservation Committee of the Council for Care of Churches. Part A is completed by the conservator before the work begins and deals with preparations. Part B is completed by the architect in charge of the building, or in consultation with an architect. It concerns the condition of the building fabric, the need for heating and/or ventilation etc. Part C concerns the work carried out on the glass, with the dates when the work started and was completed, the final cost, the sketches, photographs or rubbings of each window (or panel) after completion of the work, to act as restoration diagrams, shaded as in *Figure 7.46b* or according to an agreed scheme. Statements should also be made about the extent of releading and the types of leads used; how the glass was cleaned; whether any pieces of replacement glass were painted or stippled; which pieces were plated, and what type of plating was used (internal, external, both sides or gel-plated); whether new materials such as silicones or mastics were used, and what solvent should be used at the next restoration to remove them; whether any work was done on the T-bars or saddle bars; if any were replaced and, if so, what metal was used; and whether any wire-mesh guards were installed. If any external protective glazing was installed, it should be described, for example, isothermally or as external protective glazing, and what types of ventilation was used. Part D concerns the *photographic record* (as distinct from any photographs used as restoration diagrams in Part C). The identity of the building, the date, and the negative number must be recorded on the back of each photograph, and on the envelope in which the negative is kept. It is preferable to supply the negative and a print (or four prints if for a committee); four copies of colour transparencies or prints should be included where appropriate. These should be supplied before and after conservation and, where an interesting feature is involved, during conservation.

Protection of restored windows

The restored window is liable to mechanical damage (from vandalism, airgun pellets, hailstones, builders' ladders, branches torn from trees during storms etc.) and deterioration by weathering (rainwater and, on the inside, condensation) or micro-organisms (chiefly algae and mosses). Mechanical damage can be reduced by installing wire-mesh guards or sheets of plastic materials; and deterioration by weathering can be reduced by protective glazing methods.

Before the restoration work started, discussions will have taken place with all concerned regarding the need (or otherwise) to provide external protection against mechanical damage, and whether this should be by means of wire guards (which can cast unsightly shadows on the windows and also prevent the cleaning action of rain) or by sheets of plastic material (which can result in unsightly reflections of surrounding buildings or trees). External glazing will also provide some mechanical protection against vandalism, and it can reduce the sounds from passing traffic and save some heating bills (Simon, 1981).

Use of wire-mesh guards

In the past, external wire guards were made of copper or galvanized iron. Now, stainless steel is available. The decision whether or not to install wire-mesh guards is a difficult one and should be referred to the architect. It is preferable to provide individual wire guards for each of the main lights, and for each of the tracery openings; they should be fixed to the chamfer of the mullions in such a way that as much as possible of the stonework mouldings can be seen. Many cases are known where the stonework has been entirely covered by unsightly wire mesh guards which could have been avoided by consulting a competent wire-worker.

The cheapest guards are made from galvanized iron wire of the type known as *long-hole wire-mesh*; this consists of crimped 12 SWG (2.6 mm diameter) wire with 12 mm spacing with horizontal strands at 76 mm intervals, the outer frame being made of 4 SWG (6 mm diameter) wire. If the sections are larger than about 4 m, they become extremely difficult to transport and fix. Before leaving the workshop, the galvanized wire should be given two coats of an anticorrosion paint (such as Galvafroid), followed by a coat of dark grey paint. Unpainted galvanized iron will quickly rust at places where the zinc coating is damaged, and rust stains are difficult to remove from stonework.

Copper and bronze guards do not rust but the former can produce disfiguring bright green stains. Stainless steel guards do not corrode but are very expensive.

Wire guards can disrupt the view of the painted glass whether the window is viewed from the inside or the outside; plain glazing can also be impaired by the mesh of the guards.

Use of sheets of glass or of plastic materials

Wire-mesh guards will not protect windows against deliberate damage by airgun pellets and thrown stones, whereas sheets of plastic materials will do so although they tend to be expensive. There are various types of transparent plastic materials available. However, there are frequently valid architectural objections to their use since they may spoil the scale of medieval buildings, produce glaring reflections and mask the rich texture of leaded painted glass.

Acrylate sheet, such as Perspex and Oroglas, has an excellent impact resistance and is said to be seventeen times tougher than glass, but the surface is easily scratched. Following a serious fire, in Britain, of a building incorporating a large amount of Oroglas, doubts have been expressed about the use of such sheeting, but the areas used for protecting windows are so small and discontinuous that there should be little risk of fire. Moreover, acrylic sheet would soften and fall out of its frame before igniting; it has a Class III (medium) spread of flame when tested according to BS 746. Acrylic sheet should be fixed by clasping the sheet between battens in a frame, and not by screwing it directly to any support, because it has a relatively high coefficient of thermal expansion and the buckled sheets would give distorted reflections.

Polycarbonate sheet, such as Lexan, is tough and easily installed (provided the supplier's instructions are followed) but the soft surface seems to loose its brilliance on weathering. Laminated glass, consisting of glass with interlayers of poly(vinyl butyral), is used for anti-bandit and bullet-resistant purposes. The disadvantages of its use are that the glass tends to be rather heavy, is very expensive and has to be ordered specially to size.

Georgian wired glass can be broken but the pieces do not fall out because a mesh of wire is embedded in it. It has one shiny surface and one dimpled surface, thus it does not give coherent reflections, nor does it lack life in its reflectivity. Georgian wired glass has been installed in the Church of St John at Gouda in The Netherlands. The wire mesh is, however, visible but the material is not excessively expensive.

Protection against damage by moisture and the environment

Much thought has been given, in the last few years, to the use of external protective glazing (Ger. *Aussenschutzverglasung*) to protect medieval windows against rainfall on the outside of the window (or driven rain reaching the inside of the window), and condensation on the inside. It will also give mechanical protection, reduction of heat losses and protection against bird droppings (*CVMA News Letter*, No. 15, June 1975). There are three main types of external protective glazing: unventilated; internally ventilated or isothermal glazing; and externally ventilated (Newton, 1975a).

Unventilated external glazing

External protective glazing systems have been in use for some 130 years, protective glass having been used at York Minster since 1861 (*CVMA News Letter*, No. 13, Feb. 1975, No. 14, Apr. 1975). Large plates of rough-cast glass were inserted into iron frames, but the frames rusted and the plates fell out so that, in

1906, only one panel remained whole. In 1907 leaded glass windows were installed and these remained in place during both world wars; and were useful as replacements when the historic glass was removed during the Second World War. In 1952 the external glass was cleaned on the outside; and in 1970 part was removed from the Great East Window, revealing that 18 years after restoration the lead solder joints were still bright; thus this external window clearly gave considerable protection although an oily film of dirt had penetrated, no doubt through the gaps in cement that permit smoke to enter (*CVMA News Letter*, No. 15, p.7, June 1975). There are, on record, even earlier examples of external glazing in Britain, one being installed at Audley End, Essex, in 1782, another being *removed* from Cotehele Church, Cornwall, in 1880 (it is not known when it had been installed), and a third being used at Redbourne, Lincolnshire, before 1845 (*CVMA News Letter*, No. 13, Feb. 1975).

Perhaps the most famous example of unventilated external protective glazing is that at the church of Lindena in East Germany which was installed in 1897. The thirteenth-century glass in the window was examined in 1974 (*CVMA News Letter*, No. 7, pp.8–10, March 1974) and in 1987 (Drachenberg, 1988), when the paintwork on both sides of the window was found to be in good condition. It seems that the wooden framework was no longer airtight and it is probable that this example, and no doubt *all windows which are more than about ten years old* are actually good examples of *ventilated* windows.

[Here it should be noted that tests with smoke generators have shown that none of the windows at York Minster was airtight, even those with soldered edges (*CVMA News Letter*, No. 15, June 1975).]

Ventilated interspaces

In the cases of isothermal glazing and externally ventilated external protective glazing there is an interspace between the medieval glass and the external (modern) protective glazing in the sense that it is deliberately ventilated. This prevents condensation and encourages the evaporation of any driven rain which may enter the interspace.

The revised practice is to number the faces of the glass, one to four, starting at the outside. Consideration must be given to climatic changes at the four glass surfaces:

- *Face 4*, the outer surface of the external (modern) protective window, is exposed to rain, fog, snow, hailstones, bird droppings etc., and it is made of replaceable modern glass.
- *Face 3*, the inner surface of the external protective window, may, on cold nights, have moisture condensed on it. Such moisture will raise the dew point of the air in the cavity but is not likely to have

any effect on the medieval glass if it evaporates quickly during daylight hours.

• *Face 2*, the outer surface of the medieval glass, may bear painted decoration; even if there are no trace lines there may well be surface matting as an indication that paint was originally present. It will be desirable to avoid condensation on this glass because it could be damaged.

• *Face 1*, the inner surface of the medieval glass, bears the medieval paintwork. It must be protected from condensation. It is not actually in the ventilated cavity but condensation could occur on it if its temperature falls below that of the dew point of the air inside the church.

The next point to consider is the source of the air used for ventilation. It can be obtained from inside or from outside the building. The temperature of the air will depend on the time of the year and the weather. The moisture content of the air (humidity) will also vary with the weather and, inside of the building, with the air change rate. Here it is important to note the difference between absolute humidity, the mass of water vapour present in the air measured in $kg\,m^{-3}$ and relative humidity which is the ratio of the amount of water in a given quantity of air to the maximum amount of water which the air can hold at that temperature, usually expressed as a percentage (see Thomson, 1986).

For example, air with a water vapour mass of $10\,g\,m^{-3}$ will have a relative humidity of 43 per cent at 25°C, 57 per cent at 20°C, 78 per cent at 15°C and 100 per cent at 11°C which is the dewpoint temperature (the temperature at which condensation starts to occur). In winter the absolute humidity will be considerably lower because, if the average temperature is only 1°C then the maximum water vapour mass will be $5\,g\,m^{-3}$ (i.e. at the dew point). If this air is heated within the building without adding water vapour then the relative humidity will be lowered: 100 per cent at 1°C, 57 per cent at 10°C and 28 per cent at 20°C. However, increased water vapour will be generated by people and their clothing and from the porous structure of the building. By measuring the relative humidity and temperature within the building and the external temperature and relative humidity, it is possible to determine if and where condensation will occur within the ventilated double glazing.

In general (Lacy, 1970, 1973), condensation *in the cavity* is likely to occur *less frequently* when the cavity is ventilated to the outside. The work at York Minster, using variable apertures on an externally ventilated window, showed that the ventilation openings should be made as small as possible, preferably less than 1 mm wide, and the flow rate should be less than $10\,mm\,s^{-1}$ (Newton, 1976b). If the ventilation conditions can be arranged so that the

temperature of Face 2 is the same (or nearly the same) as that of Face 1 (the rationale of isothermal glazing), condensation on the painted face will occur only under exceptional conditions, for example, when there is fog inside the building, or when the furniture and the walls are moist and clammy. Nevertheless, if there is no ventilation to the outside, water will be 'pumped' into the cavity, and be deposited as condensation on Face 3, whenever the outside temperature falls below the dew point of the inside air; this condensation does *not* occur on the medieval glass when external ventilation is used.

Isothermal glazing

This system was intended to be used in heated buildings, and it is equivalent to placing the ancient glass in a museum environment where further corrosion will be at a minimum. Subsequent work (Newton, 1976b) has shown that the system will function equally well in unheated buildings. It seems that the first installation of this kind was in Switzerland in 1945 at Berne Minster (Hahnloser, 1972), where modern glass was installed in the glazing groove of the mullions and the ancient glass was rehung so that the warm air of the Minster can circulate on both sides; Marchini reinvented the technique in 1969 (*Proc. VII, Collogue CVMA*, Florence, 1970). One of the problems of rehanging the glass, on screwed bolts 65 mm long, inside the building is that the glass is then narrower than the space between the mullions due to the slope of the reveals. Thus, unless special precautions are taken (such as adding shields at the sides, and at the top and bottom of the window) daylight can shine around the panels. This can be troublesome when the panels are rather dark (Frenzel, 1971a,b). Detailed drawings have been published of the system used at St Maria am Gestade in Vienna (Bacher, 1973a,b), but if the panels have a clear border, then this is no longer a problem (*CVMA News Letter*, No. 10, Sept. 1974, No. 11, Nov. 1974). Hayward (1975) describes the protection of a window by this method at The Cloisters in New York City.

A comprehensive study of an experimental system, in which the spacing between the windows could be varied, has been made (Newton, 1975a) and it was found that truly isothermal conditions were never actually achieved, the air in the interspace always being slightly colder than the 'inside' air, for example, by 0.7°C when the separation of the windows was 240 mm, or 1.7°C when the space was 80 mm. If the 'building' was heated the differences were much increased. The air flows in the cavity were measured and were found to be downward at rates often in excess of $1\,m\,s^{-1}$. Measurements were made of airflows in an actual installation at St Walpurgis in Austria (Bacher, 1976a) and they were found to be upwards, no doubt because it was a bright sunny day and the sunshine caused the medieval glass to warm up. Frenzel (1972a; *CVMA News Letter*, No. 24, abstract no. 251, Feb. 1977) has been concerned about the possibility of condensation forming on Faces 1 or 2 during sub-zero nights in Central Europe, and has suggested that electric heating wires should be installed in the cavity.

There seems to be no doubt that this type of external protective glazing does afford protection to the glass because Frenzel (1971a,b) claims that unprotected windows at Nuremburg have continued to deteriorate whereas protected windows did not, and the glass at Lindena is in an unexpectedly good condition (*CVMA News Letter*, No. 7, Section 3.4, Mar. 1974). An interesting analogy is the sixteenth-century window which was found walled up: after 400 years the surface was 'quite smooth' (Bacher, 1967). Some fears have been expressed that dust from the interior of the building might be carried into the interspace and remain there, but White has inspected the interspace at Berne Minster. He found that the 30 mm interspace had collected some dust during the 30 years that the system had been installed, but this was only on Face 3 and not on Face 2 (*CVMA News Letter*, No. 15, June 1975). Dust would of course be deposited preferentially on the colder surface, and most of the material seemed to be soot (*CVMA News Letter*, No. 17, section 1.5, Nov. 1975). It would, however, be wise to incorporate simple measures for cleaning and maintenance, such as the 'hanging butts' used at the Beauchamp Chapel, Warwick. Inspection of the Berne Minster windows in 1987 showed that those which had been protected since 1946 were in much better condition than those left unprotected (Trümpler, 1988).

Apart from the problem of fitting the panels into the wider space between the mullions, there is a problem of the aesthetic treatment of the modern window, and this will be discussed under external glazing. Theft is another possibility, and anti-theft devices have been installed at St Lorenzkirche in Nuremburg. Frenzel (1981) has given detailed descriptions of twelve types of isothermal glazing.

Externally ventilated external protective glazing

In the case of isothermal glazing, the main problem is that of rehanging the medieval glass inside the church and then fitting the modern window in the glazing groove. If the protective window is placed on the outside, there need be no disturbance of the ancient glass and the ventilation air can be drawn from the outside of the building giving, in general, less frequent condensation in the cavity. Another problem is, however, created because the use of a wide space between the glazings, for example 65 mm, would involve some loss of depth of the external

mullions; the depth of a window in its reveal is of fundamental importance to the appearance of a building (*CVMA News Letter*, No. 7, footnote to p.5 Mar. 1974). Considerable attention has therefore been given to designing a glazing system where the width of the space between the windows is minimal. One arrangement, which has been used in several churches by the York Glaziers Trust, has an interspace of only 6 mm (*CVMA News Letter*, No. 33/34, Jan. 1982).

A comprehensive experiment was carried out at York Minster in which the interspace was kept constant at 65 mm, but the width of the slots at the top and bottom of the window could be altered (Newton, 1976b, 1978b). Briefly, the medieval glass was kept warmest (and therefore the least risk of condensation) when the slots were closed as much as possible (they could not be made airtight because the sill was uneven). When the slots were opened wide (150 mm), Face 2 could be some 3°C lower than the temperature of the air in the building, but when the slots were reduced to 10 mm, Face 2 was about 2.5°C colder than the air in the building. With the slots closed as much as possible, the temperature drop was only about 1.5°C. Air flows were also measured and they could be as high as 1 m s^{-1} with widely opened slots, but only some 20 mm s^{-1} when the slots were closed; clearly, plenty of air was continuing to flow when there was nominally no slot, and it would be preferable to reduce the air flow to less than 10 mm s^{-1}. It seems likely that the situation at the church at Lindena in East Germany involves a reasonable flow of air, enough to dry out any driven rain (*CVMA News Letter*, No. 7, Mar. 1974). Note: no windows are airtight, despite the many speculations that they might be sealed hermetically, or even that the interspace might be filled with a dry inert gas; the experiments at York Minster (*CVMA News Letter*, No. 15, June 1975) showed that smoke can always be introduced through a window, no doubt because movements of the stonework and the effects of gale-force winds open up small cracks in the leading or in the cementing of the leads.

The effect of daylight on the window was quite marked. The window was coldest just before dawn but by mid-afternoon the temperature had risen by some 3°C, even when the sky was overcast. The effect of sunshine was very striking, a temperature of 46°C being recorded on one day. This could give the impression that external glazing might develop temperatures which were dangerous to the glass. However, it is known that even unprotected medieval glass warms considerably in sunshine.

A warning should be given about drawing conclusions from experience with modern colourless window glass, which does not heat up much in sunshine but allows the incident radiation to pass through and heat the objects behind, thus leading to the well-known 'greenhouse effect'. Colourless *medieval* glass has a rather different behaviour because the sand contained much iron and the glass was decolorized with manganese, both of these materials absorb some visible and infrared radiation with the result that the glass heats up and less energy passes through to heat materials in the 'greenhouse'. Thermography clearly distinguishes between the two types of colourless glass, for example, in a north-facing window the modern glass had a temperature of 16.8°C whereas the medieval glass had a temperature of 18.8°C. In another experiment, with a south-facing window in full sunshine, the air temperature was 22°C and modern glass warmed up by a further 7–11°C, whereas medieval glass warmed up by 13–15°C, due to the iron and manganese it contained (Newton, 1976b).

In the experiment at York Minster, no condensation was encountered on Faces 1 or 2, but an important *laboratory* experiment carried out in Austria in 1977 (Schuecker, 1977; Schuecker *et al.*, 1978) did produce condensation, especially in conditions where there was simulated external ventilation. The details are given in the two papers, and an important difference concerned the extreme Alpine winter conditions that were simulated in one of the trials (−15°C for the outside air, and +2°C for the inside air). Not only were these conditions much more severe than anything which would be encountered in the UK but (coupled with the large ventilation holes used) they led to rapid air flows in the interspace (250 m s^{-1}) and these caused much

more chilling of the medieval glass than would have occurred in the British experiment. Nevertheless, it seems likely that internal ventilation could be suitable for the extreme climates of Central Europe whereas external ventilation would be better in the UK.

Subsequent experiments carried out at York Minster, using a north-facing window which was free from the problems caused by direct sunshine, explained why no condensation had been encountered in the earlier experiment. It transpired that the massive stonework of the Minster acted as a night storage heater. When the outside ventilation air was taken from a hole close to the sloping sill of the window (instead of the slot discussed above), the stream of air entering the interspace was heated by the warmer stonework (even in the middle of a cold winter's night) usually by about 3°C, but sometimes by as much as 7°C, with the result that its temperature was always above that of the dew point of either the inside or the outside air (Newton, 1980b; *CVMA News Letter*, No. 33/34). There is already much information about the climatological conditions which exist in various buildings. Lacy (1970) studied King's College Chapel, Cambridge; Crosthwaite and Crawford (1973) examined St Paul's Cathedral, London; Geis (1976) has reported on Freiburg Minster, West Germany; and Paterson (1974) has discussed the conditions in the Royal Albert Hall, London. These can be modified to take account of the results of the special experiments in York Minster, in France (Bettembourg, 1980) and in Austria (cited above). Newton and Bettembourg

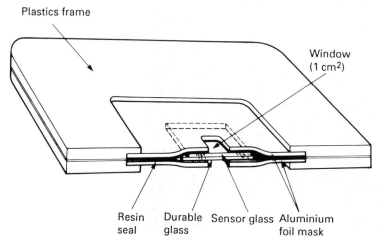

Figure 7.50 The glass-sensor (atmosphere assessment chip) is a small piece of specially sensitive glass, 0.5 mm thick, which possesses a very poor durability, so that its surface will register a measurable attack from the atmosphere in about six months. One square centimetre of the top surface of the sensitive glass is exposed through the aluminium mask which, for ease of handling and for secure positioning, is fastened into a plastics framework. The rear surface of the sensing glass is protected from the atmosphere by a piece of durable glass, and the progress of any attack can be observed through the window by transmitted light using laboratory equipment. Fraunhofer Institut für Silicatforschung.

both discovered that the greatest risk of encountering condensation was in September, and not in the depths of winter.

In 1987 a novel approach was devised by the workers at the Fraunhofer-Institut für Silicatforschung, in Würzburg, for assessing the aggressiveness of any atmosphere towards medieval glass. They have developed some *Glassensoren* — pieces of specially polished, poorly-durable 'model-glasses' which can be exposed, in their special mounts (*Figure 7.50*), to (1) the air in the church, or (2) the air in the ventilated interspace of the protective glazing, or (3) the 'polluted' atmosphere outside the church. Experiments have already been carried out in important churches in three countries, and useful results can be obtained in as little as six months.

Their effectiveness depends on three features: (a) the sensing glasses have a very poor durability so that they can readily form the hydrated surface layer; (b) they possess carefully polished surfaces so that the thickness of the hydrated layer can be measured using infra-red spectroscopy; (c) they are very thin so that the hydrated layer, though itself thin, forms an appreciable proportion of the total thickness of the glass, and thus can be measured more accurately.

The tests which have already been carried out have given the following results, the figures indicating the relative aggressiveness of the atmosphere at that point.

Building	Outside air	In the interspace
York Minster	0.40	0.07
St Lorenzkirche, Nuremburg	0.72	0.07
St Janskerk, Gouda	0.70	0.04

Thus the protection afforded by external protective glazing can easily be seen and the expected widespread use of these *Glassensoren* will greatly assist the understanding of the most appropriate types to employ in different circumstances. Further details can be found in *CVMA News Letter* No. 41/42, 1988 (which contains several important articles on the use of external protective glazing) in Newton and Fuchs, 1988 and Leissner and Fuchs, 1992.

Aesthetic treatment of the external window

The earlier systems of isothermal glazing used large sheets of plain flat glass for the external modern window, with the result that disturbing reflections could be obtained of the surrounding buildings (Ferrazzini, 1976b). An example, showing the reflection of television aerials in the windows of Prato Cathedral, has been published (Marchini, 1975). At York Minster the earlier external windows were leaded with diamond quarries, but the diagonal lines of the leading cast disturbing shadows on the painted glass at certain times of the day. These

Figure 7.51 The early experiments on external glazing schemes at Canterbury Cathedral (1977). Every alternate light has been glazed with plain glass. The second light from the left has regular rectangular glazing which still enables the reflection of a nearby tree to be seen as a nearly coherent reflection. The light on the extreme right has regular diamond quarries, and the reflection is broken up, but the window looks more like a domestic Tudor window than an ecclesiastical stained glass window, and distracting shadows were created. The third from the right is irregular diamond glazing which shows little advantage over regular diamond glazing. The fourth from the left is an abstract design which is the most aesthetically pleasing solution. Courtesy of the Dean and Chapter, Canterbury.

shadows are made worse because the diagonals are continuous, and the eye automatically follows the long lines down and across the window. Thus both flat sheets and diamond quarries are aesthetically objectionable.

An attempt to break up the reflections by the use of geometrical leading, and yet avoid the use of long continuous lines, has been made in Austria by employing pieces of hexagonally shaped glass (Frodl-Kraft, 1975, Figure 2a). The most comprehensive experiments, started in 1977, were carried out at Canterbury Cathedral. The first experiments are illustrated in *Figure 7.51* where every alternate light has been glazed with plain glass and the coherent reflections of the tree can be seen quite easily.

When a visitor approaches a cathedral he expects to be able to anticipate seeing painted glass. When it is present he can recognize it from the outside by its leading and by its patina. Hence the external glazing (which does not yet have a patina) should have leading which imparts an impression that painted glass will be found behind it. Therefore the leading should *not* consist of straight lines (like 'crazy paving') but it should simulate the window behind it; a figure window should have outer glazing which gives the impression of a figure, and a heraldic panel should have an outer panel which gives the impression of a shield. The next experiments are illustrated in *Figure 7.52*, where the external window on the left simulates the figure-window within, except that the area of the head is extra large so that the outer leading is less likely to throw disturbing shadows across the important detail of the window. Note, however, that the canopy is shown as a too-rigid detail, and the limbs have been copied too slavishly. The treatment on the right is an improvement because the details are not so rigid, yet enough indication is provided for the eye to capture the picture. The head area is again extra large.

The final approach was to adopt a compromise: where there were large pale areas (such as drapery), large pieces of glass were used in order to avoid disruptive lines (as shadows, or simply seen through the glass). The lowest rank of the final window is shown in *Figure 7.53*. The window now gives some anticipation of the treasures to be seen from within, and the presence of heraldic panels in the row at the top of the lights (and in the bottom panels of each light above) can be appreciated. Modern flat glass, for example, float glass, was not used for making the external window because the surface is flat and untextured; instead, the glass was of a type known as *French Antique*, relieved by a certain amount of *English Antique*. The contrast between *Figures 7.51* and *7.53* is quite remarkable.

The Jacobi process

Various medieval windows, but particularly those of Cologne Cathedral, West Germany, have been protected by the process invented by Richard Jacobi. It consists of embedding the medieval glass in a plastic material, rather like that used for making laminated car windscreens, and then moulding-on thin, modern transparent glass on both sides. Simple as the idea is in itself, it is extremely difficult to put into practice and the whole process demands great skill and experience, or mistakes will occur, such as can be seen in the yellow marks in the nearby church of St Kuniberts. An enormous number of individual pieces of glass are involved and only a well-coordinated workshop, with economical means of mass production, is in a position to cope with such a task.

The process has been described in some detail by Jacobi (1955, 1957, 1960, 1971, 1973), and also by the Dombaumeister (Wolff, 1975); in addition Moncrieff (1974) has prepared a detailed study of the process. In 1984 the process was no longer in use, and in 1987 windows treated by this method were being 'reversed' in workshops at Cologne Cathedral.

Use of protective coatings

In an attempt to reduce the attack by atmospheric agents (especially water), various transparent coatings have been advocated at one time or another, and these have been either organic resins or inorganic materials.

Organic resins

Many resins have been advocated from time to time as 'protective' coatings: Acrylek, Bedacryl, Vycoat (*CVMA News Letter*, No. 3, April 1973) and poly(methyl methacrylate) (Domaslowski and Kwiatowski, 1962).

Much has been written about the use of organic coatings, especially since the French Department for Historic Monuments used Viacryl VC363 (acrylic resin) hardened with Desmodur N75 (an isocyanate) on the windows of the West Front at Chartres Cathedral (Bettembourg and Perrot, 1976). The use of this resin was first proposed by Frodl-Kraft (1973, 1975), and then adopted by Bettembourg (1976b, 1977) after extensive accelerated tests of the *resin* only (i.e. not what might happen to the glass).

Experience with glass-reinforced plastics (GRP) has shown that water will penetrate to the interface and cause failure within 20 years (Bascom, 1968; Dukes and Greenwood, 1972; ERDE 1973; James *et al.*, 1968; Norman, 1973; Ryabov *et al.*, 1967; Stone, 1971; Werner, 1966; Pogany, 1976).

Some experiments suggest that there is already evidence of attack on glass which has been coated with Viacryl resin (*CVMA News Letter*, No. 24, Feb. 1977). There is much confusion in the voluminous literature because some investigations

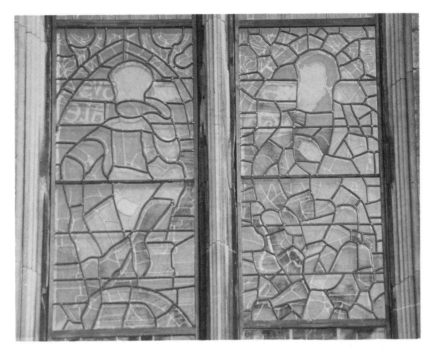

Figure 7.52 External glazing experiments at Canterbury Cathedral. On the left, the arrangement of the external glazing simulates the figure-window within, except that the area of the head is extra large so that the outer leading is less likely to throw disturbing shadows across that important detail of the window. Note, however, that the canopy is shown as a too-rigid detail, and the limbs have been copied too slavishly. The treatment on the right is an improvement because the details are not so rigid, yet enough indication is provided for the eye to capture the picture. As in the first window, the head area is deliberately made extra large in size. Courtesy of the Dean and Chapter, Canterbury.

Figure 7.53 External protective glazing of the south-west transept at Canterbury Cathedral. The final solution was a compromise between using small and large pieces of glass depending on the design in the original windows. Courtesy of the Dean and Chapter, Canterbury.

have been concerned solely with the behaviour of the resin, and whether it has deteriorated or not, and the possibility that the glass might have been harmed by the presence of the resin does not seem to have been considered. Marschner (1984) has carried out an extensive series of trials on more than 200 samples of resins, using sophisticated apparatus to accelerate weathering, and her paper should be consulted by anyone who seriously intends to use resin coatings. Other authors, although alerted to the danger that the glass might have suffered damage, have restricted themselves to removing the resin and examining the surface with the unaided eye. Thus Bauer (1984) considered Viacryl to have protected the glass, and he was also able to conclude that glass test pieces which had been cleaned with either of Bettembourg's (1972a) chemical solutions had undergone subsequent weathering that was more severe than those which had been cleaned mechanically, or with water alone. The workers at the Institut für Silikatforschung, at Würzburg, (ISC, 1982, 1983, 1985), however, using highly sophisticated techniques, concluded that none of the many coating materials tested had at that time provided convincing long-term protection but their ORMOCERS (ORganically MOdified CERamics) show much promise, see Römich and Fuchs, 1992. The work by Fitz *et al.* (1984) concluded: 'the protective coatings used accelerate the corrosion of glass instead of stopping it'. Another, but much neglected, danger lies in a too-low T_g point which will cause the resin to absorb dirt into its thickness. Bauer's conclusion that Viacryl VC363 *did* protect the underlying glass could be explained by the work reported by Pederson *et al.* (1983), in which it was stated that very small amounts of water did attack the glass, but that the attack stopped as the leachant became *saturated* with degradation products from the glass. The hypothesis was taken up by Newton (1987a) and, later, by Newton and Seddon (1992) who showed that, in fact, the attack did stop when saturation of the corrosion products was reached.

Waxes

Much interest has been created by the successful use of suitable waxes for the *refixing* of loose paint (Cole, 1979; Möller, 1980; Müller *et al.*, 1980), but the authors have insisted that only the painted line should be covered, and not the rest of the glass.

Inorganic coatings

The aim of creating a 'new glass surface' which is durable and which can protect the old glass is attractive, and many attempts have been made to coat the poorly durable glass with a more durable one. The first attempts were at the beginning of this century, using the Zettler process (overfusion, also known as Schmitz's process; Frenzel, 1969), firing on a low-melting glass at 400°C. There have been many misgivings about the process (e.g. Frodl-Kraft, 1963). In attempts to reduce the problems of heating the glass to such a temperature, radiofrequency sputtering in a vacuum has been attempted (Newton, 1974d, p.vii; Linsley, 1972). The sol-gel process has also been advocated (Schröder and Kaufmann, 1959), but all of these are plagued by the problem that poor durability is usually due to the presence of excess alkali which, in turn, leads to a high coefficient of thermal expansion; but all durable glasses have a much lower thermal expansion, and hence the coating ultimately fails through expansion mismatch. Jovanović and Zalar (1974) found that the porous surface of weathered glass could be consolidated by heating it under 50 atm. pressure in an autoclave but, even then, the durability had been increased only twenty times.

Inorganic cements

Solutions of water glass (sodium silicate) in water have been used industrially for adhering glass (Wills, 1977) but they have not been successful in conservation work. Solder glasses have been suggested (Leigh, 1978) but the problems of thermal expansion mismatch, and of adequate durability, may be insuperable.

Glossary

abraded decoration A type of decoration executed by shallow grinding on a wheel, as a speedier and less exacting process than facet-engraving, and with designs in curved lines, circles and ovals.

acid-etching Decoration on the surface of glass by the use of hydrofluoric acid, varying from a satin matt finish to a deeper rough effect. The process involves covering the glass with an acid-resistant wax, varnish or drying linseed oil, and then scratching the design with a sharp tool. A mixture of hydrofluoric acid with potassium fluoride and water is then applied to etch the exposed design into the body of the piece. The depth of etching varies with the time of exposure of the glass to the acid. The acid must then be thoroughly washed off since it is highly corrosive.

agate glass A type of decorative opaque glass made by mixing several colours (usually purple and green) before shaping a glass object, so as to imitate natural semi-precious stones, such as agate, chalcedony, onyx, malachite, lapis lazuli and jasper.

air-twists Spiral veins of air formed by the extension, by blowing, of tears in stems of drinking vessels and ornamental wares.

alkali A soluble salt, one of the essential ingredients in making glass, being about 15–20 per cent of the batch. It serves as a flux to reduce the fusion point of the silica.

annealing (1) The process of reintroducing a completed object into an auxiliary part of the glass furnace (like a lehr), in order to cool it slowly. This results in the release of any strain created in the glass during the forming process. (2) In the manufacture of painted glass windows, the technique of attaching pieces of coloured and shaped glass to a larger piece of clear glass by using solder glass, e.g. as jewels around the edge of a garment.

antique glass A hand-made window glass which has the uneven (reamy) appearance of medieval glass.

at-the-fire The process of reheating a blown glass object at the *glory hole*, during manufacture, to permit further blowing to enlarge it or alter its shape, or to permit manipulation with tools.

at-the-flame (at-the-lamp; lampworking) The technique of shaping glassware from rods and tubes of readily fusible glass, by heating and thus softening them at the flame, originally of an oil lamp, later of a gas burner. The glass is then manipulated to the required shape.

aventurine glass A type of translucent glass flecked throughout with sparkling oxidized metallic particles, simulating the appearance of brownish aventurine quartz, which is flecked with mica or other minerals.

baluster A term used to describe a type of drinking glass with a baluster stem, made in England.

bar See *cane*.

barilla Soda from calcined plants native to Spain.

backpainting See *hinterglasmalerei*.

basse taille A subdivision of *champlevé enamel*, in which a design in low relief, chased or engraved on a base plate, is covered with a transparent layer of enamel. The modelled surface is visible, and graduations in the height of the relief are reflected by variations in the depth of colour in the enamel.

batch The mixture of raw materials, generally silica, soda and lime, heated together in a crucible or *pot* to make glass. Broken glass (*cullet*) and minor ingredients such as colourants may also be added to the batch.

block A block of wood hollowed out to form a spherical recess. After being dipped in water to prevent charring, it was used to form a blob of molten glass into a sphere as an initial operation in making a globular *paraison*.

blow-pipe (blow-iron) The hollow iron tube used to take a *gather* of molten glass from the pot, and then to shape it by blowing the mass (*paraison*) into a bubble. The tube (usually up to 1.75 m long and about 250 mm in diameter) has a thickened end for gathering the *glass metal*, and sometimes wooden coverings where the workmen must handle it. The metal end is heated before use to cause the gathering of glass to adhere.

bottle glass (green glass) A common naturally coloured (dark greenish or brownish) glass. The colour is characteristic of unrefined glass including traces of iron found in the natural *silica* used as an ingredient. Sometimes additional quantities of iron, in the form of iron oxide, were added to darken the colour. Used for making bottles.

broad glass See *cylinder glass*.

bull's-eye pane See *crown glass*.

cage cups See *vasa diatreta*.

calcar (calker; caulker) A type of *reverberatory furnace*, used for calcination of the *batch* into *frit*.

came(s) Strip(s) of lead used as an integral part of glass windows.

cameo glass (cased glass) An object formed of cased glass of two colours, such as opaque white that forms an overlay on coloured glass, where the outer layer was carved on a wheel so as to leave a design in white relief on the coloured background, with the effect depending upon the extent and depth to which the white was removed. See *flashing*.

cane (rod; bar) A slender rod of glass, groups of which are bundled together and fused to form a polychrome design. The bundle is heated and drawn out to achieve the required diameter. Multiple inlays or appliqués can be sliced from each bar, each retaining the identical design.

cartoon The full-scale design for a painted glass window. Early examples were drawn on whitened boards, or on a plaster floor (tracing floor). At a later date, paper or parchment rolls were used. Cartoons were often adapted for designing several different patterns, and bequeathed from one glass painter to his successor.

cased glass See *cameo glass*.

cast glass A type of glass made either by (1) fusing powdered glass in a one- or two-piece mould (i.e. open vessels or solid objects but not hollow vessels), or (2) by the *cire perdue* process.

chair (1) The bench used by a *gaffer* while forming a glass object. It is a wide bench with flat, extended, and slightly sloping arms. The gaffer rests the *blow-pipe* with its *paraison* of molten glass on the arms and constantly rolls it back and forth so that the paraison keeps its symmetrical shape, and does not collapse during manipulation. The French term is *banc à bardelles*. (2) The team which assists the gaffer; sometimes also called the 'shop'. It usually includes five to six craftsmen and apprentices.

champlevé **enamel** A technique in which areas of the metal base are gouged out, and the hollows filled with vitreous enamel, leaving a raised metal outline.

cire perdue The 'lost wax' process originally used in casting bronze pieces, and later for glassware. A model was carved in wax, then encased in a mould. Heat was then applied to cause the wax to melt and run out, after which the mould was filled with molten glass or reheated powdered glass. *Cire perdue* was used for pieces too detailed to be effectively produced by the usual process of making in a mould.

clippings See *shearings*.

cloisonné **enamel** A technique in which differently coloured vitreous enamels are separated by narrow *cloisons*, or strips of metal, which have been soldered on to the metal base.

cold colours Lacquer colours or oil paint applied as a decoration to glassware (as to porcelain) without firing. Often much of this type of decoration has worn off antique pieces. Such colours are more effectively used when applied to the back of the surface to be viewed, and protected by a layer of varnish or metal foil, or by another sheet of glass.

cold-cutting The process of cutting a glass vessel or object from a raw block of glass which has not previously been cast to shape. The cutting is carried out by means of a rotating wheel fed with water.

coloured glass Glass that is coloured by (1) impurities in the basic ingredients in the *batch*, or (2) techniques of colouring transparent clear glass by three main processes: (a) by use of a *metallic oxide* in solution in the batch to impart a colour throughout; (b) by use of a substance in a colloidal state; or (c) by use of embedded particles of coloured material.

combed decoration A wavy, festooned, feathery, or zig-zag pattern of decoration in two or more colours which was produced on glass objects by applying threads of opaque glass of a different colour to that of the molten glass body. The threads were rolled into the glass body by *marvering*, after which they would be combed or dragged to achieve the desired effect.

composition See *Egyptian faience*.

cord See *reamy glass*.

core-forming The technique of forming a vessel by trailing molten glass over a core supported by a metal rod (or dipping the core into the molten glass). The object was removed from the rod and annealed, after which the core was scraped out.

cristallo A type of *soda glass* developed in Venice, perhaps before the fifteenth century. It was made with sea plant ashes or *natron*, and had a pale-yellow, straw-like or smokey-grey colour. By the use of manganese as a decolorizing agent, the glass was made colourless and thus resembled *rock crystal*.

crizzling (crisselling) A basic defect in the glass caused by an imperfect proportion of the ingredients in the *batch*, particularly an excess of *alkali*, resulting in a fine network of cracks and the formation of moisture on the surface. Such glass, if incorrectly stored, eventually decomposes and crumbles.

crown glass (bull's-eye pane; Normandy mode) Flat glass made by the process of blowing a bubble of glass, transferring it from the *blow-pipe* to a rod, cutting it open, then rapidly rotating it, with repeated reheatings, until, by centrifugal force, the glass spread into a large flat disk up to 1.2 m in diameter. The glass was then annealed and cut into rectangular- or diamond-shaped pieces that were fairly thin but showed slight convexity and concentric wavy lines caused by rotating, leaving the centre boss or bull's-eye, where the rod had been attached.

cullet Cleansed and broken glass from glass objects discarded during manufacture, and remnants (moil) left on the *blow-pipe* or the *pontil*, melted together with the fresh ingredients of a new *batch*.

cutline In painted glass window design, the tracing of the lead-line pattern from the cartoon.

cylinder glass (broad glass; muff glass) Flat glass made by the process of blowing a large glass bubble and swinging it on the *blow-pipe* to form a long bottle. Both hemispherical ends were then cut off; the resultant cylinder ('muff'), up to 1.5 m in length, was then cut lengthwise with shears and reheated, after which it was flattened using a wooden plane, or by being allowed to sink to a flat state. Cylinder glass showed straight ripples and retained less polish than *crown glass*. The process was called the 'Lorraine method' because it had been used in Lorraine, France, as early as *circa* 1100.

decolorizing agent A mineral, e.g. manganese oxide, used to counteract, in glass, the dark greenish or brownish colour resulting from iron particles in the *silica* (sand) ingredient, or imparted to the *batch* by iron or other impurities in the *pot* or elsewhere in the production process. The decolorizing agent does not remove the colour but acts as a chromatic neutralizer, it and the iron absorbing the light that the other transmits (if in equal quantity); if too much of both is present, little light can be transmitted, and the resultant glass, if thick, becomes grey or blackish.

devitrification The process of converting glass into a crystalline substance by heating the glass to a temperature just below its *liquidus temperature*. Under these conditions part of the glass forms a definite crystal compound, having an opaque appearance.

diamond-point engraving The technique of decorating glass by engraving, using a diamond-point to scratch the surface.

dichromatic glass Glass showing different colours depending on the angle of light falling on it, as when seen by reflected or transmitted light. This is sometimes due to the addition to the *batch* of a tiny percentage of colloidal gold (e.g. the Lycurgus Cup appears red by transmitted light and olive green by reflected light).

dividing iron A medieval tool used in the manufacture of painted glass windows, the tip of which was heated to crack pieces of glass.

églomisé A style of decorating glass by applying gold leaf (occasionally silver leaf, or both) and then engraving it with a fine needle point. Since such work was unfired it would readily rub off. It was therefore usually applied on the reverse of the surface to be viewed, and then protected by a layer of varnish or metal foil or another sheet of glass. Sometimes there is a supplementary background decoration in black or colour where the foil has been removed.

Egyptian blue A blue pigment in which the colour is due to a copper calcium silicate, a synthetic form of the mineral cuprorivarite ($CaO.CuO.4SiO_2 = CaCuSi_4O_{10}$). Silica is usually present in excess. Egyptian blue may be ground and used directly as a pigment, or moulded into objects and refired.

Egyptian faience (faience; composition) A fired silica body containing very small amounts of clay and/or alkali, and varying greatly in hardness depending on the degree of sintering. It is covered with a glaze which may or may not occur interstitially to the silica grains of the body. The term 'glassy faience' is often used to describe a 'faience' in which the degree of melting has proceeded to such an extent that the glass phase defines the visual appearance of the material. The term 'unglazed faience' is used to describe a similar body, also produced by the sintering or partial vitrification of silica particles, probably with a fluxing agent and/or colourant added. Glass may be a minor component. There is no clearly defined glass layer. (The term *frit* is a common synonym for this material.)

enamel colours Enamel colours are *metallic oxides* mixed with a glassy *frit* of finely powdered glass and suspended in an oily medium for ease of application with a brush. The medium burned out during firing in a low temperature muffle kiln (about 500–700°C). Sometimes several firings were required to fix different colours.

enamels See *basse taille*; *champlevé enamel*; *cloisonné enamel*; *painted enamels*.

engraving The process of decorating glass by cutting the design into the surface of the glass by a diamond, metal needle or other sharp implement or a rotating wheel. There were various techniques: *diamond-point engraving*; *wheel-engraving*; *stippling*. Related processes are *etching* and sand-blasting.

etching See *acid etching*.

eye (1) The centre of the *siege* of the glass furnace, the hottest part. (2) The hole (occhio) in the floor of a *lehr* through which heat is transmitted. (3) The coloured tip (pearl) on the *prunts* of some Nuppenbecher and other fifteenth- or sixteenth-century Antwerp and German glassware.

façon de Venise, à la In the style of Venice, as applied to high-quality glassware made throughout Europe, often by emigrant Venetian glassworkers, especially the thin *soda* glass, and glassware decorated in *filigrana* or with ornate embellishments such as winged glasses. It was developed in the mid-sixteenth century and flourished throughout the seventeenth-century.

faience See *Egyptian faience*.

ferramenta See *glazing bar*.

filigrana (vetro filigranato) Literally, thread-grained. A term that has been applied to glassware (with various styles of decoration) of clear glass, made originally at Murano, Italy, *circa* 1527–49, by the use of opaque white or coloured glass threads (or even, occasionally, a single white thread). However, it is now usually used to refer to all styles of decoration on clear glass that are made with a pattern formed by embedded threads of glass.

fire-clay Clay capable of being subjected to a high temperature without fusing, and hence used for making crucibles in which early glass batches were fused. The clay contains much silica, and only small amounts of lime, iron and *alkali*.

fire polish The brilliant surface condition given to glass by heating at the mouth of the furnace (*glory hole*) after the manufacture of a glass object. The process removes the dull surface sometimes imparted to glass by the mould.

firing The process of heating the *batch* in order to fuse it into glass by exposing it to the required degree of heat in a crucible or *pot*; or of reheating unfinished glassware while it is being worked; or of reheating glassware in order to fix *enamel colours* or *gilding*. The melting of the *batch* may require a temperature of 1300–1500°C, and the muffle kiln a temperature of 500–700°C.

flashing The gathering of a small amount of one glass on a much larger gather of a different glass. For example, dense copper ruby glasses were flashed on clear glass in order to dilute the effect of their colour. Flashed glass formed into vessels could have the outer layer(s) cut back to form cameo designs.

flint glass (1) A misnomer for English *lead glass*, probably arising as a result of the evolution of lead glass at a time when calcined or ground flint was substituted for Venetian pebbles as the source of *silica* for making the glass. Later, sand replaced the flint, but the name 'flint glass' has persisted, and is still sometimes used to refer to all English lead glass. (2) In the glass container industry, flint bottles are those which are colourless. (3) In the optical glass industry, flint glasses are those which have a smaller refractive index, for the same dispersion, than *crown glass*.

flux A substance added to *enamel colours* so as to lower their fusion point during firing to below that of the glass body to which they are to be applied. A flux was also added to the *batch* in order to facilitate the fusing of the *silica*. Fluxes include *potash* and *soda*.

founding Modern initial phase of heating the *batch* in the *furnace*, when the materials must be heated to a temperature of about 1400°C, before a maturing period of 12 hours, during which the *molten glass* cools to a working temperature of about 1100°C. Ancient glasses had to be fritted before they could be melted.

free-blown glass (off-hand blown) Glassware shaped solely by the process of blowing with the use of a *blow-pipe* and shaped by manipulation with the tools of the craft (as opposed to *mould-blown*).

frigger Glass objects, of various forms, made by glassmakers in their own time, for their own amusement and home decoration, or for sale. They were usually made from the molten glass remaining in the *pot* at the end of the day, considered as the workmen's perquisite.

frit The granular product of the first stage of ancient *glass-* or *glaze-making*; the raw materials are heated to temperatures around 850°C to produce solid-state reactions between them. When cool, the frit is ground and melted to produce a homogeneous material.

fritting The preheating of raw materials to initiate glass-making reactions and drive off volatile reaction products. The result is a granular material or *frit*. When the frit is ground and reheated, it melts more readily than original *batch* materials.

gaffer The master worker of the team (*chair* or shop) engaged in making glass objects. The gaffer does the most skilled and intricate work and controls the procedure of the team until the object is completed and sent to the *lehr* for annealing.

gather(ing) A blob of molten glass attached to the end of a gathering iron, *blow-pipe* or *pontil*, preparatory to forming a glass object.

gilding The process of decorating glassware, on the surface or on the back of the glass, by the use of gold leaf, gold paint or gold dust. The gilding may be applied with a size, amalgamated with mercury, fired or unfired.

glass A silicate material that has been substantially molten during manufacture, and has been cooled in such a way to remain predominantly non-crystalline. It may include unmelted *batch* materials, devitrification products and intentionally produced opacifiers. It can be formed into an infinite number of self-supporting forms and shapes.

glass forming The heating and reshaping of a piece of glass.

glass-making (fritting) The preparation of the glass *batch* from its basic raw materials.

glass-melting The preparation of molten glass by melting down fragments of *cullet* and *frit*.

glass metal The fused vitreous material, in a molten state, made up of various ingredients (e.g. *silica* and *alkali*) from which glass objects are made. The metal produces glasses of varying characteristics depending on the quality and proportions of the ingredients. The term is regarded as archaic by glass technologists.

glass-of-lead See *lead glass*.

glassmakers' tools The various instruments used by a glass-making team (*chair*) to develop and shape an object, including the *blow-pipe*, *pontil*, gathering iron, pucellas, shears, clapper, woods, pallet, blocking wood, pincers, battledore, lipper and crimper.

glass sensor A sensitive device developed at Würzburg for assessing the aggressiveness of the atmosphere, shown in Figure 7.50.

glaze A discrete layer of glass on a predominantly crystalline body, i.e. a vitreous coating applied to a core or base such as stone or clay, either to make it impermeable and/or for decorative effect.

glazing bar (ferramenta) An iron window bar used to support painted window glass panels.

glory hole A hole in the side of a glass furnace, used when reheating glass which has already been molten, and is in the process of being fashioned or decorated, or ware which having been mould-blown is fire-polished to remove imperfections remaining from the mould.

glyptic Susceptible to carving, especially gems, but also applicable to certain types of glass, as evidenced by incised relief cutting such as *hochschnitt* and *cameo* cutting.

green glass See *bottle glass*.

grisaille (1) Clear glass, ornamented in muted colours (usually including varying shades of grey), with delicate, often foliar patterns and leaded into decorative designs. (2) A brownish paint made with iron oxide that was fused on to the surface of glass to define details in painted glass windows.

grozing Biting away the edge of a piece of glass (usually window glass) with pliers or a hooked grozing iron in order to shape it in a precise manner.

haematinum (haematinon) An opaque blood-red glass in which, under a magnifying glass, the cuprous oxide crystals become visible against a colourless background. It was made in the early Egyptian period and in the Roman period, and was used in enamels and mosaics.

heel ball A black wax composition used in the process of painted glass restoration to make rubbings of glass panels on thin paper.

hinterglasmalerei **(backpainting; mirror painting)** The German term for painting on the back of glass, to be viewed from the front.

hochschnitt Literally, high engraving. The German term for all degrees of relief decoration produced on glass objects by *wheel-engraving*. It is opposite of *tiefschnitt* or *intaglio*. The process involved the making of the design in relief by cutting away the ground, in the manner of a *cameo* relief.

humpen A large and wide, nearly cylindrical, beaker frequently of tinted *waldglass*, with straight sides and a slightly projecting base, and sometimes a cover. They were made of many styles and sizes (some up to 600 mm high) and were used for drinking beer or wine.

hyalith A dense opaque glass, coloured sealing-wax red or jet-black, developed (following the emergence of ruby-red and other strong colours for glass) at glasshouses owned by Count von Buquoy in southern Bohemia from about 1803.

hyaloplastic (Greek: *hyalos*, glass) Relating to the decoration on glassware made by manipulation, e.g. by blowing, *threading*, *trailing*, pincering (rather than by moulding, pressing, cutting, *engraving* etc.).

ice-glass A type of decorative glassware which has a rough irregular outer surface resembling cracked ice. It is produced by plunging the vessel momentarily into cold water during manufacture.

intaglio The style of decoration created by engraving or cutting below the surface of the glass so that the apparent elevations of the design are hollowed out. (An impression taken from the design would yield an image in relief.) The background is not cut away, but is left in the plane of the highest areas of the design.

iridescence The rainbow-like play of different colours, changing according to the angle of view or with the angle of incidence of the source of illumination. The iridescence results from exposure of the glass to adverse conditions and is caused by the diffraction of light from several layers that have air between them.

isothermal glazing On painted glass windows, the system of protective external glazing in which the interspace is ventilated to the interior of the building, in order to equalize, as far as possible, the temperature on both sides of the medieval glass.

kelp A type of seaweed, the calcined ashes of which were formerly used as a source of *soda* in making glass, especially in Normandy (France) and Scandinavia.

kick A deep concavity in the base of a vessel where it has been pushed in by a tool, either to make sure the vessel stands vertically or to reduce the volume of liquid inside.

kiln-oven See *reverberatory furnace*.

knop A component, usually spherical or oblate, of the stem of a drinking glass, made in many styles, hollow or solid, and used either singly or in groups of the same or different types, and placed contiguously or with intermediate spacing.

lachrymae batavicae See *Rupert's drops*.

lampworking See *at-the-flame*.

larmes de verre See *Rupert's drops*.

lead glass (glass-of-lead) A type of glass containing a large percentage of lead oxide. For practical purposes it can be considered to be a late seventeenth-century English development. Lead glass is dense, soft and exceeds potash and soda glass in its brilliance and suitability for facet-cutting. When struck it emits a characteristic ring.

leading-up The act of assembling pieces of glass for window panels with lead strips.

lehr (leer) The oven used for annealing glassware. Early lehrs were connected to the furnace by flues, but the difficulty in controlling heat and smoke made it impracticable. Later the lehr was a long brick-lined separately heated steel tunnel through which the glass objects being annealed were pushed slowly; placed in iron pans on a conveyor the ware remained in the lehr for several hours, while being gradually reheated and then uniformly cooled (modern lehrs work on a conveyor belt system).

lime Calcined limestone, which, added to the glass *batch* in small quantities, gave stability. It originally occurred as impurity in the raw materials before the seventeenth-century when its beneficial effects became known.

lustre painting Painting on the surface of glass with metallic oxide pigments, comparable to lustre painting on pottery, and producing the same metallic effect.

marver (French *marbre*: marble) Flat surface, originally of stone or marble, but later of iron, on which the *gather* of molten glass on the end of a *blow-pipe* or *pontil* is rolled into a globular or cylindrical symmetrical mass. The process is known as marvering.

metallic oxide The oxide of a metal employed as a pigment to colour glass, and in making *enamel colours* to decorate the surface of glass. The resultant colour from any metallic oxide depends on the nature of the glass itself, the purity of its ingredients, and the furnace conditions, i.e. degree of heat or existence of a *reducing* or *oxidizing* atmosphere.

millefiori Literally, a thousand flowers. A style of decorating glass with slices of coloured *canes* embedded in clear molten glass, usually in flower-like designs.

mirror painting See *hinterglasmalerei*.

molten glass Glass in a melted state after fusing the ingredients at a high temperature until the *batch* has become liquid, then allowing it to cool until it reaches the stage when it is *plastic* and ductile.

mosaic As applied to portable glass objects rather than architectural mosaic embedded in cement in floors, walls and ceilings: a glass object formed or decorated with many small adjacent pieces of vari-coloured glass.

mould A form used in shaping glassware by *mould-blown* or *mould-pressed* techniques. Early moulds were of one- or two-piece construction and made of fire-clay, carved wood or stone, and later of metal.

mould-blown Glassware made by the process of blowing the molten glass *paraison* into a *mould*. The interior wall of mould-blown glass is in the shape of the outer form, so that the blown object could be reheated and further blown to enlarge its size.

mould-pressed Glassware made by the process of pressing, as distinguished from *mould-blown* glass.

muff glass See *cylinder glass*.

muffle A *fire-clay* box in which glass (or porcelain) objects were enclosed, when placed in the muffle kiln, to protect them from the flames and smoke while being subjected to low-temperature firing, especially in the process of applying *enamel colours* and fired *gilding* at temperatures of 500–700°C.

natron Sodium sesquicarbonate, obtained from the natron lakes north-west of Cairo, Egypt. It was used as the soda constituent in making Egyptian glass.

network former The material, usually *silica*, forming the parent or basic glass.

network modifier A material used to modify the basic *silica* glass, and thereby lower its melting and working temperatures.

Norman slab A type of window glass made by blowing a gather of glass into a square mould. The square is then cut so that each side becomes a small flat piece of glass. Little used at present.

obsidian A volcanic material which is the earliest form of natural glass used by humans. It is usually black or very dark in colour, but its splinters are transparent or translucent and have a bright lustre.

off-hand blown See *free-blown glass*.

opal glass A translucent white glass, partly opacified with an oxide such as that of tin. Seen by transmitted light it shows brownish or reddish tones ('sunset glow').

opaque enamel An enamel which is not transparent. It was usually produced by adding tin oxide (as in the white glaze on faience, maiolica, and delfware ceramics). When used to decorate the surface of glassware, it was applied thickly and hence palpable. It was the principal medium for decorating glass by enamelling until the development of transparent enamel, *circa* 1810.

opus sectile A *mosaic* panel made of pieces of glass which were not fused together, but were embedded in mortar. See also *revetment*.

oxidation The combination of oxygen with a substance or the removal of hydrogen from it. The term is also used more generally to include any reaction in which an atom loses electrons; e.g. the change of a ferrous ion, Fe^{2+}, to a ferric ion, Fe^{3+}.

painted enamels *Enamel colours* painted on a plain foundation of sheet metal and fired.

paraison A *gather* on a *blow-pipe* after it has been blown into a bubble.

pâte-de-verre Literally, glass paste. A material produced by grinding glass to a paste, adding a fluxing medium so that it would melt readily, and then colouring it. Objects were made of it in a mould and the material was fused by firing.

pattern-moulded glass Glassware that has been blown in a mould whose interior has a raised pattern so that the object shows the pattern with a concavity on the inside underlying the convexity on the outside.

piece-mould A mould made of two or more parts, in which glassware is made in part-size or full-size. A part-size vessel is later expanded by blowing.

plastic Susceptible to being readily modelled or shaped, as glass in a molten state.

polishing The process of giving glass pieces a smooth brilliant surface after an object has been cut or engraved.

pontil The iron-rod to which a partly made molten object is transferred from the *blow-pipe* on which the metal has been gathered, marvered and tentatively blown. When the pontil was removed it left a rough pontil mark on the glass. This mark was polished out on better glassware.

pot A crucible of *fire-clay* in which the *batch* of glass ingredients is fused.

potash Potassium carbonate. It is an alternative to *soda* as a source of *alkali* in the manufacture of glass. Potash glass is slightly heavier than soda glass; it passes from the molten to the rigid state more quickly and is therefore more difficult to manipulate into elaborate forms. However, it is harder and more brilliant and lends itself to decorative techniques of facet-cutting and wheel-engraving.

pressed glass Glassware made by the process of shaping an object by placing a blob of molten glass into a metal *mould* and then pressing it with a metal plunger or 'follower' to form the inside shape. The resultant piece, termed mould-pressed, has an interior form independent of the exterior, in contrast to *mould-blown* glass whose interior corresponds to the outer form.

prunt A blob of glass applied to a glass object as decoration but also to afford a firm grip in the absence of a handle.

purple-of-cassius A crimson-purple colour that was sometimes used to colour glass. The pigment was prepared by precipitating a gold solution by means of chloride of tin and then adding the resultant colloidal gold to the *batch*; the treated glass became ruby-red when reheated to strike the colour.

quarry Square or diamond-shaped pane of glass used particularly in *grisaille* windows.

reamy glass (cord) Irregular streaky glass made from a mixture of glass of different hardnesses and therefore differing refractive indices (its presence indicates that the glass is inhomogeneous).

reducing atmosphere A non-oxidizing condition in the furnace, rich in carbon monoxide, produced by a smoky fire. It affects glass in the crucible, e.g. a red colour is produced by the use of copper (cuprous oxide) in the *batch* in conjunction with a reducing atmosphere, in contrast to an oxidizing (smokeless) atmosphere, which produces a blue-green colour with copper.

refining (French *affinage*) Holding the molten glass at an elevated temperature (well above its liquidus temperature) so that the larger air bubbles can escape.

reverberatory furnace (kiln-oven) An early type of glass-making furnace, somewhat paraboloid in shape, made so that the heat from the burning fuel was reflected downwards from the furnace crown on to the *pots* for maximum efficiency. The pots were arranged around the inside, and above them were openings (bocche), through which the workmen inserted the rods to take out the molten glass; some had a small hole (*glory hole*) for reheating a partially made glass object, giving it a *fire-polish*.

revetment The general term used to describe glass, stone or terracotta elements applied to a wall as pure decoration. Elaborate revetments were termed *opus sectile* in Latin or *skoutlosis* in Greek.

rock crystal Natural quartz, chemically pure *silica*. It is usually colourless and translucent (or nearly so). From earliest times glassmakers sought to imitate it.

rod See *cane*.

rod-formed The the technique of winding molten glass on the tip of a narrow metal tool or wire. Used for making small beads; larger objects required a core material so that the glass did not adhere to the rod.

Rupert's drops (tears glass; *larmes de verre;* **lacrymae batavicae)** Tadpole-shaped hollow glass objects about 50 mm long, having a bulbous end tapering to a thin curved tail. They were made by dropping a small blob of fully molten glass into cold water and leaving it until cooled. They are not affected by a blow to the bulbous end but, if the tail is broken or the surface scratched, the piece, due to different internal stresses, explodes loudly into a fine powder.

sand The most common form of *silica* used in making glass. It is an impure silica, taken from the seashore or preferably from inland beds whose sand is more readily ground and is freer from impurities. It should have a low iron content, and must first be well washed, heated to remove carbonaceous matter, and screened to obtain uniform small grains.

seam mark A slight narrow ridge on a glass object which indicates that it has been made by moulding. The seams appear where the joins in the parts of the mould have permitted molten glass to seep during the process of formation. On well-made pieces the seam marks are usually smoothed away by grinding or fire-polishing.

seed Undissolved tiny bubbles of gases or air that rise to the surface while melting the glass ingredients. They show as tiny specks in the finished glass objects.

shearings (cuttings; clippings) Cuttings of waste glass formed by trimming glassware during manufacture.

siege The floor of the glass furnace on which the *pots* sit.

silica A mineral which is one of the essential ingredients of glass. The most common form of silica used in glass-making was (and still is) *sand*.

silver A metal used in colouring or decorating glass or in backing mirrors. It has been used by various techniques: (1) silver leaf laid between two layers of glass; (2) silver nitrate used to back mirrors and in making silvered glass; (3) silver sulphide used to produce deep-yellow stain or a straw-yellow colour in lustre painting; (4) silver foil; (5) silver used to make silver electroplated glass.

soda Sodium carbonate. It (or alternatively *potash*) is used as the *alkali* ingredient of glass. It serves as a *flux* to reduce the fusion point of the *silica* in making glass. Soda glass is relatively lightweight, and on heating remains plastic and workable over a wider range of temperature than other varieties. Soda glass therefore lends itself to elaborate manipulative techniques.

stannic oxide See *tin oxide*.

stippling The process of decorating glass by striking a diamond or hardened steel point against it, so that the desired image is produced by many tiny shallow dots (stipples) and sometimes short lines, indented in the surface of the glass. The graded dots provide the highlights, the intensity varies with their closeness, and the shadows and background result from leaving the polished glass untouched.

stones Specks of foreign matter, sometimes found in glass.

strain-cracking Deterioration in a glass object, having the appearance of tiny internal cracks in the wall of the object, caused by stresses and strains – sometimes due to faulty *annealing*, or to mechanical damage, but also as a result of loss of alkali from the surface by weathering.

striking The process of reheating glass after it has cooled, in order to develop a colour or an opacifying agent.

tears Air bubbles in the shape of tears, encased in the stem of some drinking glasses or other glassware, or occasionally in the finial of a solid *knop*.

tears glass See *Rupert's drops*.

tesserae Small pieces, usually roughly square, of glass or other suitable material, used in the formation of architectural mosaics.

threading (1) The process of attaching glass threads as independent decoration, to be distinguished from *trailing*, where the threads are applied to the surface of the object. (2) The process of drawing glass threads through molten glass as a method of decoration.

tiefschnitt Literally, deep carving; the opposite of *hochschnitt*. Wheel-engraved decoration on glass where the design is cut below the surface of the glass in the reverse of relief.

tin oxide (stannic oxide) A chemical used to opacify glass in making opaque white glass, and also in making tin oxide glaze for pottery.

trailing The process of applying threads of glass as a decoration on the body, handle or foot of a vessel. It is done by laying or winding softened threads on to a glass object.

twists Decoration in the stems of English drinking glasses produced by twisting a rod of glass in which air-bubbles or threads or tapes of opaque white or coloured glass were embedded.

undercutting The process of decorating glass in high relief by cutting away part of the glass between the body of a piece and its decoration, leaving an intervening open space (see *vasa diatreta*).

vasa diatreta (**cage cups**) Glass vessels in which the body is surrounded by a network or other openwork pattern of glass that is attached by small glass struts.

verre de fougère Literally, fern glass. A primitive type of greenish glass produced in France after the Roman era. The *alkali* ingredient was *potash* derived from burnt bracken (fern).

vetro filigranato See *filigrana*.

vitrification The process of changing the raw materials of which glass is made, into a glassy (vitreous) substance, by heat and fusion at temperatures around 1300–1550°C.

waldglas Literally, forest glass. A primitive type of glass (greenish, yellowish, brownish) produced in the forest glasshouses (*Waldglashutten*) of medieval Germany. The *alkali* ingredient was potash derived from wood ash.

waster A glass which was defective in manufacture, or that became out-of-fashion and hence unsaleable. It was usually discarded and reused as *cullet*.

weathering Changes on the surface of glass (caused by exposure to adverse conditions), which appear as dulling, frosting, *iridescence*, or decomposition.

wheel-engraving A process of decorating the surface of glass with pictorial or formal designs or inscriptions, by the grinding action of a wheel using discs of various materials and sizes with an abrasive in a grease applied to a wheel, as the engraver holds the object against the underside of the rotating wheel.

zwischengoldglas Literally, gold between glass. A type of decoration in which a design in gold leaf was incorporated between two vessels which fitted precisely together.

Bibliography

ACGIH (AMERICAN CONFERENCE OF GOVERNMENTAL INDUST-RIAL HYGENISTS) TLVs Threshold limit values for chemical substances and physical agents in the workroom environment, with intended changes for 1983–84, Ohio

ADAMS, P.B. (1974) Crack propagation in annealed glass during exposure to water. *Proceedings of the 10th International Congress on Glass*, Kyoto, July 1974, pp. 11–16 to 11–23 and 15–100

ADLERBORN, J. (1971) Investigation of weathered glass surfaces with the scanning microscope. *OECD Report on Science Research on Glass*, Ref: DAS/SPR/71.35

ADVF (1976) Association pour la Défense des Vitraux de France, 8-page Manifesto, 76 Rue du Bac, Paris 75007

AGRICOLA (1556) *De re Metallica*, Basle (1556), translated by H.C. & L.H. Hoover, London (1912).

AINSWORTH, L. (1954) The diamond pyramid hardness of glass in relation to the strength and structure of glass. *J. Soc. Glass Technol.* **38**, 479.T–560.T

ALBRIGHT AND WILSON LTD (1978) *The Properties and Applications of Calgon*

ALFREY, T., GURMEE, E.F. and LLOYD, W.C. (1966) Diffusion in glassy polymers. *J. Polymer Sci.* **12**, 249

AMAYA, M. (1967) *Tiffany Glass*, Studio Vista, London

ANDERSON, P.R., BACON, F.R. and BYRUM, B.W. (1975) Effects of surface treatments on the chemical durability and surface composition of soda–lime glass bottles. *J. Non-Cryst. Solids* **19**, 251–263

ANDRÉ, J.M. (1976) *The Restorer's Handbook of Ceramics and Glass*, Van Nostrand, New York; also *Keramic und Glas*, Berlin (1976)

ANKNER, D. (1965) Chemische und physikalische Untersuchungen an vor- und frühgeschichtlichen Gläsern I. *Technische Beiträge zur Archäologie, II*, Mainz

ARNOLD, L. (1978) *The preservation of stone by impregnation with silanes* (Building Research Establishment). In *Council for Places of Worship*, News Letter No. 24, pp. 4–6 and frontispiece

ARRHENIUS, B. (1973) Teknisk verksamhet. *Kungl. Vitterhets historie och antikvitets akademieus årsbok*, pp. 176–182

ARWAS, V. (1977) *Glass: Art Nouveau to Art Deco*, Academy Editions, London

ASAHINA, T-I. and ODA, S. (1954) Shaping of ancient Japanese glass beads. *Sci. Pap. Jpn Antiques* **7**, 10–13

ASAHINA, T-I., YAMAZAKI, F., OTSUKA, I., NAMADA, T., SAITO, K. and ODA, S. (1973) On the colorless glass bottle of Tóshódaiji temple ... β-ray backscattering. *Sci. Pap. Jpn. Antiques*, No. 6, pp. 14–18. Abstract in *Studies in Conservation*, I-314

ASH, D. (1975) *Dictionary of British antique glass*, Pelham Books, London

ASHURST, D. (1970) Excavations at Gawber Glasshouse, near Barnsley. *Post-Medieval Archaeology* **4**, 135–140

ASHURST, D. (1992) *The History of South Yorkshire Glass*, University of Sheffield

ASMUS, J.F. (1975) Use of lasers in the conservation of stained glass. In *Conservation in Archaeology and the Applied Arts*, IIC Conference, Stockholm, pp. 139–142

ASPINALL, A., FEATHER, S.W. and RENFREW, C. (1972a) Neutron activation analysis of Aegean obsidians. *Nature* **273** (June 9th), 333–334

ASPINALL, A., WARREN, S.E., CRUMMETT, J.G. and NEWTON, R.G. (1972b) Neutron activation analysis of faience beads. *Archaeometry* **14**, 27–40

BACHE, E. and HOLLOWAY, D.G. Spontaneous cracking of silica glass in alkaline solutions. *Glass Technol.* **31**, 126–130

BACHER, E. (1967) Die Ornamentschieben aus Spitz. *Osterr. Zeits. Kunst. Denkm.* **21**, 191–192

BACHER, E. (1973a) Aussenschutzverglasung. *CVMA News Letter*, No. 5, Abstract No. 128

BACHER, E. (1973b) Aussenschutzverglasung. *Osterr. Zeits. Kunst. Denkm.* **27**, 66–68

BACHER, E. (1974) Visit by Dr Ernst Bacher to Britain. *CVMA News Letter* No. 11, Nov., p. 2

BACHER, E. (1976a) Air flows in isothermal glazings. *CVMA News Letter*, No. 20, Section 1.3

BACHER, E. (1976b) Reversibility of processes for re-fixing of loose paint. *CVMA News Letter*, No. 24, Abstract No. 256, p.16

BACHER, E. (1978) *CVMA News Letter*, No. 26, item 3.1,5, p.6, Jan.

BACON, F.R. (1968) The chemical durability of silicate glass. *Glass Industry* **49**, 438–439, 442–446, 494–499, 519, 554–559

BACON, F.R. and CALCAMUGGIO, G.L. (1967) 'Effect of heat treatment in moist and dry atmospheres on the chemical durability of soda–lime glass bottles. *Bull. Am. Ceram. Soc.* **46**, 850–855

BACON, F.R. and RAGGON, F.C. (1959) Promotion of attack on glass and silica by citrate and other anions in neutral solution. *J. Am. Ceram. Soc.* **42**, 199–205

BACON, L. and KNIGHT, B. (eds) (1987) *From Pinheads to Hanging Bowls; the Identification, Deterioration and Conservation of Applied Enamel and Glass Decoration on Archaeological Artefacts.* UKIC, London

BAER, N.S. (1984) Risk assessment as applied to the setting of solvent toxicity limits. In *Adhesives and Consolidants*, preprints of the 10th International Congress, Paris. IIC, London

BAKARDJIEV, I. (1977a) Korrosionsuntersuchungen an Gläsern des 17. und 18. Jahrhunderts. *DGG meeting in Frankfurt*, 31 March, 1977 (Abstract No. 274 in *CVMA News Letter* No. 26)

BAKARDJIEV, I. (1977b) Stand der Untersuchungen an 'kranken' Gläsern. *Projektgruppe 'Glas' meeting in Würzburg*, 14 September (see Abstract No. 275 in *CVMA News Letter*, No. 26)

BANNISTER, F.A. (1929) A relation between the density and refractive index of silicate glasses, with application to the determination of imitation gemstones. *Mineralog. Mag.* **22**, 136–154

BARNES, I.L., GRAMLICH, J.W., DIAZ, M.G. and BRILL, R.H. (1978) The possible changes of lead isotope ratios in the manufacture of pigments; a fractionation experiment. In *Archaeological Chemistry. 2. Advances in Chemistry Series 171* ed. G.F. Carter. American Chemical Society, New York, pp. 273–277

BARRELET, J. (1953) *La verrerie en France de l'epoque Gallo–Romaine à nos jours*, Larousse, Paris

BARRERA, W.M. and KIRCH, P.V. (1973) Basaltic glass artefacts from Hawaii: their dating and prehistoric uses. *J. Polynesian Soc.* **2**, 176–187

BARRINGTON HAYNES, E. (1959) *Glass Through the Ages*, Pelican Books, Harmondsworth

BASCOM, W.D. (1974) Surface chemistry of moisture-induced composite failure. In *Interfaces in Polymer Matrix Composites*, ed. E.P. Plueddleman. Academic Press, London, p. 79

BASS, G. (1980) The wreck of the Serçe Liman. *Inst. Nautical Archaeology Newsletter* **7** (2/3), 1–6

BASF (1969) *Technical Leaflet: Ultramid 6A*

BAUER, W.P. (1967a) Untersuchungen Nr. 1. Analysen der Malfarben aus Glasproben des Chorfensters Nord II der Stiftskirche in Heiligenkreuz. *Osterr. Zeits. Kunst. Denkm.* **21**, 201–202

BAUER, W.P. (1967b) Untersuchungen Nr. 2. Analysen von acht Glasproben des Chorfensters Nord II der Stiftskirche in Heiligenkreuz. *Osterr. Zeits. Kunst. Denkm.* **21**, 203–205

BAUER, W.P. (1976) Der Einfluss von Reinigungsmethoden auf die Glasoberfläche (Vorläufige Versuche und mikroskopische Untersuchungen). *Verres et Réfract.* **30**, 62–64. A longer version, in English, is given in *CVMA News Letter* No. 18, item 2, Feb. 1976, and No. 23, Dec. 1976, pp. 12–13

BAUER, W.P. (1984) Kontroluntersuchung der testscheibe A (Viacrylbeschichtung) und der testscheibe D (reinigungsmethoden) von Maria am Gestade. *CVMA News Letter* No. 37/38, Nov. 1984, pp. 21–24

BAYNES-COPE, A.D. (1975) Fungicides and the preservation of waterlogged wood. In *Problems of the Conservation of Waterlogged Wood*, ed. W.A. Oddy. Maritime Monographs 16, National Maritime Museum, Greenwich

BAZAINE, J. and MANESSIER, A. (1976) Notes d'un peintre sur la restauration du Porche Royal de Chartres. In ADVF (1976) *q.v.*

BEALL, G.H. (1978) Microstructure of glass ceramics and photosensitive glasses. *Glass Technol.* **19**, 109–113

BECK, H.C. and STONE, J.F.S. (1936) Faience beads of the British Bronze Age. *Archaeologia* **85**, 203–252

BECKSMANN, R. (1976) Probleme der Restaurierung Spätromanische Glasmalereien. *Kunstchronik* **29**, 330–337. Long abstract (No. 251) in *CVMA News Letter* No. 24, p. 13ff.

BEERS, M.D. (1977) Silicone adhesive sealants. In *Handbook of Adhesives*, ed. I. Skeist. Van Nostrand, Wokingham, p. 628

BERLYE, M.K. (1963) *The Encyclopedia of Working with Glass*, Oceana Publications, New York

BESBORODOV, M.A. (1957) A chemical and technological study of ancient glasses and refractories. *J. Soc. Glass Technol.* **41**, 168–184

BESBORODOV, M.A. and ABDURAZAKOV, A.A. (1964) Newly excavated glassworks in the USSR, 3rd–14th centuries, AD. *J. Glass Stud.* **6**, 64–69

BESBORODOV, M.A. and ZADNEPROVSKY, J.A. (1963) The early stages of glassmaking in the USSR. In *Advances in Glass Technology*, Part 2, ed. F.R. Matson and G.E. Rindone, New York, pp. 291–292

BETTEMBOURG, J.-M. (1972a) Nettoyage par voie chimique et par ultrasons des verres de vitraux. *Compt. Rend. 8e Colloq. CVMA*, York, September, p.47

BETTEMBOURG, J.-M. (1972b) La restauration de vitraux brisés. Vieillissement accéléré de colles, 8 pp typescript, dated 11 March 1972, abstracted in Newton (1982b), Abs. No. 43

BETTEMBOURG, J.-M. (1973) Cleaning of medieval window glass. A statement of his practice in 1973 is given in *CVMA News Letter*, No. 7, item 2.4, p. 3, 7 March 1974

BETTEMBOURG, J.-M. (1975) Étude de mastics élastomeres – le masticage des panneaux de vitraux anciens. *Proceedings of the IIC Congress on Conservation in Archaeology and the Applied Arts*, Stockholm, pp. 137–138

BETTEMBOURG, J.-M. (1976a) Composition et alteration des verres de vitraux anciens. *Verres et Réfract.* **30**, 36–42

BETTEMBOURG, J.-M. (1976b) Protection des verres de vitraux contre les agents atmosphériques. Etude de films de résines synthétiques. *Verres et Réfract* **30**, 87–91

BETTEMBOURG, J.-M. (1977) Problèmes de la conservation des vitraux de la façade occidentale de la cathedrale de Chartres. *Les Monuments Historiques de la France* **No. 1**, 7–13

BETTEMBOURG, J.-M. (1978) Degradation et conservation des vitraux anciens, *Les Dossiers de l'Archéologie* **No. 26**, 102–111, Jan./Feb.

BETTEMBOURG, J.-M. (1980) Climatic factors and corrosion of stained glass windows. Preprints of the *IIC Congress on Conservation within Historic Buildings*, Vienna, 7–13 September, pp. 93–95

BETTEMBOURG, J.-M. and BURCK, J.J. (1974) Restauration des vitraux anciens. Methodes testées par le laboratoire de Recherche des Monuments Historiques, 10 pp typescript, see Abstract on pp. 8–9 of *CVMA News Letter* No. 13, Feb. 1975

BETTEMBOURG, J.-M., BURCK, J.J., ORIAL, G. and PEREZ-Y-JORBA, M. (1983) La degradation des vitraux de St Remi de Reims (Marne). *CVMA News Letter* No. 35/36, pp. 10–17

BETTEMBOURG, J.-M. and PERROT, F. (1976) La restauration des vitraux de la façade occidentale de la cathedrale de Chartres. *Verres et Réfract* 30, 92–95

BETTEMBOURG, J.-M., BURCK, J.J. and HENRY, J.-P. (1984) Effects of mastics on the behaviour of stained glass windows. Preprints of the contributions to the *10th International Congress of the IIC*, September, pp. 195–198

BICKERTON, L.M. (1971) *An Illustrated Guide to Eighteenth Century English Drinking Glasses*, Barrie and Jenkins, London

BIEK, L. (1963) *Archeology under the Microscope*, Lutterworth Press, London

BIEK, L. and BAYLEY, J. (1979) Glass and other vitreous materials. *World Archaeology* 11, 1–25

BIEK, L., CRIPPS, E.S., ANSTIE, J.W. and TEAGLE, W.G. (1955) A new impregnating chamber. *Museums J.* 54, 311–313

BIENEMAN, R.A. (1967) Drying oil caulks. In *Sealants*, ed. A. Damusis. Reinhold

BILLMEYER, F.W. (1971) *Textbook of Polymer Science*, Part II, John Wiley and Sons, Chichester

BIMSON, M. (1975) Coloured glass and *millefiori* in the Sutton Hoo grave deposit. In *The Sutton Hoo Ship Burial 3: The hanging bowls, silver vessels and domestic objects*, ed. A.C. Evans. British Museum Publications, London

BIMSON, M. and FREESTONE, I.C. (1983) An analytical study of the relationship between the Portland Vase and other Roman cameo glasses. *J. Glass Stud.*, 25, 55–69

BIMSON, M. and WERNER, A.E. (1964a) The danger of heating glass objects. *J. Glass Stud.* 6, 148–150

BIMSON, M. and WERNER, A.E. (1964b) Scientific examination of ancient glass. *Ann. 3ᶜ. Cong. Journées Int. Verre*, Damas, pp. 200–209

BIMSON, M. and WERNER, A.E. (1967) Two problems in ancient glass: opacifiers and Egyptian core material *Ann. 4ᵉ. Cong. des Journées Int. du Verre*, Ravenne-Venise, pp. 262–266

BIMSON, M. and WERNER, A.E. (1969) Problems in Egyptian core glasses. *Studies in Glass History and Design*, Sheffield, pp. 121–122

BIMSON, M. and WERNER, A.E. (1971) Notes on a suggested technique for the consolidation of fragile excavated glasses. *Proceedings of the 9th International Congress on Glass*, Versailles. *Art Hist. Comm.* pp. 63–65

BINNS, C.F., KLEM, M. and MOTT, H. (1932) An experiment in Egyptian Blue Glaze. *J. Am. Ceram. Soc.* 15, 271–272

BIRINGUCCIO (1540) Quoted by Turner (1956a) p. 48 T, translated by Smith and Gnudi (1942) *q.v.*

BISHOP, F.L. and MOWREY, F.W. (1952) Deterioration of the surface of sheet glass. *Bull. Am. Ceram. Soc.* 31, 13–15

BLACKSHAW, S.M. (1975) Comparison of different makes of PEG, and results of corrosion-testing of metals in PEG solutions. In *Problems in the Conservation of Waterlogged Wood*. ed. W.A. Oddy. National Maritime Museum Monograph No. 16, Greenwich

BLECK, R.D. (1967–79) *Bibliographie der Archäologisch-Chemischen Literatur*, Weimar, Vol. 1 (1967); Vol. 2 (1968); Vol. 3 (1971); Vol. 4 (1979)

BOCKHOFF, F., GUO, K., RICHARDS, G.E. and BOCKHOFF, E. (1984) Infrared studies of the kinetics of insolubilization of soluble nylon. *Adhesives and Consolidants, Proceedings of the 10th IIC Congress*, Paris, (London IIC), pp. 81–87

BONTEMPS, G. (1868) *Guide du Verrier*, Paris

BOON, G.C. (1966) Roman window glass from Wales. *J. Glass Stud.* 8, 41–45

BOVINI, G. (1964) Les anciens vitraux de l'église Saint-Vital a Ravenne. *Ann. 3ᵉ Cong. Journées Int. du Verre*, Damas AIHV, Liège (1965), pp. 85–90

BOVINI, G. (1967) Actualité de la mosaique. *Ann. 4ᵉ Cong. Int. Journées de Verre*, Ravenne-Venise, pp. 226–229, AIHV, Liège (1968)

BRAIN, C. (1992) Glass reconstruction materials and techniques. *Glass and Enamel Conservation*, UKIC Occasional Papers No. 11, 15–17

BRANDRUP, J. and IMMERGUT, E.H. (1975) *Polymer Handbook*, 2nd edn, Wiley Interscience, Chichester

BREWSTER, D. (1855) On the phenomenon of decomposed glass. *Trans. Br. Assoc. Adv. Sci.* p. 10

BREWSTER, D. (1863) On the structure and optical phenomena of ancient decomposed glass. *Phil. Trans. Roy. Soc., Edin.* 193–204

BRIGHTON, J.T. and NEWTON, R.G. (1986) William Peckitt's red glasses, *Stained Glass* 81, 213–220

BRILL, R.H. (1961) The record of time in weathered glass. *Archaeology* 14, 18–22

BRILL, R.H. (1962) A note on the scientists' definition of glass. *J. Glass Stud.* 4, 127–138

BRILL, R.H. (1963) Ancient glass. *Scientific American* November, pp. 120–130

BRILL, R.H. (1965) The chemistry of the Lycurgus Cup. *Proceedings of the 7th International Congress on Glass*, Brussels, paper No. 223

BRILL, R.H. (1967a) A great glass slab from ancient Galilee. *Archaeology* 20, 88–95

BRILL, R.H. (1967b) Lead isotopes in ancient glass. *Ann. 4ᵉ. Cong. Journ. Int. Verre*, Ravenne-Venise, pp. 255–261

BRILL, R.H. (1967c) Information for persons submitting samples (for lead isotope analyses). *Ann. 4ᵉ. Cong. Journ. Int. du Verre*, Ravenne-Venise, p. 261. AIHV, Liège (1968)

BRILL, R.H. (1968) The scientific examination of ancient glasses. *Proceedings of the 8th International Congress on Glass*, London, pp. 47–68

BRILL, R.H. (1970a) Scientific studies of stained glass: a progress report. *J. Glass Stud.* 12, 185–192

BRILL, R.H. (1970b) Lead and oxygen isotopes in ancient objects. *Phil. Trans. Roy. Soc. Lond.* A.269, 143–164

BRILL, R.H. (1970c) Some chemical observations on the cuneiform glass-making texts. *Ann. 5ᵉ. Cong. Journées Int. du Verre*, Prague, AIHV, Liège, pp. 329–336 (1971)

BRILL, R.H. (1970d) The chemical interpretation of the texts. In *Glass and Glassmaking in Ancient Mesopotamia*, ed. Oppenheim et al. Corning, pp. 105–128

BRILL, R.H. (1971a) A request for help in the conservation of early stained glass windows. *Compt. Rend. IXe Int. Cong. Glass*, Versailles, September, pp. 51–56

BRILL, R.H. (1971b) Scientific investigations of early stained glasses. *Proceedings of the 9th International Congress on Glass*, Versailles. *Art Hist. Comm.* pp. 307–316, 317–321

BRILL, R.H. (1971c) Chemical-analytical round-robin of

four synthetic ancient glasses. *Proceedings of the 9th International Congress on Glass*, Versailles. Art Hist. Comm. pp. 93–110

BRILL, R.H. (1971d) In discussion. *Proceedings of the 9th International Congress on Glass*, Versailles. Art Hist. Comm. p. 90

BRILL, R.H. (1972) Incipient crizzling in some early glasses. *Bull. Am. Group Int. Inst. Cons. Hist. Artistic Works* 12, 46–47

BRILL, R.H. (1973) Analysis of some finds from the Gnalić wreck. *J. Glass Stud* 15, 93–97

BRILL, R.H. (1975) Crizzling – a problem of glass conservation. *IIC Congress on Conservation in Archaeology and the Applied Arts*, Stockholm, pp. 121–134

BRILL, R.H. (1978) The use of equilibrated silica gel for the protection of glass with incipient crazing. *J. Glass Stud.* 20, 100–118

BRILL, R.H., BARNES, I.L. and ADAMS, B. (1974) Lead isotopes in some ancient Egyptian objects. In *Recent Advances in Science and Technology of Materials*, Vol. 3, ed. A. Bishay. Plenum Press, New York, pp. 9–25

BRILL, R.H., FLEISCHER, R.L., PRICE, P.B. and WALKER, R.M. (1964) The fission-track dating of man-made glasses: preliminary results. *J. Glass Stud.* 6, 151–155

BRILL, R.H. and HANSON, V.F. (1976) Chemical analyses of Amelung glasses. *J. Glass Stud.* 18, 216–238

BRILL, R.H. and HOOD, H.P. (1961) A new method of dating ancient glass. *Nature* 189, 12–14

BRILL, R.H. and MOLL, S. (1961) The electron beam probe microanalysis of ancient glass. *Recent Advances in Conservation*, Butterworths, Guildford, pp. 145–151. (Also in shortened version *Advances in Glass Technology* (1963) pp. 293–302.)

BRILL, R.H., SHIELDS, W.R. and WAMPLER, J.M. (1970) New directions in lead isotope research. *Application of Science in Examination of Works of Art*, ed. W.J. Young, pp. 73–84

BRILL, R.H. and WOSINSKI, J.F. (1965) A huge slab of glass in the ancient necropolis of Beth She'arim'. *Proceedings of the 7th International Congress on Glass*, Brussels, paper No. 219

BROCKWAY GLASS CO., INC. (1967) *US Patent* No. 3314772, 18 April (Abstract No. 78 in Newton, 1982b)

BROMMELLE, N.S., PYE, E.M., SMITH, P. and THOMSON, G. (eds) (1984) *Adhesives and Consolidants*. Preprints of the 10th Int. IIC Congress, Paris

BROOKS, J.A. (1973) *Glass: 100 masterpieces of crystal and colour*. Sampson Low

BROOKS, R.R. (1972) *Geobotany and Biogeochemistry in Mineral Exploitation*, Harper & Row, New York

BROWN, S.L. (1928) The structure of lead as related to stained glass. *J. Br. Soc. Master Glass Painters*, 2, 123–128

BROWNE, T.D. (1974) The treatment of hydrofluoric acid burns. *J. Soc. Occup. Med.* 24, 80

BROWNING, E. (1965) *Toxicology and Metabolism of Industrial Solvents*, Elsevier, Amsterdam

BRUCE, J. (1979) *Work in progress: Glassblowing – a manual of basic techniques*. Crafts Council and Jane Bruce

BRUCE-MITFORD, R. (1975) *The Sutton Hoo Ship Burial, 3: The Hanging Bowls, Silver Vessels and Domestic Objects*. British Museum Publications, London

BRYANT, G.F. (1973) Experimental Romano-British kiln

firings. *CBA Research Report No. 10*, pp. 149–160

BRYDSON, J.A. (1989) *Plastics Materials*, 5th edn, Butterworths, Guildford

BUILDING RESEARCH ESTABLISHMENT (1977) *Control of Lichens, Moulds, and Similar Growths*, Building Research Establishment, Garston, Watford

BUDD, S.M. (1975) ESCA examination of tin oxide coatings on glass surfaces. *J. Non-Cryst. Solids* 19, 55–64

BURRELL, H. (1955) Solubility parameters, I and II. *Interchem. Rev.* 14, 3, 31

BURRELL, H. (1970) Solubility of polymers. In *Encyclopedia of Polymer Science*, Vol. 12, p. 618

BURRELL, H. (1975) Solubility parameter values. In *Polymer Handbook*, eds J. Brandrup and E.H. Immergut. Wiley Interscience, Chichester, p. iv–337

CABLE, M. (1979) Personal communications

CABLE, M. and SMEDLEY, J.W. (1987) Liquidus temperatures and melting characteristics of some early container glasses. *Glass Technol.* 28, 94–98

CALEY, E.R. (1962) *Analyses of Ancient Glasses, 1790–1957*, Vol. 1, Corning Museum of Glass, New York, Monographs

CALLMER, J. (1977) *Trade Beads and Bead Trade in Scandinavia, ca 800–1000 AD*, Acta Archaeologica Ludensia, Lund, Sweden

CAMERON, G.M. and MARSDEN, J.G. (1972) Silane coupling agents. *Chemistry in Britain* 8, 381–385

CANN, J.R. and RENFREW, C. (1964) The characterization of obsidian and its application to the Mediterranean region. *Proc. Prehist. Soc.* 30, 111–133. Reprinted with new introduction in Renfrew, C. *Problems in European Prehistory*, Edinburgh, pp. 65–86

CASSIDY, P.E. and YAGER, B.J. (1972) Coupling agents as adhesion promoters. In *Reviews in Polymer Technology*, Vol. 1, ed. I. Skeist. Dekker, New York, p. 1

CAVINESS, M.H. (1971) *Report on the Conservation of the Stained Glass of Canterbury Cathedral* 22 pp typescript, unpublished (Abstract No. 82 in Newton, 1982b)

CAVINESS, M.H. (1972) Saving Canterbury's medieval glass. *Country Life*, September, pp. 739–740. (Abstract No. 83 in Newton, 1982b)

CHAMBON, R. (1963) L'evolution des procedes de fabrication manuelle du verre a vitres du dixieme sièle a nos jours. In *Advances in Glass Technology* Part 2, eds F.R. Matson and G.E. Rindone. Plenum Press, New York, pp. 165–178

CHANCE, H. (1968) The Nailsea Glassworks. In *Studies in Glass History and Design*, Sheffield, pp. 33–39

CHANCE, J.F. (1919) *A History of the Firm of Chance Brothers & Co., Glass and Alkali Manufacturers*, privately printed, London

CHAPPELL, R.A. and STODDART, C.T.H. (1974) An Auger electron spectroscopy study of float glass surfaces. *Phys. Chem. Glasses* 15, 130–136

CHARLES, R.J. (1958) Static fatigue in glass, I. *J. Appl. Phys.* 29, 1549–1553

CHARLES, R.J. (1971) The origin of depression constants of glass thermometers. *Glass Technol.* 12, 24–26

CHARLESTON, R.J. (1958) Glass. In *A History of Technology*, Vol. III, *From the Renaissance to the Industrial Revolution, c. 1500–c.1750*, eds C. Singer et al. Oxford

CHARLESTON, R.J. (1959a) English glass-making and its spread from the XVIIth to the middle of the XIXth

Century. *Ann. 1ᵉʳ Cong. Int. Journées du Verre*, Liège, pp. 155–165

CHARLESTON, R.J. (1959b) The Luck of Edenhall. *The Connoisseur*, February, p. 35

CHARLESTON, R.J. (1960) Lead in glass. *Archaeometry* **3**, 1–4

CHARLESTON, R.J. (1962) Some tools of the glassmaker in medieval and renaissance times with special reference to the glassmaker's chair. *Glass Technol.* **3**, 107–111

CHARLESTON, R.J. (1963) Glass 'cakes' as raw material and articles of commerce. *J. Glass Stud.* **5**, 54–67

CHARLESTON, R.J. (1964) Wheel-engraving and -cutting: some early equipment. I. Engraving. *J. Glass Stud.* **6**, 83–100

CHARLESTON, R.J. (1965) Wheel-engraving and -cutting: some early equipment. II. Water-power and cutting. *J. Glass Stud.* **7**, 41–54

CHARLESTON, R.J. (1967) The transport of glass in the 17th–18th centuries. *Ann. 4ᵉ Cong. Journées Int. du Verre*, Ravenne-Venise, May, pp. 183–192, AIHV, Liège 1968

CHARLESTON, R.J. (1972) Enamelling and gilding on glass. In *Glass Circle 1*, eds R.J. Charleston, W. Evans and A. Polak, Newcastle, pp. 18–32

CHARLESTON, R.J. (1977a) Introduction to the catalogue. In *The James A. De Rothschild Collection at Waddesdon Manor, Glass and Enamels*, eds R.J. Charleston, M. Archer and M. Marcheix, Fribourg, pp. 31–34

CHARLESTON, R.J. (1977b) A brief survey of the history of glass and glassmaking. In *An Illustrated Dictionary of Glass*, ed. H. Newman. Thames & Hudson, London, pp. 9–14

CHARLESTON, R.J. (1978) Glass furnaces through the ages. *J. Glass Stud.* **20**, 9–33

CHARLESWORTH, D. (1968) The dating and distribution of Roman cylindrical bottles. In *Studies in Glass History and Design*, Sheffield, pp. 6–8

CHARLESWORTH, D. (1977) Roman window glass from Chichester, Sussex. *J. Glass Stud.* **19**, 182

CHASE, W.T. (1971) Egyptian blue as a pigment and ceramic material. *Science and Archaeology*, ed R.H. Brill, MIT Press, Cambridge, Mass., pp. 80–91

CHEMICAL DURABILITY COMMITTEE of the Society of Glass Technology (1966) The effect of temperature on the water-extraction of alkali from glass. *Glass Tech.* **7**, 35–41

CHIRNSIDE, R.C. and PROFFITT, P.M.C. (1965) The Rothschild Lycurgus Cup: An analytical investigation. *J. Glass Stud.* **5**, 18–23; *Proceedings of the 7th International Congress on Glass*, Brussels (1965), Paper No. 222

CIBA-GEIGY (1970) *Epoxy Adhesive Resins*, Instruction Sheet No. A26F

CIBA-GEIGY (1978) *Araldite Bonding, Surface Preparation and Pretreatments*, Instruction Manual A-15

CLARK, D.E., PANTANO, C.G. and HENCH, L.L. (1979) *Corrosion of Glass*, Books for Industry, New York

CLARK-MONKS, C. and PARKER, J.M. (1980) *Stones and Cord in Glass*, Society of Glass Technology, Sheffield

COHEN, A.J. (1963) Fossil glasses produced by meteorites and asteroids with the planet earth. In *Advances in Glass Technology*, Part 2, eds F.R. Matson and G.E. Rindone. Plenum Press, New York, pp. 360–375

COLE, F.W. (1972) The state of 'Adam Delving'. *Compt*

Rend 8e Colloque CVMA, Canterbury, September, pp. 31–32 (Abstract No. 95 in Newton, 1982b)

COLE, F.W. (1975) Reversibility of an epoxy resin. *CVMA News Letter*, No. 15, Section 1.6, June

COLE, F.W. (1979) Problems of conservation and restoration at Canterbury Cathedral. *CVMA News Letter*, No. 30, pp 2–3 (Abstract No. 412 in Newton, 1982b)

COLLONGUES, R. (1974) Sur le phénomène de corrosion des vitraux. *ENSCP Convention*, March, 11 pp typescript

COLLONGUES, R.W. (1977) La corrosion des vitraux. *Les Monuments Historiques de la France*, No. 1, pp. 14–16

COLLONGUES, R. and PEREZ-Y-JORBA, M. (1973) Sur le phénomène de corrosion des vitraux: Part I (Abstract No. 182 in *CVMA News Letter*, No. 13, February

COLLONGUES, R., PEREZ-Y-JORBA, M., TILLOCA, G. and DALLAS, J.-P. (1976) Nouveaux aspects du phénomène de corrosion des vitraux anciens des églises francaises. *Verres et Réfract* **30**, 43–55

CONRADT, R. and SCHOLZE, H. (1984) Glass corrosion in aqueous media – a still unsolved problem. *Riv. della Staz. Sper. del Vetro* **15**, 73–77

COOVER, H.W. and WICKER, T.H. (1964) 2-Cyanoacrylate adhesives. In *Encyclopedia of Polymer Science*, eds H.F. Mark, N.G. Gaylord and N.M. Bikales, Vol. VI. p. 337

CORNING, (1976) *Conservation of opus sectile panels from Kenchreai*, unpublished work report

COWARD, J.N. and TURNER, W.E.S. (1938) The clouding of soda–lime–silica glass in atmospheres containing sulphur dioxide. *J. Soc. Glass Technol.* **22**, 309.T–323.T

COWELL, M.R. and WERNER, A.E. (1973) Analysis of some Egyptian glass. *Ann. 6ᵉ. Cong. Assoc. Int. Verre*, Cologne, pp. 295–298

COX, G.A. and COOPER, G.I. (1995) Stained glass in York in the mid-sixteenth century: analytical evidence for its decay. *Glass Technol.* **36**(4), 129–134

COX, G.A. and FORD, B.A. (1989) The corrosion of glass on the sea bed. *J. Mat. Sci.* **24**, 3146–3153

COX, G.A. and GILLIES, K. (1986) *Archaeometry* **28**, 57–68

COX, G.A. and POLLARD, A.M. (1977) X-ray fluorescence analysis of ancient glass: the importance of sample preparation. *Archaeometry* **19**, 45–54

COX, G.A., HEAVENS, O.S., NEWTON, R.G. and POLLARD, A.M. (1979) A study of the weathering behaviour of medieval glass from York Minster. *J. Glass Stud.* **21**, 54–75

CRAMP, R. (1968) Glass finds from the Anglo-Saxon Monastery of Monkwearmouth and Jarrow. *Studies in Glass History and Design*, pp. 16–19

CRAMP, R. (1970) Decorated window glass, and millefiori, from Monkwearmouth. *Antiq. J.* **50**, 327–335

CRAMP, R. (1975) Window glass from the monastic site of Jarrow. Problems of interpretation. *J. Glass Stud.* **17**, 88–95

CRONYN, J.M. (1987) Principles of conservation of enamels. In *From Pinheads to Hanging Bowls; the Identification, Deterioration and Conservation of Applied Enamel and Glass Decoration on Archaeological Artefacts*, eds. L. Bacon and B. Knight. UKIC, London

CROSSLEY, D.W. (1967) Glassmaking in Bagot's Park, Staffordshire, in the sixteenth century. *Post-Medieval Archaeology* **1**, 44–83

CROSSLEY, D.W. (1972) The performance of the glass industry in sixteenth-century England. *Economic History*

Review, 2nd ser. **25**, 421–433

CROSSLEY, D.W. and ABERG, F.A. (1972) Sixteenth century glassmaking in Yorkshire; excavations of furnaces at Hutton and Rosedale, North Riding, 1968–71. *Post-Medieval Archaeology* **6**, 107–159

CROSTHWAITE, C.D. and CRAWFORD, A.S. (1973) *A study of the internal environment of cathedrals with particular reference to St. Pauls*. Paper to British Association for the Advancement of Science, August

CROWLEY, J.D., TEAGUE, G.S. and LOWE, J.E. (1966,1967) A three-dimensional approach to solubility. *J. Paint Technol.* **38**, 269; **39**, 19

CULLIS, C.F. and HIRSCHLER, M.M. (1979) Emissions of sulphur into the atmosphere. In *International Symposium on Sulphur Emissions and the Environment*. Society of Chemical Industry, London, pp. 1–24

CUMMINGS, K. (1980) *The Technique of Glass Forming*, Batsford Press, London

CVMA (1958) Corpus Vitrearum Medii Aevi, *Directives de 1958, Système de hachures pour les dessins schématiques*. Table p. 28, Comité International d'Histoire de l'Art, Union Académique Internationale.

DABBS, M.D.G. and PEARSON, E.F. (1970) The variation in refractive index and density across two sheets of window glass. *J. Forensic Sci. Soc.* **10**, 139–148

DABBS, M.D.G. and PEARSON, E.F. (1972) Some physical properties of a large number of window glass specimens. *J. Forensic Sci.* **17**, 70–78

DAMUSIS, A. (1967) *Sealants*, Reinhold

DANIELS, V.D., PASCOE, M.W. and HOLLAND, L. (1978) Plasma reactions in the conservation of antiquities. *5th Triennial Meeting of the ICOM Committee for Conservation*

DANNEBERG, H. and MAY, C.A. (1969) Epoxide adhesives. In *Treatise on Adhesives*, Vol. 2 ed. R.L. Patrick, Dekker, New York, 78–23–1

DAS, C.R. and DOUGLAS, R.W. (1967) Studies on the reaction between water and glass. Part 3. *Phys. Chem. Glasses* **8**, 178–184

DAVIDSOHN, A. and MILWIDSKY, B.M. (1978) *Synthetic Detergents*, 6th edn, Godwin, London and John Wiley, New York

DAVIS, D.C. (1972) *English Bottles and Decanters 1650–1900*, Charles Letts, London

DAVIS, P. (1949) *The Development of the American Glass Industry*, Harvard, Cambridge, Mass.

DAVISON, S. (1978) The problems of restoring glass vessels. *The Conservator* **2**, 3–8

DAVISON, S. (1981) New materials in the service of glass restoration. *Annales du 8ᵉ Congres Int. d'Etude Histoire du Verre*, Liège, 369–375

DAVISON, S. (1984) A review of adhesives and consolidants used on glass antiquities. *Preprints of the contributions to the 10th International Congress of the IIC*, September, pp. 191–194

DAVISON, S. (1988) Cut glass chandeliers; dismantling, cleaning, recording and restoring. *Preprints of the contributions to the UKIC 30th Anniversary Conference*, 90–93

DAVISON, S. (1992) The conservation of a Louis XIV glass table top. *Glass and Enamel Conservation*, UKIC Occasional Papers No. 11, 3–5

DAVISON, S. and JACKSON, P.R. (1985) The restoration of flat glass: four case studies. *The Conservator* **9**, 10–13

DAWSON, P.T., HEAVENS, O.S. and POLLARD, A.M. (1978) Glass surface analysis by Auger electron spectroscopy. *J. Phys. C: Sol. Stat. Phys.* **11**, 2183–2193

DAY, R.K. (1953) *Glass Research Methods*, Industrial Publications Inc., Chicago

DE BRUYNE, N.A. (1976) *Extent of Contact Between Glue and Adherend*, Aero Research, Tech. Notes, Bull. 168, Duxford, Cambridge: quoted in Wake (1976) p.38

DEKÓWNA, M. (1967) Remarques sur les méthodes d'examen de perles de verre du Haut Moyen Age, trouvées en Pologne. *Ann. 4ᵉ Cong. Journées Int. du Verre*, Ravenne-Venise, AIHV, Liège, pp. 147–161

DEKÓWNA, M. (1980) Methods of examining ancient glasses. *Unconventional Archaeology: New Approaches and Goals in Polish Archaeology*, 213–233

DEKÓWNA, M. and SZYMANSKI, A. (1970) Recherches sur les techniques d'exécution des objets du verre anciens par les méthodes pétrographiques. *Ann. 5ᵉ Cong. Assoc. Int. Verre*, Prague, 337–351

DELMONTE, J. (1965) *The Technology of Adhesives*, Hafner. Reprint of 1947 edition

DE LOLLIS, N.J. and MONTOYA, O. (1967) Mode of failure in structural adhesives. *J. Appl. Polymer Sci.* **11**, 983

DE WITTE, E. (1975) Soluble nylon as a consolidation agent for stone. *Studies in Conservation* **20**, 30–34

DE WITTE, E., GOESSENS-LANDRIE, M., GOETHALS, E.J. and SIMONDS, R. (1978) The structure of 'old' and 'new' Paraloid B-72. *5th Triennial Meeting of the ICOM Committee for Conservation*, 78–16–3

DIDEROT (1751–71) *Dictionnaire Raisonné des Sciences, des Arts, et des Metiérs*, Diderot, Paris

DILLON, E. (1907) *Glass*, London

DIMBLEBY, G.W. (1978) *Scientific Treatment of Material from Rescue Excavations*, Report of the Working Party of Ancient Monuments and Buildings, Department of the Environment

DODWELL, C.R. (1961) *The Various Arts*, Nelson, London. (Translation of Theophilus' *De Diversis Artibus*.)

DOMASLOWSKI, W. and KWIATOWSKI, E. (1962) Probleme der Konservierung von Glasmalereien. *Ann. 2nd Cong. Journées Int. du Verre*, Leyden, June, AIHV, Liège, pp. 137–151

DOPPELFELD, A. (1965) Die Kölner Glasöfen vom Eigelstein. *Proceedings of the 7th International Congress on Glass*, Brussels, New York, Paper No. 236, 4 pp.

DORAN, W.E. and HODSON, F.R. (1975) *Mathematics and Computers in Archaeology*, Edinburgh

DOREMUS, R.H. (1973) *Glass Science*, New York

DOSSIE, R. (1758) *The Handmaid to the Arts*, London (1758 and 1764)

DOUGLAS, R.W. (1958) Some comments on indentation tests on glass. *J. Soc. Glass Technol.* **42**, 145.T–157.T

DOUGLAS, R.W. (1966) Glasses and time. *Br. J. Appl. Phys.* **17**, 435–448

DOUGLAS, R.W. and FRANK, S. (1972) *A History of Glassmaking*, Foulis, Henley-on-Thames

DOUGLAS, R.W. and ISARD, J.O. (1949) Action of water and of sulphur dioxide on glass surfaces. *J. Soc. Glass Technol.* **33**, 289–335

DOVE, S. (1981) Conservation of glass-inlaid bronzes and lead curses from Uley, Gloucestershire. *The Conservator* **5**, 31–35. UKIC, London

DOWMAN, E.A. (1970) *Conservation in Field Archaeology*,

Methuen, London (out of print)

DRACHENBERG, E. (1988) Les vitrages protecteurs en RDA. *CVMA News Letter* No. 41/42, pp. 15–17

DRAKE, M. (1912) *A History of English Glass Painting, With Some Remarks upon the Swiss Glass Miniatures of the 16th and 17th Centuries*, T.W. Laurie, London

DUKES, W.A. and GREENWOOD, L. (1975) An adhesive system for an appliqué glass screen out of doors. *Aspects of Adhesion*, Vol. 8, Ch. 5, pp. 92–111

DUNCAN, G.S. (1960) *Bibliography of Glass (from the earliest records to 1940)*, Dawsons, London

DURHAM, K. (1961) *Surface Activity and Detergents*, Macmillan, London

DURRANS, T.H. (1971) *Solvents*, Chapman & Hall, London

DUVE, G., FUCHS, O. and OVENBECK, H. (1975) *Hoechst Solvents*, 5th edn, Hoechst

EEC (1976) European Economic Commission, *Directive relating to materials and articles intended to come into contact with foodstuffs*, Reference: 76/893/EEC, November; this has now been followed by other Directives

EL-SHAMY, T.M. (1973a) The chemical durability of K_2O–CaO–MgO–SiO_2 glasses. *Phys. Chem. Glasses* 14, 1–5

EL-SHAMY, T.M. (1973b) The rate-determining step in the dealkalization of silicate glasses. *Phys. Chem. Glasses* 14, 18–19

EL-SHAMY, T.M. and AHMED, A.A. (1977) Corrosion of some common silicate glasses by aqueous solutions. *Proceedings of the 11th International Congress on Glass*, Prague, July, Vol. III, pp. 181–195

EL-SHAMY, T.M. and DOUGLAS, R.W. (1972) Kinetics of the reaction of water with glass. *Glass Technol.* 13, 77–80

EL-SHAMY, T.M., LEWINS, J. and DOUGLAS, R.W. (1972) The dependence on the pH of the decomposition of glasses by aqueous solutions. *Glass Technol.* 13, 81–87

EL-SHAMY, T.M., MORSI, S.E., TAKI-ELDIN, H.D. and AHMED, A.A. (1975) Chemical durability of Na_2O–CaO–SiO_2 glasses in acid solutions. *J. Non-Cryst. Solids* 19, 241–250

ELVILLE, E.M. (1951) *English Table Glass*, Country Life, London, Ch. 14, pp. 256–266

ELVILLE, E.M. (1953) *English and Irish Cut Glass, 1750–1950*, Country Life, London

ELVILLE, E.M. (1961) *A Collector's Dictionary of Glass*, London

EMELEUS, V.M. (1960) Beta-ray backscattering: A simple method for the quantitate determination of lead oxide in glass, glaze and pottery. *Archaeometry* 3, 5–9

ENGLE, A. (1973a) 3000 years of glassmaking on the Phoenician Coast. *Readings in Glass History*, No. 1, Phoenix Publications, Jerusalem, pp. 1–26

ENGLE, A. (1973b) A semantic approach to glass history. *Readings in Glass History*, No. 1, Phoenix Publications, Jerusalem, pp. 81–84

ENGLE, A. (1974a) The De Gands of Ghent. *Readings in Glass History*, No. 4, Phoenix Publications, Jerusalem, pp. 42–54

ENGLE, A. (1974b) Mayer Oppenheim 'de Bermingham'. *Readings in Glass History*, No. 4, Phoenix Publications, Jerusalem, pp. 61–71

ENGLE, A. (1975) The glassmakers' charter. *Readings in Glass History*, No. 5, Phoenix Publications, Jerusalem, pp.18–22

ENGLE, A. (1978) *Readings in Glass History*, No 10, Phoenix Publications, Jerusalem

ERACLIUS (pre AD 1000) Eraclius, *De coloribus et artibus Romanorum*. See Merrifield (1849), *Original Treatises, etc.*

ERDE (1973) Explosives Research and Development Establishment, How they saved the Churchill Window. *Plastics and Rubber Weekly* March 9, p. 12

ERNSBERGER, F.M. (1959) Attack of glass by chelating agents. *J. Am. Ceram. Soc.* 42, 373–375

ERNSBERGER, F.M. (1977) Mechanical properties of glass. *Proceedings of the 11th International Congress on Glass*, Prague, *Survey Papers*, Vol. I, pp. 293–321

ERNSBERGER, F.M. (1980) The role of molecular water in the diffusive transport of protons in glasses. *Phys. Chem. Glasses* 21, 146–149

ERRETT, R.F. (1972) The repair and restoration of glass objects. *Int. Inst. Cons., Amer. Gp.* No. 12, 48–49, Washington

ERRETT, R.F., LYNN, M. and BRILL, R.H. (1984) The use of silanes on glass. In *Adhesives and Consolidants, Proceedings of the 10th IIC Congress*, Paris; IIC, London, pp. 185–190

ESCRITT, J. and GREENACRE, M. (1972) Note on toxic gases in polyurethane foam. *Studies in Conservation* 17, 134

ETHRIDGE, E.C., CLARK, D.E. and HENCH, L.L. (1979) Effects of glass surface area to solution volume ratio on glass corrosion. *Glass Technol.* 20, 35–40

EUROPEAN SCIENCE FOUNDATION (1976) *Report 1976*, Strasbourg, France

EVANS, D. (1982) *A Bibliography of Stained Glass*, Boydell & Brewer, Woodbridge, Suffolk

FELLER, R.L. (1967) Research on durable thermoplastic polymers. *Estatto dagli atti della Riunione della SIPS*

FELLER, R.L. (1971a) Solvents. In *On Picture Varnishes and their Solvents*, eds R.L. Feller, N. Stolow and E.H. Jones, 2nd edn. Case Western Reserve University Press

FELLER, R.L. (1971b) Properties of a mature varnish. In *On Picture Varnishes and their Solvents*, eds R.L. Feller, N. Stolow and E.H. Jones, 2nd edn. Case Western Reserve University Press

FELLER, R.L. (1972) Problems in the investigation of picture varnishes. In *Conservation of Painting and the Graphic Arts*, Proceedings of the IIC Conference, Lisbon, pp. 201–209

FELLER, R.L., STOLOW, N. and JONES, E.H. (eds) (1971) *On Picture Varnishes and their Solvents*, 2nd .edn, Case Western Reserve University Press

FEMENELLA, A.J. (1994) Restoring stained glass paint. *Stained Glass* 89(1), 42–47, 54–58

FERRAZZINI, J.C. (1974) *Die Überwachung der Korrosion mittelalterlicher Glasgemälde – Ein Vorschlag*. (Abstract No. 138 in Newton, 1982b)

FERRAZZINI, J.C. (1975) Reaction mechanisms of corrosion of medieval glass. *IIC Congress on Conservation in Archaeology and the Applied Arts*, Stockholm, p. 135

FERRAZZINI, J.C. (1976a) L'influence de la corrosion sur la vitesse de décomposition des verres du Moyen Age. *Verres et Réfract.* 30, 26–29

FERRAZZINI, J.C. (1976b) Eine neue Methode zur Konservierung von Glasgemälden. *Weltkunst*, No. 6, 15 March, p. 508

FERRAZZINI, J.C. (1976c) Vorteile und Technik der Anwendung von Cyanoacrylat-Monomer-Klebstoffen zur sicherung der Malerei von Glasgemälden. *Glastech. Ber.* 49, 264–268

FERRAZZINI, J.C. (1976d) Die Anwendung von Cyanoacrylat-Monomer-Klebstoffen in der Glasrestaurierung. *Inf. Bull. Assoc. Museums in Switzerland* **16**, 5-10

FERRAZZINI, J.C. (1977a) Untersuchungen über eine neue in Chartres angewandte Methode zur Reinigung von mittelalterlichen Glasgemälden. *Maltechnik* **83**, 145-154. (Abstract in *CVMA News Letter*, No. 23, item 3.2, 3 December, 1976

FERRAZZINI, J.C. (1977b) Chemische und Physikalische Aspekte des Zerfalls mittelälterlicher Glasgemälde. *DGG Meeting in Frankfurt*, 31 March. (Abstract No. 279 in *CVMA News Letter*, No. 26.)

FIORENTINI-RONCUZZI, I. (1967) Traditions et progrès dans les materiaux vitreux de la mosaique. *Ann. 4e Cong. Int. Journées du Verre*, Ravenne-Venise. AIHV, Liège, pp. 230-238

FIORENTINI-RONCUZZI, I. (1970) Dating and analysis of mosaics. *Ann. 5e Cong. Assn. Int. Hist. du Verre*, Prague. AIHV, Liège, pp. 353-356

FIORENTINO, P. and BORELLI, L.V. (1975) A preliminary note on the use of adhesives and fillers in the restoration of glass. *Studies in Conservation* **20**, 201-205

FISHER, P. (1988) Advances in the restoration of glass vessels. *Preprints of the contributions to the UKIC 30th Anniversary Conference*, 81-83

FISHER, P. (1992) HXTAL NYL-1, an epoxy resin for the conservation of glass. *Glass and Enamel Conservation*, UKIC Occasional Papers No. 11, 6-9

FISCHER, P. and NORMAN, K. (1987) A new approach to the reconstruction of two Anglo-Saxon beakers. *Studies in Conservation*, 32. IIC, London, pp. 49-58

FITZ, S. (1981) A new method of cleaning browned Medieval glass. *Proceedings of the ICOM Committee for Conservation, 6th Triennial Meeting*, Ottawa

FITZ, S., FITZ-ULRICH, E., FRENZEL, G., KRÜGER, R. and KÜHN, H. (1984) *Die Einwirkung von Luftverunreinigungen auf ausgewählte Kunstwerke mittelalterliche Glasmalerei*, Deutsches Museum, Munich

FLETCHER, W.W. (1972) The chemical durability of glass. A burial experiment at Ballidon in Derbyshire. *J. Glass Stud.* **14**, 149-151

FLINDERS PETRIE, SIR W.M. (1894) *Tell el Amarna*, London

FLORIAN, M.L.E. (1979) letter to R.G. Newton, dated 16 February (1987)

FOLEY, K. and HUNTER, K. (1987) The Lincoln Hanging Bowl. In *From Pinheads to Hanging Bowls; the Identification, Deterioration and Conservation of Applied Enamel and Glass Decoration on Archaeological Artefacts*, eds L. Bacon and B. Knight. UKIC, London

FORBES, R.J. (1957) *Studies in Ancient Technology*, Leyden

FORBES, R.J. (1961) Glass throughout the ages. *Philips Tech. Rev.* **22**, 282-299

FOWLER, J. (1881) On the process of decay in glass, and, incidentally, on the composition and texture at different periods, and the history of its manufacture. *Archaeologia* **46**, 65-162

FRANK, S. (1982) *Glass and Archaeology*, Academic Press, London

FRANK, S. (1984) Gold ruby glass. *Glass Technol.* **25**, 47-50

FREIMAN, S.W. (1974) Effect of alcohols on crack propagation in glass. *J. Am. Ceram. Soc.* **57**, 350-353

FREMERSDORF, F. (1930) Die Herstellung der Diatreta. *Schumacher Festschrift*, Mainz, pp. 295-300

FRENZEL, G. (1968) Glasgemälderestaurierung. Die Instandsetzung des Kaiser-Fensters und des Rieter-Fensters aus der St Lorenzkirche zu Nürnberg. *News Letter of the Society for the Restoration of the Lorenzkirche, N.S.* No. 9, July, pp. 3-16. (Abstract No. 150 in Newton, 1982b.)

FRENZEL, G. (1969) Die Instandsetzung des Kaiser-Fensters und des Rieter-Fensters aus der St Lorenzkirche zu Nürnberg. *Osterr. Zeit. Kunst. Denkm.* **23**, 75-85. (Abstract No. 151 in Newton, 1982b.)

FRENZEL, G. (1970a) La conservation des vitraux anciens. I. Les causes de dégradation - développment et importance. 5 pp typescript. (Also in *Glas-Email-Keramo-Technik* **22**, 168-171, 1971.) (Abstract No. 152 in Newton, 1982b.)

FRENZEL, G. (1970b) La conservation des vitraux anciens. II. Le nettoyage 4 pp typescript. (Abstract No. 153 in Newton, 1982b.)

FRENZEL, G. (1971a) Umweltgefahren bedrohen mittelalterliche Glasmalerei. *Kirche und Kunst* **49**, 58-60. (Abstract No. 154 in Newton, 1982b.)

FRENZEL, G. (1971b) Die letzen Zeugnisse mittelalterlicher Glasmalerei in Untergang. *Glasforum* **6**. (Abstract No. 155 in Newton, 1982b.)

FRENZEL, G. (1972a) Gutachen über den Erhaltungszustand und Vorschläge zur Sicherung der Mittelalterlichen Glasmalereien, Munster zu Ulm. *Report to the Department of Works of Ulm Minster*, 11 pp, 24 photographs (6 June 1972). (Abstract No. 156 in Newton, 1982b.)

FRENZEL, G. (1972b) Preventative and conservational methods for preserving the Augsburg Propet windows of 1130. *Compt. Rend. 8ᵉ Colloq. CVMA, Canterbury*, October, p. 54. (Abstract No. 157 in Newton, 1982b.)

FRENZEL, G. (1975a) Comments by Dr G. Frenzel on Fräulein Rausch's Report. *CVMA News Letter*, No. 15, item 1.2, 23 June

FRENZEL, G. (1975b) Restaurierung und Konservierung mittelalterlicher Glasmalereien. *Freiburg Exhibition Booklet*, 15 June to 31 August, pp. 5-10. (Abstract No. 159 in Newton, 1982b.)

FRENZEL, G. (1981) Probleme der Restainierung, Konservierung und Prophylaktischen Sicherung mittelalterlicher Glasmalereien, *Kunstspiegel* **3**, 173-209

FREY, P. (1973) Luftverunreinigung oder Verwitterung? *Umwelt* (Dusseldorf) **3**, 22-23. (Abstract No. 160 in *CVMA News Letter*, No. 8.)

FRIEDMAN, I., SMITH, R.L. and CLARK, D. (1963) Obsidian dating. In *Science in Archaeology: A Comprehensive survey of progress and research*, eds D. Brothwell and E. Higgs. Thames and Hudson, London, pp. 47-58

FRODL-KRAFT, E. (1963) Das Problem der Schwarzlotsicherung an mittelalterlichen Glasgemälden. *Inst. für Osterreichische Kunstforschung des Bundesdenkmalbates*, 23 pp. (Abstract No. 162 in Newton, 1982b.)

FRODL-KRAFT, E. (1967a) Restaurierung und Erforschung. I. Die Südrose von Maria Strassengel. *Osterr. Zeits. Kunst. Denkm.* **21**, 192-197. (Abstract No. 164 in Newton, 1982b.)

FRODL-KRAFT, E. (1967b) Restaurierung und Erforschung. 2. Heiligenkreuz, Chorfenster der Stiftkirche. *Osterr. Zeit. Kunst. Denkm.* **21**, 197-200

FRODL-KRAFT, E. (1970) 'Konservierungsprobleme mittelalterlicher Glasmalereien. *Ann. 5ᵉ Cong. Int. Hist. du Verre*, Prague, July, AIHV, Liège, pp. 357-370

FRODL-KRAFT, E. (1971) Zur Restaurierung und Sicherung. Die Bildfenster der Wassenkirche in Leoben. *Osterr. Zeits. Kunst. Denkm.* **25**, 70–73

FRODL-KRAFT, E. (1973) Untersuchungen und Praktische Erfahrungen in der Konservierung mittelalterlicher Glasmalereien. *Osterr. Zeits. Kunst. Denkm.* **26**, 55–65

FRODL-KRAFT, E. (1974) Mittelalterliche glasmalerei-Erforschung, Restaurierung. *Osterr. Zeits. Kunst. Denkm.* **28**, 200–209

FRODL-KRAFT, E. (1975) Mediaeval stained glass corrosion – conservation – restoration. *IIC Congress on Conservation in Archaeology and the Applied Arts*, Stockholm, pp. 105–110

FRODL-KRAFT, E. (1976) Einige Bemerkungen zu Wissenschaft und Handwerk in der Glasgemälde – Restaurierung. *Verres et Rèfract.* **30**, 73–76. (See also the illustrations in *CVMA News Letter*, No 19, Fig. 1, 5 Apr. 1976.)

FROHBIETER-MUELLER, J. (1979a) Lead poisoning – a word to the wise. *Stained Glass* **73**, 285–286

FROHBIETER-MUELLER, J. (1979b) The author replies. *Stained Glass* **74**, 59–60

FUCHS, D.R. and LEISSNER, J. (1992) Environmental monitoring using glass sensors: relevant features for small-scale mapping at monuments. *Third International Conference on Non-destructive Testing*, Sienna, 4–8 October 1992

FUCHS, O. and SEIHR, H.-H. (1975) Solvents and non-solvents for polymers. In *Polymer Handbook*, eds J. Brandrup and E.H. Immergut. Wiley Interscience, Chichester

FURON, R. (1967) *The Problem of Water*, trans. P. Barnes. Faber, London

GAIROLA, T.R. (1960) *Handbook of Chemical Conservation of Museum Objects*, Department of Museology, Maharaja Sayajirao University of Baroda

GARLAKE, M. (1969) Recovery and treatment of fragile artifacts from an excavation. *S. Afr. Archaeolog. Bull.* **24**, 61–62

GASPARETTO, A. (1958) *Il vetro di Murano dalle origini ad oggi*, Venice

GASPARETTO, A. (1965) Les fouilles de Torcello et leur apport a l'histoire de la verrerie de la Vénétie dans le Haut Moyen Age. *Proceedings of the 7th International Congress on Glass*, Brussels, New York, paper No. 239

GASPARETTO, A. (1967) A proposito dell' officina vetraria Torcellana – Forni e sistemi difusione antichi. *J. Glass Stud.* **9**, 50–75

GASPARETTO, A. (1973) Verres Venitiens du Moyen Age. *Proceedings of the 10th International Congress on Glass*, Kyoto (1974), pp. 9–21 to 9–29 and 15–90

GEDYE, I. (1968) Pottery and Glass. In *The Conservation of Cultural Property, XI. Museums and Monuments*, UNESCO, pp. 109–113

GEE, E.A. (1969) The painted glass of All Saints' Church, North Street, York. *Archaeologia* **102**, 151–202

GEFFCKEN, W. (1939) Der Angriff von alkalischen Lösungen auf Glas und seine Beeinflussung durch gelöste Ionen. *Kolloid-Z.* **86**, 11–15

GEILMANN, W. (1956) Beiträge zur Kenntnis alter Gläser. IV. Die Zersetzung der Gläser im Boden. *Glastech. Ber.* **29**, 156–168

GEILMANN, W. (1960) Beiträge zur Kenntnis alter Gläser. VI. Eine eigenartige Verwitterungserscheinung auf römis-

chen, Glass-scherben. *Glastech. Ber.* **33**, 291–296

GEILMANN, W. and BRUCKBAUER, T. (1954) Beiträge zur Kenntnis alter Gläser. II. Der Mangangehalt alter Gläser. *Glastech. Ber.* **27**, 456–459

GEIS, K. (1976) Raumklima und Schwitzwasserbildung im Freiburger Münster. Pamphlet, Freiburg-im-Breisgau. (Abstracted in *CVMA News Letter*, No. 24, Section 4.2

GEUSKENS, G., BURSU, M. and DAVID, S. (1972) Photolysis and radiolysis of polyvinyl acetate. III. *Eur. Polyer J.* **8**, 1347

GIBSON, P. (1992) The conservation of stained glass. *Glass and Enamel Conservation*, UKIC Occasional Papers No. 11, 10–14

GIBSON, P. and NEWTON, R. (1974) A study on cleaning painted and enamelled glass in an ultrasonic bath. *Br. Acad. CVMA Occasional Papers*, Part I, pp. 70–78

GILARD, P. and DUBRUL, L. (1937) The calculation of the physical properties of glass. III. The index of refraction. *J. Soc. Glass Technol.* **21**, 476.T–488.T

GLEDHILL, R.A. and KINLOCH, A.J. (1976) Weathering of epoxy-resin adhesives. *Plastics and Rubber Institute Conference on Weathering of Plastics and Rubbers*, June, 11 pp typescript. (Abstract No. 237 in *CVMA News Letter*, No. 22.)

GODFREY, E.S. (1975) *The Development of English Glassmaking 1560–1640*, Oxford

GOLDSTEIN, S.M. (1977) Forgeries and reproductions of ancient glass in Corning. *J. Glass Stud.* **19**, 40–62

GOODMAN, C.H.L. (1987) A new way of looking at glass. *Glass Technol.* **28**, 19–29

GORDON, J.E. (1975) *The New Science of Strong Materials, or Why You Don't Fall Through the Floor*, Pelican, Harmondsworth

GRANT, J. (1936) 'Ultraviolet test as an aid to the glass industry. *Ceram. Ind.* **26**, 420, 422

GREEN, P. (1979) Tracking down the past. *New Scientist* **84** (1182), 624–626

GREENFIELD, S., JONES, I.LL. and BERRY, C.T. (1964) High pressure plasmas as spectrographic emission sources. *Analyst* **89**, 713–720

GRIFFITHS, D.R. (1980) *The Deterioration of Ancient Glass*, unpublished BSc thesis, University of Wales, Cardiff

GRODECKI, L. (1978) Sauvons les vitraux anciens!. *Les Dossiers de l'Archéologie* **26**, Jan.–Feb., pp. 12–25

GROSE, D.F. (1977) Early blown glass. *J. Glass Stud.* **19**, 9–29

GUFFEY, S., MCKINNEY, R. and WOODCOCK, R. (1979) Lead exposure and its control in a stained glass studio. *Stained Glass*, **74**, 49–53

GUIDO, M. (1977) *The Glass Beads of the Prehistoric and Roman Periods in Britain and Ireland*, London

GUL', V.E., CHANG, YIN-HSI, VIKULA, V.L. and VOYUTSKII, S.S. (1962) *Vys Soed.* **4**, 294. (Adhesion of polymers to silicate glasses, II) (Abstract in *Polymer Science, USSR* **3**, 533, 1974.)

GÜNTHER, R. (1961a) Die entwicklung der Glasschmelzwannenofen. *Glastechn. Ber.* **34**, 471–482

GÜNTHER, R. (1961b) Rauchgaskegel auf alten glashütten. *Glastechn. Ber.* **34**, 559–562

HABEREY, W. (1963) Die Glasindustrie im römischen Rheinland. In *Advances in Glass Technology, Part 2*, eds F.R. Matson and G.E. Rindone. New York, pp. 349–358

HAEVERNICK, T.E. (1960) *Die Glasarmringe und Ringperlen der Mittel- und Spätlatenezeit auf dem Europäischen Festland,* Bonn

HAEVERNICK, T.E. (1961) Beiträge zur Geschichte des antiken Glases. VI. Die Aggryperlen; VII. Zu den stachelfläschchen. *Jahrb. des romisch-germanischen Zentralmuseums, Mainz* 8, 121–138

HAHNLOSER, H. (1972) Restaurationsbericht von Konrad Vetter, Bern, betr. Scheiben von Hans Acker, 1441, Sowie Biel & Burgdorf. *8th Colloq. CVMA,* York, 15 pp typescript and 16 illustrations (*not in the Compte rendu*). (Abstract No. 193 in Newton, 1982b.)

HAHN-WEINHEIMER, P. (1954) Über spektrochemische Untersuchungen an römischen Fenstergläsern. *Glastech. Ber.* 27, 459–464

HAJDAMACH, C.R. (1991) *British Glass 1800–1914,* Antique Collectors' Club

HALL, E.T., BANKS, M.S. and STERN, J.M. (1964) Uses of X-ray fluorescent analysis in archeology. *Archaeometry* 7, 84–89

HALL, E.T. and SCHWEIZER, F. (1973) X-ray fluorescence analysis of museum objects: a new instrument. 1. A non-dispersive X-ray Isoprobe. *Archaeometry* 15, 53–57, 74–76

HALL, J.A. and LEAVER, V.M. (1961) Stabilization of thermometers of borosilicate glass for use at high temperatures. *J. Sci. Instrum.* 38, 178–185

HANSEN, C.M. (1967) The three-dimensional solubility parameter key to paint component compatibilities and affinities. *J. Paint Technol.* 39, 104–105

HANSEN, C.M. (1968) A mathematical description of solvent drying by solvent evaporation. *J. Oil Colour Chem. Assoc.* 51, 27

HARDEN, D.B. (1936) *Roman Glass from Karanis Found by the University of Michigan Archaeological Expedition in Egypt 1924–1929,* University of Michigan Press

HARDEN, D.B. (1956a) Glass and glazes. In *A History of Technology,* Vol. 2, eds C. Singer *et al.* Oxford (reprinted with corrections in 1957), pp. 311–346

HARDEN, D.B. (1956b) Glass vessels in Britain and Ireland, AD 400–1000. In *Dark-Age Britain: Studies presented to E.T. Leeds,* ed. D.B. Harden. London, pp. 132–167

HARDEN, D.B. (1958) Glass-making centres and the spread of glass-making from the first to the fourth century AD. *Ann. 1. Cong. Journées Int. du Verre,* AIHV, Liège, pp.47–62

HARDEN, D.B. (1959) New light on Roman and Early Medieval window glass. *Glastech. Ber.* 32K, VIII/8–VIII/16

HARDEN, D.B. (1961) Domestic window glass, Roman, Saxon and Medieval. In *Studies in Building History: Essays in Recognition of the Work of B.H. St. J. O'Neill,* ed. E.M. Jope. Odhams, London, pp. 39–63

HARDEN, D.B. (1963) The Rothschild Lycurgus Cup: Addenda and corrigenda. *J. Glass Stud.* 5, 9–17

HARDEN, D.B. (1968) Ancient glass. I. Pre-Roman. *Archaeolog. J.* 125, 46–72

HARDEN, D.B. (1969a) Ancient glass. II. Roman. *Archaeolog. J.* 126, 44–77

HARDEN, D.B. (1969b) Medieval glass in the West. *Proceedings of the 8th International Congress on Glass,* Sheffield, pp. 97–111

HARDEN, D.B. (1971) Ancient glass. III. Post-Roman. *Archaeolog. J.* 128, 78–117

HARDEN, D.B. (1973) In *Excavations at Shakenoak Farm, near Wilcote, Oxfordshire,* Part IV, eds A.C.C. Brodribb, A.R. Hands and D.R. Walker. Privately printed and available from Dr A.R. Hands, Exeter College, Oxford

HARDEN, D.B. (1974) Window glass from the Romano-British bath house at Garden Hill, Hartfield, Sussex. *Antiquaries J.* 54, 280–281

HARDEN, D.B. (1978) Anglo-Saxon and Medieval glass in Britain: some recent developments. *Medieval Arch.* 22, 1–24

HARDEN, D.B., PAINTER, K.S., PINDER-WILSON, R.H. and TAIT, H. (1968) *Masterpieces of Glass,* Trustees of the British Museum, London

HARDEN, D.B. and TOYNBEE, J.M.C. (1959) The Rothschild Lycurgus Cup. *Archaeologia* 97, 179–212

HARDING, G.W. and MACNULTY, B.J. (1961) The embrittlement of polyamides. *Thermal Degradation of Polymers,* Society of the Chemical Industry Monograph No. 13, p.65

HARRINGTON, J.C. (1952) *Glassmaking at Jamestown,* Richmond, Va.

HARTSTHORNE, A. (1897) *Old English Glasses. An account of glass drinking vessels in England, from early times to the end of the eighteenth century, with introductory notices, original documents, etc.,* London. Reprinted as *Antique Drinking Glasses,* New York (1968)

HARVEY, J.H. (1968) The tracing floor in York Minster. *Fortieth Annual Report to the Friends of York Minster,* pp. 9–13

HARVEY, J.H. (1972) *The Medieval Architect,* London

HARVEY, J.H. (1975) *Medieval Craftsmen,* Batsford, London

HAWTHORNE, J.H. and SMITH, C.S. (1963) *On Divers Arts: the treatise of Theophilus,* 2nd edn, University of Chicago Press

HAYNES, D.E.L. (1964), revised edn 1975 *The Portland Vase,* Trustees of the British Museum, London

HAYWARD, J. (1975) Installation of the medieval stained glass at The Cloisters. *Verres et Réfract.* 30, 77–79

HEALTH AND SAFETY EXECUTIVE (1984) *Threshold Limit Values for 1984, Guidance Note EH 40,* HMSO, London

HEATON, N, (1907) Medieval stained glass: its production and decay. *J. Roy. Soc. Arts,* pp. 468–484

HEDGES, R. and NEWTON, R.G. (1974) Use of the 'Isoprobe' for studying the chemical composition of some 12th century glass from York Minster. *Br. Acad. CVMA Occasional Papers,* Part I, pp. 79–93

HEDVALL, J.A., JAGITSCH, R. and OLSON, G. (1951) Über das Problem der Zerstörung antiker Gläser. II. Mitteilung. Über die Belegung von Glasoberflächen mit Schutzfilmen. *Trans. Chalmers Inst. Tech.* No. 118, Goteborg. (Abstract No. 200 in Newton, 1982b.)

HEJDOVÁ, J. (1965) Comments on archaeological finds in the field of glassmaking in Czechoslovakia. *Czechoslovak Glass Rev.* 12, 353

HENCH, L.L. (1975a) Characterization of glass. In *Characterization of Materials in Research Ceramics and Polymers,* eds J.J. Burke and V.I. Weiss. Syracuse, Ch. 8, pp. 211–251

HENCH, L.L. (1975b) Characterization of glass corrosion and durability. *J. Non-Cryst. Sol.* 19, 27–39

HENCH, L.L. (1977) Physical chemistry of glass surfaces. *XI Congress of the International Commission on Glass,* Prague, July, *Survey Papers* Vol. II, pp. 343–369

HENCH, L.L. (1982) Glass surfaces. *J. Physique Colloque* C.9, Supplement to No. 12, 43, C9-625 to C9-636

HENCH, L.L. and CLARK, D.E. (1978) Physical chemistry of glass surfaces. *J. Non-Cryst. Sol.* **28**, 83–105

HENCH, L.L., CLARK, D.E. and YEN-BOWER, E.L. (1979) Surface leaching of glasses and glass ceramics. *Proceedings of the Conference on High Level Radioactive Solid Waste Forms*, ed. L.A. Casey. US/NRC, pp. 100–235

HENCH, L.L. and MCELDOWNEY, B.A. (1976) *A Bibliography of ceramics and glass*, American Ceramic Society, New York

HENCH, L.L., NEWTON, R.G. and BERNSTEIN, S. (1979) Use of infrared reflection spectroscopy in analysis of durability of medieval glasses, with some comments on conservation procedures. *Glass Technol.* **20**, 144–148

HENCH, L.L. and PASCHALL, H.A. (1973) Direct chemical bonding between bio-active glass-ceramic materials and bone. *J. Biomed. Mater. Res. Symp. No. 4* pp. 25–42

HENCH, L.L. and SANDERS, D.M. (1974) Analysis of glass corrosion'. *The Glass Industry*, Feb. and Mar. pp. 12, 13, 16, 18, 19

HENDERSON, J. (1987) The Iron Age of 'Loughey' and Meare: some inferences from glass analysis. *Antiq. J.* **67**, 29–42

HODGES, H.W.M. (1965) *Artifacts: an introduction to early materials and technology*, John Baker, London

HOGAN, L. (1993) An improved method of making supportive resin fills for glass. *Conservation News* **50**, 29–30

HOLDEN, A. (1988) Stained glass conservation today. *Preprints of the contributions to the UKIC 30th Anniversary Conference*, 94–95

HOLLAND, L. (1966) *The Properties of Glass Surfaces*, Chapman and Hall, London

HOLLISTER, P. (1964) *Encyclopaedia of Paperweights*

HOLLISTER, P. (1974) The glazing of the Crystal Palace. *J. Glass Stud.* **16**, 95–110

HOLLOWAY, D.G. (1973) *The Physical Properties of Glass*, Wykeham Publications, London

HOLLOWAY, D.G. (1984) Letter to RGN, July

HOMER, P.N. and CRAWFORD, B.J. (1970) The microstructure of etched glass surfaces. *Glass Technol.* **11**, 10–14

HORIE, C.V. (1981) Cyanacrylate adhesives in glass conservation. *CVMA News Letter*. (Abstract No. 212 in Newton, 1982b.)

HORIE, C.V. (1987) *Materials for Conservation*. Butterworths, London

HOWARTH, J.T., SYKES, R.F. and TURNER, W.E.S. (1934) A study of the fundamental reactions in the formation of soda–lime–silica glasses. *J. Soc. Glass Technol.* **18**, 290.T.–306.T.

HOWDEN, C.R., GERMAN, B. and SMALLDON, K.W. (1977) The determination of iron and magnesium in small glass fragments using flameless atomic absorption spectrophotometry. *J. Forensic Sci. Soc.* **17**, 153–159

HREGLICH, S. and PROFILO, M.V. (1980) Study on the corrosion and colour of potassium glass–church of SS Giovanni and Paolo, Venice. *CVMA News Letter*, **31/32**, pp. 16–23

HUANG, W.H. and WALKER, R.M. (1967) Fossil alpha-particle recoil tracks: a new method of age determination. *Science* **155**, 1103–1106

HUDSON, A.P. and NEWTON, R.G. (1976) A means for the *in situ* identification of medieval glass by the detection of its natural radioactivity. *Archaeometry* **18**, 229–232

HUGGINS, M.L. and SUN, K.-H. (1946) Calculation of density and optical constants of a glass from its composition in weight percentage. *J. Soc. Glass Technol.* **30**, 333–342

HUGHES, M.J. (1987) Materials, deterioration and analysis. In *From Pinheads to Hanging Bowls; the Identification, Deterioration and Conservation of Applied Enamel and Glass Decoration on Archaeological Artefacts*, eds L. Bacon and B. Knight. UKIC, London

HUGHES, M.J., COWELL, M.R. and CRADDOCK, P.T. (1976) Atomic absorption techniques in archaeology. *Archaeometry* **18**, 19–37

HUME, I.N. (1976) Archaeological excavations on the site of John Frederick Amelung's New Bremen Glassmanufactory, 1962–1963. *J. Glass Stud.* **18**, 138–215

HUNTER, J.R. (1977) Glass fragments from the vicarage garden, Brixworth. *J. Br. Arch. Assoc.* 104–107

HUNTLEY, D.J. and BAILEY, D.C. (1978) Obsidian source identification by thermoluminescence. *Archaeometry* **20**, 159–170

HURST-VOSE, R. (1980) *Glass*, Collins, London

HUSBAND, T.B. (1972) A new type of mending lead. *Compt. Rend. 8e Colloq. CVMA*, York, September, p. 28

HUSSONG, L. and WIHR, R. (1954) Ein wichtiger Fortschritt im Nachbilden und Ergänzen antiker Gläser. *Trierer Zeitschrift* **23**, 231–238

HUTCHINSON, M.E. (1981) An experimental method for consolidating excavated medieval glass. Contribution to the Seminar *Medieval Glass Technology and Medieval Glaziers*, Urban Research Committee of the Council for British Archaeology and Corpus Vitrearum Medii Aevi, 17 October. (Abstract No. 416 of Newton, 1982b.)

IBRAHIM, L., SCRANTON, R. and BRILL, R.H. (1976) The panels of *opus sectile* in glass. *Kenchreai – Eastern Part of Corinth* 2, Brill, E.J. (Leiden)

ICI (1977) *Polyurethanes, General, Isocyanates, hazards and safe handling procedures*, 4th edn, ICI Technical Information U93, London

IGARASHI, T., KONDO, S. and KUROKAWA, M. (1979) Contractile stress of epoxy resin during isothermal curing. *Polymer* **20**, 301

ILIFFE, C.J.A. and NEWTON, R.G. (1976) Using triangular diagrams to understand the behaviour of medieval glasses. *Verres et Réfract.* **30**, 30–34

VON IMHOFF, H.C. (1978) *A Basic Bibliography of Conservation*, Fribourg, Switzerland

INTERNATIONAL COMMISSION ON GLASS (1972–79) *The Chemical Durability of Glass; a bibliographic review of the literature*, Inst. Nat. du Verre, Charleroi, Belgium. 3 Vols, Vol. 1, 1972; Vol. 2, 1973; Vol. 3, 1979

ISARD, J.O. (1963) The determination of composition from routine physical property measurements. *Glass Technol.* **4**, 45–51

ISC (1982) (Fraunhofer—Institut für Silicatforschung) Untersuchungen zum Schutz mittelalterlicher Glasfenster. *Tätigkeitbericht, 1982*, 95–100

ISC (1983) Untersuchungen zum Schutz mittelalterlicher Glasfenster. *Tätigkeitbericht, 1983*, 78–83

ISC (1985) Untersuchungen zum Schutz mittelalterlicher Glasfenster. *Ergänzende Versuche* (H. Patzelt, G. Tünker and H. Scholze). Forschungsbericht 10608005/01, Berlin, obtainable from the Bundesministers des Innern, Berlin

JACKSON, P.R. (1982a) A dowelling technique for glass restoration. *The Conservator* 6, 33–35 (UKIC)

JACKSON, P.R. (1982b) Resins used in glass conservation. *Proc. Symp. Resins & Conservation* 10.1–10.7 SSCR

JACKSON, P.R. (1983) Restoration of an Italic glass oinchoe with Technovit 4004a. *The Conservator* 7, 44–47 (UKIC)

JACKSON, P.R. (1984) Restoration of glass antiquities. *Preprints of the 7th Triennial Meeting of ICOM*, September, pp. 84.20.13–17

JACKSON, P.R. (1985) Restoration of the Auldjo Jug. *Annales de 9 Congres de l'Association Internationale pour l'Histoire du Verre*, Liège, Belgium, 77–87

JACOBI, R. (1955) Das Konservierungsverfahren für die Obergadenglasfenster des Kölner Domes. *Kölner Domblatt* 9, 122–130

JACOBI, R. (1957) Die Konservierung alter Glasmalereien des Kölner Domes. *Glastechn. Ber.* 30, 509–514

JACOBI, R. (1960) Fehlurteile über die Restaurierung der Domfenster – Entgegnung auf einen Aufsatz von G. Frenzel. *Kölner Domblatt* 18/19, 167–170

JACOBI, R. (1971) Ein Konservierungsverfahren für mittelalterlicher Glasfenster auf der Basis der modernen Sicherheitsglastechnik. *Glas–Email–Keramo Technik* 22(5), 172–174

JACOBI, R. (1973) Zur Frage der Erhaltung alter Glasmalereien. *Maltechnik Restauro.* 2, 114–120

JAMES, D.I., NORMAN, R.H. and STONE, M.H. (1968) Water attack on the glass–resin bond in GRP. *Plastics and Polymers* 36, 21

JANTZEN, C.M. and PLODINEC, M.J. (1984) Thermodynamic model of natural, medieval and nuclear waste glass durability. *J. Non-Cryst. Sol.* 67, 207–223

JOHANNSON, O.K., STARK, F.O., VOGEL, G.E. and FLEISCHMANN, R.M. (1967) Evidence for chemical bond formation at silane coupling agent interfaces. *J. Composite Mater.* 1, 278

JOHNSON, J.R. (1965) *The Radiance of Chartres*, New York

JOHNSTON, N.W. (1974) Microstructure and macroproperty relationships of coatings and adhesives. *Pigment and Resin Technol.* 3(12), 4–7

JOHNSTON, R.H. (1975) Master glassblowers of Herat, Afghanistan; some archaeological relationships. Paper presented at the *77th General Meeting, Archaeological Institute of America*, December, p. 22

JONES, S. (1988) The conservation of three 14th-century stained glass lancets. *Preprints of the contributions to the UKIC 30th Anniversary Conference*, 84–89

JOVANOVIĆ, M.A. and ZALAR, R. (1974) Einige Möglichkeiten zu verbesserung der chemischen Beständigkeit der Glasoberfläche. *Proceedings of the 10th International Congress on Glass*, Kyoto, July, pp. 9–100 to 9–104

KÄMPFER, F. (1963) Kranke Gläser. *Neue Museumskunde* 6, 211–214

KÄMPFER, F. and BEYER, K.G. (1966) *Glass. A World History. The story of 4000 years of fine glass making*, Studio Vista, London

KARL, F. (1970) Behandlung korrodierter geschliffener Gläser. *Arbeitsblätter für Restauratoren*, Heft 2, Gruppe 5, 17–19

KENYON, G.H. (1967) *The Glass Industry of the Weald*, Leicester University Press

KERPER, M.J. and SCUDERI, T.G. (1964) Modulus of rupture of glass in relation to fracture pattern. *Bull. Am. Ceram. Soc.* 43, 622–625

KERPER, M.J. and SCUDERI, T.G. (1966) Relation of fracture stress to the fracture pattern for glass rods of various diameters. *Bull. Am. Ceram. Soc.* 45, 1065–1066

KERR, J. (1988) Repair and maintenance of historic glass. In *Practical Building Conservation, English Heritage Technical Handbook 5, Glass Resins and Technical Bibliography*, ed. J. and N. Ashurst, Gower Technical Press

KEULEN, N.M. and DISSEL, M. (1993) Temperature dependence of indentation cracking. *Glass Technol.* 34(5), 200–205

KING, D.G. (1971) Winchester College stained glass. Part II. Technical report on the restoration of the glass. *Archaeologia* 103, 166–174

KING, D.G. (1972) Methods of cleaning medieval painted glass. *Compt. Rend. 8^e Colloque du CVMA*, York, September, pp. 15–16

KING, R. (1989) Personal communication dated 2 February. CAPSIS, UMIST

KINLOCH, A.J., DUKES, W.A. and GLEDHILL, R.A. (1975) Durability of adhesive joints. In *Adhesion Science and Technology*, ed. L.H. Lee. Plenum Press, New York, pp. 597–614

KNIGHT, M.A. (1945) Glass densities by the settling method. *J. Am. Ceram. Soc.* 28, 297–302

KNOWLES, J.A. (1929) Ancient leads for windows and the methods of their manufacture. *J. Br. Soc. Master Glass Painters* 3, 133–139

KNOWLES, J.A. (1935) Letter to Bernard Rackham, of the Victoria and Albert Museum, 28 May. (Abstract No. 241 in Newton, 1982b.)

KNOWLES, J.A. (1959) Decay of glass, lead and iron of ancient stained glass windows. *J. Br. Soc. Master Glass Painters* 12, 270–276

KNY, E. and NAUER, G. (1977) Devitrifikation alter Gläser – Grundlagen, Möglichkeiten und erste Ergebnisse. *Contribution to the DGC Meeting in Frankfurt*. (Abstract No. 285 in CVMA News Letter No. 26.)

KOOB, S.P. (1979) The removal of aged shellac adhesive from ceramics. *Studies in Conservation* 24, 134–135

KOOB, S.P. (1981) Consolidation with acrylic colloidal dispersions. Preprints of the *9th Annual Meeting of AIC*, Philadelphia. AIC, Washington, pp. 86–94

KOOB, S.P. (1982) The instability of cellulose nitrate adhesives. *The Conservator* 6, 31–34

KORN, U.D. (1971) Ursachen und Symtome des Zerfalls mittelalterlicher Glasgemälde. *Deutsche Kunst und Denkmalpflege* 29, 58–74

KREUGER, B.E. (1994) Belcher mosaic. *Stained Glass* 89(1), 20–30

KUCHEL, A. (1987) Glass adhesives. *Profess. Stained Glass* 7, 10–12

KUNCKEL, VON LOEWENSTERN (1679) *Ars Vitrarii Experimentalis*, Leipzig

KURATA, M., TSUMASHIMA, Y., IWAMA, M. and KAMADA, K. (1975) Viscosity – molecular weight relationship and unperturbed dimensions of linear chain molecules. In *Polymer Handbook*, 2nd edn, eds J. Brandrup and E.H. Immergut. Wiley Interscience, Chichester, p. IV-1

LABINO, D. (1966) The Egyptian sand-core technique: a new interpretation. *J. Glass Stud.* 8, 124–127

LACY, R.E. (1970) A note on the climate inside a medieval chapel. *Studies in Conservation* 15, 65–80

LACY, R.E. (1973) *Estimates of Frequency of Condensation on the Windows of a Large Church or Cathedral*, Building Research Station Report, unpublished, 12 March. (Abstract in Newton, 1982b, No. 249, and CVMA News Letter, No. 4, Abstract No. 104, p. 8.)

LADAIQUE, G. (1975) The glassmakers of the Voge. *Readings in Glass History*, No. 5, pp. 1–17

LAFOND, J. (1969) Was crown glass discovered in Normandy in 1330? *J. Glass Stud.* **11**, 37–38

LAL, B.B. (1962–63) Chemical preservation of ancient glass. *Ancient India* **18–19**, 230–280

LAMB, A. (1966) A note on the glass beads from the Malay Peninsula. *J. Glass Stud.* **8**, 80–94

LAMB, A. (1970) Some observations on glass beads in Ghana, West Africa. *Ann. 5ᵉ Cong. Journées Int. du Verre*, Prague, pp. 247–250

LAMBERT, J.B. and MCLAUGHLIN, C.D. (1978) Analysis of early Egyptian glass by atomic absorption and X-ray photoelectron spectroscopy. In *Archaeological Chemistry 2. Advances in Chemistry Series* **171**. American Chemical Society, New York

LAMM, C.J. (1941) *Oriental Glass of Medieval Date Found in Sweden and the Early History of Lustre-painting*, Kungl. Vitterhets Hist. och Antik. Akad. Handlingar, del 50:1, Stockholm

LANCASTER, O. (1976) What should we preserve? In *The Future of the Past*, ed. Jane Fawcett. London, pp. 65–73

LANFORD, W.A. (1977) Glass hydration: a method of dating glass objects. *Science* **166**, 975–976

LANFORD, W.A. (1986) Ion beam analysis of glass surfaces: dating, authentification and conservation, *Nucl. Inst. and Meth.* B **14**, 123–126

LANG, J. and PRICE, J. (1975) Iron tubes from a Late Roman glassmaking site at Mérida (Badajoz) in Spain. *J. Archaeol. Sci.* **2**, 289–296

LANMON, D.P. and PALMER, A.M. (1976) John Frederick Amelung and the New Bremen Glasmanufactory. *J. Glass Stud.* **18**, 14–137

LARNEY, J. (1975) *Restoring Ceramics*, London, pp. 100–102

LAVOISIER, A.L. (1770) Action of water on glass. *Mem. Acad. Sci.* (Paris) **73**, 90

LEE, H. and NEVILLE, K. (1967) *Handbook of Epoxy Resins*, McGraw-Hill, Basingstoke

LEE, L. (1977) *The Appreciation of Stained Glass*, Oxford

LEE, L., SEDDON, G. and STEPHENS, F. (1982) *Stained Glass*, Mitchell Beazley, London

LEE, L.H. (ed.) (1975) *Adhesion Science and Technology*, Plenum Press, New York

LEIGH, D. (1978) *First Aid for Finds*, Rescue Publication No. 1, 2nd revised edn

LEISSNER, J. and FUCHS, D.R. (1992) Glass sensors: a European study to estimate the effectiveness of protective glazings at different cathedrals. *Congreso Internacional de Rehabilitacion del Patrimonio, Arquitestonio*, Islas Canarias, 1992

LEONARD, F., KULKANNI, R. K., BRANDES, G., NELSON, J. and CAMERON, J.J. (1966) Synthesis and degradation of poly(alkyl α-cyanoacrylates). *J. Appl. Polymer Sci.* **10**, 259

LEWIS, G.D. (1973) *The South Yorkshire Glass Industry*, 2nd edn, Sheffield City Museum

LEWIS, M.D.S. (1953–54) The history of paste, Parts I, II and III. *The Gemmologist* **22**, 193; **23**, 53, 91

LILLIE, H.R. (1936) Stress release in glass, a phenomenon involving viscosity as a variable with time. *J. Am. Ceram. Soc.* **19**, 45–54

LINSLEY, G.F. (1972) A possible method of conserving ancient glass. *Compte rendu du 8ᵉ Colloque du CVMA*, York, p. 51

LINWOOD, S.H. and WEYL, W.A. (1942) The fluorescence of manganese in glasses and glazes. *J. Opt. Soc. Am.* **32**, 443–453

LOUBENGAGER, A.W. (1931) Weathering of glass. *J. Am. Ceram. Soc.* **14**, 833–836

LOWE, J. (1975) The conservation of stained glass. In *Conservation in Archaeology and the Applied Arts*, IIC, London, pp. 93–97

LOWE, W. (1960) The conservation of stained glass. *Studies in Conservation* **5**, 139–149

LUCAS, A. (1962) *Ancient Egyptian Materials and Industries*, London

LUNDSTRÖM, A. (1976) *Bead making in Scandinavia in the Early Middle Ages*, Kungl. Vitterhets Hist. och Antik. Akad., antikvariskt arkiv **61** 19 pp offprint

LUSKIN, L.S. and MYERS, R.J. (1964) Acrylic ester polymers, *Encyclopaedia of Polymer Science and Technology*, Vol. 1, Mark, Gaylord and Bikales, Wiley, Chichester, p. 299

LYLE, A.K. (1943) Theoretical aspects of chemical attack of glasses by water. *J. Am. Ceram. Soc.* **26**, 201–204

MACLEHOSE, L.S. (trans.) (1907) *Vasari on Technique – Georgio Vasari*, Dover Pub. Inc., New York, pp. 253–257

MCGRATH, R., FROST, A.C. and BECKETT, H.E. (1961) *Glass in Architecture and Decoration*, Architectural Press, London

MCCRONE, W.C. and DELLY, J.G. (1973) *The Particle Atlas*, 2nd edn, Ann Arbor Science, Michigan

MCKENNA, J.F. (1961) Fracture analysis. *Bull. Am. Ceram. Soc.* **40**, 61–65

MacLEOD, C. (1987) Accident or design? George Ravenscroft's patent and the invention of lead-crystal glass. *Technology and Culture* **28**, 776–803

MADSEN, H.B. (1972) A new product for mending glass. *Studies in Conservation* **17**, 131–132

MAJEWSKI, L.J. (1973) Conservation of archaeological material at Sardis, Turkey. *Bull. Am. Inst. Conservation* **13**, 99–104

MALLOWAN, M.E.L. (1949) Excavations at Brak. *Iraq* **9**, 33

MANDELKERN, L. (1972) *An Introduction to Macromolecules*, Springer-Verlag, Berlin

MÅNSSON, P. (c 1520) *Glaskonst*. Modern translation by R. Geete, Stockholm, 1913–15

MARCHINI, G. (1972) L'affaiblissement de la grisaille de long des plombs. *Compt. Rend. 8ᵉ Colloque CVMA*, York, September, p. 46

MARCHINI, G. (1975) La vetrata ed il suo restauro. *Mitteilungen des Kunsthistorischen Institutes in Florenz* **19**, 181–196

MARCHINI, G. (1976) La restauration de la grisaille. *Verres et Réfract.* **30**, 65–68

MARK, H.F., GAYLORD, N.G. and BIKALES, N.M. (1964) *Encyclopedia of Polymer Science and Technology*, Wiley, Chichester

MARSCHNER, H. (1977) Zur Lochfrasskorrosion an mittelalterlichen Fenstergläsern. *DGG Meeting in Frankfurt, 31 March*. (Abstract No. 289 in *CVMA News Letter* No. 26.)

MARSCHNER, H. (1984) Prüfung von kunstharzen zur malschichtkonservierung mittelalterlicher Glasfenster. *CVMA News Letter*, No. 37/38. pp. 13–20

MARSDEN, O. (1963) *Solvents Guide*, 2nd edn, Cleaver Hulme

MARSDEN, J.G. and STERMAN, S. (1977) Organo-functional silane coupling agents. In *Handbook of Adhesives*, ed. I. Skeist. Van Nostrand, Wokingham, p. 640

MARTIN, F.R. (1977) Acrylic adhesives. In *Developments in Adhesives*, Vol. 1, ed. W.C. Wake. Applied Science, London, p. 157.

MARTIN, J.H. (ed.) (1977) *The Corning Flood: Museum Underwater*, Appendix IV, iv–x

MARTIN, L.C. and JOHNSON, B.K. (1962) *Practical Microscopy*, 3rd edn, Blackie & Son, Glasgow

MARYON, H. (1971) *Metalwork and Enamelling. A practical treatise on gold and silversmiths' work and their allied crafts*, 5th revised edn, Dover Publications Inc, New York

MATHESON, L.A. and BOYER, R.F. (1952) Light stability of polystyrene and polyvinylidene chloride. *Indust. Eng. Chem.* **44**, 487

MAURER, E. and GRATWOHL, S. (1986) Silbergelb in Königsfelden. *Osterr. Zeits. Kunst. Denkm.* **40**, 191–192

MEHLMAN, F. (1982) *Phaidon Guide to Glass*, Phaidon Press, London

MEIGH, E. (1972) *The Story of the Glass Bottle*, C.E. Ramsden & Co., Stoke-on-Trent

MELLAN, I. (1970) *Industrial Solvents Handbook*, Noyes Data Corpn., New Jersey, USA

MELLOR, E. (1924) The decay of window glass from the point of view of lichenous growths. *J. Soc. Glass Technol.* **8**, 182.T–186.T

MELUCCO, A. (1971) Vetro-materiali vitrei. *Problemi di conservazione*, ed. Urbain, Section IV. Uff. de Min. per il coordinamento della ricerca scientifica e technologica, Bologna

MERRETT, C. (1662) *The Art of Glass*. (Translation of Antonio Neri, *L'Arte Vetraria*), London

MERRIFIELD, M.P. (1849) *Original Treatises dating from the C12th to the C18th on the Arts of Painting (etc.)*, London

METCALFE, A.G., GULDEN, M.E. and SCHMITZ, G.K. (1971) Spontaneous cracking of glass filaments. *Glass Technol.* **12**, 15–23

MILES, F.D. (1955) *Cellulose Nitrate*, Oliver and Boyd

MILLS, A.A. (1987) The conservation and restoration of medieval stained glass windows by 'gel-plating'. *Studies in Conservation* **32**, 122–136

MILLS, J.F. (1964) *The Care of Antiques*, London

MILLS, J.S. and WHITE, R. (1977) Natural resins in art and archaeology. *Studies in Conservation* **22**, 12

MISRA, G.S. and SENGUPTAL, S.C. (1970) Shellac. In *Encyclopedia of Polymer Science and Technology*, Vol. 12, eds H.F. Mark, N.G. Gaylord and N.M. Bikales. Wiley, Chichester, p. 419

MÖLLER, R. (1980) Sicherung der Schwarzlotmalerei – Material und Methode. *CVMA News Letter*, No. 31/32, December, pp. 12–15

MONCRIEFF, A. (1971) Polyurethane foaming resins. *Studies in Conservation* **16**, 119

MONCRIEFF, A. (1974) Lamination of stained glass at Cologne. *Studies in Conservation* **19**(1). 3–6 of Supplement

MONCRIEFF, A. (1975) Problems and potentialities in the conservation of vitreous materials. *Conservation in Archaeology and the Applied Arts, Proceedings of the IIC Conference*, Stockholm, pp. 99–104

MONCRIEFF, A. (1976) The treatment of deteriorating stone with silicone resins: interim report. *Studies in Conservation* **21**, 179–191

MONEY, J.H. (1976) Fourth Interim Report on Excavations in the Iron Age Hill-Fort and Romano-British Iron-Working Settlement at Garden Hill, Hartfield, Sussex, Fig. 8

MOODY, B.E. (1977) *Packaging in Glass*, 2nd edn, Hutchinson, London

MOODY, B.E. (1980) Prince Rupert, glass technologist. *Glass Technol.* **21**, 223–224

MOODY, B.E. (1988) The Life of George Ravenscroft. *Glass Technol.* **29**, 198–209

MOORE, H. (1944) Retrospect and Prospect. *J. Soc. Glass Technol.* **18**, 92.T–104.T

MOORE, H. (1948) Reproductions of an ancient Babylonian glaze. *Iraq* **10**, 26–33

MOORE, W.R. and MURPHY, M. (1962) Viscosity of dilute solutions of poly(vinyl acetate). *J. Polymer Sci.* **56**, 519

MOREY, G.W. (1954) *The Properties of Glass*, Reinhold

MORGÓS, A., NAGY, J. and PÁLOSSY, L. (1984) New silicone rubber mould – making materials. The addition-type silicone rubbers. *Preprints of the Contributions to the 7th Triennial Meeting of ICOM*, Copenhagen, September, pp. 84.20.19–84.20.20

MOSER, F. (1961) A study of glass surface deterioration by moisture. *Glass Ind.* **42**, 244–248, 286

MÜLLER, W., POUILLON, H., BOCHYNEK, G. and MEHNER, H. (1986) Extreme Dunkelung von Glasmalareien, *Glastech. Ber.* **59**, 272–278

MÜLLER, W., DRACHENBERG, E. and POUILLON, H. (1980) Untersuchungen zur Schutzwirkung organischer Beschichtungen auf simulierten mittelalterlichen Gläsern. *CVMA News Letter*, No. 31/32, pp. 7–12

MUNNIKENDAM, R. (1978) Consolidation of fragile wood with low viscosity aliphatic epoxy resins. In *Conservation of Wood, Proceedings of the International Institute of Conservation Conference*, Oxford, p. 71

MUNSELL (n.d.) *Munsell Book of Color*, 2 vols, Munsell Color Co., 2441 North Calvert St, Baltimore 18, Maryland, USA

MURGATROYD, J.B. (1942) The significance of surface marks on fractured glass. *J. Soc. Glass Technol.* **26**, 155–171

MURRAY, B.D., HAUSER, M. and ELLIOT, J.R. (1977) Anaerobic adhesives. In *Handbook of Adhesives*, 2nd edn, ed. I. Skeist. Van Nostrand, Wokingham, pp. 560–568

MUSTY, J. and NEVINSON, J.L. (1974) Sixteenth century stained glass from Rycote Chapel, Oxfordshire. *Antiq. J.* **54**, 297–299

NELSON, P. (1913) *Ancient Painted Glass in England*, Methuen, London

NERI, A. (1612) *Dell 'Arte Vetraria*, Firenze. Translated by Christopher Merrett, *The Art of Glass*, London

NEWMAN, H. (1977) *An Illustrated Dictionary of Glass*, Thames & Hudson, London

NEWTON, R.G. (1966) Some problems in the dating of ancient glass by counting the layers in the weathering crust. *Glass Technol.* **7**, 22–25

NEWTON, R.G. (1969) Some further observations on the weathering crusts on ancient glass. *Glass Technol.* **10**, 40–42

NEWTON, R.G. (1970) Metallic gold and ruby glass. *J. Glass Studies* **12**, 165–170

NEWTON, R.G. (1971a) The enigma of the layered crusts on some weathered glasses, a chronological account of the investigations. *Archaeometry* **13**, 1–9

NEWTON, R.G. (1971b) A preliminary examination of a suggestion that pieces of strongly-coloured glass were articles of trade in the Iron Age in Britain. *Archaeometry* **13**, 11–16

NEWTON, R.G. (1971c) Glass trade routes in the Iron Age? *Proceedings of the 9th International Congress on Glass*, Versailles, *Art Hist. Comm.* pp. 197–204

NEWTON, R.G. (1972) Stereoscan views of weathering layers on a piece of ancient glass. *Glass Technol.* **13**, 54–56

NEWTON, R.G. (1973) Bibliography of studies on the deterioration and conservation of stained glass. *Art and Archaeology Tech. Abstracts* (Suppl.) **10**, 132–178

NEWTON, R.G. (1974a) Cathedral chemistry – conserving the stained glass. *Chemistry in Britain* **10**, 89–91

NEWTON, R.G. (1974b) The spontaneous surface fracturing of some medieval window glass. *10th International Congress on Glass*, Kyoto, July, pp. 11–32 to 11–38

NEWTON, R.G. (1974c) The deterioration and conservation of painted glass. A critical bibliography and three research papers. *Br. Acad. CVMA Occasional Papers*, Part I, 93 pp. (The completely revised version is Newton, 1982b, but the three research papers were not repeated.)

NEWTON, R.G. (1974d) Recovery of lost or faded decoration on painted glass. *Br. Acad. CVMA Occasional Papers*, Part I, pp. 68–69, 87–89

NEWTON, R.G. (1975a) Conservation of medieval windows (isothermal glazing). *IIC Conference, Conservation in Archaeology and the Applied Arts*, Stockholm, pp. 111–114

NEWTON, R.G. (1975b) The weathering of medieval glass. *J. Glass Stud.* **17**, 161–168

NEWTON, R.G. (1976a) The unusual weathering of one of Dr Jane Hayward's samples. *Verres et Réfract.* **30**, 35

NEWTON, R.G. (1976b) Experimental studies of the protection of medieval windows using external glazing. *Verres et Réfract.* **30**, 80–86

NEWTON, R.G. (1976c) First report to the Royal Society on cleaning stained glass with the airbrasive equipment. 26 pp typescript and 60 coloured photographs. (Abstract No. 257 in *CVMA News Letter*, No. 24, and abstract No. 284 in Newton, 1982b.)

NEWTON, R.G. (1976d) The effects of medieval glass paint. *Stained Glass* **71**, 226–230

NEWTON, R.G. (1978a) Colouring agents used by medieval glassmakers. *Glass Technol.* **19**, 59–60

NEWTON, R.G. (1978b) A general discussion of the scientific aspects of external protective glazing (Aussenschutzverglasung). *CVMA News Letter*, No. 28, pp. 1–4

NEWTON, R.G. (1979) Sulphur dioxide and medieval stained glass. Society of Chemical Industry, Water and Environment Group. *Sulphur Emissions and the Environment*, London, May, pp. 311–313, 500–501

NEWTON, R.G. (1980a) Recent views on ancient glasses (review paper). *Glass Technol.* **21**, 173–183

NEWTON, R.G. (1980b) A study of conditions in five ventilated double windows in cathedrals. IIC Congress, *Conservation Within Historic Buildings*, Vienna, pp. 89–92. The illustrations are reproduced in *CVMA News Letter*, No. 33/34, Jan. pp. 12–19

NEWTON, R.G. (1981a) A summary of the progress of the Ballidon glass burial experiment. *Glass Technol.* **22**, 42–45

NEWTON, R.G. (1981b) Medieval methods of attaching 'jewels' to stained glass. *Stained Glass* **76**, 50–53

NEWTON, R.G. (1982a) Unusual effects of the weathering of ancient glass. In *Crown in Glory*, ed. P. Moore. Jarrold, pp. 73–80

NEWTON, R.G. (1982b) *The Deterioration and Conservation of Painted Glass. A Critical Bibliography*, British Academy and Oxford University Press, Occasional Papers, II. (This is a completely rewritten and extended version of Newton, 1974c.)

NEWTON, R.G. (1985a) The durability of glass: a review. *Glass Technol.* **26**, 21–38

NEWTON, R.G. (1985b) W.E.S. Turner: recollections and developments (The Eighth Turner Memorial Lecture). *Glass Technol.* **26**, 93–103

NEWTON, R.G. (1987a) What do we really know about 'protective coatings?' *Prep. 8th Triennial Meeting ICOM Comm. for Cons.* Sydney, Australia. III, pp. 1009–1012

NEWTON, R.G. (1987b) Air pollution damage, *Profess. Stained Glass* **7**, 14, 15, 17, 19, 21

NEWTON, R.G. (1987c) *Caring for Stained Glass*, Ecclesiastical Architects and Surveyors Association

NEWTON, R.G. (1988) Who invented covered pots? *Glass Tech.* **29**, 49–50

NEWTON, R.G. (1992) The future of the Ballidon glass burial experiment. *Glass Technol.* **33** (5), 179–180

NEWTON, R.G. and BETTEMBOURG, J.M. (1976) Effects of repeated condensation, *CMVA News Letter*, No 22, 9–10

NEWTON, R.G., BRIGHTON, J.T. and TAYLOR, J.R. (1989) An interpretation of Peckitt's eighteenth century treatise on making glasses and stains for them. *Glass Technol.* **30**, 33–38

NEWTON, R.G. and FUCHS, D. (1988) Chemical analyses and weathering of some medieval glass from York Minster. *Glass Technol.*, **29**, 43–48

NEWTON, R.G., HOLLOWAY, D.G. and HENCH, L.L. (1981) A note on the 'spontaneous cracking' of ancient glass samples. *Ann. 8e Cong. Assoc. Int. du Verre, London & Liverpool*, AIHV, Liège, 355–367, 385

NEWTON, R.G. and PAUL, A. (1980) A new approach to predicting the durability of glasses from their chemical compositions. *Glass Technol.* **21**, 307–309

NEWTON, R.G. and RENFREW, C. (1970) British faience beads reconsidered. *Antiquity* **44**, 199–206. Reprinted with a new introduction and a larger bibliography in *Problems in European Prehistory*, ed. C. Renfrew, Edinburgh University Press, pp. 293–303

NEWTON, R.G. and SEDDON, A.B. (1992) The durability of a silicate glass in the presence of a saturated leachant. *Corrosion Science* **23**, 617–626

NEWTON, R.G. and SHAW, G. (1988) Another unsolved problem concerning weathering layers, *Glass Technol.* **29**, 78–79

NEWTON, R.G. and TAYLOR, J.R. (1990) Peckitt's eighteenth century treatise: staining glass with red tones. *Glass Technol.* **31**, 69–71

NEWTON, R.G. and WERNER, A.E. (1974) Definition of the term 'devitrification'. *Br. Acad. CVMA Occasional Papers*, Part I, No. 100

NISHIMURA, S. (1971) Fission track dating of archaeological materials from Japan. *Nature* **230**, 242–243

NIXON, W.C. (1981) Safe handling of frosting and etching solutions. *Stained Glass* **75**, 215–216

NOBLE, J.V. (1969) The technique of Egyptian faience. *Am. J. Arch.* **73**, 435–439

NOLL, W. (1968) *Chemistry and Technology of Silicones*,

Academic Press, London

NORMAN, R.H. (1973) The significance of the interface in glass reinforced plastics. *11th Ann. Conf. on Adhesion and Adhesives*, April. (Abstract No. 296 in Newton, 1982b.)

NORMAN, R.H., STONE, M.H. and WAKE, W.C. (1970) Resin–glass interface. In *Glass Reinforced Plastics*, ed. B. Parkyn. Iliffe, p. 206

NORTHWOOD, J. (1924) Noteworthy productions of the glass craftsman's art. I. The reproduction of the Portland Vase. *J. Soc. Glass Technol.* **8**, 85–92

NOTMAN, J.H. (1973a) Questionnaire about adhesives. *CVMA News Letter*, No. 3, pp. 5–6

NOTMAN, J.H. (1973b) Restoration of a stained glass roundel. St Anne with Virgin and Child. Early 16th century: Flemish. *Scottish Art Review* **15**(2), 10–13

NOTMAN, J.H. and TENNENT, N.H. (1980) Conservation and restoration of a seventeenth century glass roundel. *Studies in Conservation* **25**, 165–175

NOVIS, W.E. (1975) The lifting of mosaic pavements. In *Conservation in Archaeology and the Applied Arts*, Stockholm, pp. 143–146

NYLÉN, E. (1975) Documentation and presentation. *Fornvännen* **70**, 213–223

OAKLEY, V. (1992) The deterioration of glass. *Glass and Enamel Conservation*, UKIC Occasional Papers No. 11, 18–23

OAKLEY, V. (1992) Vessel glass deterioration in the museum environment: a quantitative study by surface analysis. *Victoria and Albert Conservation Journal* **3**, 6–10

OBERLIES, F. (1956) Elektronenoptische Untersuchungen an Verwitterten Glasoberfläschen. *Glastech. Ber.* **29**, 109–120

O'CONNOR, D. and HASELOCK, J. (1977) The stained and painted glass. In *A History of York Minster*, eds G.E. Aylmer and R. Cant. Oxford, p. 377

OECD (1977) *Long-range Transport of Air Pollutants*. (Abstract No. 294 in *CVMA News Letter*, No. 26

OGDEN, P.H. (1975) A new glass adhesive. This paper was presented at the *IIC Conference on Conservation in Archaeology and the Applied Arts*, Stockholm, but was too late for inclusion in the published volume. (Abstract No. 191 in *CVMA News Letter*, No. 15 but the material is not now available.)

OHTA, H. and SUZUKI, Y. (1978) Chemical durability of glasses in the silica–calcium oxide–sodium oxide–R_mO_n. *Am. Ceram. Soc. Bull.* **57**, 602–604

OLIN, J.S., THOMPSON, B.A. and SAYRE, E.V. (1972) Characterisation of medieval window glass by neutron activation analysis, in *Development in Applied Spectroscopy*, ed. A.J. Perkins *et al.*, Plenum Press, pp. 33–75

OLIN, J.S., SALMON, M.E. and SAYRE, E.V. (1976) Neutron activation and electron beam microprobe study of a XIV century Austrian stained glass panel. *Accad. Naz. Lincei.*, Rome, 99–110

OLSEN, D.A., JOHNSON, R.E., KIVEL, J. and ALBERS, F.C. (1969) Kinetics of leaching of lead glass by ethylenediamine tetraacetic acid. *J. Am. Ceram. Soc.* **52**, 318–322

OLSEN, D.A., JOHNSON, R.E. and OLSEN, K.H. (1970) Thin film formation on etched lead glass surfaces. *Glass Technol.* **11**, 119–122

OPPENHEIM, A.L. (1973) A note on research in Mesopotamian glass. *J. Glass Stud.* **15**, 9–11

OPPENHEIM, A.L., BRILL, R.H., BARAG, D. and VON SALDERN, A. (1970) *Glass and Glassmaking in Ancient Mesopotamia*, Corning Museum of Glass

ORGAN, R.M. (1957) The safe storage of unstable glass. *Museums J.* **56**, 265–272

ORGAN, R.M. (1968) *Design for Scientific Conservation of Antiquities*, Butterworths, London

ORGAN, R.M. (1975) The organization of an integrated facility for conservation of museum objects. *Bull. Inst. royal du Patrimoine artistique* **15**, 283–301

OUTWATER, J.O. and MURPHY, M.C. (1970) The influences of the environment and glass finishes on the fracture energy of glass-epoxy joints. *J. Adhesion* **2**, 242

PALLANT, R.J. (1973) The response of some leaded windows to simulated sonic bangs. *Royal Aircraft Estab. (Farnborough, Hants), Tech. Rept. 73111*, 22 pp typescript and 26 diagrams and photographs.

PANEK, J.R. (1977) Polysulphide sealants and adhesives. In *Handbook of Adhesives*, 2nd edn, ed. I. Skeist. Van Nostrand, Reinhold, p. 368

PAPE, T. (1933) An Elizabethan glass furnace. *The Connoisseur*, 172ff

PATERSON, M.P. (1974) The atmosphere of the Royal Albert Hall – a study of the internal atmosphere of a natural draught building. *Air Pollution Research Group*, Imperial College, London, 28 October, 12 pp typescript

PAUL, A. (1977) Chemical durability of glasses; a thermodynamic approach. *J. Mater. Sci.* **12**, 2246–2268

PAUL, A. (1978) Influence of complexing agents and nature of the buffer solution on the chemical durability of glass. Part I. Theoretical discussion. *Glass Technol.* **19**, 162–165

PAUL, A. and YOUSSEFI, A. (1978a) Alkaline durability of some silicate glasses containing CaO, FeO and MnO. *J. Mater. Sci.* **13**, 97–107

PAUL, A. and YOUSSEFI, A. (1978b) Influence of complexing agents, and nature of the buffer solution, on the chemical durability of glass. Part 2. EDTA, ethyl alcohol and sugar in the leach solution. *Glass Technol.* **19**, 166–170

PAZAUREK, G.E. (1903) *Kranke Gläser*, Reichenberg

PEARSON, C. (1975) On-site conservation requirements for marine archaeological excavations. *Proceedings of the ICOM Sessions on Conservation*, Venice, 75/13/2

PEDERSON, L.R., BUCKWALTER, C.Q. and MCVAY, G.L. (1983) The effects of surface area to solution volume on waste glass leaching, *Nuclear Technology*, **62**, 151–158

PEASE, M. (1964) Report of the Murray Pease Committee: IIC American Group Standards of Practice and Professional Relations for Conservators. *Studies in Conservation* **9**, 116–121

PELOUZE, T.J. (1867) Sur le verre. *Compt. Rend. Acad. Sci. Paris* **64**, 53–66

PELTENBURG, E. (1971) Some early developments of vitreous materials. *World Archaeology* **3**, 6–12

PEREZ-Y-JORBA, M. and DALLAS, J.-P. (1984) Composition et altération des grisailles anciennes. 3 examples de grisaille du XIIIe siècle étudiés par rayons X et microsonde électronique. *CVMA News Letter*, No. 37/38, 8–12

PEREZ-Y-JORBA, M., DALLAS, J.-P., BAUER, C., BAHEZRE, C. and MARTIN, J.C. (1980) Deterioration of stained glass by atmospheric corrosion and micro-organisms. *J. Mater. Sci.* **15**, 1640–1647

PEREZ-Y-JORBA, M., DALLAS, J.-P., COLLONGUES, R.,

BAHEZRE, C. and MARTIN, J.C. (1978) Etude de l'alteration des vitraux anciens par microscopie électronique à balayage et microsonde. *Silicates Industrielles* **43**, 89–99

PEREZ-Y-JORBA, M., TILLOCA, G., MICHEL, D. and DALLAS, J.-P. (1975) Quelques aspects du phénomène de corrosion des vitraux anciens des églises françaises. *Verre et Réfract.* **29**, 53–63

PERROT, P.N. (1971) A 'tank' furnace at Somelaria (Es-Samariya) Israel. *Proceedings of the 9th International Congress on Glass, Art Hist Comm.* pp. 51–61

PERSSON, H.R. (1962) Improvement of the chemical durability of soda–lime–silica bottles by treating with various agents. *Glass Technol.* **3**, 17–35

PETERMANN, R. (1969) Nachbildung antiker Gläser. *Arbeitsblätter für Restauratoren*, Heft 1, Gruppe 18, pp. 9–14

PETRICIOLI, S. (1973) The Gnalić Wreck: the glass. *J. Glass Stud.* **15**, 85–92

PEVSNER, N. (1976) Scrape and anti-scrape. In *The Future of the Past*, ed. J. Fawcett. London, pp. 35–53

PEVSNER, N. (various dates) *The Buildings of England*, Pelican Books, Harmondsworth

PEYCHES, I. (1952) The viscous flow of glass at low temperatures. *J. Soc. Glass Technol.* **36**, 164.T–180.T

PHILIPOTT, P. and MORA, P. (1968) Conservation of wall paintings. In *Conservation of Cultural Property*, UNESCO, p. 169

PIERCY, R.C.M. (1978) Mombasa wreck excavation. Second preliminary report. *Int. J. Nautical Archaeology and Underwater Exploration* **7**.4, 301–309

PILKINGTON, A. (1971) Float: An application of science, analysis, and judgement. Third Turner Memorial Lecture. *Glass Technol.* **12**, 76–83

PILKINGTON, A. (1976) Flat glass: evolution and revolution over 60 years. *Glass Technol.* **17**, 182–193

PINDER-WILSON, R.H. (1968) Pre-Islamic Persian and Mesopotamian, Islamic and Chinese. In *Masterpieces of Glass*, eds D.B. Harden *et al.* Trustees of the British Museum, London.

PIPER, J. (1968) *Stained Glass: Art or Anti Art*, London.

PLENDERLEITH, H.J. (1934) *The Preservation of Antiquities*, Museums Association

PLENDERLEITH, H.J. and WERNER, A.E.A. (1956) *Conservation of Antiquities and Works of Art*, 2nd edn, Oxford University Press, Oxford

PLENDERLEITH, H.J. and WERNER, A.E.A. (1974) Oxford University Press, Oxford

PLINY (AD 77) *Natural History*, Book xxxvi. Translated by Eichholtz (1962) Loeb Classical Library, p. 190

POGANY, G.A. (1976) Anomalous diffusion of water in glassy polymers. *Polymer* **17**, 690

POLAK, A. (1969) Economic and social aspects of European glassmaking before 1800. *Proceedings of the 8th International Congress on Glass*, pp. 155–161

POLAK, A. (1975) *Glass, its Makers and its Public*, London; the same book is published in New York as *Glass – its tradition and its makers*

POLLARD, A.M. (1979) *X-ray Fluorescence and Surface Studies of Glass with Application to the Durability of Medieval Window Glass*, unpublished PhD thesis, University of York, January. Permission to use material from this thesis is gratefully acknowledged

POLLITZER, S. (1936) Sandblasting and other processes for decorating glass. *J. Soc. Glass Technol.* **20**, 724–734

POWELL, H.J. 1875) Toughened glass. *J. Roy. Soc. Arts* **23**, 638

POWELL, H.J. (1923) *Glass-making in England*, Cambridge

PRESTON, F.W. (1973) The post-instantaneous creep of long-loaded glass specimens. *Glass Technol.* **14**, 20–30

PRICE, C.A. (1980) Note on the surface contamination of glass specimens held at constant relative humidity over saturated salt solutions. *Glass Technol.* **21**, 306

RADLEY, J.A. and GRANT, J. (1954) *Fluorescence Analysis in Ultra-violet Light*, Van Nostrand, New York

RADO, P. (1976) The effect of detergents on porcelain. In *Conservation in Archaeology and the Applied Arts, IIC Conference*, Stockholm, pp. 47–53

RANA, M.A. and DOUGLAS, R.W. (1961) The reaction between glass and water. Part 1. Experimental methods and observations. *Phys. Chem. Glasses* **2**, 179–195; Part 2. Discussion of the results, *ibid.* **2**, 196–205

RÅNBY, B. and RABEK, J.F. (1975) *Photodegradation, Photo-oxidation and Photostabilization of Polymers*, Wiley Interscience, Chichester

RATHOUSKY, J. (1957) Experiments with the restoration of glass objects. *Zprávy Památkové Pece* **17**, 154–159

RAUCH, F. (1985) Applications of ion-beam analysis to solid state reactions, *Nucl. Inst and Meth.* **B10/11**, 746–750

RAW, F. (1955) The long-continued action of water on window-glass: weathering of the medieval glass at Weoley Castle, Birmingham. *J. Soc. Glass Technol.* **39**, 128.T–133.T

RAWSON, H. (1984) *The Properties and Applications of Glass*, Elsevier, Amsterdam

RAY, N.H. (1976) Sulphur dioxide and glass. *CVMA News Letter*, No. 20, No. 21

REES-JONES, S.G. (1963) A simple vacuum impregnation tank for pottery and other objects. *Studies in Conservation* **8**, 67–71

REISMAN, S.N. and LUCAS, D. (1978) Recommendations for the treatment of glass objects retrieved from an underwater environment (unpublished report)

RENDELL, R. (1975) Who was George Ravenscroft? In *The Glass Circle 2*, eds R.J. Charleston, W. Evans and A. Polak). Old Woking

RENFREW, C., CANN, J.R. and DIXON, J.E. (1965) Obsidian in the Aegean. *Ann. Br. School Arch. Athens* **60**, 225–247

RENFREW, C., DIXON, J.E. and CANN, J.R. (1966) Obsidian and early cultural contact in the Near East. *Proc. Prehist. Soc.* **32**, 30–72

REYNTIENS, P. (1977) *The Technique of Stained Glass*, Batsford Press, London

RICHARDSON, J.H. (1971) *Optical Microscopy for the Materials Sciences*, Dekker, New York

RICHEY, W.D. (1975) Chelating agents – a review. In *Conservation in Archaeology and the Applied Arts, International Institute of Conservation Conference*, Stockholm, pp. 229–234

RIEFSTAHL, E. (1972) A unique fish-shaped glass vial in the Brooklyn Museum. *J. Glass Stud.* **14**, 11–14

RITTER, J.E. (1973a) *Stress Corrosion Susceptibility of Polymeric Coated, soda–lime glass*, University of Massachusetts Report No. UM-73-5

RITTER, J.E. (1973b) Stress susceptibility of polymeric-coated soda-lime glass. *J. Am. Ceram. Soc.* **56**, 402–403

ROBERTS, J.D. (1984) Acrylic colloidal dispersions as pre-consolidants for waterlogged archaeological glass.

Preprints of the 7th Triennial Meeting of the ICOM Committee for Conservation, Copenhagen. September, 84.20.21–84.20.24

ROBSON, M. (1986) Clear, colourless adhesives for glass. *Conservation News*, July 1988, UKIC, 14–15

RÖHM and HAAS (1974) *Acryloid Resins for the Adhesives Formulator*

ROMICH, H. and FUCHS, D.R. (1992) A new comprehensive concept for the conservation of stained glass windows. *Bol. Soc. Exp. Ceram.* **31–C**, 137–141

ROOKSBY, H.P. (1959) An investigation of ancient opal glasses with special reference to the Portland Vase. *J. Soc. Glass Technol.* **43**, 285.T–288.T

ROOKSBY, H.P. (1962) Opacifiers in opal glasses throughout the ages. *Gen. Elec. Coy., Sci. J.* **29**, 20–26

ROOKSBY, H.P. (1964) A yellow cubic lead tin oxide opacifier in ancient glasses. *Phys. Chem. Glasses* **5**, 20–25

ROOSMA, M. (1969) The glass industry of Estonia in the 18th and 19th century. *J. Glass Stud.* **11**, 70–72

ROTTENBERG, B.L. (1981) Care and display of glass collections. *History News* **35**, 11

RULE, L.G. (1967) *The Flame of the Lamp*, Glass Manufacturers Federation, London

RUSH, J. (1973) *The Ingenious Beilbys*, London

RYABOV, V.A., BORISOVA, I.I., KULIKOVA, E.N. and KALUGINA, G.S. (1967) Protecting the surface of silicate glasses with silicone compounds. *Steklo i Keramika* **24**, No. 4, pp. 4–8 in Russian. *Glass and Ceramics* **24**, 175–179 English translation

RYDER, S.H. (1975) Comments on his experience of a cameo-cut vase made by J. Northwood, and quoted on p. 104 of Newton. *Glass Technol.* **16**, 102–106

SALVA, M. (1977) Epoxy resin adhesives. In *Handbook of Adhesives*, ed. I. Skeist. Van Nostrand, Reinhold, p. 434

SANDARS, N.C. (1977) *The Sea Peoples. Warriors of the Ancient Mediterranean 1250–1150 BC*, Thames & Hudson, London

SANDERS, D.M. and HENCH, L.L. (1973a) Mechanisms of glass corrosion. *J. Am. Ceram.Soc.* **56**, 373–377

SANDERS, D.M. and HENCH, L.L. (1973b) Environmental effects of glass corrosion kinetics. *Ceram. Bull.* **52**, 662–665

SANDERS, D.M. and HENCH, L.L. (1973c) Surface roughness and glass corrosion. *Ceram. Bull.* **52**, 666–669

SAUNDERS, K.J. (1977) *Organic Polymer Chemistry*, Chapman and Hall, London

SAVAGE, G. (1965) *Glass*, Weidenfeld and Nicolson, London

SAYRE, E.V. (1963) The intentional use of antimony and manganese in ancient glasses. *Advances in Glass Technology*, Part 2, eds F.R. Matson and G.E. Rindone. New York, pp. 263–282

SAYRE, E.V. (1965) Summary of the Brookhaven program of analysis of ancient glass. *Application of Science in Examination of Works of Art*, pp. 145–154, Seminar, Boston, September 7–16

SAYRE, E.V. and SMITH, R.W. (1961) Compositional categories of ancient glass. *Science* **133**, 1824–1826 (No. 3467)

SAYRE, E.V. and SMITH, R.W. (1974) Analytical studies of ancient Egyptian glass. In *Recent Advances in Science and Technology of Materials*, Vol. 3, ed. A Bishay, Plenum Press, New York, pp. 47–70

SAX, N.I. (1975) *Dangerous Properties of Industrial Materials*, 4th edn, Van Nostrand

SCHÄFER, F.W. (1968) Two pragmatic views on 'Vasa Dietrata' 1. *J. Glass Stud.* **10**, 176–177

SCHÄFER, F.W. (1969) Wiederherstellung eines Diatretglases in römischer Schlifftechnik. *Studies in Glass History and Design*, Sheffield, pp. 125–126

SCHENK ZU SCHWEINSBERG, E. (1963) Contributions to the sociology of glass – an attempt. *Advances in Glass Technology*, Part 2, eds F.R. Matson and G.E. Rindone. Plenum Press, New York, pp. 252–262

SCHMIDT, C. (1976) Zur Restaurierung der Glasmalereien in Mühlhausen. *Denkmalpflege in der DDR* **2**, 42–51

SCHOFIELD, P.F., CRESSEY, G., HOWARD, P.W. and HENDERSON, C.M.B. (1995) Origin of colour in iron and manganese containing classes investigated by synchrotron radiation. *Glass Technol.* **36**, 89–94

SCHOLES, S.R. (1929) Density factors for soda–lime glasses. *J. Am. Ceram. Soc.* **12**, 753–755

SCHOLZE, H. (1977) *Glas. Natur, Struktur und Eigenschaften*, 2nd edn, Springer Verlag, Berlin

SCHOLZE, H. (1978) Characterisierung 'kranker' Gläser. Contribution to the *Projektgruppe 'Glas'* Meeting in Bonn, March. (Abstract No. 336 in *CVMA News Letter*, No. 28.)

SCHOLZE, H. and CORBACH, R. (1971) Study of properties of glass in acidic aqueous solutions. *OECD Report on Scientific Research on Glass*, Ref. DAS/SPR/71.35, pp. 156–175

SCHOLZE, H., HELMREICH, D. and BAKARDJIEV, I. (1975) Untersuchungen über des Verhalten von Kalk-Natron Gläsern in verdunten Säuren. *Glastech. Ber.* **48**, 237–246

SCHREINER, M. (1987) Analytical investigations of medieval glass paintings. In *Recent Advances in the Conservation and Analysis of Artefacts*, Proceedings of the Institute of Archaeology's Jubilee Conservation Conference, University of London, pp. 73–80

SCHRÖDER, H. (1953) Über die Angriefbarkeit des Glases durch Lösungen mit pH Werten nahe 7. *Glastech. Ber.* **26**, 91–97

SCHRÖDER, H. and KAUFMANN, R. (1959) Schutzschichten für alte Gläser. In *Beiträge zur Angewanten Glasforschung*, ed. E. Schott. Stuttgart, pp. 355–361

SCHUECKER, G. (1977) Klimatechnische Versuche im Zusammenhang mit dem Schutz mittelalterliche Glasfenster durch Aussenschutzverglasungen. *Report No. 404576 440/383* from Vienna. (Abstract in *CVMA News Letter*, No. 28, pp. 6–8, 1977, and Abstract No. 338 of Newton, 1982b.)

SCHUECKER, G., BAUER, P.W. and BACHER, E. (1978) Discussionsbeitrag zum Thema Aussenschutzverglasung. *CVMA News Letter*, No. 28, sections 2.6–2.11, pp. 4–5, 22 December

SCHULER, F. (1959a) Ancient glassmaking techniques. The molding process. *Archaeology* **12**, 47–52

SCHULER, F. (1959b) Ancient glassmaking techniques. The blowing process. *Archaeology* **12**, 116–122

SCHULER, F. (1962) Ancient glassmaking techniques. The Egyptian core-vessel process. *Archaeology* **15**, 32–37

SCHULER, F. (1963) Ancient glassmaking techniques. Egyptian fused miniature mosaics. *Advances in Glass Technology*, Part 2, eds F.R. Matson and G.E. Rindone. Plenum Press, New York, p. 206

SCHULZE, G. (1977) Chemisch-analytische Untersuchungen an Glasfunden aus der Kunckel-Hütte. Contribution to the DGG Meeting in Frankfurt, 31 March. (Abstract in *CVMA News Letter*, No. 26, 23 January 1978, Abs. No. 297.)

SCHWARTZ, M.D. (ed.) (1974) *American Glass from the pages of Antiques*, I *Blown and Moulded*, The Pyne Press

SCHWEIG, B. (1973) *Mirrors: A Guide to the Manufacture of Mirrors and Reflecting Surfaces*, Pelham Books, London (out of print)

SCOTT, A.S. (1932) Apparent decay of ancient glass at Wells Cathedral. *J. Br. Soc. Master Glass Painters* 4, 171

SCRANTON, R. (1967) Glass pictures from the Sea. *Archaeology* 20, 163–173

SEELA, J. (1974) The early Finnish glass industry. *J. Glass Stud.* 16, p. 65, Fig. 3

SELLNER, C. (1977) Untersuchungen an Waldgläsern mit Elektronen-spinresonanz. Contribution to the *Projektgruppe 'Glas'* Meeting in Würzburg, 14 September. (Not published but abstracted in *CVMA News Letter*, No. 26, 23 January 1978, Abs. No. 298.)

SELLNER, C., OEL, H.J. and CAMARA, B. (1979) Untersuchungen alter Gläser (Waldglas) auf Zussamenhang von Zusammensetzung, Farbe und Schmelzatmosphäre mit der Elektronenspektroskopie und der Elektronenspinresonanz (ESR). *Glastechn. Ber* 52, 255–264

SEMENOV, N.I., PAPLAUSKAS, A.B. and RYABOV, V.A. (1972) Effect of surface microstructure on the strength of glass. *Glass Technol.* 13, 171–175

SHAND, E.B. (1958) *Glass Engineering Handbook*, New York

SHAW, G. (1965) Weathered crusts on ancient glass. *New Scientist* 27, 290–291

SHELL, (n.d.) *Relative evaporation rates of solvents using the Shell liquid film evaporator*, ICS/69/1

SHIELDS, J. (1984) *Adhesives Handbook*, Butterworths, London

SICONOLFI, C.A. (1968) Polyester resins. *Mod. Plastics Encycl.* 45, 265

SIMON, W.E. (1981) Heat loss through stained glass windows. *Stained Glass* 76, 123–125

SIMPSON, H.E. (1951) Measuring surface durability of glass. *Bull. Am. Ceram. Soc.* 30, 41–45

SIMPSON, H.E. (1953) Some factors affecting the testing of surface durability of flat glass. *J. Am. Ceram. Soc.* 36, 143–146

SKEIST, I. (1977) *Handbook of Adhesives*, 2nd edn, Van Nostrand, Reinhold

SLOAN, J.L. (1987) A historical overview, *Profess. Stained Glass* 7, 7–9

SMITH, R.W. (1963a) Archaeological evaluation of analyses of ancient glass. In *Advances in Glass Technology*, Part 2, eds F.R. Matson and G.E. Rindone. Plenum Press, New York, pp. 283–290

SMITH, R.W. (1963b) The analytical study of glass in archaeology. In *Science in Archaeology*, eds D. Brothwell and E. Higgs. Thames & Hudson, London, pp. 519–528

SMITH, C.S. and GNUDI, M.T. (1942) *The Pirotechnia of Vannoccio Biringuccio*, American Institute of Mining and Metallurgical Engineering, New York

SMITHSONIAN INSTITUTION (1969) *Glass Goblet Excavated from Privy*, Conservation – Analytical Laboratory

SOCIETY OF GLASS TECHNOLOGY (1951) *Glass and W.E.S. Turner*, Sheffield

SPITZER-ARONSON, M. (1974) La distribution du cuivre dans les verres rouges des vitraux médiévaux. *Compt. Rend. de l'Académie des Sciences* C.278, 1437–1440

SPITZER-ARONSON, M. (1975a) Étude de vitraux rouges médiévaux à l'aide de microscope optique, microscope à balayage avec image par électrons rétrodiffusés et microsonde électronique a rayons X. *Verres et Réfract.* 29, 145–153

SPITZER-ARONSON, M. (1975b) Contribution à la connaissance des vitraux du Moyen-Age. La présence du plomb et du cuivre et leur diffusion sélective dans les vitraux rouges des cathédrales françaises. *Compt. Rend. de l'Académie des Sciences* C.280, 207–209

SPITZER-ARONSON, M. (1975c) Diffusion sélective du cuivre et de l'arsenic dans les vitraux rouges médiévaux. Étude quantitative de la concentration du cuivre pour des 'plaques' de techniques differentes. *Compt. Rend. de l'Académie des Sciences* C.280, 1343–1346

SPITZER-ARONSON, M. (1976) Contribution à la connaissance des vitraux du Moyen Age. Insuffisance de la diffusion pour expliquer la non-concordance stricte entre la presence du cuivre et la couleur à l'interieure des verres des vitraux rouges. *Verres et Réfract.* 30, 56–61

SPITZER-ARONSON, M. (1977a) A note on the nature and origin of early ruby glasses from York Minster. Unpublished, but read to the Crafts Advisory Council Stained Glass Symposium held in York on 9–11 January 1977. (Abstract No. 273 in *CVMA News Letter*, No. 25, 22 April, 1977.)

SPITZER-ARONSON, M. (1977b) La repartition 'initiale' du cuivre retrouvée et calculée dans certains vitraux rouges médiévaux. *Compt. Rend. Acad. Sci.* C.285, 269–272

SPITZER-ARONSON, M. (1978) Titan als möglicher Indikator mittelalterlicher gemalter Gläser. See *CVMA News Letter*, No. 28, Abstract No. 339

STACPOLE, A. (ed.) (1972) *The Noble City of York*, Cerialis Press, York, p. 169 and Plates 3A and 4A

STAFFORD, R.D. (n.d.) *Ultrasonic Cleaning Techniques*, 2nd edn, Dawe Instruments Ltd

STAHL, C.J. (1915) *Dekorative Glasmalerei, Unterglasmalerei und Malen auf Glas*. In *Chemisch-technisch Bibliothek*, Vol. 354, Wien and Leipzig

STAINED GLASS INDEX (1979, 1980, 1981) *Stained Glass Index 1906–1977* with Supplements

STANFORD RESEARCH INSTITUTE (1968) *Sources, Abundance, and Fate of Gaseous Atmospheric Pollutants*, Stanford Research Institute Report, PR-6755, February

STANWORTH, J.E. (1950) *Physical Properties of Glass*, Oxford

STAUDE, H. (1972) Die Technik des Zusammensetzens und Ergänzens antiker Gläser. *Arbeitsblätter für Restauratoren*, Heft 1, Gruppe 5, pp. 20–27

STEVELS, J.M. (1948) *Progress in the Theory of the Physical Properties of Glass*, Elsevier, Amsterdam

STEVELS, J.M. (1960) New light on the structure of glass. *Philips Tech. Rev.* 22, 300–311

STEVENSON, R.B.K. (1954, 1976) Native bangles and Roman glass. *Proc. Soc. Antiq. Scotland* 88, 208–221 (1954); see also *Glasgow Archaeol. J.* 4, 45–54 (1976)

STOCKDALE, G.F. and TOOLEY, F.V. (1950) Effect of humid conditions on glass surfaces, studied by photographic and transmission techniques. *J. Am. Ceram. Soc.* 33, 11–16

STOLOW, N. (1971) Solvent action. In *On Picture Varnishes and their Solvents*, eds R.L. Feller, N. Stolow and E.H.

Jones. Case Western Reserve University, p. 45

STONE, M.H. (1971) A new test for the glass-to-resin bond life in GRP; comparison of typical systems exposed to water. *Japan Plastics*, April, 15–21

STONE, J.F.S. and THOMAS, L.C. (1956) The use and distribution of faience in the ancient East and prehistoric Europe. *Proc. Prehist. Soc.* **22**, 37–84

STRABO, (1st century BC) *Geography*, book XVI, chap. II, sec. 25. English translation by H.L. Jones in Loeb Classical Library, London, New York, Vol. VII, p. 271

STRAUSS, J. (1977) Use of the archaic word 'metal' for glass. *J. Glass Stud.* **19**, 186

STRONG, D. and BROWN, D. (1976) *Roman Crafts*, Duckworth, London

STUCKER, N.E. and HIGGINS, J.J. (1977) Butyl rubber and polyisobutylene. In *Handbook of Adhesives*, 2nd edn, ed. I. Skeist. Van Nostrand, Reinhold, p. 16

SYKES, R.F. (1965) The preparation of glass grain samples for durability tests. *Glass Technol.* **6**, 178–183

TABACZYNSKA, E. (1968) Remarks on the origin of the Venetian glassmaking centre. *Proceedings of the 8th International Congress on Glass, Studies in Glass History and Design* pp. 20–23

TAIT, H. (1968) Glass in Europe from the Middle Ages to 1862. In *Masterpieces of Glass*, ed. D.B. Harden *et al.* Trustees of the British Museum

TAIT, H. (1979) *The Golden Age of Venetian Glass*, British Museum Publications

TARALON, J. (1962) Le Colloque International d'Erfut et la sauvegarde des vitraux anciens. *Les Monuments Historiques de la France*, No. 1, 2–6

TARNOPOL, M.S. and JUNGE, A.E. (1946) Resistance of plate glass to alkaline solutions. *J. Am. Ceram. Soc.* **29**, 36–39

TAVAS, I. (1975) Glass restoration – in Hungarian. *Múzeumi Mütárgyvédelem.* **2**, 195–198

TAYLOR, T.H. (1984) *In situ* repair of architectural glass. *Preprints of the Contributions to the 10th International Congress of the IIC*, September, 202–204

TAYLOR, H.E. and HILL, D.K. (1952) *The Identification of Stones in Glass by Physical Methods*, Glass Delegacy of the University of Sheffield. Now out of print, and replaced by Clark-Monks and Parker (1980)

TEAS, J.P. (1971) *Predicting Resin Solubilities*, Ashland Chemical Corp., Box 2219, Columbus Ohio, USA

TENNENT, N.H. (1979) Clear and pigmented epoxy resins for stained glass conservation: light ageing studies. *Studies in Conservation* **24**, 153–164

TENNENT, N.H. (1981) Fungal growth on medieval glass. *J. Br. Soc. Master Glass Painters* **17**, 64–68

TENNENT, N.H. and TOWNSEND, J.H. (1984a) The significance of the refractive index of adhesives for glass repair. *10th International IIC Congress*, Paris, *Adhesives and Consolidants*, September, pp. 205–212

TENNENT, N.H. and TOWNSEND, J.H. (1984b) Factors affecting the refractive index of epoxy resins. *ICOM Committee for Conservation, 7th Triennial Meeting*, Copenhagen, pp. 84.20.26 to 84.20.28

TERWEN, P.A. (1981) The mending of stained glass – a Dutch approach. *Conference on the Restoration of Stained Glass*, Lunteren, Netherlands, February

THEOBALD, W. (1933) Technik des Kunsthandwerks im zehnten Jahrhundert des Theophilus. Berlin

THEOPHILUS, P. (c 1140) *On Divers Arts*, translated by Dodwell (1961) and by Hawthorne and Smith (1963)

THOMPSON, R.G. (1925) *On the Chemistry of the Ancient Assyrians*, London

THOMSON, G. (1986) *The Museum Environment*, 2nd edn, Butterworths, London

THORPE, W.A. (1929) *A History of English and Irish Glass*, London

THORPE, W.A. (1935) *English Glass*, A & C Black, London

THORPE, W.A. (1938) The prelude to European cut glass. *J. Soc. Glass Technol.* **22**, 5.T–37.T

THORPE, W.A. (1961) *English Glass* 3rd edn, London, p. 99

TICHANE, R.M. (1966) Initial stages of the weathering process on a soda–lime glass surface. *Glass Technol.*, **7**, 26–29

TITE, M.S. (1972) *Methods of Physical Examination in Archaeology*. Academic Press, London

TITE, M.S., BIMSON, M. and FREESTONE, I.C. (1983) Egyptian faience: an investigation of the methods of production. *Archaeometry* **25**, 17–27

TITE, M.S., BIMSON, M. and MEEKS, N.G. (1981) Technological characterization of Egyptian Blue. *Actes du XX Symposium Internationale d'Archaeometrie III* (et Analyse): Review d'Archaeometrie Supplement, pp. 296–301

TITE, M.S. and BIMSON, M. (1987) Identification of early vitreous materials. In *Recent Advances in the Conservation and Analysis of Artefacts*, Proceedings of the Institute of Archaeology's Jubilee Conservation Conference, University of London, pp. 81–85

TONER, J. (1985) The sound of making glass. *New Scientist*, 3 October

TONINATO, T. (1984) Technology and tradition in Murano glassmaking. *Glass in Murano*, Vicenza, pp. 29–40

TOOLEY, F.V. (1953) *Handbook of Glass Manufacture*, Ogden, New York

TORRACA, G. (1968) Synthetic materials used in the conservation of cultural property in UNESCO. *Cons. of Cultural Property*, 303–308

TORRACA, G. (1975) *Solubility and Solvents for Conservation Problems*, ICCROM, Rome

TRANTER, G.C. (1976) Patination of lead: an infra-red spectroscopic study. *Br. Corrosion J.* **11**, 222–224

TRIBE, H.T. and MABADEJE, S.A. (1972) Growth of moulds on media prepared without organic nutrients. *Trans. Br. Mycol. Soc.* **58**, 127–137

TRÜMPLER, S. (1988) Experience with protective glazings in Switzerland. *CVMA News Letter*, No. 41/42, pp. 19–22

TUMMALA, R. (1976) Stress corrosion resistance compared with thermal expansion and chemical durability of glasses. *Glass Technol.* **17**, 145–146

TURNER, W.E.S. (1930) The scientific basis of glass melting. *J. Soc. Glass Technol.* **14**, 368.T–393.T

TURNER, W.E.S. (1949) That curious word Lehr. *J. Soc. Glass Technol.* **33**, 278.T–288.T

TURNER, W.E.S. (1954a) Studies in ancient glass and glass-making processes. Part I. Crucibles and melting temperatures employed in Ancient Egypt at about 1370 BC. *J. Soc. Glass Technol.* **38**, 436.T–444.T

TURNER, W.E.S. (1954b) Studies in ancient glasses and glass-making processes. Part II. The composition, weathering characteristics and historical significance of some Assyrian glasses of the eighth to sixth centuries BC from Nimrud. *J. Soc. Glass Technol.* **38**, 445.T–456.T

TURNER, W.E.S. (1956a) Studies in ancient glasses and glass-making processes. Part III. The chronology of the glassmaking constituents. *J. Soc. Glass Technol.* **40**, 39.T–52.T

TURNER, W.E.S. (1956b) Studies in ancient glasses and glass-making processes. Part IV. The chemical composition of ancient glasses. *J. Soc. Glass Technol.* **40**, 162.T–186.T

TURNER, W.E.S. (1956c) Studies in ancient glasses and glass-making processes. Part V. Raw materials and melting processes. *J. Soc. Glass Technol.* **40**, 276.T–300.T

TURNER, W.E.S (1957a) Antichi vetri opali, il supposto effeto oppalizzante del biossido di stagno. *Vetro e Silicati* **2**, 27–30

TURNER, W.E.S. (1957b) Ancient sealing-wax red glasses. *J. Egyptian Arch.* **43**, 110–112

TURNER, W.E.S. (1959) Studies in ancient glasses and glass-making processes. Part VI. The composition and physical characteristics of the glasses of the Portland Vase. *J. Soc. Glass Technol.* **43**, 262.T–284.T

TURNER, W.E.S. (1962) A notable British seventeenth-century contribution to the literature of glassmaking. *Glass Technol.* **3**, 201–213

TURNER, W.E.S. (1963) The tercentenary of Neri-Merrett's 'The Art of Glass'. *Advances in Glass Technology*, Part 2, eds F.R. Matson and G.E. Rindone. New York, pp. 181–201

TURNER, W.E.S. and ROOKSBY, H.P. (1959) A study of the opalizing agents in ancient opal glasses throughout three thousand four hundred years. *Glastech. Ber.* **32K**, VIII/17–VIII/28

TURNER, W.E.S. and ROOKSBY, H.P. (1961) Further historical studies, based on X-ray diffraction methods, of the reagents employed in making opal and opaque glasses. *J. Röm.-Germ. Zentralmuseums* (Mainz) **VIII**, 1–6

UEBERREITER, K. (1968) The solution process. In *Diffusion in Polymers*, eds J. Crank and G.S. Park. Academic Press, London, p. 219

UHLMANN, D.R. and KOLBECK, A.G. (1976) Phase separation and the revolution in concepts of glass structure. *Phys. Chem. Glasses* **17**, 147–157

UNWIN, M. (1951) A treatment for the preservation of glass. *Museums J.* **51**, 10

UPSHER, F.J. (1976) Microbial attack on materials. *Proc. Roy. Aust. Chem. Inst.* **43**, 173–176

VAN DER MERWE, R. (1979) Notes on the use of epoxy resins for restoring glass and porcelain. *JCCM Bull.* **5**, 27–28

VAN LOOKEREN, K. (1993) Sticky wax and the restoration of flat glass. *Conservation News* **52**, 29–30

VASSAS, C.D. (1971a) Chemical, thermal-analysis, and physical study of glasses of medieval stained glass windows. *Proceedings of the 9th International Congress on Glass, Art and Hist. Comm.* pp. 241–266

VASSAS, C.D. (1971b) Colorimetric study of glasses of medieval stained glass windows. *Proceedings of the 9th International Congress on Glass, Art and Hist. Comm.* pp. 267–294

VINCENT, J. (1556) *La Pyrotechnie ... traduite d'Italien en Français par feu Maistre Jaques Vincent*, Claude Fremy, Paris, p. 90

VIOLLET LE DUC, E.E. (1868) *Dictionnaire Raisonné de l'Architecture Française du XIᵉ au XVIᵉ Siècle*, Vol. 9, Paris

VON SALDERN, A. (1970) Originals – Reproductions – Fakes. *Ann. 5 Cong. Assoc. Int. Hist. Verre*, Prague, pp. 299–318

VON SALDERN, A. (1974) *Gläser der Antike*, Museum für Kunst und Gewerbe, Hamburg

VON WITZLEBEN, E. (1968) *French Stained Glass* (English edition)

VOS-DAVIDSE, L. (1969) Note on the reversible gluing of broken glass objects. *Studies in Conservation* **14**, 183

WAGNER, G.A. (1978) Archaeological applications of fission-track dating. *Nuclear Track Detection* **2**, 51–64

WAKE, W.C. (1976) *Adhesion and the Formulation of Adhesives*, Applied Science, London

WAKE, W.C. (1978) Theories of adhesion and uses of adhesives: a review. *Polymer* **19**, 291–308

WAKEFIELD, H. (1963) Methods of packing in the Victoria and Albert Museum. In *Recent Advances in Conservation*, ed. G. Thomson. Butterworths, London, pp. 16–18

WALTERS, H.V. and ADAMS, P.B. (1975) Effects of humidity on the weathering of glass. *J. Non-Cryst. Sol.* **19**, 183–199

WARREN, P. (1970) *Irish Glass*, Faber, London

WATKINSON, D. and LEIGH, D. (1978) Polyurethane foam: a health hazard. *Conservation News*, IIC–UKG, **No. 6**, 7–8

WATTS, D.C. (1975) How did George Ravenscroft discover lead crystal. *The Glass Circle 2*, eds R.J. Charleston, W. Evans, and A. Polak. Old Woking, pp. 71–84

WEBB, D.R.B. (n.d.) *Background Research on Leaded Light Windows in Support of Cathedral Survey*, Royal Aircraft Establishment document (undated, but c 1969)

WEEDEN, C.E. (1987) Dr Syntax in the glasshouse. *Glass Circle*, 4–14

WEIER, L.E. (1973) The deterioration of inorganic materials under the sea. *Bull. Inst. Arch. (London)* **11**, 131–163

WEINBERG, G.D. (1975) A medieval mystery: Byzantine glass production. *J. Glass Stud.* **17**, 127–141

WEINTRAUB, S. and GREENLAND, M. (1984) Field application conservation techniques. *Preprints of the Contributions to the 10th International Congress of the IIC*, September, 199–201

WENTZEL, H. (1954) *Meisterwerke der Glasmalerei*, Berlin

WENTZEL, H. (1958) *Die Glasmalerei in Schwaben von 1200 bis 1350*, Berlin

WERNER, A.E. (1958) Problems in the conservation of glass. *1ᵉʳ Cong. Journées Internat. du Verre*, Liège, pp. 189–205

WERNER, A.E. (1964) New materials in conservation of antiquities. *Museums J.* **64**, 5–16

WERNER, A.E. (1966) The care of glass in museums. *Museum News Technical Supplement*, No. 13, pp. 45–99

WERNER, A.E., BIMSON, M. and MEEKS, N.D. (1975) The use of replica techniques and the scanning electron microscope in the study of ancient glass. *J. Glass Stud.* **17**, 158–160

WEXLER, H. (1964) Polymerization of drying oils. *Chem. Rev.* **64**, 591

WEYL, W.A. (1951) *Coloured Glasses*, Society of Glass Technology, Sheffield

WEYL, W.A. (1975) Structure of sub-surface layers and their role in glass technology. *J. Non-Cryst. Sol.* **19**, 1–25

WEYL, W.A. and MARBOE, E.C. (1967) The constitution of glasses, a dynamic interpretation. *Surface Chem. of*

Silicate Glasses. Wiley, New York, 3 vols, **23**, 1010–1270

WIEDERHORN, S.M. (1967) Influence of water vapor on crack propagation in soda-lime glass. *J. Am. Ceram. Soc.* **50**, 407–414

WIEDERHORN, S.M., EVANS, A.G., FULLER, E.R. and JOHNSON, H. (1974a) Application of fracture mechanics to space shuttle windows. *J. Am. Ceram. Soc.* **57**, 319–323

WIEDERHORN, S.M., JOHNSON, H., DINESS, A.M. and HEUER, A.H. (1974b) Fracture of glass in vacuum. *J. Am. Ceram. Soc.* **57**, 336–341

WIHR, R. (1963) Repair and reproduction of ancient glass. In *Recent Advances in Conservation*, London, pp. 152–155

WIHR, R. (1968) Möglichkeiten der Restaurierung und Nachbildung antiker Gläzer, mittels giessbarer Kunststoffe. *Arbeitsblätter für Restauratoren*, Gruppe 5, 1–12

WIHR, R. (1977) *Restaurieren von Keramik und Glas*, Munich

WILLOTT, W.H. (1950) The hardness of glass. *J. Soc. Glass Technol.* **34**, 77–79

WILLS, J.H. (1977) Inorganic adhesives and cements. In *Handbook of Adhesives*, ed. I. Skeist, p. 117

WILSON, M.J.G. (1968) Indoor air pollution. *Proc. Roy. Soc.* **A.307**, 215–221

WINBOLT, S.E. (1933) *Wealden Glass*, Hove

WINBOLT, S.E. (1934) A window glazed with medieval glass fragments. *J. Soc. Glass Technol.* **18**, 307

WINTER, A. (1965) Alteration des surfaces des verres anciens. *Proceedings of the 8th International Congress on Glass*, Brussels, paper No. 229, 12 pp.

WOLFF, A. (1975) The conservation of medieval stained glass according to the Jacobi method of laminating used at Cologne. *International Institute of Conservation Conference on Conservation in Archaeology and the Applied Arts*, Stockholm, pp. 115–120

WOLFF, A. and LUCKATT, S. (1973) Untersuchungen zur Einwirkung von Luftverunreinigungen auf die Baumaterialen des Kölner Domes. *Conference on Air Pollution*, pp. A90–A92. (Abstract No. 166 in *CVMA*

News Letter, No. 8.)

WOOD, E.S. (1965) A medieval glasshouse at Blunden's Wood, Hambledon, Surrey. *The Surrey Arch. Collections* **62**, 54–79

WOODFORDE, C. (1954) *English Stained and Painted Glass*, Clarendon Press, Oxford

WOSINSKI, J.F. and BRILL, R.H. (1969) A petrographic study of Egyptian and other cored vessels. *Studies in Glass History and Design*, (Proceedings of the 8th International Congress on Glass, Sheffield) pp. 123–124.

WULFF, H.S., WULFF, H.W. and KOCH, L. (1968) Egyptian faience, a possible survival in Iran. *Archaeology* **21**, 98–107

YABUKI, H., YABUKI, S. and SHIMA, M. (1973) Fission track dating of manmade glasses from Ali Tar Cavern vestiges. *Scientific Papers of the Institute of Physical and Chemical Research* **67**, 41–42

YALOURIS, N. (1968) An unreported use for some Mycenaean paste beads. *J. Glass Stud.* **10**, 9–16

YPEY, J. (1960–61) Das Bergen von stuck angegriffen Glas während einer Ausgrabung mit Hilfe einer Kunstharzlösung. *Ber. van de Rijksdienst voor het oudheikundig Bodemonders.* **10–11**, 363–369

YPEY, J. (1965) The conservation of disintegrated glass during the excavation. *Proceedings of the 7th International Congress on Glass*, Brussels, paper No. 227, 3 pp

ZACHARIASEN, W.H. (1932) The atomic arrangement in glass. *J. Am. Chem. Soc.* **54**, 3841–3851

ZECCHIN, L. (1968) Two pragmatic views on 'Vasa Dietrata' II. *J. Glass Stud.* **10**, 178–179

ZECCHIN, L. (1987) Il Ricettario Dardvin; Un Codice Vetrario del Seicento Transcritto e Commentato. Staz. Sper. del Vetro. Venice, Italy

ZISMAN, W.A. (1975) Recent advances in wetting and adhesion. In *Adhesion Science and Technology*, ed. L.H. Lee. Plenum Press, New York, p. 58

ZISMAN, W.A. (1977) Influence of constitution on adhesion. In *Handbook of Adhesives*, ed. I. Skeist, Reinhold, p. 33

Subject index

Name index

Pantano, C.G., 288
Pape, T., 122
Paplauskas, A.B., 302
Parker, J.M., 189f
Paschall, H.A., 135
Pascoe, M.W., 289
Paterson, M.P., 270
Patzelt, H., 294
Paul., A., 137, 144, 149, 151f, 157, 166f, 251
Pazaurek, G.E., 174
Pearson, C., 201
Pearson, E.F., 190
Pease, M., xi, 299
Peckitt, W., 100
Pederson, L.R., 274
Pellat, A., 83
Pelouze, T.J., 153
Peltenburg, E., 19
Penrose brothers, 49
Perez-y-Jorba, M., 142f, 151, 160f, 163, 194
Perrot, F., 167, 171, 248, 272
Perrot, P.N., 110
Persson, H.R., 138
Petermann, R., 181, 239
Petricioli, S., 35
Petrie, W.M.F., 66, 107, 109
Pevsner, N., xi, 242
Peyches, I., 13
Phidas (Maker of Zeus glass statue), 66
Philippot, P., 176
Piercy, R.C.M., 215
Pilkington, A., 101
Pinder-Wilson, R.H., 72, 87
Piper, J., 248
Plenderleith, H.J., 153, 206
Pliny 19, 24, 56, 58, 60f, 109
Plodinec, M.J., 144
Pogany, G.A., 272
Polak, A., 39, 51
Poli, F., 53
Pollard, A.M., 139, 194f
Pollitzer, S., 73
Pouillon, H., 297
Powell, H.J., 100f
Powell, J. and Sons., 48
Preissler, I., 41
Prestereau, J. and L., 83
Preston, F.W., 13
Price, C.A., 152
Price, J., 24, 78
Price, P.B., 287
Proffitt, P.M.C., 10
Profilo, M.V., 151
Pye, E.M., 287

Rabek, J.F., 173
Radley, J.A., 192
Rado, P., 166
Raggon, F.C., 167
Rana, M.A., 136
Rånby, B., 173
Rathousky, J., 219

Rauch, F., 194
Ravenscroft, G., 11, 44, 60, 143, 189
Raw, F., 149, 155, 196
Rawson, H., 190ff
Ray, N.H., 151,160
RCHM (Royal Commission on Historical Monuments), 242
Rees-Jones, S.G., 210
Reisman, S.N., 201, 212
Rendell, R., 45
Renfrew, C., 18, 63, 195
Reyntiens, P., 96
Richards, G.E., 286
Richardson family, 48
Richardson, J.H., 187
Richey, W.D., 167
Riefstahl, E., 84
Ritter, J.E., 171
Roberts, J.D., 213, 215
Roche, P., 48, 134
Rohm and Haas, 176
Rooksby, H.P., 10
Roosma, M., 125
Rottenberg, B.L., 240
Rousseau, E., 52
Rule, L.G., 82
Rush, J., 85
Ryabov, V.A., 272
Ryder, S.H., 72

Sabellico, M., 77
St Agnes, 103
Saito, K., 284
Sala, J., 53
Salmon, M.E., 299
Salva, M., 174
Salviati, A., 3
Sandars, N.C., 22
Sanders, D.M., 136, 140
Sang, J., 43, 71
Sargon (King of Syria), 69
Saunders, K.J., 170
Savage, G., 44
Sax, N.I., 168
Sayre, E.V., 8, 55, 60, 105, 195
Schäfer, F.W., 69
Schaper, J., 39, 85
Scheele, C.W., 73
Schenk zu Schweinsberg, E., 18
Schmidt, C., 153, 247
Schmitz, G.K., 301
Schofield, P.F., 8
Scholes, S.R., 15
Scholze, H., 136, 142, 150, 189, 191f
Schreiner, M., 142, 192
Schröder, H., 136, 222, 274
Schuecker, G., 270
Schuler, F., 66ff, 76, 78
Schulze, G., 10, 131
Schurterre, J., 30
Schwanhardt, G., 71, 73
Schwartz, M.D., 50
Schweig, B., 73, 89, 198
Schweizer, F., 194

Scolting, H., 43
Scott, A.S., 159
Scranton, R., 90
Scuderi, T.G., 191
Seddon, A., 298
Seddon, G., 296
Seela, J., 123
Seihr, H-H., 168
Sellner, C., 8, 195
Semenov, N.I., 192
Senguptal, S.C., 176
Shand, E.B., 192
Shaw, G., 159, 197
Shell Co., 168
Shields, J., 170
Shields, W.R., 287
Shima, M., 305
Siconofli, C.A., 175f
Siebel, F.A., 85
Simon, W.E., 266
Simonds, R., 294
Simpson, H.E., 137, 152, 248
Skeist, I., 170
Sloan, J.L., 252
Smalldon, K.W., 294
Smedley, J.W., 123
Smith, C.S., 59, 89, 91, 96, 118f
Smith, P., 287
Smith, R.L., 291
Smith, R.W., 55, 186, 195, 222
Smithsonian Institution, 159, 200, 206
Society of Glass Technology, 100f
Sowerbys Ellison Glass Works, 48
Spiller, G., 40
Spitzer-Aronson, M., 96
Stacpole, A., 257
Stafford, R.D., 249
Stahl, C.J., 86
Stained Glass Index, 302
Stanford Research Institute, 151
Stanworth, J.E., 192
Stark, F.O., 295
Staude, H., 183, 219, 222, 226
Stephens, F., 296
Sterman, S., 171
Stern, J.M., 293
Stevels, J.M., 7
Stevens and Williams (glassworks), 48
Stevenson, R.B.K., 62
Stiegel ('Baron'), 50
Stockdale, G.F., 152
Stoddart, C.T.H., 195
Stolow, N., 168
Stone, J.F.S., 63
Stone, M.H., 272
Strabo, 24, 60
Strauss, J., 3
Strong, B., 24
Stucker, N.E., 180
Sun, K-H., 190
Suzuki, Y., 142
Swan, J., 101
Sykes, R.F., 137
Szymanski, A., 65